Joyce Grenfell

Joyce Grenfell is fondly remembered for her varied work on stage and in film. As an actor, writer and comedian she delighted audiences around the world. Sceptre also publishes Joyce Grenfell's celebrated collections, THE TIME OF MY LIFE, *Entertaining the Troops*; TURN BACK THE CLOCK, *Her Best Monologues and Songs* and DARLING MA: *Letters to her Mother*.

Janie Hampton's mother and Joyce Grenfell were close friends and Joyce became a 'fairy godmother' to the family when Hampton's mother was widowed. Janie Hampton has written ten books on travel and health and has been a journalist in Zimbabwe and a producer at the BBC World Service.

∫

SCEPTRE

Joyce & Ginnie

The Letters of Joyce Grenfell
& Virginia Graham

Edited by JANIE HAMPTON

SCEPTRE

For my mother Verily Anderson
who taught me to laugh
and introduced me to Joyce Grenfell

First published in 1997 by Hodder and Stoughton
First published in paperback in 1998 by Hodder and Stoughton
A division of Hodder Headline PLC
A Sceptre Paperback

10 9 8 7 6 5 4 3 2 1

British Library Cataloguing in Publication Data

Grenfell, Joyce, 1910–1979
    Joyce and Ginnie: letters of Joyce Grenfell & Virginia Graham
    1. Grenfell, Joyce, 1910–1979 – Correspondence 2. Graham, Virginia –
    Correspondence 3. Women entertainers – Great Britain – Correspondence
    4. Entertainers – Great Britain – Correspondence
    I. Title II. Graham, Virginia III. Campbell-Preston, Frances IV. Hampton,
    Janie
    828.9'14'009

    ISBN 0 340 67193 9

Typeset by Palimpsest Book Production Limited,
Polmont, Stirlingshire
Printed and bound in Great Britain by
Mackays of Chatham PLC, Chatham, Kent

Hodder and Stoughton
A division of Hodder Headline PLC
338 Euston Road
London NW1 3BH

Contents

List of Illustrations

Endpapers: 'Old Time Dancing' by Joyce Grenfell and Richard Addinsell (*courtesy of Claremont Fan Court School*)

Section One

Joyce at Clear View School, 1925
Reggie Grenfell and Joyce soon after their engagement was announced, 1929
Joyce and Virginia with other students in Paris, 1927
Virginia, Lord Dundonald and Eben Pike in Luxor, 1937
Virginia went up the Nile to Aswan on this steamer, 1937
Joyce's brother, Tommy Phipps, at Cliveden, 1934
Joyce and her mother, Nora Phipps, outside 21 St Leonard's Terrace, 1931
Virginia Graham marries Tony Thesiger at St George's, Hanover Square, 1939
Joyce and Reggie all dressed up for Virginia's wedding, 1939
Virginia and Tony's co-respondent feet on honeymoon, 1939
Maria Brassey, Stephen Potter, Reggie, Att (Mary) Potter, Bertie and Joan Farjeon at Parr's Cottage, 1939
Virginia driving Ford V8 van, 1940
Joyce and Renée Easden at Parr's, 1940
Percy Thesiger, Virginia, Alec Thesiger and Tony at Greystones, 1940
Joyce teaching embroidery to Canadian soldiers at Cliveden, 1941
Viola Tunnard and Joyce relaxing with British troops in Baghdad, 1944
Tony and Maria Brassey painting the railings of the Thesiger home, 1945
Rupert Hart-Davies, Celia Johnson and Tony Thesiger, 1945
Joyce and Princess Margaret, St Paul's, 1948
Virginia and Joyce on holiday with Tony and Reggie in Venice, 1949
Joyce and Terry Thomas in *Blue Murder at St Trinian's*, 1946

Section Two

Joyce and Richard Addinsell on *RMS Mauretania*, 1955
Joyce brings her Christmas shopping back from New York, 1957
Joyce helps in a nursery school in Oldham, Lancashire, 1952
Virginia and Joyce in a meadow near Brighton, 1956
Joyce, Reggie and Miriam Grenfell birdwatching in South Africa, 1955
Virginia on her way to Scotland, 1955
Reggie and Joyce and their new Ford Zephyr, 1958
Christmas with the Grenfells, 1961. Reggie, Richard Addinsell, Joyce, Virginia and Victor Stiebel
Joyce rehearses with William Blezard at the Theatre Royal, Haymarket, 1962
Joyce reads Beatrix Potter on 'Jackanory', 1969
Virginia, Joyce and Reggie in Austria with Tony, 1957
Dilys Tugwell on Virginia's balcony at Hyde Park Gardens, 1970
Joyce with her niece and nephew, Sally and Lang Phipps, in their New York flat
Paul Paget marries Verily Anderson, 1971
Joyce, Virginia, Simon Bowes-Lyon and Queen Elizabeth the Queen Mother, 1972
'Face the Music', BBC2, 1976. Joseph Cooper, Walter Todds, Joyce, Robin Ray and David Attenborough
Virginia and Athene Seyler at Joyce and Reggie's golden wedding party, 1979

Acknowledgements

The most important person in helping to produce this book has been Dame Frances Campbell-Preston, Reggie Grenfell's youngest sister. She has provided the background to countless Grenfell and Graham friends and relations. Also Reggie Grenfell's niece, Lady Susan Hussey, who added many footnotes.

I would also like to thank Sir Hardy Amies; Verily Anderson; the staff of the Bodleian Library; Lady Brassey; the staff of the Church of Christ, Scientist in London and Oxford; the staff of Claremont Fan Court School; Viscount Chelmsford; Alison L. Cross of the US Embassy; J.D. Drew; Vere Fane; Wieland Giebel; Sir Rupert and Lady June Hart-Davis; Sheila Haughnessy of A.P. Watt Ltd; Michael Hines of Harrogate Festival; Dr Kim Jobst; Freda Levson; Jenny Naipaul of the *Spectator*; Barry Norman of the Theatre Museum, Covent Garden; Tommy and Mary Phipps; Barry Russell; Nina Thesiger; Heather Thompson of Scale Hill, Loweswater; Wendy Trewin; Dilys Tugwell; John Villiers; Alex Walker; Jean Webster; Vanessa Whinney and Dr Patrick Woodcock for their invaluable help in providing background information.

And Jane Gaul, Judy Hammond, Angela Herlihy, Nick Lee, Carol Milner, Mick Norgrove and Teresa Thompson for their practical assistance.

And Roland Philipps for his editing, even while on paternity leave.

And my family – Charlie, Daisy, Pamela, Orlando and Joe – for their emotional support, cooking and gin and tonics.

The following books have been useful references: *The Noël Coward Diaries*, edited by Graham Payn and Sheridan Morley, Weidenfeld & Nicolson, 1982; *Dictionary of National Biography; Debrett's Peerage* and *Debrett's Handbook; Halliwell's Film Guide* and *Halliwell's Filmgoers Companion; The Letters of Nancy Mitford* and *The Letters of Nancy Mitford and Evelyn Waugh*, both edited by Charlotte Mosley, Hodder & Stoughton, 1993 and 1996; *Whitaker's Almanack*, 1968; and *Who's Who*.

Chronology

Joyce Grenfell	Virginia Graham
1903 Reggie born on 1 November	Tony Thesiger born
1910 Joyce born on 10 February	Virginia born on 1 November
	Lived in West End, London
1914–18 First World War	
Joyce lived in Chelsea	
1917 Joyce and Virginia met	
Joyce to Francis Holland School	
1924 Joyce to Clear View School	
1927 Joyce met Reggie	

Joyce and Virginia to finishing school in Paris

1928 Joyce sent to America to get	
over Reggie	

Joyce and Virginia did debutante season

Joyce Grenfell	Virginia Graham
1929 Reggie and Joyce married	
1935 Virginia and Joyce went to USA.	
	First poem in *Punch*
1936 First poem published	Harry Graham died
1937 Radio critic for the *Observer*	Virginia to Egypt
1938	*Heather Mixture* published
1939–45 Second World War	
1939 First theatre performance:	Virginia and Tony married
Farjeon's Little Revue	
1940 *Farjeon's Diversion*, revue	Virginia joined Women's Voluntary Service
1941 *Farjeon's Diversion*	
*A Letter from Home**	
1942 ENSA tours of UK	
Light and Shade revue	

1943 *This Demi Paradise**
 *The Lamp still Burns**
1944 ENSA tours of India and
 Middle East
1945 ENSA tours of India
 Noël Coward's *Sigh No*
 More revue
1946 UK tour of *Sigh No More*   Left WVS
 *While the Sun Shines**   Articles in the *Daily Sketch*
1947 *Tuppence Coloured*, revue   Film critic for the *Spectator* (to 1956)
1948 *Tuppence Coloured*, the Globe Drama critic for
 *Designing Women**   the *Sunday Chronicle*
 *Alice in Wonderland** (soundtrack)
1949 *Poet's Pub**   *Say Please*
 *A Run for your Money**
 *Happiest Days of Your Life**
 *Scrapbook for 1933**
1950 *Stage Fright**
 *The Galloping Major**
1951 *Penny Plain*, revue   *Here's How*
 UK tour with *Penny Plain*
 *The Magic Box**
 *Laughter in Paradise**
1952 *The Pickwick Papers**
 Penny Plain UK tour
 ENSA tour of Middle East   Film and book critic for *Evening*
     Standard
1953 ENSA tour   Columnist for *Homes & Gardens*
 *Genevieve**   (until 1982)
 The Million Pound Note
 (*The Man with a Million* in USA)* *I Said to my Wife* (translated
     from French)

1954 *Joyce Grenfell Requests*
 the Pleasure, first solo
 show
 *The Belles of St Trinian's**
 *Forbidden Cargo**
1955 *Joyce Grenfell Requests the*
 Pleasure on Broadway

1956 *Joyce Grenfell At Home*, tour of
USA and Canada

1957 *Blue Murder at St Trinian's**
*The Good Companions**
Tour of UK with *At Home*

1958 *Happy is the Bride**

1959

1960

*The Pure Hell of St Trinian's**

1962 *Seven Good Reasons*, revue
*The Old Dark House**

1963 Solo show, London
Tour of Australia and New
Zealand

1964 *The Yellow Rolls-Royce**
*The Americanisation of Emily**

1966 Solo show, London and UK tour
Tour of Australia and New
Zealand

1967 Tour of UK
Tour of Canada and USA

1968 Tour of UK

1969 Tour of Australia

1971 *Face the Music* – until 1975

1973 *Nanny Says*
By Special Request
Retired from stage

Nikki the Sky and the Stars (translated
from French)

Sahara boom-de-ay
A Cockney in the Country
To the Gondolas (translated
from French)
Say I'm in Conference (translated
from French)
Daybreak (translated from French)
The Spanish Tulip (translated
from French)
The Story of the WVS
Everything's too Something
Ready Revenge (translated
from French)

Tony died

*denotes films.

VIRGINIA GRAHAM'S FAMILY TREE

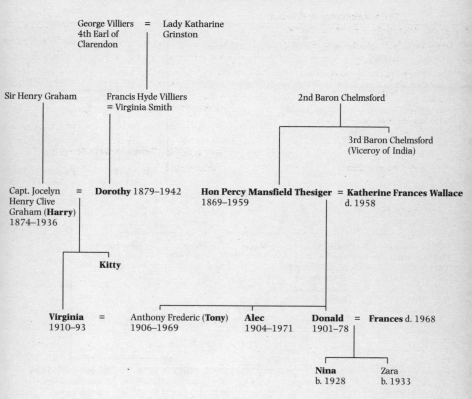

George Villiers
4th Earl of
Clarendon
= Lady Katharine
Grinston

Sir Henry Graham

Francis Hyde Villiers
= Virginia Smith

2nd Baron Chelmsford

3rd Baron Chelmsford
(Viceroy of India)

Capt. Jocelyn
Henry Clive
Graham (**Harry**)
1874–1936
= **Dorothy** 1879–1942

Hon Percy Mansfield Thesiger
1869–1959
= **Katherine Frances Wallace**
d. 1958

Kitty

Virginia
1910–93
= Anthony Frederic (**Tony**)
1906–1969
Alec
1904–1971
Donald
1901–78
= **Frances** d. 1968

Nina
b. 1928
Zara
b. 1933

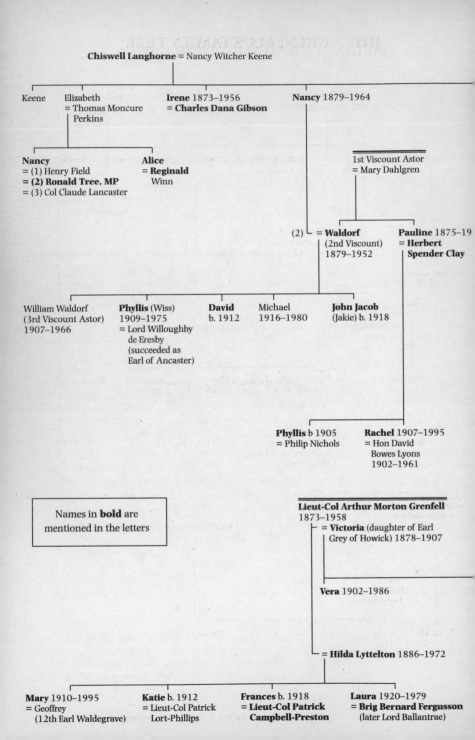

Chiswell Langhorne = Nancy Witcher Keene

Keene Elizabeth **Irene** 1873–1956 **Nancy** 1879–1964
= Thomas Moncure **= Charles Dana Gibson**
Perkins

Nancy **Alice**
= (1) Henry Field = **Reginald**
= **(2) Ronald Tree, MP** Winn
= (3) Col Claude Lancaster

1st Viscount Astor
= Mary Dahlgren

(2) = **Waldorf** **Pauline** 1875–19
(2nd Viscount) = **Herbert**
1879–1952 **Spender Clay**

William Waldorf **Phyllis** (Wiss) **David** Michael **John Jacob**
(3rd Viscount Astor) 1909–1975 b. 1912 1916–1980 (Jakie) b. 1918
1907–1966 = Lord Willoughby
de Eresby
(succeeded as
Earl of Ancaster)

Phyllis b 1905 **Rachel** 1907–1995
= Philip Nichols = Hon David
Bowes Lyons
1902–1961

Names in **bold** are
mentioned in the letters

Lieut-Col Arthur Morton Grenfell
1873–1958
= **Victoria** (daughter of Earl
Grey of Howick) 1878–1907

Vera 1902–1986

= **Hilda Lyttelton** 1886–1972

Mary 1910–1995 **Katie** b. 1912 **Frances** b. 1918 **Laura** 1920–1979
= Geoffrey = Lieut-Col Patrick = Lieut-Col Patrick = Brig Bernard Fergusson
(12th Earl Waldegrave) Lort-Phillips **Campbell-Preston** (later Lord Ballantrae)

JOYCE GRENFELL'S FAMILY TREE

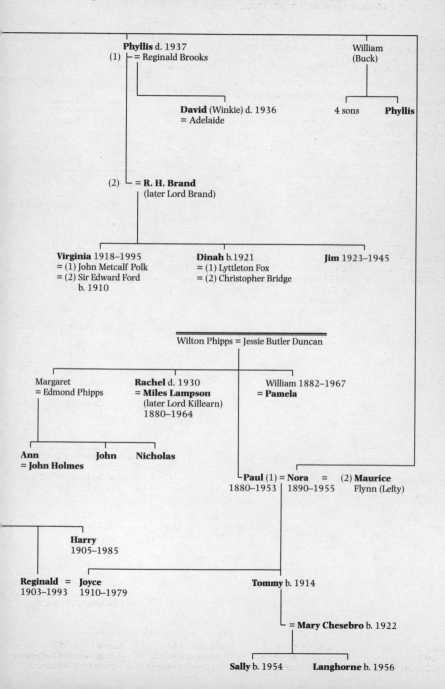

Phyllis d. 1937
(1) ├ = Reginald Brooks

William
(Buck)

David (Winkie) d. 1936
= Adelaide

4 sons   **Phyllis**

(2) └ = **R. H. Brand**
(later Lord Brand)

Virginia 1918–1995
= (1) John Metcalf Polk
= (2) Sir Edward Ford
b. 1910

Dinah b.1921
= (1) Lyttleton Fox
= (2) Christopher Bridge

Jim 1923–1945

Wilton Phipps = Jessie Butler Duncan

Margaret
= Edmond Phipps

Rachel d. 1930
= **Miles Lampson**
(later Lord Killearn)
1880–1964

William 1882–1967
= **Pamela**

Ann
= **John Holmes**

John   **Nicholas**

└ **Paul** (1) = **Nora** = (2) **Maurice**
1880–1953 │ 1890–1955   Flynn (Lefty)

Harry
1905–1985

Reginald = **Joyce**
1903–1993 1910–1979

Tommy b. 1914

└ = **Mary Chesebro** b. 1922

Sally b. 1954   **Langhorne** b. 1956

Preface

Joyce Grenfell, actor, writer, comedian and musician, was admired all over the world. Her autobiographies have introduced the public to her private side – her fifty-year marriage to Reggie Grenfell; her relations on both sides of the Atlantic; her friendship with both famous and ordinary people. Joyce's best friend Ginnie (the writer Virginia Graham, alias Ginny, Gin, Winsome, Aunt Aggy) was less famous, but just as funny and observant. Virginia was the daughter of playwright and comic poet Harry Graham. A prolific journalist, she contributed regularly to *Punch*, was the *Evening Standard*'s film and drama critic and wrote several books.

Joyce and Virginia first met when they were seven, and became close friends in their early teens: they found each other funny and entertaining. When they were both in London, Joyce rang Virginia every morning at 8.20 sharp. When apart, they wrote almost daily. These letters illuminate the lives of the writers from nineteen-year-old girls to Joyce's death at sixty-nine years. Joyce wrote in her diary: 'Gin writes gaily of nothing. She pens a really pretty letter, she really does.'

The love that Joyce and Virginia had for each other is refreshing in its old-fashioned honesty. Few happily married women nowadays would wax so lyrical about each other as Virginia: 'with fondest love and reeking of sentiment' (1937), or Joyce: 'your letter has filled me with glows and heart thumps' (1941). When Joyce married, the friendship didn't falter, nor when Virginia married nine years later. They adored each other's husbands almost as much as their own.

Joyce believed that loved ones should be spared burdens and confidences. However, she and Virginia did write to each other to sort out problems and worries. By the end of a letter they would say, 'Now I've got that off my chest I can see it more clearly and it isn't as bad as I thought.'

They didn't agree on everything: Virginia did not like the countryside, except as a place in which to have house parties and dances. While Joyce enjoyed watching birds, Virginia preferred visiting houses. Virginia grew less fond of the cinema after being film critic for the *Evening Standard* for some years. Joyce preferred making films to watching them.

In her autobiography, *In Pleasant Places*, Joyce wrote:

My only continuous practice of putting words to paper was in the diary-letters I wrote to my mother and in the letters I had written to Virginia ever since we were about fifteen and one of us was away from London. These were unedited communications; they rambled on, were sometimes graphic, occasionally funny, sad, 'holy', thoughtful. Their main merit was their liveliness. Virginia told me they read as I spoke. It is amusing to compare how differently in the war, I described the same incident to my mother in America and to Virginia, then living in Bristol to be near Tony who was with an anti-aircraft battery. Because I knew my Ma was agonised about my being in and near London under the bombing, I was gentle about what I told her, played down the unpleasantness of the raids and made light of the damage done. To Virginia, undergoing her own noisy nights in the West Country, I was not so delicate. You would hardly think the letters were about the same events, or from the same pen.

A few weeks after Joyce's death, Virginia wrote in *Joyce by Herself and Her Friends*:

An irrepressible correspondent, Joyce's pen pals were spread in layers across the globe, and to each she gave her interest and attention. Her letters to me are full of the minutiae of daily living, for she was a great lover of detail. Concurrent with her views on the contemporary scene, or on the plight of friends, or on something fascinating she had read or heard, there would be news of how she and Reggie had gone into Cockermouth at 10.10 a.m. and bought a reel of cotton, some peppermints, another toothbrush and two apples; or of how her hotel bedroom in Leeds was furnished, or what they had had for luncheon in a restaurant in Sydney. These letters, written daily when she was not in London, provide a thorough survey of the world development over the past fifty years in all fields save the political (in which she was only marginally interested), and as fodder for future historians they are surely invaluable. Joyce wrote at great speed and just as she spoke; if anyone wants to know the price of a Melton Mowbray pie in 1962 or what one wore to go to a wedding in 1949, it is all here. Here too, in detail, a whole assortment of people and birds and flowers, all of which she loved. Incidentally, in writing letters she not only demanded of herself full particulars, but also accuracy, once going so far as to put an asterisk against the word Dreft and a footnote reading, 'It wasn't Dreft I bought, it was Flash!'

The success of Joyce's theatre sketches demonstrated her extraordinary ability to listen, observe, and then recreate characters and vignettes. Whether she was portraying Shirley's girlfriend or a keen opera fan, they were funny and often touching, but never unkind. As she matured as a writer and a performer, the sketches often commented on the social injustices of the world. In South Africa she met a young black driver who was held back by apartheid but had discovered that he could travel in his mind with books. This inspired her talking-song 'Nicodemus'. Her own favourite sketch was a sad story told by an old Virginian woman on a rocking chair about her friend 'Lally Tullett'. The sources of many of Joyce's sketches are in these letters: her first Women's Institute meeting; cocktail party characters and a school reunion.

Joyce's letters to Virginia reveal a committed Christian Scientist; and a secret philanthropist; someone who revelled in nature; who was terrified of her audiences, and worried about her increasing fame; depressed by other people's poverty; shocked by lax morals and indignant about selfishness.

Both women were shy about their emotions. Joyce had all the normal feelings of jealousy and irritation. Her autobiographies merely hinted at her Christian Science and never mentioned her generosity, her depressions and her illnesses. Virginia was also a publicly optimistic and happy person who had her private tragedies, including the slow demise of her husband Tony with Alzheimer's Disease.

As a young woman Joyce benefited from the generosity of her aunt, the millionaire Nancy Astor. But she found the strings that were attached to Lady Astor's gifts often took away their pleasure. In 1941 she wrote a sonnet:

> If ever I am rich enough to make
> Generous gestures let me hide my hand.
> Let me give freely lest my giving take
> With it freedom. Not the frailest strand
> Of obligation must go with my gift,
> Nor must the comfort glow of being kind
> Be used to lend a foolish head a lift.
> Grant I may bring a clear and seeing mind
> To work in wisdom, giving with a touch
> So light that never breath of power blow
> Across the crystal of my sharing much
> That is lovely. Pray I may mark and know:
> Beauty dies like linnet in a cage,
> Beneath the bruising hand of patronage.[1]

Joyce kept to her word, and Virginia had the same philosophy. Neither of them expected praise or publicity for their generosity. Joyce and Reggie supported several nephews and nieces through school and bought houses and dishwashers for friends. Virginia had few relations, so she spread her wealth among friends and her servants' families. Before Joyce earned her own money, Virginia would surprise her with cheques to tide over difficult times, enable a treat or even keep Joyce's early shows afloat.

Joyce didn't lend money – she gave it, and then no more was to be said about it. When my mother was widowed with five children, Joyce took us on. Ready cooked meals were left on the doorstep, or she'd whip round the kitchen on the way to a performance, and she had us all over for Christmas. Her Christmas presents were carefully chosen to suit each person (and her lists ran to at least a hundred people). Usually she gave my sisters and me sensible cardigans from Marks and Spencer's, but one Christmas Joyce realised that what I really wanted was a frilly frock from Dickins & Jones. To my delight I got it – but she had cut out the label and put the frock in a C&A bag!

Joyce and Virginia enjoyed being traditional wives to Reggie and Tony, who were both well off. But both women were grateful for the financial independence that their own incomes brought them. 'Thank goodness I don't have to ask a man before buying anything,' wrote Virginia after buying an eighteenth-century desk while out looking for a table lamp.

Neither woman was able to have children. Although sad at first, they both became grateful for the opportunity to develop their own careers. They both started writing short stories and articles in their early twenties, and struggled with rejection slips for many years. Joyce's breakthrough came when she was asked to be the *Observer*'s radio critic – a new idea and considered safe for an unknown young woman. When Joyce began performing in public, Virginia wrote many of her songs.

Joyce was a working woman who travelled all over the world. Her priority was Reggie and their marriage, but when the Second World War broke out she volunteered to entertain troops in the Middle East. Reggie always encouraged her. In later life he accompanied her on theatre tours, acting as her assistant stage manager.

'I really am lucky to have a husband who is, apparently, entirely interested in all my doings, enjoys my career for me and is enthusiastic about all my attempts,' wrote Joyce after fifteen years of marriage.

The war brought out Joyce's ability to organise, but as she grew older she wished she could resist the urge to put things right. Even when she had learned to stop organising people, she could still be quietly bossy with her opinions and advice. Virginia had less of that urge and was happier to muddle along.

Central to the lives of both Joyce and Virginia was their faith as Christian Scientists. They had both been brought up in this faith and apart from a few years of rebellion in adolescence, they adhered to it all their lives. Because it entailed a certain amount of ridicule from others, they rarely spoke about it in public. Joyce enjoyed the acceptance of Christian Science that she found on her visits to the United States.

Christian Science teaches that people are in the image of God and that their identity is spiritual and not material. All creation exists as spiritual ideas, man and woman being the highest, animals and plants being lesser ideas. Christian

Scientists endeavour to live their lives as the reflection of God, and since they understand that God is Love, then only Good is their true reality. So sin and disease are no part of their true selves. A cold or a headache is just a wrong idea – make something of it, and you give it life. People often get the idea that Christian Scientists ignore illness in the hope that it will go away, but they actually strive to overcome sickness by praying to get a clearer view of themselves as the perfect children of a perfect Father/Mother God. God does not get colds or headaches, so neither can his reflection. Christian Scientists are not interested in medical diagnoses, preferring to treat the person with prayer. The nineteenth-century founder of the Church, Mary Baker Eddy, wrote: 'Christianity is the basis of true healing. Whatever holds human thought in line with unselfed love, receives directly the divine power.' Joyce and Ginnie strove to lose their 'false material selves' in order to gain spiritual wholeness. This requires considerable self-discipline: every day a committed Christian Scientist 'does the lesson'. This entails studying prescribed readings from the King James Bible, plus relevant extracts from *Science and Health, Key to the Scriptures*, by Mary Baker Eddy. Sometimes Joyce or Virginia commented on the difficulty in understanding the message of the lesson. Church services led by elected lay members would usually clarify the lesson. Joyce attended First Church of Christ, Scientist in Sloane Street and Virginia attended Eleventh Church near Edgware Road.

Non-Christian Scientist friends of Joyce or Virginia would sometimes ask to be cured of painful or chronic illnesses. Reluctantly they would be told that little could be achieved without belief, and hard work. It saddened both women that few of their close friends and neither of their husbands were Christian Scientists. Virginia gave a lot of time to Church work: administrative meetings, arranging flowers and staffing the Reading Room. Joyce and Virginia were comfortable in Anglican churches – which share many hymns – but were suspicious of Roman Catholics.

Joyce and Virginia were both tall, elegant women who liked to dress well. Joyce always smelled fresh and soapy and never had that cloying over-perfumed smell that children dread kissing. Her skin was as soft as a kid glove. The only clue to her theatrical profession was her eye make-up – not heavy, but worn every day. Joyce's hair, which she called Maud after Queen Victoria's granddaughter, was very fine and silky. She wore it in an original and distinctive style – fringe, short on top and a bun at the back. She once told me that when it was loose she could sit on it.

Virginia was described by Joyce in *In Pleasant Places* thus:

A recent objective scrutiny of Virginia's appearance confirmed that her always attractive rounded face, with a finely wrought nose that tilts at the tip, blue eyes that go up at the corners and eyebrows that put in the expression as she thinks and speaks, is still evident. The mouth is well-drawn, slightly, charmingly crooked and has the lower lip that I was once told signified a performer – which Virginia isn't. She is the least dramatic person I know. Now that I have looked more clearly at my oldest and dearest friend I see that her appearance presents a restoring kind of comfort, a sense of confidence without hauteur; and with her great height she has become a most handsome woman. Feature by feature she is not conventionally beautiful, but the whole, the invisible and the visible, has something more than physical beauty in it.

In January 1939 Joyce wrote:

Riding up Regent's Park in a bus on my way to lunch with Ginnie I made a mental list of the things I don't know how other people manage without.
    Christian Science
    A husband like mine
    Virginia's London flat to soar up to for warmth, rest and cuppers.
    With, of course, Ginnie there
    A raccoon coat
    A René [Joyce's cook]
    Music.

Joyce believed that 'friendship is the most precious privilege that this earthly experience can offer'[2] and in Virginia she had a true friend.

[1] *Turn Back the Clock*, Joyce Grenfell's best monologues and songs, Macmillan, 1983.
[2] *In Pleasant Places*, p. 241.

Editor's Note

Joyce and Virginia kept nearly all their letters. Sometime in the 1970s, Joyce sorted both sets of letters into bundles bound with string. Virginia put them in boxes stamped 'The Mayfair Laundry – box charged 45/- if not refunded' and they sat in her cellar, getting a bit damp, until 1995.

Virginia's heir, on hearing that I was interested in writing a book about the unknown side of Joyce Grenfell, suggested I read them. The letters revealed that there was no need to write a book about the inner Joyce: she had done it herself. There are nearly 4,000 letters from Joyce to Virginia and over 2,000 from Virginia to Joyce.

These letters begin in 1929, when they were nineteen years old and Joyce was just engaged to Reggie. They continue for fifty years right up to a few days before Joyce's death in November 1979. In the early days, sending letters was a fast and efficient business: there were five deliveries to homes a day. A letter posted at breakfast-time reached its destination by tea-time. In spite of the telephone, Joyce preferred letters for communicating events, feelings and ideas. Sometimes they wrote to each other to comment on a telephone call.

Any collection of letters is a haphazard record of a life – these as much as any. When they could, Joyce and Virginia met or telephoned each day. Only when they were separated, or had something special to say, did they write. They admit that their letters contain things they could not say out loud – their mutual admiration or gratitude for surprise presents.

Some of the pre-war and wartime letters have been lost. During the war Virginia's home was bombed, and she moved house several times. However two million words survived and the biggest problem was what to leave out. I have removed most of the daily weather reports, the references to their bowels and menstrual cycles, the menus and flower arrangements of every meal eaten, what every woman wore and daily comments on *The Times* crossword and the Christian Science daily lesson. Where initials were used for people's names I have supplied them in full. If a person appears once only they are explained in a footnote. Frequent characters have a biographical note on pages 483–6. A few people remain a mystery.

The Joyce Grenfell archives held in Esher, the published books of Joyce and Virginia, and interviews with surviving friends, relatives and colleagues have served to fill in gaps about personalities and events. Missing dates from footnotes are those of entertainers, noble ladies or Christian Scientists who do not record their birth dates.

The letters from Joyce to her mother – *Darling Ma* – were published in 1988 and her wartime diaries – *The Time of My Life* – in 1989. These letters between Joyce and Virginia, covering a much longer period, have never been published before.

Janie Hampton
Oxford, 1997

Introduction
1910–29

Joyce Grenfell was born in London on 10 February 1910. Her father, Paul Phipps, was educated at Eton and Oxford, and worked as an architect in the practice of Sir Edwin Lutyens. Joyce's mother, Nora Langhorne, was born in Virginia, USA, the youngest of the eleven children of a self-made millionaire.

Paul's father was English and his mother American, so Joyce was three-quarters American by birth, and English by upbringing and residence. By the time she was four years old she had crossed the Atlantic six times.

Joyce and her younger brother Tommy grew up in a happy, stable home in an eighteenth-century house in Chelsea, London. They had a nanny called Lucy who then became their nursery-governess, supervising school homework, piano practice and bedtime.

Joyce's father taught his children self-reliance and an appreciation of art and music. From the top of a No 11 bus he pointed out the notable buildings, while she eavesdropped on the passengers' conversations.

Joyce was stage-struck at the age of seven when she went to see a wartime revue at the Hippodrome. Her Granny Phipps also lived in Chelsea, and her six indoor staff provided Joyce with her first audience. They felt obliged to applaud her songs, riddles and conjuring tricks.

A plump, gawky little girl, she really wanted to be a ballet dancer. She practised in secret with Schubert on a wind-up gramophone, though never progressed beyond hanging on to the table edge. By the age of twelve, she was in love with both Noël Coward and Ivor Novello and wanted to be an actress. She did not actually want the *job* of acting, she just liked the look of the chocolates and parma violets they brought to her glamorous mother.

Lucy stayed until Tommy went to prep school and Joyce went to Clear View, a Christian Science boarding school, where she won a certificate for elocution and cried when she was rejected by the tennis team. At seventeen, Joyce was sent to Mlle Ozanne's, a 'finishing school' in Paris where she learned the skills needed to acquire a well-bred husband: needlework, hosting a dinner party, good conversation and French.

Virginia Graham was born on 1 November 1910 in London. Her father was

Harry Graham, a successful playwright and lyricist. She had a half-sister Kitty Fraser by the first marriage of her mother Dorothy.

Virginia and Joyce first met in the summer of 1917 when they were six and seven. Their parents were tennis- and bridge-playing friends who often stayed at Cliveden, the home of Joyce's aunt Nancy Astor in Buckinghamshire. It was not until their early teens that they became 'staunch and everlasting friends', sharing a sense of humour and a love of observing people.

Dances were hard work for both Joyce and Virginia. Joyce learned to dance on the arm of her father. He and Waldorf Astor introduced the daring 'reverse waltz' to the ballrooms of London. Mothers warned their daughters about the men who changed direction while spinning. But Joyce was too tall and gawky for most young men and Virginia was too shy. They spent a lot of time in the ladies powder room or watching the others dancing. They had little idea about kissing, and even less about sex.

In 1957 in a BBC radio series called *The Laughtermakers*, Joyce and Virginia talked about their childhood:

Joyce: As a family we laughed a great deal – always good-natured laughter. But I hadn't realised then, as I did so clearly later on, that making people laugh is the greatest possible luxury. My mother and I used to play at 'Ladies' and talk in various voices to each other from when I was quite small. But I never had the remotest idea of going into the theatre. When I did eventually become an actress I'd never been on the stage in my life – not even as an amateur. I knew I had quite a knack of imitating people, talking like them, and so on: but that was all. Those imitations used to make my mother and our friends in Chelsea laugh: friends like Virginia, who has her own special kind of fun and is one of the cleverest humorous writers we have.

Virginia: That's a matter for argument. But it is true that I've known Joyce Grenfell since we eyed each other suspiciously at the same parties. I didn't get to know her really well until we were thirteen or fourteen. She was so lucky to have been born into a gay, light-hearted and very unpompous family.

As a teenager she was a stout, upstanding child – big for her age, well, *fat* really. It didn't in the least deter you from impersonating Pavlova. Do you remember, Joyce?

Joyce: In a pair of red bedroom slippers! I was rather good.

Virginia: Even then she was always passionately interested in people: and I don't necessarily mean people she knew, but people she met on buses or in the street. She was a terror for listening to other people's conversations – and still is.

Joyce: I'd have you know this is my *friend*.

Virginia: In those leisurely days we used to go to rather a lot of matinées.

Joyce: Rather a lot! You had some fantastic record.

Virginia: One year I went to eighty-seven. Anyhow, we used to sit in the pit and before we went we would always keep up our strength with a lunch of poached eggs and baked beans at a Lyons Corner House. Of course, we were at the age when girls got rather intense and discussed with their intimate friends things that were worrying them. Subjects like God, and the problem of 'What's it all *for?*' But so often, just as I was embarking on a profound metaphysical argument, Joyce would say: 'Did you hear what she said – that woman behind us?' She hadn't been listening at all and I would get fearfully cross. After tea she'd recite the balcony scene – a very plump Juliet leaning over the banisters.

There were *some* signs that she was going to be a singer – at least she was always singing. We never went away for a holiday or for the weekend without first making quite sure we had packed our ukeleles. One of my cherished memories is of Joyce singing like Evelyn Laye in *Bitter Sweet* to the strains of her uke. She would, at the drop of a hat, imitate any one of the stars at the time – Dorothy Dickson, Jessie Matthews and so on. But I wouldn't say that Joyce impressed me then as someone who was going to be 'musical' in the sense that she would ever sing well, or broadcast and make records. She used to play the piano, but only knew one tune properly.

We never really lost sight of each other. We still go out together – only now we take our husbands with us. We stayed fast friends even when Joyce married, and went off to live in a little cottage in the country.

To me, Joyce has always been the old reliable: exactly the same since I first knew her. She is both good and funny. This is a very rare combination and a very good thing for a friend to be. Even in her extreme youth, and youth is often cruel, when she took people off – which she did a great deal – it was always without a trace of malice. I don't know how to put it, but she gives you that sort of 'safe' feeling.[1]

The friendship of Joyce and Virginia was such that neither could imagine life without the other. They probably wrote to each other as schoolgirls, but those and all Virginia's between 1929 and 1936 are lost. The first letters to have survived are from when Joyce was first married.

[1] *The Laughtermakers and the Art of Joyce Grenfell*, produced by Tom Ronald, transmitted on the BBC Home Service, 26 March 1957.

1929

~~~

April 1929

11 Gloucester Place
London[1]

Darling Joyce,
   As you know, I am a woman of few words as regards feelings – and
so I can't possibly tell you how incurably pleased I am about your
engagement. Somehow, I feel just a tiny bit sad too, because, although I
know there can be no real 'parting of the ways' between us, I can't help
realising that in this new life of yours, then the innumerable little joys
and secrets none of your girlfriends will be able to share – and indeed,
why shouldn't there be? I hope you feel just a spot sorry too, at leaving
us plodding round the ballrooms, casting despairing glances at eligible
young men.
   When I see you, I shan't be able to say anything I want to – but
you know exactly how I feel about Reggie – and forsooth, about your
own sweet self; and so take it for granted that I'm *terribly happy* that
you should be happy & forgive me for my inability to express myself in
suitable words.
   With fondest love and reeking with sentiment, yrs Gin

[1] The Graham family home in the West End of London.

Joyce and Reggie first met at her aunt's home, Ford Manor, in Surrey. Joyce was
seventeen and Reggie a trainee chartered accountant aged twenty-three. Joyce's
father had been at school with Reggie's uncles and he was startled by Reggie's
likeness to them. Not handsome, but charming with a delightful smile. During 1928
they met at dances and weekend house parties. When Joyce's parents realised their
attraction they packed her off to stay with her aunt Irene Gibson in America. Joyce
was considered too young for commitment. Joyce pined for Reggie and when she
came back he proposed – or at least wrote to her with the two reasons why he
could *not* marry her: he had no money and no prospects. Joyce replied she could
wait for ever. They waited until 12 December 1929.
   Joyce and Reggie were married on a cold, blustery day at St Margaret's Westminster
by the Bishop of Bradford. Joyce's dress was made by the family dressmaker and she
wore it with velvet evening sandals brought from America. *The Times* reported that
'her tulle was held by a halo of green leaves and orange blossom.' Virginia and three
of Reggie's five sisters were among the fifteen bridesmaids, wearing dresses designed

1

by Joyce – white velvet with long medieval sleeves lined in green, fastened at the back with green ribbon streamers. Of the 400 guests who attended the reception at the Astors' London home in St James's Square, over half had titles.

Reggie Grenfell came from a large family. His mother, Lady Victoria Grey, died when he was only five, leaving Reggie, Harry and their sister Vera. His father, Lieutenant-Colonel Arthur Morton Grenfell, a financier, then married Hilda Lyttelton, and they had four more daughters. Hilda brought them all up with equal devotion. She was beautiful, tough and usually got what she wanted but was neither a wicked stepmother nor a wicked mother-in-law. Joyce and Hilda soon became not only friends but truly devoted. Joyce felt that she got on well with all her in-laws because they liked each other, so life with them was 'restful and nourishing'.

Joyce's life as a young wife consisted of entertaining, visiting, parties, shopping and dancing. Reggie had been promised a good job, but as with so many men during the depression of the 1930s, it never materialised. He was lucky to have work as a junior accountant in the City and the newly weds got by with help from relatives.

1930

10 January 1930

Hotel Wardaus
Sils-Maria
Engadine

Darling Ginnie,

Your very nice letter has just arrived and has filled me with glows and heart-thumps.

Reggie has passed his exam – ain't it swell – and now we are all set for a Rolls. So if you see a rather prosperous looking lady dressed in Chanelish clothes alighting from a train in about ten days' time you will say, ah ma, an erstwhile mate now doomed to riches. But you'll be wrong sister, mighty wrong.

It is with a good deal of sadness that I think of you. Because where you really ought to be is here with us all. You'd be very funny on skis, ducks, as am I. The sight of the slightest decline in the ground makes me swallow hard and-know-that-God's-arms-are-round-about-me, and then I shut my eyes and go bum. If you were here we could plod hills hand in hand and slither down gracefully – till comes a corner – and then suck a whack as down we'd come.

The hotel is rich and big and awfully nice. 'Now I'm in Love' oozes out of the phonograph or talking machine.

There is a huge girls' schools here from Lausanne. They are supposed to talk French all the time and this is the sort of thing you hear in the passage – 'Betty avait vous voo my writing case je l'ay laysay don the lavabo et maintenont sayt partee completely.' A Canadian girl was skiing very fast down a steep hill and tripped and fell head first in the snow. There was a good deal of consternation and some people hurried towards her to help. She emerged and said, obeying all school rules – 'Il y a un trou là.'

Oh, life's swell if you don't weaken.

We dance of a night and Reg and I created a sensation by dancing the tango! And Tom and I jazz 'em up hot and don't mean maybe. We skate but *leetle* because you can do that in London – a big town full of nondescript people and nobility where you can go to museums or cinemas if you pay enough. How is your father, your mother, your sister and the flea that hides in your vest?

Don't you hate paper that's folded queer?

16 January 1930   Engadine

Darling Ginnie,

So you've been reading Katherine Mansfield[1] too. Isn't it all marvellous. That girl could certainly wield a pen and convey all the right ideas. She seems to me to be the perfect medium to all my own ideas that I've longed to be able to express. I almost know her letters by heart having read them several times over. At the early age of twelve I was given *Dove's Nest* and I used to try and understand what was obviously marvellous but seemed odd. There's something awfully lump-in-the-throat about every word she utters. I'd love to have known her. She did so struggle against God to be with Him. I was once told that she could have been healed of her 'wing trouble' but that she would let things slide, always believing that things couldn't be as bad as they seemed and yet not doing anything to stop them. She never gave up hope.

Such a lovely humour. What about this, apropos of the bright young writers – 'the trouble is that nobody will ever kick their little derrieres for them because they haven't got 'em to kick – seulement deux globes d'ivoire.' Vulgar but so neat. She loves a good W.C. joke and yet can just fill a page with more sheer beauty than anyone I know.

Isn't it funny how we all allow the crowd to pick our great men for us? One feels almost apologetic in saying that Katherine Mansfield gives one more pleasure than any one other person. But it's true and so says all of us.

You will wonder what bug has bit your old gel friend. Just a cold cold night and the world made more beautiful with heavy snow than anything ever has been. It's funny, but there's no one – not even anyone – that I could write what I really feel of to – but you. It's a pretty big compliment because I sometimes get so constipated with things I *must* say or bust and you're the only crittur I can say 'em to. It's queer that. But you know how much I love and adore Bungs[2] – well I can't tell her somethings because she can't give 'em back. I feel they've gone right away when I've said 'em, and with toi – I just don't know but they seem to revolve so nicely and warmly and gain such a lot on their circular route.

O how I do wish I could write. I hope to one day when I've provided a suitable family for R.P.G. and can lay aside the last layette with a sigh. I shall then buy me a luverly small room somewhere where sun tickles up everything but don't hurt me eyes and then I shall write on and on and on. And some will be so bad and now and again I hope a little bit of what I mean to say does appear. Then I shall take me first money and spend it all on movies for me and you and Reggie in our old ages.

I think perhaps you may burn this letter. It's written after dark and I just go on saying things that have probably embarrassed you and will do so in the future. So just give it a last look and plop! into the fire it shall go, and think of us before and not all loose tongued. Aren't people funny.

I'm longing to see you. We get back tea-ish on Monday. We're going to Wilts to stay with an uncle and an aunt for the Bowood dance on Friday. May't be fun.

From your loving little niece Aggie.

[1] New Zealand writer of the Bloomsbury Group (1888–1923). Author of *The Garden Party*, 1922.
[2] Catherine Fordham (1910–69), a school friend.

1931

From the age of thirteen to sixteen Joyce attended Clear View, later renamed Claremont Fan Court School, a Christian Science girls' boarding school. In 1931 she attended a reunion, with a foretaste of St Trinian's . . .

9 April 1931   36 Chesham Place, SW1[1]

Darling Ginnie,

We spent the afternoon with Bungs who was her nicest self and we chose her a little navy number for all occasions at Rita where I was trying on my useful thin wool [suit]. Aunt Nancy called me to meet her at Chez Beth[2] this morning for she had found a dress for me. And it's a beauty. It's pale blue moire faille and is stately and frigid. I'm dying to wear it.

On Sat. I got awfully over excited and went down to Claremont where I played left back for the Old Girls vs. the Present Girls in the hockey match. We old girls borrowed togs and I was a plitty picksher in my borrowed plumes. The knickers were too long and the tunic didn't help at all. I played with frenzied enthusiasm during the first half and attacked wildly with both eyes tight shut. But 'twas of no avail for the present girls, organised little blighters, had it all over us and knocked up 9 goals to our 0. I didn't do much in the second half, but an old friend whom I'd not seen in 8 years was goalkeeper so we leaned against the posts between attacks and asked each other questions. After high tea with meringues we had an abridged version of the *Mikado* done by the Dramatic Club which includes both staff and girls. So it was fun to see the headmistress in a leading part and dear old Ebby who took stinks [chemistry] and gum [gym] as Ko-Ko. It was surprisingly good and un-school-girlish, well rehearsed and thankfully swift.[3]

I've found a lovely Handel called 'Spring is Coming' which is better than it sounds.

I *must* go, drat it.

[1] Reggie's parents' home.
[2] Nancy's dressmaker who was employed to copy the designer models. A dress cost £1.10 to be made and a coat cost £2.
[3] In 1980 Claremont School built a theatre in Joyce's memory.

Avril le dix-neuf [1931]   21 St Leonard's Terrace
                                                                              Chelsea, SW3[1]

Darling Ginnie,

On Tuesday we went up to house warm Maria's[2] flat. We cooked bacon and eggs and ate largely of bread and cheese. We took Maria bouquets of cauliflower, carrot, spring onions, radish and lettuce instead of flowers, and Pen gave her a cucumber surrounded by onions and a lettuce leaf. Very taste-full. Afterwards we went to a flick in the King's Road.

This is a lousy letter. Goodbye, ducks. Please hurry home. You're missing England's Spring.

[1] Joyce and Reggie's wedding present from Nancy Astor and Joyce's parents – a four-bedroomed house in Chelsea.
[2] Mary Brassey (1910–88), Christian Scientist and lifelong friend.

4 November 1931   St Leonard's Terrace

Darling Ginnie,

I've been having a nawfully [*sic*] exciting time with a *Daily Mail*
man who came with his little camera and took pickshers of my ouse.
He was a dear little man, and talk – he never stopped. 'The *Daily
Mail* is a rotten paper,' he said, 'but that's not saying it's not done the
public some good, beneficial good. Think of the Yadil scandal – why I
remember – it was before our summer holiday, and we set a store by
our summer holiday, my boy, he was only a little chap then – nine or
ten – then had measles at his school, well, I said to the wife, what about
Yadil. Do you know it never did him a bit of good, not a bit – he had
measles same as all the other kiddies had. But then the *Daily Mail* put a
stop to it. Uncovered everything – it was all a lot of onion water. If the
Mail hadn't uncovered everything people'ud still be putting studd down
'em. I *must* get on with this study.'

And he replaced his spectacles and dived under the black velvet to
see what he was doing and came up a moment later with his back hair
all on end, like a little boy's.

As a matter of fact this letter has a purpose. Will you come to
dine here next Monday – latish – After we're going on to the Bryan
Guinnesses[1] but not till 11.15.

[1] Poet, novelist and playwright (1905–92), later Baron Moyne. Diana Mitford's first ·
husband, 1929–34, before she married Oswald Mosley.

[December 1931]   St Leonard's Terrace

Darling Ginnie,

I've just seen a pretty good thing in the shape of an almond
tree against the glow of the West End as I came in from the
King's Road.

That's all, really. Only there are so few people I can tell this to
without blushing that I had to put it down quickly before I became
ashamed. It was black – not one single leaf on it.

I went to the cinema alone, as is my wont, to see Gertie Lawrence[1] in
a picture called *The Battle of Paris* – I can't think why. It is rather fun.
She looks supreme and wrings the heart a good deal in a high necked
white blouse and beret.

Must post this quick or it will never go.

[1] English actress (1898–1952) and close friend of Noël Coward.

<u>1932</u>

Joyce and Reggie went by Atlantic liner to see her mother Nora in the States. Before they married, Joyce's father described Nora as 'very original, has her own ideas and looks at things from her own point of view . . . extremely sensitive and artistic person . . . She has an observation which is quite uncanny.' She was the kind of woman whose arrival made any party a success. Nora gave Joyce a taste for light, sunshine colours and fresh flowers. The Phipps marriage started to crumble early on. Nora's positive outlook had a downside – she always expected happy endings, so did not plan the middles. She imagined bills paid themselves and that taxis were provided just for her, even to pick up her shopping. Because she forgave everyone, she assumed they would too.

Nora stayed with Paul until 1930 when she ran away with Maurice 'Lefty' Flynn, a glamorous American. Joyce and Reggie were on their honeymoon and had to return to cope with the great trauma. A year later Nora and Lefty married and moved to Connecticut, USA. A former film actor and football hero, he was called Lefty because of his left-footed kicking skills. At first Joyce was resentful and critical of her stepfather, but she gradually became fond of him, because he made her laugh and made her mother happy.

22 June 1932   Greenwich Conn USA

Darling Ginnie,

Here peace reigns. We both get deeper and deeper in colour and I'm losing weight. We live and bathe and play tennis and dine and go to the movies, and I've bought some pretty dashing cotton frocks in the Sales. Clothes are dirt cheap here though expenses are *very* high, 15/- for an ordinary shampoo and set in the village here! But it's all fun and you'd love it for a holiday, as we do. People are so nice to us and we go from house to house getting more and more spoilt.

There's a sort of pre-English Jazz movement on here. They all rave over Mona Lisa and Blase and the like. All the people we adore on the gramophone are daily on the radio. It's such fun.

Last night Winkie[1] took us to dine to see *Show Boat*. It's been revived in a grand manner. Robeson[2] and masses of real niggers with grand voices. Helen Morgan – of gramophone – sings the part of Julie and couldn't be more fascinating. They say she's a dope fiend and of course that adds to the glamour. Anyway she's very good, and Norma Terriss who plays Magnolia is really quite superb. A lovely voice, figure, and delicious face, and she looks right in all the periods beginning with the bustle, going through 1910 up to the present day.

I saw a humming bird the other day. Thrilling, about the size of a large butterfly but a real bird. Nature is certainly interesting.

I'm longing to see you, blessed female, soon but I hate the thought of settling down again for goodness knows how long. I've missed you a good deal and it's the truth. You laugh so much at all that's damn silly and love all that's fun.

This is a real heat haze letter.

[1] David Brooks, Joyce's first cousin, Aunt Phyllis's son.
[2] Paul Robeson (1898–1976) Afro-American singer.

3 July 1932

700 Acre Island
Dark Harbor
Maine

Darling Ginnie,

Whew! if you could only see this island. Rocky and wild with spaces here and there for fields, and trees in blobs and on the edge. The house is comfy to a degree and the food perfect, and it all belongs to Aunt Irene[1] and Uncle Dana Gibson.[2] It's 45 minutes in a motor boat from the mainland and the sky is windy and air fresh and we all feel super.

This morning R. and I went for a walk over the back of the Island and home by the rocks and beaches. Very perilous in places and fat old Fipps[3] needed a good deal of assistance from her man. But it helped the appetite and how. After chicken broth, chops and strawberry ice cream I'm feeling pretty good. And this borrowed fountain pen fairly slips over these dazzlin' blue papers.

We are browner than is decent, and I've cut a fringe. It looks so queer just now with the wind in it. But in towns and drawing rooms it has the real 1880 flavour and adds dignity to the profile.

Oh dear, oh dear, we've only got $3\frac{1}{2}$ more weeks. It's such fun travelling. Broadens the mind I feel, and besides we've had such kind friends that we've only had to pay for one bus ticket from Greenwich to Providence at 6 dollars for two the whole time we've been here. We've motored the rest and seen 12 States in the doing. From Virginia right up North to Maine. Fetch your Atlas, little Gertrude, and you shall see where your friends are, one, two three!

This must cease. It is really only to give you love, and slight news. Mama goes on the radio next Thursday to sing. We are all thrilled, none so much as she. Tomorrow is the 4th of July. Not a tactful moment for us, but we'll hide while the fireworks go down and pretend to be nonshallont [nonchalant].

[1] Joyce's mother's older sister.
[2] Irene's husband Charles Dana Gibson was a society portrait painter.
[3] Joyce's maiden name was Phipps.

Joyce returned to London with no ambitions other than 'a lovely padded rut with a salary at one end and a pension at the other. No worries and no adventures.' Reggie's salary was not large, so Joyce designed Christmas cards which she sold to W.H. Smith.

Before the Second World War servants were still the norm in Britain. Joyce and Reggie felt very progressive when Joyce's father designed a staff flat for their two full-time maids. They had a bedroom each and their own bathroom and sitting room. Only when the Grenfells visited the house after the war did they notice how small and cold the rooms were, and that neither the bathroom nor the sitting room had windows.

27 October 1932   St Leonard's Terrace

Darling Ginnie,

I'm nearly dotty, really nearly dotty. For three solid days I wrote a story – it's not too bad and you shall read it – and then feeling wuzzy and feeble I discover that Miss Ivy, the house-parlour-maid here, is in the family way and with no gold band to make the condition respectable. She hasn't told me but I've discovered it and it's all too awful. The cook tells me she is going to give me notice (Ivy I mean) so I shall wait for that, as Heaven knows, I can't cope with girls who go with boys, who don't do right by our Nell. I hope she will get married as soon as she leaves. But oh, aren't people bloody and fools and back to bloody again.

My cook is on the verge of a nervous upheaval, for she has been bottling this all up for weeks. I think Ivy's about 6 months gone, as they say. This is no letter for a virgin as you, darling, but I must tell someone. Don't go telling it though, please. It looks so sort of sordid and awful. I expect we've not been strict enough but she seemed such a quiet serious sort of girl that I thought her head must be set firm on her square shoulders. Oh blast, blow, blast.

P.S. I've purposedly refrained from writing to you what I felt for you re. Dick. You know how very much I care and I can't bear to see you miserable. It must be a case of good riddance. You are to marry the world's best man very soon, I'm sure. Have a good time and don't be sad.

1933

13 August and a Sunday, 1933   Warmwell House
                                                           Dorchester
                                                           Dorset[1]

Darling Ginnie,
    I came across country. In a way five train changes are less boring
than one long sit. The company were so very different and I got deeply
attached to two farmers between Taunton and Yeovil. They took me to
their bosoms and we discussed every possible topic including bathrooms.
It took me eight hours to cover 100 miles!
    Here I found various Grenfells of different generations. They have
taken this house with a truly lovely facade but the inside is quite
hopeless and very barely furnished. It belongs to a family with four
beautiful daughters, no money and no sense of cleanliness or taste.
    They inherited this lovely Jacobean home from some cousin and it's
quite out of keeping with our way of living. Dust and cobwebs and
dirt everywhere when we arrived, and all the linen and blankets were
threadbare and the curtains ragged, and yet in the gallery upstairs
is the very latest radio-gramophone with an eight record changer
which costs about £200. They didn't even tidy the drawers before they
left, and there are old stockings, a necklace, hairpins and lipstick all
hotchpotched together in a very nasty way.
    They came over to pick flowers on Friday evening wearing scarlet
trousers and bringing two young men wearing sandals and shorts and
curly hair. Not so tasty.
    I must stop. We are off 'to the sea again, the lonely sea and the sky',[2]
with tea in a basket and rather a damp bathing suit under me arm.
We plunge from the rocks into clear green pools. It really is lovely and
when the boys aren't there bathe naked which after all is the only really
satisfying way to bathe.

[1] House taken by the Grenfell family for a summer holiday.
[2] *Sea-Fever* by John Masefield (1878–1967).

21 September [1933]   St Leonard's Terrace

Darling Ginnie,
    Those gay little sketches made me laugh ever so. Especially the one
entitled 'View under the bed'. *So* bizarre.
    You did ought to take up arting. I showed your work to Mr Gutta[1]

and he said 'Too utterly too and *such* sordid form'. So you see even great minds like Mr Gutta agree with me.

Dear Gutta, he was lying on a mother-of-pearl trombone when he saw your sketches. He finds he can forget himself better that way. He loses himself in the lower notes which issue forth from time to time, as he sleeps with his nose on the mouthpiece and his breathing makes music. Quaint.

I bought 4 tickets for the opening of the new Dietrich[2] film, *Song of Songs* for the night before I sail. John and Nicholas[3] came home from Austria in the same train as Marlene and managed to sit at the table across the aisle from her and they never took their eyes off her. She was younger than she looks on the screen: in fact they were agreeably surprised by her whole appearance. She ate only le Roastbiff and cheese.

There's a joke in the *New Yorker* in the form of a dictionary for the East Side of New York as a result of the Crime Wave. My favourites are –

Guilt = a short pleated petticoat worn by a Scotsman in place of trousers

Foil = to wrap flag close to the mast

Judge = the name of the King of England

Posse = pet name by which you call a cat

Gosh how the pen skids in wet weather. The tea cosy you sent Auntie makes a splendid lampshade. Hardly any light shows at all. Just a little circle which escapes from the bottom. Fancy you making it all by hand. It's everso original making it like a Gladstone bag. And all those flannel labels. Auntie loves her initials.

I'm less actively miserable about going [to USA] and even though the rain is pouring down I'm quite capable of picturing myself on board in a cold grey fog and I don't actually whimper. If I begin thinking of R. sitting here alone and forgetting to buy flowers, mend the fire or even change his library books, I *do* feel queer. But after all 2 months isn't very long and the ecstasy of return will be so terrific that I'm all shaky as I think of it.

You will have a care of R. won't you? You and Maria are about the only females he really likes to see. So do ask him to go movies etc. Try a concert on him for fun. Result not guaranteed.

[1] Spaniel dog.
[2] Marlene Dietrich, German singer and actress (1901–91), born Maria Magdalene von Losch.
[3] Phipps cousins.

Joyce went to America to stay with her mother, accompanied by an eleven-year-old American cousin, Betsy Perkins.

1 October 1933   on board RMS *Majestic*

Darling Ginnie,

It's Sunday afternoon and we've had a huge lunch and now I'm in the tea lounge waiting for that meal. I'm not fat though – I mean I'm not fatter than usual. Sea air makes one hungry, but then exercise should cancel out the eating. 11 times round the deck completes a mile. I've already done a mile and a half and shall do more before bed.

Everyone goes to the movies and so far they have been very unsuitable for the young, being either very sexy or else murder. But I believe they float over Betsy's head, so I just don't discuss them. Yesterday's movie opened in a morgue. Every child in the place was heard asking what a morgue was. I tried to make it sound like a lovely place, but I don't know what Betsy thought.

In the evenings when there are no movies there is racing with toy dogs – a sort of gambling steeplechase. Very dull. We add an hour every day to our clocks, and so Betsy has to stay up to 9.30 to make it really 8.30. She's very sweet and very easy, and I like having her enormously.

Betsy has made a tough pal called Mary with an accent that hurts. They exercise Betsy's dachshund puppy on the toppest deck of all, and then they play patience and ask each other personal questions –

'How late's the latest you've ever sat up?'

'What's your second name?'

'What's your best friend called?'

Half the dining room is divided into Kosher tables, and there are Germans and Russians and two aged French women with very little hair and a lot of silver jewellery.

There was a thrill on Friday morning when a small boy disappeared. Everyone looked for him – sailors, stewards, waiters and passengers. The mother was frantic. He was eventually found playing behind his mother's trunk under her bed. He'd heard everyone calling him but just didn't answer. A clear case for psychoanalysis.

There has also been a whale. I didn't see it. And someone got stuck in the lift.

We make up stories about our fellow passengers and our conversations are dotted with references to 'The fat girl in the Russian blouse', 'The Loving Couple', 'The man Hope refused to dance with'. (She is about 16 and refused a nice young man's invitation to dance by saying 'No thank you'. Poor man, he blushed scarlet and said 'I'm really very nice' and went away, never to reappear on the dance floor!) Then there is 'The man Who Sings' and 'The Monkey faced man'. I sat next to a pudding of a woman at lunch. No bounce to her. A sort of apple that tasted of knitting.

See R and let me know how he is. I miss him so much that I hurt when I think of him. I'm glad I feel that way. He's pretty nice.

10 October 1933

c/o Flynn
Box 942
Greenwich
Connecticut

Darling Ginnie,

Whew! what goings on. The trip really was quite fun. Ma and Lefty were on the dock at New York to meet me. Ma in black velvet hat and coat with gardenias. We caught sight of each other 40 mins. before we could hear each other, for it takes ages to dock a big liner, and we got all worn out with smiling and gesticulating.

After Customs we drove off to the Barclay Hotel where we ate lunch. Just to make me look particularly attractive that day, I had started a noisy and hellish cold. So the nose was a dull rose and the voice thicker than a thief. But Ma and Tommy,[1] who dashed in for five minutes from the *New York Times* on which he works, seemed glad to see me so I was cheered.

This house is delicious. In a wood that is now turning gold and on top of a tiny hill. My bedroom has pink unglazed walls, chintz curtains and a green and white quilt on the bed. A huge cupboard and private bathroom. de Luxe in every detail.

All the friends we made last year came rallying around to see me and all brought flowers and one a bed jacket!

Really America is the most hospitable place on earth. I've been feted like a movie star, and the second evening I'd been here Ma gave a party for me: 24 for supper and silly games afterwards. It was the greatest fun, and some unknown has sent me orchids! I've already been to three other parties in my honour. The food is gorgeous here.

I'm in grave danger of being spoiled and I love it. I miss R. like hell. But I'm happy at the same time and gosh how time flies.

We saw Katharine Hepburn [2] in *Morning Glory* on Sunday evening. You must see it when it comes to London. The film itself is punk, but she is incredible. The girl can certainly act.

Ma is marvellous. Younger than ever, very cosy and miles advanced in [Christian] Science. She has just come in from the garden and is reading the weekly *Daily Sketch*, which was my present to her last Christmas. She says to tell you that if she saw you now she would rush up, put her arms around you, and through long years spent in the wilds would say 'How's tricks?' instead of 'How are you?' Actually she couldn't be more English.

Life is such a bowl of cherries here just now and I'm all of a walnut whirl. Do let me know how R. is.

---

[1] Joyce's brother, four years younger.
[2] American film actress (1907–).

Nora and Joyce went to Virginia, where Nora had been born. Her father's family, the Langhornes, had been established in Virginia since the late seventeenth century and were involved in Virginian politics before the American Revolution. Chillie – Joyce's grandfather – made his fortune building railroads. In 1892 he bought Mirador near Charlottesville – a country estate for hunting, fishing, and entertaining, with plenty of black servants. Granny Langhorne taught herself the piano and to paint and had eleven children. The adult survivors were: Keene, Elizabeth (Lizzie), Irene, Harry, Nancy, Phyllis, William, known as Buck, and Nora, the youngest. Keene and Harry both died young of drink. The six Langhorne sisters were beautiful society belles. Irene married the American artist Charles Dana Gibson and was the model for his portraits of Gibson Girls. Nancy married the millionaire Waldorf Astor, and became Britain's first woman Member of Parliament.

Both Nora's parents died before Joyce was born, but she inherited from her grandmother the ability to sing and play the piano, and determination from her Grandfather Langhorne.

Tuesday, 17 October 1933   537 North Wolfe Street
                                                                    Baltimore
                                                                    Maryland

Darling Ginnie,

Ma and I went down to Virginia on the train to stay for four days for Phyllis Langhorne's wedding.[1]

Virginia was lovely. It's the only part of America that I've seen that strikes me as being solid and with any sort of permanence to it at all. Being settled by the English may have something to do with it. Several of the families down there are still living on the land that was granted to them when Virginia was first settled in the Seventeenth Century. These houses are very lovely: red brick and almost all of them have white pillars on the front. Some still have the furniture and even the doors and mouldings that their ancestors brought with them from England. I'm glad my American blood is Southern. Very very glad. There is something about Yankees which is very hard to get over. Not that they aren't kind and generous: they are, but at the same time they are very worldly. You never get a man in the street up North to call you madam or touch his hat – I mean a working man, a chauffeur or your butler or anyone. They call you 'Mrs Grenfell' as familiar as you please. (I suppose the answer is 'Why not?')

The wedding was quite fascinating. It took about three days to marry Phyllis. For two days before the ceremony there were parties for the bride and what is called the bridal party. This means the bridesmaids, maid and matron of honour, and the corresponding groomsmen. There were two dinners, dances, a luncheon and a tea party. We went to the two dances and I was quite amused to find myself cut in on. And very flattered too. The weddings in the South are the cause of as much wet celebration as possible, and whisky flowed with the usual results. Rather a bore that was. Especially when one saw a lovely young girl really tight and unable to walk. But fortunately neither the bride nor her attendants were that way, though as much cannot be said for the ushers. Very silly and not very attractive.[2]

The actual wedding took place at four o'clock in the garden of the bride's home. It was a glorious day, hot and still and very clear. Uncle Buck's house is white with columns, miles from town.

Do you remember how tiny Phyllis is? Well, she looked like a child of 12 in her wedding dress. It was dead plain, white velvet. Her bridesmaids wore green velvet dresses with big velvet hats and carried enormous yellow chrysanthemums. I know it sounds like Ealing but it really was lovely. I've never seen a garden wedding before. It strikes me as a far better idea than a church one for people who don't actually go to church. There's something very false about Christian ceremony and prayers and bishops and choirs all of a sudden when the bride never goes to church. I agree that one does want to have a little God-ness. Personally I like a lot, but for someone like Phyllis who is naturally religious only in climax situations and who lets Sunday after Sunday go by, a garden wedding is more appropriate.

The bridal procession, headed by 8 ushers in twos, followed by 6 bridesmaids also in twos, and then the matron and maid of honour in single file, and lastly Phyllis on Uncle Buck's arm, came down the front steps of the house, across the lawn to where the flower-built altar stood. The congregation stand on either side of a path marked with white ribbons and baskets of flowers. A four piece orchestra played 'Because' in a whisper during the ceremony.

After the actual marriage there were kisses and congratulations and much toasting. As you may well imagine I was busy with my camera so you will see all the results when I get home.

I miss Reg something cruel. If I allow myself the luxury I can weep without the least effort.

[1] Daughter of William (Buck), Nora's brother.
[2] Joyce, like several of her aunts, was a teetotaller and unsympathetic to alcohol. Drunkenness was 'inexcusable and boring'. As a child Joyce had been terrified by a drunk man lying in the gutter outside Harvey Nichols: she thought immediately of

his children. On special occasions she drank a thimbleful of champagne. Her father gave up drinking during the First World War as an example to his men, and never started again.

2 November 1933   New York

Darling Ginnie,

This is a wonderful place. It's *so* exciting. Lots of it is horrid: the drinking and general public necking, but the youth and vitality of it are both such exciting qualities. And it's such fun to see it as a stranger.

Tommy, mon frère, took me around the town on Tuesday night. We dinner-danced first at his hotel – he lives in a residential part of a huge hotel, and then we went on to see Roland Young[1] in *Her Master's Voice*, which was fun and light and packed with people.

From the dressing room of Mr Young who Tommy knew well in California, we walked a few blocks up Broadway to the Hollywood Restaurant where Mr Rudy Vallee[2] holds sway. This is a huge tough joint. You go up some fairly narrow and definitely tawdry stairs to a huge and rather low room. It's decorated in no taste with a good deal of orange around. There are very small tables packed as closely as possible to each other and the food is terribly foul. The management obviously feel that music and entertainment are more important than victuals. T and I sipped orange juice and let supper go.

But the music –! There was Mr Vallee himself, all curls and shyness and with a lovely voice. There was a floor show which is more like a real stage revue than a cabaret, which began at 12 and went on till 2.45. All of it good. There is a beauty chorus in less clothes than is quite nice. About five different female singers, one serio-light tenor, two marvellous dancers – a man and girl – and numberless tap dancers.

And all around the room were gangsters and their molls. The molls are unique. A tart in England is obvious and yet possible. Over here the molls are different. To start with they belong to one man and they are richly turned out. Nearly all blondes, all beautiful, all with superb figures and the average age about 19. They make up as if they were sitting under the most powerful stage lights and they mostly wear evening hats, tulle and sequins or velvet and aigrettes. They are quite fascinating. Rudy is absorbing too. He's so coolly indifferent with such an obviousness that it's quite fascinating. In fact condescension is the general air. The chorus all dance as if they didn't really have to and have dropping insolent eyelids. It's more fun to watch than a picnic.

Tom and I looked horribly conspicuous, as all the rest were so obviously gangster or Tired Business men or generally toughs. The chorus were nearly naked most of the time and it was such obvious nakedness that one lost interest.

Golly it was funny. And the compere – Host he's called – announced the various girls with 'Ceeum on Foiks, geeve the leettle gel a big hand. Come on – geeve!'

I'm collecting some swell tunes for you, cutes. Have you got 'This is Romance'? It is dandy.

I adore your letters. Keep on.

[1] American actor (1887–1953).
[2] American character comedian (1901–86).

1934

Joyce and Reggie often went with the Grenfell family to Nannau in north Wales which they rented several years running for holidays. Nannau was a large Queen Anne house much loved by all the family. During the Second World War a girl's school was evacuated there.

1 October 1934

Nannau
Dolgelly
N Wales

Darling Ginnie,

I'm pink all over with Pride and Pleasure after reading your lovely letter, and I wish you were here that we might sit in silence to show how much affection we feel, you with a Times Library Book, and I with a humbler W.H. Smith Library book concealing our faces.

The old place ain't the same without you. As soon as the tail light of the Rolls turned the corner the rain came down and stayed down all day and on into the night. And it blew too.

There is a lovely atmosphere of Olde Worlde Butter drops, wool work, knitting and 'One's Company' here. Just what I like.

We took the dogs and R. and I went for a walk around the loch. On our way we found that one of the home farm cows had just, literally just, calved. There stood the offspring, covered in tight black curls and very wobbly at the knees. The Ma looked most surprised and rather proud. If cows have pride.

This afternoon I re-read *Private Lives* and was amazed at its appalling badness. It had no sincerity and no distinction. I think that's Noël Coward's whole trouble. He's not sincere and he's too clever. Then I dipped into a novel, and finally I ended up with the *Ladies Home Journal* which I read from cover to cover.

After dinner we played letter games to soothe us, for at dinner feeling had run sky high on the subject of War and Pacifism. I loathe discussions. I get so over excited and miserable and I almost cry all the time, and that's embarrassing, and I never convey in words what I'm feeling inside. It was most exciting and I got hotter and hotter.

17 October 1934   Eydon Hall[1]
                                                                        Eydon
                                                                        Rugby

Darling Ginnie,

I've just had breakfast in bed (first time for years) and a very hot very deep bath, and I've skimmed *The Times* and scorned the *Mirror*, and now I'm writing to you.

I met old Lady Antrim just inside the Station after you dropped me yesterday (thank you). So we travelled down together in a very shaky Third, plumb over a pair of very loose wheels and full of draughts. There was an elderly woman in with us who made cooing overtures to Gary[2] and tried Dog Conversations with me, but I was mean and wouldn't play.

This house is enchanting. Full of lovely things, light rooms with big windows, great bowls of autumn flowers, and a wireless. I found Aunt Phyl looking very sweet in a childish woolly suit, playing out Bridge problems from *The Times*.

We dined at eight, Aunt P in a pale blue woolly dressing-gown, and I in the old black velvet which has now got a lace collar (left by Grannie) instead of the silver sequins of former years. After I sang a bit, and it felt like making noise under water for there are bookshelves by the piano and they soak up the sound like sponges instead of tossing it from wall to wall, as it was at Nannau.

I was thinking about your not seeing properly and I do seriously think that it's important not to let things rip in [Christian] Science. If you don't meet it alone, get onto a practitioner.[3] Please do. It's awfully silly to wait till it gets really bad before you do anything about it. Don't be a mug, duckie, and do get onto it, won't you? After all, it's only a question of realising that one is Complete. Now, this instant. There's no Perfect State, to be reached ultimately: we must realise it is *now*. Ever Present.

(Are you hot and angry about this outburst? I'm sorry but I do love you and I think you ought to be spanked sometimes, for you are a marvellous person in everything you do and you mustn't let down for a single moment.)

---

[1] Country home of Phyllis, Joyce's aunt (1881–1937) and Bob, later Lord, Brand (1878–1963).
[2] Gary Cooper, a black spaniel dog.

[1] Christian Scientists do not have ordained ministers. Instead they have trained and licensed men and women practitioners to help members of the Church with prayer and understanding.

Tuesday, 23 October 1934   Eydon Hall

Darling Ginnie,

Australia in three days – isn't it incredible?[1] Aunt P. and I listened in to a broadcast from Melbourne and were very much moved.

I spend the morning in re-writing old stories, in trying to feel a little satisfied with any one of them. But somehow after the second reading they all seem hopelessly 'bright' or else desperately dull.

When I see the sun shining on this lovely house, hear the gardener humming while he arranges the flowers for the drawingroom, then I feel I must write. I can observe all right. My mental picture is clear down to the minute pleated underneath of the mushroom I picked yesterday. But when I try to put it into a story, it leaves me blank. I twist my pen, draw daisies up the margin and go in search of an apple. But Golly, how I long to do it.

I've been trying to construct that idea of the conventional family 'going' Bohemian, but it won't be done. Actually it's the sort of thing you could do far better than I can. If you want to use it, please do. While I'm in bed, unhampered by pen and paper, I can visualise the whole thing and I laugh to myself at some of the things I see. But I *can't* tighten it up into words and paragraphs.

This outburst is only for you. I just feel that way today. As I read these two pages through I see the whole thing looks mighty self-conscious; as if I had an eye on my biographer. Anyone would think we had a Shakespeare in our midst! I know that you understand these things and that's why I don't edit my thoughts when I write to you.

Mrs Romilly was here for Sunday. She is Mrs Winston Churchill's sister. A queer cup of tea. Good looking but running to fat, practically a chain smoker, rather sloppy but with alert and somewhat witty mind. Her sons, aged 19 and 16, are both rabid Socialists, and the second one was expelled from Wellington for editing and writing a magazine called *Out of Bounds*. In this paper he advocated Freedom for All. No restrictions of any sort. He's pretty hopeless and entirely lawless, and now, aged 16, he is forbidden to darken his father's door and lives where he can for £1 per week. Quite impossible he sounds and his mother agrees that he is and, what is more, that he always has been. He's brilliantly clever and writes really well. But no fun to have around the house.[2]

Mr Beud-Smith, about 50, a bachelor, is coming to stay today. He's a musician and has a wide repertoire, which he renders rather woodenly but very correctly, sitting bolt upright at the piano and never showing any expression in either his face or his fingers. His love of Bach and Handel endears him to me. And *they* sound almost as well without expression. He also composes delicate little imitations in the style of John [*sic*] Sebastian B[ach] or even Wagner. He will play as long as is required and is very obliging in that way.

I've sung quite a lot since I came here. I found that by turning my back on the absorbent books I could get clear sounds.

Aunt P. has arrived from her hut, hatted and caped in red tweed, date pre-war – we are going for a short walk. This conversation has been awfully one-sided. Do you mind these rather egotistical frothings?

P.S. Aunt P is sculpting me while I read to her. So far it's a very fat girl but she says that time will fine her down.

[1] Twenty aeroplanes had raced from Norfolk in England to Melbourne in Australia. The winners were C. Scott and T. Campbell-Black who flew 11,300 miles in two days and forty-eight minutes.
[2] Esmond Romilly (1918–41) and Giles Romilly (1916–67) were notorious for their socialist and pacifist views and published *Out of Bounds* 'against Reaction, Militarism and Fascism in Public Schools'. They both fought in the Spanish Civil War. Esmond married Jessica Mitford (1917–96) and they emigrated to the USA in 1939 where he worked in a bar and wrote articles. In 1941 he joined the Canadian Air Force and was killed in action. Giles was a prisoner of war in Colditz.

9 November 1934   Nannau

Darling Ginnie,

What a grand place this is, we arrived last night, Frances, Laura, Harry[1] and I to find the Col., Mrs and V.[2] all ready for us. Big fires everywhere and narcissus in pots in the drawing and dining rooms. Forced by Godwin[3] to be ready for us. And they smell so lovely.

My room is a dream. Lovely chintz, a comfy chair by a roaring log fire. Vera had fixed a painting of pale yellow, white and creamy pink chrysanthemums and a few marigolds by the bed. The same colours as the chintz and the bed hangings and one wakes up in a warm golden glow.

I've been lousy for two days but I think that after a long solo walk this morning through the deer park, that I'm more oke. It's all a muddle. Partly because I've just heard that Ma has been going through rather awful hell. It's all been a good deal bloodier than Ma led me to think, and oh gosh, what can I do?

And the second thing that's got me a bit is that I've just heard that Katie[4] is going to have a baby and I'm horribly jealous and I wish it were me. And it's all very silly of me I know and I'm really getting on top of it. But oh, damn damn damn, and at the same time, God God God. The Gs are all so tactful about me not having children that they hardly ever mention Katie at all, which is almost worse than if they asked me point blank in the drawingroom why I hadn't any. (All this, duckie, is very horrid and rotten of me but just for a moment I'm feeling that way and while I do *know* that none of it's true and that I ought to be spanked hard, I'm feeling sort of homesick – what for? I don't know – and teary and, oh dear, low. Mark you, it will be quite another cup of tea by tonight when R. gets here I'm sure. Perhaps it's the altitude.)

On Tuesday we dined at the Gros House[5] with a darling little American called Cameron. Harry, R., and a couple called Grant completed the party. Mrs Grant and I were danced off our feet owing to the scarcity of women. I adored it. I love dancing and fortunately all present were able to do so, and Mr Cameron who is shorter than I and has a stomach floated over the floor in good old college style, and I enjoyed bouncing at the corners with him no end. The band there was awfully good. The Monte Carlo Follies appear at one moment in brassieres made of flesh pink net, garni de rubies! and a brief loin cloth similarly adorned. From the back they appear to be starkers, but of course they aren't tho' they might as well be. They are quite pretty but a dull lot we thought.

P.S. Since writing this letter I'm feeling a good deal oke-er. By counting my blessings and thanking God for not giving me protruding teeth or black hair, I'm feeling better. There are lots of new deer in the deer park. Tinies with matchstick legs.

[1] Reggie's younger brother and half-sisters.
[2] Reggie's parents and his sister Vera.
[3] The gardener.
[4] Reggie's half-sister, two years younger than Joyce.
[5] Grosvenor House, a hotel in Park Lane, London.

Joyce and Reggie went to Yugoslavia for the opening of Allatini Mine, recently bought by Reggie's father's company.

5 December 1934   Skopje
                                                       Yugoslavia

Darling Ginnie,

Top hit in here. Stove in the corner is very Russian and, oh boy, does it warm the room. R and I are bright pink all over, each having emerged from a boiling bath after a heavenly day, me i' the saddle and R half i' the saddle and half i' the shanks leather.

Oh foreign travel is fun. All through Italy we stared and stared, and when we saw our first Yugo peasant at 8 a.m. on Sunday morning we really did feel we were seeing the world. We arrived at Skopje at tea time and spent the night 5 miles out of the town, where the managing director and his assistant live and have an office. Next day we came up here, 25 miles away, in a tiny little wooden carriage tacked on the end of the empty trucks going back to be filled again. For there is no road. One can ride or else rock one's way up in the mine train.

Here we found unexpected luxury. A largish stucco house in which live 2 couples (mining engineers and their wives), 3 bachelors, and 3 spare rooms. A de luxe bathroom, and the hottest stoves possible, We all eat in a mess room a few steps down the garden and the food (good) comes from a kitchen a few steps below that. It's all built on rock and there are office buildings near the kitchen house. The country is barrenish but impressive. Big Alp-y mountains covered with snow at the back, and nearer are big brown mountains with just a little scrub on them. One rides up these and sees marvellous views.

Everyone in the colony is Austrian, so of course 'Das ist eine Kuh' can be brought into general conversation with ease. But I murmur 'Schone' and point at pretty things and my 'Danke' is full of meaning.

The people are very Biblical: oxcarts, asses, and wooden ploughs. Mostly Turks and a few Serbs. The Turks are very handsome and clean looking and full of smiles, and have few complexes, they tell me here.

My new jodhpurs are lovely. I was in a movie all day today: riding in Arizona, on a sleek white horse with distended nostrils. Actually my pony was pale mudcoloured and a real armchair.

But oh God is good to me, for yesterday was the 1st day of the curse and we rose at 7 for breakfast, followed by a 5 mile train trip, a 3,000 feet climb on foot, a 2,000 feet descent on foot, the opening of a new mine head by me and a ride home, some 8 miles! I gave myself a bit of 'thinking'; and we got as far as opening the mine. Then we started to ride back and the return climb of 2,000 feet was done fairly easily. But then we had to walk the 3,000 feet down as it was too steep for the ponies. And was I bursting to sit down? (nursery meaning) So I told R. to ask for me, and I was escorted by a charming Capitaine Durrigl (Do-wriggle!) to a cottage . . . Then came God's Good Deed – a passing peasant offered a lift in his cart and he was going the whole way back here. I was on horseback almost all today too and it was hardly uncomfortable at all. God ist Gut.

10 December 1934   Belgrade

Ginnie Darling,

No one can say I'm not the letter writing wizard. Actually I'm forced to write this letter or bite my nails for in three quarters of an hour's time R. and I will be speeding through the town on our way to take tea with the Queen of Roumania![1]

Aunt N[ancy] wrote her that I was coming here and she got in touch with the British Legation who we visited this morning, and we in our turn let the Palace know of our arrival, and now, here we are, in the lounge of Belgrade's best hotel (3rd rate in Eng.) awaiting the Royal car which is coming to fetch us. Very Ruritanian and exciting. I had my hair washed for 2/- this morning and when the girl had finished it, she put it up in a veritable pagoda of twirls and twists, and I had to sneak into the Ladies Cloaks to dismantle it before I could dream of getting my hat on. Most foreign it was, and very insecure.

Nothing could be duller on paper than a record of the sights seen by a pal abroad. But in reality they are thrilling. Last night we dined in a Serbian cellar. Very rough looking: literally cellar with wine vats all around, and the food, all grilled, was delicious.

This is an incredibly provincial town to be a capital. Poky little Edgware Road shops and no traffic and not one museum, picture gallery or even interesting church. The Danube looks muddy and Thames like. Nevertheless abroad is abroad and I like just looking.

I've fluffed up my suede shoes and I need a manicure badly, but my hair is clean and my stockings are new and my pearls are real. R's hair is practically plaitable but he doesn't dare risk a Serbian razor. R met an old Ballioll-er in the diningroom today. A Yugo-Slavian. Isn't the world small, Effie?

Ooo-er I don't care what the world says. I'm thrilled by Royalty. Already my palms are wet and I want to go to the W.C.

R. pretends indifference – but I know better.

[1] Queen Marie of Romania (1893–1938), granddaughter of Queen Victoria and Tsar Alexander II, first cousin of George V. Mother of the Queens of Yugoslavia and Greece and King Carol II of Romania. Friend of Waldorf Astor, had stayed at Cliveden.

1935

5 January 1935   Nannau

Darling Ginnie,

Here we miss you a lot. Incidents have been few since your
departure. One evening Mary and John[1] conducted a really first class
argument about disarming, 'Do we want the Empire' and war. Mary
is the only woman arguer I've ever seen who never alters her voice or
her face during even the most palpitating moments. And that combined
with John's rather clear and orderly mind gave the audience a most
educational and really amusing evening. It began with the soup and
went on till midnight. The audience one by one slipped off to bed but
the principals went onto the end, neither of them getting hot and
crying, as I always do in an argument, and both of them remaining
cool and tidy to the last.

Today was a water colour day. Sudden splashes of sun lit up a tree
at a time in very Cochran manner, and down in the valley where we
rode the buds on the bushes were really fat and quite green.

Yesterday afternoon in a raging gale we all climbed Moelofrren
(phonetic spelling) and were all but blown off the summit. The sun
setting down the Estuary showed a most Holy light being split by a
small cloud and falling in wide Biblical rays. I leaned on a wall and
watched with urban wonder while a man in a blue shirt ploughed a
furrow with the aid of two enormous coal black horses. It was lovely.

Frances is staggering through the hymn book on the hall piano.
'Worship the King' in jerks right now.

The meals here are suffused with a rosy atmosphere, for none of the
girls[2] is addressed without they glow, from the bottom of the throat, a
deep rich pink. It extends, while attention is on them, to their smooth
young foreheads. It's the pinkest thing you ever saw. Being young they
are all in rather the swollen stage and their skin tight jerseys reveal all,
and they are miserable and stand with arms crossed. Today's lesson is
so nice and affirmative, 'God, the *only* Cause and Creator'.

Did I tell you about Aunt Nancy's present of an evening
dress?[3]

I am making your bright blue seersucker into a blouse. But the
needling urge left me yesterday, so it's still very embryo.

---

[1] Reggie's sister, Mary Waldegrave, and Joyce's first cousin John Phipps.
[2] Reggie's teenage sisters, Frances and Laura and their friends.
[3] Joyce's extended family shared each other's houses, couturier clothes, money, and children
in the holidays. At least twice a year Aunt Nancy Astor sent suitcases of clothes from
Lanvin, Chanel and Shiaparelli for Joyce and her cousins.

In the autumn, Joyce and Virginia went to America together and Joyce returned on her own, in time for Christmas. This was to be the last time that she went to the USA until 1946.

15 December 1935   on board Cunard White Star, *Aquitania*

Darling Ginnie,
    On Friday Tommy and I went to dinner at the St Regis, where I heard my rival Eve Symington who is definitely good. She sings rotten songs however! We stayed there till 10.30 and then moved off to the Montmartre where B Lillie[1] performs. The orchestra is the best I've almost ever heard. Most American dives are lit by one candle but this wasn't gloomy. B Lillie was only *quite* funny. The trouble was she'd been drinking and kept giggling and forgetting her words. Her chief charm is her neat, precise aloofness, and when she's loose it's just not very funny. Afterwards we talked to her and she was in a definite fog.
    I've come to the conclusion that, oddly enough, I do go through emotions. In a big way. I've never been homesick for Ma before and could be now if I didn't battle. I think I'm growing to be a bit more understanding. I hope so, tho' in a way it's hell. I miss you too, blast you.
    It has been fun though, duckie, hasn't it? I've never enjoyed anything so much. It's so satisfactory to find Ma and Lefty in such fine shape.
    The movies are now shown in a theatre! No craning around pillars or sitting on the backs of sofas. Last night we had a perfectly lovely thing called *The Face of England*. Lovely views of Cotswolds and cornfields, cloudy skies and a good deal of factory chimneys. To prove that now we have a chance to make England clean and beautiful once more, by electricity. Pylons on the downs *are* preferable to sooted squalor in villages near mines.
    I'm glad of this week to adjust myself in, for except for seeing R. again I don't in the least want to go home.

[1] Beatrice Lillie (1898–1989), British revue star.

Monday, 16 December [1935]   *Aquitania*

Darling Ginnie,
    In spite of not having you to handicap my social side, I've not spoken to a soul! I'm being a woman of mystery, sitting always alone. I feel remote and unattached in any feeling today. England and America seem, naturally enough since it's about true, equally far away. R is coming more and more into focus as we progress Eastward. But you

and Ma and Lefty are still rather brightly outlined in Carolina sunshine. My inclination is to dash for England, grab R and return speedily to Tryon, NC.

Gosh, we're rolling suddenly. The entire window of this lounge filled with sea!

Later

I spoke too soon of my blessed silence. After writing the above I went on deck for the air. Here I paused a moment thinking to observe the faint sinkage of light where the sunset should be. One Owsley Gray Junior, very young with pale orange hair, speaks to me re the rolling. I speak back. Owsley says 'I'm Mr Gray'. We chat. He's an engineer en route for a gold mine in West Africa. Almost mutual interest. We chat of cricket, of American football, of enthusiasm. I go below to my bath.

(While actually in the tub every light went out. Furious, I struggled out wildly. Dry in spots, I put all my underclothes on inside out and emerged to find it's only been a local fuse and no one has noticed it!)

Back in my cabin there is a minute card in a minute envelope. Owsley himself: 'Would you allow me to join you for dinner tonight?' (He is 1st class and may come slumming but not allowed to ask me aloft.) I was furious. It meant dining in bed unless I wished to be blatantly rude. Poor Owsley meant well, but I did want my solitude. So I dashed him off a note saying, 'I'm afraid the lure of my novel and a tray are too tempting and I've succumbed. Yours, etc.' Which will do for tonight but I'm afraid that tomorrow will bring renewed invitations for there is a dearth of young women aboard, and in spite of my haggard expression I seem to rate as a young woman. (Tho' only just, for I heard a man say there were no young girls up in first 'they are all 27 and up.' A narrow shave.)[1]

[1] Joyce was then almost twenty-seven.

Wednesday, 18 December 1935   *Aquitania*

Darling Ginnie,

I went up to the top promenade deck to look again in vain for a sunset. I thought I was hidden by a huge funnel thing, but up comes Owsley Junior to apologise for his audacity in last night's invitation. He looked so callow and so remorseful that I was nicer than I meant to be, and after 20 mins. chat he asked himself for tonight! But I'd hardened my heart by then and said that as I eat *so* little he'd far better come down after dinner and take me to the movie! It was my only alternative and I couldn't face eating with him. He's a type that only exists in

America I think. Very big and healthy, crazy about his mother, little kids, rough seas, and is naively proud of staying up late at night. Last night he didn't turn in until 4.30, oh boy. I don't know whether he thinks I'll do the same this evening, but if he does he'll get a rude shock for I'm the early bird type, unless really roused. He's never been abroad before and is thrilled by everything, which is rather endearing.

Thursday, 19 December [1935]   [*Aquitania*]

Darling Ginnie,
    Don't ever go to see a movie called *Transatlantic Tunnel*. Ozzy – his friends call him that – took me last night and it's quite horrible. Half naked men suffocating in gases. Ugh. Afterwards we repaired to the smoking room for a coupla lemonades and were soon joined by three boy friends of Ozzy's. We chatted on Travel, Theatre and Customs Officials, and then I went to bed. Ozzy is on the wagon on account he's got a good job and he's going to keep it. Rather touching and movie-ish.
    I've been reading *Romeo and Juliet* and the Sonnets, and you *can't* think Shakespeare boring. It's *so* lovely. There's a good library on this ship.
    Happy New year, ducky, and see you soon.

P.S. I, too, am happy in our palship. It never varies which is perfect. Bless you.

Sunday, 22 December 1935   St Leonard's Terrace

Darling Ginnie,
    I had a grand lunch with your family today. Mom, Pop and Kate. All flourishing. Revelling in your letters and popeyed while I told of your conquests, success and altogether pretty-niceness. I jawed for 2 hours and then came home to shop. For alas, I am not too late to get presents for the relations at Cliveden.
    Please, if time, go to Kresses on Fifth Avenue and buy me six 25 cent white lampshades. Quite plain white paper with a white cotton fringe edging. I brought 4 in this trip with no trouble. I put 'em in my hat box with the hats arranged around them. I had an easy time at Customs and paid 12/- on the things from Betsy Bird shop. I'd be mighty grateful for they cost 4 times that here and then are hideous.
    Fog held us up for 16 hours, just 2 hours off Southampton. There we sat, fuming. R had to spend the night in a hotel, among the miserable

passengers en route for America. R was a bit fatter, very sweet, and seems pleased to see me.

Long conversations with Aunts N and Phyllis. Aunt N *is* going to give Ma a house. Isn't it thrilling. I'm *so* pleased.[1]

It's too cold here, and oh gosh the bathroom with no heating. If it weren't for R I'd hate being back. But by the time you get this I'll be in harness once more, woolly vested and back to normal. I can't wait to see you for I'm starving for lack of Tryon talk. Oh I did love it all so.

Peter Fleming married Celia Johnson last week, hurray.[2] That's all I know, darling.

The old Wolseley is practically on its deathbed. Clutch trouble R says. It just sighs its way along and has palpitations on hills. Where we'll get another one, God alone knows. Doubtless He'll provide.[3]

[1] Nancy Astor gave her youngest sister Nora Flynn Little Orchard, Tryon in North Carolina.
[2] Peter Fleming (1907–71), brother of writer Ian, was already making a name for himself as an explorer and author of *News from Tartary*. Joyce first met Celia Johnson (1908–82) in 1929 when Joyce attended the Royal Academy of Dramatic Art (RADA) for one term. Joyce's father, Paul Phipps, designed an eight-bedroom neo-Georgian house called Merrimoles for the Flemings on their estate in Oxfordshire.
[3] Nancy Astor provided: a two-door Ford for £100 plus £6 tax. Reggie taught Joyce to drive in two days, before driving tests were introduced. Her first solo journey took 45 minutes to drive two miles, stalling at every bend in the road and at the sight of every oncoming vehicle. After that she became a safe, but always slow, driver.

1936

Sunday [February] 1936

Hall Barn[1]
Beaconsfield
Bucks

Darling Joyce,

I can't possibly write you a proper Collins[2] but I look forward to my cossets with you with an almost unholy violence and look backwards on them with affectionate longing. The Cottage is the only place where I lead the sort of country life I should like to lead if I lived in the country – if you see what I mean. The rest of my rural life is bound to be weekendy and uncrunchy, & I do so appreciate those fierce aimless walks among the snowdrops, & those long deep hours of silence when I don't even raise my head to listen to your spiritual arguments – much less make polite replies. And I like not doing my hair for tea, &

worrying a little over Gary, & seeing the stars through the bedroom window – a lot of things I like about your home, in fact.

I went with Sue to the House of Lords yesterday. The Archbish made a most moving & beautiful speech. My heart is so constantly called to 'go out to the Queen' that there is none left for anything else.[3]

Many thanks, darling, for your enormous coeur, your ridiculous espirit & your profound aimé.

Love Winnie

[1] Home of Lord and Lady Burnham (Fred and Enid Lawson), owner of *Daily Telegraph*.
[2] Thank-you letter.
[3] George V had died on 10 January and Edward VIII succeeded to the throne.

Joyce and Reggie decided they could no longer afford to live in London. Nancy and Waldorf Astor offered them a cottage on their Cliveden estate, twenty-five miles west of London, 'until such time as they were better off'.

Cliveden was bought by William Astor, an American millionaire who emigrated to England in 1890 and spent millions of dollars on houses, a castle and newspapers. Waldorf was heir to one of the largest fortunes in the world and sent to Eton and Oxford. Like his father, he had little sense of fun. Physically weak, Waldorf gave up sports and went into politics as a left-wing Conservative MP for Plymouth (Sutton). When, in 1919, Waldorf inherited his father's peerage he had to resign from the House of Commons. Undeterred, Nancy fought the by-election and became the first woman to sit in the British House of Commons. She was American by birth and upbringing, but had received an English-style education and British citizenship by marriage.

Waldorf and Nancy were given Cliveden as a wedding present in 1906. Designed by Charles Barry, the Victorian architect of the House of Commons, the vast house had 'splendid gloom'. Nancy livened it up with books, chintz curtains and flowers. Joyce described Cliveden as a great liner, with Nancy as the engine that kept it going – without her everything stopped. Waldorf had 'a sort of self-bestowed sense of Host of England that makes him collect celebrities, he thinks it's his duty,' wrote Joyce to her mother. Entertaining was on a grand scale, with guests from all walks of life: aristocracy, media and society celebrities, British and American politicians, cousins, foreign royalty, tycoons, Christian Scientists, social workers, and 'lost souls' that Nancy took a fancy to. Nancy's reaction to a huge party of ambassadors and international politicians was to make them play musical chairs. The young Kennedys stayed at Cliveden when their father was US Ambassador to Britain. The King and Queen of Romania were frequent guests. The large and efficient staff had to carry cans of hot water and buckets of coal to each bedroom every morning – a hundred tons of coal was consumed a year.

Nancy Astor was noted for her biting wit, advocacy of women's rights, strong views on temperance and fierce temper, combined with a warm heart. She somehow blended both outrageous talk and strictly moral behaviour. She was intensely possessive of all her relations, particularly her own six children, but had to buy their allegiance with lavish presents. Joyce was 'scared to death' of Nancy, who could not praise or pay compliments, but she was amusing, generous and treated everyone as equals.

Joyce's father drew up the plans to renovate Parr's Cottage – named after the Astors' butler – and Nancy gave them £100 to buy furniture from Heal's. René Easden, a local girl, was employed as cook and another woman as 'daily'. Joyce settled down to life as a country wife, involved in local activities such as ladies' sewing circles and helping Aunt Nancy with Cliveden house guests. Reggie commuted by train to the City, and at weekends they played tennis, gardened, and danced up at the Big House.

Telegrams: 'HARRIGRAM, LONDON'[1]

June [1936]   5 Montagu Square, W1

Darling Joyce,

I find it rather deplorable the way I go on writing to you, and you go on not paying any attention whatsoever, but I know of course that there is always un qui donne et un qui recoit.

I feel delirious, having just returned from a *Bridge* dinner at the Glyns consisting of Sir Guy Dornville, Lady Ribblesdale, the Ray Athertons, the Northamptons, the Rabens, Lady Gosford, Crinks Johnstone, and a few more besides!

Today I have also bought three strings of pearls, backed two wrong horses in the Derby, lunched with Moira and Oonagh, taken Ma to Victoria Station, tried on two dresses, gone to bed for an hour, and had a headache.

God, the strawberries and asparagus I have eaten these last days.

I am furious with Deirdre, as she tells me she is taking me to a dance at Sutton Courtney on Saturday, at which I shall not know a soul.

Yrs truly, The Hon Joy

---

[1] Virginia's father was Harry Graham (1874–1936), author of *Ruthless Rhymes for Heartless Homes*, 1899. A code-name given to the post office saved on words and allowed telegrams to be delivered straight to the door.

During the summer of 1936, Harry Graham, Virginia's father, become very ill and Joyce wrote to her mother, 'Virginia drives him around and is cheerful and gay, and underneath she is about all-in. But her Christian Science is better and she writes such good letters and is learning so much that I feel she'll emerge about a hundred per cent better, if that were possible.'

Joyce gave Virginia weekend breaks away from home, reading, talking and 'being girlish' together.

[June 1936]   Montagu Square

Darling Joyce,

I loved staying with you. Last night in bed I started writing the
words of my new cottage song – it begins:

'Whiter than any Polar bear, or soft Angora rabbit's hair; whiter
than apple blossoms blow, or arum lilies in the snow; before my
something eyes – the Grenfell cottage lies. The little door is painted
green, so are the window ledges; the honeysuckle lays her head
upon its emerald edges' – that's as far as I got and no music yet! But
undoubtedly it's going to be *frightfully* good.

I wish I were with you.

Enid's plot has worked so well that John G really *is* rather in love
with me now! He came and quaffed sherry here on Tuesday evening
and is taking me to do the same tonight. He has got to the stage of
saying *if* he were older, *if* he wasn't in the Irish Guards, *if* he wasn't
going to Egypt and a few more ifs, he'd ask me to marry him, but
wouldn't insult me now with such an offer! Sweet, isn't it? The more
things like that he says, the younger he becomes. Oh, the intolerable
steadiness of my heart beats.

Tell Harry I am deeply conscious of the fact that I owe him 5/- and
that it is stamped like a brand on my brain!

Bless you darling, Love Ginnie

18 June 1936   Parr's
                                                             Cliveden
                                                               Taplow
                                                                Bucks

Darling Ginnie,

I can't tell you how strong you sound over the telephone. By which
I mean CLEAR. This thing is a hideous dream but you are awake in it.
Nothing can alter an idea. Do hug that. An infinite idea, all nice and
harmonious. That's your Pa. Nothing has or ever will alter this.

We dined up at t'big house [Cliveden] last night, and when we gals
came out of the dining room we wandered onto the terrace and it was
that silver moment when colour is almost washed out and when Delius'
music is indicated. A great white star, which I think is Venus, hung
over the woods on the left and the trees became spinach green and very
feathery so that I felt to fall on them from an aeroplane would be an
exquisite delight. (And talking of 'planes, my serious and pince-nez'd
Uncle Bob Brand landed from a gyro-scope on the Polo Field during
yesterday afternoon. I can't quite understand why, but there was

some business connection. Perhaps Lazards are financing a new sort of gyro.)

While the beauties of nature were tearing out my vitals I gave the other nose powderers the slip and went down the stone steps from the terrace onto the gravel below. As I picked my sandalled way over the grit, I tried to see the infinite man in his relation to beauty. By this time some more stars had come out and I was almost in tears. The gramophone began to moan and my gloom soon evaporated and for a flash I saw a bit about Infinity. So I squeezed the lemon verbena in my hand and the delicious smell of it translated me to this planet once more, and I arrived back on the terrace un-noticed.

Nothing much happened then. Sydney Herbert[1] and Harry Wyndham[2] pretended to jump the parapet and to hide my nausea I skipped les-girlishly down the terrace arm in arm with Bill [Astor] to the strains of 'Top Hat'. The Debs looked longingly at the lights of Maidenhead but even my entreaties failed to move their mothers.

I'm so glad about *Punch* and the book reviewing possibilities. Activity, that's the thing. I'm going to start processing my Kodak pictures – I think. But while there's the possibility of a game of tennis I'm tempted to stray from duty.

I can't say all I want because it's a mortal mind feeling, but if I could, I'd be going through all you're going through instead of you.

Bless you.

---

[1] Lord (Sydney) Herbert (1906–69) succeeded his father as Earl of Pembroke in 1960.
[2] Hon. Harry Wyndham (1915–42), son of Lord Leconfield.

30 June 1936   Montagu Square

Darling Joyce,

You must be having a lovely weekend, and I can picture you at every moment of the day, playing some very hot tennis, bathing, drinking tomato juice, inventing excuses not to dine at Cliveden, & lying in a somnolent posture with your eye-shade over your nose. A lovely life, and one that I delight to share.

Life like an ever rolling stream bears all its buns away, & in particular this bun, who can barely keep pace with the tide! I would like to get into bed and stay there for ages, snoring decorously though my faintly distended nostrils, & breathing out through my rosebud mouth. Instead of which tomorrow I go for my Glyndebourne weekend, with much motoring hither and thither, & intelligent conversation. However, I shall enjoy it a lot I know. Last weekend's *Don Giovanni* was *marvellous*.

I had a nice Sunday and there was 16 persons there, who I mostly didn't know. A military looking Colonel Hare sat knitting socks all the time. We played tennis, and the hardiest bathed and in the evening we played Lexicon. There were a lot of bad watercolours the size of postage stamps hanging on long wires from the ceiling!!

Yesterday I lunched with Maria, and feeling better went to Wimbledon. There I nearly died of excitement, and much enjoyed myself.

I look forward to my stay with you with parched longing – Ginnie.

While in America the year before, Joyce had met a poet called Elliott Coleman a few years older than her. He had inspired her to write poetry and she sent some verses to Virginia who had already had some poetry and articles published. Without telling her, Virginia sent them on to *Punch* magazine.

Friday summer 1936   Montagu Square

Darling Joyce,

How are you, lambkin?

I am crazy with excitement over the new Vauxhall 10. It looks a *stupendous* car. I can get £155 for mine and this costs £182 – so that means a new car for £27. But it really isn't much smaller – and it goes 40 to the gallon – and the tax is smaller – & – hush dear, there's no need to get so excited. Joyce has other things to do . . .

Tomorrow we go to Granny to see her 84th birthday in. She insists on my giving her a hideous flower vase which pinches the flowers round their throats until they're sick over the edge.

A peculiar happening: Mr Watt[1] writes to say will I accept £10/– for 'Finished with Fun'. *No* I write back furiously, because I didn't write it, & will he please apply to Mrs Grenfell. I suppose they got the Gs muddled up. He also calls it an article. I thought it was a poem. Anyway, congrats old top.

lots of love, darling, and thousands of thank yous for being vous
Winnie Grimes

[1] Literary agent, was either A.S., W.P. or Hansard Watt, who were all working for A.P. Watt at the time.

Reggie's job in the City was precarious and Joyce worried about his future and their finances. She decided to get herself a job, but 'What? I dunno' and they discussed working in America.

13 August 1936   Parr's

Darling Ginnie,

How right you are about me needing a kick in the pants. I'm having the first two pages of 'Governess' re-typed by R's stenographer and I'm going to mail it across the ocean blue to the *Atlantic Monthly*. If I fail there I'll submit it to the *Ladies Home Journal* etc. etc ETC. Meanwhile I'm floundering in the middle of a rather well written story about a heartless widower and try as I may I can see no conclusion. I've also done a sort of Women's Page article which might be made useful. So you see, in my way, I'm being gently active.

We had your exquisite tongue for dinner last night. Did you get our telegram? R's idea. The telephone girl thought we were dotty for we were all laughing at our own wit while I tried to dictate it. 'Tonguek you.' It's delicious and quite one of R's favourite foods.

I've just spoken mit you on the telephone.

Tuesday [August 1936]   Montagu Square

Darling Joyce,

Is it just that wild streak of American blood in you that makes you write on thin sheets of Bromo?[1]

Things 'ere have been much better. Daddy hasn't been sick and has been far stronger. Sleeping is still atrocious, & last night he tried without drugs. Unfortunately, a failure and at 4 he had to take an Aspro. Still, he was very brave and good, & it's all a step in the right direction. I cannot say life has been very folichon [much fun], but at least it has been emotionally calm.

On Friday I took a train for Cambridge and there saw Humphrey[2] act Hamlet with such passion & manliness & beauty I would have fallen over had you but breathed on me. He was marvellous. It seems quite inexplicable. I stayed in fusty lodgings & breakfasted with Humph in his rooms at Trinity. Then a tour of King's C. Chapel where I thought of you because they were playing Toccata on the organ. Home with Mr Butler in his open Austin, so I had to wear his Homberg to save my curls. Then it rained, & we had one of those hood fights.

Yesterday Kitty and I got onto a large sailing boat in the middle of Regent's Park, & with dozens of ragged children floated hither and thither! It cost us 2d & was rather pleasant, but queer, undoubtedly queer.

Could go on writing for ever, but the gong gongs for tiffin.
Oceans of amour from Flopsie

[1] Shiny lavatory paper.
[2] Virginia's cousin, Humphrey Whitbread.

1 September 1936

Ardgowan[1]
Inverkip
Renfrewshire

Darling Ginnie,

I've just come off the moors having walked half way home in the
warm rain. My hair was like a yardstick, so I'm now full of combs and
curlers waiting for it to dry.

We came yesterday in Vera's[2] old Chrysler and it took us 11 and
a half hours. It's 335 miles and I must admit I felt fairly silly by the
time we arrived. We were nabbed for speeding when we were just
over the Border. A very young pink policeman with two confederates
holding stop watches did the job. Very tiresome. We were only doing 37
m.p.h. too.

Here we find a pleasant party. Earl Grey[3] and his mixture: wife,
daughter Molly and a dozen or so others.

I awoke at 4 a.m. feeling strangely theatrical and found the moon
spot lighted directly through the window into my cold-creamed face.
What a moon. White as marble and nearly full. The sea and the distant
hills were lit up in various blues and the silver birches in the garden
below had shadows more definite than themselves. I was glad to be
awake.

The household here is old world enough to segregate the sexes
for tea!

I wish I were at Nannau but seeing R's look of ecstasy as he lets off
his gun makes up for quite a lot. I'm afraid I've been a bit queer lately
and given you to think I wasn't entirely happy in the home. But forget
it. I'm terribly happy. R is perfect and I'm the luckiest woman alive.
He's being so sweet too and we've all sorts of plans for a new job and a
lovely future. I don't mind a bit about not having children and as I now
know for certain that I am essential to his lordship I'm quite content!
Inexplicable I'm afraid, but then so are many other things.

Have a fairly nice time at Lightwater and come to me in October.

[1] Home of Sir Hew and Lady Shaw-Stewart.
[2] Reggie's sister.
[3] Reggie's uncle.

Joyce and Reggie had been married nearly seven years, and there was still no sign of a child. As a Christian Scientist Joyce was not interested in consulting a doctor. Her childlessness was also a regular reminder of the day when her beloved nanny left. Lucy had been with Joyce since she was one month old, and she had 'perfect understanding' with her, the 'ever-fixed-star' she loved and relied on. Joyce's parents decided that the time for Lucy to leave would be when Joyce's periods began. 'I went to school in the morning and when I came home at tea-time she had gone. It was meant to make it easier for me; no goodbyes. I felt a desolation that was hard to bear. The day that Lucy left me and the night I learned my mother had left my father were times of wilderness.'[1] So every month she was also reminded of this desolation with what she called 'little deaths' which sometimes only lasted a few minutes.

Twenty years later Joyce wrote that not having children 'was a sadness when we were young, then one got used to it, now I am almost grateful, for there have been many compensations. Our particular companionship over and above love, and that as well; and the need to canalise the various little talents that I'd played with as a child. I must say I would like to have *grand* children.'[2]

[1] *Joyce Grenfell Requests the Pleasure*, 1977.
[2] Letter to Katherine Moore, 18 January 1959, in *An Invisible Friendship*, 1981.

3 September 1936   Lightwater Manor
                                                          Lightwater
                                                              Surrey

Darling Joyce,
    I'm so awfully glad about Reggie, darling. The trouble about men is that they persist in taking everything for granted, & when, after years of goading, cajoling, & prompting they say 'of *course* I love you, you know that quite well' one can only say 'then why in the *hell* didn't you say so, or *look* as though you did, or *behave* as though you did?' Woman, among her many other qualifications is supposed to have the gift of clairvoyance as well! At least, that is what I have found with my last two husbands.[1] The first one, Fred, only once said he loved me, & that was one night – May 4th 1893, I think, just after we'd gone to bed – he was talking in his sleep. 'I love you' he said; & then a few seconds later added 'darling Josephine', which as you know is not my name.
    Bertie, my second man, used to say 'Can't you see I adore you?' as he came in at the front door every evening, so as to prevent me asking him if he did. This was maddening. Eventually, & keep this between somebody & the bed pan – I murdered him. At this very moment he lies beneath my feet, ruining the drainage system, & making the installation of central heating an impossibility.

Did you listen to the Bach prom? I'm quite sure that you didn't, so don't bother to answer. We listen every night, & I can't tell you what a joy the wireless is to an old folk like myself, I just sit, listening, & trembling & dribbling and having a lovely time.

Schieben weeden bittee, luf, Hyasquinth

[1] Virginia was not yet married.

16 September 1936   Drummond Castle[1]
                                                                          Crieff

Darling Ginnie,

I wish you had seen Wiss, Sally H[2] and I yesterday in the Auction Rooms at Perth. It is a fascinating game. I was so afraid of winking or moving my head lest the auctioneer bring down his hammer to sell me some colossal bibelots for £100. Most of the stuff was Lord Esher's. Lots of Empire furniture with brass decor and a number of inlaid Spanish pieces which I wouldn't have accepted as a gift, my dear. Sally H has bought a large property in Sussex and is buying furniture for it. We nearly went dotty bidding for two strange desk cupboard things of Empire date, for a bald fat man, probably a dealer, raised us by half a crowns to £32 the pair! Lady Sally didn't bat an eye. She got a bargain in mirrors. I left a 10/- bid on two hunting prints that would do for Lefty's Christmas present.

I'm not mad about Her Ladyship. She's a cat, and perhaps, a troublemaker. She has very little good to find in anyone. Calls people like Aunt Pauline a bitch! I mean it's *too* silly, Aggie, ain't it? She loathes my ma-in-law: says she's a viper beneath her Golden Gate exterior, which is strange and goes back to the old Vienna days when she did something she didn't orter when under Mrs G[renfell's] chaperonage. You'd be proud of me. I haven't spoken back once. A smiling face and a smooth answer tho' I must admit my heart has hammered and I've longed to scratch her. But they say she's an idea of God's, Trixie, don't they? At least the *real* she is.

This sounds much more heavy on paper than it is in life. She's really just an ordinary gal with a mean side and fat little hands. Rather chic and a soft breathless voice that is fascinating. There's probably *quite* a lot that's good in her.

Brrrr.

Priscilla[3] is awfully attractive I think. There's an illusive quality about her which is boyish without being masculine. She goes shooting with the men wearing a plus four suit of Willoughby tweed and today, a non-shooting day, she came to breakfast in a kilt and green aertex shirt, looking a treat. She's a strange mixture. At night she's dolled to the eyes with satin and fur and jewellery and knitting. By day she's tweed and collar and tie. R finds her very attractive and she's easy to talk to.

[1] Home of the Earl and Countess of Ancaster, parents-in-law of Wiss Astor.
[2] Countess of Hardwick (died 1965).
[3] Lady Priscilla, daughter of the Earl of Ancaster.

18 September [1936]   Lightwater Manor

Darling Joyce,

I am in a most terrible quandary! Either I must buy a new attaché case or I must tear up some of your letters. I tore up hundreds of other people's letters last month – ones which I used to consider proved I was the most popular girl in the Upper Fourth, some which were merely chatty, & a few strays from my beaux asking me to meet them at Bell metti's at 7.30 sharp. Still, however, it is necessary for me to lean on the case to shut it, & the problem becomes more acute every day, as another Grenfell letter is stuffed in to swell the flood.

Perhaps it would be an exaggeration to say that I live for your letters, but they are certainly one of the major joys of my existence. You have an amazing way of transmitting yourself to your pen, so that when I read I can picture you all the time – walking along the seashore in your brown Standen & Tudor shoes, or talking to Lord Ancaster about the Ring and Napoleon about neither of which subjects I feel you can know more than I (which is nil).

The circles I move in get smaller & smaller, but God, they get higher & higher! I had luncheon with the Gathorne-Hardys[1] yesterday & met the Duke of Connaught[2] & Princess Patsy.[3] The old boy was sweet. He talked a lot, which is unusual in a masculine eighty, and had pimples on his chin. The other side of me was a youth called John Nelson, engaged to Jane FitzRoy. Pink, or rather mauve, he seemed to be about $12\frac{1}{2}$ but presumably he knows best. We stood for hours after luncheon while the old Duke tottered about looking distinguished & senile, & Princess Patsy, dressed in dove grey tied herself into a series of incredibly sly knots. Why are/is the Royal family so acutely self conscious? She had a grey umbrella too.

There seems to be a dearth of good new novels – not that you care because you are so Proud & Prejudiced & easily Persuaded.[4]

I am rather depressed about my literary activities. Mr Watt has about four of my articles now, & nothing seems to happen to any of them. As they are intensely topical, hope dies in the human breast, sizzling faintly and letting off clouds of steam. I thought the Scotch one & the Deb one rather good, didn't you? Well, I don't care if you did! Nobody else does.

I sometimes wish I were 2[1]2, sitting in a pram with pneumatic tyres, bobbling up & down, waving my arms about, & tossing teddy bears over the side – being unreasonable but strangely attractive, saying gagagaga & chewing the ribbons of my white bonnet. Ah well . . .

Love Ginnie

[1] Edward (1901–78) was a historian and his brother Robert (1902 –) a writer. Sons of 3rd Earl of Cranbrook.
[2] Field Marshal HRH Prince Arthur (1850–1942), seventh child of Queen Victoria.
[3] Second daughter of the Duke of Connaught (1886–1974).
[4] Jane Austen was one of Joyce's favourite writers.

25 September 1936   Nannau

Darling Ginnie,

Well, we got Katie[1] married on Wed. and, my *deer*, what a place it was at. The old great aunt is 75 and was one of Queen Victoria's maids of honour. The house is Balmoral cum Sandringham, neat. Built about 1840, a great stone castle – castellations along the top and a tower and several blank shields, let in above the windows. A view of the sea below the house is all right at high tide, but mud flats are never very alluring at low, are they? The hall where we eat is painted dark thick red and stag and deer glare down with glassy eye. I've never quite changed from my childish certainty that their bodies were through the wall, quite whole. We had two organs – both wheezy and hand blown, *and* a piano, a forest of palm trees in brass pots, and I had my cup of tea off a small round table whose legs were three stuffed deer's legs!

All the engravings and prints that one knows were hung on the walls. *The Retreat from Moscow, The Doctor* (you know that child on two chairs with a sober faced doctor holding her pulse. Mrs G[renfell] said she knows for a fact that the child *does* recover!) and we had two Aberdeen dogs with labels over our washstand called *Passengers*. I'm sure that *Dignity and Impudence* and *Stag at Bay* were there somewhere.

None of us had ever seen the old aunt and Katie had said she was fierce, frank and allowed no smoking and was super punctual. Mrs G did her best to impress us and we promised to do our best, but by the time we got there we were so giggly that none of us had any control. Reg kept murmuring under his breath and Frances replied with giggles, so no wonder Mrs G had nerves. And so had poor Katie who came rushing out to meet us and jumped on the running board and pushed her head into the car 'Now you've all got to behave because my entire future depends on it.' So we came in like lambs, all tidied and gloved – we'd stopped half a mile away for that – and soon we were having tea at little tables in the frightful hall. The in-laws are all of the Plum Monk variety. Hearty and jolly and most awfully nice.

(Mrs G told me a story of going to stay at a huge house party for some ball in the county when she was a deb. and as she sat at her dressing-table before dinner the daughter of the house pushed her head in and said 'Don't forget to be cheery in the Bus.' She said this to all the girls and the result was, of course, Utter Gloom and one Mlle. Spring-Rice was sick out of the door at intervals all the way there!)

There was a white tie dinner party that night! Reggie of course hadn't got one and he was the only one. 26 of us sat down at a dinner table decorated with pink rambler roses, tiny potted palms and rucked up jap silk like a stormy sea. The entire village was standing in the hall to see us go in to dinner arm in arm! My dear it was so feudal and serf-y. The men were rustic and rather blond and the women were shy and dropped curtseys! When we arrived they were hanging flags over the gateway and a huge poster saying 'God Bless the Bride & Groom' in silver ornamented with Union Jacks hung over the Church door. Under the porch there were paper decorations obviously left over from the servants hall Christmas box. It was superb.

We had speeches at dinner and toasts, and a young Baron de something made a very amusing and rather near-wind one to his Great Aunt. The relations sat with scarlet faces while he told her some home truths, so the Grenfells were all quite at ease and much amused. As was the old lady. He said that this was the first time he'd ever been able to stand up and talk to Great Aunt without her talking back at him. She was heard to murmur – 'And it's the last'. She was dressed in purple with marabou, and she is tiny and pointed and rather nice. Quite incredibly unprogressive. Won't allow Girl Guides or a Women's Institute in her village as she thinks that woman's place is in the home!

After dinner we stood about in the hall for a while, then one Robert put a roll onto organ number 1. (Honeysuckle and the Bee.) Meanwhile his sister had gotten out her concertina and was playing the Eton Boating Song. At organ no. 2 the Best man who is 5 feet high was playing scales. A third young man was doing chopsticks on the piano, and the old lady was beaming.

The Grenfells became motionless and if you knew them at all you could tell they were miserable. This noise went on for about 20 mins when at last at my suggestion we danced Sir Roger. It was a stroke of genius I can tell you. Elizabeth played the piano and never by any chance hit the right notes in the bass altho' she did rather well in the treble. Reg did some magnificent fielding and caught the young Baroness after she'd been knocked for six by an old Lord who was by this time definitely mellow. (They say the champagne at dinner was

40

superb.) However, there were no casualties and we finished the dance. The others were *mad* to do an eightsome but none of us could help.

Soon we thought it wise to send the bridegroom away to the neighbouring house where he was to sleep the night (trad.). Then began a series of jokes in the hall, in the cars, in the hall again, and finally amid roaring cheers and a cloud of dust he drove off with the best man. And so, finally to bed. Gas and candles, but a lovely bed.

The service was short and simple and we boomed 'All people that on earth do dwell' and 'Love divine all loves excelling'. Katie wore a yellow dress and a small brown velvet biretta like a RC priest! She looked pretty but very white. I wonder what feelings she went through.

We had lunch afterwards and at 2.30 they drove off under fire of confetti to catch the train to London. Oh, I forgot to tell you that the car was pulled by men of the Estate from Church to House. And that the head-keeper stood with his back to the Church just outside the gates of the churchyards, firing blanks into the heavens to celebrate the occasion!

[1] Reggie's half-sister whose first husband had died two years earlier.

In the autumn of 1936 everyone in Britain was talking about the affair between Edward VIII (1894–1972) and the American Mrs Wallis Simpson (1896–1986). The King wanted to continue with his mistress and be crowned King. As he would be head of the Church of England and she had been divorced twice, this was not allowed. He had to choose and the country was on tenterhooks.

[September 1936]   The Bees
                                                                  Watford[1]

Darling Joyce,

I am in a fearful fuss & there's something I have *got* to ask you & I know you won't mind, only don't tell anybody else will you? I mean *promise*. I know it's frightfully silly of me but . . . really this is awfully difficult . . . I hardly know how to begin . . . Well, here goes, I'll burn my boats. Look . . . (oh the embarrassment . . .) Now *promise* you won't tell. But who *is* Mrs Simpson? I've heard so much about her lately, & everybody seems to know all about her, but I never have, & I can't imagine who she is! I feel an awful fool not knowing, so do tell me. Actually, I'm pretty sure, judging from people's conversations, I've a shrewd suspicion I mean, that she's the Duke of York's mistress.[2] My dear, what a scandal that would be, with the sweet little innocent girls and everything. But maybe I'm being beastly and it's not that at all. I hope not for all our sakes. Perhaps you would be so kind as to set my mind at rest – I hate uncertainty.

This is supposed to be a) a letter of thanks and b) a letter of condolence, but Satire took me on her wings, & flew me to the Realms of Irony, the old cow! I loved my weekend, darling. You do me so much good, I feel permanently safe with you, & life appears to be the simple thing it really is, & insurance policies assume more correct proportions.

Love from Winnie.

---

[1] A joke address.
[2] The Duke of York was Edward VIII's brother, later George VI (1895–1952), already married to Elizabeth Bowes-Lyon and father to Princesses Elizabeth and Margaret.

Edward VIII chose to marry Mrs Simpson and abdicated the throne on 10 December. They married and lived in exile as the Duke and Duchess of Windsor.

26 September 1936   Nannau

Darling Ginnie,

There's a nip i' the air and I feel a sort of pleasant internal stirring: like New Year's Day. Last night the heavens opened and while we sat in dinner the wind suddenly raised itself and blew in the right direction. Result: a good clean laundered morning with Cader in full view and yards of blue to make pants of all the Dutchmen in Holland. The sun isn't in residence yet but he's to-ing and fro-ing with the pantechnicon of small firm clouds and will settle as soon as he's cleaned things up a bit.

Have you read *Lolly Willowes* by Sylvia Townsend Warner? Your drop. How's this –

'I shouldn't think young Billy Thomas would make much of a footman,' said Laura. 'I don't know,' he answered consideringly, 'he's very good at standing still.'

Yesterday afternoon Mrs G and I went to call on a neighbour, Mrs Lee, aged 85, who lives in that Tudor-esque monstrosity below Precipice Walk. It was a rather cosy and completely novel-ish visit. We arrived on the doorstep with Canon and Mrs Watkin Davies who had also come to call. The Canon has an eye for a young face and a double row of pale blue shams set in a rosy mouth. Baby pinkness and snowy hair. Interminable anecdotes, one about how he'd aided a young woman whose car had backed over a four foot drop. His efficiency, heart and calmness. 'Couldn't leave a little woman in distress', was his charming excuse for gallantry. Honestly. It's true.

Mrs Lee's daughter-in-law, Mrs Charlie and her nobbly husband were there for the fishing. Mrs Watkin Davies, like a huge Pekinese, goggled at old Mrs Lee about weather and neighbours. Tea was in the garden room. Wicker chairs, begonias in green glazed pots, portraits of all the young Lees in uniform, wedding kit, or naked bearskins. There were exquisite eclairs filled with Devonshire cream. The Canon saw that our plates were never empty and Mrs Charlie, who is half Dutch, rolled her slow kind R's at Mrs G in defence of the Fascists in Spain.

See you at Paddington on Monday, love.

Harry Graham died on 10 October 1936. His wife and daughters Kitty and Virginia had to move out of their house to pay death duties on Harry Graham's musicals. In January they found a flat in Portman Square, off Oxford Sreet. Virginia's first book had been commissioned – *Heather Mixture* – a collection of witty articles from *Punch*, *Vogue*, *Night and Day* and *Design*.

Tuesday [October 1936]   Beaulieu

Darling Joyce,

Here I am in a nice house with a ruin at the bottom of the garden, & it is raining immensely hard. There are only two other guesties, so we have help yourself meals and absolutely *no* powder on the nose.

My whole life is bound up in ' marks and ~ marks. I have finished the first Chapter and I really don't know what to make of it, but then I've read it so many times I wouldn't! I'm feeling creative, I don't know where to begin – a new song called Swinging in a Hammock – very much in embryo, a Guide song for you rather more advanced, & of course the book!

I did love my ten days with you, but they went so fast.

I miss you very much. I feel strange, as though I were in a foreign country. Although my body is here, my spirit is still apparently with you (or else on the way to bedlam). Last night when Lady M.B. said 'we have got pancakes coming' I said 'That sounds disgusting' instead of delicious! Mercifully only Joscelyne heard, but I frightened myself to death.

I love to think of you going about your tasks – tidying up the lawn & making lavender bags!!

Yrs Aff,V

23 October 1936   Parr's

Darling Ginnie,

How are you duckie? When you are here I find it hard to tell you to your face how *grand* I think you are being and how I admire your peace and calm in the face of such bloodiness. Yes, I know it's all God's doing but then you are an idea of his, aren't you? Anyway, darling, you are being wonderful.

From the above thoroughly un-English attitude I'll slip back behind a Britannic mask and chat to you of the day's doings. Yesterday I had my hair washed in Maidenhead very successfully done by a Miss Church from Liverpool with lovely hands and definite ideas. Then to lunch with Miss Skimming. We chatted of clothes and books and I've said I'd join a sewing circle of local girls. 'We young ones must get together,' she said. I must confess I enjoy it. The local belles have a pretty thin time of it I gather, and Sylvia is anxious to introduce some of the lonely Burnham girls to the lonely Taplow girls over a dish of tea and a flannel nightie.

Today I determined to accomplish something, so I set myself to write from 10–12, and tho' I did no new stuff at all that was worth anything I did polish up some elderly pieces. A dialogue-ish one to Mr Watt, 'Governess' to the *Atlantic Monthly* and one called 'Finishing school' to the *New Yorker*.

Reg, darn him, has finished reading his thriller and wants to play rummy à deux.

I've completed $2^1{}_2$ flannel vests for the poo-er and seek at King's College Hospital.

Ma writes that the 3 day visit went well and that Aunt N continued to be nice to Lefty. Grace à dieu.

6 November [1936]   Montagu Square

Darling Joyce,

Ta for yours of the mpth inst. I am looking forward to Monday night like nobody's business, but if I am irritable, or worse still, *queer*, you are to forgive me, because I feel both irritable & queer.

There is a most odious feeling that all of you have gone miles away – you're there as large as life, & yet I can't quite focus on what you're saying, I can't make contact sort of, you don't seem to me to be substantiated in any way. I seem to have known you a long way back, & now I haven't met you for years & must start all over again getting to know you! Mercifully, I also know that this isn't true, & that it'll pass – at least I hope to God it does.

Anyhow, there it is, & if I am whimsey, or slashing you across the face with sausages, you must just lump it. What would I do without you & the Cottage – one the sustaining Infinite & the other so infinitely sustaining!!

I have seen 15 flats today. Don't ask me about them, if you value your life.

Yrs royally blue, Ginnie

6 November 1936   Parr's

Darling Ginnie,

Maria is quite right. You are true blue through and through. (Tho' I don't like the idea much. I mean blue legs and blue tails and blue teeth. I'd have you a double distilled 'brick'. Or perhaps you'd prefer to be a 'corker'. Or what about 'solid gold'?) Anyway you are doing fine, love, and I can't tell you how impressed I am by your courage. I mean it.

Yesterday I went to my first Women's Institute meeting. 20 of us met in the recreation room by the tennis court. Diana Smith is the sec. and an elderly Miss Serocold from Taplow is the president. We began with 'Jerusalem' played on a not very well Decca portable and in a key almost beyond human hearing. I'm sure we went above top C octave. We all sang it and I was able to come in occasionally with certain words. 'Dark satanic mills . . .'

Then we did the day's business, the minutes, a report or two, and the formal welcoming of our new member. I stood up, said nothing, and sat down again. Probably not quite adequate.

Mrs Millar from Burnham then made a pork pie and some of us took notes and some followed her with their own ingredients at a separate table. This took nearly an hour. I chatted to Mrs Dance from the Lodge and Mrs House from the Dairy.

Then we had tea. Buns, brown bread and butter and confectioner's cakes: the sort that look unreal and taste worse. Chat goes with tea and after tea I was called upon to propose my Xmas party scheme, which is to make the kiddies entertain their parents and others on the afternoon of the Xmas tree! So next Thurs, dear, while you are here, I'm 'at home' to the young at 6 p.m. to discuss what we shall do. Could you make us a song for us to sing? A simple ditty about 'Cliveden at Christmas Time'?

I came home armed with a membership card and the W.I. magazine which is full of fascinating reading. I've missed some wonderful demonstrations in the past year. 'The use of salads and how to make them' in June, and in August 'Herbs in myth, magic, medicine and meals'. January taught us 'Care of the Feet'.

It took us 20 mins to start the Ford today. I pushed my guts out getting it up the drive and onto the road.

If you had one match and you had to light a gas mantle, a candle, a cigarette and the fire, which would you light first?

. . . the match, ha! ha!

The Christmas tree party at Cliveden was a great success. Every year the Astors gave a children's party and a dance for the domestic and estate workers and their families. Joyce dressed the little girls in flowered Kate Greenaway frocks and the boys

45

in matching shirts and ties. They sang popular songs, including one written specially by Virginia, performed amusing sketches and the Astor children recited poetry. At the fancy dress dance afterwards, Waldorf Astor's valet dressed as a pantomime fairy and Old Jeffries, a gardener, as 'Old Mother Slipper Slopper'.

1937

11 January [1937]   Montagu Square

Darling Joyce,

This is just a last letter from the old homestead, which is now in a state of degradation. Bishop's[1] men traipse about with bits of china in their corrugated paws, & large bits of the wall hang down where the shelves were. It is repulsive. However, we shall soon be safely tucked into our new nest – sans curtains or carpets, but still.

Oh, the rich, Joyce! Sue telephones last night to say she was just leaving for Switzerland, so would I please buy them a suitable dining room suite. It must be done immediately. I weakly acquiesced, & spent the whole morning struggling with gate leg tables at Waring's. Why can't the rich do a single thing for themselves except write cheques? I am vexed beyond measure.

I don't wish to *hint*, but I know a nice young girl, with apple-green cheeks who could do with a couple of quiet days on a farm somewhere in the country. Perhaps you would let me know if you hear any suitable place?

Bless you, darling.
Love Winnie

[1] House removal firm.

12 January 1937   Parr's

Darling Ginny,

I found this in a local paper and thought maybe it would soot yoo:

'Tall blonde female guest welcomed in happy couple's simple home. Must play piano, rummy, tennis, the Game[1] and be fond Spaniels. Food adequate, bath, H & C. Two wenches kept but one whistles a bit. House set in beautifully appointed pleasure grounds. Gravel sweep. Rose bed, garage, shed. Apply by Phone Burnham 460 or WRITE.'

Of course I don't know at all if it's the thing you want but I've met the owner who struck me as being quite nice. She is the motherly type and he hums to himself. They have a room for you free for at least a week. Do drop them a p.c. and book EARLY.

Lindbergh[2] and his wife were here for Friday night and there's a good couple! He's not a bit disappointing. Long and strong, with those sea or air blue eyes and more charm than is good for any one man. But needless to say I don't believe he knows about it. She is little and still looks haunted. Almost very pretty. Looks delicate and dreamy but I believe she's the only one who didn't crack up during the kidnapping. Her ma, his ma, him, etc. etc. all went under, but Mrs Lindbergh was quite marvellous throughout.

I sent a short article to EV Knox[3] and I got a good, probably constructive, criticism in his own handwriting from E.V.K. himself. It was that conversation in the Pit. When I wrote it I didn't feel actually superior to the people I was writing about. In fact I felt affectionate towards them, but he read it – and I expect, probably, everyone would read it – as superior disdain. He says 'I think you have been too merciless here – it's hard, of course, to write about such people without seeming disdainful, but that's what has to be attempted.' However, I'm not down about it, because I'm sure he's right.

They had Queen Marie of Yugoslavia[4] for the weekend at Cliveden. Fat as a house and very good company. I shouldn't think it's much fun being her. She knows her life is always in danger.

With love and see you soon. I may come to London on Fri. to have my hair cut. Could we lunch?

---

[1] Version of charades, often played at Cliveden.
[2] Charles Lindbergh, (1902–74), American aviator, made first non-stop solo transatlantic flight from New York to Paris in 1927. Won the Pulitzer Prize for autobiography with *The Spirit of St Louis* in 1954. His wife Anne was his co-pilot and an author. Their baby son was kidnapped for ransom and murdered in March 1932. A German-American carpenter was found guilty and executed. In December 1935 the Lindberghs and their second child moved to England, to avoid the harassment of the media.
[3] Editor of *Punch* magazine from 1932 to 1937 (1881–1971).
[4] Great-granddaughter of Queen Victoria, daughter of Queen Marie of Roumania and wife of King Alexander I of Yugoslavia, who was assassinated in Marseilles in 1934 (1900–61).

27 January 1937   Montagu Square

Darling Joyce,

This is to say goodbye. You won't see me for a long long time, for I am off on Tuesday to Egypt!

I couldn't possibly be more bored or annoyed about it, but I can't get out of it – so there. Here is the saga. Olive and Eben Pike, and Lord Dundonald and Viola Dundas were going and then Viola chucked, they asked me. As I only know Olive, and but slightly, and it costs £100, *and* I don't want to go to Egypt, I rightly decided that I would prefer to spend my money elsewhere – say, the Tyrol – with people I like, say you. So I wrote a charming letter saying that owing to very heavy expenditure lately I feared I couldn't come, although it would be *divine* to. Then je laved les mains.

On Monday evening Lord Dundonald telephones and says 'Ah, Miss Graham, I hear you are coming on this trip with us.' 'No indeed I'm not' I say. 'Well, that's mighty odd' answers the noble Earl, who I believe incidentally is quite poopsy [dotty] 'because I've just this moment talked to Olive, and she gave me your telephone number so that I could arrange cabins with you.' I repeat again that I definitely *cannot* come, and return rattled to the fireside. Of course, you have guessed. They are *giving* me the trip. I think it's perfectly perfectly sweet and charming of them, and absolutely too nauseating for words. I know that most girls would leap at a trip down the Nile, but I wish to God they'd offered it to most girls. I am now resigned.

I tell myself that it will be nice to see the sun.

I buy silk dresses at Fenwick.

My summer clothes have been hauled out of their trunk, and look decrepit.

Passport troubles are rife. I have to visit the Egyptian Legation tomorrow.

My hats are non-existent.

Oh dear.

I feel too disheartened to go on now. Anyhow, the new radio-gram is going full blast – and I simply *have* to go & twiddle the knobs.

lots and lots of love, Ginnie

Monday, January 1937   Parr's

.Darling Ginnie,

WELCOME TO YOUR FLAT.

I should think you would have plenty of material for articles out of The Move.

I'm practising my typing on you as you may see. Are you a two finger typer? I am. You are an angel to lend me this one.

Yesterday was a good day as I managed to write two poems one of which is in four parts and is called 'Monday Morning's Mail' and is about – or is, actually – four different letters. One is from a small boy at prep school; the next is from a cook in answer to an advertisement. I'm rather fond of the third which is from the next-door neighbour complaining of noise, and the last one is an invitation to a cocktail party. The other poem is written with real feeling and is all about the sleepless night I spent last Saturday with a Corgi puppy! When I've done this letter I shall run out and post them.

So you're off to the Land of the Camel and the Sphinx. You'd be a great ass to refuse so fair a gifte and there's sun out there. Think of it. A round yellow thing that makes you feel good. How very kind of the Pikes. Who is Lord Dundonald?

I'm smoothed like a shore pebble by a lovely sea of Mozart. Did you hear it? I'm all ironed out, clean and young. I don't think Mozart's intellectual. I don't know why you say he is. He's architectural – like all the good ones – and hearing one of the slow movements was like looking at a wrought iron gate.

I'm sad tonight with a luxurious sense of surface melancholy. A gentle gloom that the Mozart has produced. I've read some Housman[1] too, which might also account for it.

[1] A.E. Housman (1859–1936), English poet, wrote 'A Shropshire Lad'.

Friday night   [Montagu Square]

Darling Joyce,

Yes, I listened to the Mozart *and* enjoyed it, but I do think they make a mistake in having all one composer. One gets so seeped in it that the appreciative senses become benumbed. I couldn't take the Jupiter, and switched to Radio Luxembourg for a spot of Horlicks.[1]

Your ignorance of the peerage is crass. Lord Dundonald is, I should judge from his appearance, a relative of Lord Dundreary. He came to tea yesterday and talked exclusively of disease, and how the cold tickled up his lung. I took the gloomiest view of him – but I think he was shy. He is 50-ish, tall and rather like a Cubist to look at. And he wore a yellow leather overcoat with a fur collar. However, as my host, I must, I suppose, be pleased with him.

It has been snowing here all the day, and I have been skidding to and fro. *To* the Egyptian legation, and *fro* Messrs Harrods, who strangely enough, produce rows of excellent summer gowns in palest pink. I have also been studying works on Egypt, by defunct archaeologists, and I would like to read you a little bit: 'Osiris, King of the North & South, Men-Kau-Ra, living for ever! The heavens have produced thee, thou wast engendered by Nut (the sky), thou art the offspring of Seb (the earth) the mother Nut spreads herself over thee to be a god, as a divine mystery.' Osiris' father, of course, was a Kernel. Also: 'The Kiosk, or Pharaoh's bed is one of the most graceful objects on the island.' Well, well. I had luncheon with Reggie yesterday. We stoked ourselves up with Scotch Broth and he was very sweet.

Nell, I set off on Tuesday by the 11.0 boat train – get to Marseilles the next day, then board a minute ship called *El Nil* – only 7,000 tons and remain puking thereon until the 8th! Could get to America in that time. On the 10th we start down the Nile until we get to Aswan. There the men leave us and rush into the wilds to shoot animals. After simmering there in the sun we shall all start back again.

Take good care of yourself, and think a great deal of me, and write lots of poems for *Punch*.

lots and lots of love from Winsome

¹ Horlicks a hot, milk drink, was frequently advertised on Radio Luxembourg, the only commercial radio station then in Britain.

Thurs, 28 January 1937   Eydon 'all

Darling Ginnie,

For heavens sake don't go too far down the Nile because you'll have to come all the way back up the same old river and beside which I don't at all like the idea of you seeing foreign parts – new ones – without me. Is it a cruise? Even my feelings for 'Abroad' could be stifled if I thought we'd stare at a pyramid together.

My hair is a riot of curls seeing as how I spent the morning kneeling in front of a colossal pyre in an effort to dry it. Now pleasantly smelling of tar and lemon rinse. A nursery smell, like knees that have been covered in woollen stockings.

France's house is just our drop. (Not as to decor; but as to warmth, light, books, an open piano under a suitable light in a getatable position, a jar of Parkinson's Humbugs, the *New Yorker* and a *Tatler*, and a good radiogram. Table full of photograph books, a royal blue cinararia, a tangled Yorkshire terrier, and a table set with much too good tea.)

Have a lovely sunny time, darling. Please flirt a bit: preferably non-Army but I don't forbid the services. Relax and enjoy it.

P.S. If it is a cruise you'll have to take part in the deck games. Yar! Yar!

5 February [1937]   SS *El Nil*

Darling Joyce,

I have just had a nice café complet, and am now sitting on deck pretending that it is a good deal warmer than it is! We have had an excellent journey so far. From Marseilles to Genoa it was really hot, and the sea was a deep blue. And flat as a pancake. We sat basking in the sun, trying to read Egypt and the Nile in various forms, and ending by merely falling asleep. We reached Genoa amid a terrific din and much bangings & shoutings which were rather a bore. We took a rather dreary walk along the quayside. Olive wished to buy some stockings, and we eventually found a taxi driver, showed him our legs, and he drove us to a shop! Every word of Italian has left me except for Voi che Sapete[1] and Aspetto un momento[2] (which is a more useful phrase).

Now, about the company. Olive is really charming – very kind and gentle, and we have already had long discussions on Sex, and the Art of Bringing up Children, on both subjects of which of course, I am most knowledgeable! Eben is sweet, and so far hasn't been at all grandiery.

Lord D joined us just five minutes before the boat sailed, having motorised 150 miles in a taxi from somewhere. The stewards call him Your Excellency. He is very quiet, and with rather a good sense of humour. So far hasn't taken any pills, but he talks a lot about inoculation, & would, I think, like me to get inoculated in Cairo, for typhoid or the plague! Nobody's told me about their operations yet, which is something.

The other inmates of this floating asylum are old ladies with oldish daughters, old ladies with old companions, or old ladies with their old husbands. The stewards wear crimson accordion pleated pants, red & gold pea-jackets, & fezes. They seem to be straight out of musical comedy. If one says things backwards they understand – Juice orange? has much more effect than orange juice. We have a pathetic band after all meals. It plays awfully badly, but we clap it a lot.

Viola Tree's mother-in-law is also with us. She is very dictatorial and tiresome, and I hear her telling people about Peter and Celia – 'she was just a doctor's daughter you know.'

I wonder what you are doing love? I miss our singsongs in the cabin of an early morning – our awful bouts of giggling – It doesn't seem at all right to be without you on the high seas – I perceive incidentally that they are getting a trifle higher. And I *do* wish you were here.

In the Lounge there is a trout playing the piano – rather well, except that she divides the chords, and plays with *far* too much feeling.

The Nile steamer is very white and houseboatish. Lord D is doing us proud, with a bathroom to every bedroom: it takes us 10 days to get as far as Aswan.

Well, well duckie, lots and lots of love from Ginnie

[1] Aria from *Marriage of Figaro*, meaning 'You who know'.
[2] Wait a moment.

7 February 1937   Parr's

Darling Ginnie,

Maria and I spent an enjoyable half hour in the Maidenhead PO
yesterday morning sending you 10 birthday cards which we discovered
in Woolworth's.[1]

You left on Tuesday. I came up from Eydon that afternoon on a four
o'clock train and from Paddington went direct to 4 St James Square[2]
to bring the latest from the girls. Aunt Nancy looked a wreck; very
tired and rather nervy, and it's all taken her far harder than you'd
have thought possible.[3] Of course, she and Aunt Phyllis were very
close, but even so and with C.S. [Christian Science] Aunt N oughtn't
to be minding so much. Wiss has got the new hair-do which consists
of a roll right around the head so that the face looks quite naked and
rather page boy like. She was in gay and sparkling mood and rather
a good tonic for the rest of the party. I followed Aunt N upstairs after
tea where she was to have her hair washed. Miss Hammond who has
a famous 'system' was overalled and ready, with an egg shampoo in
a little jug and half-a-dozen bottles of distilled water lined up on the
floor. As soon as she'd got Aunt N's hair wet, Miss Brew, a political sec.
came in with dope on the Child Nutrition Bill, due in the House next
day. Then Rose, the maid, announced a dressmaker, her tailor and an
ornamental assistant who hustled in with much foreign under-whispers
and milady-ing and they proceeded to put minute tweed coats on me to
show Auntie![4]

Meanwhile Wiss was trying to change her curl and I, tweeded and
all, was reading a very good C.S. letter from Ma to Aunt N on the
subject of Death. How the Great survive is beyond me! Before the room
had cleared M. Ernest from Antoine had arrived with a drier and a
bottle of setting lotion. Quelle vie.

R collected me and we drove down here through rain, as usual: and
gosh I was glad to see the homestead once more. There was a potted
azalea of a deep ruby red, fires everywhere, a pale smile from René and
liver and bacon for supper. A couple of *New Yorkers* and the *Reader's
Digest* and two Brandenburgs from Manchester kept me busy until
bedtime.

Next day I went to the Strachey[5] class, which was on Tennyson. A
small circle of five women and me. Tennyson seems to be rather good in
spite of some much quoted horrors. He had great religious wars going
on in his own mind. The good warring with evil.

I was invited for lunch and it was good, with a fine Brie cheese at
the end. Over the table Miss Strachey discoursed on Psycho-Analysis.
I think her brother James[6] is a professional one. It sounds frightful and

altogether wrong. You would have hated it. It's far more ridiculous, from our point of view, than I'd even imagined. The PA has to get the patient so confident in him that he causes a 'transference': by which the patient thinks of and treats the PA as he would his parent – 'half in love with him' said Miss Strachey, 'and half hating her or him'! Anyway it's all bound up with sex and dreams and those way back terrible nursery days when one was repressed! I was thankful to escape, and to take the taste out of my large mouth I took myself to the New Gal. Cinema to see *Sweet Aloes* and watch Kay Francis suffer maternal thwartings.

Next day after that it was the Annual Birthday Party of the Women's Institute, Taplow branch. So I spent the morning in Maidenhead buying one doz. candles, a pastry board, one packet wax tapers, one package of dry peas (!) and a bundle of lemonade straws. You stick the candles, all cut to different lengths, on to the pastry board and light them. Then you sit on a chair 1 $\frac{1}{2}$ yards away and, with your hands behind your back and your feet off the ground, you see how many you can blow out. See? The dried peas are moved from a bowl to a teacup by means of suction *through* the lemonade straw. How many can *you* move? I had early lunch so that Alice, the cook, could get off in time too, for we are fellow members.

Can you play 'Jerusalem'?[7] It's got all the sharps and great gaps between the octave chords and is hideously difficult. However, by eliminating the introduction I managed to scrape through on that Institute piano, damp and half silent. Then we had Community Singing and because the professional who was to have taken it had 'flu, I did my best from the *Daily Express Song Book*. They like sad things best and we droned the 'Londonderry Air' and 'My Bonnie lies over the Ocean', getting slower and slower. I tried to beat time with me head but found it got me dizzy. Finally Miss Serocold, our elderly president, genteelly conducted us and we romped ahead with 'Robin Adair' and the 'Vicar of Bray'. Then tea, competitions and games.

On Friday morning I walked down to Jeffries to enquire after the old man.[8] He had a stroke about three days after Aunt Phyllis's funeral. He was very devoted to her and terribly distressed when she died. Connie was hanging up the washing and her sister-in-law, Bert's wife, was peeling potatoes and soon little Mrs J joined them carrying a hot water bottle and looking amazingly cheerful. The old man is not expected to 'last' long. He's over 80 and has had a good life. The family are philosophic about it but, as they say, 'it won't be the same when Dad's gone'. His garden is so brave. Full of green spikes and the polyanthus he bedded out are flowering feverishly. I shall miss him awfully. Passing by his cottage I always went in. He'd sit on his barrow and fill his pipe with an earthy hand, slap them on his green baize apron and talk about mummy. 'Tell 'er I asked after 'er when you wroite,' he always said.

I had a particularly good and instantaneous healing when I was at Eydon. One evening I got a real penetrator of a headache. The sort that makes you feel you daren't stand up or even move. Agony. The girls teased me for laziness when I lay on the sofa. I couldn't even think: but I particularly didn't want them to know I didn't feel so good. In the bath I did some automatic denying. You know the sort of thing. Next thing I knew I was down at dinner feeling like a daisy. Not a sign left! I was so pleased, I must have shone.

I miss you awfully. Even when I don't see you I like to know that you are at the end of the telephone wire. I want to hear all the details. R is angelic and the damp weather has turned up his footman's lock and he looks fascinating. I'm in *Punch* this week. My book is stuck and I seem dry somehow.

Have a happy time.

[1] Virginia's birthday was on 1 November.
[2] The Astors' London home.
[3] Phyllis, Nancy's younger sister, had just died of pneumonia.
[4] Joyce was several sizes larger than Nancy and much taller.
[5] Marjorie Strachey, known as 'Gumbo' (1882–1964). Teacher and writer, member of the Bloomsbury Group, she lived in Gordon Square. Described by Virginia Woolf as 'vivacious and commanding', she gave obscenely comic renderings of nursery rhymes. Younger sister of writer Lytton Strachey (1880–1932), whom Joyce met at Cliveden and of James Strachey.
[6] James Strachey (1887–1967). Psychoanalyst trained by Sigmund Freud and translator of *The Complete Works of Freud* in twenty-four volumes.
[7] The Women's Institute anthem. Joyce was a proficient pianist.
[8] The Jeffries family had worked for the Astors for many years. Bert was Waldorf Astor's second chauffeur.

11 February 1937   Parr's

Darling Ginnie,

Radio has been poor except for a first class 20 mins. by Philip Lothian[1] on 'God and the Common Life'. It's a series in which prominent laymen are airing their views on the relationship of the Church, Community and the State. Philip spoke simply but convincingly, and he made it a living thing. R listened spellbound. Needless to say it was all pure C.S. Positive statements of truth that would make anyone think if they were at all interested. Not a bit aggressive, but exactly what was needed. (C.S. wasn't mentioned of course.)

Yesterday comes next and was my birthday. R and I drove up to London to deposit our bags at 4 St Jas. Sq. Lee [the butler] told me Aunt N wanted to see me upstairs. And there she gave me a pair of pearl and diamond ear-rings like the ones I had stolen only even bigger and more exquisite, isn't it angelic of her to always give me such lovely presents? I'm certainly lucky.

At 12 I attended Miss Strachey's class and we went on with Tennyson, who wrote a good deal of complete rot and a certain amount of 'flat' poetry. Of the eye and not the stomach. Have you ever read 'Dora'? She was adopted by her uncle, who wished her to marry his son William; but William 'the more he saw her the less he liked her'.

Lunch with Pa and he gave me a tenner. Wasn't it good of him, and again, aren't I lucky? He was in rosy form and we chewed in a happy glow and he told me about a good healing he'd had.

After lunch I banked my cheque and then feeling expansive and uplifted I wafted into First Church and flipped some £.s.d. into the smiling aperture of the Church Funds box and came away feeling smug.

We had supper at the Savoy Grill where we saw Arthur Rubinstein,[2] who'd just played at the Queen's Hall under Beecham. Lots of people we know there. A good entry by a certain lovely actress who I thought knew better. She came in wearing a Garbo-ish felt hat, black right over one eye, a very chic grey lamb fur coat, and in hands a colossal bunch of parma violets which she held against her face and peered over with this one enormous and much mascarr'd eye. It was good, yes, but as it was Diana Wynyard[3] I was rather sickened. It was too easy: a slow entry, smothered in violets. Gosh she looked lovely.

In the restaurant I banged straight into Carroll Gibbons[4] who was watching the cabaret. He immediately and hurriedly apologised for not answering either of my notes and promised then and there to hear and help me. I'm to ring him up on Monday. I'm not counting on it at all, so don't worry. But it *could* be exciting.

Back down here I made lunch for 8 before poor old Jeffries funeral. It was terribly sad. No music and a huddle of little, skinny, black clothed Jeffries in paroxysms of tears. Lovely flowers. Oh! how I cried too, of course. I *loathe* funerals. Don't let me have one will you. Just hire a professional man to get rid of my body and then you and a few right thinking friends can make some statements about Life, and leave it at that.

Mama sent me a superb pair of country gloves from Fortmason!
I realise had you been here I'd have received my annual Rolls. But I
understand perfectly, Mopsie. Next time will do. Bless you darling.

[1] Lord Lothian of Blickling, formerly Philip Kerr (1882–1940). Founder member of the
Cliveden Round Table, which Phyllis called The Tabloids. Converted to Christian Science
from Roman Catholicism. British Ambassador in Washington at beginning of the Second
World War.
[2] Concert pianist (1888–1982).
[3] British stage actress (1906–64). Began her career in Hollywood, and returned to work in
Britain when she married director Carol Reed.
[4] An American pianist and bandleader. Financially insecure, Joyce hoped to get a job
as a singer.

11 February [1937]   SS *Egypt*

Darling Joyce,
    I suppose it is true that I am now sailing up the Nile in a steamer,
but hardly! We have just had a large luncheon & are sitting on deck.
Felukas, with their lovely curved masts are sailing merrily by.
    Looking at me in rather a *snweery* way from the bank is a camel.
Eben is fast asleep, his feet on the white rail, and on his head balanced
precariously, a green felt sporting hat! Cocky [Lord Dundonald] is
reading the *Sporting and Dramatic*, & Olive is striving to disenravel the
mysteries of Egyptian history, the ramifications of which are, like God,
past all understanding.
    Everything is very harmonious, and we travel in great style. In Cairo
we went out to the sphinx & the pyramids after dinner. It was most
impressive – absolute dead stillness except for distant dogs barking, the
sky riddled with stars, & these immense objects glimmering faintly, like
ghosts in the blue night. The Sphinx is far bigger than I supposed, and
they have lately excavated more of it, so that it has two immense paws!
    We also saw Tutankhamun's treasures, which are unbelievably
beautiful.
    We boarded yesterday and the only other person we know is Lady
Howard de Walden.[1] Yesterday afternoon we staggered about in the
sand from one tomb to another, and then we saw the best sunset that
I have ever seen – yellow, pink, blue, orange, mauve, *everything*. The
boat ties up all night which is very nice of it, it is divine to know that
it simply *can't* move about. It is also divine to travel with men, who do
everything tiresome, like the tickets, etc.
    Cocky is an extraordinary fellow – clever, and yet vague, very kind
about everybody, ugly to the point of unattractiveness, but has a nice
warm smile.
    We all have tremendous jokes – several of which are undying, such

as the KittyKat which was on the Menu one night on the *El Nil*. Olive and I have extraordinary fits of giggling, born we know not how. They are so good for me, and I really feel as though I were coming alive again. The sun, of course, enhances everything.

I hope you are having a swell time in your little cottage. It is queer to think of you taking brisk walks in the nippy air and it does seems a pity that you can't be here with Winnie Grimes. I believe, with all your hatred of abroad, you would like the East, the colours would catch you a bit.

When we went ashore yesterday we had Egyptian policemen on white Arab ponies, flicking the beggars with their whips. It felt tremendously Pasha Bashy Bazook, and rather dreadful, but it saved us a lot of exhausting work, shouting oaths in Arabic.

Tomorrow we are climbing onto donkeys and are going for a ride into the desert to see a Tomb of a Sacred Cat (or Kitty Kat).

yards of love from Ninnie

[1] British society hostess, married 1912, died 1974.

18 February 1937   Parr's

Darling Ginnie,

I wrote a couple of poems this afternoon both of which have gone to Watts. 'Thames Valley Floods' is the best. 'Fetch down the album' I like a little less. But not much less.

On Saturday I lured handsome R on to the indoor court and we played for nearly two hours and felt much better at the end.

Tommy [Phipps] told me a story I'm delighted to know. Two char ladies went into a pub. No. 1 said 'Going to have one, duck?' And her friend replied 'No, dear, it's the way me coat's buttoned up.'

Now I'm back in the drawing room where an orchestra in Ireland are rollicking through the Fifth Brandenburg and I'm swaying with the intoxication of it. Next we're to have some Handel and lastly a Concerto Grosso by Brent Smith, who was a friend of Aunt Phyllis and played at her funeral. He looks like a question mark but is full of nice things.

There, the Bach is over and the Belfastians are clapping away. There's a 'cello near the microphone and it's being tuned – vim, vom, veem, veem.

After Sunday lunch R and I threw some evening clothes into a bag and drove over to Ditchley to tea and dinner, between which there was a quartette concert for Aunt Irene.[1] Various other Astors, Philip Lothian, Virginia and Dinah [Brand] over from Eydon – nice party. In the white and gold drawing room with its gold and crystal chandeliers lit with real candles. The four strings were squared together in a corner. A great bowl of white freesia and another of hyacinths filled the air with a delicious scent and the windows were still unshuttered, and the grey of the gloomy day was turning into a thick bright blue.

First some Mozart and then the slow movement of Faure that was like a lovely sensation. After dinner we drove sleepily through a fine rain. We found a dundrearied young man in Bourne End who'd run out of gas, so we took him in search of a station. The two girls he'd had with him were sent back to the car to wait. It took us half an hour to locate a pump, wake up the owner and get a canful. We then discovered he'd never seen the girls before, he'd met them at 'Binnie's' in Maidenhead, which is quite a Spot. He had to be back at Andover later that night. Not an attractive boy but quite grateful.

Next day R and I went up to London for two nights. I went to the dentist in the afternoon and came away with a stiff jaw owing to an injection, but I'd had four cavities filled so I felt pretty glad.[1] At John Lewis I found a very good plain black crepe evening dress for $3\frac{1}{2}$ guins. A 'safe' sort of dress.

Aunt N had a huge reception and dinner for the 10 year Nursery School Plan that night. Waldorf couldn't be there, so Bill[2] was host and I was a helper. I had one Ramsbottom MP on my left and Terence O'Connor on my right. I felt somewhat light-headed from the dope and we talked of white slaves and drug traffics.

After dinner a great crowd of Earnest Women and MPs and their wives came in to hear Julian Huxley[3] speak on the importance of environment for Leetul Cheeldren Etc. Etc. The upstairs room was arranged as an exhibition of photographs showing conditions and some of the improved schools. It was rather exciting and I saw that if I let myself go I should probably get bitten with the Nursery Schools bug. Owing to wonderful self-control I wasn't. I wish you could have seen Bill, Dame Edith Lyttelton[4] and Julian Huxley squeezed on a platform about a yard square. They had to concentrate to remain on it!

Maria has had a windfall of an unexpected £250 so she took me to lunch at the Berkeley Grill, where she had gnocchi and I had sweetbreads, and it was very comforting and warm. We indulged in manicures after a movie and then I hurried back to 4 St James Squ to change. The house was quite empty but for me. Rather gloomy except that in my room was a roaring fire and the evening paper.[5]

Then I went to Jimmie's concert where I saw your Ma and Jim sang with professional finish and great restraint. A very difficult programme including two unheard Purcell songs from a m.s.s. found in the British Museum. Then four songs by Holst for voice and fiddle. No piano. Lovely but excruciatingly difficult.

Aunts Nancy and Irene left that afternoon for 10 days snow and sun in St Moritz. I'm glad, for Aunt N needed it badly.

(miss you *somph crool.*)

[1] Christian Scientists are allowed to use dentists.
[2] Waldorf and Nancy Astor's son and heir (1907–66).
[3] Eminent scientist (1887–1975), brother of Aldous the writer.
[4] A rather stout cousin of Hilda Grenfell and great friend of Nancy Astor.
[5] Laid on by a retinue of servants.

21 February [1937]   Cataract Hotel
                                                                    Aswan

Dearest Joyce,

You put me to shame with your glorious long letters. I got one yesterday, which I simply loved. I tucked up in bed and read it very slowly, picturing you in every attitude of your busy life.

Darling, this is paradisical spot. I am sitting on an enormous verandah overlooking a backwater of the Nile – over the edge of which hangs deep purpoile bougainvillaea. In the background there is a range of hills the colour of sand (just between you and me, they are sand) and over the other side the Sahara stretches for hundreds and thousands of miles as far as Timbuctoo. The sky is pale Eton blue and there is a tigsy breeze. I am wearing a dress I bought at Fenwick, a blue guernsey, and a flywhisk.

We were awfully matey with everybody at the end of the trip. Riding donkeys seems to bring one together like nothing else can. Lady Howard de Walden was *very* nice, if somewhat forceful, and her friend Mrs Fitzclarence was nice too, but of the gin and tonic, Camel cigarette order.

We also became embroiled with a large family – Poppa, Mama, Harry, Angela and two maiden aunts as like as two pins. They were very hard to place. They know people like Phoebe Houston-Boswell, and they are just *not* quite quite, but rich.

There were two tough American boys who thought it would be nice if I could drive across the Sahara with them in a car, and there were lots of old trout of course and old buffers.

We did an awful lot of sightseeing, mostly very early in the morning which made the day rather long. Our dragoman was called Gaddi Morgan, and we never understood a word he said. His pal we christened Grenfell. Our expeditions were a triumph of organisation, what with policemen to beat off the beggars and sailors to dust our shoes with feather brooms on our return! At Luxor we got taken by an Egyptian honeymoon couple on a launch down the river to a garden. There we met a snake charmer and the most alarming cobra. He magic-ed it in a truly wonderful way, denouncing neither mesmerism, hypnotism nor animal magnetism, but using them all with great success.

The honeymoon couple were pathetic. He was very showy-off young man, splashing about with laurels and dinner parties on shore, and she was quite silent except for a few words of French, and had a rash on her cheek. I think the young man was already bored with her, judging by his desire to entertain all of us at every opportunity. She had extraordinary almond eyes, plonked onto her face.

This is the swankiest hotel ever and I bet it costs £1 a minute. Anyway it costs 3/6 to have a dress ironed.

Eben and Cocky took us to the Races! You ought to see camels racing. It is extremely droll. The whole thing was rather like a fete at Horsham. The local regimental band played, and would you believe it, they had 6 Irish pipes, like the Irish Guards, and they were dressed in Khaki and wore red tarboush fezzes. The audience was just pukka, in printed crepe de chine!

Frank, Cocky's manservant, is about to iron Olive's nightdress. Cocky is called The Lord by the Egyptians. They are always saying 'The Lord awaits you in the trolley!'

Thank you for your lovely letter darling.

Love Virginia

23 February 1937   Parr's

Darling Ginnie,

You'll have to bear with me for I'm in a very Lamb and Cloud mood. Gary and I have been out in the wood for two hours and it's all so new and bursting and exciting and soft, that I'm all of a tremble and have seen most of the loveliness through a haze! By the time we'd arrived at the big oak tree with the river views I was quite worn out through exaltation. The river was Lady Mendl's favourite beige in colour. Through the willows was a very Nash-like landscape. Did you know that oak trees in February are a rich rose in colour? Well they are.

While plopping in puddles with Gary I thought up an idea for a jingle. Its title won't come but here it is for you:

> Please need we go to the Mildewy-Maddows
> Who live in a house which the Albert Hall shadows?
> They will play very deep intellectual games
> And no one will ever discover our names.
> It wouldn't insult them for they'll never know.

So I really don't see why we bother to go.
Let's sup by our fireside instead,
Oh let's.
Let's sup by our fireside instead.

My love we *must* go to the Mildewy-Maddows
Who live in a house which the Albert Hall shadows.
They are giving a dance, for their daughter, in June
And remember our Millicent's coming out soon.
So we've got to be nice – and you mustn't be silly –
To people who might send an invite to Milly.
Get up from your fireside you must
My pet.
Get up from your fireside you must.

Now *why* did we go to the Mildewy-Maddows
Who live in a house which the Albert Hall shadows?
I spoke to a duchess, who's well over eighty,
And fed a jam puff to your own sister Katy,
Our hostess mistook me for old Colonel Slaughter
Is this how I'm helping to launch my dear daughter?
I won't leave my fireside again
Oh no!
I won't leave my fireside again.

(The orchestra has gone all Hungarian – that harp instrument being beaten into a frenzy of tin plonks. It's driving me crazy.)

On Saturday R, Frances Grenfell and I drove over to Oxford for the Grind!!! *ME*. We went direct to Michael's [Astor] room where we were invited to drink champagne. We picked up Hugh Fraser[1] who is an amusing RC bloke with a big nose and a lovely sister, Magda Eldon. At Little Tea – where the point-to-point takes place – a lovely position at the top of a hill overlooking about six fields, we drove into the 10/- car park and got out into the teeth of the wind. We collected at Bill Astor's Bentley, and here we ate well of smoked salmon, plum cake and coffee. Bill rode in a race and came third. It was sunny and gay, and I actually enjoyed myself a lot. I enjoyed seeing the teddy bear coated debs, with their Joan Crawford hair cuts and silly pretty faces, with pillar box mouths and thread-wide eyebrows. I was photographed staring vacantly at the list of starters and the result came out in yesterday's *Daily Mail*. Not so good.

(The orchestra is now pirouetting to a Tango. Sunny, Funny, Spain.)

I spent yesterday morning writing another pome but it got too tricky and R thought it a 'tacky' metre. I'm going to re-do it after this letter. It's about a girl who can't understand why she wasn't a belle at the party last night. She looked lovely and had her hair newly washed etc. When she gets home she goes to the bathroom to clean her teeth and sees a great wreath of spinach cleaving to a molar, and realises why she was such a failure.

(Brahms waltz now.)

I believe you may get back in time for the daffodils.

Much love and I miss you.

[1] Hon. Hugh Fraser (1918–84), elected Conservative MP at twenty-seven, knighted in 1980, first husband of writer Antonia Fraser *née* Pakenham.

2 March 1937   Luxor Winter Palace
                                                  Luxor

Darling Joyce,

Two gloriously long letters today from you, full of poems and fun. The pome about not going out to drinks made me laugh out loud.

This morning Cocky and I rode a couple of donkeys to Karnak to have another look at the Temple there, and a mosquito chewed large chunks out of my left thigh. I dare not scratch in case Cocky produced a bottle of iodine and insisted on applying the mixture to the spots.

This afternoon we watched a Visitor's donkey race. The Visitors are a family called Soames, consisting of a typical guardsman father, a mother and 2 girls. The latter three dress as though they were just off to Buck House Garden Party – in enormous hats, and white gloves & Ma carries a parasol!

We called on Mrs Ronnie Greville[1] in her cabin in the Nile Steamer the other day. I had never met her before and found her fascinating. She had, needless to say, just dined alone with the K & Q [King George VI and Queen Elizabeth] and was full of gossip. She was extremely funny and not a little catty about Lady Cunard,[2] her rival in the social field. Not only did she have a maid, but a maid to look after that maid, & a manservant.

I *wish* you were here to see the sights. They range from compleat English clergyman's wife abroad, to women dressed liked pre-war film stars in riding breeches, beaded gauntlets and a scarf tied round the head with a hanging tassel behind the ear! It would be six times more amusing if you were here, you dirty dog!

My love to darling Reggie and the black boy [Gary].

Yrs Aff Gin

[1] British society hostess (*c.* 1870–1942). Owned Polesdon Lacy where King George VI and Queen Elizabeth took their honeymoon.
[2] American society hostess (*c.* 1870–1948). Married Sir Edward Cunard, shipping magnate, in 1895. Friend of the Duke and Duchess of Windsor.

Carroll Gibbons auditioned Joyce singing and they made a gramophone record together in Billy Higgs's studio in Tottenham Court Road. Gibbons hinted that she might be offered a job as a weekend singer at the Hotel de Paris, Bray in Wales.

6 March 1937   Semiramis Hotel
                                                                                    Cairo

Darling Joyce,

What a lion-hearted creature you are! I've never heard of anything so brave as your Gibbons adventures! I can picture myself crawling in a half faint about Totters Court, and being sick into the piano – but I have no doubt you thought it a picnic. I can't help thinking Auntie [Nancy Astor] won't absolutely like you being the cabaret at Bray, but I do hope you'll waive her objections aside, unless this would cause a rupture in family relations.

And your *Punch* stuff too! You certainly are going it, darling, and I *am* so hugely pleased. We'll spend hours in the gramophone place practising your vowels – wouldn't it be grand if you became the Grammy Queen – like a Frances Langford. What is there to stop you?

Last night we went to *The Importance of Being Earnest*, acted by the Dublin Gate Theatre people. They do a new play every night, and so they don't not 'arf know their words.

Howard Carter[1] took us round the Museum this morning, which was passionately interesting. He has been treated shabbily by everyone, but he doesn't complain over much.

Must stop now, darling. Oh the blizzards I must meet before I meet you!!!

Love Winsome

[1] British archaeologist (1873–1939) who discovered Tutankhamun's tomb in 1922.

Joyce's quest for a job came by chance when she sat next to J.L. Garvin, the editor of the *Observer* at lunch at Cliveden. They talked about the radio and how much Joyce enjoyed listening to it, especially dramas and classical concerts. Garvin had no idea that anyone listened to this machine which had been transmitting programmes for fifteen years. Some months later he invited Joyce to write six trial radio reviews.

Good Friday [1937]   40 Orchard Court, W1

Darling Joyce,

I was so glad to get your wire telling me of your successful audition
with old Popeye Garvin. Now just you rise in the strength of spirit –
hold on to everything, especially grammar – & write two absolutely
knock out articles, won't you, duckie?

My God, once you're a critic in the *O.* there's *no* looking back, &
you're *going* to be a critic in the *O!* I am sure of it, in fact I insist.

This morning I have been doing headings in my book, & am now
going to stand headdownwards in a drawer seeking a Sun Insurance
Policy for the car.

It is fine, cold & I am looking forward to my Easter.

Now darling, for God's sake concentrate on your construction
of sentences which I sometimes think are a bit unwieldy, & you've
got this job in your lap. I love, adore and worship you, but I like
Gary more.

Yours Tootsie

After a three-week apprenticeship, Joyce's 'Broadcasting Review' first appeared on
11 April, for which she was paid £10 – more than Reggie was earning. It appeared
weekly until newsprint was rationed at the start of the Second World War.

In May, Britain was preparing for the coronation of George VI.

[May 1937]   Orchard Court

Darling Joyce,

I just thought you'd like to know that in our courtyard there are
two sparrows who are building a nest behind a drain pipe, using
for their bricks & mortar all our bunting! Any piece of string lain
down is immediately removed, & this morning they took a small
Union Jack which is now peeking out of their nest! Mr Edgson & his
slaves are in despair, but notwithstanding, the creases in their faces
soften as they crane their necks backwards to look at the culprits –
chasing about with bits of geranium & hydrangea in their mouths!)
They are the sweetest birds you could imagine, and patriotic to
the core.

I lunched with Rachel,[1] heavily made up, but without any nail
varnish! We went to see the King's crown, & on to the Academy. This
morning I raced to Westminster Hospital & got seats for the rehearsal
tomorrow for the maids. Meanwhile I've got the grammy charged with
records, & am sticking in photographs. Gosh, I wish you lived in a

drawer in my writing table. It would really be quite snug, & I would so
love to have you there!

[1] Rachel Spender Clay (1907–95). Waldorf Astor's niece, later married to Sir David
Bowes-Lyon, the brother of Queen Elizabeth, the Queen Mother. She remained a close friend
of Virginia all her life.

Sunday, 16 September [1937]   Orchard Court

Darling Joyce,

It has been a drab day, which I have enjoyed. I went to Church,
and after a rather disgusting luncheon of rolypoly pudding, I smothered
myself in Grip-fix and photographs, & scissors, & blotting paper, &
paints, & toothmugs filled with green water – you have guessed?
My book.

I put on *all* the gramophone records I possess, without looking at
them first.

Mummy and Kitty went to Hayling Island and found a marvellous
antique shop in which a peculiar young man lived, moved & had his
being. On the refrigerator were bits of Bristol china & a bust of Byron;
& there was some Crown Derby on the stove, & his brush & comb &
toothglass on a Queen Anne commode. Ma found at last the garniture
de cheminée [fireplace decoration] that we have been seeking so long for
the drawing room. Two Empire objects of great monstrosity but eminent
suitability! 'It' is a woman (bronze) with gold breasts & a dolphin's
tail holding an immense gold shell on her head. It does sound dreadful
doesn't it. There are two of them.

I have just read a horrid book which you would hate, called *No
Pockets in a Shroud* written by the man who wrote *They Shoot Horses,
Don't They?*[1] It is probably damned good – in fact I'm sure it is, but
somebody's always lying naked in somebody else's bed, not to mention
abortion, castration, & other follinesses. I felt quite queasy last night
after I'd finished it, but I had to finish it. Do you think there is a morbid
side to my nature? Thanks, I thought you did, you egg-faced thing.

I long to see you. I realised when I was away that 'coming home'
for me means coming home to you, & I was suitably horrified at the
discovery!! I think it must be the nanny in you, or else the gypsy in me.

Yours loving ever, Virginia

[1] By Horace McCoy.

Joyce did voluntary work at the Infant Welfare Clinic in Slough and met a family of
six children. At Christmas she bought them clothes and toys at Marks and Spencer
and Woolworth's and wrote to her mother, 'You can't imagine what wonders can be
achieved for £2.0.0. Of all the forms of self-indulgence, giving is the pleasantest.'

1938

6 January [1938]

Beaufort
Hexham
Northumberland

Darling Joyce,

My life progresses happily enough in this dazzlingly beautiful weather. Yesterday Anthony Coates[1] and I hurled ourselves down an immense slope on a toboggan – by far the most terrifying thing I've done for years. One appears to be going 60 miles p.h. and owing to flying snow, it is impossible to see. We had one colossal spill in which I lacerated my knee and poor Anthony scratched his face to ribbons, & we felt most frightfully dashing & heroic.

Well, darling, the dance wasn't too bad. Lovely Georgian Assembly Rooms in Newcastle in which we both dined and danced. I sat next to the Duke of Northumberland[2] & Harold Nicolson's son.[3] The former was like a very aristocratic looking but oh such a depressed carrot, & the latter hadn't had a haircut for weeks & talked all the time about the appalling slum conditions in the North! At 12.0 the Dook said, very pathetically, 'I do wish I could go home now, don't you?' I am assured by others he is intelligent, noble, amusing and altogether delightful!

As for my loves, dear heart, of which I have so many as you know – the major love is in Scotland killing things & it is rather restful & nice because however gratifying it may be to be beau-ed it is extremely fatiguing what with keeping myself smart looking and eating rich foods at restaurants every other day I feel as though I had been living in Paris for years – rather scented and gorged. It is useless to ask me whether I am enamoured of the creature, because I haven't the faintest idea – I wish I had.

We had a wonderful time last night, dipping dead mullions in a bath of whitewash. The whole room became like one gigantic Heath Robinson contraption. We are hoping, that arranged with pampas the effect will be staggeringly beautiful!

Anthony has just come in to say that our toboggan run is even more perilous than yesterday, & that I must come at once! help!

Love from Virginia

[1] Son of Lady Celia Coates, killed in action in the Second World War.
[2] 8th Duke, then aged twenty-six, owner of Alnwick Castle, killed in action in the Second World War in 1940.
[3] Nigel Nicolson, then aged twenty-one, author and Conservative MP. Son of Vita Sackville-West and Harold.

Joyce was promoted to president of the local branch of the Women's Institute.

28 March 1938   Parr's

Darling Ginnie,

We came in second at the Women's Institute Dainty Tea Competition on Thurs! What's more, those stuck up Taplowites were disqualified for showing 9 plates instead of the stipulated 8! Ha. Ha. Ha. What a day it was. I made the trips to Loudwater four times – 8 ways – that morning – 56 miles! A woman in homespun tweeds called Digby talked to us about International Affairs. So diplomatic and anxious to avoid controversy was she that even the astutest among us couldn't get a hint of what she was talking about. And there was an hour of this.

The weekend at Cliveden for the P.M.[1] went very well. Instead of long secret corner discussions after dinner they played musical chairs and The Game. Mrs Chamberlain put her heart and soul into being the racehorse 'Battleship' winning the National, on all fours, at moderate speed.

On Sunday Dr Tom Jones[2] deserted the Big House to tea in comparative cosiness down here. We heard Myra Hess's[3] broadcast: the Mozart was exquisite.

This has been one hell of a long day. Took R to station at 9. With Aunt N to Greenwood Cottage to see what needed repairing. 11. Committee at Enid's till 1 o'c about the Grand WI Rally. (Too much time is wasted on WI activities I think: there are plenty of idle pussy cats who love the committees and chit-chat. But not me.) Lunch at Cliveden at 1. Slough Infants School from 2 to 5. Then R's train again. So I'm ready for sleep. lots of love for yourself darling. Have fun.

[1] Neville Chamberlain (1869–1940) Prime Minister.
[2] Secretary to the Pilgrim Trust and former Deputy Secretary to the Cabinet.
[3] British pianist (1890–1966). Awarded DBE in 1944 for organising the wartime National Gallery concerts.

In March 1938 Hitler invaded Austria and was threatening to take over Czechoslovakia. Prime Minister Chamberlain believed that war could be averted by reasoning with Hitler. The threat of war hung over 1938 and in order to eliminate panic, civilians were taught how to make a room gas-proof, and issued with gas masks, to be carried at all times.

[June 1938]   Orchard Court

Darling Joyce,

Thank you for the veggies. It's been hot this week, hasn't it? I went to a deb dance, and met some charming Blimps. Their views are so superbly ordinary, one could lay a huge bet as to what they were going to say next. *Nice good worthy* people though!

I went to the Theatrical Garden Party[1] with my deb cousin Fortune.[2] It was bedlam, & I spent fortunes. We had tea in the Lunts 'compartment', & Noël Coward played to us very prettily while Gladys Cooper sat at his feet. *Everything* cost 5/-. I met Nicholas who wants us to go and see his play and supper with him afterwards.[3] When? Next week is Glyndebourne. I am going to the Test [cricket] this morning & Wimbledon this afternoon, which is lovely for me.

[1] Held in Chelsea Old Hospital Grounds every year to benefit the Actors' Orphanage. A year later Joyce ran a penny rolling game as a member of *The Little Revue* Company and made £23. Noël Coward called it the 'Theatre and Film Balls-Up' because so many famous actors appeared, and so little money was raised.
[2] Possibly Fortune Smith, later Duchess of Grafton.
[3] Nicholas Phipps, Joyce's cousin, was playing in *Spring Meeting*, a comedy, with Margaret Rutherford (1892–1972), English character actress.

[June 1938]   Parr's

Darling Ginnie,

I had a p.c. from a Liverpool fan yesterday stating that of all the good things in the *Observer*, he first sought mine! I do hope the *Obs.* read the p.c. before they forwarded it to me!

It's a drome day. Three hideous aeroplanes have just zoomed low and slowly over this house. I went all cold when I saw them. Horrid.

[July 1938]   Lake End House
                                                               Taplow
                                                                Bucks

Darling Joyce,

Will you please not be silly. I want you to accept this trifling – & it is trifling honestly, because I'm extremely rich these days – gift, & take yourself & Reginald a few miles nearer Tryon and your mama?

It seems so absurd, when you are offered a lovely trip like that to be unable to take it simply for the sake of a few pounds I should so love you to have. Maria feels the same way, darling, & I do hope you won't have 'feelings' of any kind, & will accept our joint present.

You have already repaid it a million times.

Mr Watt tells me I have sold 471 copies of *Heather Mixture*. I haven't the faintest idea if that is good or bad, but anyway it surprises *me*!

Lots of love from Ginnie

18 July 1938   Parr's

Darling Ginnie,

I keep coming all over a-glow at the thought of you thinking about me in that partickler way. That you should want to do it touches me so very deeply; the present itself is beyond words exciting. I feel rather a cheat not using it as it was intended. But the V.G. and M.B.[1] Sinking Fund is going to carry out that purpose in the nearest possible future.

I am *so* lucky to have you and M for friends, and R for my husband, this house, the dogs – oh *everything*.

Oh dear, I could blub about it right now about it all, but it would be tears of that peculiar sort of happiness induced by other people's niceness.

Gosh – but I am grateful, and humbly surprised at you wanting to do such a thing for me.

Much love and *thank you*.

[1] Virginia Graham and Maria Brassey.

Virginia spent her twenties yearning for a husband. Many young men are mentioned in her letters, but none was what she wanted. Then, on a ship returning from India, Joyce's cousin Barbara Bevan met a handsome bachelor. Barbara thought he would 'do' for Virginia and invited them both to Scotland.

Wednesday [August 1938]   Waverley House
                                                                          Gullane
                                                                     East Lothian

Darling Joyce,

Such lovely cloud effects on the way up here. I immediately thought of you & those lambs. Even at 6.30 the North Road was bunting with little cars; prams and suitcases strapped to their backs. I ate my usual bun and tomatoes just the other side of Scotch Corner, under a draughty-ish hedge.

Tony Thesiger was here, but he went on Monday. I have played some bad golf – I shall have to have lessons. The courses are very alarming: there is always the feeling one is being pursued by at least 4 players who are dying to get through.

We've all been for picnics on the beach and long walks. The children are largely invisible, but when seen, are nice.

The plan worked and Virginia and Tony Thesiger spent the autumn courting, meeting for frequent lunches, dinner and twosomes in theatres.

16 August 1938   Parr's

Darling Ginnie,

Did you hear Alistair Cooke[1] this afternoon? He made a fine
job of the Mr Sears story. 'I have here a letter from Miss J.G. of
Buckinghamshire, etc. etc.' Of course he got the actual Toccata wrong
but that was hardly the point; any way it made sensational hearing and
I felt as pleased as if I'd done the whole thing myself.

Meanwhile I'm missing you a whole lot. The old place just don't feel
the same. So strong was your influence, that I was forced quite against
my will to exercise the damned dogs.

It has taken me twenty-four hours not to resent Fougasse's letter[2]
and criticism of my *powm* about Singing Before Breakfast! It came
yesterday while you were still here but I was too sore – in the literal
sense – to expose it even to you. He obviously thought it terrible.
Whimsy and just plain bad. He decorated the edge of my manuscript
with facetious drawings and wrote me a long and laboured analysis of
why it was soo so much waste of time. Or so I thought yesterday. After
a good night's sleep and the lesson, I looked at it again with fresh eyes.
Time has done much to heal my wounds and I must say I thought he
was rather funny and probably fairly right. But he had quite missed the
'mood' of the thing and only saw the ridiculous side. It is silly to mind
such treatment for I even asked for it. But all the same I do, a bit. I had
liked it rather a lot and written it in all sincerity. Well there it is and it
doesn't in the least matter. I wrote him a very nice letter and I'm sure
he hasn't an idea that I minded. You needn't tell anyone about any of
this; not that there is anyone who would be remotely interested.

I heard from Phyllis Nichols[3] today. She is working at an
International Camp in Breconshire, where she tells me the Jew is
working side by side in complete harmony with the Nazi. Did you hear
Harold Nicolson on the radio? he was nice and gloomy I must say. Oh
dear. So vivid is my imagination that I wear widow's weeds at least
twice a day!

René made me do all my clothes this morning and had all my winter
stuff out on the bed for my inspection. Oh the gloom of last year's
black felt.

[1] British journalist working in USA, (1908–).
[2] Editor of *Punch*, 1937–49.
[3] Lady Nichols (1905–90) niece of Waldorf Astor.

<u>1939</u>

January 1939 was the month in which both Joyce and Virginia's lives were changed

After an autumn of busy courting, Tony Thesiger proposed to Virginia on 12 January. In hopeful expectation, she had had her hair permanently waved the day before. Tony had lived for ten years in Burma as manager of a tea plantation for Wallace Brothers, a merchant trading company owned by his mother's family. He had returned to London as one of the Directors in charge of recruiting suitable young men from British public schools and universities to be managers in the Far East.

Tony was thirty-two, tall, handsome, charming, and rich. Virginia's mother noted that Tony was the exception to her belief that '*no* nice man ever had more than £500 a year'. Joyce wrote to her mother that Virginia was 'aglow all over and looks so pretty and radiant and is so romantic and altogether heavenly. She is quite dazed and can't believe it is true. She never thought she would fall in love and has like a ton of bricks.' Tony lived in 'a very grand flat near the Ritz', drove a Bentley, enjoyed dancing and had a sense of humour to match Virginia's. Joyce found him thoroughly tolerant, honest, sweet, and silly enough to play bears. The friendship between Joyce and Virginia was further strengthened by this union and both couples adored each other.

22 February [1939]   Orchard Court

Darling Joyce and Reggie,
    I can never thank you enough for that enormous quantity of gramophone records. I have simply refused to allow myself to *count* the number of them, as I know it is far more than either of you can afford! At each turn of the disc I think oh so happily of you both. We shall be sitting in our little sitting room with our Philoc green line bus full on, and the whole of Cambridge Square will ring with 'How Jovial is thy Laughter'.
    I am longing to see you. I am practically unrecognisable under a *welter* of diamonds.
    Aff. Yrs, Ginnie

Virginia and Tony married in March and Tony's parents bought them a flat for £3,000 in Cambridge Square, near Marble Arch and they employed a cook, Mrs Westaway, and a parlourmaid, Mary. They were lent a villa in Italy for their honeymoon.

Sunday [March 1939]   Ventimiglia

Darling Joyce,
    It's nice to think of you sitting there typing away in the sunshine, looking out onto that pregnant border, thinking of me. Life here is good. Every morning we walk down the garden past beds of pansies, a field of

freesias, a bank of arum lilies, past the roses over a wall of geraniums to the orange grove. There we pick ourselves each a *blood* orange warmed in the sun. Like the idea?

We have been into Monte Carlo every day – which, as you know is a musical comedy town with policemen dressed as Ruritanian hussars, & not a single butcher's or baker's shop in sight.

We had a gamble in the casino, losing a fiver & winning 200 francs respectively. You would simply *hate* it. Electric light, suffocating heat & smoke, frightful old harridans & bejewelled tarts, & a quite unbelievable quantity of octogenarian men, with curly white moustaches & white beards. I haven't the faintest idea what's happening! And whatever does happen, happens quick!

We tried not to look too honeymoonish but our *shoes*! We have taken a snap of them – the newest co-respondents ever to leave Dolcis & Harrods. As for our luggage, we completely disown it. The first day was the worst – it was gleaming white and submerged in large coronet-ed Claridges labels.

Tony sends his love. He is wearing blue corduroys and is infinitely alluring.

I must fly – to Monte Carlo of course!

Love Virginia

Joyce's membership of the Women's Institute gave her the material on which her new career was based. On Friday, 13 January, she and Reggie were invited to supper with a young radio producer, Stephen Potter (1900–69). After supper she told the guests about the WI talk that week on 'Useful and Acceptable Gifts – How to Make a Boutonnière from Empty Beech Nut Husks'. Without thinking, she took on the voice and character of the lady speaker. The party roared with laughter. She was asked who had written the piece.

'No one wrote it. I made it up.'

A few days later she was phoned by one of the guests, Herbert Farjeon, who wrote and directed London theatre revues. He wanted Joyce to perform the sketch in his next revue. Joyce had sung a bit with her mother and had been the school comic after lights-out in the dorm, but she had never acted before. She could 'become possessed' and turn into a character, but she had never stood in front of an audience, nor learned lines.

Farjeon was also interested in using Virginia's songs. Joyce was bewildered by the offer and decided to 'put the whole problem to God'. She did not think she was the right type for the stage and honestly believed that Farjeon would realise this and change his mind.

Rehearsals for *The Little Revue* began in April and went well. Joyce signed a three-month contract, joined Equity and received a salary of £11 a week (US$55 at the time). She had written further sketches for the revue and she was able to continue her reviewing for the *Observer* by installing a radio in her dressing room.

Joyce found that she could overcome her fear if she saw the audience as part of herself, with no 'outside difficulties'. She found theatre people strange, especially the men, who she believed were all 'queer' with a 'complete lack of standards'. She found she liked them in small doses but disapproved of their apparent inability to think of others or read books.

The show opened in April, to rave reviews and full houses. Tony and Virginia gave her an eighteenth-century amethyst brooch as a first-night present. All Joyce's relations came, sent flowers and even Nancy Astor eventually approved. Joyce was astonished by her success.

By the summer of 1939 Joyce was commuting to the theatre in London for eight performances a week. During the day she continued to live as a country wife, attending WI meetings and lunches at Cliveden.

In July, Joyce performed at a private party held for King George VI and Queen Elizabeth. Although very nervous, 'great surgings of loyalty kept going up and down my spine as I looked at their sweet little faces'.[1] The fifteen-guinea fee was spent at Harrods sale on a black flared coat with Persian lamb collar which she wore throughout the war.

In August 1939 income tax was increased from 4/6d to 7/6d in the £1 and the Astors went on an economy drive. Servants and gardeners were laid off and Cliveden house was closed indefinitely. Joyce was saving for a trip to the USA to see her mother and claimed that 'it don't smell like a war to me'.

The tabloid newspapers created the idea that the 'Cliveden Set' were appeasers and therefore pro-Nazi. But most people with some influence in British society visited Cliveden. The Astors and some of their friends did at first hope that war could be averted by negotiation with Hitler. But once the war began, they all threw themselves into the fight and Nancy Astor was soon proud to be on Hitler's Black List.

War against Germany was declared on 3 September and all theatres immediately closed. Rationing of food, clothing and petrol was introduced and Joyce laid in emergency supplies of six pairs of silk stockings, two new sweaters and a black skirt. Virginia ordered two cases of Bromo lavatory paper, which turned out to be so much that it became her standard Christmas present for several years. Newsprint was also rationed, so the *Observer* reviews were cancelled. Two girls evacuated from London were billeted on Joyce who enjoyed their company for three weeks. Evacuee children went everywhere wearing labels and gas masks.

Reggie was turned down by the army because of his varicose veins and his job with British Non-Ferrous Metals was evacuated to Wales. Joyce missed him, but was also relieved that he was safe from both enlistment and bombing. Determined to 'do his bit' he returned to London for treatment for his legs and worked in the Deciphering Department at the Foreign Office. Joyce was thrilled to have him home, while secretly hoping that the treatment would not work.

The Little Revue reopened with non-stop performances between 1.15 and 6 p.m. Between appearances, Joyce sewed clothes for evacuee children and knitted socks for sailors. She often stayed with Virginia in her new London house.

Virginia joined the Women's Voluntary Service as a driver. Her uniform was a bottle-green tweed suit and overcoat with wine-red shirt in which Joyce thought she looked most attractive. Virginia described the barrage balloons over London as the loveliest thing she ever saw. 'When the sun has set and the city is dusky the balloons remain rose pink, high above the grey buildings.' Tony had joined up with an anti-aircraft unit in Bristol and received an officer's commission in December 1939 but was too old for a posting abroad.

¹ *Darling Ma*, July 1939.

1940

At the declaration of war all the paintings were removed from the National Gallery in Trafalgar Square, and daily lunchtime concerts were performed to raise everyone's spirits. Joyce made friends with the pianist Myra Hess (1890–1966) and was soon part of the sandwich-making team. On New Year's Day Joyce played the water whistle in a joke concert of famous musicians playing Haydn's Toy Symphony.

On Joyce's thirtieth birthday she made 1,500 sandwiches for 1,280 people listening to Myra Hess playing Bach duets in the National Gallery.

Telegrams: TONIGRAM, LONDON
10 February [1940]   Cambridge Square

Darling Joyce,

I was unable, last night, to make suitable cosseting noises to you, because Kitty was in the room, but believe me, I yearned over you like a cow over its calf (or some other appropriate simile).

Doubtless today you are feeling immensely well & cheerful & fully realise with what incredible wholeheartedness you have lived your thirty years. I hope so, darling, because honestly, if I'd given one quarter the amount of joy you have given to all of us I would have nothing to complain of. I can think of no thirty years more usefully & disinterestedly spent – & I find it particularly clever of you, now that you have attained such a large measure of success, to have changed not one morsel. Perhaps it is because, unlike others, you attribute your success to God, although I confess I am loathe to give Him any of the kudos! Anyway, whatever it is, you have managed to remain consistently Joyce, & for this we love you (although *really*, if you became a drugged cocotte with an odious temper I should still love you).

Now, what do you want for your birthday? Material for undies, or some money for a hat, or a book or record or what? It's no use shaking your head dolefully, as you were last night, because unless you're careful I shall give you the lot, see?

Lots of love you poor *old old* thing, Gin

The Little Revue closed in March after a successful run of nearly a year. Much to Joyce's surprise she had loved theatre life, learned a lot and missed it terribly.

In April 1940 the 'phoney war' ended and the Blitz began. The National Gallery concerts became an important part of Joyce's and other Londoners' lives.

'I do love music – more and more and more. The only thing I would like to have a child for would be to watch it grow up with music. But it might hate it so I wouldn't care to risk anything so awful,' she wrote to her mother. Both Joyce and Virginia were relieved not to have children as they watched many of their friends and relations evacuating theirs to Canada.

Monday night [May 1940]   Claridge's Hotel

Darling Joyce,

Ma & I have evacuated here as all the maids, except Mary [maid] who won't, left in a fine flurry yesterday, I must say it is much easier and calmer without them, as one feels responsible for them. Mary insists in sitting in the house alone as she is in love with the grates & the blankets & professes neither loneliness nor fear. She tells me she put on her *hat* during last night's do.

I wish you could have seen us in our air raid shelter – an Italian waitress, people from Orchard Court, & an American Jewess who deemed it her mission in life to prevent a non-existent panic! She implored us to play round games, & we could only gaze at her through sleep glazed eyes, & yawn incessantly. Our shelter is everso cosy – with a crisp white nurse, & carnival chairs of tasteful design. No-one could say that a siren is good for the nervous system.

A lot of people dining here tonight – the Cromers,[1] Lady V Bonham Carter,[2] Crinks, the Nacindoo girls & the Murrays – strangely social.

Bless you V

[1] Lord Cromer (1877–1953) married Lady Ruby Elliot in 1908. She was Dame Grand Cross of St John and the inspiration for Joyce's 1940 sketch, 'Canteen in Wartime', about a grand lady running a WVS canteen for troops.
[2] Violet Bonham Carter (1887–1969), Liberal spokeswoman and orator, daughter of the Liberal Prime Minister Herbert Asquith.

Chamberlain resigned as Prime Minister in May and was replaced by Winston Churchill. Joyce and Virginia's Christian Science helped them rise above the fear and horror. 'We know that none of this is real and that there's only the now and that is harmonious and eternal,' Joyce wrote cheerfully to her mother. 'Thanks to what I understand of Christian Science and a nice solid constitution, I don't mind the noises and bumps.'

In June Reggie was passed fit to join the King's Royal Rifle Corps in Wiltshire, with talk of a posting behind the lines in Belgium.

During the First World War, Cliveden had been converted into a hospital and once again the Astors offered it to the Canadian Red Cross. New wards and offices were built to accommodate a luxurious, modern hospital with 480 beds. Nancy and Waldorf Astor spent most of the war in Plymouth, as MP and mayor respectively.

Nancy insisted that if Joyce was to remain in Parr's cottage, she would have to organise the voluntary workers at Cliveden. If Joyce wouldn't do the job, then she would have to move out. Joyce was torn between having a home to live in, and the promise she had already made to tour troop camps with *The Little Revue.*

Joyce chose to be a welfare worker at Cliveden Hospital, and threw herself into befriending patients, writing letters for them and doing their shopping. She felt that this was the only war work that she could do really well. She had two wards of 35 Canadian patients to care for. Joyce also sang songs in hospitals, gun-sites, barracks and canteens.

In October Bertie Farjeon assembled a new variety show called *Diversion* with Edith Evans (1888–1976), Peter Ustinov and Dirk Bogarde, both nineteen years old. Joyce was thrilled to be sharing the stage with Edith Evans whom she had first seen at the Old Vic in 1926. However, she was disappointed to find her a 'seething mass of self-interest'. Joyce performed two sketches and sang some of Virginia's songs. As the show was a matinée, Joyce managed to continue her hospital work by shopping for patients before the show in London and then visiting them straight from the station before she returned to Parr's cottage for supper and early bed. *Diversion* was another success – partly because there was very little competition.

Virginia moved to Bristol to be near Tony, taking her domestic staff with her. But Bristol was not much safer. None of Joyce's letters has survived from this period.

16 August [1940]   Druid's Garth
                                                    Bristol

Darling Joyce,
    Last night we had the bangiest of raids – the house shook like a blanc-mange, & a couple of bombs fell quite near. Did I tell you we had two in our street? I simply couldn't believe my *ears* when I heard them whistling down. My only reaction was to shut my eyes tight & avert my face. Oh well, I thought, that's got us, but somehow I survived.
    Tony is fearfully *shleepy* – he is up every night from 9.30–5 pooping off his gun. The blasted things come earlier every day now, but he seems to thrive on it and of late has taken to hitting them, which adds a macabre spice I suppose.

Virginia returned to London for a few days to collect a Ford Utility van donated by the American Red Cross for the Women's Voluntary Services.

October [1940]   [Bristol]

Darling Joyce,
    I went to Cambridge Square where I found the stairs covered in glass from some bomb or other. Was I *kloss*? I brushed the stairs madly with a broom, & then had a fearful time trying to get some of Mrs Westaway's plum puddings out from the back of a cupboard filled

with Bromo. I then had tea with Mrs T[hesiger] who was having awful servant troubles.

Then I went shopping at Harrods. I sent a wire to Tony which he didn't get for 24 hours so thought I was dead, & the maids sat up all night imagining things. Seeing all the old familiar things here in London makes me feel I have deserted London in her hour of need – I feel exactly like a traitor.

How thrilling about the Gent!!¹ I really can't believe it will endure the rehearsals, but if it does, it will entirely be due to you. So I give it to you as a birthday present, & may both of you prosper.

¹ Joyce broadcast for the Ministry of Information on the BBC Overseas Service to America, Canada, Australia, South Africa and New Zealand thanking them for their war support. Virginia's song, called 'Gentleman', was performed by Joyce in radio broadcasts and in *Diversion 2*.

2 December [1940]   Bristol

Darling Joyce,

Forgive me for not writing sooner, but mon Dieu, LIFE!!

We are having rather a noisy raid at the moment, with the garden gun working busily and the walls quivering. Oh dear, this is a bloody war, & I am so sick of it, aren't you? I try to see myself as perfection with a capital P & protection with another capital P – a Being unto whose light all must come for comfort; & then I hear a bomb drop, & whizz. I'm out of bed & downstairs in a second! However, I must not yield to discouragement I suppose.

Last night was rather bad – very noisy booboos on the way to Birmingham. I suppose now they've had such success with Coventry they'll take every industrial town in turn. I expect Maria told you of the horror of her day here, of how she tried to light a primus stove in a trailer while I drove her, swaying like a ship!

However, thank God, the worst is over now. The roads are passable and the firemen have gone home. Only the demolition boys remain, working in a cloud of dust, and of course, the homeless. Bristol looks fearful, & the poor Bristolians wander about in a daze, hardly daring to believe their eyes. The three main shopping streets have quite disappeared, & there is the usual complication about food. Our tempers have remained admirably equable, though frequently strained further than they have been for years!

I shall be 'up to town' to buy some Xmas gifts, because there isn't a gifte shoppe left in this poor fired burg.

In December Joyce began rehearsals for a second edition of *Diversion* in which she performed new sketches and two of Virginia's songs. She wrote the sketch 'Local Library' in the train from Paddington to Taplow – a journey of about forty-five minutes. She found the noise of the train's wheels an incentive to work.

Neither Reggie, Virginia nor Tony got leave over Christmas 1940 and Joyce spent the time at Cliveden Hospital. She gave presents to all the men and staff on 'her' wards and was in tears when they presented her with an engraved silver plate. Aunt Nancy gave a party with a jazz band and a Father Christmas for the 300 patients who were mobile. Joyce performed her sketches to her bed patients.

1941

The new edition of *Diversion* began on New Year's Day, to more excellent reviews and full houses and ran until the end of April. When John Gielgud said on the radio programme *Curtain Up* that 'brilliant people like Ruth Draper and Joyce Grenfell are the true exponents of make-believe kind of theatre', Joyce was amazed. Ruth Draper (1885–1956), the original American monologue artist, was a distant cousin of Joyce's father. Joyce was inspired by Ruth Draper, but she never imagined she could ever be as good as her at conjuring up a whole crowd while opening a village fete or filling an entire railway station just by telling a story.

The blitz on Bristol continued unabated. The WVS was responsible for distributing second-hand clothes sent to Britain by the Canadian and American Red Cross Societies.

January [1941]   WVS Civil Defence
                                                                                    Bristol

Darling Joyce,

Friday night the planes came over steady from 6.15 p.m. to 6 a.m. and tried to set the whole place on fire – like London on Sunday. They pretty well succeeded & this time chose the part of the city where they should have been aiming for with the original raids – the warehouse & docks. (I don't imagine anyone will read this on its way to you? Hope not.) Our nerves were stretched like banjo strings for 12 weary hours, but it wasn't the worst blitz.

Last night's blitz was at the port two miles west, which was *mighty* pretty to look at, & then they went south & blitzed the seaside town where *all* the people who are frightened of living in Bristol have run to! I'm sick of the sound of guns & the smell of burning houses & the sight of second-hand clothes, & longing for a sight of you!

Toad is enjoying his new work which at the moment consists of sticking pins into enormous maps.

The whole office is stacked with Cadbury's milk chocolate, destined for our Brave Lads in Khaki.

love from Ginnie

February [1941]   Bristol

Darling Joyce,
   I always forget your birthday. Why don't you remind me? I bet your
joints are creaking & your little face crinkling up like that proverbial
apple. Darling, here is a gifte from Toad & me. Please don't buy Savings
Certificates with it, however patriotic you feel; buy something rather
silly, or exciting. Actually it's practically impossible to buy anything
except baked beans or sardines.
   How dashing you are, having Edith Evans to stay! And Val Gielgud[1]
imploring your services! Where will it end, I ask myself? Shakespeare at
the Old Vic? I'll be tagging along duck, holding your bouquet & smiling
possessively!
   Tony excelled himself by standing up in the bath, scratching his
back, & falling in a dead faint out of the bath onto the washbasin,
thereby cutting his eyebrow open! Obviously going to have a baby. I
have got mild whooping cough & don't sleep much – so we are fairly
drab. However, yesterday I healed T of a cold instantaneously – it seems
peculiar that I can't heal myself.
   Oh dear, I never saw your pome in the *Observer*, and now Mary
has lit the fire with it! Will you remember it for me please & coo it into
my ears.

[1] Head of BBC Drama, brother of actor John Gielgud.

The winter of 1941 was so cold that Joyce 'pushed aside prejudice' and wore trousers,
though only in the privacy of her own home. In March she performed in the plastic
surgery hospital at East Grinstead for young RAF officers with severe facial and
hand burns.

20 March [1941]   Bristol

Darling Joyce,
   How *awful* that hospital must have been! I know how foul it is
suddenly to come up against the war, one can be so untouched by
it. Somehow the houses are tidied up so quickly & the rubble neatly
stacked, & the people dug up or out, in streets closed to the public, &
the homeless housed – all apart, away from one. And then suddenly,
like this morning, I flaunted into our Housewives office with a crocus
in my buttonhole, & there was a little queue of poor people outside,
the men deathly pale & tired looking, & the women in tears or looking
desperately calm, waiting to get death certificates for their relatives.
I *really* felt as though somebody had slapped me in the face. And yet,

one must be gay if one can, & try not to get one's thoughts hopelessly embedded in war affairs.

I have been to Plymouth for a few days – depressing in the extreme, & yet the people are so wonderful one is vaguely cheered. I had an awful time tracking your Aunt Nancy – Elliot Terrace was surrounded by exploded & unexploded bombs, & we eventually found her lunching at Admiralty House. She seemed strangely calm, considering everything, & we stood in the sunshine & gossiped. She told me that England was full of the rumour that Tothill Street[1] is riddled with lesbians! Behind us buzzed wonderful sailors covered in braid, & I did so envy Lady N. She kept on sending despatch riders out. Wouldn't you adore to despatch a despatch rider?

Love Winsome

[1] Headquarters of WVS, near St James's Park.

Between performances of *Diversion*, Joyce appeared in her first film, *Letter from England*, directed by Carol Reed. It was a Ministry of Information propaganda film for the United States, telling the story of a British woman living an ordinary life through the Blitz. Joyce played an American woman fostering two children evacuated from Britain, and Celia Johnson played the lead, their mother. Joyce had been convinced that she would not get the part because of her upturned nose.

23 April [1941]   Bristol

Darling Joyce,

Please send me your poem in *The Times*. Mummy mentions it in laudatory tones. She has been staying with the Oonaghs/oogans/Organs/orgahs, & they have sold their house for a vast sum & are terribly depressed. They have *no* servants. Joan cooks for 14 people – 2 evacuee women, 7 children & her own brood, & Oofah buttles.

Did you hear about poor old Esmé Glyn?[1] She & a 70 year old butler put out 45 incendiaries on her roof, & they were just leaning against the railings at 5 a.m. when the raid was nearly over, when a plane came & dropped a single incendiary on Lord Cannon's house next door, & the *whole* shoot went up! All Esmé rescued were her bedroom slippers, her library books, & her unpaid bills. Isn't Greece *awful*?[2] Isn't Plymouth *awful*?[3] Isn't life sanguinary [bloody]? And yet I am happy really, with my man & my plum blossom. Heigho, I must away to Gloucester with some canned carrot cubes!

[1] Worked in the WVS with Virginia (1908–85).
[2] British and Commonwealth troops were being evacuated from Greece as the Italians overran it.
[3] Plymouth had suffered heavy bombing.

When *Diversion* came off, Joyce took on a third ward at Cliveden Hospital and gave more troop concerts. Two army officers were billeted on her at a time. Reggie was promoted to captain and as he was based in Wiltshire he got occasional leave weekends at home.

Bristol

Darling Joyce,

Oh we did enjoy ourselves! Friday night we leapt out of the train at 9.45, hurled ourselves to the Cumberland to wash, & then on to Hatchett's where we danced. It was fun; with a super band. The pianist is quite ga-ga & a genius on the keys. Tony & I walked home through Berkeley Square, in which we sat & kissed.

Next morning we went to Lock's and bought To a new hat, & then we had *two* ice cream sundaes at Selfridge's.

Back in Bristol I removed all four wheels of Vauxy, & had a lovely time with the *inches* of thick oozy mud behind. Unfortunately I climbed under the car, with the result that my luscious blonde curls were black as pitch & had to be paraffined. It is hard to be a mechanic & a lady.

4 August 1941 Much too late at night   Parr's

Darling Ginnie,

Look, d'you know what I've spent the entire evening doing? Reading a batch of your old letters – a big batch of 1936–37 ones. And they are *so* wonderful. I've been roaring with laughter all by myself in here; and crying a little bit too. One thing I beg of you – don't never you write to me in pencil because it gets so hard to read after four or five years have gone by.[1]

There are also a lot of my own written to the family from Paris 1927. They are touching and a bit priggish and ever so earnest about everything. C.S. played a large part in my life even then. Like all letters home from school mine are full of beggings. 'Could I *possibly* have my May allowance (£3.0.0.) in April as I've got masses of music, stockings, pencils, etc. to buy and I *must* have it soon.'[2]

[1] From now on Virginia's letters were written in ink, and later in ballpoint pen.
[2] These letters are now all lost.

13 August 1941   Salisbury

Darling Ginnie,

I'm here to Entertain the Troops – 3 concerts in 3 days. Florrie St Just[1] is my hostess, remember her?

We had dinner in the Officers Mess – good it was too – and then I changed in her room and went to the R.A. [Royal Artillery] Gym, where the concert was being held. It was a very grand affair with the R.A. Band and lots of Cols. in front. The Band is a good sized combination with strings and brass and a xylophone and a terrific conductor who compèred with heavy 1900 pomposity.

All adored 'The Gent' which I rendered very nicely, although I couldn't hear the pianist who was 6 feet below me at a faulty upright. Getting on to the platform was an Alpine climbing feat and had to be done from steps at the back of the stage. Progressing around an unrailinged edge to get to the side was tricky and induced a 'vertigo' that had to be mastered by – I'm sorry to say – Will rather than Truth. All went well, even the sketches. Never ceases to surprise me that the Forces enjoy – or at any rate appear to tolerate – them. I've an idea that they regard it as a sort of magic that hypnotises them into thinking it's clever. That must be the reason because most of the jokes aren't quite down their alley.

Finally I was driven back here, where I came into a world of trouble. Poor Florrie! Her footman, who isn't a soldier because he has brainstorms, took her car and drove it neatly into a tree. A dog made a mess on a carpet. Olivia Baring's extremely enjoyable mother came in at 1 from saying goodbye to a son about to go East today and was locked out, so had to howl like a dog on the lawn till she was let in. The boiler burst. The cook has concussion from falling off her bike. The kitchen maid's mother has died. Fortunately I'm out for all meals, which will, I trust, ease things.

Tomorrow we do another concert at Larkhill Y.M.C.A. It's a busy life, hein? I do wish it ever included you, duck. Seeing so many dear old familiar faces makes one realise what a blank sort of existence it is among strangers and new friends. Though nice they can't be as warming as those who knew one when . . .

I've just eavesdropped on a good conversation as to whether it 'looks bad to advertise for a footman these days?' They feel one can do it discreetly by the use of a Box Number in *The Times*. As the footman is wanted to feed chickens, lug coals, do heavy chores no female can, and will be welcome at any age over 15, and unfit at that, I cannot think Florrie need feel ashamed to want him. This is a largish house and the butler is over 70 and deaf, so I do see her need. I've brought my rations and René has firmly labelled all my stuff, so that my jam jar with Mrs R.P.G. on it stands among the other private hoards on the sideboard. How strange it all is, isn't it!

Val Gielgud, Drama Dept. B.B.C., has written to tell me I'm to have a 20 min. recital of my works in the not too distant future over the Home

Stations, so that's glowing.[2] The O [*bserver*] are just sitting on my sonnet
it seems. *So* silly because it'll be out of date – being about summer
storms. Oh I almost forgot – I sang your 'Stays' song last night and it
was much admired. Let it be confessed that the accordion is hell to sing
to really. But Eve is so good and so nice that it's fun at the same time.[3]

[1] Wife of Edward Charles Grenfell, Lord St Just, director of the Bank of England, a cousin
of Reggie.
[2] Joyce broadcast seven sketches live on the Home Service in October, produced by
Stephen Potter.
[3] Eve Clarke accompanied Joyce on the accordion.

18 August 1941   Parr's

Darling Ginnie,

The Cap. [Reggie] came home Fri. night even healthier than ever
because he's taken to doing P.T. at 6.45 a.m. every day! He's only done
it for a week but swears he'll stick to it because he feels so good from it.
We had a lovely quiet and completely uneventful weekend.

George Bernard Shaw is at C[liveden]. Also his wife, who is *much*
nicer than him and even older. I took him for a 45 min. tramp in the
pouring rain – up banks, down hills, through dripping shrubberies, and
we emerged damp but undaunted, and he said he could go for more but
I dissuaded him. Then he came to tea in my humble cott.

Lots of love. Oh why don't we ever see each other, dammit.

Joyce first met George Bernard Shaw (1856–1950) at Cliveden when she was fifteen
and he had encouraged her to sell her Christmas cards. He was now eighty-five and
brought his pure wool Jaeger sheets and vegetarian food with him.

René Easden, aged twenty-three, Joyce's 'maid, secretary and friend' for five years,
was called up to join the ATS – the Auxiliary Territorial Service. Joyce was 'laid low
by the parting'.

Mrs Proctor came as housekeeper with her two daughters Truda, eleven, and
Shirley, six. They were a great success and stayed until the end of 1942.

16 September [1941]   Bristol

Darling Joyce,

That's the most awful thing I've ever heard! I am so sorry. What
will you do? You know that Mrs Urquhart, well she solved her servant
problem by going to a Something of Moral Welfare & getting an
unmarried mother *with* baby. I gather the home she got hers from is
an excellent one & prides itself on the fact that none of its girls has
ever slipped up again. Mrs U's girl is certainly very nice, & was a
parlourmaid somewhere.

Enclosed is the nonsense waltz, which you can hack about as much as you like.

Tony heard you on Monday night, sitting with the maids in the kitchen, & he loved you & so did they. Mrs Westaway couldn't imagine how you *thought* of such things, & Toe couldn't tell her.

I hope Ma Proctor turns out well – but she will never replace dear René, whose absence you must feel acutely. No more of that gay whistling, as the beds are made.

My new German poem is in this week's *Punch*.

In tearing hurry, just off to Gloucs with 24 urns.

12 October 1941   Parr's

Darling Ginnie,

It's a heavenly work. I dote on't. Thank you so much and bless you my duck. The Bedroom Song will be a good alternative to the Gent when it's done, don't you think? Goody.

Such a super duper day. R. is gardening like mad. I can hear the clink of his spade as he frees the fruit trees from grass at their roots. The Grieg Concerto makes lovely lush background music.

René goes tomorrow. We don't mention it much and I feel lead heavy and homesick about the whole thing. I go to London at 9 to get a perm; am interviewed for the *Radio Times* at 12.30; lunch at the Ivy with Stephen Potter. When I get home after the broadcast (about 9) Mrs Proctor will have taken over. Oh I do dislike it all. Reg. is very well and sweet. Wish I ever saw you.

Much love and many thanks for the Waltz.

26 October 1941   Bristol

Darling Joyce,

I remembered to listen in to your broadcast, and I *loved* it. You seemed to be rather far away at the beginning – I don't know why – but after a short while, you became nice and Joyce-ish. If you *must* know, when they played 'You'd be so easy to love' I cried. I can't imagine why. I was doing a jigsaw puzzle at the time, & we have since discovered there were 92 pieces missing, so my nerves were undoubtedly strained . . . still it wasn't very moi was it?

3 November [1941]   Bristol

Darling Joyce,

How *heavenly*! How unutterably celestial! I have never had a pair
of Nylon stockings before, so my excitement can only be described as
intense. Thank you darling, so very much – you couldn't have given me
anything more desirable.

I had such a happy birthday. Oysters & a matinée & *Citizen Kane*[1] &
supper at Quaglino's. All hideously expensive & unpatriotic, but highly
delightful. After such an orgy, I am pursued by visions of enraged
Defence Bonds & glowering Savings Stamps – but though remorseful I
am not repentant.

The leave couldn't have been more perfect, & I hope you *know* how
much we loved every blessed moment. Such a tremendous joy & relief to
be really silly again, & to be silly for a long time at a stretch – because
when To & I meet, although we are fairly silly, a lot of time is spent in
talking about coal, or the cleaners, or the boiler.[2]

Thank you darling for giving us such a heavenly leave. I feel
fearfully forlorn here. It is cold & triste, & I miss you & your little red
carpet slippers so. The memory of boiled contentment by the fire is
undimmed.

I was thinking last night that *honestly*, there isn't much to choose
between my love for you and Tony! I mean, if you were hit by a bomb,
there are some things not all the Tonys in the world could give me
back. So take care, won't you, & keep your head under cover!

Would it be possible for us to spend Chrissymas Day & a portion of
le Box with you? Perhaps you are staying at Cliveden, or entertaining
relatives?

I am very fretsome these days – torn between the urge to go &
make munitions & really *do* something, & realising that spiritually, that
is doing less than nothing! If only I could be sure that I would make
uniform pockets or something, I would probably go; but I still have a
distaste for actually making weapons of destruction myself, although I
am *all* for others doing so. If one starts to think about it scientifically,
one wouldn't do anything at all – not even W.V.S. . . . . oh dear,
sometimes the right & the wrong get so confused.

xxx love from Gin

---

[1] Film directed by Orson Welles (1915–85).
[2] Joyce described Virginia as the Queen of Sillies.

13 November 1941   Parr's

Darling Ginnie,

How completely perfect! There isn't anything I could possibly look
at with more pleasure than your letter proposing a Yule visit. There's
a slight snag which doesn't bother me but it might spoil your fun, so
I shall *perfectly* understand if you feel it would be a bore – that is, Mrs
Proctor is going home for the feast and I'll be here alone. But I'm alone
here every Sat: from lunch time till Sunday at 11 a.m. (Mrs P's go to
Windsor each Sat. – Sun.) and I'm *that* good at keeping the boiler in,
doing the Aga, throwing together meals, re-lighting fires next day,
and if you didn't mind the alfresco-ishness of it, darling, it would be a
downright treat for me to have you. But maybe To. would prefer un peu
de luxe for his few hours off, and darling I couldn't understand more
if you feel you'd rather be somewhere with more comforts. *Honest.* I
suspect we'd have at least one meal on Xmas Day up at C. anyway, and
in between we could tuck in by the fire and pretend it wasn't Christmas
at all, at all. (I'll have to be in the hosp. a goodish bit I suspect.)
However there it all is and it's just exactly as you fancy, and I shan't be
offended if you don't come and I'll rejoice like MAD if you do. (So *do.*)
Oh well, think it over.

R. is being moved to Cheltenham which we both view with distaste.
It's an honour so far as the job is concerned, but it's so very out-of-
the-wayish and so far from his pals, and he'll be billeted in a house and
miss what has been to him fun – the Officers Mess.

Today I did a *Starlight to India* and it was recorded, and you can hear
it next Weds. *A.M.* at, I *think*, 9.30. But look it up in the *Radio Times*.
You just must be late at the Office that morning because I'm doing *your*
'Do you Remember?'. The accompanist blew in 15 mins. before we went
on air and we had no run through at all, and I felt hurried and worried.
So I should think it was probably lousy. Darling, I do so love doing your
stuff and I hope I've done justice to 'em.

Celia Johnson wrote me last week and asked tenderly of you and
said she was having a screen test for N. Coward's new movie but not to
mention it as she felt sure she wouldn't get it. I do hope she has.[1]

Mr E.V. Knox [*Punch*] has accepted a new poem called 'Tribute to a
Treasure' about – guess? – dear René.

I feel equally fretsome about one's duty in this darned old war. All
you say is indeed true. I'm as illogical as you are and just as muddled.
I've a feeling that this job I do in the hosp. *is* a good thing because you
do feel needed and are able to help 'em a bit: on the other hand any
motherly old body could do it on her head. But I WON'T make a bomb
tho' I hope lots of other people make millions of 'em.

P.S. Celia thinks all is o.k. about the film. She's to be Noël Coward's wife! Small part – it's mainly a naval action story.

[1] *In Which We Serve* with John Mills (1908–), directed by Noël Coward and David Lean (1908–96).

16 November [1941]   Bristol

Darling Joyce,
    What fun! perhaps I might even be allowed to cook, a thing which Mrs W[estaway] never permits, & I shall love making the beds with you & flicking at the ornaments with a duster. I'm sure it is terribly boring if one has to do it for ever, but in bursts it must be fun.
    Maria is here, very bonny, but as distraught as I am about war work.[1] Cheerfully going off with a letter saying one is indispensable to the W.V.S. pricks the mind into fuller consciousness! Maria has an urge to be a Wren, but her mother has seriously said that if she joins the Forces she will throw herself in the Thames!
    If Tony is posted to London then I shall ask God to lead me to a nice petite factory in Bryanston Square – quiet, warm, sunny where they make rubber dingheys, or parachutes, or dainty toys for export. I have had a parcel of cheese, tea & marmalade from New York. No name on the package which is maddening.
    Sorry about Reg, but Cheltenham isn't a bad place.
    When are you registering, love? Because if it's Dec: 6th you better start pulling those strings . . . oh no I forgot – we army wives can't be made to lift a finger, isn't it bizarre?
    Maria has just read a morsel from the *Express* saying that all letters saying members of the W.V.S. are indispensable are now invalid!
    I must now go & stick pins into flags to aid Russia.
    Love from Gin

[1] Women were now being called up.

10 December [1941]   Bristol

Darling Joyce,
    I really was thrilled to hear you singing my songs – you make them sound so *awfully* good.
    A hideous day yesterday. I rose at 6.30 & drove a large lorry to London. It was designed for terrier legs & I arrived paralysed from the waist down.[1] Had lunch at Prunier's with Maria and then caught an imaginary train from Paddington, which went to a small station in Bristol's suburbs. Walked for miles from there, while To waited for 2

87

hours at the big station without discovering that trains can't get in there now!

What have you decided about war work? Can you get exempted for stage work, & would you if you could? If we weren't such lousy [Christian] Scientists, the idea of making Hurricanes would never enter our heads – nor would we be forced to make them! I see wives of soldiers can work near their homes, so I expect to be led to a canning factory in Shepherd's Bush 'ere long.

Those ruddy Japs have done more damage in two days than the Germans have in 2 years – however think no evil of thy brother as I read in the lesson this morn – nice Japs, loving Japs, God's Japs . . .

xxxx Gin

---

[1] Virginia was nearly six feet tall.

The Japanese bombing of Pearl Harbor brought the USA into the war which pleased Joyce who had been complaining to her mother about this since the war began.

There was no leave for Reggie this Christmas, but Virginia and Tony joined Joyce. She sent 175 telegrams from patients at Cliveden Hospital to Canada and bought twenty-three presents for $7\frac{1}{2}$d each.

1942

Sunday, 18 January 1942   Parr's

Darling Ginnie,

How are you and is the letter answering getting too much for you?[1] If so, remember I can and will with pleasure deal with the ones who don't know your writing.

R. came on Fri. night and we're snug as can be in the dining-room whence we've moved for the cold weather. It's so cosy and so warm, we feel a bit as if we'd spent the day in bed! The chairs are wedged in by the fire, and by supper time the place was cluttered to the top with writing paper, magazines, candies, my hosp. basket, the *Observer*, R's feet in fur-lined bed-slips. (I had a pome in today's *Ob.* – did you see't? or are you faithless and read the *Sunday Times*. ??)

No special news. I've been ever so busy at the hosp. but I'm slowing down for two days tomorrow, when R. and I go to Lon. to stay at the Cumberland and attend numerous movies, plays and places of good feeding.

I've been giving R. a free show of all the intended monologues I've sketched out in the past six months. He made an indulgent audience and laffed quite hard at my costume piece 'Lady's Maid'. So with two dispassionate appreciators to go on I think I'm right to count that one in. (You did like it, didn't you?)

I've got a new rather pathetic one. It's about a woman begging a Domestic Agency just to allow her to get on to the waiting list of those waiting to get on to the Agency's book looking for a housekeeper. I've made her rather exaggeratedly emphatic: but inside she's you and me.[2]

I slipped a bit as a wife this week in that I didn't get a thriller in for R's weekend, so it's sort of sad to see him reading the *Ladies Home Journal* with what appears to be true interest.

I got a wonderful box from Macey's yesterday – no name, no card, dammit – full of butter, slab choc. and cooking choc. too. Ma has lately sent me a dressing gown and 2 vests and 2 panties made of angora and silk. How clever they are in the U.S. about things like this.

Lots of love, darling, and lots of nice thoughts.

[1] Virginia's mother had just died.
[2] 'Situation Vacant' was first performed in *Light & Shade*, 1942.

10 February 1942   Bristol

Darling Joyce,

I go on writing and writing letters. I've done over eighty now and I think I'm writing the most awful rot by now.

I have just eaten a lovely hard-boiled egg prior to couching me down on the old lielow [air-mattress]. Beyond me stretches a vast vista of blackness filled with crates, which it is my duty to defend single handed against bombs, firebombs & other warlike impedimenta.

Prior to wrestling with my army blankets I send you greetings. Also, the top notes of 'News' & a lyric which I still maintain belongs to another song. Everything rhymes though, & if you approve, we can go ahead on these lines.

Oh I forgot, on Sunday we have got a man called Joe Cooper[1] to come and meet you, because he has written the most lovely song imaginable. You will swoon with it. I am struggling with the words at the moment. Did you see my poem in Feb 4 *Punch*?

XX Ginnie

[1] Joseph Cooper (1912–) was a fellow officer of Tony's and a pianist by profession. He became a firm friend of Joyce's and chaired the television series *Face the Music* from 1966 to 1984.

26 February 1942   Parr's

Darling Ginnie,
    The lovely pink Shelley came yesterday afternoon and is most
decorative as well as a nourishing mental gift. Thank you my darling,
velly much indeed for Shelley. He's quite a hard poet, don't you find?
Too prolific but there are moments of terrific beauty. I use the adjective
literally for once. Thank you for a beautiful gifte.
    Lunch with Bertie [Farjeon] in Frith Street. He is full of ideas for
Our Show. He's got a man called Max Adrian[1] and various others.
Tentatively called *Farjeon's Eleven*, which is good, don't you think? It's
all a *dead* secret, so-cross-your-heart-and-hope-to-die-if-you-tell.

[1] British comic actor (1903–73).

2 March [1942]   Bristol

Darling Joyce,
    Here is the Baby song.[1] It is deathly simple, as you see, but I think it
has a touch of lump in the throatishness. The chorus demands a repeat,
as the whole thing is *such* a queer shape.
    We celebrated the third anniversary of our wedding by going to Bath
to buy a game of Snakes & Ladders.
    Maria is staying here, & she tells me that your Aunt Nancy is
indulging in that blackmail stunt peculiar to her. I do beseech you to be
in no wise acquiescent to it. If it is a question of acting in the revue, &
having your own life to do as you please with, giving up the Cottage, or
staying at the Cot as a sort of feudal vassal, do not hesitate to make a
stand for the former. Because your aunt knows full well she cannot bear
to lose you, & I bet she is pulling a big bluff. Even if she isn't, it will be
her loss, not yours; & I really cannot let her buy you, either with money
or appeals to your higher nature. It would be perfectly silly of you to
go into the ATS[2] or WAAFS.[3] If there is any importance in the morale
of a nation, you are the one person to sustain it. By helping apart from
the war in its beastliest sense, you are inevitably a beacon set on a high
hill, & people will come to you, as indeed they do now, to be fortified &
refreshed. Don't lose the idea, & above all, don't think you're not adding
to the war effort. Nobody in the world works harder than you do now.
    It would be hellish to leave the cottage, but I often think the price
you pay for it is too high. Even, darling if you are considered the most
ungrateful & hateful of nieces I should say point blank 'This is blackmail
& I'm sorry but I must live as I see fit even if I starve so nuts, aunt, to
you.' She won't dream of taking the cottage away from you really.

I am now covered in crumpet margarine.
Would you care for a visitation over Easter?
Isn't this paper lousy, just like blotting paper.
Masses of love, darling from Virginia.

[1] Virginia wrote the words 'No news is good news' to Cooper's music and Joyce performed it in *Light & Shade*.
[2] Auxiliary Territorial Service.
[3] Women's Auxiliary Air Force Service.

Once again Joyce was torn between the hospital and theatre. Her work in the hospital had expanded to being liaison officer between the British and Canadian Red Cross Societies and also teaching the patients to embroider, which was now called Occupational Therapy. Farjeon wanted Joyce in his new revue but after much heart-searching Joyce decided to remain with the hospital. When the show flopped in July, she agreed to try and help rescue it, but after three weeks it quietly closed.

Tony was transferred to the War Office in London and the Thesigers moved back to London.

18 April 1942   Bristol

Darling Joyce,
    Tremendous packings going on. Tony has left for his tour of the gunsites, & I feel very bereft & peculiar. *And* busy. What with tidying up m'files, & giving a final lick & polish to m'van, & delivering the last loads, & saying goodbye, I am *rushed*.
    Bristol is really looking the best – blossoms & chestnut greenery glowing between the stucco homestead, & enormous *trees* of forsythia. I cannot say, though that I am sorry to go.
    I find I am missing Mummy very badly these days. Shock & winter freeze the senses, & spring brings an unwelcome thaw. I would like so much to tell her about the move – about anything, really. I lie in bed & cry very quietly so as not to disturb To, who would be devastated if he knew. It is a pity, & it gives me a headache, & doesn't do anybody any good, & I don't know why it should happen now, so many months after, unless, as I say, it's the spring.
    Ah well. I think this is a dreary letter. Sorry. xxx

20 April 1942   Parr's

Darling Ginnie,
    Oh my heart did bleed for you darling when I read your Saturday letter. Spring is a sad time. Much more so than autumn. Wish I was with you to cosset and nanny you, my duck. Don't be lonely and sad,

will you? Even though I've seen nothing of my Ma for 5 years I still can't bear to think what it must be like not to have the one person in the world who really cares deeply about one – because even tho' the Regs and Tos are quite perfect as husbands they haven't known us since we were that first uneasy early morning discomfort and they don't fill the place one's Ma has had for ever. Oh lor. This is a hard and beastly world and if I could I'd try to protect all the people in it I love from its horridness.

We've had 2 hospital weddings in 3 days and one of my nice English R.A.F. patients died last night and I've been looking after his very courageous but miserable mother.

The officiating clergy was the kind who like to make the wedding address good and loud and personal. It was, fortunately, quite short but it boomed out about the hardship of matrimony, the difficulties of remaining constant etc., and I could have sniped the old man with any of the handy arums that stood about in church shaped green vases.

It's time for my supper but Mrs P[roctor] is just having a bit of a wash I think. Oh no, here it is. She's had a *bath*, that was the delay. A strangish time maybe. Dear René was home for 7 days and spent one of 'em – her own idea – doing out my cupboard and putting away my heavier winter wear. Last year's summer stuff looks a little faded from the trunk. And much too thin. Still chilly, ain't it.

Lots of love, love, and don't be sad.

P.S. I've just re-read this and it's not a bit the letter I meant to write to make you feel how important you are to me, your favourite friend. I mean it.

9 June 1942   The Castle Hotel
                                                                      Bangor[1]

Darling Ginnie,

Do you recognise this ink? I stole it from your desk at dawn yesterday morning and much as I appreciate it I can't say I find that it flows in *my* pen.

On the train here there was a spy – obviously – who must be kin to Lord Castleross.[2] Just the same outline and going Eire-wards, so it all adds up. He took snuff from a gold snuff box, wore 2 pairs of *tinted* glasses, and had pale pink hands totally unmarred by any form of exertion, and lots of luggage all unlabelled. The spy read from a 4 day old Zeitung [newspaper] and a paper printed in no known tongue. It wasn't Greek, Russian, Norwegian, Swedish or Hungarian. It could have been Romanian I suppose. He didn't actually smell of scent, yet you knew he used it. I saw him making a list of something and the first two words, obviously a code!, were 'Elizabeth Arden' and 'Max Factor'!

I ate breakfast vis-à-vis with a 2nd Lieut. of at least 48 with a Midland accent, who was coming up here to collect his evacuated family back to Hayes in Kent. We had bright rose coloured sausage of the most un-pig like taste.

Had tea in a bunnery with a local lady who told me all about the Bangor Blitz (one bomb). Acting on a sudden impulse I got onto the first bus that came along and took a ticket to the end and back. This turned out to be an excellent idea, and we crossed the Menai (pronounced quite simply as MANY) Bridge into Anglesey, followed the coast road and ended by a remote tin Chapel on a hill, where the conductress told me they'd wait for 10 mins. or so if I'd like to get out. So I did and started walking back into the delicious evening light, with great mauve hills lolloping along the mainland and little Welsh fields in all sorts of greens. The bus picked me up about 2 miles later.

The B.B.C. boys are a bit frightening in their pale green corduroys and hatless long hair. Had an amusing evening with some of them and then a piping hot bath in lovely soft Welsh water.

I feel a million miles from everywhere and it's rather refreshing.

Thank you, love, for having me to staydle. Lots of love.

[1] The BBC had a recording studio in Bangor, Wales.
[2] Lord Castleross (1891–1952), portly gossip columnist on the *Daily Express*, and friend of Lord Beaverbrook.

Soon after this, Joyce was 'called up'. Her designated war work was to be an entertainer with ENSA – the Entertainment National Service Association, the official entertainment organisation for the armed services, based in Drury Lane Theatre and directed by Basil Dean. After two demanding years working at Cliveden Hospital Joyce was glad of a change. Nancy Astor tried to dissuade her with a new tactic of Deep Disappointment, saying that anyone who knew about God should not go near the stage. Joyce retaliated with Plain Silence.

So Joyce set off for Northern Ireland on an eight-week tour with 'The Music You Love' company of 'rather refined second rate musicians'. Joyce compèred the classical concerts in troop camps, village halls and barns to British and American troops. Joyce's monologues were not easily understood and she soon replaced them with Virginia's 'silly' songs.

Reggie was posted to Yorkshire, so they would have rarely seen each other anyway. Joyce's parting gift to Virginia was a precious bag of bulb fibre.

12 October 1942   Somewhere in Northern Ireland

Darling Ginnie,

It is 9.20 p.m. and our night off. I am sitting up in bed wearing the blanket dressing-gown Ma sent me last year, with a hottie at my feet, for this is a cool little room. This is a medium sized country town with one large rambling hotel, and we are in it.

The proprietor is a cissie who fixes the flowers himself and sees that the food is good: it is. But my bed is harder than concrete and 'owing to the water shortage' (what water shortage? It never stops raining here) 'guests may take only one bath, hot or cold, ONCE A WEEK!' Just to sock 'em I've had 4 basins full of peaty hot water – luke – and washed myself *all* over, rinsed out my stockings ('Guests may NOT wash clothes in the bedrooms') and cleaned my teeth under a running tap. Water shortage indeed.

I've homified it with my large folding photograph frame full of pictures of Reg and you and Ma and Pa and Lefty, and Tommy! When I came to wash before supper there was an untuneful male voice far too near singing about cow-boys in the sky. The great snag of the whole business is this communal life. I never knew how much I went for solitude. It's a bit much being branded with the insignia of ENSA but to move in bus loads of nine is almost worse.

Our chief trouble – and really rather a serious one – has been our Manager, a tough little non-Aryan East Ender. He doesn't begin to understand us or our programme, thinks only in terms of gate, is unbelievably rude, crude, and now malevolent. I've been vaguely trying to love him: like him you could NOT. One of the jobs of the Manager is to get in touch with the place we are to do that night and arrange for fires in the dressing-room and about the piano, etc., AND to tell them about the show. Our pal doesn't do any of these things and when he contacts the entertainment officer says to him that the boys won't like our show because it's all high-brow and dull!! Not a help. He was so rude to me on the first day that we mutually avoid each other, for I ticked him off like a duchess! After one really successful concert ending with cheers all round (even I went Beeg!) the Station Padre told him what a lovely treat it had been and how much everyone had enjoyed it, and he said 'But it only brought in 33 and a third of the Station; that's no good!' The whole point is that we are here specifically to entertain the minority and aren't expected to do more. Thirty three and a third is damned high for Beethoven, Bach and Mozart. And how they loved it all.

After a week's total silence from R. I finally telegraphed him and got a telegram back. He is a pig of a correspondent.

Our contralto, who is built like the prow of a ship, has a lemon yellow petticoat with two black butterflies embroidered on each bosom!

I'm glad I came. It is full of interest if only one can keep on top of the gloomy parts. And I can.

Now I'll lay me down to sleep on this old meanie of a mattress. It has the personality of a granite hard spinster in a Victorian novel. Oh Lord . . . Lots of love.

16 October [1942]   Northern Ireland

Darling Ginnie,

Time goes on and there's not a lot to tell you. At the moment we are going through a slight crisis because our sop[rano] has gone very temperamental on us and developed persecution mania in the first stages. She is like a house, with blonde corkscrew curls, and I had thought she was at least 44, but I'm appalled to find I'm 10 years wrong and she's only 34. It's a ghastly revelation. She has become a victim of inferiority complex for no special reason and is sure we none of us like her, that her singing's awful and that we laugh at her. No one dreamt of it until she suggested it, but now it's getting to be a little funny because it's so damned silly. The trouble with all the singers – no, Maud Mountain is o.k. – is that they are like spoilt children, cry if they don't get more applause than each other. I know you think I'm exaggerating but I'm not. They come off the stage in a fury if they haven't got the applause they think they deserve and sulk all the way home and say they are going back to England! Rather pathetic, but one can't go on and on building someone up eternally. It's too much like hard work. She *has* got rather a lovely voice but she's scared of it or something. I dunno.

Anyway I haven't helped matters because, in all innocence, I apparently stepped in with both feet last night when announcing her. She followed the 'cellist and I had to move her chair. I always keep up a running commentary while I do the furniture removals and it seems that last night I said: 'And now I'll move the chair to make room for our soprano'! As her sensitiveness mainly concerns her shape this was *not* a good idea. I don't remember doing it and of course I didn't do it on purpose; but, oh dear, it has cut deep and she suspects me of saying 'funny' things about her! As if I cared to waste the time.

So the atmosphere is a leetle tense. And there is also trouble because all the singers seem to want to sing the same songs! This really is quite funny. 'Largo' is arranged for tenor, baritone, sop. and contralto it seems, and it's wrestled for by all the quartet! They have now arranged to take turns, like nice children. I couldn't have believed all these things unless I actually witnessed them. For exhibitions of uncontrolled egotisms I do recommend a group of singers. Instrumentalists seem to be more rational. Though the fiddler has his problems because he is slow as dripping cream and cannot be hurried, and it gets us down to watch him stand on the stage for what feels like hours while he tunes and retunes and makes up his mind what to render. Poor showmanship there. And he is stubborn as a mule. But quite sweet.

We are staying in a strange hotel and I can't say I like the atmosphere. It's run by a pansy R.C. with a sinister feeling about him, and all day yesterday the place was overrun by drunken little doughboys on 24 hr passes.[1] The 'cellist and I had to *almost* literally fight 'em off in the lounge where we'd gone to read before tea! One of 'em wanted me to sit on his knee and was about to enforce his pleasure when I moved off! Most unattractive. The poor little wretches are from the most remote provincial one horse towns in the Mid-West and they haven't a thing to do, too much money, weak heads and homesickness. They just pour it down from morning to evening and are not fit for anything. Of course it's lining the local pockets and they are not averse to that.

Last night we entertained a U.S. unit in an underground room under an old dis-used water mill. There *just* weren't any rats. Small audience but appreciative and very touching. Miles from anywhere and as usual nothing for them to do. They were very sweet and pathetic somehow. It's such a strange way to fight a war. And it rains and rains. I'm so sorry for 'em. It slightly explains the drinking. But you'd think their welfare officers could do *something*. They seem to have gone completely native and the girls they conjure up out of the ground are really alarming. Oh dear. Life – with a big L – is very sad sometimes!

I'm finding it all rather hard to cope with. I feel all muddled. And it isn't a help to go around bearing the stigma of ENSA! I'm not a bit used to being unwanted and looked down on! Very galling and while good for the soul, mebbe, it's hard – vurry hard.

Letter from R. today: he hasn't *yet* heard from me! Dated Oct. 12th too. I've been writing every two days. He is *still* at Chiseldon, poor old thing, with nothing to do and no one to do it with.

Walter Legge[2] still thinks it's a good idea for Dick[3] to come, so he is. I can only just pray that things work out all right. I don't wish to anticipate trouble but the manager is a bit resentful of the whole idea. Truth is we are far too many already and the concerts go on and on. The baritone is going home at the end of next week, which is a help, but when D. comes we'll have three pianner players! I'll be doing quite a lot of praying from now on.

The general verdict on the day is that it's a 'pure' (poor) one but even so I'm going to pin up dear Queen Maud and wear my fetching little red oil-silk pixie hood and walk and walk. They don't pick their blackberries here and they are wonderful and so *sweet.*

Lots of love

[1] American forces were in Northern Ireland building airfields. A 'doughboy' was the American equivalent of a British Tommy – private soldier.

[2] Head of music for ENSA.

[3] Film composer Richard Addinsell (1904–77) first met Joyce after a National Gallery concert early in 1942. He was already well known for his *Warsaw Concerto* and the music to the film *Dangerous Moonlight.* Joyce and Addinsell had the same taste in music and sparked off each other with new compositions. They were soon firm friends and were writing songs together. Joyce described Addinsell in *Darling Ma* as a 'somewhat pale young man with a lovely touch on the piano. We laugh at the same things – he is the perfect giggler. Very sweet and long and gangling and sort of un-sexed and not a beau in any way. *Very* shy and C3 [not physically fit for the armed forces]. He isn't the least interested in me as a gal and that's easy.'

Joyce and Addinsell had already performed some troop concerts together and broadcast their song '*Nothing New to Tell You*'. He wrote all the music for Joyce's songs until he retired.

28 October 1942   Northern Ireland

Darling Ginnie,

I'm writing this in a Nissen hut Naafi. We've got a decent row of army blankets suspended between the boys and ourselves. I mean our boys. There are a couple of little stoves doing noble work and it's snugger than it often is. The light is one bare bulb too high for any use, and I can hardly see this page at all. The hall is freezing cold and already half full of wretched men.

Our week in Belfast was quite fun and a pleasing escape from communal life for Gwen and I stayed at the Grand Central in comfort and expense. In the afternoon we went over to the Amer. Red Cross and tea-danced for two hours with the troops. A fine time. I was taught how to Jitterbug by a large blond sailor who had heard me at a concert and thought the rest of the programme rotten but loved me!

I attended Church on Sun. Pure musical comedy. Outside white Spanish style. Inside rose pink walls and curtains and baby blue ceilings. The First Reader,[1] if you please, in a snow white dinner dress, draped bodice, Greek style. She put in such a lot of expression that I couldn't listen to a word she said. The soloist in amethyst velvet was doll sized and I nearly burst when she let out a deep rolling contralto voice! Fortunately the Second[2] was nice and normal in a gent's natty swallow tail.

Our concert has started and is one of the small, dear, little quiet ones that I find so well worth while but which the others – specially the singers – are bored by. They like large resonant halls and lots of officers. I like officers too because they like me, but these are the people I came to entertain. Last night was a nice good 'un. Large, resonant, and we all went well. Afterwards at supper I had the Major, 5 foot 6, a motor salesman from Liverpool, misunderstood by his wife, and he took to me terrifically! Begged me *please* to dine one night to *talk*. I told him all about R. and even showed him his photograph but it was no good. He had fallen. He has given me his tel. number which I need hardly say I shall not use!

I feel better about the nasty hotel and even rather like it now. Was badly confused there last time but feel clearer now. Lots of love to you and To and Maria.

---

[1] A lay man or woman elected for one to three years by the church members to conduct Christian Science services.
[2] The Second Reader is the opposite sex to the First, also elected and reads selections from the King James Bible.

1 November 1942   Northern Ireland

Darling Virginia,

Had a happy birthday today? I hope my dainty p.cs. got to you. I talked to R. on the telephone and he likes it well up there in York. Was going to play golf this afternoon he thought.

Dick is coming over on Monday next, so send any messages with him. It will be heavenly to have him because really the company are the very abyss of dumbness. Tomorrow we go to what everyone says is the very End of Everything. It's 15 miles from a railroad and is damp and deadly and is, of course, just exactly the sort of place I came over to work at. The others are very vexed about it. If only there is room enough for us not to jostle each other all the time. I'm afraid the others find Gwen and I very snooty. We aren't in the least but we do get asked out and we accept and go! It's sour grapes of course, but the rather thinly veiled remarks about some people always seeking excitement do make us giggle.

Later: At the concert. It is extremely cold. But it always is. True, there is a war on but it wouldn't hurt the few halls we find unwarmed to put in an oil stove or something for us. I've got a shawl over my shoulders and I can just hold the pen. Hardships of an entertainer!

We are still having hideous piano problems. Gwen has decided – and rightly – that this is the last night she is going to play on it. We hope that a firm stand may stir London. I know Dick won't play on it: and why should he? It's a great pity and makes each evening a new trial. Occasionally we find a piano that isn't any worse than ours and then we use it.

The audience, so far, is tiny. We can only hope it's a musical group. They are all Americans and *look* less wide-open-spaces than some we've met. Gosh, I hope so. What they'll make of me I do not know. Well it's all the same in a 100 years.

I've just been on and they have been *so* nice. They are a high brow lot I think. Oh Lor, I've just announced the soprano's solo and forgot its name, which isn't going to help her confidence any! She's the very sensitive barrage balloon I told you about. Poor gal. However she is singing nicely and they are being attentive, so I hope she is happy. Later – she got good applause, so she is. She is now rendering the Jewel Song, Faust. Coo.

This letter is a little unconnected on account of how I keep having to nip up and announce. Lillian is now doing 'Valse Triste' and in a minute our mountain Maud is to give 'em 'Elegie' by Massenet. (Lillian is Hungarian Rhapsodising now. How I hate that little numero.)

Great waves of longing for Cambridge Square come over me and I crave the smell of a B.B.C. Studio and the pleasure-pain of doing a new song on the air. I feel as remote as a sedan chair but I'm not unhappy. It's being good for me, I know. These little human problems one has to face in communal life do need coping with continually. Living alone at Parr's or with you and To puts no strain on a gal's nature, and I'm learning day by day – I think and hope. But I never was a one to suffer fools gladly and seems I've got a lot to learn! Never have there been so many assembled in a group as in our Company.

I'd give a whole lot to be with you and To around the fireside on your birthday, instead of on a dusty stage somewhere in Ulster.

P.S. Nov 2nd, Fivemiletown

This letter is getting slightly out of hand and is turning into a book. Sorry. We came here through Dutch picture landscape, mostly half hidden in a faint frosty mist. This is literally only little street with the Valley Hotel plonk in the middle. The shops have got oranges for sale to adults, and we've found a laundress and I've made an appointment with the coiffeuse in her small green hovel, and we're settled in. There's an elaborate print over the mantelpiece called *Love's Whispers* depicting an ill proportioned young Roman with a tiny Novelloesque head, colossal calves and great feet in sandals whispering to a Romaness in flowing draperies with big rolling eyes.

7 November 1942 Cambridge Square

Darling Joyce,

I read your lovely letter over breakfast in Lyons, after taking what are called 'early morning babies' to the station.[1]

You seem to be having quite a few pleasant interludes with Majors & Captains, but oh dear on the whole, how miserable it sounds! I dare say it is quite good for you to see the seamier side of vaudeville life & gather pithy sayings for future monologues. I never know why it is supposed to be so good for one to do unpleasant things – I'm always so much nicer when I'm doing things I like, & things like cold, damp, discomfort, jealousy, temper, etc. bring out the very worst in me. However, it is a theory that is hard to quash.

Had a bad week and so took Saturday morning off – had my hair washed, paddled to Richoux for my sweet ration, to Selfridge's to cash a gramophone record token (I got 2 Stefan Grappelly's![2]) & eat a double decker smoked salmon sandwich; bought a book called *Cooking for the Middle Classes* and so home to slippers.

Queenie[3] attended a huge WVS service in St Paul's [Cathedral] – I don't know what we were giving thanks for or dedicating or remembering, but I know I sang quite beautifully, because I was against the brick wall covering Cromwell's tomb, & it echoed so pleasingly I appeared to be the only person singing, & that effortlessly! We nearly died of cold – a drenching day & the big doors flung open for Queenie. On the way out the 10 WVS Regional administrators followed in pairs behind like little bridesmaids & all registering the most acute embarrassment – oh, we girls in green!

I wish I could go to sleep in a warm white cottonwool nest, circular in shape & warmed by constant pink fire. Just a few strains of music could be seeped through to me, & a few plates of delicacies, & just occasionally a short rather moving poem read to me . . . can this be what we are fighting for?

News is good innit?[4] lots of love Gin

[1] WVS accompanied evacuated babies and children under five to the countryside.
[2] Jazz musician (1908–). He later changed the spelling to Stephane Grappelli.
[3] Queen Elizabeth.
[4] On 7 November the Allies landed and advanced in North Africa.

17 November 1942 Northern Ireland

Darling Ginnie,

Last week goes down in the annals as Big Experience, learning all the way and emerging triumphant in Harmony! We were a big success, you see, and the Company hated it. Gwen turned on me and let go, ending with 'God damn you', which was velly plitty, hein? I minded dreadfully. Partly because it was hatred unmasked and very ugly and partly because it was getting at Dick by attacking me. Things like: 'The songs you used to do were far subtler than these'! Nice for you, love, but hard to take for D.! I may say that I was low as a bass that night and got on to God like anything – on the lines of harmonious man. And from that moment onwards not only did we continue to go even bigger than ever but the rest of the company went well too, and a beautiful time was had by all. Our success isn't mentioned but it's accepted now, so it is all turning out like a well-set jelly. But I hope I never have to see faces and feel feels and sense horrors as I did again.

I'm enjoying having Dick here. We've laughed a very great deal and he is a most cosy companion. And to have someone who ticks is so restful after the clods. The rest of the comp. are very guarded with D. but civil. He is nervous as a kitten with 'em. What I've been through in my role of maternal guardian and protector!

Gosh! He is full of complexes and is far too sensitive and not at all well, but as I'm naturally a sort of nanny I don't mind. We got talking about God last night and he believes in just nothing and in no life after death, but would like to but can't.

We are staying in a café-cum-bakers and it is surprisingly comfy.

The tour officially ends next week. Dick and I are going to do a few days work for the Amer. Red Cross in hosp, clubs, where they want us here. It seems silly not to do all we can while we're over here, because we'll never get permits again. When I get home can I stay a spotty with you??

Joyce returned home via a visit to Reggie in York, with her thirteen pieces of luggage. During December Joyce rehearsed the new *How to . . .?* radio series which she and Stephen Potter wrote together, and appeared in the film *The Lamp Still Burns*, shot at Denham studio. Joyce decided that, with more work for ENSA and Reggie based in York, they should leave Parr's Cottage and take a small flat in London.

The Grenfells and the Thesigers had a last Christmas at Parr's Cottage together before moving out.

1943

Joyce moved into her Aunt Pauline's flat in London on St Valentine's Day. She had some small parts in films, including one as a doctor in a blood tranfusion unit, which amused her as a Christian Scientist, and wrote more songs with Richard Addinsell.

Virginia continued to work for the WVS, while the rest of Joyce's year was filled with long train journeys to concerts in troop camps, hospitals, canteens and Land Army hostels.

[August 1943]   Cambridge Square

Darling Joyce,

The upstairs rooms have disappeared under yards of check cotton.
Everything – pictures, chairs & tables – is swathed, & I have lost my
knitting, newspapers, books & bull's eyes.

I have had rather a funny day. I took a nice woman with cancer
to St Thomas' for treatment, & she was so sweet – quite young & full
of brave remarks about the weather & the crops, so I couldn't resist
suggesting C.S., & she said it was queer like, there was a Christian
Scientist lived upstairs who'd suggested *just* the same thing. Well, you
ask her about it, I said.

After work I came home, washed, changed did the X word & then
sallied out to sup with Joyce[1] at you'll never guess which restaurant.
It is terribly difficult to carry on a lucid conversation at the Ivy, isn't
it? So many people to look at & so many people for Joyce to wave at
– but we had good salmon & ice cream. There was a v. frightening
party next to us – Arthur Macrae, Ivor Novello, Terence Rattigan,
Vivian Ellis & Bobby Andrews, five petals of a pansy.[2] Having been
the Mecca of my childhood days – I was taken there by Daddy
on all birthdays & festivals – I now have become full of allergy to
the place.

It is 11.15. I wish I could find the bull's eyes. I love you.

[1] Joyce Carey (1898–1993), actress starring with Noël Coward in *Blithe Spirit*.
[2] Arthur Macrae (1908–62), comic dramatist, appeared in Noël Coward's *Cavalcade*;
Ivor Novello (1893–1951), actor, composer and film star; Terence Rattigan (1911–77),
playwright; Vivian Ellis, composer, and Bobby Andrews (1895–1976), actor who lived with
Ivor Novello.

9 August 1943   Village Hall
                                                       Clitheroe
                                                         Lancs

Darling Ginnie,

It would seem we are entertaining the Licentious Soldiery tonight
in lieu of the sick. I don't quite know why but we are. I'm glad to
report that Preston is a decided cut above Manchester. The Park Hotel,
however, is as bizarre as possible, a mere spit from the station, the
goods yards, the many junction points and all the va-et-vien-ing of
the life mobile locomotif. There are three black satins in a large glass
cage called recep.; two smilers, and a fierce grouch who deals with the
clients.[1]

The company has altered slightly since last week. The old violinist has now returned. He is by way of being a comic too . . . has a comedy violin case with SECRET WEAPON written on it. He had a false moustache for his act made of a piece of old mole on a wire pincer! He is unbelievably un-funny and the boys love him. Or so I'm told. I need hardly say that I precede him on the bill! *Leon* insisted on reciting his lyrics to me. He told me he had a little rhymed monologue *just* right for me – dedicated to the sons of the fallen men who go to fetch their fathers' medals from the King at Buckingham Palace. 'It'ud be nice' he said 'against some soft music.' It was, of course, quite unbelievable. A real collector's item. I only remember one line which was to this effect: 'They left behind their life-like mould.' 'This,' said Leon, 'is a very beautiful thought. You see it's their sons are the life-like mould they've left behind. See?' I said I did, and glibly said it must be done by a man. He is a terrific braggart, is Leon. He knows everyone *very* well; Jack Warner[2] is his very *best* friend. If he'd a known I was seeing Jack Warner yesterday he'd a got me to tick him off good and proper for turning down one of his good ideas. He showed me the good idea – a poem about a man being a 'goose-gog cutter offer fuzzer!'

Leon tells me he can write anything in 5 minutes. It's getting the idea takes the 75% of the time. He writes more for a hobby like – it comes *so* easy to him, see.

I was almost entirely in the train yesterday – to and from Bristol. I queued for 45 mins. in Pad. and was lucky in the end. But only just and the corridors were all full.

I've just been on here and it was *very* nice. Three rows of officers made the right noises for the monologues, and all the songs went well – specially, as usual 'My Bonnie'. Ta ever so for that. I do wish you could see this programme we are doing.

The 'cellist is a mild, silent, worried little man who is developing, I'm afraid, a sort of unspoken fan feeling for me, which sounds conceited but is really rather saddening. Clearly his life has been pretty gloomy. Maybe I stand for West End Theatrical Glamour in his eyes! Who knows. Anyway he doggedly watches my act from the wings and claps each item with touching enthusiasm.

I can hear our comic violinist going on to do his piece. He goes on with the coat hanger still inside his coat, wears only one sock, and tries a sort of Max Millerish – 'Nah, wait a minute' technique. But I can't raise much of a smile somehow, though, in all fairness, I can hear delighted roars from the house as he does his bit.

The comic has just come off and says he wasn't able to crack his best gags tonight as they weren't up to it! He has then swiped 6 shortbread

and 4 choc bics. from the delicious supper hamper provided by the
Regiment we are entertaining. He urged me to fill me pockets too or
there wouldn't be none left! Primitive behaviour you'll note. I priggishly
said I'd had *one* already thanks and I mustn't be greedy. He didn't get it.

[1] Possibly the inspiration for Joyce's hotel receptionist in the film *Genevieve*.
[2] British character actor (1894–1981), music-hall comedian, later PC Dixon of Dock Green
on television.

12 August 1943   Cambridge Square

Darling Joyce,
     Tops in letter from you this morning! Wish I could do justice to it,
but I am everso tarhed tonight. Work is fearfully heavy what with all
these'ere Americans rushing about. I don't quite know what they're
doing. Ostensibly they are looking into women's work, but a great deal
of the stuff they see won't ever be of any use whatsoever. I mean, *will*
there by incendiaries on New York? Je m'en doubte.
     Mrs Whitehurst, queen bee of 2,000,000 club women gave a little
intimate dinner party last night at the Savoy. Seven women sitting at
the best table on the edge of the dancing floor with a specially motifed
flower arrangement. It went on for nearly 4 hours and I got home at
midnight, just exhausted . . . both spiritually & physically. I sat next
to an American war correspondent called Ruth Cowan who had been
in Africa for some months, & had come back a wreck, my dear, but
a wreck. She spoke in modest tones of bombardment and days spent
hiding in fox holes. This latter assertion shook me somewhat, as I think
she was confused with Bataan – wrong army, wrong war – perhaps it
was the gin.
     Just waiting for your broadcast – so far the programme is the lousiest
ever . . . here you come . . . ah, that's better! What a heavenly sketch &
a heavenly song!! I can absolutely see that flatlet that only needs a wipe
over. The song will grow more lovely with usage. At the moment it is
wafty & Debussy & lovely, but rather ungetatable. Incidentally, darling,
whoever it was said 'Joyce, Consonants' was right . . . couldn't quite get
all the words, but oh, you do *sing* pretty.[1]
     Reg & To went to a movie together last night. Forgive if I
write no more, but my eyes feel like hot boot buttons, masses of
love, Gin

[1] Joyce performed a new sketch about flat hunting and a song of Addinsell's in
a musical variety radio show, *Jack's Dive* with Jack Warner, and Ivy Benson &
Her Girls.

14 August [1943]   As from the Adelphi, Liverpool,
                                            whence I go tomorrow

Gin Darling,

Ta for yours. Damn about my consonants. I fondly thought I was
spitting 'em out like anything. Oh blow.

I like Preston but enough is as good as whatnot and I'll be pleased
to move on tomorrow. The Park Hotel is dead quiet socially and *FFFF*
physically on account them trains. But in a way they are sort of sweet.
There's one that coughs just like an old man. And another whistles and
they puff and shunt like Reginald Gardiner's gram record, and are sort
of companionable in a way. There's a Col's wife here who recognised
me and has paid me comps. Which is always a help.

Our comic fiddler, who is Arch Bore No. 1, lost his son in Sicily this
week and that, as you can imagine, has cast a gloom. Oh dear. But
not for long. He is resilient, as are all show people I find! His jokes are
as bad as *Jack's Dive* – if not worse. He's very pleased with himself and
wherever we go he writes on the wall of the dressing room among the
other ENSA artists: 'LEON, The Fiddling Funster! What a lad!'

I swear that's true. The other companies have names like Cheery
Chappies, Cheerful People, The West-Enders, Etc. Etc. Oh ENSA!

Ta for wiring. Do it again please. Love to To, and Maria, and Laura –
and most, of course, for you'dle.

20 August 1943   Adelphi
                                                    Liverpool

Darling Ginnie,

I'm indulging in the unusual beauty of a morning in bed. Got the
curse yesterday morning and did 2 enormous Lunatic Asylums in
the afternoon and evening, so I felt a little luxury was merited. I'm
not quite clear why ENSA entertains loons but it does, and we found
them good. The first lot were very nice – 600 of 'em in an exquisite
hall with a lovely stage, full lighting, perfect acoustics, comfy dressing
rooms, and a Bechstein concert grand in excellent condition. We don't
often find such things. At the second, a mile or so outside the un-lovely
city of Warrington, there was the biggest hall I have ever played in –
enormous. And bad for sound, with another concert grand below pitch
and minus two essential notes, and a semi-dark dressing room lit by a
single naked bulb high in the ceiling. Here they had military casualties
as part of the place was turned into an emergency war hospital. We
had the first half of the hall full of beds and stretchers, and they didn't
begin for 50 feet because of an outsize orchestra pit (why?). The pit was

surrounded by a high wooden balustrade so the patients had to be put far enough back to be able to see over it. So we had a great blank for yards before the audience of 500 began. My intimate style didn't mean a thing. However they liked and knew 'I'm going to see you today',[1] so we sang it together and it saved the day for me! But it was what you might call a slight effort. I took your consonant criticism to heart and fair barked out my Ts and Ds and, according to a kindly clergyman who went to the far end of the place in order to see if they could hear, I was entirely audible without effort. So it can be done.

Our comedy violinist is conducting a really terrific affair with our contralto. Things have reached boiling point and on Weds. night they didn't come into the ENSA hotel all night! Didn't even bother to disguise their absence by ruffling their beds. No one is supposed to know but it's keeping 'em all agog. He is 50 and over; she is what Marian (concertina) calls 'Well on'. About 40–45. The ENSA Matron asked our Managing Major to 'speak to them' about their behaviour. We await further developments in rather horrified eagerness. At least I do. Marian says: 'It's disgustin', reelly. At *their* age.'

She was talking to me yesterday about her husband Herbert, who is our accordionist: 'He's got one very poor eye but the other's got double vision it's so good'(?). 'His heart and all his organs, really, are on the wrong side. Makes him more of a Freak of Nature than anything.' She is one long joy to me.

Oh, Marian has warned me to watch my things as Leon (the Fiddling Funster) 'lifts' things. Don't I see Life?

Yesterday the accordion's wife dropped this gem: 'I'm always thinkin', I can't help thinkin' that's why I can't read because I'm always thinkin'.'

P.S. I suppose if I was a practising Christian I wouldn't have observed any of these things!

Lo o Lo to oo and Too.

[1] Written by Joyce and Richard Addinsell in 1942 and recorded by Gracie Fields (1898–1979).

[August 1943]   [London]

Darling Joyce,

Maria and I lay in the Park today at lunchtime & listened to the band playing 'The Gondoliers' & ate our cheese sandwiches & queen cakes in rhythm. A nice feature of the war. Do you think after the war we shall be able to lunch on the grass, or will fashion dictate that we lunch again sitting at tables *every* day?

Go on having a sparking time, old girl, & masses of love to you both, from Gin

By September Joyce's professional life had become so complicated with ENSA concerts, broadcasting and recording songs, that she engaged an agent, Aubrey Blackburn.

At Noël Coward's recommendation, ENSA asked Joyce to go on a two-month tour of North Africa. She had hoped to go with Richard, but he was still convalescing from hepatitis. Victor Stiebel designed the first of many stage frocks for her.

'ENSA is notorious for being third rate, inaccurate and a mess. We all hate it and it's a great pity it's so rotten for it ought to be so good. But it's run by fifth rate people and their standards are low. It is peopled by little inefficient ex-variety managers who are scared to death they'll be found out. It's a wonderful thing really and a great scandal. It would take years to sort out,' Joyce wrote to her mother.

In spite of Joyce's misgivings about ENSA, she saw this tour as a job she could and should do as part of the war effort.

Viola Tunnard, a professional pianist, was engaged as her accompanist. They played together for the first time in the Elizabeth Garrett Anderson Women's Hospital on Christmas Day.

Joyce wrote of Viola: 'She speaks my language – good sense of humour and quiet, intelligent and *nice*. She has a true gift and has a lot of sensitivity. She is very shy and almost too humble but her playing is heavenly and everyone loves it.'

1944

After waiting impatiently for several weeks for their ENSA tour, Joyce and Viola finally boarded a cruising liner in Liverpool in mid-January. For security reasons, Joyce could not tell anyone where she was going. This period is covered in detail in Joyce's diaries, *The Time of my Life, Entertaining the Troops – Her Wartime Journals*.

13 February 1944   Villa Desjoyeux
Algiers[1]

Darling Ginnie,

Life is very full and I'm, off the record, very tired. 39 concerts of an hour each in 15 days! But there is so much to do and when you pass a ward and they yell out: 'Ain't you coming in here?', you just have to go on. We average three a day.

Staying here with Roger (Makins)[2] has made the whole difference. We've had hot bottles, meals in and carpets and warmth – all the things you don't find in this town. Working at this pressure these comforts have made a lot of difference. Tomorrow, though, we get off on our one or two night stands, which will be different to say the least. The trimmings – tea, and good transport, billets, etc. – do help *so* much to the final entertainment. I know now why the big stars have stooges to fend for them and clear the way for them. It leaves you free to 'give your all'! I mean it quite seriously.

ENSA out here is better than at home; but even so it is a poor thing. However Nigel Patrick[3] – remember him in *George and Margaret?* – has taken over here and really has its interests at heart and knows how to cope with the players, so all is in good hands. And by dint of hard work I've made them understand that I'm not just a fuss-pot but anxious to do the job really well. They now see I mean it and take me seriously as a worker and not just a London star flitting by on a lady-bountiful tour! These hosps, are *the* jobs to do. It's *so* needed and (sh-sh) I can do it.

I think I'll get less tired as I go on. At the moment I'm sort of whacked and that's because we've *had* to do a certain amount of social life as well and that involves sparkling, and really you can't do both. I'm o.k. though. I miss you all in bad patches and get awful waves of homesickness, but truth to tell I'm so busy I don't get time to think much. D.V. And I'm so b–y lucky to be here doing this job and seeing this beautiful country, and being full of fruit and sun (and soon, I gather, *snows!*). We finish with the N. African Continent about the end of the month. Then Malta, Sicily and sunny Italy.

Hilda [Grenfell] has just sent me a mysteriously arrived letter from Cairo addressed C/o Brit. Embassy and written in Baghdad. It says *please* go to Baghdad and round there because they are so far off and feel so forgotten and have, some of 'em, been out there for 4 or 5 years. So I'm now seriously toying with the notion? That means staying out another month, which makes the return about May 1. *If* we do Baghdad it means a quick shopping trip in Cairo to buy a cotton or two, as we're all equipped for the early weather here. I don't *know*.

As I write Viola is playing Chopin for Roger and it's high time we both went to bed, as it's 11 p.m. and we leave at 8 a.m. for 175 mile drive up mountains. I don't look forward to it – hair pin bends.

Danced last night with some young American diplomats on a tiled floor to a very British band, mainly brass! The night before Jock Whitney[4] and I sang *very* beautifully to each other on a *straw* sofa for a long time in harmonies of such exquisite purity that we swooned!

---

[1] The official residence of Harold Macmillan (1894–86), British Resident Minister, Allied Forces HQ, Algiers. Later Conservative Prime Minister and Earl of Stockton. Joyce and Macmillan shared a birthday, and they all went on a flower-picking picnic together.
[2] Old friend of Reggie's and assistant to Harold Macmillan 1904–96. Later British Ambassador to Washington and was created Lord Sherfield.
[3] British actor (1913–81).
[4] Captain Jock Whitney, American Air Force Combat Intelligence Division.

Joyce and Viola encouraged their audiences to sing along, sing their own solos, do conjuring tricks and pull funny faces. They learned to handle every sort of audience from the terminally sick and fatally wounded to drunken officers. Audiences ranged from a few men at a gun site to halls with several hundred. Their 'ideal' audience was a small ward of convalescent patients – bored but not so ill they couldn't join in. They felt their job was first and foremost to cater for bed patients, in an intimate and friendly style. The most difficult audience was a hall in Iraq with 800 men, including three front rows of non-English-speaking Italian prisoners of war.

Joyce's repertoire of popular and favourite songs grew, and Viola could pick up an accompaniment by ear.

They discovered that Nissen huts were perfect for sound and tents were especially difficult – the only solution was to get all the patients to sing along as loud as possible, and then no one noticed the acoustics. Viola had to cope with a range of 'bloody' pianos – some had missing notes, others played double notes, nearly all were out of tune, one had a scorpion in it and many were just 'barking brutes'. She was usually asked to play Richard Addinsell's *Warsaw Concerto*.

After performing, Joyce and Viola would go round the wards chatting to the patients. Joyce spent many evenings writing letters to the wives, mothers and sweethearts for the very badly wounded patients. She also learned that one of her jobs was as 'a useful piece of blotting paper' to lonely and homesick young officers.

27 February [1944]   Cambridge Square

Darling Joyce,

It all sounds fun, but mighty vigorous. Toe & I saw a Carmen Miranda film the other day & it depressed T terribly as it contained a lengthy ballet devoted entirely to the adoration of bananas!

We have had a fairly sticky time this past week, & both days & nights have been far too busy to be pleasant. Mercifully the raids have been very short. I have come to the conclusion that half one's fear is that one may be asked to *do* something about something – put out an incendiary or rescue someone from a burning building, neither of which I could actually do.

Oh, how lovely the raids are! The flares turn the sky green, the phosphorescent bombs drop out of it like Mr Brock's best fireworks, & our red sausages of tracer bullets lazily go upwards. Reg lost the top of his office just near us.

We all dined at Maretta's the other night, & Reg was in fine form, dressed in his little battlesuit. We were all fearfully funny, which did us a lot of good.

When we got home we had the usual raid & gave a spirited exhibition of studied British Phlegm, sitting in little heaps & asking each other general knowledge questions! Today Mary & I motored two doubly blitzed babies to Reading. I have not enjoyed taking our two

Canadian WVS women round & round the 'bad' areas. They simply
adore it of course, & I know it does a lot of good, but it always seems
a bit ghoulish. The US Military Police now wear enormous white hats
& white spats & white gloves. Their advent coinciding with Spring they
have been christened 'snowdrops'.

They are plugging 'I'm going to see you today' like anything, but
always at half tempo so it sounds like a dirge!

We have nearly been married for 5 years! Coo.

Joyce, Viola and their mini-piano were driven around Algiers by M. Grassin, whom
they nicknamed Joli Garçon. At the end of February they drove to Tunis and then
took their first ever flight to Malta where they performed in military hospitals.

Joyce grew more and more fond of Viola, and 'her funny gaucheries'. There were
times when they exasperated each other – Joyce's constant optimism sometimes
clashed with Viola's sudden black moods of depression. Joyce was always grateful
to Viola for teaching her how to listen to music properly and introducing her to
birdwatching.

By mid-March they had reached Naples, where Vesuvius was erupting, covering
whole villages with molten lava. Viola was relieved to meet up with her brother
Peter who had survived the Battle of Anzio. The hospital wards were full of 'far
the illest people I've seen as yet', casualties from the Battle of Monte Cassino as
the Allies pushed up Italy. Even in wards full of dying and screaming casualties,
they sang requested sentimental songs quietly in a corner.

19 March [1944]   Cambridge Square

Darling Joyce,
    Reggie dined on Tuesday evening and remarked how much
quieter the nights were. Of course half an hour after he'd gone we
had a whopping raid. I lay on the sofa with my eyes closed, mentally
murmuring hymns & psalms, until the awful moment came when it was
apparent the Ts would have to use their little stirrup pump for the first
time! A whole bagful of incendiaries fell in the street, & proceeded to go
off with a deafening noise. We nervously peered out of the front door &
saw the two corner houses of Sussex Place alight. Not an encouraging
spectacle.
    Clutching a large white slop pail & the pump we made a sortie, &
just as we were passing the Air Vice Marshal's house opposite, his wife
opened the door, snow white from head to foot from falling plaster, &
said, quite conversationally, 'I'm afraid my house is hopelessly alight!
Have you got a stirrup pump?'
    'Indeed yes' we said. You never saw such a mess! The Marshal
was trying to squash the flames with his best Persian rugs & his wife's

bedclothes, to no good effect. Well, T pumped away in the bath & we saved the house, & felt justifiably proud.

Avid for more action, we then became one of a team of at least 12 stirrup pumps which were holding at bay a huge fire in a garage in the Mews. It was a wonderful sight. About 50 men pumping in turns while their wives held the nozzles from which came the feeblest streams of water imaginable. Still, I am *amazed* to see what a stirrup pump *can* do! Bebe,[1] in full Panama Hattie make-up devoted herself to a wounded warden in her house, & when I saw her was kneeling with his head in her lap giving him tea. The poor chap has had to have his leg off since. He has written Bebe *the* most touching & British letter, mostly concerned with how sorry he was he messed up her carpet!

[1] Bebe Daniels was an American film actress who had settled in England.

29 March 1944   British Embassy
                                                                              Cairo

Darling Ginnie,

Picture if you can, travel stained me lying on a chaise longue in a wonderful bedroom giving, as they say, onto the Nile. There is a trolley with tea, silver pot, and thin savoury sandwiches at my elbow. My hair is newly washed and Maud is bristling with pins pending dinner with H.E.[1] and the royal box to see a flick. C'est la guerre!

Just listen to this and reel a bit: Monday, lunch at dear old Naples, then dinner on the brave little island of Malta.

Next day, Tues, whirring off at 7.30 a.m. (together with a sick man on a stretcher being hurried to a specialist here for a brain operation) and coming down in time for an early lunch in the middle of the desert at a little cluster of R.A.F. Buildings somewhere in Libya. Here there were sand storms ahead and Cairo said visibility is nil. So we spent the night and met such kindness and hospitality as I have never before met with. Tradition of the desert they tell me. We were the only women, until a Free Francaise loomed up in a sort of paper moth with the tri-colour on it, and they put us into the transit mess dining room miraculously made into a bedroom. Rugs made from blankets by our beds, hot water in jugs, hot cocoa to go to bed on, hot bottles, a huge mirror to see ourselves in, and oranges in a basket to help ourselves from. They asked me to perform and so I did – to a huge audience culled from the surrounding distances (just tented camps smack in the desert – awful for them) and it went good, thank heavens.

We left there at dawn today, Wednesday and arrived in the middle of another desert 20 miles from here, where I rang up Uncle Miles to see if I was expected and it seemed I was. So V. and I were dropped here by the airport truck, looking very exhausted and dusty, and found it was five to one and there was a big lunch party at one! So we scratched the surface and made a leisurely descent in order to get our breath again. Of course our clothes are all wrong and by now all dirty and crumpled.

My golly, they *dress* for dinner here, and all I've got is a couple of old stage numbers that only get by at a distance and under lights. There it is. I'll have to take my old fur coat because it's all I *can* do in the evenings, and by now it is so full of Vesuvius ash and Saharan sand, and I can't in any sense be thought to be smart. But it's been so faithful, on me bod. all day and me bed all night.

We had a fairly gruelling time in Italy and saw far too much war and horror for me ever to quite forget it. The selfish relaxation I'm indulging in here makes me feel a mite guilty, I *must* say. But even so it is balm, and in contrast to rooms sans windows, bathrooms sans water, and one or two other minor grizzles, I do find this very restoring! The only snag is that I wish you and R. and To were all here wallowing too. There were 6 or 7 real strawbs asitting atop the mousse!! And I used fresh limes to rinse my hair just now. Hope it doesn't turn green. (It didn't.)

Later. I have just had a bath – a real hot lounging-about-in-bath. The first in 2 weeks. I have made up the face with great leisure at a real dressing table with lights, and now in my old gray lace smellin' pretty of White Lilac I'm ready for the royal box – unless you look too close. I'm in need of a darn here and there, and V. is going to weld the needle on me in half a jiff when she's finished her face. Lace is so practical but it's frail too, if you see what I mean. This is a mad life and a crazy world. Sitting under Vesuvius blowing her top off, I heard of raids on London and I worry a bit about you all. Is it being very hellish? Oh dear.

I remember that you were here once and that's a cosy thought. Please wear your tin bonnet and get under cover. Lots and lots of love to you both and a million thanks for lovely letters.

[1] Miles Lampson (1880–1964), Lord Killearn, British Ambassador to Egypt from 1934 to 1946, widower of Joyce's paternal aunt Rachel Phipps.

3 April 1944   Cambridge Square

Darling Joyce,

Sorry to hear you are going on to Baghdad but I expect you know best. As long as you're not tired and stale. I'm sure it is a good thing to do, particularly as I hear news on every side of your success.

We saw *Madame Curie* which is excellent but does not seem to be a suitable theme for a film. After all, Madame C spent her whole life sitting in a dripping shed staring at a pipette, & though the result was dramatic, staring is in itself not a very exciting thing to watch.

I have got a lovely, Joycey bunch of spring florets in a bowl before me – I wish you were here to give it a sniff.

Joyce and Viola flew on to Baghdad and spent a month touring Iraq by train and truck. After touring for three and a half months and undertaking 155 performances, they had to wait over three weeks in Cairo for an aeroplane home. During this time they socialised, danced and Joyce endured a flirtation from Prince Aly Khan (1911–60), heir to the Aga Khan and leader of Ismaili Muslims, who later married the film star Rita Hayworth.

Joyce and Viola arrived back in London in mid-May, exhausted and 'miserable and lost and cold'. Reggie had been promoted to major and was based at the War Office in Oxford. He was Joyce's constant and loving linchpin as she came back down to earth.

Joyce lived with her Aunt Pauline and spent the summer 'getting ironed out' with her closest friends: Virginia and Tony; Richard Addinsell and Victor Stiebel; Joyce Carey and Myra Hess. Joyce lunched at the Ivy, danced at the Ritz, visited friends in the country and wrote new sketches, songs, and radio broadcasts with Stephen Potter for the *How* radio series. The night raids and doodlebugs continued over London and Joyce was relieved to do some concerts with Viola in country hospitals.

ENSA suggested another tour with Viola. As Reggie was expecting to be posted to Belgium, Joyce agreed. They set off again together on 27 September for what was to be a tour of six months, covering nine countries, including India.

30 September 1944   [Minister's Residence]
Cairo

Darling Ginnie,

Yes, it's as lovely as I'd remembered it. Shall I skim over the beauties or make your mouth water? It don't hardly seem fair with your shuttling to Totters each day on buses in rain and wind and inclemency.

Word got round quite quickly that we were here and the kind invitations began, but we've fended most of 'em off and are only seeing the chosen few!

Last night one of my Coptic admirers took us dining on a roof under a great white moon with stars and a faint breeze and fed us nectar, and then swept us along in a Lincoln Zephyr through brilliantly lit streets to the new open air dance place Anzona, where we swung in delight to a good band wearing white and were given bracelets of wonderful jasmine strung on cotton and smelling of heaven.

In between times Viola and I have worked like beavers on new songs and are getting a fine smoothness over the routines. At last, for the first time since we left here last May, I really do feel ready and capable of doing the job. It's a lovely feeling. Between you'n me I've felt awful these past months, sort of grey inside and selfish and rather too tired all the time, and now in a flash I feel better. I think I rather dreaded doing it all again for a great many reasons, but now I'm laying ghosts and getting rest and time to sort out and I do believe it's going to be o.k.

I must now take a bath in a marble pool 8 feet square! We dine at *9.30!* Wish I could send you some sun and a banana. I can't, so I'll send L.o.L., and write often to the add. you've got.

4 October 1944   Cambridge Square

Joyce Darling,

We dined at the Joy on Monday night with Dick & Victor.[1] Somehow we were all in good form & cracked some merry jokes. We were all very cross *indeed* with Dick because he had had a letter from you.

T & I went to see *Richard III*, which I only half enjoyed but this maybe because I was feeling sick and sad from having had tea with 25 faceless pilots. Olivier[2] gives a brilliant performance, but I cannot believe Shakespeare intended the part to be played à la Victorian villain? O. was constantly about to crook his finger over his nose and twiddle his moustaches, & played the part for laughs! Surely Richard was sincere in his villainy? A fearfully bad play really, & oh the confusion of Queens!! At least four, & all cursing.

Jimmy Hambledon-Smith took me to see Yehudi[3] on Sunday. A Lalo Symphony & the inevitable Beethoven, played to bring the tears to eyes. I wonder how he makes the violin sound like another instrument?

[1] Victor Stiebel (1907–76), dress designer and later owner of a couture house where he designed clothes for royal princesses. Became close friend of Joyce and Virginia.
[2] Laurence Olivier (1907–1989), British actor.
[3] Yehudi Menuhin (1916–), American born violinist living in Britain.

ENSA lent Joyce and Viola a NAAFI mini-bus with room to carry the piano and hang their stage clothes. Viola tuned the piano with a piece of lead tubing with a nail through it, made by a soldier. The bus broke down frequently, and on very slow journeys Viola practised in the back as they moved. They both felt more confident on this tour and had a 'more rounded' programme of original songs by Joyce, Richard and Virginia; Joyce's monologues; piano solos by Viola and old favourite and popular songs for the audience to sing along to. From Cairo Joyce and Viola went by bus to Gaza, Jerusalem, Amman and Haifa.

14 October 1944   [Haifa, then Palestine, now Israel]
                                                      PAIFORCE[1]
                                                      ENSA HQ

Darling Ginnie,

Well, it is going well and is unbelievably hard work. I'm just about dead but tomorrow is an off day so I'm looking forward to that to breathe in. It's these long journeys and one night stands that make it more of a chore than the last tour where we averaged at *least* 3 nights in the same bed. We were literally off the map most of the week. *Miles* off. Just grit and grit and more grit. Heavenly little units and such hospitality and kindness. As usual the social side is fairly heavy. We make chat with the boys and with their officers, and we are expected to go to a mess after the show for drinks, when of course all we long for is bed. But it's all part of the job so must be done.

Last night was, if I say so myself, a real triumph and I don't believe even Noël could have done it any better. 500 rather tough blokes on a stiff battle training course confined to their camp because it is all so hush-hush. Out of *doors*, dear, and *no* mike. The olive trees looked lovely in the bright lights they'd erected around my canvas stage. Above were the stars. For full one hour and a half I held 'em, as in the palm of me hand too! They were wonderful – got all the jokes, were moved when I wanted 'em to be moved, gay with me and they sang and were silent all at the right times. Goodness it was fine. The hardest work, I suppose, I've ever had to do because of acoustics. They were the friendly kind who answered back but do it pleasantly and not smart-alicky.

It was the second show of the day too, for I'd yielded to an impulse (I'm glad to say) and given an impromptu show at a town we passed through at lunch time [Nazareth], when I discovered they were only a handful and never got shows. So I saw the Town Mayor. He circulated the various little groups and an hour later, having changed from our cotton frocks into silks in our 'bus, we did a slap up show for them. I'm glad to say it went nicely. Lots of cockneys. They are always the nicest, the quickest, the easiest to play to. I love 'em.

Tomorrow I hope to see Comfort's mother: if you remember who she is you'll know where we're going.[2]

Sunday. This is bar none the noisiest town in the world. Not just Eastern noises of cocks and donkeys and cries, but cars and bells and Lord knows what. I write at 7 a.m., wide awake from it all for at least an hour.

[1] Allied forces in Iraq and Persia.
[2] The mother of Comfort Hart-Davis was Lady Spears whose husband Major-General Sir Edward Spears was then First Minister to Syria and the Lebanon.

30 October 1944   [Damascus to Baghdad]
                                                ENSA HQ

Darling Ginnie,

Writin' in an aeroplane! Can't use my pen; because of some scientific reaction to altitudes it spurts all over everything.

We adored Syria and hated to leave. Dined with Bryan Guinness[1] who is liaising with the French. He is going to be a *fat* man! Most extraordinary. He has improved except that he is sort of vague and draws in his breath in saying 'Yes' all the time one is talking, which means he isn't taking anything in at all. We talked of home and then he said let's go and dance. I was having a bit of Death,[2] but he was so eager that off we went, and we tango'd and waltzed and I stood heads over all the little wags dancing in their zoot suits with funny little women on wedge soles with pompadoured hairdos.

Damascus under a moon is wonderful, and V. and I leaned on our balcony rail and watched the life go on in the big square below, while the moon lit up all the square houses and played on the domes of mosques and made the whole place a faded smokey sapphire blue.

Talking of hair. I had a Lebanese coiffage in Beirut. It was most glamorous and I looked very unlike me but a bit Loretta Youngish.[3] A huge fat roll all round my head. It was a miracle of engineering and stayed up too. Done by backcombing and skilled rolling and the use of at least 100 invisible hairpins. It was a treat while it lasted.

We are due in 20 mins at where there was a fictitious Thief once. Ged it?

[1] The father of Bryan Guinness was Baron Moyne, Minister Resident of Cairo until November 1944 when he was assassinated by a Jewish terrorist group.
[2] Short-lived depression.
[3] Star of over ninety films (1913–).

6 November [1944]   Cambridge Square

Darling Joyce,

You certainly are being a very fine correspondent. I had a letter from you today written in an airplane! I feel if I was in an airplane I should be leaning back with my eyes closed, & very occasionally biting into a dry biscuit. Presumably you are not allergic to heights. I have been battling against claims of nervous exhaustion, so my leisure moments have been spent in repose with *S & H*.[1]

[1] *Science & Health with Key to the Scriptures*, by Mary Baker Eddy, 1875. The textbook for Christian Scientists.

5 November [1944]   [British Embassy, Baghdad]
                                                      ENSA HQ

Darling Ginnie,

Stepping from my two seater plane today I was greeted with a
couple of letters and one was from you! Many tas. Sorry you've been
death-ing. Me too. However, I think mine is o.k. now, and I hope yours
is too, darling? And not too cold at Totters. I write in a silk dress with
all windows wide to the Tigris and it's 6 p.m., dark and mysterious
with the lights of Baghdad springing on the opposite bank and making
quivery daggers in the water. I do wish you could have a bit of this
life. You'd hate the travel and the shows I suspect, but the in betweens
are lovely.

Today, for instance, we flew back from a northern town [Mosul]
and we cruised at around 300 feet and saw Arab village life like a toy
model. A Bedouin gal in scarlet, bowed double under a load of camel
grass. And I saw a fine sheikh crossing the shallow cream-green river
on a white horse, making a long arrowing design in the water.

No social life because of pore ole' Princess Beatrice conking it so
conveniently and casting the circle into official mourning.[1]

Viola has had a series of b–y pianos but is very good about it and
we have lots to laugh at. She is a sweet companion and watches over
me in a fine nanny way. I suspect I'm more of a gov. to her. She is *not*
punctual – and you know me!

I must say I'm glad I came! Lots less tired now. Take care of
yourself love.

[1] Queen Victoria's youngest child, born 1857.

They drove about 150 miles a day from Iraq through Persia to Abadan. Whenever
they found a British army signal post they stopped for a chat or to sing a few songs.
In the evenings they stopped at hospitals where they performed and slept. They then
flew to the United Arab Emirates where they performed to mixed audiences of the
British navy, Royal Air Force, American oil workers and Indian sailors.

25 November, 1944   [Sharjah, United Arab Emirates]

Darling Ginnie,

Do get out your atlas and look up Sharjah. Look for the Persian Gulf
and on the left, palest possible brown, is Arabia and down at the end of
the Gulf is Sharjah. There is an Arab village with a Sheikh's Palace and
a great many mud huts.

What else is there here? – well, a few palm trees and heavily veiled girls squatting in black rags under them, and idle camels poised for silhouette effect or folded for sleep, and thousands of little children with giggles, tummies, engaging grins, and flies. There is, of course, as well, the object for which we are here, but that's careless whatnot, so I'll leave you to guess just why we happen to be on this buff bit of the map.[1]

Constant slaves fold everything into little teensie squares. I lay in bed this morning while mine folded up all my underwear and stockings and scarves into minute folds.

I think we've got to abandon further isolated places and that's a thing I hate to do but there is no plane this week.

No letters for *far* too long. It's rather a headless feeling, not knowing nothing. Don't like it. A pilot passing through here two days out from London said rockets were falling consistently, and my heart and tummy turned over for the loved ones and I felt sick for you all. Damn and blast the bloody things.

I did an outdoor show on an unnamed island [Bahrein] in these parts two nights ago, in a high wind. It was coming at me from the right so carried my voice out to at least half the house, who sat and shivered but kept on asking for more and more, so we stuck it. But it was extremely funny singing with my hair coming down and blowing like a moustache across my mouth and my skirt swirling about my ankles till they were quite sore! Vi's piano swayed away in it and when she played 'Warsaw' I thought the whole thing might take off.

[1] British military base.

29 November 1944   Cambridge Square

Darling Joyce,

It is strange to think of you just approaching Mother India, it seems terribly terribly far away . . . I cannot visualise you, expect perhaps against a background of a picture postcard of Taj Mahal. Do not, I beseech you, come home with a diamond embedded in your right nostril, *nor* with the intention of writing a book called 'What I Should Do with India', *nor* with an ayah, *nor* clapping your hands. Any orientalisation of your good self would irrefutably strain my love for youdle, much love . . .

How to Woo was on last night, almost better than *How to Keep a Diary*. It was everso queer hearing your old voice, & of course I minded. I know T did too, because he closed his eyes & pretended he was asleep which he always does when he thinks his big blue lamps might show too much emotion!

Yesterday I went quite berserk. I happened to go to the Private View at the Leicester Galleries of Epstein's[1] recent paintings. There were about 10 people there, & they were frantically buying everything . . . the little man was rushing about with those red spots. So I became panic stricken & thought, God, I *must* be quick, they're taking *all* the best, heavens!! So I bought *TWO*. In fact I was subject to mass hysteria. I hope I like them when they come. One of waterlilies and the other Epping Forest. I really *am* rather extravagant.

I hear Harry [Reggie's brother] is on the seriously ill list. The lad hasn't got here yet . . . oh dear.[2]

[1] British Cubist artist (1880–1959).
[2] Harry Grenfell lost his lower leg in Burma and later had to have his other leg amputated.

6 December 1944

ENSA HQ
Greens Hotel
Bombay

Darling Ginnie,

Such a wonderful mass of mail met us here five days ago. We fell on it in contented silence and only the odd 'oh' or 'ah' came out of either of us for about an hour. Wonderful. Darling you are an old faithful, and if you could but guess how lovely it is to get your fair hand on an envelope you'd not stop writing for a single second.

Well India is very *big* and, contrary to the map, not really very pink when you look at it close to. More buff tones really. I feel that I can stagger through two shows a day in a place where I'm not travelling, and one of the beauties of this phase of the job is that things are very centralised so that we stay in one bed for several nights together, which helps a lot.

I've been racing here. It was *so* lovely to look at I nigh swooned. The ladies in their saris are divine and all are lovely and slim and have liquid eyes and diamonds and high welsh voices, and there was sun on the grass which was miraculously emerald, and the horses gleamed in purple flashes of best Lyons satin, and the beds were full of tiny little yellow button chrysanths, and it was all velly plitty indeedle. I picked a horse for its kind face and placed 10 rupees on its back, but it didn't win. Eric Dunstan took us. He's a friend of all the Toyes, Enid, Barbara Back, Bruce Ottley and Oglander Asp, world. Rather fierce and in fact an organised bully but good at the job, and it needs a bully I'm afraid. Anyway he's raised the status of ENSA up here so that one is no longer ashamed of being associated with it, which is big change I can tell you.

We are in the process of assembling our kit for up country! *Not* a pith helmet but a canvas bath, bucket, bed and blankets, and a bag containing cutlery and beetleware plates and cups. A device for the killing of flies is – 'Flaps, Fly' on the label. And an enamel bucket is charmingly called 'Pails Slops'.

Now don't blanche or anything, but I think I'll stay out till March *if* Noël doesn't need me before.[1] There is such a really important job of work to be done out here, and so huge is it that I feel having got here at last I must complete it if I possibly can. I've cabled Noël and await his answer.

V. and I were taken to the opening of the Navy's own show here, running for 10 nights, called *Men Only*. It's wildly ambitious and rather touching and not very good. One of the Indian ratings is a fakir (on the side) and he did an act of horrifying awfulness by throwing himself on a pile of broken glass, eating an electric lamp bulb and a Gillette razor blade, and finishing by appearing to enjoy a pudding of fire. He was a handsome creature and the alarming exercises and contortions he went into between eats was very creepy. Animal mag. I suppose. Yogi anyway. Very queer. Me no like.

We are both very fine and giggle constantly. Our English settlers here are exactly like the jokes and caricatures. It's hard to credit them. Coo, I'm late. Haven't read the lesson yet. Oh dear. Go on writing *constantly please*.

Happy Noodle Year.

[1] Noël Coward had invited Joyce to join the new revue he was planning for 1945.

15 December 1944   Cambridge Square

Darling Joyce,

How glorious it sounds. Bathing & fruit drinks & sunshine & Foreign Legion forts all folded to the size of a napkin.

Oh dear, I knew you wouldn't come home when you ought to of! I am praying Noël C[oward] will demand your presence forthwith.

Harry is back and Laura says he is in wonderful spirits. Reg came up to see him and was quite green at the thought of a wrecked & crippled Harry. But the latter was so jolly, it set Reg up to the skies. He went out & bought Harry an orange dressing gown with pink facings! It is *the* most awful thing, but H is mad about it. If they can fit him up with a foot & he can manage crutches he is going home for Christmas.

We had *such* a big bang my dear, which rocketed us in our beds ever so. It fell between the flat where I used to live and THE big street nearby

[Oxford Street]. It is distressing these things coming this way. Ah well, it is a very democratic war.

Can you sing this?

> I'll see you again
> Wherever there's a queue again
> Tho' life & love come to naught
> The fish we've bought is past forgetting.
> In my dreams I'll see
> You waiting Oh so patiently,
> Haddocks eyes may lie between
> Flabs of turbot intervene
> You'll be close as a sardine – to me.

love to Viola and you

From Bombay Viola and Joyce travelled by train to Poona, where they continued to perform in hospital wards. Noël Coward did not need Joyce until March, so she and Viola happily carried on their tour of hospitals.

28 December 1944   Cambridge Square

Darling Joyce,

A very happy New Year to you & may it bring peace *for Heaven's sake*! I'm fair fed up with this war, aren't you, although God knows I've had a cushy one. Wonder what you're doing? We've just eaten a very big piece of Christmas cake covered with US *icing* and now we feel sick again.

Before Christmas our lives were complicated by the daily arrival of some thousands of toys for Belgian children. They were packed loose in huge railway containers and somehow we had to distribute them. We then got letters from old gentlemen to say their sons sent a little blue painted handcart with a red stripe, and would we please find and return it! O là là, la vie!

How perfect it is not to work! I really think that after the war I must make a short but very determined effort to get an Act passed whereby nobody works more than 4 days a week.

Dick has rung & asked us to a little New Year's Eve party, which we have accepted with alacrity, only to be a little depressed at the idea of staying up so late!

Harry was home for Christmas & in huge form. He insisted on going to The Messiah at the Albert Hall. Laura says he heaves himself around on his hands, & is persistently gay.

Here is a little religious poem for the New Year

> Lift up your eyes
> Unto the skies
> The Parson said.
>
> O weary one,
> Sorrow is done,
> Lift up your head.
>
> Lift it up high,
> Heaven is nigh,
> Look, and you'll see
>
> Bombers, she said
> Fighters, she said
> And a doodlebug coming for me.

A very happy new year, darling, and of *course* you can stay here.

29 December 1944   [The Gables, Secunderabad]
                                                        ENSA

Darling Ginnie,

We've met with wild enthusiasm. Not, which is flattering I think, at first. They are very cagey out here. So much has been promised to them for so long and none of it has materialised that they are very diffident. Often we find groups of them lurking the far end of the ward and not going to co-operate: just browned off with things in general. But almost entirely without exception they have slowly joined the circle and at the end have become our most enthusiastic audiences, and they listen so beautifully: not just let it drip over them. I feel as if I'm learning a lot, not only as a human bein' but from the technical side too.

Our Christmas day was heavenly. We'd taken pains to conceal that we were alone here, feeling that some hospitable local would bid us join their family ring. I woke up and saw a bulky silhouette hanging from my mosquito net – V. had got a pair of child's socks, red and white striped ones, and filled them with bits and pieces from the bazaar. I never heard Santa hang it up at all: complete surprise. I had some items for her and they were wrapped in giddy paper from the village and hung with tags of my own devising. We were garlanded at our bedside breakfast by our bearer, white chrysanthemums and pink roses. A gardener in a puce turban came in through our french windows across our little lawn with a bouquet for each of us. The cook lost his head and went mad over breakfast, garnishing everything with bits of greenery with passion fruit and yoghurt. It was unlike any Yule I've ever had.

Ghulam – our bearer – presented us each with a large coconut as well as the garlands. We went up to one of the hosps. at 5 and visited quietly in the bed wards for nearly three hours.

We are mostly far too busy to dwell long on unhappy things but now and then we hear the news and it's none of it much good. However we are sorry for you all. Darling, let's hope next year *is* Peace.

Joyce and Viola had reached 'that comfortable state of sympathy when silences are often more articulate than speech. Added to which she is almost as silly as Gin, and that's high praise.'

1945

2 January 1945   Cambridge Square

Darling Joyce,

Here we are in New Year, very cold and bleak. I wish you could have seen Tony & Me on Sunday night, waiting for Dick's party. We really didn't want to go, after a nice dinner at home, toes in the fender & all, and seriously thought of falling down the stairs & injuring ourselves everso slightly. Needless to say we enjoyed it hugely. Noël [Coward], Gladys [Calthrop],[1] Victor [Stiebel], Winifred [Clemence Dane], the Lunts,[2] and several people I never deciphered. I must say Noël is extraordinarily friendly, and was determined the Ts should feel thoroughly at home. We talked about you, of course, and ate chicken and drank Dick's boiling red brew which I believe is full of tea, treacle and cloves. Alfred Lunt told us about Bea Lillie singing the first Act of *Carmen* at the Met Opera House, which must have been superb. We thought him thoroughly delightful and completely kind about everyone. Winifred and Noël had what I take to be their usual discussion on Shakespeare 'Think of Corialanus . . .' 'My *dear* Winifred, I am *always* thinking of Corialanus from morning till night . . .' I became slightly tight and thought everyone entrancing. At 12.0 we sang Auld Lang Syne, & then kissed each other separately, regardless of sex. Tony feels tremendously bucked at having been kissed by Noël Coward!

Here is an extract from the *Observer* from Miss Lejeune:[3] 'What else happened in 1944? Frank Sinatra happened. Gaunt & hollow eyed, he came riding on the clouds to tell us He hadn't slept a Wink last night. We believed it. The celestial choirs had a busy year. Errol Flynn died for his country (France) and George Raft died for his organisation (U.S.O.

Camp Shows). Phyllis Calvert died for purity in Florence, & Margaret Lockwood near as died from exposure in Cornwall, on a rock in mid-winter with a weak heart in a bathing costume. Claude Rains went slowly mad in baby blue, Boris Karloff kept an embalmed prima donna in his bedroom . . .' Isn't she a sweet writer?

The bumps [bombs] go on rather tiresomely, but the first bunches of narcissi are in the shops price 12/6 a bunch dear, so spring is on its way tra-la. Love to Viola, all love from Gin.

---

[1] Gladys Calthrop (1897–1980) designed many of Coward's shows and had been a friend of his since 1921.
[2] Alfred Lunt (1892–1977), American actor, and his English wife Lynn Fontaine (1882–1983) acted together in many of Coward's plays.
[3] Caroline Lejeune was a film critic.

New Year's Day, 1945 saw Joyce and Viola Tunnard travelling down India by train from Hyderabad to Bangalore. Joyce found Indian trains made her 'angrier and angrier about the heat and dust and the length of journey and dullness of scenery seen through the eye-dazzling mesh of fly screens'. In Bangalore they performed three times a day in the British Military Hospital, and shocked the Polo Club by wearing day dresses for dinner.

Joyce, Viola and Ghulam Mohd, their manservant, continued by train to Madras, which was 'hot and depressing', with 'more bullocks sitting in more ponds, more brass pots on the heads of more willowy women and endless naked children'. The hospital piano was the usual nightmare for Viola who went through 'one long hell never being able to make a sound to satisfy the ear'.

12 January 1945   ENSA HQ
                                                     Greens Hotel
                                                          Bombay

Darling Ginnie,

So faithful am I that I can't even remember what I wrote in the last letter – seeing as I write so frequent. I don't think I'd told you about our night in the train with the Hindu lady and 'her children'? When we got to the station we were told we were sharing a four berther from Bangalore to Madras with a Mrs Tanejee and her two children. V. and I, now all too aware of the horrors of Indian travel, were, mercifully, all tucked in with our books when Mrs Tanejee arrived. The 'children' turned out to be a couple of adolescent boys of 16 and 13, and one had a heavy black moustache! They were no trouble, I must admit. The elder peered down at me through steel rimmed glasses till I arranged my suit on a hanger as a protective curtain. Mrs Tanejee was talkative and pretty but disappointed us badly by hiding in a corner to take off her saree, for we did so want to know how it went on. There was a beetle as big as a matchbox in the compartment at one moment. With deadly accuracy I wonked it and then of course wished I hadn't. Very messy.

Madras is faintly attractive because it's historical. Clive was here, and Napoleon! There's an old fort and a lovely Colonial white club of enormous proportions. We've met rather nice people, too, who seem to be leading fairly realistic lives and to have character. Rare out here. It's a land of British mediocres.

Viola is now playing on the hotel grand which is, literally, a whited sepulchre. She's a glutton for work that gal. Practises almost every morning and sits solid at b-y pianos for two or three hours every afternoon. Did I tell you about the sweet fan who remembered me from Paiforce last year and who is in a hosp. here now. He said 'The minute I saw your poster I knew it was you.' We go to Calcutta on Sunday.

16 January 1945   Totters

Darling Joyce,

Victor came to dinner last night. He was off to Scotland on leave today, to the bonny paps of Fife. We gave him some pre-war ice cream! I hadn't realised that Mr Walls literally froze his ices when the ban was put on. But this is so, and London is dripping with the most divine vanilla of a heavenly velvet texture at the moment, which we are lapping up in great gulps, regardless of the weather or the fact that we do not like it very much in peace time!

Masses of love, darling, from Gin

From Madras, Joyce, Viola and Ghulam flew to Calcutta by DC3 where they stayed in the Government House, which was camouflaged with 'strawberry jam'-coloured paint.

They performed in more hospitals, and Joyce lost a contest between her voice and the trams' clang and scream, and found the RAF audiences more flattering and discriminating than the army. At one army hospital they performed in the drive, with their audience hanging over two high balconies, and a second audience of parrots and crows behind them.

26 January 1945   Cambridge Square

Darling Joycey,

Talked to Dick and he said 'All Our Tomorrows'[1] is being sung quite a lot in concerts and the radio by Anne Shelton, and Decca is recording it with her and Ambrose. He said she sings it very slowly, very rich and very gloomy! 'You know what she thinks her tomorrow's going to be all right, all right.'

Celia is starting on the film which necessitates going for a fortnight to a remote railway station in the North somewhere.[2] As we are still deep in snow, and the *sea* has been frozen for 3 days at Folkestone, it will not be jolly.

Isn't the war news *wonderful*? We hardly dare believe it, & it seems impossible they should whisk right through to Berlin. In the mean time I take Australian ladies to hover on the brink of craters & Canadian ladies to photograph Acton children forced into jerseys much too small for them; & today I take around an Indian lady from East Africa called Lady Abdullah who was trying to get to Switzerland & doesn't quite know how to pass the time.

God Bless xxx Gin

[1] Song by Richard Addinsell and Joyce.
[2] Celia Johnson was filming *Brief Encounter*, co-starring Trevor Howard (1916–88), originally written as a play called *Still Life* by Noël Coward.

Joyce and Viola toured north-east India giving two or three performances a day in hospital wards and then another hour talking to the patients. Joyce managed to be both sister and mother to the wounded young men, while Viola played them their favourite pieces.

9 February 1945   Calcutta

Darling Ginnie,

Tomorrow I'm 35 and it's far too old. Very depressed about it, and I know one oughtn't to record ages and all that, but as I look at my poor old face and take a frank look at my wrinkles it all seems sad. However I'm really in good form after two weeks off map, doing hard work but with little travelling and fresh food.

We all went to a B.O.R's[1] dance and were worked to our knees. I had a Shepherd's Bush partner who just reached to my nose. He danced like F. Astaire only more twirly and he whirled me all over the floor and taught me a smashing new glide and dip movement. He booked every alternate dance and I've seldom had more exercise or enjoyed it more. He was about 20, Tank Corps, had been in one of the hosps. and thought me a 'wizard singer', and he wore his beret on the very back of his head, kept on purely by suction I think. Conversation was sparse: we kept our minds on our work. It was a very good evening and I slept like a log after it.

Are you a leetle warmer now? It must have been awful. Dick writes that Noël has put off the revue till the autumn. Tant pis. Maybe I'll go to Australia instead? O.K. then I won't.

[1] BOR: British Other Ranks. Joyce said they dance 'far, far better than their officers'.

11 February 1945   Cambridge Square

Darling Joyce,

There hasn't half been a gap since I last wrote, and I feel everso bad about it, my badness only assuaged by the knowledge that you haven't found time to write either.

Last Sunday we walked across the Park and had tea with Harry. Reggie was there too, and also a jumble of elderly ladies and gentlemen, the former wearing far too long fur coats and round hats pulled down over their ears, and the latter avuncular and moth eaten. I have never seen anyone look so as well as Harry! He is very brown and very talkative. He has, however, no legs from the shins down. This is disconcerting because he waves them about, either because the muscles get stiff or simply to startle one. He crosses them repeatedly, & flip goes his trouser leg & flap goes the other! He is so gallant, & goes off to all plays, concerts etc.

Tell me when to stop writing to you and then my heart will rise like a young bird!

We have solved the coke problem by hiring a *pantechnicon*, & going to Fulham to *fetch* it. We are only allowed 4 cwts, so Tony went off with 4 little sacks in this enormous vehicle and came home gleaming with triumph.

xx Gin

Joyce received a telegram from Noël Coward saying that she must come home as soon as possible for his revue. Unperturbed, she replied that she planned to fly back in mid-March. She felt alarmed by her lack of inspiration or energy to tackle a revue so soon. She was embarrassed by a photograph in the *South East Asia Chronicle* which captioned her as Cabaret and West End Singer, with no mention of either Viola nor the hospitals they had performed in.

At the Ranchi Central Military Hospital she was conscience-stricken when she realised that her monologues were causing the facial injury patients considerable pain but they urged her to carry on, even the 'newly done tonsils who went on bleeding cheerfully'.

Joyce and Viola arrived back in London in mid-March after being away for six months. They both 'dreaded England and the difficulties ahead . . . it's been a heavenly six months. Lots of it hard going – I'm fairly dead now, but all of it was worth it. I dread the business of coping, without Ghulam or the sun to help, for I've grown soft in those ways.' Reggie was on leave and they stayed at Virginia's.

On 2 May 1945 Germany surrendered to Russia and a week later the war was over in Europe.

Saturday [June 1945]   Cambridge Square

Darling Ginnie,

Here is a wee gifte in the Victorian manner for wearing with black
sometimes. It has a certain faint far off charm but you may hate it.
Anyway it brings beaucoup de love and is the thinnest possible end
of the most vast colossal wedge of thanks I'd like to say for ALL you
have DONE for me. Words fail. I think you must catch a blinding flash
from the lovelight in my eye now and then, and possibly this may hint
at my gratitude. How hard it is to convince on paper. But in all truth
I'm deeply and eternally thankful for you – FOR BEING YOU – and for
all your sweet and loving hospitality. I bet it's a bore having a third
presence even when out. A sort of occupant seed in an otherwise quite
sound space by two teeth! If you get my meaning.

For the next few months Joyce stayed with Virginia, gathering her strength and
writing new material for the Noël Coward revue *Sigh No More*. Rehearsals began
soon after the Victory in Europe celebrations in May. Working on a revue with Noël
Coward turned out to be both emotionally and physically hard work. All the eight
numbers written by Joyce and Richard Addinsell were cut, but for one song and one
monologue. Coward either raged or praised, and the actors never knew whose turn
it was for praise. Heading the cast were Madge Elliot (1898–1955) and Cyril Richard
(1898–1978), a husband and wife team who had starred in many musical successes.
Also appearing were Graham Payn (1918–), later editor of Coward's diaries, and Edith
Evans, who was better known for performing Shakespeare.

Two days before the show opened in Manchester, Coward wrote in his diary: 'I am
horribly worried about Richard's and Joyce's material. It is all pretty amateurish and
gets nowhere.' Virginia and Tony saw the show a few days after the first night.

16 July [1945]   Cambridge Square

Darling Joyce,

It is before dinner, & I have had a bath & am listening to *Forces
Favourites*. You will just have finished Du Maurier,[1] you glamorous
creature you, & Manchester will be sitting back dazzled & breathless.
You really do it *swell* – all the gestures to perfection – crisp, elegant . . .
I could eat you!

As soon as the train got in yesterday we dashed off to the Club & ate
with the others.[2] They were having champagne to celebrate nothing at
all except possibly Winifred's escape from her nursing home & Victor's
farewell to his GHQ. He had spent the day crying at a goodbye parade
& was suitably emotioné. Of course we talked exclusively of the revue.
I was somewhat confused by the feeling they engendered that you had
had a very rough time indeed the week before – that Noël had been cold

& beastly to you & Dick, that *you* had been wonderful etc etc. They had quite a mother complex about you, a sort of tiger for her cubs attitude. I assured them that tho' tired, you were not miserable – I hope to God I was right. I imagine that darling Dick, super-sensitive as he is, minds things that much more than you do. I simply can't believe that Noël who is one of your greatest fans, should have given you a rough time, but if he has, here come the Ts with the tongs!!

I rang up your Pa. He was sweet.

[1] Oh Mr Du Maurier', song written by Joyce and Dick Addinsell.
[2] Victor Stiebel, Winifred Ashton (Clemence Dane), and friends.

Three weeks later Noel Coward wrote in his diary: 'Saw the show. Joyce G is first rate, but some of the others are really no good. I told the company that, whereas before I wanted them to be happy and efficient, now I was not remotely interested in their happiness but determined that they were going to be efficient.'[1]

[1] *The Noël Coward Diaries*, edited by Graham Payn and Sheridan Morley, Weidenfeld and Nicolson, 1982.

Sunday, 22 July 1945   The Midland Hotel
                                                       Manchester

Darling Ginnie,

It's 11 and I'm still abed and NOT going to Kirk. My chamber maid tells me it's a wild day. Life is a little on the lonely side. I remain bedded till I've read the lesson, *The Times*, written my letters and killed off most of the morning.

Being islanded like this throws things into a horrid clarity and I find it, humanly speaking, of a tragicness quite colossal! Thank God, and I mean it, for my job. At least that uses up a lot of me and it seems to be one I can do. (Noël said to me yesterday, in obvious surprise, that he'd never met such an uncanny theatre sense as I seemed to have.) One must trust in the Lord, that's obvious. And not try to plan or circumvent. Right places are right places and one can't get into wrong 'uns.

Lovely Bach on the radio. Today I take lunch with His Eminence [Noël Coward] in the Royal Suite to talk over the new plans for Hat.[1] I'm in High Favour at the moment: it's quite fascinating to watch the needle swinging round and picking on certain people for a time and then veering off in quite another direction. I'm growing used to it.

I'm reading *Brideshead*.[2] It's a little sinister I think but highly readable. What a skilled and altogether fascinating work. For subtlety and pro Papish propaganda it's the slickest thing ever. Most people I find are fooled into thinking it's anti-Roman, which is the cleverest of all.

Sundays in strange cities are not the thing. Wish I was at 32 with my FRIENDS I love. The boring thing is I must wash my hair. That's a terrible depressin' thought and all.

¹ One of Joyce's sketches that Coward cut.
² *Brideshead Revisited*, by Evelyn Waugh, published in 1945.

25 July 1945   Women's Voluntary Services for Civil Defence
41 Tothill Street
London SW1

Darling Joyce,

Following a new policy I went to the office out of uniform today! I have decided that when I am lunching out or going to a play I shall do this – I feel it is the thin edge of the wedge! Had luncheon with Barbie at the Dorchester and qua food it was disappointing – spam and stewed plums. Barbie is tremendously happy, & her bust has got so large I think she must be going to have a baby, although her tum doesn't show it. Perhaps it's just happiness swelling her bosom.

This evening I went to Nancy's [a cousin] reception, she having been wed at Caxton Hall at 5.30. It was all very slap up, in one of those superb houses in Queen Anne's Gate. A most extraordinary conglomeration of people ranging from exotic tarts through aunties to Muswell Hill. Aunt Titsey was there, rather bent now with shreds of carrots & white striped hair roistering from under a flowered straw planted straight on the forehead. She still has a pawky wit. Extraordinary how few members of my family are gentlemen! The bridegroom is about 4 ft high, but has a nice innocent face & shaggy friends.

XX Virginia Margaret Thesiger

30 July 1945   The last Monday at Midland in Manchester

Darling Ginnie,

Last week in Lancs, which is a pleasing thought to one who cares not for cobble and soot and train and treeless civic pridelessness. I daresay behind those cultured, sane facades there will always lurk autumnal tinted Kidderminsters in modernistic squares and angles, figurines of Scottie dogs with lolling red tongues, and *Radio Times* covers emblazoned with crinolined ladies in Clark's silk.

Viola and I got to a more rustic district than I'd achieved the week before and while we were there we picked a lot of wild flowers and saw a wood and cows, and there were no pavements or buses and only a very few cars. It was wonderfully tiring and we staggered home to tea in my room. Hated to see her go off this morning. To Notts, poor girl, with yet another ensemble of unblended musicians.

Stephen [Potter] writes that *Vogue* is full of a huge photograph of me. I've not seen it. Have you? I don't know anyone who takes *Vogue*, do you? And I know you can't buy it anywhere. In common gratitude for the ardours of climbing to their dirty old studio and standing about in draughts they ought to send me a copy but they won't. I bet they don't.

Write again please. I send Felicitations and Affection.

Your close friend

Grace Gumshell

On 26 July Conservative Prime Minister Winston Churchill lost his premiership in the general election with a landslide victory to Labour, led by Clement Attlee.

2 August [1945]   Cambridge Square

Darling Joyce,

I have been dilatory (or dilapitory) in writing, owing to various things, chiefly playing golf & tennis.

Going backwards a bit, we went to the Ivy on Election Night, so we all felt a bit giggly – because somehow it really *was* funny. All the letters I'd written the day before which mentioned the probably small Conservative majority had to be written again, & we'd had a gay day calling each other Comrade & setting off to get tea for our stooges & pretending to be rather afraid of them & sucking up to them! They entered beautifully into the spirit of the thing, & refused to answer the telephone etc. I suppose that even if the tumbrils are coming they make so much less noise than bombs we can't treat them seriously.

Tony has been in seething rage all morning because his Ma, standing on the doorstep had pointed at a small child & said to To 'Why don't you adopt something like that? Lots of people *do*!' She really is top notch for tactless remarks. T just turned away. But there was a lot of 'I wish she'd mind her own bloody business' & a lot of soothing & loving from me as we drove away.

I must now to bed. I am looking forward to this as our last two nights were spent in a *small* double bed & we are *big* people.

3 August [1945]   [Manchester]

Darling Ginnie,

I hereby award you the Hawthornden Prize for Utter Beautiful
Silliness. It was your Peke on Dareen that did it. Oh and the music by
Du-Faure-ier. Lil ol' Grenfell laffed and laffed.

In answer to enquiry: so far I've got through the show beautifully
though it wasn't very comfy last night. An unpleasant restrictive sense
and rather laboured breathing. But after a very peculiar start this a.m.
all seemed lots more under control. Noël did a meanie on us and sat in
the back row of the stalls so we didn't know where he was and thought
he was absent. He rang me this morning (how my grandmother would
curl up at that phrase! Quite right too) to say he could hear every
syllable of me to perfection. I'm still, pro tem, teacher's pet, Pollyanna
the Glad Girl. Long may it endure!!

Stephen [Potter] came up last night. He rather enjoyed the show
and we had dinner afterwards and dissected the programme until it
was time to go rather im-morally to my bedroom and hear our *How* on
my radio.

There is literally no news. Out of the 24 hrs I worked out that I'm
spending 15 $\frac{1}{2}$ in or on bed! I've a suspicion that I'm Fattening slightly
on it, which is very fine except that it feels more tum than bust and bust
is the urgent place.

6 August 1945   Southsea

Darling Joyce,

How you must have sweated in your theatre these past few
days. Fairly fresh here owing to the sweet sea breezes, but scorching
temperatures in London.

Yesterday afternoon we took the maids to the sea, & after depositing
them with an immense picnic basket bulging with orangeade bottles
on the pebbly shore, we paddled – extremely painful. Then we drove
to Brighton to see if we could buy an ice cream. Brighton was pretty
tremendous – yards of pink bodies prone on the beach,[1] & queues,
strung about with damp bathing dresses & damp babies patiently
waiting outside the tea shops.

T. battled into an Ice Cream parlour & returned with two objects we
decided were frozen flour & water. I do love Brighton. You would have
enjoyed the conglomeration of tarts, gigolos, racing tipsters, mixed up
with very old ladies & Colonels in boaters.

When do you return, darling? It will be nice to see your old dial
again. Incidentally, I did see your picture in *Vogue* – the *dress* looks all

right, but you look ghastly – rather a blurry famine child. I shouldn't make any *sort* of effort to get a copy.

All my love X Gin

[1] The first time the beach was accessible since before the war.

7 August 1945   Cambridge Square

Darling Joyce,

I feel quite upset that you want to get a flat. I'm sure it is a good thing and all that, but it has given me the WILLIES (who was WILLY?). We haven't half enjoyed having you around. Still, I suppose if Reg comes home I should be even more worried about the bath water than I am now. But you *must* come HOME first *please*, & then you must leave lots of bits & pieces behind so that you have to come back every single day to fetch something.

Back to work today – very boring and distasteful. It is getting like the ten little nigger boys – only two out of 12 left in the Department. I went to Gypsy Hill this p.m. to attend the opening of a Darby & Joan Club – for derelict old ladies & gentlemen who have nobody to look after them. It was oh so depressing & tear jerking. They'd all put on their best bits & bobs – little cameo brooches & white cotton gloves, & oh their feet! We are going to set up lots of these clubs all over London where these moribund old people can come for a game of whist & a cupper.[1]

Uncle Ronald dined & we discussed the Atomic Bomb, which was clever of us considering the extent of our knowledge.[2] I must say I am pretty horrified by it aren't you, & yet on the other hand it is a sock in the eye for Matter, rubbishy old thing!

Tony gets out of the army on Sep 7th!! Wish to God I was getting out of mine.

Much love from Winkie

[1] The WVS set up Darby and Joan Clubs all over Britain. 'Darby and Joan' was northern dialect for an elderly couple of humble background, often depicted in eighteenth-century china figures.
[2] The Americans had dropped the first atom bomb on Hiroshima the day before, and the next day a second bomb was dropped on Nagasaki, thus ending the war in the Far East.

Tuesday 7 August [1945]   Adelphi [Liverpool]

Darling Ginnie,

Items of interest: I've used up almost a whole Waterman's ink since July 8th when I came away! Liverpool took to us in a big way last night. Today's press say nice things. In the *Post* I 'dazzle'. In the *Echo*

I 'delight', and they go on to say how much they liked my singing and *dancing*! In the *Evening Express* I am 'one of the Show's big hits'.

Write to me please, s'il vous plaît.

Ton amie spéciale J.

Friday, August [1945]   Totters

Darling Joyce,

When a little hole appears in this letter, it will denote that I have run up against a Basil Seed! A lady called Miss Cora Harris of Charlote N.C. has sent us innumerable packets of this herb & I have spent the morning dividing them into twelve, which is the number of Civil Defence Regions. There is now no cranny or nook in my person or my desk which is not impregnancted with Basil seeds! The joke is that nobody has the faintest idea what one eats Basil with. The only thing we know for *certain*, is that it should be in a pot!

Am so bored with my work today, it does seem so futile, but I suppose somebody has to do it.

Up at two this morning to sit on my tin hat on the doorstep. Lucky I did because a warden came along, took down all the names of the others who were supposed to be firewatching and weren't, & went cheerfully away saying that last month a chap had got 14 days with no option of a fine for defaulting! Wouldn't it be ignominious to land up behind bars for such an offence?

Back to the seeds.

Thursday 9 August 1945   Adelphi

Darling Ginnie,

I'm all for the Atomic Bomb, but not to drop it much. I'm quite sure the only reason the Russians have declared war on Japan is because they want a share in it, but I hope we'll hug it closely in case . . . I don't trust the Russians, I don't.

Hope this finds you as it leaves me in my pink dressy gown. Lots of . . . to both, speshully you.

(When I was interviewed the woman said 'Thank you for being you'! Wasn't it splendid.)

12 August 1945   Cambridge Square

Darling Joyce,

I tried for 3/4 hour to get through to you this a.m. as I fanced hearing your golden voice, but I gave it up as a mauvais job.

Tony & I are reeling with fatigue having been a-dancing till 2 a.m. chez Howard de Walden.[1] Tremendous preparations for our dinner party before. The morning spent in buying flowers & a most expensive bunch of grapes. It did look so lovely. We all dressed up to the nines – me in m' old maize bought at Olga Fernande in 1938 – shoulder strap trouble skilfully pinned by T – Kitty in blue, Sheila in silver with a purple flower, Priscilla in borrowed organdie, chaps in dinner jackets & white waistcoats. We couldn't get over ourselves.

The dance was great fun & very Resurrection morning-ish. All those old faces quite unchanged save for a few medals on the bosom, recapturing a whiff of youth. Lots of boys & girls whose faces looked vaguely familiar, resembling their elder sisters or occasionally, their *mothers*. Oh the years! We weren't quite sure about the young. Rather dim, on the whole, we thought, but I'm not sure 18–20 isn't a bit dim anyway. And of course, they haven't had much chance to dress decently. Priscilla had *never* been to a dance like this before! She is simply sweet: very pretty & very gay & silly like us.

Princess Elizabeth[2] was there. She is tiny & wore an ugly-ish white dress; but one can see she has all her Ma's charm & has the same ravishing complexion. She danced with one Guardsman after another, each of whom appeared like clockwork to claim her the moment the dance started. I wonder how it is organised?

Well, it was quite a novelty number & we feel everso tired today.

I am longing to see you next Sunday, when you 'hit town'. By then we shall I trust, have finished with VJ celebrations. Already nights are a bit rowdy, & people are gaily overturning cars, & I really think after last night I have danced enough for one week.

XXXX
Ginnie

[1] Lord and Lady Howard de Walden lived in Berkeley Square.
[2] Aged nineteen.

Sunday, 12 August   Liverpool

Darling Ginnie,

Now I'm sitting in my bedroom slippers with the radio on, having written a huge letter to my Ma on Politics and why England isn't in the danger she thinks it is.

I've never been so alone for so long in all my life. I expect it is excellent for me but I can't say I like it. Yes, I could easily mix with the others, but the sole topic would be the Show and I think a Good Book is more to my taste. I dined with Madge and Cyril on Fri. night to celebrate the Jap news. We had claret: it was scrumptious!

Lots and lots of love to you'dl and To'dle.
from J.I. Grenville

Sigh No More opened in London on 22 August. Noël Coward wrote; 'Notices good for box-office but patronizing for me. Joyce and Graham [Payn] as predicted, made the outstanding hits and have really got away with it. Evening papers enthusiastic.' The show ran for six 'unsettled' months until the spring of 1946.

Joyce and Reggie stayed with Virginia while they searched for a flat. They eventually moved into a maisonette in King's Road, Chelsea, over a toy and sweet shop where they lived for ten years. Mrs Anna Gavrieldes ('Mrs Gabe') from Frankfurt became Joyce's much loved housekeeper from now until 1964.

1946

After *Sigh No More* closed, Joyce flew to America to visit her mother whom she had not seen for nine years. Richard Addinsell accompanied her, in the hope of making theatre contacts for future work.

24 April [1946]   Hotel Le Gink
                                                          Goose Bay
                                                          Labrador

Darling Ginnie,
    Please take in the above address for it has something. We were grounded there for 12 hours today and are now off on the last lap.
    Dick was recognised and interviewed by Dublin pressmen at Shannon. I was recognised by two fans and had to sign autographs also at Shannon; and by a U.S. pilot at Goose Bay! World famed you see! I heard 'Warsaw' and the Greig Piano Concerto swung by Freddie Martin on the radio – both were awful.
    If only flying wasn't so *difficult*! I far prefer boats and shall come back that way.

28 April 1946   In the train to Little Orchard
                                                          Tryon[1]

Darling Ginnie,
    Shades of 11 years ago. Do you remember coming in the train to Spartanburg and waking up and seeing the country, red with little shacks? It is just what I'm doing and it's very exciting. Everything is new green, banks of honeysuckle, dogwood in flower and red roses on front porches.

I'm slightly dazed after N.Y. and the trip and all. I shop gazed and bought myself a roll-on and two brassieres and some gloves. Whew. It is so intoxicating to see the shelves laden with things. The hats here are divine. The little silly is gone but in its place wonderful madnesses with over life size cabbage roses and frothings and entire flower beds. The stocking question is very tricky. There are none.

This next bit is private so don't read it aloud!

Yesterday Elliott came up from Baltimore to lunch with me.[2] I dreaded it rather because of so many things but I needn't have. He had grown out of all recognition in strength and character and was terribly nice and easy, and while I flatter myself he is still fond of me, as I am of him, it is the very nicest warmest undifficult affection, and that is really something to be grateful for. When a situation has been very emotional and tense and indeed unhappy – for I did love him terribly I'm afraid – it is lovely when it ends quietly in real friendship. I don't think I'm being over confident of this! We lunched and went to see Laurette Taylor in *The Glass Menagerie*, which is an enchanting little play – very delicate with a new technique. I loved it. He then rode down as far as Baltimore with me last night and we dined on the train. He is now Head Prof. of a new dep. of creative working at the JohnsHopkins Univ. Jolly good job I gather.[3]

[1] Joyce's mother's home in North Carolina, built for her by her sister Nancy Astor.
[2] Elliott Coleman (1905–71), poet who introduced Joyce to poetry. Joyce met him in a pub in North Carolina in 1935. 'The next day,' she wrote in his obituary, 'every leaf, blade of grass and face seemed edged in light; every sound rang with meaning. Everything I saw, heard and felt became a poem.'
[3] This may have been the inspiration for 'The Past is Present I', a sketch about a grandmother from Virginia meeting a boyfriend from forty years before on Waterloo station.

29 April [1946]   [Tryon]

Darling Ginnie,

Well here ah is! Lefty and Tommy were at Spartanberg to meet me. Mummy couldn't stand the strain and was at Little Orchard plumping up the cushions. L. is unchanged and in top form – he looks wonderful. T. is thinner and looks bonny too. He is writing like mad, just sold a short story to Colliers for 750 dollars, has two more on the way to the agent who is very confident in him.[1]

This house is fascinating. It has taste and light and Mummy's special touch. Full of flowers – white mountain laurel frothing in huge bowls everywhere – log fires in all the rooms, a low table heavy with magazines, the piano waiting to be played on, books inviting from the shelves, the view inviting through the windows, and *such* peace and happiness. It really is a spot. I was greeted in tears, so we all had a let down and blubbed a little!

Mum is pleasantly surprised to find I'm not tubercular or starving, for Aunt N. had led her to believe I was in poor shape and very Belsen. What a woman for sowing seeds of peace in the heart.

Write soon and give R. a hug now and then. Have I ever said a proper thank you for my party on the 16th? I do so now. It was jolly good. Love to To. I smell divine of Blue Grass. Eliz. Arden from Elly. Love, of course, from All here.

---

[1] Tommy went on to write plays for television and Broadway.

Tuesday, 11 May [1946]   Tryon

Darling Ginnie,

I've, at last, begun to un-spin and I'm ironing out jolly well and starting to feel quite as I used to, instead of always being tautly aware of time and obligations. The house is a dream of comfort and the food . . . the flowers . . . the views.

Dick is now here and is under the magic of this place too. We go for little saunters in the pine woods and stop and laugh – for it's so hard to take in. That we are here, in N.C., in the U.S.A., and the war is over and we've had orange juice for breakfast and we shall have tomato juice and maybe steak and certainly strawberries for lunch and cream from Lefty's jersey cow Daisy.

On Sunday night the neighbours came in to hear Dick and me. About 40 of them. We were nervous as witches. But it went with a graceful swing from start to finish and we had 'em in tears of emotion and amusement at the proper times. Very peculiar. We imagine that they all imagine the most romantic situations for us together. There am I singing my heart out about love and there is D. playing his heart out on the piano, so the illusion is understandable. One neighbour telephoned Mummy and asked if we knew each other very well?

Write, you beast. Lots of love.

13 May [1946]   London

Darling Joyce,

Victor & I have decided that the Addinsell–Grenfell letters are in rotten bad taste! You both seem to have given yourselves up unreservedly to the cult of the body & we think you might at least have the grace to apologise. Anything more like a pagan heaven it would be hard to visualise. What anybody thinks or feels in America you do not mention, any trend in public affairs you disregard. Bless you, my darling, & eat all you can & drink in the sun & the flowers & the warmth & the love & come back all bonny, fat & glowing.

We took the grass widowers [Reggie & Victor] to see *Sweeter & Lower*. Gingold[1] is better than ever. Reggie looked well & primed with a little whiskey boomed happily about cricket & high finance. I always find this very pleasant – I am not really interested in either subject, but it stands for constancy & immutability & timelessness & makes me feel peculiarly *safe*. I think he is missing you a lot, but who isn't?

We have a new kitchen maid! Called Gladys, from the Waifs & Strays, very demure & pink & with the toothache. The household seems strangely happy & calm & most people seem to be speaking to each other, which is singular.[2]

Toad is wearing the pink tie you brought from Cairo. It is ever so bright. X Gin

[1] Starred Hermione Gingold (1897–1987), English actress.
[2] Virginia and Tony had three full-time domestic staff.

Sunday, 19 May 1946   Glencove
LI
NY

Darling Ginnie,

No flashy news. Life in N.Y. was hectic and enjoyable. D. and I saw *Oklahoma, St Louis Woman*, and I saw Ray Bolger in *Three for the Money*. The two first are *superb*. Even more miraculous than I'd hoped. *St Louis Woman* is all negro and a joy from a to z. The revue *Three for the Money* was a let down except for Bolger who dances jolly well even if he isn't Astaire. Charm and a certain wit. It was also rather comforting because while *Oklahoma* and *St Louis Woman* made us gasp with awe they depressed us a little for our own inadequacy, whereas the revue was below even our London standard. Not even as good as *Sigh No More!* So I felt rather cheered and longed to tackle N.Y. myself. And so I will some day . . .

We've seen various publishers and I've sung to Dreyfus of Chappell-Harms, who was enthusiastic and sweet. Parchment faced old gent of 70 with gentleness and humour.

D. has had some purely prestige meals with big music blokes. It is all the building up technique for the future. Where I come in is fairly obscure but it seems I do! You see I'm not here to sell ME this time but to sell the songs.

I have lost my pore old head and bought three hats! One is o.k. and passes even Addinsell's censorious eyes. But the others . . . Well one is a soup plate entirely made of black net, and the third is a sort of coal heaver number also noire.

R. writes reams, which makes me think he is lonely and un-busy. O damn the heartstrings. They twang in so many directions always.

I lunched with Elliott while in Baltimore and found myself performing monologues in his office at 3 p.m. to four fellow professors!

Lots of love to you darling and to old To. Write soon.

21 May 1946   Cambridge Square

Darling Joyce,

Life is considerably more than somewhat at the moment as yours truly is almost entirely living with Peter Pan & 4,000 Dominion's & Colonial troops in Kensington Gardens! I send out dozens of cars & dozens of guides daily, & really the 'human element' is so provoking I could scream. Either there are too many guides & not enough Fijis or else there are hundreds of Malayans left over. I am surrounded & surmounted by bits of paper which I flutter round the Albert Memorial, & I have to think a great deal about Harmony to survive! Everybody is roped in, including To & we ran a fearful shuttle service on Sunday to the Zoo which all but killed us. In the morning we took 65 Malayans round London in the dripping rain, & was constantly meeting To in peculiar places like Lombard St, his Macintoshed arm pointing out of his window at buildings of no historic importance whatsoever! Incidentally the lads knew far more about London than we did!

Celia [Johnson] stayed last night. The babe is a week overdue & poor C is terribly bored. We were very apprehensive, not being too skilled in obstetrics. All I know is that one must boil gallons of water & have a pair of scissors handy. C says she notices that people say Hullo & Goodbye simultaneously these days, casting nervous glances & twitching a bit.

Celia's baby, Kate, was born a week later and Virginia was made her godmother.
  Joyce received a telegram from Reggie which read 'CLEM SAYS GEORGE WISHES GIVE YOU THREE-QUARTERS LENGTH ROBE REGGIE.' Using her *Times* crossword puzzle skills she deciphered it as Prime Minister Attlee (Clem) had asked the King (George) to give her an OBE (three-quarters of a robe) for her war work.

25 May 1946   Cambridge Square

Joyce DARLING!!

This is *the* most gorgeous news! Reg told me last night, & To & I could have kicked ourselves for not guessing, as the letter came here, & we looked at it in amazement & said what *can* the P.M. be writing to Joyce about? Oh darling, I am glad – no-one deserves it more than you, & we are all going to bask in your reflected glory for years & years. I bet your Ma's pleased, bless her!

Celia has had a daughter, called Kate. Peter is doing a film on Scott & we feel he will probably debunk him so much that the whole expedition will seem like a stroll on the nursery slopes!

Oh! a woman pushing a baby in a pram & leading a *horse* has just passed by! Do you think she just met the horse, or did someone say: 'Here, you're passing the Mews, so just hand this in?'

A million congratulations. I am terribly proud of you & beaming from stern to stem, tho' mum at the moment of course.

XXX Gin

31 May 1946   Tryon

Darling Ginnie,

Goodness me this is a heavenly place: it's a great tribute to my Mum. She has progressed no end. True she is still covered in lipstick and she is still extravagant. But she has achieved a real core of understanding in C.S. and her radical reliance on it has been well rewarded. It's a perfect place to do nothing in for there is so much nothing to do.

I'm working on a second short story. I sent one off to the *New Yorker* on Weds. My hopes are very slim but I thought it would be fun to try. I ought to be working on radio scripts but I cannot conjure up a British radio public and I can't remember anything about Shirley and her girl friend,[1] so I've quite given up and am expressing myself in a new form!

Last night we sat on the terrace after supper and sang – just Lefty and Mum, and me. We watched the sky turn black behind the mountains and we sang both with the guitar and without. The stars prickled through one at a time and the air was delicious with gardenia and white jasmine. Golly.

The thing about hammocks is how uncomfy they are, and the least movement turns one over.

O, having been rather glib about Eliz. Arden's leg stuff not coming off, I now see it's all over my dress. Damn.

---

[1] 'Shirley's girl friend began as a series of radio sketches and then appeared on the stage in 1957. Silent Shirl and her talkative girlfriend from south London went to the fun fair, then on picnics and by 1964 they had been to a music festival, rather like the one at Aldeburgh where Joyce brought them to life.

31 May 1946   Cambridge Square

Darling Joyce,

I wish to G. I was with you, as life is 'un peu fort' here what with
Cypriots & Aden laddies & fat black gentlemen from Bazutoland & rain
– gallons of it all the time. I get soaked every day shovelling these men
into cars by the Albert Memorial & they do look so desolate & damp
poor dears.

We went to *The Kingmaker*[1] last night & really it is excellent, the
whole thing carried out with much verve & go-ness. The intervals were
spent by everyone trying to disentangle their history: remarks like 'I
think you will find it *was* Henry VIth' or 'Why did they all marry people
called Neville?' or 'No darling, the Black Prince was ages before' rang
round the theatre.

Totters is absolute bottoms. However, only a few more weeks &
I shall but be visiting it twice a week praise the Lord & pass the salt
please. I was very forcibly struck by the terrible tiredness of the other
girls' faces – that awful sort of wan dogged appearance they have
which is so touching. In Holland, where for years & years they have
been sitting doing nothing – it being unpatriotic to move a finger,
& refreshed by the fact that each day's food still seems miraculous,
they are bright & busy as bees – plotting & planning & digging &
delving & painting & building & sowing & reaping. We who are faced
with a prospect of black bread & even more fish don't seem to be
quite so bonny, & on returning to this dear island I was considerably
saddened.

London is a mass of latrines & mess, but sort of gay.

Peter [Fleming] was telling a guards officer how interesting it had
been to see the plans of what Hitler was going to do when he conquered
England – men deported, women in farms, children down the mines, a
ghastly picture. The man sat brooding for a while, & then said 'Yes, we
were well out of that.'

---

[1] Starring husband and wife actors Kay Hammond (1909–80) and John Clements
(1910–88).

10 June 1946   London

Darling [Joyce],

Just to show you that I can write on wobbly things too, I am writing
this on m' old knee, which is particularly wobbly today, as is the whole
of my frail body – Victory having played the devil with it. Before I
embark on a full & lurid description of the perils & adventures we have

endured, the sights we have seen & the miles we have walked, let me first thank you warmly for the belt for the body bulgy, which arrived about the same time as your hammock letter. The pull-on is Heaven. I feel a new woman – my present misfit is held together with adhesive tape & loving but obscene stitches. I can never decribe to you the joy I felt in hurling it in the w.p.b.

Now let me go back to the past week, which has all but killed me. On the Thursday we had the Millers & the Actons to dine, all of us dressed to the nines & feeling frightfully naked. We went off to the dance at the Dorchester, the Ts groaning & moaning like fog horns. There were two bands, Ambrose & a terribly noisy rumba band, & proper sit down supper – all very pre-war. There was nobody under 30 there, & it was just like sleepwalking – all the old friends but all slightly changed, with the addition of a few medals on the bosom. Cosmo a little less good looking, Rosemary a bit thinner, Bill rather greyer, Margaret a bit blonder – one could go on for hours. Being of an age however, we all looked well dressed & sort of sparkling, & radiated a certain 'chien'[1] which is lacking in deb dances. For Maggie Dufferin it was a case of touch & go whether her dress actually fell off or not – every time I looked it had slipped an inch further down her bust & I have no doubt by the party end she was naked to the waist.

Joan Assheton Smith looked like a Canterbury sheep, in a black cartwheel hat & black lace mittens. She talked in that way I had quite forgotten about. 'My dear, you *must* come & see the flat – it's *the* most awful mess.' One longs to say that's awfully kind of you but it doesn't sound particularly inviting.

I found I was greeted effusively & warmly by all sorts of people who used to cut me dead – like Christopher Sykes[2] – can't make out why can you?

At 7.45 a.m. on Saturday we set forth for Nurse Cavell[3] where we had the offer of a window in the Colonial Club. The crowds were huge, Joyce, but really *huge*. Most of the people had slept in the streets all night, & been rained upon, but there they were, paper caps & all, fainting like flies, cheering every horse or dog or policeman, as merry as grigs. We stood on a balcony from 8.30 to 12.30 & saw the whole caboodle, & very impressive it was too, only strangely enough not terribly moving. I really don't know why. Of course Kingy & Queenie in that superb state landau drawn by the Windsor greys & escorted by those feverish clanking foam flecked Life Guards brought tears to the eyes, & the great roar that went up nearly knocked one down.

Victor & I have decided that we are not fit to describe processions as we get so emotioné we go dizzy & can't really see – but somehow the rest was glorious without being heartbreaking. Khaki is, of course, a very drab colour, & I noticed as the hours went by that we cheered more vociferously whenever a splash of colour appeared – the Indian band in café au lait uniforms & blue turbans, the Transfordians in pink chiffon hats, the U.S. Navy in their white gaiters, our own pipers. We were in a bad place in as much as the powers that be had evidently said to all the bandmasters: 'When you see Nurse Cavell, *stop* playing!' Of course when I saw that green wodge of WVS coming round the corner I nearly burst, & for the first time I remembered there had been a war on & I felt suddenly desperately sad. There were 144 WVS & really they marched remarkably well considering their varying ages & shapes. One old girl was 70!

We reeled back home about 1.30, & looked at the flypast through the scaffolding – squadron after squadron submerged in the clouds & not, I think, flying anywhere *near* the Mall. After luncheon Tony & I went to bed.

Up again, & off to Victor for din. Victor had had various adventures in the Park & had carried a heavy iron chair about with him, running back & forth with it with varying degrees of success, & he was ever so tired. Undaunted however, we went forth again – it had stopped raining, but oh my, I forgot to tell you it deluged the whole afternoon & thousands retired into the Tube with their sodden sandwiches poor devils – & we repaired to Westminster. A good few million people had the same idea! However, having stood entranced by a floodlit Abbey we then literally *fought* our way onto Lambeth Bridge. Having got half way across, it was apparent that we weren't so mad about the crowds, so we fought our way off it again & stood in Millbank, where we saw the fireworks to perfection. They were *oh* so pretty.

All sorts of things were taking place on the River too. What a perfection of symmetry the illuminations were. And the river looked so mysterious & frightening under a grey sky. There were fire floats spraying about in multi-coloured plumes of water & it was all very gay.

We then podged to Buck House [Palace], which was lit an unbecoming cerise colour, which was quite a pity, with a large V sign in search lights behind. I wish you could have seen St James Park lake tho'. There were most inappropriate gondolas bobbing about in the dripping rain, fountains & a *waterfall*.

Everyone shouted for the King with the approved style. We wished you had been with us darling – we really missed you. We knew if you'd been with us you would have been dancing eightsome reels till dawn. As it was we picked our way across the park over dozens of prostrate bodies lying in *deep* mud in loverlike embraces & got home about 1.30. And Oh m' poor feet!

I heard one woman say 'I don't care if they floodlight Mr Churchill 'iself, Dad, I can't go a *step* further!'

[1] A Virginia word – both *chic* and *bien*. Joyce and Virginia used the word *bien* to mean 'well bred'.
[2] Novelist and journalist (1907–86).
[3] St Martin's Lane, overlooking Trafalgar Square.

21 June 1946   Train back to Tryon

Darling Ginnie,

The net result of my U.S. visit is satisfactory. (a) The four songs are being published: (b) it is quite probable that Dwight Norman will use one or more in his new revue next year, and (c) Guthrie McClintic wants to do a very special revue and would like me for it season after next. So it is all highly nice to dwell on. I don't suppose any of it will come off; you know my pessimistic streak. Anyhow it's nice to be wanted. And by Guthrie especially, for he is a rather high-brow theatre director, husband of Kit Cornell[1] and way up in the heavenly regions of theatrical N.Y.

My social life was very chic. Supper with Lynn and Alfred Lunt one night cooked by Alfred and eaten at 12.30 by Larry Olivier and Vivien,[2] Jack Wilson,[3] and D. and me. One of those over life sized Mae West shaped bottles of champagne chilled to a nicety and I had a snifter. Jolly good too. So was the froth of fish and mushroom and cream that Alfred whipped up for us. No ordinary Fish Pie that!

Conversation was theatrical and absorbing to me and poor Larry looked as if he'd die if the Old Vic season didn't stop soon for he'd done 9 perfs. a week of the rep. and a full length radio play each Sunday and he was silenced by it. I sat between him and Alfred and didn't bother but was femininely appreciative. Or so I fondly hope! I'm more than slightly amoureux de lui – de les deux as a matter of fact. A.L. has the nicest manners and I think a divine sense of humour, and he flatters me by appearing to listen. Larry is always kind to me, so you see I had a happy soirée, and was very touched somehow by the sight of Lynn's white nightie (un-pressed) and scruffy little red bed-slippers on one side of the bed and Alfred's white pyjamas and similarly worn bed-slippers on the other side of the bed.

D. and I went to a very grand party at '21' for Jennifer Jones. At one moment I found myself sitting at a table against a wall between Kit Cornell and Helen Hayes (oh this b— pen, I HATE IT). This is better. The Lunts were at the party and Marg. Sullivan, Dame May Whitty, Ralph Bellamy, Ruth Hussey, Tilly Losch and Jennifer Jones with tousled hair and a natural charm. Kit Cornell is wonderful looking. Serene and beautiful and quite out of the world. I liked her too. Helen Hayes is a little teensy somehow but friendly and nice and intelligent too. For looks tho' Marg. Sullivan won the laurels. Her natural fair hair is thick and shiny and she wears it with a thick fringe. She wore a slightly arty black topped number with plaid greeny blue taffeta skirt, bare legs and sandals, and she was a good smooth gold all over as far as one could see.

Will you please let me know *at once* if you want me to bring you another roll-on belt. If so, do you want two way stretch: no zip? or zip? satin panel? Do you like panty girdles for wearing without stockings? I've sent you the album of *Carousel* from Mummy and *Annie Get Your Gun* from me. I'll write soon again, and sorry for long pause this time. I'm looking forward to getting HOME soon.

Lots and lots of love.

Your plump chump. J

[1] Katherine Cornell (1898–1974), actress.
[2] Vivien Leigh (1913–67), British actress.
[3] American theatre manager (1899–1961), had been Noël Coward's business manager.
[4] Jennifer Jones, American film star (1919–); Helen Hayes, American stage actress (1900–); Margaret Sullivan, American actress (1911–60); May Whitty, British actress (1865–1948); Ralph Bellamy, British actor (1904–91); Ruth Hussey, British actress (1914–); and Tilly Losch, American actress (1901–75).

24 June [1946]   Cambridge Square

Darling Joyce,

Yes *please* darling, I'd love another pull-on. Exactly the same. I'm not mad on satin insets as they always seem to mean bones & as I always take the bones out, this means the satin heaves over and lies in folds on my Michelin.

This afternoon we played hooky and went to Wimbledon, which was kinda fun, & felt, smelt and sounded very pre-war.

I sent in my resignation from WVS today, for October. I am not very afraid they will be difficult about it, as they know I want to write. I pointed out that for the past 7 years I have only produced some piddling poems & that, although it was probably very doubtful that I could produce anything else, I would like to have the chance to try.

When I clear my things out of the drawers I may get a soupçon of a pang. But oh how lovely to be free! What *shall* I do? I can't imagine. Nothing perhaps. But *think*, I can meet you for a cupper coff in the morning, & go to the movies in the afternoon!

Lunched with Noel Streatfeild[1] today who was very funny. A week or two ago she sacked a rather indifferent 'little woman' who mended for her, & when the woman left she said to Rose, Noel's maid 'I'm afraid Miss Streatfeild will regret dismissing me, as I am a witch.' Rose, in repeating the conversation said 'I don't believe in witches, Miss, but somehow I wish she hadn't said it.' 'Oh, well,' said Noel airily. Nevertheless, the whole chandelier fell from the ceiling on the Monday, the telephone wires became so entangled that the men who worked on them for three days said 'Almost looks as tho' someone 'ad been tampering with these,' vases full of flowers fell from the table and are found on the other side of the room, Noel's coffee pot keeled over & emptied itself into her bed – the accidents, tho' minor, never end. Noel says she has found a clergyman who will come with a bell, book & candle if things get worse.

The *Spectator* has asked me to continue reviewing until the end of the year, so I shall be closeted in a theatre of some sort nearly every day. I shall have to do some Holy Work about my eyes, as I find pretending to be able to see is a great strain on them.

The maids don't get back until Monday, so will you come and do a lot of eating with us at the Aperitif please? Oh gummy good drop, am I looking forward to seeing yew!

[1] Children's novelist (1910–86). Author of *Ballet Shoes*.

4 September 1946

Tornashean[1]
Aberdeenshire

Darling Joyce,

Before anything else, would you like a brace of grouse? I don't know if your Mrs could pluck & disembowel them, & I don't believe poulterers will do this for one now.

We had the usual sleepless journey up in very comfy first class sleepers, met by Admiral Sir Bertram & Lady Thesiger with a very old Rolls. It's all family save for a nice old spinster called Alice. The Admiral is a rather dear furry little man who irritates Tony. The wife Violet is one of those extremely nice women, faded to a paper white, in both mind & body, by much living in the East. She wears good pale blue tweeds & is gentle & Kind & simple. Everyone is simple here. They love the good, they hate the bad, they mistrust foreigners, they rejoice in the scenery, they cannot abide Osbert Sitwell,[2] & they are mad about fresh air. Everything is as expected. It is frightful.

I believe someone once told me it was in very poor taste to be rude about people under whose roof one was nestling. Perhaps if I started by being nice it wouldn't seem so ungracious? On the credit side we have hot brown bath water, comfy beds, strawberries, cream, new peas, dropscones & grouse. On the debit side we have freezing rooms, rain, the most banal conversation known to man, breakfast at 8.30 a.m. & constant family tension. My mother-in-law is, as you know, the kindest woman in the world, & her kindness spreads right down the Valley of the Don, causing endless friction & irritation, turning man against man, disrupting happy homes, & sowing seeds of doubt & mistrust.

Yesterday Tony shot well, which was nice for him but not so nice for the grouse. We had a perfect pre-war lunch, all the guns sitting in a long row against a wall – the gallant Colonel from Braemar, three bouncy girls, & a police superintendent from Malaya. Grouse pie & potatoes, apple turnovers & cheese. Six Labradors: 'Get *back* Sir, at once!' Cider & sloe gin, photographs, the beaters round the corner, the good solid tweeds, the shooting brake full of macintoshes . . . you can see it all I know.

---

[1] Thesiger family home in Scotland, used during the grouse shooting season.
[2] Author, poet and biographer (1892–1969).

8 September [1946]   Tornashean

Darling Joyce,

We went to the Fancy Dress dance in the village hall which was swathed in plaids intertwined with antlers & was extremely cold. It was all very feudal. The gentry sat on a platform *next* to the Band, which was indescribably bad & noisy, and the hoipolloi leaped about at our feet. Tony & I had great difficulty in judging the dresses, mostly because we couldn't make out what anyone was supposed to be! Although the entrants were masked, & we really didn't recognise any of them, we inadvertently contrived to give prizes to Tornashean's cook, chauffeur, second housemaid & head keeper's wife! I fear this may have caused 'feeling': but we have received no threatening notes as yet. Some of the dresses were home-made & others hired from Aberdeen, & there were three classes – historical, fancy & comic. You will see how undecided both the entrants & ourselves were when I tell you that 'Sweet Lavender' won the *historical*, & 'Cleopatra' the *fancy*. The comic was easy. A man dressed as Traffic Signals with lights that went on & off!! After watching them dance an eightsome – & I must say it is an invigorating sight – we were driven home by Davis the chauffeur who removed an enormous bushy beard & a turban to do so. He still retained, however, a pair of cerise balloon trousers, & these under a blue macintosh & was wearing a chauffeur's hat which gave him an exquisite appearance.

It was fine yesterday but nobody could kill anything because an ex-game keeper had died & all the other keepers had to go to the funeral. All the chaps were very disappointed & cross, & they are equally cross today as now it is Sunday & even finer.

It is wonderfully boring here.

8 September 1946   149 [King's Road, Chelsea]

Darling Ginnie,

Oh yes, *please, grice*. They can be plucked at the butcher who is R's friend, and I'm getting to be such a dashing cook that I am anxious to tackle them. So if they can be spared, darling, how jolly nice.

Victor supped last night and I cooked a chicken! R. got it in the Kings Road perfectly legally and over the counter, so things are improving. And R., in carving second helps, flung the whole pan, carcass and grease all over the kitchen and me! I counted ten and rose slowly to cope, a Christian smile on my lips. Victor and R. both roared with joy.

Oda Sloboskaya is singing a revolting song by Glazounov called 'Chatterbox' that has to be translated first and is coy and Russian and unfunny but meant to be a delicious giggle.

Yesterday Pa, R., Ann and I went to see *Cleo and Caesar*[1] and we enjoyed it. Miss [Vivien] Leigh is so feline and alarmingly attractive. Isn't it queer the way there is no sex in it? I mean there she is lovely and alluring, and there he [Laurence Olivier] is, susceptible one thought after that first starlight meeting on the paws of the Sphinx, but no one cares and it's all a little dead. You can't believe any of it, can you? Even when she rolls her eyes and talks of Marc Antony it is all theatrical – a *conception* of a woman infatuated – not a woman infatuated. Shaw is so cool and distant. I don't believe he ever even enjoyed the hurly burly of the chaise longues with either Mrs Pat [Campbell] or Mrs G.B.S. He's a paper lover. Lovely words. But was he in fact a lover? He seems to me to know so little about it. Get me? The Great Loveress!!

Sundays are wearying I find, rather, and there's time to sit and mope and think even more than usual of self, and what folly that is. As Victor says: I'm a work person and should be working all the time. Goodness knows I'm not idle, but it's all rather bitty. The nicest is to be working *for* something. That's why I loved my war job – it used up every inch of me there was and I felt all stretched and springy. Sounds like an old tennis raquet.

Oh Ginnie, how horrid I am – so much to be grateful for and I moan and groan like an old ship in a gale. I *am* grateful, actually. It's just a sadness that's whisperin' in me heart for absolutely no reason except tempus fugiting and wet weather.

Love to silly old To and silly old Gin both of whom I dote on –
Silly old J

---

[1] By George Bernard Shaw, written in 1900.

1947

Early in 1947 Joyce began work on a revue called *Tuppence Coloured* written by herself and her cousin Nicholas Phipps, supported by Max Adrian (1903–73) and Elisabeth Welch (1904–). The dress rehearsal in Cheltenham in August was a disaster. Virginia, Tony, Reggie, Richard, Victor and Winifred were there and pronounced the next morning that the show must be entirely redone before it moved to London.

7 August [1947]   Cambridge Square

Darling J[oyce],

This must be the most odious bank holiday weekend you have ever spent, & the influx of your loving pals must have made it truly memorable!

I can *never* tell you how bloody I thought it was this morning when Winifred brought those heavy verbal guns to bear on your prostrate exhausted person – you looked so terribly touching lying there with that old piece of toast & that freezing tea – about 10 years old & as forlorn as a waif & stray.

Darling one, you mustn't mind too much all these emotional positions, these hideous post mortems, this tidal wave of adverse criticism. As you know they are all involved by a love of you, & by a lively distaste for you to be involved in anything short of perfection. That the whole gang should have descended on you in one fell swoop, was a dommage [shame], because they (we?) infect each other & whip one another into a frenzy of words & feelings. The stage atmosphere is so fraught with emotionalism & so totally out of proportion with the rest of the world, & yet so terribly infectious that even Tony & I felt we had been away for *years* visiting a strange island, cut off from all knowledge of real life.

I wish so much you had had only one visitor, say Winifred, who would have forcefully but calmly pointed out the necessity of a new producer & so forth, instead of five temperamental whales thrashing about with their tails & all but submerging you. No, we behaved like wolves. God knows we made our point, but with supercharged blunderbusses.

There is a *lot* of good stuff & it is only a question of sifting the wheat from the chaff. *You* have never been better, which I know is no consolation to you, but is a great joy to us.

Winifred talked the whole way home – about Hamlet, hats, endives, Hadrian's Wall, rosehip jam & corsets. Tony & Reg preserved a happy sullen silence, occasionally saying: 'Have a cigarette?' 'No thanks' or 'Guinness have got a big factory haven't they?' 'Ar.' I could have knocked their silly heads together I was so envious.

I will ring you tomorrow morning to see if we actually killed you or not.

XX Gin

Tuppence Coloured was rewritten by the company and after a short tour it opened in London. Even at that dress rehearsal Reggie and Virginia had their doubts. But somehow the revue came together in time for the first night in London.

9 September 1947   Lyric Theatre
                                                             Hammersmith

Darling Ginnie,

I'm in my 2 by 4 hutch of a dressing room waiting to go on.

Well it is certainly a hit. We are sold out tonight again and the advance is terrific. We are definitely moving to the Globe in Oct. So you see it's just one of those dream things. Even the *Daily Worker* says it's good.

Do you remember how bad you thought Bertie's *Little Revue* was when you and To came to the dress rehearsal; and what a hit that turned out to be? I begin to think it's a jolly good sign to get you to dress rehearsals and have you hate it!

I love my toy theatre and it adds much to this little hutch. Ta ever so.[1]

---

[1] Printed paper cut-out theatres were sold in the nineteenth century and cost one penny plain, or tuppence (two pennies) coloured.

1948

Tuppence Coloured ran for a year in London, followed by a tour of Scotland.

1 July 1948   Edinburgh

Darling Ginnie,

I'm jolly keen on Edinb'. And Edinb' is *jolly* keen on us! The Lyceum
is packed to overflowing every night and they are the most wonderful
quick enthusiastic and warm audience I ever did play to. It is *most*
pleasant. And what a glorious city it is. I like the way you look down,
or rather up, any side street off Princes Street and there is always a big
black statue riding the sky at the top of the incline.

I'm mad about the accent and *cannot* get it. Miss Williamson brought
me some mail and one letter had O.B.E. on it. 'Och' she said 'I dinna
know you had the ooh-be-ay.' It sounded like a lot of cooing doves as
she said it.

9 July 1948   Glasgow

Darling Ginnie,

Bonnie Scot. has been a lot nicer than I ever thought it could be.
They are a very listeny public. Never miss a point. I suppose it's true
that all Scots are educated.

My dinner at Holyroodhouse will have to wait till I see you, but in
brief: I got a telephone message on the Sat. matinee to ring up Peter
Townsend[1] at the Palace,[2] so I wondered what was up, daring to dream
it might be to say come to tea with Princess Margaret. Anyway it
was an invite to dine with the K. and Q. on Sunday night! Within half
an hour of the telephone conversation my formal pasteboard arrived
and excitement was intense, for of course I told *everyone*, and I must
say they were wonderful about it, sharing the emotion and interest.
No evening dress or bag with me and only a mac. for a cloak! So I
borrowed my red finale dress Victor built for me, and my dresser ran me
up a little silver lamé Dorothy bag! as a surprise, between the mat. and
the evening, and I borrowed the lady pianist's red fox fur cape!

It was a smashing outing. Very small party. K.Q. and Princess M.;
Mima Harlech, Jean Rankin, Ed. Ford, Peter Townsend, Tom Harvey,
John Elphinstone and sister Jean, and five outside guesties, Lord and
Lady Harrington, and me.[3] I sat on the K's left. It was *very* cosy and
easy. Lots of jokes and Princess M. did her stuff, briefly, in a contralto
voice. We saw all the lovely historic parts of the Palace in the twilight,

and then I was asked to do a monologue so did three and they really laughed till the tears ran down their royal cheeks. They were *so* nice to me. I was quite dead when it was over, with a sort of stiff neck from nervous excitement! It was *gorgeous*. The cosy vicarious pleasure enjoyed by the housekeeper, hall porter, lift boy and manageress at the Old Waverley was very touching and sweet. That one invitation did give a lot of pleasure and most of it to *me*.

[1] Group Captain Peter Townsend RAF (1914–95). Fighter pilot in World War II and equerry to King George VI 1944–52.
[2] Holyroodhouse, Edinburgh.
[3] King George VI; Queen Elizabeth; Princess Margaret; Lady Mima Harlech and Lady Jean Rankin, the Queen's ladies-in-waiting; Sir Edward Ford, the King's assistant secretary, married to Joyce's first cousin Virginia Brand; Lord Elphinstone and his sister the Hon. Mrs Wills, the Queen's niece and nephew and the Earl and Countess of Harrington.

27 July [1948]   Cambridge Square

Joyce Darling,

I wish you'd stop jumping about like this, I haven't set eyes on you for well over a month & I don't like it one little bit.

Lefty & Nora lunched today. It seems nigh incredible but your Ma was picked up by a taxi driver who was an old friend – he really was. She knew all about his sons & daughters & everyone cried. The taxi driver was so enchanted at meeting Nora again after all these years (at least 15) that he came back after luncheon to pick her up. She is in smashing form, did a dance for us & looked as young as twenty four. Lefty & To went to the Olympics.

Your tweed has arrived. There is 9 yards, so you ought to be able to be very New Look.

25 August 1948   149 King's Road
                                                           Chelsea

Darling Ginnie,

We had a good evening at the ballet and, while some of the dancing and all the orchestral playing was jolly bad, there was some really thrilling stuff done. Mr Egjlevsky twiddles his feet more often in the air than any other living dancer, so it was of interest. And how I do love that house! The dark red stripes and the slow fade of the house lights. Real theatre glamour as one first knew it.

Victor had a heart attack on Sun. but looked more or less all right when I lunched with him on Mon.

Yesterday was summer. Lots of little local chores such as looking at my very old coonskin fur coat at Peter Jones and deciding to have it turned into a boxy jacket at a fairly reasonable price. 'Cheaper than a new one' is my cry.

27 August [1948]   Tornashean

Darling Joyce,

It is exactly like it always has been here. We went straight from the night train to luncheon in a wooden hut through which the wind blasted. I was so sleepy I could barely see. However I saw enough to depress me, & I snatched at the cherry brandy with unholy abandon & a lovely wildness. Now it is raining like hell, & the shooters are sitting about reading & yawning, raising wistful eyes to the dark & drooping hills.

I have moved to the bedroom because Ma-in-law constantly interrupts even the most boring thoughts.

How these maids survive up here I don't know, as we sit down 12 to every meal.

2 September 1948   King's Road

Darling Ginnie,

Tornashean sounds pretty grimski-korsakov and staying with elderlies is hardly ever very relaxing.

On Monday Johnnie Bevan[1] took us to see the very top secret Cabinet Offices underground where he worked all through the war. Churchill's little bed-sit with candle and torch and hot water can just as it was. The map room still stuck with little flags and pins showing what went on everywhere every minute by sea land and air.

[1] (1904–84). Worked in War Office intelligence. His wife Barbara was Waldorf Astor's niece.

Virginia was appointed film critic for the *Evening Standard*.

23 November 1948   Cambridge Square

Darling Joyce,

M'films upset me – they are always taking me to Texas or Wyoming, they make Mayfair seem rather tiring. After the film this morning all about cattle raising & red Indians & nearly everyone got shot, I had the novel experience of lunching mid-week with my spouse. Then *another* film called *Another* Shore. I simply can't see how film critics dare to criticise anything! How can one come to a film with a fresh eye &

an unbiased mind when one has spent the whole morning looking at another film? Tomorrow I have *two* more to see, & unless the fourth is very out of the ordinary I don't see how I can fail to find it tedious.

We have a schizophrenic staying the night. He is a wretched young man who was captured by the Japs & worked on that railway in Burma. After the war T's firm took him back but he was so poopsy they sacked him. The plan is to pay his passage out to India to join his parents. But he doesn't want to go, so Tony has to physically put him on the BOAC plane tomorrow morning. He appears to me to be as mad as they make them – non-sequitur after non-sequitur & lots of twitchings. It is so sad – he was a brilliant young man, & all this is as a result of Japanese imprisonment.

25 November 1948   Bryn High[1]

Darling Ginnie,

Thank you for your good biro letter. Yours is the only hand I know that retains at least *some* of its character with a Biro in it. I think they are a horrid invention, though, coming out as they do in strokes all the same in spite of characteristic pressures.

I'm havin' a fine time. Now all the wisps have wiped away and it's a very Emmet of an emptiness, palest blue with a faint rose in it left by the sunk sun. I quite see that if ever I am to write that great novel or those startling short stories, this is the sort of life one has to lead. So far I've completed five Shirleys, and several in between bits for the series. I also finished off an awful poem about my Pa as I remember him and now, that is terrible and possibly rather good.

This afternoon I explored the town and I saw a series of sordid sights that really are a short story in themselves. Add four ragged little children collecting old tins off the beach and pretending to drink out of them, two large rough dogs assaulting a small creeping black bitch, and a party of six or eight very little, very old idiots, the men in berets and the ladies in knitted pixie hoods, and you will get quite a sum total! Tomorrow I will take to the wild hills again I think.

I had a nightmare last night in which I went on to the stage without knowing my monologue and made it up as I went and it was utterly pointless and bad. Woke me up sweatin' it did.

[1] Home of Dr Thomas Jones, near Aberystwyth. 'T.J' was a mentor to Joyce. Among his correspondence that he left to the National Library of Wales are all the letters that Joyce wrote to him over several decades.

1949

24 March 1949   King's Road

Darling Ginnie,

Here's a letter. I think it's going to be about cocktail parties but you never know. Nina[1] had one tonight and I went.

I think I must make myself go to more cocktail parties and practise at being nicer. I'm *horrid*. I want to avoid everybody and I think I've got an increasing fear (very conceited) that people want to talk to me now *because* I'm an actress and it's glamorous! But now *why* should I make an effort *not* to see Iris and Daphne when I see them goggling eagerly in my direction? I cannot see why I should be so unkind and snooty. And yet I am. Plainly I need to be more Christian.

But how nice Nina is.

Cocktail parties require a lot of spiritual equilibrium to behave well. As usual the noise was animal and enormous. I find all my nastiest side soars to the surface and I want to be unkind, and am, about people's hats and faces. I think it's about time: you gotter score fast and it seems quickest to be cruel. I don't like myself at all tonight. I've been snooty and mean and I'm afraid it boils down to some form of conceit that I wasn't aware I had. It's so unnecessary to be unkind where only a few words and some gentleness was required. It's been quite a shock to know how horrid I can be.

The practicality of giving such parties is plain. But oh the hell. We stood close together face into face yelling while a butler wove his way among us with trays of drinks and the twins with red bows wobbled plates of savoury mouthfuls and asked people to take two. It's frightening to see our contemporaries. To suddenly see Rosemary again with a middle-aged face and hat and figure, and pretty people like Primrose grown plump and usual looking, is sort of sad.

R. is coming home only just in time.[2] I'm enjoying my independence and these early to bed evenings altogether too much. I do hope I'm nice and kind when he gets back. The thing to do is remember it takes two to re-adjust to a union!

Wasn't it a pretty day? But oh the *sadness* of spring. A little man with badly fitting teeth and a professional cheery smile came to the door to try and sell me a very reasonable little mink cape. He looked so wretched and seemed to need the money badly, so I felt a beast to send him away as I did.

Spring shows up the flaws by being so perfect and eternal in a transient world. I wish I'd been nicer at that party tonight.

---

[1] Nina Lucas, née Grenfell – a favourite cousin.
[2] Reggie had been in South Africa for several weeks.

3 September 1949   Edinburgh Festival

Darling Joyce,
    Thanks for the press cutting. I tremble to think that the reporter to
whom I reported on *The Third Man*[1] put zephyr instead of zither as a
musical instrument! I wonder how many people will write & tell me
how stupid I am.
    We went to *Cosi* last night. As I had dress circle seats I didn't bother
to change into a dress & went in m' grey flannel. Felt sure the Queen
would be in a box, but no, there she was, en grande tenue, with us
exactly behind. I compliment Arthur Penn[2] on his good manners in not
cutting us dead. Oh dear, how Mrs Thesiger would have loved it . . . she
could have watched Princess Margaret trying to get some extraneous
matter out of her teeth without resorting to using her fingers, she could
have assisted the Queen in the arrangement of her sapphires, she could
have stroked the Royal hairs & breathed down the Royal necks, & she'd
have been happy for months to come. The Ts however, blobs of flannel
in a sea of chiffon, rather wished they weren't fated to meet the Queen
at every performance they attended. One can't get into the theatre or
out again in under an hour, & I always think Queens have a dampening
effect on an audience, don't you? Still, the opera was ravishing.

[1] Written by Graham Greene, directed by Carol Reed and starring Orson Welles, Joseph
Cotten and Trevor Howard. Virginia was film critic for the *Evening Standard* until 1952.
[2] The Queen's Comptroller.

9 September 1949   King's Road

Darling Ginnie,
    Reg & I went and saw *The Third Man. Excellent*. We loved it. The little
unmentioned subtleties like when you realise how well she knows Harry
Lime's flat by her automatic playing with the dice as she telephones.
And his initials on her pyjamas. Orson Welles is first class. So is Trevor
Howard. So are they all.
    (I'm now *covered* in ink from refilling my pen. Every finger is
navy blue.)
    We had a Proper Adventure coming home from dinner last night.
We hailed a taxi in Piccadilly and it drew into the kerb just beyond us.
Two spivs and their girls darted at the cab and one of the spivs got in.
R. said 'Sorry but it was our taxi' and the driver said he'd seen us first.
But the spiv at the door said 'Don't be silly it's our cab.' R. then said
'Don't be an ass' and the spiv hit him! Hard enough to knock his glasses
off and shatter them on the pavement. R. kept his temper and his head
and told the creature to stop it, the spiv's girls tried to drag him away,

he would have hit me too but I ducked. He then hit R. twice again and then the girl friends pulled spiv No. 1 away and the second spiv got out of the cab: we got in and the driver said 'Keep your eye on them and I'll drive you to a policeman.' Which he did. We got one, explained all and we then swung up Regent Street, swung round outside the Café Royal where the policeman nabbed No. 1. We then all – Reg, the Spiv, the Copper and me – drove round Eros and to the front of Swan & Edgar where a police van miraculously sprung out of the ground. The policeman asked R. and me to go with him and the spiv, and so we let the taxi go! Then followed 1 $\frac{1}{2}$ hrs at the police station off Sackville St., where R. was examined by the Police-Surgeon to see if he could charge the spiv with assault and battery (the police wanted this) and it seemed he certainly could. Very minor injuries really but in fact a cut on the eyebrow, a bruise on the neck and jaw – nicely swollen by now! – and a blistered lip. A statement was taken and signed, R. went and charged the spiv. who denied the whole thing with the innocence of a new born baby, and then we came home leaving him, presumably – yes, in a cell overnight. We got to bed at 1.15. This a.m. R. went to Bow St. and has sent me a message to say the spiv got fined 5 guineas.

Wasn't it eventful? I wasn't very shaken: nor was R. oddly enough. But I did find my teeth chattered rather, about an hour later. However it was sheer citizen-ship that made us persist. So much easier to have gone home really. But I think it was the right thing to do because it is a bit thick to have people behaving like that over nothing and getting away with it. We neither of us felt particularly revengeful but it was pretty maddening for R. to lose a very expensive pair of tortoiseshell glasses and be hit at too. And the bland smoothness of the little man *was* maddening.

I've just talked to R. and find the boy had a record – gambling, burglary, etc. – and is a bookie's assistant earning £5 a week. He has one lung and was invalided out in 1944. R. says he looks rather nice today in the light! He has to pay 25/- to the doc. but R. gets nothing for his glasses. So there you have the full drama.

12 September 1949   Moorlands Hotel
                                                     Hindhead
                                                     Hants

Darling Ginnie,

On Saturday, I wrote a new Sydney[1] and I've got a skeleton done which is something. Lunched with Pa and then I spent the afternoon packing in order to come down here for filming *St Trinian's*.[2] First it was Thurs. for Friday, then Sat. for Sun. and that not certain. No wonder fillum stars get paid so well. The undermining all this sitting about does is incalculable.

This is a very comfy large manorial sort of hotel 'set in its own grounds'. I've got a very secluded corner room overlooking the gardens and bang next to a lav. and Margaret Rutherford.[3]

Yesterday, a beautiful day, ideal for working, I was made up at 9.30 and off in a car with Margaret and several others, to Byculla a girls' school at Liss. It's a *very* attractive place with fields and woods round it, and the headmistress and her number two are there to help and encourage and are both enjoying the whole adventure enormously. Hundreds of children were being used yesterday for lacrosse scenes, and football scenes. There's a lot of new stuff in the script concerning a progressive school with unruly children and a pair of bearded masters, who were played by naval ratings from Portsmouth and Liss village's wilder young. Everyone is having such fun that I must say I enjoyed it too. And then Muriel Aked[4] arrived and is a darling, very funny and intelligent and excellent company. I supped with her last night and enjoyed it. She told me a long fascinating saga about her first engagement which was a year's tour to the Far East. Someone called 'Win' killed herself and about the laying out and the carrying of the coffin down in a lift. She and a girl called Blossom were pursued in a Madras hotel by two whispering Englishmen who hissed through their keyhole 'Let us in' and they said 'What do you want' and they said 'What you've got, girls'! All this in 1920.

I did about 6 shots yesterday, one in a gym dress which caused some laughter. I rather think the picture may be overburdened with laughs for with Margaret, Muriel, Alastair[5] *and* me it's going to need some rigid directing. I'm not quite sure how I'm to play the part but Lauder seems very good and I'm leaning on him for guidance. I think I shall be innocent and keen at the same time. Margaret is splendid. She is now *enormous*. Quite blown up, but it adds to the whole thing.

---

[1] The 'Nursery School' sketches starring Sidney and George began on the radio in 1944 in *How to Talk to Children* as a short piece called 'What Flower are You?' Six nursery school sketches were published in *George – Don't Do That* by Macmillan in 1977.
[2] *The Happiest Days of Your Life* was the first of the five St Trinian's films directed by Frank Launder, based on the books by Ronald Searle about a horrific English girls' boarding school. In this one, Joyce played a gym mistress, Miss Gossage, with the immortal line 'Call me Sausage'.
[3] British comedy actress (1892–1972).
[4] British character actress (1887–1955).
[5] Alastair Sim (1900–76), Scottish actor.

1950

Joyce, Reggie and Victor went on holiday in France. They were later joined by Virginia and Tony.

30 April [1950]   Hôtel du Touring
                                                                  St Céré (Lot)

Darling Ginnie,

This is a charming small French town – or overgrown village. A sort of Burnham with those noble buildings one finds in France – all old, pale golden stone. Small green hills around, patchwork of vineyards. Victor is dazed with delight and R loves it too.

Madame is youngish, chic and beadily efficient. Giggles throatily and bows to us with a side smile. Odette aged 20 is the femme de chambre, pretty as paint and sturdy as a pony. Pinot, about 16, is the Bar, in a white jacket and bright pink cheeks.

We watched a match of le Rugby on the town field (a yard long in hay!) and tonight the teams have a banquet in our bar. 100 of them. It was the best entertainment you could wish. Not much Rugby, but such a wealth of gesture and swearing and laughter and jeering and applause. The 1st of May

The banquet last night was wonderful. The men soon removed their coats and they put away yards of bread and wells of wine. They were hard at it in the bar. We took an evening walk by moonlight. The crickets were 'singing well with their legs' (C. Fry) and the frogs were very woodwindy. It was enchanting catching glimpses of highly polished copper hanging in kitchens. When we got back here the banquet had become a concert. Speeches were made and applauded with spoons on the table. Then songs. Many solos and some choruses. We sat on the terrace looking in with the rest of the village who weren't inside. I fell asleep to the sound of distant singing as they went home through the moonlit streets.

This *is* Nightingale Wood. They sing all day and all night and are so intoxicating I can't do anything but stop and stand and try to stare.

4 May [1950]   Cambridge Square

Darling Joyce,

Your letter arrived by the afternoon post, and we were just beginning to think you had hit a ditch or run off the rails.

I feel so cross & depressed today, really fed to the back teeth – I interviewed Peter Cheyney[1] yesterday in his 'well-appointed' flat which smelt of scent & had a large Mrs Spry as a centre piece and distorted glass trees & a wife in a tartan skirt. He was the most conceited man I have *ever* met in my life – I was completely hypnotised, fascinated like a rabbit before a boa constrictor. He talked, without interruption, for one solid hour, not only about his triumphs, but also telling me outlandish tales about the underworld & how truth was so much stranger than fiction etc. In a way he was simply splendid, so utterly spivish & braggart, & he rather endeared himself to me in the end by asking me not to paint an awful picture of him – 'I know I look a cad & I sound boastful but I'm not really.' I reeled away with a signed copy of his latest & spent the afternoon writing my article.

I'm pretty fed up with these articles. Curran[2] says Beaverbrook is always going on at him about how everything must be controversial, & this week he wants me to tackle some tripe-ish novels & try to analyse why the public like them. I don't see how I can do this without either insulting the authors or the public, & this of course is just what he wants. It's so destructive, & I hate it. If things go on like this I shall try & break my contract. Curran isn't satisfied with what I wrote because I've failed so far to be controversial, & I was under the impression I had been contracted to write book reviews. I don't mind if the *subject* is controversial – should babies be given kippers – but when it comes down to personalities I hate it. Who am I to say Ursula Bloom writes tripe? I can see I am going to have a stinking weekend.

Tell old Vic I spent the afternoon at Jacqmar trying on that dismal elephant's breath dress & the spotted shirt which practically throttles me!

[1] British mystery film writer (1896–1951).
[2] Charles Curran (1903–72), assistant editor of the *Evening Standard*.

6 May 1950   St Céré

Darling Ginnie,

We have acquainted ourselves with a completely Charles Adams family who run the Café du Commerce in the main street. We go there after supper and we get to know Madame and Anny and, by repute, Monsieur who is malade en haut. Madame is more or less normal. She is pretty and plump and had her 49th birthday on Thursday, when she gave me a share of her floral tributes (long roses tastefully ruined by maidenhair ferns). But Anny looks like a frog and is 12. She also has one eye smaller than the other which seems a source of pride. Also she is much trop intelligent so is kept from school to calm down. But the most Adamsy of all is the invisible Monsieur, who mysteriously swelled up like a balloon on Sunday. We had a complete account of his troubles which are very dramatic and include a trepanned skull, intestines as small as a six month old child, and no appetite at all ever. Monsieur is getting better so we hope to see him soon. Madame has hinted that he is not very tall, so we expect a midget and possibly an oriental one to account for Anny's strange looks.

10 May [1950]   France

Darling Joyce,
    You will get this just about the same time as you get me, with my new permanent wave & my new coat and my old face.
    I was most frightfully ill yesterday driving through Paris. Very tiresome and nose blowy and congestion of the lungs. I think it is maddening to be ill with non-Scientists, however sweet & non-aggressive they are because one knows how irritating it must be for them – one little pill, a sniff of this & a sup of that & they are quite sure one wouldn't be suffering at all, & I must say at times it's very hard not to be believe they are right! One could sense my hosts' alarm lest I should develop pneumonia & insist on dying of it. I *do* see how maddening it must be!
    Our only adventure has been putting out a fire in an antiquated Citroen, which we did by making mud pies in a ploughed field & laying them reverently on the burning parts. It was amazingly successful. The owner, a stalwart farmer's wife, was trying to extinguish the flames with *pebbles* & her bare hands. She was quite determined to lie down on the car if necessary!
    Sing well, darling. *Mahsses* of *lerv* from Gin

After appearing as a folk dance enthusiast in the film *Poet's Pub* in 1949, Joyce was cast as a cockney milk maid in *The Galloping Major*. She did not mind being cast as a gawky butt of womanhood, but she did wish that the public realised that she was acting and did not look like this all the time. Her fans were often surprised to find how normal and attractive she was in real life.

12 July 1950   As from 149, but in fact
                                                father-watching in Sloane Avenue

Darling Ginnie,
    I don't at all like it when you aren't here. Weeks may go by without the sight of your dear old face but there are those morning gossips and I miss them badly. I go to dial Pad 9942 and then realise it's no good. Buck up and come back. (Have a good time first though.)
    What is there to tell you. Well now all of Monday, I was on Wandsworth Common right by the Victoria Line Railway Station.[1] It was a sequence showing us training our syndicate horse and there's a bit of the common running parallel to the line, so we show the horse

galloping like mad at a jump, locally made of old iron bedsteads, a pram, a lot of greenery and a towel horse, while electric trains whizz by beside it. We – that is Mr Matthews,[2] Rene Ray,[3] Jimmy Hanley[4] and me watch from a point by the fence. All the shots that day were crowd shots and there was a lot of standing about, some of it in rain. I went and fell over a tussock and heard and felt something unpleasant go on in my ankle. I did a quick think and was able to walk on it all day with *no discomfort*. Jolly good. It's still painless unless I wiggle it in a certain direction, so I don't.

I did a very quick rush and got to Drury Lane to meet R. and Viola to see *Carousel*. It's very slow and oh so sentimental but we liked it. Lovely songs and good principals. The men's chorus, both vocal and dancing, is pitiful. When I remember the (apparent?) virility of all those bronzed Adonises in New York and then see our undersized bad-toothed little lot, I'm saddened. But in spite of these impoverished moments I enjoyed the evening.

My Ma sails into Southampton next week for about two months.

R. and I dined in last night and I designed another chair seat to use in my television *Woman's Hour* programme next week when they come to my home (in the Studio of course) for half an hour and I show 'em my handwork, your chair seats, and make a salad dressing!

Pa is reading *Punch*, Mozart is filling the air, and I'm writing to you. Tomorrow I probably film in Hyde Park.

I miss you no end. It was a good party, wasn't it. I don't remember laughing so hard and so often for a long time. But as a matter of fact, as a four, we do laugh a great deal. Your ears, and To's, should of burned scarlet after the love speeches made about you and the others.

Have a lovely time and over-eat and all that. Love to silly old To and lots to you.

[1] Filming *The Galloping Major*.
[2] A.E. Matthews (1869–1960), British actor on stage from 1886. Later famous for his crotchety cheerfulness. Worked until he was ninety-one years old.
[3] British writer and actress (1912–93), played downtrodden women.
[4] British actor (1918–70), made his film debut at sixteen.

1951

Joyce and Stephen Potter continued to write and broadcast together for the BBC Home Service and American radio. Joyce also collaborated on series for the Light Programme.

In early 1951 Laurier Lister risked another revue, with no financial backing. Virginia offered to invest in it if necessary. *Penny Plain* opened at St Martin's Theatre and once again the company included Elisabeth Welch and Max Adrian, playing a St Trinian's schoolgirl.

16 May [1951]   Cambridge Square

Darling Joyce,

I'm sorry you had rather a tough time on Monday, but I imagine
a Bank Holiday audience at any time & in any place is lousy, the
determination to enjoy oneself as noisily as possible being the first
consideration. By the time you get to London you'll have overcome so
many problems & handled so many audiences you won't turn a hair
on opening night at St Martin's. Still, I expect these things are rather
shaking.

I am wading on with m' book.[1] Oh, it's so unfunny & oh I hate
having to write to schedule!

Love & a bun from Gin

[1] *Here's How*, Harvill Press, 1951. Amusing essays on 'How to Sing', plumb, knit, etc. few
of which skills Virginia had. The final chapter, 'How to cook', says simply: 'I do not know
how to cook.'

Wednesday, 11 June 1951   2nd House
                                                          Interval. Whew

Darling Ginnie,

From you to me – from me to you. I love our battledore
correspondence.

Last night was up on the week before but tonight is down £3 which
is hard to explain. Another very appreciative audience and so it is fun
to play to them, but of course it's not enough. I don't know quite what
to think. The get out figure is about £1,200 and we did £1,050 last
week. It looks as if it will be about the same this week and that won't
do. I shan't mention your generosity to the management till it gets
desperate! Again and again ta darling, *so* much for your offer.

18 June [1951]   Cambridge Square

Darling Joyce,

We had a happy weekend, with one sortie to see the polo at Cowdray
– *such* a different world & *so* strange to be in it again. Angela[1] playing
with great gusto amid a whirl of people called Smith Ryland or Prior
Palmer, & a visiting team of Argentines with grooms in black pea
jackets, & Lord Blandford[2] & debs in imprimés & dozens of dogs attached
to horsey looking youths – *so* queer.

Another heavenly day which I shall, alas, spend in the cinema
staring at David Niven[3] in the a.m. and Maxwell Reed[4] in the p.m.

Joyce at Clear View School, 1925 (*Courtesy of Claremont Fan Court School*)

Reggie Grenfell and Joyce soon after their engagement was announced, May 1929 (*Private collection*)

Wanda Holden, Joyce, Diana Mitford, Buena?, Angela Neville, Pam?, Lesley? and Virginia attending Mme. Ozanne's finishing school, Paris 1927 (*Private collection*)

Virginia went up the Nile to Aswan on this
steamer, 1937 (*Private collection*)

Joyce and her mother, Nora
Phipps, outside 21 St
Leonard's Terrace, Chelsea,
May 1931 (*Private collection*)

Virginia, Lord Dundonald ('Cocky') and Eben
Pike watching a camel race in Luxor, 1937
(*Private collection*)

Joyce's brother, Tommy
Phipps, at Cliveden, 1934
(*Private collection*)

Left: Virginia Graham marries Tony Thesiger at St George's, Hanover Square, 1939 (*Private collection*)

Below: Joyce and Reggie all dressed up for Virginia's wedding, 1939 (*Courtesy of Thomas Phipps*)

Virginia and Tony's co-respondent feet on honeymoon, 1939 (*Private collection*)

Maria Brassey, Stephen Potter, Reggie, Att (Mary) Potter, Bertie and Joan Farjeon at Parr's Cottage, Whitsun 1939. Photo taken by Joyce (*Private collection*)

Virginia driving Ford V8 van donated to the Women's Voluntary Service by the American Red Cross, 1940 (*Private collection*)

Joyce and Renée Easden at Parr's, 1944 (*Courtesy of Claremont Fan Court School*)

Percy Thesiger, Virginia, Alex Thesiger and Tony at Greystones in Scotland, April 1940 (*Private collection*)

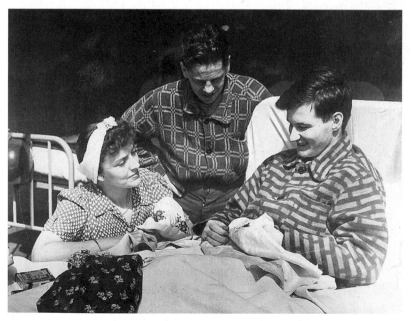

Joyce teaching embroidery to Canadian soldiers in the military hospital at Cliveden, Buckinghamshire, summer 1941 (*Private collection*)

Viola Tunnard and Joyce relaxing with British troops in Baghdad, 1944 (*Courtesy of Claremont Fan Court School*)

Tony and Maria Brassey celebrating victory by painting the railings of the Thesiger home 'a luscious pale green', 1945. Photo taken by Virginia (*Private collection*)

Left: Rupert Hart-Davis, Celia Johnson and Tony Thesiger, 1945 (*Private collection*)

Below: Joyce and Princess Margaret looking at photographs, St Paul's, summer 1948 (*Private collection*)

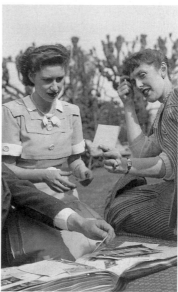

Virginia and Joyce on holiday with Tony and Reggie in Venice, *1949* (*Private collection*)

Joyce loses her heart to Terry Thomas in *Blue Murder at St Trinian's*, 1946
(*Courtesy of Claremont Fan Court School*)

My back was much better over the weekend, but not quite so well today. Mrs Plaister[5] is so nice, a sort of hockey player type, but her line is the CHURCH, service to & everything radiating from it. She may be right, of course, but J.C. wasn't particularly keen on Church organisation if I remember rightly.

Hear your mum arrives tomorrow. I'll cosset next weekend like *anything*.

Wow, I must be off to *Show Boat*.

[1] Angela Campbell-Preston, sister of Lord Cowdray.
[2] Then heir to the Duke of Marlborough (1926–) and Blenheim Palace.
[3] British leading actor (1909–83) just opened in *Happy Go Lucky*.
[4] Irish leading film actor (1920–74).
[5] Mrs Plaister was a Christian Science practitioner.

Takings for *Penny Plain* were not enough to pay all the wages, and Virginia gave £330 to keep the show going.

9 July 1951   St Martin's Theatre
                                                              London

Ginnie Darling, words really do fail me about that money. I am touched *beyond words* and so warmed by your thought and generous feeling. All I can say is thank you, and I hope it won't have to be used. And among other things *thank you for being you*. What would it be like not to have a pal like you I wonder? All down the years you have been kind and generous and good, and I may not say much – or enough – but I do feel it and am very grateful. Thank you darling *so* much.

Lunch today with Stephen Potter after writing all morning. He and I are to do a series of talks to N. America – sort of chatty news letter. He is in good form and had a wonderful time in America.

Ma and I go to see Gielgud on Weds. afternoon. I can't stay all through but I'll manage two acts. Tomorrow I'm being photographed again by McBean.[1] As Maud.[2] He failed last time and is to do a large one. Also of Victor's green dress.

The King is better. There's a snap in the *Star* ce soir and he looks quite a lot bonnier.[3]

Thank you darling. With love from your fliend J.

[1] Angus McBean, photographer (1904–90).
[2] Joyce's song 'Maud Won't Come into the Garden', based on Tennyson's poem 'Come into the Garden, Maud'.
[3] George VI was suffering from lung cancer and died in February 1952 aged fifty-six.

18 July [1951]   Cavalie
                                                              South of France

Darling Joyce,
    You are a good gal to keep me so happily posted – not that it's
happy news I fear. Somehow I thought you'd cover last week. What I'm
hoping & believing is that the holiday public, the visiting firemen, will
all want to come & see their Joyce, their radio Joyce, & will love you &
force their aunts in Penge to stop pruning the roses to take their uncles.
An unsophisticated audience is obviously your best bet now.
    Tony is wearing an orange shirt & pale blue slacks & blue tennis
shoes, & a spotted kerchief round his neck, & he has a gin fizz at hand.
    Bar life goes on & on, some people don't dream of starting dinner
till 10.0, the English being the exception! At 8.30 the Holies[1] canter to
their table, & we try desperately hard not to follow. The Holies come
from Woodstock & we haven't quite disentangled them yet. Though
we converse on a number of topics, I haven't mentioned C.S. One
wouldn't normally talk about religion & I feel that just because I've seen
a *Sentinel*[2] I needn't make some Masonic sign like a Great Elk. By the
way, isn't it a pity, that all C.S. people one knows or meets seem to be
crippled or ailing! They are bent in every direction.

[1] Virginia and Joyce's word for other Christian Scientists.
[2] Monthly Christian Science journal.

Sunday, 22 July 1951   King's Road

Darling Ginnie,
    As the revue is in my mind – on my mind – in my hair – etc. I write
to say that after a smashing start last week we dropped sadly on Friday
and Saturday, and I don't see how we can possibly survive, which is as
can be. For myself it isn't all that important. I am always ready for the
next step, but for the others it really is hell and I am sad about it.
    We were well up until Thursday and looked as if we'd do a really
good week, but then, wallop, we dropped like anything on Friday and
Saturday, and it just isn't going to be possible to continue because it's
no good wasting money on hope. I think they will know more after this
week, and IF the weather changes and IF we do go up it may work out.
But I personally am gloomy about it. So there it is. Oh well.
    Ma went to Nancy [Joyce's cousin] yesterday after a major nonsense
of a row with Aunt N who was intolerable. I took a firm line and sent a
message via Lee [Nancy Astor's butler] that Mrs Nora Flynn was going
elsewhere. Aunt Nancy said she'd said she'd go to Cliveden. She hadn't

and I knew so couldn't be fooled this time. It isn't as if Aunt N cared. It's just show of power. Oh *dear*. Poor Ma looked white and small and mis. and I wasn't going to have it! For a so-called C.S. Aunt N really does make a silly noise.

Darling I should think your £330 has gone smartly down the drain and I'm so sorry. It may not have but I don't know. Thank you, *thank you* – for your spontaneous gesture.

Penny Plain limped along for a few more weeks in London, but continued more successfully as a provincial tour the following year.

1952

Joyce played in *The Pickwick Papers*, based on Charles Dickens's book, directed by Bob McNaught and starring James Hayter, Hermione Gingold and Nigel Patrick.

21 July 1952   King's Road

Darling Ginnie,

I'm writing while I have my brekky before going down to Pinewood to post-synch the Pickwick picture.

Saturday was a *grooling* day here. I took lunch with Pa who was heavy and silent. Today is *greije* in colour and leaden in weight. But yesterday was divine – blue-gold-light with a tittuping breeze.

Lunch with Victor who was dear and not too tired.[1] The boys' criticisms always fascinate me. I'm a constant victim – for being too this or that or wearing a scarf for a hat. You know. It comes from love, that's sure; anyway one must settle for it because there's no choice. He was gay and nice, and as ever I enjoyed my outing.

In the afternoon Norman Wisdom[2] came here to work on 'I don't 'alf love yer', which we are to record. The arranger came too and you will find it hard to believe that his name is Norrie Paramore. Dick came too and hard work went on for 1½ hrs.

To my pleasure and relief *Everywoman* is cutting my article out as from October.[3] Re-organisation of policy. I've enjoyed it but now it's gone on too long. So I'm glad not to do it any more.

---

[1] Victor Stiebel was semi-paralysed in both legs, awaiting a diagnosis. He and Richard Addinsell were close friends.
[2] British comedian and film star (1920–).
[3] Since 1950 Joyce had written a monthly article 'Joyce Grenfell on . . .' parties, eating habits, buying a dress, etc. In 'J.G. on Letter writing' she reveals: 'Bed, with a hot bottle at the feet and a smooth pen in the hand is the perfect place to write the few letters we really enjoy;

the ones where we don't bother about style but just say what we want, to the people we want
to tell it to.' She quotes an entire letter from Virginia which read, 'Hullo! Love Gin'.

8 August 1952   Arduagashel House,
                                                                          Bantry
                                                                         Co Cork

Darling Ginnie,

We flew over very easily on Weds. and were, as arranged, in Dublin
by 10. The car met us. It is a huge whalenosed Ford v.8., very battered,
with its bonnet that won't quite shut and its doors that won't lock and
my window that won't wind. But it goes and is excellent on hills.

After setting off from Dublin to the South, two hours off and miles
from anyone the car quietly spluttered and stopped. R. said: 'Now what
do we do? You'd better do your work.' Which I had already done but
even I hadn't expected the answer as quickly as it came! Lo, over the
brow of the hill loomed a young A.A. Scout on his yellow motorbike
to do the job successfully in about twenty mins. On and on we drove.
Going through Waterford at the discreet hour of 6.30 when all is
respectable and the world is tidying up for the evening R. touched
the horn and it stuck. There is no noise like it for screaming, ruthless
penetration. People ran to their windows and doors. I made signs of
agony and helplessness and called out 'Garage?' We found one and it
was shut but a feller with red hair riding by on his bike leaped off and
tore out a wire and a glorious silence was restored. Both R. and I had
helpless giggles while it went on because it is such an *awful* sound and
there just didn't seem to be a thing to do about it that we knew. Can't
say I called on the Lord that time.

Tramore is rather like Barmouth on the Welsh coast. The Grand is a
battered grey block with rain splashed windows.

The place was full to the brim with priests. They came in all shapes
and sizes, mostly alone, and flirted in a holy-ish way with the waitresses
who spoiled them with little extras. We commented on their number
and were told 'Oh yes, they all come here for their holidays because it's
so quiet for them. In July the place was full and there was 2 Bishops
too.' As dinner cost us 23/- without drinks I can only think the Church
of Rome must pay its boys better than the C. of E.

Much love darling and write to O'Dowds.

Maud is at her least controllable.

11 August 1952   Cambridge Square

Darling Joyce,
   This morning I lost my head and bought an angelic Regency
worktable. I was really looking for some yellow material for the
drawingroom chairs. As I was buying it I thought what a joy it is to
have money of one's *own*! So many wives would have to apologise to
their husbands for buying a Regency worktable, or implore them to *let*
them buy one – I'm really damned lucky being able to puddle about
with the National Provincial [Bank] on my own!
   The Times is bothering me to write an article on the WRAC for some
supplement – I have already refused once but now they have returned
to the charge. And I'm supposed to be writing an article for *Homes &
Gardens*[1] on Weddings, illustrated by Bateman. Funny how when you
have nothing to do how hard it is to do anything.
   A curious thing – my right leg is going through 'The Change'. My
calf keeps on flushing. I *thought* you'd be amazed!

[1] Virginia wrote for *Homes and Gardens* regularly from 1951 to 1982.

Last day – 12 August 1952 (for poor grouse too)   Arduagashel

Darling Ginnie,
   We went to Kilgorin and The Puck Fair – a pagan rite held by the
tinkers from all over Eire. It's really just a drunken orgy. The so-called
wild mountain goat is a cosy old tamer, tethered and put in a basket
on top of a fifty foot pole, and crowned with laurel. There he stays for
three days while much drinking and gladdery goes on, as well as a
cattle market and a wild horse sale. The streets were two inches deep in
running cow dung. The drunks were of the glassy eyed, pickled variety.
We saw little gaiety. Crowds of smallish farmers in cloth caps, very
few women, and some shoddy side shows. The tinkers' caravans very
colourful and hung with tawdry curtains, and filled with bits of cheap
china. The tinkers' girls pretty, the children filthy. Old tinker grannies
dancing in black boots.
   Today we blackberried up the river and got 10lbs. and R. found a
huge amount of mushrooms, which the whole place had tonight on
toast. Delicious.

14 August 1952   Cambridge Square

Darling Joyce,
   My dress came from Jacqmar's at lunch time. Jane[1] was here and

she said: That's the loveliest material I've *ever* seen – held it up to the light & saw a hole. We made further investigations & the whole of the net skirt was absolutely *riddled* with holes!! Wherever the gold had been appliqué-ed the net has 'come away'. I raced back with it & poor Jacqmar curdled like sour milk, spun like a top & keened like a banshee. Everybody went & got someone else & stood bouche bée[2] in horror. Now they've got to start all over again – faulty bit of net presumably & my heart bleeds for them. Still, I don't think one can *start* with a hundred pounds worth of holes do you?

Went to a v. congested cocktail party last night – a mixture of Military attachés & pansies. It was, well, just like all cocktail parties. The room looked lovely, eats were scrummy & we were glad to get away.

[1] Jane de Jongh, Dutch friend of Virginia.
[2] Bouche béante – open-mouthed.

21 August 1952

O'Dowd's
Co Galway

Darling Ginnie,

Last night I was on the air in *Leisure Hour* and we sat in the kitchen to hear it. Mrs O'Dowd, who is so lovely to look at, gentle and delicately featured, with a fine skin and beautiful eyes. Four of her five daughters were there: Eithne, Mary-Therese; Letitia Moynsham with Sheila, Niall, and Diarmid. And our Miss Bennet from Oldham and her friend Frank. The only light came from the ever burning little red light under a holy picture. The announcer said something nice about me and off I went doing a new Sidney and singing 'Light as Air'. It went a treat, particularly with Sheila (10) who giggled with delight as Sidney got more difficult. She is like a Kate Greenaway drawing. Hair cut nearly as short as a boy, and really enchanting features and, of course, the O'Dowd skin and beautiful eyes. Kindly remarks were passed: 'a dear sweet voice', 'most enjoyable', '. . . so lively and all'. When it was over they all clapped!

(Pause while I sit up in bed and see R. setting off with Capt'n Hazel for a day's mackerel fishing on a glassy sea in a silver morning. He is a symphony of yallery greens as he sits on a stump awaiting the Capt'n – and the Boy, who is called Raymond.)

Well this is part of the cure. There just is no time here and learning to do without it has helped iron out that almost permanent tightness at the back of my neck.

It's hard to explain a place like this. I'd never dare recommend it anyone except perhaps Viola. I'd never have recommended it to me, ever.

Had my hair washed, thank heaven. It cost 2/6 and is really clean. Then tweeding, nothing for To or Reg so far. Irish tweed isn't really for boys unless they are living in Chelsea or Hampstead and like looking hairy or Donegally.

We then went to the Galway Horse Show in the Greyhound Track. Very haphazard. Children's jumping. One little girl with huge scarlet taffeta bows under a black velvet cap rode bare-back! One winner was Miss Danny Curley, 14, in a faultless black habit, velvet cap, and on a pony like a Siamese cat – cream with black trimmings. Very pretty. We clapped her.

The crowd was enjoyable. Galway en fete wore imprimés and cardigans. There were the most wonderful old seedies in cloth caps and broken shoes; ex-military types in riding breeches; endless children of all castes.

While I was spending a penny at the hotel a group of three dashers, checks and horse life written all over them, asked R. to settle a wager. Was I or was I not on the fillums? A pound changed hands.

Home latish Mon. I'll ring you (how my grandmother must be spinning in her grave to hear me say 'ring'!).

Penny Plain went on a tour of the provinces.

2 September 1952   Cambridge Square

Darling Joyce,

Yesterday was a golden blowy day & I spent it entirely in the movies – two French films both devoted to squalor – prostitutes & wet pavements, face slappings & beaucoup d'amour on tousled beds. Good they were, but depressing. Then the *Spectator*'s monthly cocktail party.

Reg has just rung to say you had a smashing first night. Goody goody.

The boys [Richard & Victor] took me to the ballet – Sadler's Wells – & I enjoyed it thoroughly. The wonderful thing about me going to the ballet is that I have so little to compare it with I'm absolutely bound to like it – like a country cousin at her annual play outing. I don't know anybody's names so that I feel abroad, & I'm all dewy & starry eyed. How odd that all balletomanes prefer sitting in the front row. In Covent Garden this cuts them off to the knee! But how wonderful Fonteyn is! Even without any legs.

I go out with Reginald Pascoe this eve – he's suggested a Bob Hope at the Pally.[1]

---

[1] London Palladium theatre.

12 September 1952   Liverpool

Darling Ginnie,
   My day at Oldham before the show was so touching. Evidently a big
occasion. I was fetched in a small Morris that swung most interestingly
whenever a brake was touched. We got there at 12 and saw the
infants having their dinner. They sang grace, eyes tight shut and hands
clenched. Certain characters peeped but kept blinking to pretend they
weren't. Later they sang 'The Kin-G of Luv ma Sheppud is'. You can
imagine how much I loved it. I had 'School dinner' in the Office – which
arrives in heated containers. It was very good, oddly enough. A sort
of meat pie followed by a really delicious hot sweet rice pud. The local
press came to meet me and I was snapped sitting on the floor with a
wonderful party of six year olds, who told me about the pantomime
they'd been to last year – 'with all fairies – and they were flyin-g with
win-gs. And they 'ad coloured glasses on.' It seemed some fairies had
sequins on their eyelids! The staff came in for after-dinner tea and of
course I was soon doing a sketch for them. Then two. They were very
shy and I made bright chatter mostly with myself. But I think it was all
right. I came home in a grand taxi and had a lie down before coming
to work.
   Now to do 'Life and Lit.'[1] Ta-ta for now.
   Darling, you didn't have to pay any duty on the tweed did you? If so,
WHAT? Bags me know, see. And pay. I hope you'll have a j.d.hol. but I
bet it'll be cold. It's hell here.

[1] Life and Literature was first performed at a party given by Sir John Gielgud at the Royal
Shakespeare Company, Stratford in 1950. It is about a keen fan meeting a thriller writer.

12 September [1952]   Cambridge Square

Darling Joyce,
   Victor lunched & we talked personalities. He was a little naughty
about La Fairbanks who keeps on sending messages asking if *Lady*
Fairbanks can come & see the collection, & he always answers in
writing so as he can put *Mrs*!
   Poor old V is so madly bored at being a dressmaker he feels he's
going to scream if someone asks him to raise another shoulder strap!
   Noël, though genuinely upset about Gertie, is finding his role as
bereaved Prince Consort somewhat overpowering![1]
   I shall be happy to hold Toe's damp & frozen little mitt in Scotland.
How long I shall cope with the nest of Generals, knitting needles and
stories about the Queen we shall see. I shall have to concentrate very

hard on the beauty of draughts – they always leave all the doors open up there. But I shall be damned glad to see T. Grass widowhood has its advantages, but only for a very very short time.

I've caught a parlourmaid! She's apparently very quiet & nice. Whether she will be influenced to be otherwise remains to be seen. So far she is diffident, aquiline & splendidly smiling. This morning she has made many obliging noises & seems to be going about her work quietly and efficiently.

I visited your Pa on Friday & he was in bed – for what reason nobody was sufficiently unholy to tell me – propped up with dozens of pillows & having a cupper with a nice emaciated member of 11th [C.S. church]. Mrs Gabe was bustling about radiating warmth & happiness. She seems now to 'do' for everybody & I really expect her to open *every* door.

[1] Gertie Lawrence died in New York on 6 September.

Friday, 26 September 1952   Harewood Arms
                                                             Leeds

Darling Ginnie,

As an example of stinking weather this day is 100% perfect. Wet, wind and gnawing coolth.

Last night I gave prizes at a juvenile Olde Tyme Dancing contest. Because the manager is an old friend from Paiforce 1944. He was the Sgt. in charge of Viola and me for a month. Did all the organising and escorting. To my horror all 30 pairs competing in the two classes, under 12 and 12 to 16, were in full evening dress. The boys all wore white tie and tails, white carnations and white gloves. One old man was $4\frac{1}{2}$! His lady was 4. I must say it was fascinating, but awful too.[1]

Wonderful business. We are packed out every time and tonight they are a wonderful house too. Sometimes a bit pudding-y but not ce soir.

Haven't told Viola or Dick or Vic, but the War Office, having *asked* me to go to the Middle East or Malaya or Korea, now don't think it's practical and suggest Germany. To which I make a rude noise and say No. So we'll see. I *think* it's just Middle East Command can't be bothered to organise the transport. Anyway high level action is being taken so we just sit back and wait. I don't mind personally, if you see what I mean, but if there is a job to be done in the M.E. and if I'm ready to go, surely it can be arranged?

[1] May have been the inspiration for the song 'Stately as a Galleon'.

29 September [1952]   Nottingham

Darling Ginnie,

   There's radio-diffusion, no telephone, but gas fires which swallow
only *pennies*.

   Great dramas here. The wardrobe mistress, an hysterical ex-hoofer
blonde would be more accurate, went to London on Sat. evening and
hasn't returned. She took all her stuff and all our keys, which made
things tricky I need hardly say. Mercifully my Nellie is on hand and
with a local lady has done all the Monday pressing and coping. But it's
downright wickedness on Babs White's (glorious name) part. She sent a
telegram saying 'Can't return, keys, float and loan in post Tues.' She's
having a large love affair and has two children and isn't divorced, so it's
a charming little mess. Nellie will take over.

   Yes, *v.* small dinner on Nov. 2. How about just D. and V. and us, with
no one else?

13 October [1952]   Cambridge Square

Darling Joyce,

   Yesterday was such a wonderful day one could have *eaten* it!
It almost looked like a caramel too. Mighty cold today & I've
put on a pair of woolly knickers which I find comforting but
cloying.

   Tony is deathly tired all the time which is a spot worrying.

   Glad the Middle East is *settled*. Can't say it fills me with delight
because I always miss you, but I know it's a job you like doing & do
superlatively well so I mustn't be selfish.

   I haven't written since I took Dick to lunch with Charlie Chaplin.[1]
He was so sweet – whitehaired & smooth cheeked, just like his
photos, but with the liveliest eyes imaginable. I was tremendously
titched up for the occasion, so it grieved me slightly to find,
when I got home, that I had failed to do up the zip of my dress –
but I mean *failed*! There was a broad broad band of pink nylon
showing!

   I'm lunching with my publisher Marjorie Villiers,[2] who wants me to
write another book, but about what I demand myself?

   Jane lunched yesterday. She is driving in one of those gorgeous
royal carriages tomorrow, following her new Ambassador on his
pilgrimage to present his credentials at Buck House! I've offered her a
paper bag![3]

   I'm going to buy your record today – keep on forgetting to
– *silly*![4]

Lovely to be creeping down your list of hotels – only two more to go now.

[1] British-born silent film star (1889–1977).
[2] Author and co-founder in 1947 of the Harvill Press, which published many of Virginia's books. Wife of Virginia's first cousin.
[3] The ancient springs of the royal horse-drawn carriages are said to cause travel sickness.
[4] *Keepsake,* EMI, a collection of songs by Noël Coward, Richard Addinsell and others from *Penny Plain.*

23 October 1952   Glasgow

Darling Ginnie,

I read your A.T.S. article in *The Times* yesterday and admired you for it. Clever.

Business is good but not the smash it's been elsewhere. Lots of competition from Betty Hutton and *Rosemarie on Ice!* Both are taking our cheap seats. I expect our noses are out of joint for we all feel a bit depressed here. However it's a wonderfully gay house ce soir. Frankly I've had enough hotel life and I've been under the carpet for days now. A sort of dull gloom. And yet out of one corner of my blueish eye I can see the light. This is a very sordid town and one sees so many spivs, toughs and undersized cripples, tarts, pansies and flotsam and jetsam that it tends to get a girl down. Liz [Welch] and I walk home after the show for the air. There are a lot of cases about and I'm always glad to be behind the bolt of my own door. What sheltered lives we've lived, you and me. Latterly mine's been a bit less so I suppose, but even so the seamy side gives me the same horrors I got from *Reading Without Tears, Book II.* Did you ever have it? Disaster from p. 1 to the very end.

Got route today for our trip. Viola will come. Malta – Tripoli – Canal Zone. I begin to feel a sense of spinning at all there is to be done before we go. I'm doing a lot of word rehearsing here and feel, as I always do at this point, how 'special' my material is and how much I wish I was broader for the boys. Maybe a Shirl's Girl Friend is the response?

Joyce, Viola Tunnard and Joyce Sharpen, their stage manager, set off for a six-week tour of British troops garrisoned in the Middle East.

18 December 1952   In the air Malta – Benghazi, 7.30 a.m.

Darling Ginnie,

Here we are riding over a lot of cotton wool with sun on it.

The officer O.C. the plane is about 3 years old. *All* the troops on board are about 2. We must brush up our Nursery Rhymes. This is going to be a different sort of job this time but should be interesting and we're lucky to be doing it.

22 December 1952   Tobruk [now Tubruq, Libya]

Darling Ginnie,

Sorry for hurried note but no time. Written in Officers Mess before lunch, before flying to Fayid.

It is very hard going and truth to tell (but not to be passed on please) I'm really dead today. Five shows and long journeys in three days. Voice a bit off today but health good. Nothing rest won't cure.

Terrible pianos all the time but V. being so good about them and managing well. Tobruk where I write from is so awful. Thank God we came. Second show they've had in a year. Last night 350 in a battered hall, all hung with sacking and draped with Arab cotton. Such trouble taken, such kindness and appreciation.

Hellova night in the Salvation Army leave hut. A battered villa, broken windows, doors not fitting. Viola, Joyce and me in one room on tin beds. Hot water in an urn. We locked the front door when we came in to change for the show and couldn't unlock it. Hysterics. There we were, all tee-ed up and couldn't get out to do the show! But a man came and we passed key through broken pane!

Tell Dick 'Wish you were here' very successful. Noël's 'End of the News' no good. They don't like it, but they adore 'I don't 'arf love yer'. Really love it.

Feel a long way off I must say. It's a terrible country most of it. Dead, flat, brown, bare, dry and hideous. Some of the men have been here three years.

23 December [1952]   Cambridge Square

Darling Joyce,

It all sounds wonderfully inefficient & depressing.

Maria brought me my (late) birthday present – a smart little box marked Parker Duofold with no pen inside! Wasn't it sweetly typical? I have also had, for a reason known only to God, a card from the Princess Royal, & this has entailed a heap of telephoning as I gather I have to answer it with a letter. Robins won't do.

Reg has been round & had a gossip and collected Edy, the animated hipbath. As she never goes further than Leicester Square, anything may happen.[1] Mrs Gabe has entirely decorated your flat with holly & Mistletoe!

Masses of love to darling Viola & tell her to be good & obedient to Nanny Grenfell.

¹Edy was a Morris Minor. The Thesigers also had a Bentley called Gussie.

25 December 1952. Christmas Day   Fayid
                                                                    Egypt

Darling Ginnie,
     Happy Christmas Day to you. Here we are sitting on our little front porch with dappled sun coming through a vine on us.
     After I'd written my last letter we lunched with the Officers in their sad little mess. They are babies there – everywhere, come to that. These all come from Mill Hill, Sydenham, etc. and are the salt of the earth: kind, polite, and infinitely touching. It really is the hellova place. No redeeming feature except the bathing and a perpetual breeze.
     Viola and I are sharing, a little 'chalet' in the Grand Hotel. Joyce Sharpen is next door. She is 25 from East Ham and very alive and intelligent and an amusing little sparrow. Her hair is mouse so she's henna'd it – to be more striking she says – to stand out more. She paints her eyebrows in a thick splash of henna, so far removed from nature that one is fascinated. She is a sucker for carved camels and leatherwork. We found her some pale blue satin mules with silver brocade on them as a Christmas present and they are a huge success.
     The job is so very different this time. So much more organised and far less 'al fresco'. This is probably a good thing but I did rather like the old informality – shows in messes with the boys. Now it's all little stages and *lighting*, and a *curtain*, even. I think this probably gives the boys more fun. I change my dress half way through the programme and this evokes calls and whistles, and of course I say 'Well it makes a change', and *that's* a good joke too . . .
     We've now had lunch, turkey and Xmas pud. The Ronnie Ronalds Show are eating en masse at another table and telling their Arab waiter that 'Knees up Mother Brown' is a carol!

30 December 1952   J.G. somewhere in the Middle East

Darling Ginnie,
     The Bitter Lake is salty and said to be nice to swim in.
     Had an interesting experience yesterday. We were warned that our audience for the evening, Tanks, were the toughest in the Command. They had been hell for the last show and had more or less made it impossible for them to go on. Calling out, being funnier than the comic,

etc. So that was a gloomy thought. Then I decided to love them! I thought about it as I sat in the sunlit dapple of our little patio in the afternoon while Viola practised indoors. (She's at it now.) It was quite a long drive by moonlight to the camp. The lake shone one side and the sandhills were still quite pink, so strong was the moon. When we got there it was draughty and rather rough. Broken windows. A sad little stage. Joyce Sharpen had rigged up unbleached canvas as a backcloth. As a safety valve Viola had taken a lot of extra pop. songs with her in case . . . You can guess what happened. Easily the best, quickest, warmest, gayest audience we've had. The ways of the Lord *are* remarkable. Driving back, pleasantly tired, I felt jolly grateful I can tell. It's so *practical*, isn't it.

Happy New, my darling, and have a happy Jan.

1953

2 January 1953   Another place in the Middle East [Egypt]

Darling Ginnie,

G.H.Q. Theatre is *open* air. Well, it's got walls, *then* a two foot gap and then the roof. Nights here are *really* cold. Not actually freezing, but nippy as can be. All the audience brought rugs and overcoats. Being G.H.Q. it isn't a regimental theatre, so it's no one's job to look after it. It's a shambles. Dirty and cold and dusty. I was a bit cross and have done another complaining job to the General. As Joyce Sharpen, our Manager, says without cease: 'To be quite honest it's just not good enough.'

However the audience was superb. Acoustic good. So a lovely time was had by all. *Wonderful* laughs. People are astonished that we are funny without being dirty. Aren't people extraordinary. Dirt is hardly ever *funny*. It may make night club people laugh over their gin, but not audiences who pay to see and hear and be amused in the normal way.

Prokoviev has changed for Bach and lovely it is too. I've just darned a mammoth hole in a pair of pink woolly pants and the music helped a lot.

Suez tonight and it's *miles*.

2 January [1953]   [Cambridge Square]

Darling Joyce,

Our morning has been made glorious by the news that Walter

Midgley,[1] while singing in *Rigoletto*, inhaled half his moustache, the sticky nylon of which glued itself to his larynx. Like a true trouper he sang through the tangle of hairs till the end of the act, when a surgeon was procured to perform an operation.

Glad you're stuck in one place for a bit, but still I have the impression there's too much beer & not enough skittles.

We took Maria & Reg to *For Better or For Worse*,[2] a comedy about exactly nothing but somehow extremely endearing. I don't know why we like Geraldine McEwan so much as really she has the most irritating voice, & I think in real life one might kill her.

[1] Opera singer (1914–80).
[2] Directed by Kenneth Harper, starring Geraldine McEwan (1932–), Dirk Bogarde (1920–) and Athene Seyler (1889–1990).

Wednesday, 7 January 1953   Middle East

Darling Ginnie,

Khamsin again, and an incipient cold. Ah me. V. is down, low as a snake on ice. Her bloody piano has now developed a new menace, so that the hammers are half an inch out. It needs constant nursing, and no run is a normal exercise but a variety of tricky manoeuvres. This is all depressing. Otherwise as gay as grigs. What *are* grigs?

I keep thanking my stars Dick didn't have to come. Of course he'd have given up long since I think. There are so many small trials which we really can disregard, or any way laugh at together. We are beautifully fussed over but the conditions are so much more pretentious than in the war and so much less satisfactory. V. says she thinks all this entertaining of troops is really redundant, and mostly I think she's right. But we've decided it isn't the entertaining we're here for but for the Compliment of coming out to do the job. But it is hellish hard work in these big 'halls' and I must confess to you and *to you only* that Ah's tah'd! As a matter of fact I need to get things sorted out a bit. I get scared by the demands and not feeling 100% isn't a help.

I was spoiled in the war when we did it all so informally and far more spontaneously. Also, dear heaven, was I not ten years younger! But it's not so much fun. That's it. It's just a routine job. I've an idea there isn't quite enough imagination used in routing us. We just follow the usual tour instead of being sent into the blue as I'd asked. And why? Because now-a-days Combined Services Entertainment is a business concern and must pay its way. Therefore big halls, big audiences. Seems silly, don't it.

There I feel better after that big grouse.

When Viola has done with joining 'Bali Haiwai' on to 'Wash that Hair' we are going to walk in the wind because we're bursting for exercise.

P.S. Feel *fine* since this was written. Very gay too.

7 January [1953]   Cambridge Square

Darling Joyce,
    Wow it's cold! Yesterday was blue murder.
    After a fried plaice in Hammersmith Broadway we went to see *Richard*.[1] Frankly it was lousy. A fearful disappointment. Everyone dressed in pastel shades of a Neapolitan ice flavour, & Gielgud has turned them into beautifully elocuting dummies. The result is disastrous. There's no life, no fire, no breath in anyone. Scofield, whom I adore as you know, might be reciting at a charity matinée – wonderfully sonorous but with a face as expressionless as a mark. Perhaps actors shouldn't be producers? Back, disgruntled, to some Ovaltine.
    Reg & I mourned over the weather & wished we were baking in Fayid. I think we could get an act together – I could play the recorder and R the cymbals.

[1] *Richard III*, by Shakespeare, directed by John Gielgud (1904–), actor and director. With Paul Scofield (1922–).

When Joyce returned to Britain she accompanied Reggie to Messina, the copper mine in South Africa owned by his family firm. His cousin Harold Grenfell was the manager there, with his wife Miriam.

Sunday, 15 February 1953   On board aircraft *Princess Margaret*

Darling Ginnie,
    This is an extraordinary world. The Alps are just sticking up through a floor of ruffled cotton wool on my left. We had lunch at Frankfurt while the loud speaker called passengers to board their aircraft for Tokyo – for Buenos Aires – Copenhagen – Bombay – Jo'burg. We all look extraordinarily alike. American film influence I suppose? Dutch and Swedes and Englishers and Germans have a strong resemblance. Oh details vary – externals I mean – bow ties, silk scarves, beaver felt hats, brief cases; but so often the bones give nothing away. It makes war seem too *idiotic*. Even so I was ashamed to feel a bit funny about the Huns at Frankfurt! And all of it hearsay. No German has ever directly done me wrong. My old theory of love has to be practised on Germans, even as it is on audiences!

Now it's next day and I've had a lovely flat out night in m'sleeper, getting warmer and warmer as we get souther and souther. At Nigeria – 4 a.m. – I knelt up in the dark of my bunk and watched the goings on. Coloured boys re-fuelling, men in white shorts checking details, all under great fat stars. We fly high and at one time were *above* some stars! There they were down below us winking away. I had the bottom bunk and R. the top. Just like U.S. trains only roomier.

Sh. sh. – I had half a glass of champagne last night with me dinner.

20 February 1953   Messina (Transvaal) Dev. Co. Ltd
                                       Transvaal
                                      South Africa

Darling Ginnie,

Picture a sort of Californian house with white venetian blinds, green covered white tin porch furniture and a light breeze stirring the really warm air. That's Harold's house and the stoep[1] where we sit a good deal.

This afternoon looms a little menacingly ahead of us. Miriam and I have to attend the Reformed Dutch Church to attend a women's service. This means hats, stockings and gloves, and a solid hour of Dutch we suppose. Well, I plan to think me own thoughts and it's a nice idea I daresay. But a hot one.

We've been to our first dinner party and it wasn't too bad. I'd no idea how terrible S. African voices are! They take the vowels, iron them flat and then squeak them – E is always an I sound. Thus terrible is – tirrible. And a cool drink is a cuil drink. Daown and Raound Abaout are even worse than in Sidcup or Penge.

We went in our clean cottons with white shoes and bags, and our boys were in clean white shirts and coatless, and there we met twelve of the locals under a flamboyant tree, beneath the stars. Mixed as can be. Afrikaans, Irish, Austrian, American. Simplicity is the note. I think there are depths to be plumbed and some of them are very knowledgeable about this country, which goodness knows is a fascinating place. It is far more beautiful than I imagined. The views are enormous and there are lots of clouds which are rather becoming to the sky and do relieve the eye.

After drinks under the tree we moved into a boiling little house and ate a boiling dinner. It was a great effort on the part of the hosts. Borrowed china and glass from neighbours and lots of jokes about recognising it. Coal black 'boys' in loose cotton gloves served us with a lot of nervewrack and heavy breathing, and we ploughed our way through pink melon, beef with tinned peas, and some sort of yellow squash.

It's much too hot to play tennis or move really. Miriam and I sit and sew on the stoep a good deal. Lots of nature to observe so I'm happy. The insect life is rather frightening tho'.

¹ Afrikaans for verandah.

22 February 1953   Messina

Darling Ginnie,

Today is Sunday and Church bells of rather an aggressive tone have vied with each other to call us, and quite unsuccessfully too! Our afternoon praying with the Reformed Dutch was very giggly indeed. It turned out to be a Women's Call to Prayer for Peace service.

The Church is nice and bare, as are ours. Only some fierce orange candytufts spiked together on wires broke the bareness. Many white hats – end of season C. & A. style – with lace veiling and ribbon choux and feathers rising often all on the same lid. Printed silks, corset ridges and bulges, and many many pore tired feet in bursting white shoes. In fact the Great Middle Class anywhere warm. The service began with the entry of ten little scrubbed girls in frilly Sunday dresses and pigtails, carrying lighted candles. They sang after three false starts 'Jesus bids me shine' – in Afrikaans.

Then three ladies in turn addressed us. Two in Afrikaans and one in guttering Englische. There was a homily on not gossiping, not being unkind, not being martyrs, not being stuck up, and the advice, a little late in view of all this, to be Positive. It was slowly spoken and repetitive, and seemed to have little to do with peace. Then the pastor's wife, sounding exactly like Ruth [Draper] doing her spoof mittel-European language, spoke for twenty mins. and we understood two words and these were 'John Bunyan'. He cropped up throughout. The final lady wore hot brown buttoned modestly to the adam's apple, an Austrian man's felt hat with eagle's wing at the back, and no make up. She enjoyed herself far too much for far too long. Later we learned she was smacking her lips about sex, but alas we missed it all. It went on for an hour and a quarter. When we got back to the car it was practically on fire.

Back on our hill Miriam and I tore off our clothes and had the most welcome cuppers with our shoes off. We have now acquired a pet chameleon who remains bright green even when we put him on the red floor.

Yesterday it rained, like a movie rain storm. It simply poured down quite vertically beating into the ground. It was lovely!

24 February 1953   Messina

Darling Ginnie,

In an hour I'm to go down a mine! Hope this isn't my last letter. Don't want to go much but it's foolish not to Experience I suppose, and think R. wants me to go, so there it is – I go.

On Sunday evening we took tea with the Magistrate over the border in S. Rhodesia. Here we are in the Union of S.A. and Afrikaaners are the rulers. *Not* nice or attractive. Narrow, middle class, very prejudiced against the blacks, through fear of course, and most semi-educated. They want full Afrikaans spoken only – all Englishmen and their language banished. But oh the difference when we crossed the Limpopo and were in British S. Rhodesia! It sounds ridiculous to say so but there is a feeling of truth and order and freedom as soon as we got to the other side of Beit Bridge. And it was jolly nice to see the Union Jack waving against a pale blue sky. Mr Sherlock is a bachelor from Grimsby, which he left 25 years ago. He keeps up with things like mad and quite innocently said to me that V.G. is far the best film critic writing today. He never misses her.

26 February 1953   Messina

Darling Ginnie,

We went down 1,000 feet in the mine on Tues. and it got hotter and hotter. Had on khaki drill shirt and pants and a fine helmet. We walked for miles, shedding pounds. The great caverns down there are impressive and rather beautiful. There was an acetalene flare lit to show us the 200 foot hall with its copper walls and 300 foot high roof. Tiny specks of light below us were natives with lamps on their hats working on the loosened stuff blasted earlier when the place was empty! We were down there for two hours and emerged whacked. But I'm glad to have done it.

Miriam and I went to a ladies tea at 4 and it was exactly like a W.I. party at home. Same ladies in art silks, mopping same beads on upper lips, same dainty tea, same pore feet, same hard work for M. and I.

In the evening there was a quiz to aid the T.B. fund, and Harold took the Chair. We sat under the stars at the Bioscope. It was quite good. Second half of programme was a 'Cabaret'. A chorus of hula hula girls made up of the oddest shaped gents the community could assemble. They were quite awful and *very* funny. There was a blacked-up face comic (NOT) and a folk singer, *quite* good. Then, like a bolt from the starry blue, they announced I was present and asked if I'd favour them with a song. So holding down my wind-blown skirt, I went up on to the stage, accepted the accordionist's suggestion that 'Tipperary' would go over big, and sang it! They wanted more, so we did 'The more we are together' – only we weren't. I thought of it as a slow 1 2 3 and he thought of it as a fast 1 2 3. We ended up more or less ensemble.

4 March 1953   Messina

Darling Ginnie,

This morning an excellent outing to the native school with the R.C. padre. He is called Father Shearan and is blond and plump with a high woman's voice and a hairless face. Rather unattractive but quite nice. The children sang and danced for us and it was fascinating. The girls were mostly in very ancient navy blue gym slips with white *satin* blouses. Bare feet and white berets on their heads. The boys wore any old shirt and shorts and mostly bare feet. The seniors sang really well in a rather hideous way. Faultless pitch and rhythm and their feet beat time as they sang. All of it jazz rhythm and very contagious. They did dances for us with tom-toms and got frenzied, writhing on the floor – shouting and clapping their hands.

We are having serious ant troubles and on Mon. evening a host of them climbed up a table leg and paraded across the table. We had to move aside till they went. And white ants, $1\frac{1}{2}''$ long and very greedy, got into a cupboard of one Capt. Kelly here and ate all the left sleeves of all his garments hanging there in one night!

I am incensed about colour problems.[1] At the school today M. and I made a point of shaking hands with the two native schoolmasters. The other ladies with us didn't follow suit. I know if I lived here I'd be in constant trouble because the racial discrimination drives me dotty. And they are all by way of being so religious in S.A. Lot of . . . hypocrites.

[1] Apartheid (separate development) laws had been passed by the nationalist government in 1948.

9 March   Cambridge Square

Darling Joyce,

I'm not absolutely sure where to send this darling, but I hope it will catch you somewhere.

Yesterday I flogged out to a *Spectator* party – Peter [Fleming] rugged in tweeds, a lot of intellectual boys three feet high, Ken Tynan[1] with a child wife. Wilson Harris[2] has got the sack – very badly managed I gather & a lot of hard feelings. I confidently expect to get the sack too, as new editors invariably dismiss the previous staff, don't they?[3]

Vic moderately ill, as usual & we sat, cooing sympathetically & being very gentle & sad, which was delightful.

Tonight I've got a dinner party, chiefly to amuse the maids, who get bored giving me scrambled eggs on a tray.

[1] British drama critic for the *Observer* and *New Yorker* (1927–80).
[2] Editor of the *Spectator* from 1932 to 1953 (1883–1955).
[3] Virginia was not sacked. She was the *Spectator's* film critic from 1947 to 1956 and contributed to their Notebook under the pseudonym 'Glaux'.

9 March 1953   Jo'burg

Darling Ginnie,

We went to hear Alan Paton speak (*Cry the Beloved Country*).[1] Very moving. I wish I could *do* something about this apartheid nonsense.

We are glad to be shaking the dust of Johannesburg from our pore feet. It is a very bad place. Physically it is tough on account altitude (over 6000'). It makes me feel a mixture of tiredness and gloom and I do not like it. There are a lot of really very attractive and nice people living just outside and I can see that it *might* just be possible to be fairly happy there. But I wouldn't like it much. Isn't it funny the way things seem to balance out. There we are living in Eng. with horrid climate and certain constant difficulties either with or without servants, but *oh* the compensation of pals and stimulation, theatre, music, ballet and *antiquity*. That's one of the things I miss here. No roots. Here they've got heavenly weather, lavish foods, servants (£3 a *month*), immense American cars, and exactly nothing else. The political situation is tricky as can be. No one dares trust their houses un-burglar-proofed.

In spite of all the money people live in *tiny* little houses. It surprised me no end. Cottages with just one bathroom. But usually a big garden and a lot of life is lived in the garden. And there is usually a swimming pool. And they read quite a lot. Novels mostly.

I've done two unscripted interviews at the S.A.B.C. and they are a nice slightly defeated lot. They are even more wary of saying the wrong thing than the B.B.C. boys, and I longed to say in my broadcast how enormously impressed I was by the beauty of some of the native women and the almost regimental plainness of the Afrikaaners. You will be glad to know that I resisted the temptation which was very powerful.

We've all been photographed by a very clever and charming little Lithuanian Jew called Leon Levson. They are excellent. L.L. is married to a very brave and very nice girl called Freda Troup, who must be

25 years younger than he is and who is working very hard to do something for inter racial relations, and got arrested for walking through a native location without a pass! She is now out on bail. She has the backing of Bishops and all thinking people here, but it's a very frightening and despairing situation. I do so understand apathy and that's why I admire Freda for going on as she does.[2]

[1] First published in the USA in 1948, a novel exposing apartheid.
[2] Leon and Freda Levson were involved in anti-apartheid activities such as the Defiance Campaign and in 1962 were forced to leave South Africa for Malta where Leon died in 1968. Freda continued her work against apartheid in London, where she still lives.

14 March 1953   Government House
                                                  Salisbury
                                                  S Rhodesia

Darling Ginnie,
    This is lovely country. Very verdant. We flew in at sunset and all the trees and all the cows had long blue fluffy shadows four times their own lengths.
    Bungs and His Excellency[1] were on the steps to meet us. She looks older but is just the same. Speaks in an urgent well-bred voice, with 'splendid' and 'divine' occurring constantly. I should think she is the success in the job: bright and a good hostess and sensitive to the job. She is still very Bungsy. 'Go on – tell me more' she says, sitting bolt upright. He is a nice friendly teddy bear, a pillar of the Empire, but not very clever. I'd say between them they do it all jolly well and seem to enjoy it. It finishes at the end of the year and then home to the sink and the chores, but meanwhile all is de luxe and superbly comfortable. Bungs looks curiously 'bien' and slightly old fashioned now. Her dress was long last night and both M. and I and the sec. were in ballet length!
    This is like staying in the most perfect Eng. country house. An Irish maid looks exclusively after visiting ladies. She whisks away garments and tidies up everything so it is lost for ever!
    Bungs has to have the Queen Mum and Princess M. for two whole weeks this summer, so that's a major project to plan for.

[1] Joyce and Virginia's childhood friend Catherine Fordham (Bungs) had married Major-General Sir John Kennedy, Governor-General of Southern Rhodesia.

16 March 1953   Government House

Darling Ginnie,
    Yesterday I went to the C.S. Church in Salisbury – touching and simple. A wooden tabernacle, washed blue within. I was welcomed

afterwards by a fat lady from Richmond, Surrey, now domiciled here where, she told me, supply was so beautifully ample and opportunity so wide. She's right, it is. And in a *way*, if I was young and not too imaginative I could start a life out here I think. It's *far* happier than the Union of South Africa.

We took tea thirty miles away after a lovely bird watching journey, with John and Daphne Acton and their *nine* little Roman offspring.[1] They live in complete squalor. She is still handsome but very drawn and worn and has lost a lot of side teeth. He is apparently a superb farmer and does wonders with his pigs. These live in far superior conditions to the family. *They* are very dirty and unkempt, highly intelligent and rather attractive under their dirt. But it is living without any Grace. No flowers, no colour, no air. Instead Daphne has turned the garage shed into a school for natives, complete with crucifix, and her dream is to fill their valley with Holy Romans, black and white!

Two little boys in grubby white passed the cups with concentrated attention. They were 4 and 5. I must admit they all seem very happy. Her eldest child Pelline is 20 and engaged to a Hungarian who escaped the Iron Curtain and is learning to farm. It's quite a quiver full. She looked so jolly tired.

Today I meet Miss Dulcie Bell who is to play for me tomorrow when I do a few items for the servants (white), staff and some local chums. Ah me. But one must sing for one's supper I think.

[1] Lord Acton, Sir John Emerich Lyon-Dalberg-Acton (1907–89), married Daphne Strutt who was a girlhood friend of Joyce and Virginia. They ran a multiracial farm in Rhodesia until 1967 when they took their ten children to multiracial Swaziland.

10 July 1953   King's Road

Darling Ginnie,

Ma and I lunched with Alice [Winn], and Virginia Ford[1] was there with a truly hair raising and horrifying story about an American friend of hers who went to Blenheim for the weekend. The Duchess didn't address one word to her the entire time she was there. The Duke,[2] who was writing letters in the library where she was reading the papers on Sunday, got up from the desk and went over to the fireplace where he relieved nature! She didn't know whether to get up or pretend she didn't exist. Oh the Ducal houses! Oh the Aristocracy!!

We saw *The Seven Year Itch*[3] on Sat. It's well written but not quite well enough done. I rather enjoyed it though in a mild way, but I wouldn't dare recommend it to anyone.

Princess Marg. has a bad cold and has cut out some of her tour to go to bed at Gov. Hse. Salisbury. The papers are *full* of letters and leaders about how she cannot marry Peter Townsend because of the divorce, and I think she must be very unhappy and mis. all on her own with her pore cold and all. My heart bleeds for her I must say.[4]

[1] Cousin of Joyce, *née* Brand, wife of Edward Ford.
[2] 10th Duke of Marlborough (1900–72). This story may have been apocryphal.
[3] Play at the Aldwych Theatre, written by George Axelrod (1922–), directed by John Gerstad with Rosemary Harris and Bunny May.
[4] Princess Margaret, aged twenty-three, was in love with Group Captain Peter Townsend, who was eighteen years older than her and divorced.

16 July 1953   King's Road

Darling Ginnie,

I'm in a beautiful daze from having had three hours with my hero, Walter de la Mare.[1] He is so much more attractive, fascinating, gay, interesting, mysterious, alive and charming than all the other boys put together. That he is eighty simply doesn't occur to one. His eyes are young and bright, like stones under water. A paralysed friend of his called Mrs Ladd came to tea and was carried upstairs in her chair. She was attractive, too, nearly seventy, with serenity and wisdom and interest in life. That's the thing they both shared – this *interest* in everything. Enquiring minds. Delicious little cakes and home made brown bread. He sang several splendid music hall songs at tea.

When Mrs L. left, W.J. – as he asked me to call him – said 'Don't go. Come up to my sitting room, there is so much to talk about.' And so we talked about time, imagination, the personality of keys in music, birds – about memory and how it works. He holds that the world is entirely negative and that it is only the things of the mind that are real. So of course I was in my happiest climate! He spoke of Presences – with a capital I think – and we decided they are simply aspects of oneself. We touched on death and life and poetry, and he said he talked too much – it was old age – but of course he didn't. I talked too! He kept asking questions and seemed to want to know about my views. He asked about the characters I do. Did I get them 'whole' or did they have to be built? I said that what they *said* had to be built but what they *were* came whole. He wondered if I improvised them on the stage & I said no but that I re-thought them every time.

He said that talking was difficult to stop, and now and then he'd notice a beautiful peace and then realise he'd stopped talking!

I said 'do you think about death?' and his face lit up like a child asked about a happy time. 'All the time' he said. He enjoyed going to Buck House for his Order of Merit medal. 'I always enjoy talking to the Queen. I talked too much of course but she was so nice.' Lucky Queen.

R. has got another cold and is red and hot and uncomfy, so has gone early to bed with hot whisky and aspirins.

[1] Poet and author (1873–1956).

24 July 1953   [London]

Virginia and Tony
WELCOME HOME to you both.
This is the only piece of paper I've got with me at the Studio,[1] where I was unexpectedly called today, so I will write small to get it all in.

R. flew off on to Messina Weds. and I did not like that. It's very horrid and it gets worse as time goes by. Pa took to being very odd for at least four days, he was very muddled and frail and we all thought . . . I asked him if he was all right (what idiotic things one says in stress!) and he opened his eyes and looked at me and said 'I love you', which of course undid me. But then yesterday he was gay and voluble.

Did you know there'd been a talk on the 3rd Prog. about C.S. by someone from the *Monitor*? I hear it was really very well done. Factual, clear and not in the least 'loving' if you see what I mean. I wonder how many un-converted heard it? I missed it on acc. I was reciting at Bedford College with C. Day Lewis.[2] Festival of Spoken English. Also reading were Michael Hordern[3] (good, specially Wordsworth), C. Day Lewis who did a beautiful new poem called 'Pegasus'. I did a lot of Betjeman and, on account of my new love, C. Day Lewis' poem to honour W. de la Mare on his 75th birthday 'Who goes there?' I didn't do it a bit well on account I was so self conscious with C.D.L. being there. In fact I broke out with anxiety.

Yesterday I went to the Buck House Garden Party with Miriam Grenfell and we enjoyed ourselves no end. Wait till you see my new pink red dress with its organza collar and cuffs. Plitty. We *just* saw the Royals and, hurrah, they saw ME. Both the Q. and Prince P. smiled most kindly, and Princess M. stepped out of the procession and greeted me most warmly. So that was very pleasing for Coronation Year 1953. Such funny people in such funny clothes. We were there for hours.

Darling, it is good to know you'll soon be back on the same island. I don't like it when my loved ones are on other bits of ground.

[1] Filming *Genevieve* at Pinewood Studios. Directed by Henry Cornelius, starring Dinah Sheridan, Kenneth More, and Kay Kendall.
[2] Left-wing poet (1904–72), then Professor of Poetry at Oxford.
[3] British actor (1911–94).

12 September 1953   Welcombe Hotel
                                                  Stratford-upon-Avon

Darling Ginnie,

We saw Peggy[1] as Portia and Michael Redgrave[2] as the Jew last night.[3] Most lovely performances both. He makes the Jew into a Golders Green refugee and it is very successful and sometimes a little moving. He don't half spit when he acts! I saw great jewelled blobs flung from his lips and noticed that Peggy stood well back in the Trial Scene. How good she is and how radiant. She looks remarkably young. Except for a new tendency to poke her head forward which somehow thickens that bit at the back and isn't young. But her voice is lovely and she moves enchantingly. Thought the production dull and sometimes a bit contrived, and didn't like the sets all the time. But it was a rich evening and we enjoyed it enormously.

Cecil Beaton[4] is here too. He is so nice and now looks like a most distinguished eighteenth century marquise. He wore a white satin tie but was otherwise discreetly furnished.

We dined in the restaurant and my fan head waiter was most welcoming and whispered 'And how is father?', and I had to say 'Well, he died I'm afraid', which wasn't quite adequate and made him feel miserable, and so I spent the rest of the time trying to make him not feel he wished he hadn't said it!

[1] Peggy Ashcroft (1907–91), British actress. Joyce and Virginia knew her when she was married to publisher Rupert Hart-Davis, whose sister Deirdre had been Joyce's bridesmaid.
[2] Michael Redgrave (1908–85), British actor. Father of actors Vanessa, Corin and Lynn.
[3] Shakespeare's *The Merchant of Venice*.
[4] British society photographer (1904–80). He had recently photographed Joyce.

1954

During 1953 Joyce and a group of colleagues had tried to put together another stage revue. Joyce had a file full of new monologues and songs with music by Richard Addinsell. But the project never took off.

A few months later, Laurier Lister approached her and suggested that he produce a show with Joyce as the main performer with a collection of her sketches and songs, and three dancers as support. During rehearsals William Blezard, the musical director, fitted in his wedding to Joan, also a musician. From 1946 until he retired in 1963, Victor Stiebel made all Joyce's stage dresses, including six for this new show. They were all beautifully styled and fitted with masses of satin, netting and corsetry in deep interesting colours. One of these creations ended up in the Victoria and Albert Museum, and another became a luxurious sofa cover in Norfolk.

Joyce Grenfell Requests the Pleasure opened well in Cambridge but Folkestone was harder work. Joyce and her theatre troupe of orchestra, stage staff, performers, costumes and props flew to Dublin somewhat nervously.

11 May [1954]   Cambridge Square

Darling Joyce,

I hope your thoughts have not been concentrated on the aching cultural void that is Folkestone? Do all the quick changes make you come out into a sweat?[1]

No sign of a parlourmaid, slightly worrying as zero day is in a week and as Mrs Westaway and Evelyn don't speak I visualise certain problems. However, what the hell!

Did you see our feeble hanky flutterings, they were a token of real friendship – rigor mortis had set in long before you rose from the ground!

[1] During the performance of eight monologues and sixteen songs, there were thirteen costume changes.

Monday, 17 May 1954. Tea time   Shelbourne Hotel
                                                                Dublin

Darling Ginnie,

Ta so much for coming all the way to Northolt [aerodrome]. We had a lovely flight full of sun, only $1\frac{1}{2}$ hrs in a Viscount. I'm feted like mad. Flowers, press conferences, the manager of the hotel offered me a party on Fri. night! (*No.*)

I'll write again more after the first night. It's a big theatre, was variety, and has very ornate boxes of an 'amusingly' Victorian style. I'll be glad when we've done it tonight. Tum is full of butterflies.

Pen refilled and the first perf. over. It was TREMENDOUS. I mean *really* big. Cheers and such warmth and enthusiasm. It's a large house and it was wonderfully full. The contrast from last week is *very* funny. £30 last Mon. £246 this, for one thing, and then all those lovely, long, well-savoured laughs. I began by feeling soggy and a bit scared, and then I shifted the whole burden and got it clear in my head just where it all came from – strength, joy, harmony, etc. After that -- whizzo!

24 May [1954]   Cambridge Square

Darling Joyce,

Laurier rang up last night & said you'd broken all records in Dublin – wow! Goody gumdrops!

The June opening in London was equally successful, heralding the beginning of Joyce's career as a solo performer. Joyce received sixty-nine telegrams and rave reviews, but even after fifteen years on the stage she was still overawed by this attention. From now until her retirement in 1973, Joyce's shows were composed of monologues and songs. The sketches were one side of a conversation told by fictional characters commenting on society, or telling a story. Joyce wrote all her own material, and apart from suggestions for improvements from Reggie or Virginia, she never used scriptwriters. She also wrote all her own songs, with music by Richard Addinsell and later by William Blezard.

<u>1955</u>

In April Nancy Astor went to visit her sister Nora and learned that Nora had cancer. Joyce was on tour with *Requests the Pleasure*.

22 April 1955   The Queen's Hotel
                                                                    Leeds

Darling Ginnie,
    The only difficult part is getting accusing letters from Aunt Nancy saying she doesn't see how I *can* not come over. That I've done 'very well by the stage manager'! (I love her grasp of the set up) and that my mother is more important. In the same breath she says the doctor is quite happy about her. What can it mean? I suppose he feels 'it's' not hurrying. Aunt N. says she *is* better and that she may get a healing. But she is *so personal* and always wants things her way. Very dual – man and God quite separate.
    I've asked R. to go and see Aunt N. and explain to her a little my obligations and the principle of the thing. She is due home early next week. But I don't believe she is capable of taking it in.
    Re Ma, I am sure I have got to stop being a person with a mother and just *being* one thing. Which is of course what she is too.

24 April [1955]   Cambridge Square

Darling Joyce,
    I think your Aunt Nancy must be getting senile. Even if you could go to Nora now – stop the show, break your contracts, let everybody down – it would be the stupidest thing to do. Nora's suspicions would be thoroughly roused, in fact she'd probably be frightened for the first time. People do make such silly suggestions. I remember one old holy telling me I must sit by Kitty's bedside & sing C.S. hymns to her! Anything more guaranteed to frighten Kitty I couldn't imagine – I mean *so* unlike me.[1]

When your tour is over, go out and be with her. That would be quite natural.

[1] Virginia's half-sister Kitty had recently died of cancer.

Joyce took Virginia's advice and flew out to America as soon as the tour was over.

31 May 1955   In the air, 11 p.m. and broad daylight

Darling Ginnie,
   You do make a difference to my life and I am so grateful to you –
and to To – for taking me to the plane and cosseting R. afterwards. It
was a very kind thing.
   I hated leaving. Low. But I'm full of gratitude for the new light
shed on C.S. for me and it's *practical*, which is so glorious. I *feel* instead
of just thinking. Even now when I don't relish the trip and leaving
and all the unknown ahead of me – I feel the certainty of Mind. Now
they are going to make up my bed and I shall get to it. More in the
morning. Love.

[May 1955]   Cambridge Square

Darling Joyce,
   More movies this week. *Children of Hiroshima*, in which I had to
shut my eyes, & *Above Us the Waves* – one of those brave pictures
about brave men in midget submarines which are becoming, alas, so
wearisome.
   There's a secret view this evening of the Marlon Brando film that has
been banned – the one about thugs taking over a town.[1]

[1] *The Wild One* was banned in Britain until 1969.

2 June 1955   Tryon

Darling Ginnie,
   Ma looks far better than I feared. Thin and a little pale but a good
colour and pretty. No grey hairs showing. The doctor's wife gave me
all the news. Apparently she is less ill than she thinks she is and the
trouble seems to be one of fear.
   I had rather dreaded arriving and seeing her, but I had done a lot
of thinking and it was taken care of quite perfectly. No emotion, no

sadness. Just nice to see each other. Even Ma only just cried! So that's to be grateful for. She is dotty about your nightie and jacket and this is her thank you I am now writing. She lies and dozes mostly, doesn't read and isn't interested much in the world.

When the C.S. prac. in N.Y. wrote that he was giving up the case it nearly killed her.[1] One sees his point – orthodoxy and all that – but it was a cruel blow. She is *so* scared of pain that she asks for pills more than are necessary.

[1] Some Christian Science practitioners will not treat patients who are also receiving medical treatment.

8 June [1955]   Cambridge Square

Darling Joyce,

Freezing here & I'm involved in a domestic crisis. Mrs Evans [cook] will have to go. She does literally nothing but cook for us – won't wash up, won't feed the boiler, & gives the maids filthy food – they had the same bit of meat hotted up for a week – otherwise tinned stuff. When we're away she just stays in bed & leaves the others to look after themselves. Her doctor, very unattractive, called yesterday & said she merely eats too much. Georgie & Evelyn are nervous wrecks, as they even have to dish up. Soon they think they will be cooking.

Reg rang up, sweet boy. We exchange your news a great deal & have complicated chats about *Wild Thyme*. We are going to see it at Golders Green next week.[1]

[1] Musical composed by Donald Swann (1923–94), designed by Ronald Searle. Reggie and Virginia each invested £200.

9 June 1955   Tryon

Darling Ginnie,

You are an old faithful. Ta. Really almost nothing to report. It just goes on. Sometimes Ma is better than others. The doctor says she is deteriorating. It isn't visible. She looks extraordinarily pretty. It is such hell for her, Gin. Whew. You've had much practice in the game of pretending. Not easy tho', is it. Ma is planning new covers for the chairs and that sort of thing. Ah me.

You know people here are wonderfully relaxed and intelligent and kind and well read and civilised. Why do we get the ideas we get about Americans? Very odd.

June [1955]   Cambridge Square

Darling Joyce,

My heart does bleed for you darling – I know it shouldn't & it doesn't help. But I know so well what you're going through. Frankly I know no other greater hell, & although you are infinitely stronger sunburst than me & can bear the strain better, I would love to be with you holding your hands – I hate you having to do all this alone. This is all very unscientific, isn't it. But human!

12 June 1955   Tryon

Darling Ginnie,

All you say is absolutely true and I couldn't care less about the medical side of the picture.

Today church was a dignified good service. We sat in the front and felt nice and un-surrounded, and Miss Capps piped away at the Bible and we sang 'O Gentle Peace' to a really terrible tune, one I've never heard or wish to hear again. I'm against new tunes to old hymns.

You know I am *amazed* at the really remarkable kindness and imagination of Ma's pals. You know Americans are *FAR* less selfish than we are. Far kinder and more constant. They go *on* doing it, too. Endlessly.

16 June [1955]   Cambridge Square

Darling Joyce,

We enjoyed *Wild Thyme*, tho' the first act drags terribly still. They have pruned and altered, but one can feel the audience drooping. The decor is so gloriously fantastic & the music so enchanting. It's a lovely evening but whether it isn't just a bit too naive, too saccharine for the cynical West End I'm not sure. Reggie was angelic. He has such a passion for the play he positively glows with amour for it, & it's a charm to watch him watching it.[1]

Hyde Park is a dream today & I strolled to Harvey Knickers for some earrings.

[1] *Wild Thyme* lasted for seven weeks, battling against a heatwave. At the end of the run Joyce did the washing-up at the wedding of Donald Swann to Janet Oxborrow.

17 June 1955   Tryon

Darling Ginnie,

Here things are improved. The doctor doesn't know if she'll still be here or not when I return in September. She might easily.

If she isn't, there it is. We've had some very good talks and I think she really is rather less scared than she was, and that is very good.

I'm remarkably free of the *mood* of the illness. I feel quite remote: which is much more useful. I really have been at least 95% free of *personal* – what? – misery? emotion? Wonderfully detached, but not heartless. Free, really. I don't believe I am ever very afraid these days. And wonderfully free of actual glooms. Sometimes a small gnaw of sadness. But never gloom as I have known it.

22 June [1955]   Cambridge Square

Darling Joyce,

Victor dined. He was tired, and broke. He worries about always living beyond his income. He'd been to the Oliviers for the weekend, driving down with Danny Kaye[1] who he says has absolutely *no* sense of humour whatsoever. Queer innit? We're being taken to see him tomorrow.

Next day

At first I thought Danny Kaye had lost something a bit, or that we'd got too accustomed to his craziness. But then the old magic began to work, & he sat on a chair embracing a mike & lulled us into enchantment. At one moment he made everybody light a match or a lighter & hold it aloft in a blacked out theatre. It was the *prettiest* thing.

[1] American comedy actor (1913–87).

26 June 1955   Tryon

Darling Ginnie,

Ta for writing so faithfully, dear pal. Makes the whole difference. I've got the radio on and now rather a good sermon is going on and the preacher has just said 'We all need a friend'. Well, I thought, I got me one! Hooray.

I thought Danny Kaye had no humour too. R. and I, with Vic, spent four hours in his room at the George V Hotel in Paris. There's another Ego! I remember Vic tried to interest him in me and my art and I performed. He barely tolerated it and didn't smile at all.

Ma is out on a chair on the terrace.

When Joyce returned to London, her mother told her, 'When I die, promise me you won't grieve. You know I'll be all right. Go to the movies and know I'll be glad you've gone.' Nora died two weeks later. Although Joyce believed intellectually that 'death is not an end, but a continuation', she still grieved.

While Joyce was in America she went to an audition in New York. Much to her surprise, the producers invited her to perform *Joyce Grenfell Requests the Pleasure* on Broadway. In September the three dancers and Richard Addinsell accompanied her, to be joined later by Reggie and Victor Stiebel.

8 September 1955   King's Road

Darling Ginnie,

Now the two trunks have gone to the hold and the bedroom looks as if a bomb had hit it. I have assembled another seven pieces! Oh one is a music case, one is for stage make up, but the others are solid luggage.

My new hats are Sensational. The pink velvet muffin is astonishing, and the black wool plate is a surprise too. R. roared with laughter at *first*, then said 'Jolly pretty'. I think they are, too. I travel in the plate.

Write a *lot*, and please cossett old R. when you can. He's wonderfully independent and seems to manage all right on his own, but I don't like the idea for him. Isn't it lovely to mind so much after 26 years. And I do – more than ever. Much more actually. So that is nice.

10 September 1955   RMS *Mauretania*

Darling Ginnie,

Lully roses here for me! The most glorious golden backed rosy pink centred beauties. Lovely. Thank you darling. And for the books. And for the compact which is in *constant* use.

The press were in force at Waterloo and I was snapped with R., with D., with Vic. D. and R., and solo. And I don't suppose any of them will ever be printed.

R. has sent me froots, and mitts and a long, dear letter saying if it is a flop in N.Y. the fault won't be mine but the failure of American appreciation! Very nice. And comforting.

The other shipmates look fairly dull as usual but they will slowly emerge as personalities no doubt as the days go by. Several solitary bien ladies with 'good' jewels and dark dresses. I'm listed as Miss so I flash my wedding ring for R's sake!

Dick is a charming companion, so solicitous and wonderfully funny too. We have laughed a lot and we plan to dance a lot!

17 September [1955]   Carlton House
                                                 New York

Darling Ginnie,

Ta for *oh* so welcome letter. When I got here yesterday morning
with all the luggage and no Mrs Gabe, no R. or you or Viola, and all
the emotion I'd gone through in this bedroom before flying back in July
leaving Ma, I had a moment of full Self Pity and blubbed. But it passed
and I tidied my face for the press!

Flowers and a bottle of champagne greeted me and it would all be
exciting if I was younger! As it is I can't wait for some more sleep and
to get the Opening over. I must say people here are nice and *kind*. All
the press I met were so *quiet*! Maybe their pens scream loudly!

N.Y. is very rushed and tiring but useful. I had a v. good session
with George Bauer, the mus. director, in his attractive garden level
apartment. He has a lovely Steinway, so we had a good go at
everything. Now that we've broken the back, as it were, we get on fast.
I like him and have confidence in his work.

Tommy and Mary were here and Sally slowly remembered her aged
aunt and said 'puppy', so that was good.

17 September [1955]   Cambridge Square

Darling Joyce,

I'm having a battle at the moment, though I am trying not to fight it,
but more relax around it. I either have anthrax, mastoids, meningitis or
toothache.

Our dinner party went off well. The young really seem to be awfully
nice these days, & oh dear how enchanting they look! Oh those unlined
faces & creamy shoulders & crisp bouffante dresses! They're a tonic. And
they seem tremendously talkative, although they haven't acquired the
art of 'turning' at dinner, so that when T & I turned we found ourselves
talking in threes. The dance after was fun, & we talked to the other
grown ups exactly like our parents used to . . . 'isn't that Margaret's
elder boy?' . . . 'she isn't a patch on her mother' etc.

It is very peculiar but we have all felt you were leaving for Siberia to
do a stint in the salt mines! When really you're going to glory and a fat
Hollywood contract!

29 September 1955

Hotel Laurelton
West 55th
New York

Darling Ginnie,

We had another run-through today (*and* tomorrow). You see the poor locals have to learn the show and it takes time. Today was gloom day. No reason. It just was. Routine repeats get very hard to do with no comeback from the house.

Oh thank God for Dick! He is an absolute *pillar*. So unselfed, so *kind*, so cosy and so wonderfully funny. In fact, the perfect person for this experience. Close, but apart: involved, but clear seeing. And I am very grateful to him and FOR him. He's been an angel to me.

After supper we all watched the *$64,000 Question* on T.V. This week a grandmother called Myrtle, aged 74, answered questions about baseball and won $32,000! She was very endearing. Face like a dried prune and a southern accent. She was absolutely natural and relaxed: not cocksure or showing off. You loved her and pined for her to win. Next week she will decide whether to try for the $64,000 or keep her $32,000. If she risks the final question and fails she loses *all* but gets a 1955 Cadillac consolation prize! Hope she'll stick at $32,000.

I just made a wonderful discovery when I went to try on my new period satin slippers for 'Coteley'. They have long, thin toes and low Louis heels. You know the sort. And *somehow – someone – somewhere* has equipped them with little steel taps, so I can tap dance in them! I long to know how that happened.

Cecil Beaton has sent me two very nice pictures he took of me in the summer. As a first night present. Kind.

3 October 1955

Bijou Theatre
Broadway
New York

Darling Ginnie,

A long drawn out dress-cum-lighting rehearsal.

The stage is a mess of hammering men and electrics with miles of wires. For a progressive country this system of lighting cum dress rehearsing is archaic. In Eng. we do it separately *first*. Then put it all together. But it's so expensive here they have to do it all at once. I feel sure it will all work out in the same price in the end because it must take the same long time in the end.

I'm working on a revised version of 'Travel Broadens the Mind' – the ENSA girl, remember?[1] I've turned her into an entertainer of occupying forces all over the world, kept in most of the jokes and cut out all local references and war time specialities. It always was a funny sketch and it may be a good idea. Half the people I meet – the ones I love – say don't change too much, don't broaden, don't underestimate N.Y. audiences. Half are fearful creatures who say you must HIT hard here. Now I must stop and make up my pore ole face.

¹Written in 1945 for *Sigh No More*.

8 October [1955]   Cambridge Square

Darling Joyce,
    With ALL of you loved ones away, nobody needs cosseting. In a way I'm rather envious of everybody being 'in' on the big night & sharing in your triumph. On the other hand a distant view has its enchantments too, I feel more relaxed and therefore probably more helpful.

11 October 1955   Hotel Laurelton

Darling Ginnie,
    Well, it was quite an evening. I'd spent the day very quietly. A solitary totter to Central Park, where I was picked up! But I soon put an end to that.
    At the theatre there were mountains of cables and a forest of flowers from all sorts of surprising people I don't know. Flowers too from you, from Joyce Carey, Noël [Coward], Mary Martin,¹ Oscar and Dorothy Hammerstein,² Mr Allan of Jacqmar, telegrams from Cecil Beaton and Princess Margaret! Max [Adrian] flew over at the invitation of millionaire friends!
    From the word go tremendous warmth. The place full of pals but they couldn't have accounted for the length and quality of the sustained applause when I came on. It was *for ever*! Didn't know how to stop it – paced about smiling. 'Three Bros.' my biggest moment I think. They loved 'Songs my Mother taught me'. They laughed at all the monologues but I don't know which was the best. The dances went *very* well.
    I was calm as a pool and *wonderfully* free. Thanks be to God. The general view is that I did it all right. I wished Ma could have been there – in a way I felt she was. It really was a huge ovation with a roar of cheers through it. Amazing. People seemed pleased. Those who saw it in London say it is 100% improved. I think they are right.

Darling, *much* to be grateful for. How I loved your and To's
superb cable: 'Bijou Good or Bijou Bad We Love You'. Thank you for
everything. More sensible letter in a day or two. Much love.

[1] Texan musical comedy star (1913–90).
[2] American lyricist of stage musicals with Richard Rodgers (1895–1960), notably *The Sound
of Music*.

13 October [1955]   Cambridge Square

Joyce Darling,
   I *am* glad you had such a happy relaxed evening. The glass seems
set very fair now, & I must resign myself to not seeing you for at least
six months, damn you. It really sounds a most glorious occasion. Victor
said you had never in your life been better – nor had the dancers – &
that from first to last it went uproariously well. You *brilliant* old thing.
   I had a hectic evening too – everyone rang up. All delighted of
course, even your Aunt Nancy saying she thought it was the bravest
thing *ever*. She went on to say she couldn't understand your attitude
about Nora as you didn't seem to miss her & *she* missed her desperately
– to which I replied that you did miss her, particularly her letters. She
seemed pleased!! She was then very funny telling me she was off to
Cumberland to unveil a plaque to George Washington's *grandmother*!
'What are you going to say?' I asked. 'Can't imagine, except that I wish
she'd lived nearer London!'
   She was sucking a toffee & in a gay mood, & she was *genuinely*
happy about you.
   Fancy a wire from P. Margaret! We are still waiting for what must
be an 'announcement', Mr Townsend having called at Clarence House
yesterday & stayed two hours. Photos of the Princess looking radiant &
pages of the life of the hero.[1]

[1] Princess Margaret had to decide whether to accept Group Captain Peter Townsend's
proposal of marriage.

14 October 1955   Hotel Laurelton

Darling Ginnie,
   Alistair Cooke wants me for his *Omnibus* Sunday T.V., but I say No
to all things that involve time and work. Guest appearances are easy
but *Omnibus* is a huge rehearsed thing seen by 14 million and I couldn't
spare a Sunday. Nice being asked tho'.

The idea is that if we do make a success, then at the end of it we do a T.V. 'Spectacular'. This is an hour and a half show which pays vast sums and then clears off all costs and leaves us all rich. So we are therefore not going to do any small T.V. – as yet.

The audiences are absolutely amazing. I hate – loathe – loathe – *mind* saying it, but – sh. sh. – they are better, subtler, quicker than at home. Isn't it bloody of them. Every flick of the eyelash, every little nuance, is detected and responded to.

This is the noisiest and most irritating city in the world. Drivers just lean on their horns and these are of a piercing loudness. It does get me down a bit and I can see one has got to be clear and keep quiet to cope. To withdraw in fact.

R. says the worst part of N.Y. is the newspapers. A hundred pages a day and printed in loose black ink that leaves the hands pot black. The theatre page is always difficult so you can never find it – or anything else.

I'm fighting – no I'm not, I'm *overcoming* homesickness. R's departure is probably Nov. 1st, so you will get your birthday pres. a day late. I wish I was going home too. But you know me. Inside I'm secure as a rock and full of gratitude. Just surface ruffles of sadness you know. But I'm o.k.

R. is busy as a bee seeing brokers and taxmen for me and doing chores generally. He is an angel. He even bought me a hat we saw in an advertisement from Lord & Taylor!

15 October [1955]   Cambridge Square

Darling Joyce,

I shudder to think what your papers are saying about Princess M. Today everyone's very restrained. I feel so sorry for the Queen, for it has got such a Windsorish smack to it – such a kick in the pants for the Throne & the Church. We were all plunged into gloom yesterday. I suppose there'll be a great sentimental surge up to the wedding – & where is that to be for heaven's sake, & can the Queen go to it? – & then a big fade-out. Oh dear.

Our opera evening was so dreary & boring we left at the interval, only to find the car had disappeared! So we pogged off to Bow Street, & they broadcast the number – rather fascinating – & then somehow discovered that the police had moved it because it was in the way! And there it was, 50 yards away from where we'd left it!

I am polishing up my bottom to sit it on your growing head.

21 October 1955   Hotel Laurelton

Darling Ginnie,

Cooler and sharper and nicer. Yesterday Noël [Coward] asked me and the dancers, and I took R. and Tommy (Mary was baby sitting), to see the run through of his big spectacular Ford T.V. Show with Mary Martin. Ninety minutes of it! He's done three new numbers, all good. The first, which they sing in dressing gowns outside their dressing room doors, is called 'Ninety minutes is a long long time'. It is repeated two or three times later. Then there is a pretty song called 'Together to Music'.

And he's done a terrible one for himself – 'What will happen to the Children when there aren't any more Grown-ups?' All about people being injected and doped and kept young. Not a very pretty idea but it's fast and fearful and, of course, done by him it's jolly funny. He does 'Mad Dogs', a medley of his own songs, and a *superb* medley of old songs. Mary is superb. Voice rings out and she can do *anything* with it.

All in all a most skilful programme, brilliantly polished and rich in vitamins. I was proud for old Eng. with Noël, but I swear I don't see how anyone in Nebraska, Kentucky or Omaha will understand *anything* he says. No concessions made. All of it high satire and of course done to perfection.

When I went to buy my evening paper from Gaston in the hotel newsstand he said 'God is right out there enjoying you too'. I said tentatively 'Are you interested in such things', and he said 'Sure, I'm a C.S. Look'. And he opened a little cupboard behind a stand of cigarettes and showed me all the works of M.B.E. [Mary Baker Eddy]. He has a dear face. I'm so glad he's here. I must say the C.Ss here shine out with their inner peace.

Papers here full of Meg and Peter. Wish they'd decide. Sad whatever they do. Poor girl.

Church here is *so* smart. Jewel coloured velvet hats and mink in the million.

You needn't practise sitting on my head, it's not one bit affected I swear. It's all so silly.

26 October 1955   Hotel Laurelton

Darling Ginnie,

R. and I. and D. had a conference with my agent Joe Magee about what I was going to do. The answer was Nothing – no Cabaret, T.V. or Sunday Shows! Except, of course, Mr Ed Sullivan, whose show is a MUST and he loves me, so on Nov. 20th, both I and the three dancers are on. In confidence the sum is 5,000 dollars for us all. This is *small* but it's our first T.V. here! I get two-thirds of this, so I'll hope to do some shopping for Christmas, and even if you get it late you'll get a gorgeous gifte via Ed. Sullivan and me. Now what would you like? A glorious set of super nylon underwear? Stockings by the gross? White nylon gloves? Records? *What?* Tell me, pretty maiden, and I will do my best.

28 October [1955]   Cambridge Square

Darling Joyce,

I've had a terribly social day – ladies luncheon party. Then off to cosy drinks with Mary Roxburgh.[1] Turned out to be a vast cocktail party with an extraordinary assembly ranging from Gilbert Harding[2] to the Duke of Argyll.[3] We reeled back to dinner. Perhaps from too much gin, poor Tony turned ashy after dinner & nearly fainted.

Feelings are quite violent about Townsend, some saying that the moment he fell in love with P.M. he should have disappeared for good; or that at least a grand gesture of renunciation would have been appropriate. Others say he is a cad.

In the meantime we wait while SHE goes to see the Archbish & HE goes shopping. The Press is pretty awful. They (the unhappy couple) dined chez Jennifer[4] & when they came out they found searchlights had been rigged up in the street. It's lamentable.

I know you will disapprove, but I'm translating another book – the memoirs of Albert Prijeau, the French film star. Very light & pleasant & not nearly so difficult to translate as the last one.[5]

I should *adore* for Ed Sullivan & you to give me a nylon slip! Wow!

[1] Mary, Duchess of Roxburgh (1915–), Virginia's neighbour.
[2] Television personality (1907–60).
[3] 11th Duke (1903–73).
[4] Jennifer Lowther, Princess Margaret's first lady-in-waiting.
[5] Virginia was fluent in French and translated several books.

Princess Margaret decided to put duty to her country, Church and the Common-wealth before her love for Townsend, and announced that she was not going to marry him.

2 November [1955]   Cambridge Square

Darling Joyce,

Feelings about Princess M are very mixed here – including mine – but she is undoubtedly the heroine of the hour, & I feel all the tributes being laid at her feet must be a comfort to her. It is so amazing nowadays to find someone *not* doing what they want to do that one really does feel morally strengthened. And certainly the girl has come into a very different category of person. On the other hand, it does seem dreadfully cruel & inhuman. The Beaverbrook press, of course, is whipping up an anti-Monarchy anti-Church campaign – *vile* it is. One feels that the example of someone putting duty above love must be beneficial. In the meantime we feel emotional & sad – which is more than Mr Townsend *looks*. Very jolly & smiling he is today & to rumours that he is too upset to speak he says 'What rot!'

5 November 1955   Hotel Laurelton

Darling Ginnie,

I saw Edith Piaf;[1] she is absolutely wonderful and I know just what you mean about the wonderful feeling of seeing something perfectly done. She is rather dumpy and small, wears a plain black day dress. And her charm and her magic and her way with a song defy pen and paper. It was very exciting to see her do exactly what she wanted with a heavy load of drinking business men and dim suburban types. She is not at a smart place but rather a shoddy very expensive one. But she was above it all and a real treat.

At tea today – high tea, that is – a complete Jewish wedding came into the restaurant. Bride and groom, two grown-up bride's maids and two little girls in apricot, one matron of honour in green, and three ushers and a best man. *No* parents or outsiders. The bride in full white satin and he in a white tie. My eyes popped. They sat there among the public drinking highballs and toying with *celery*, waiting for the main meal. Somehow it was dreadfully sad and cost so much I feel!

[1] French cabaret singer (1912–63).

5 November [1955]   Cambridge Square

Darling Joyce,

You must be ABSOLUTELY MAD! A whole PILE of grammy records, each more exciting than the last!!! You seemed to have lost your head completely, which couldn't be more delightful. I really couldn't believe my eyes last night, when Reggie staggered in with all those offerings.

Reg was bonny – & it was lovely to see him fresh, as it were, from you.

I have to go & quack to ladies about *Waiting for Godot*.[1] In *Punch* there was a drawing of the usual London No Parking sign which read NO WAITING NOT EVEN FOR GODOT.

Good grief, I must go to the movies!!

¹Play written by Samuel Becket in 1953, which had just had its first performance in London.

Sunday, 13 November 1955   Hotel Laurelton

Darling Ginnie,

Sundays *should* be spacious but this one has had Ed Sullivan's show and so no time. It is a very pop, *the* most pop TV prog. from 8 – 9 on Sundays – estimated viewers 50 *millions*. Not all tonight. Some, as in Canada, see it transcribed later, so do other places here. Tonight it had Edith Piaf on first singing her great heart throb 'If the stars would only cry' – or some such. Then a long commercial about Mercury cars. Then me in the opening dress doing the opening – *slightly* cut. Then the dancers in a pretty, new finale with very gay music: then me back in me green silk to do 'The Nursery School'. When I'd gone off – after a call back – Ed said 'That is the most charming actress we've ever had on Broadway'. He gave the show a boost. Everyone *delighted*. After me a negro singer (blind I think) sang 'Unchained Melody',¹ then a ventriloquist from Manchester. And finally a college choir from Indiana – very good, indeed superb.

It's *the* top tourist attraction in N.Y. and they let the public in to watch rehearsals all day long in relays. I came home as soon as it was over and thought how funny it was, here I am, being what is known as a Great Success on Broadway, just appeared on The Top TV programme, for which I was paid 3,000 dollars (£900!) – there was I walking up Broadway, going to make myself a cup of hot choc on a primus stove in a hotel bathroom, when all the world expect I've gone boozing with rich admirers! I *was* asked to go to three places afterwards. But the lure of me rest was strong.

I dote on Sally. She's really edible – so pink and white and *so* funny and so independent, and already a character.

¹Probably Ray Charles (1930–) 'Unchained Melody' had been released in May by Al Hibbler (1915–), and was in the US charts for seventeen weeks.

15 November 1955   Hotel Laurelton

Darling Ginnie,

Today I was on a panel game called *Make up your Mind*. A situation is presented and a panel gives its views on the line to take. 'If your husband was a gambler and gave you the money to place but you never did, saying when he lost and paying out when he won, so you got enough money together to buy the home you both desired – would you tell him how you'd done it or not?' I said I wouldn't have married him in the first place. Consternation. 'What sort of man would I have married?' I told them what sort of man I had married and it was all thought to be so bright and witty! *Really.* We were sponsored by a maker of Cup Cakes! I loved the grand trade language of the producer – 'You can angle the question to reveal your view point' etc.

3 December 1955   Hotel Laurelton

Darling Ginnie,
    Well here we are, last day – sold out – rather gala and a good way to finish. New York is furious at our finish and say it's a disgrace that quality isn't widely appreciated, etc. All very comforting to the ego!
    The tour is probably *not* on. With the get-out costs of about $18,000 a week and me unknown it is not very likely to work. I'll stay on for T.V. so, Look out – I'll be home soon after Xmas!!!
    Next week is my hols. – I've got three theatres and two parties arranged and I feel as if I'd been let out of school.
    I am writing this in a shoe shop waiting for a pair of white satin shoes to be dyed. Prompt work! (Black.)

12 December [1955]   Cambridge Square

Darling Joyce,
    Your last night sounds tremendous – a lovely way to end. In fact you began & ended with a colossal bang, dinner yer?
    Personally I think it is jolly well time you came HOME, you silly old thing. I've hardly got time to do a petit point mat with WELCOME on it, but I intend painting it in lipstick on my tummy & laying down in the King's Road.
    I rather envy you seeing New York at Noel. I've always been told it is out of this world, & I shall think of you clapping your little woolly gloves together at the sight of all those fairy lights.
    Look after yo'self, darling, & don't be blue.

13 December 1955   Hotel Laurelton

Darling Ginnie,
    The T.V. on Sun. went well and I was in Saks yesterday and got recognised all over the shop. Last night I ushed at the Gala Premiere for

the Actors Studio Fund and mixed nonchalantly with Marilyn Monroe, Joan Crawford, Marlon Brando (tiny and pale), and Leslie Caron, etc. etc. Amusing to be a looker-on but very noisy and crowded, and not a very spiritually minded group!

I saw *Chalk Garden* with Tommy and Mary. It's an enchanting, dotty, non sequitur play.[1] I think you'd love it. Cecil Beaton's set is exquisite – a house in Sussex. Absolutely perfect. Gladys Cooper[2] plays over life size and without *much* wit but full of vitality, and it comes off. A happy theatre evening.

Darling, I AM COMING HOME. Ed is having us four again either Jan. 8th or 15th, and then it's me for the high seas. Very high no doubt in jolly January. Can't wait.

[1] By Enid Bagnold, English writer (1889–1981), author of *National Velvet*.
[2] Gladys Cooper (1888–1971), English actress. Created a Dame in 1967.

16 December [1955]   Cambridge Square

Darling Joyce,
THE most superb nighties have just arrived. I have NEVER felt anything like them. I want to lie down & bury my head in them & retire in them for the whole winter. I wrote m' film review with one hand stroking their softness. They're like sort of voluptuous bunnies, & I simply can't wait to go to bed. THANK YOU.

And Darling! You must think me quite poggle for not mentioning the piece de resistance among your Xmas gifties – your grammy record. I've played it a dozen times, & oh how good it is! Darling, I never thought your voice could improve, but it seems to have – higher range & a tremendous professional patina which enhances but does not disguise your natural charm. The first time I played it my eyebrows shot up to the top of my head & stayed there. Brought you right bang slap into the room, which was both agreeable & terrible.[1]

[1] From 1953 until her retirement, Joyce took weekly singing lessons.

26 December 1955   Hotel Laurelton

Darling Ginnie,
Wasn't our non-telephoning frustrating. Oh well. This letter won't make much sense for I've written actually twenty letters this evening. Christmas you see. Whew.

I went to see Cecil Beaton in his flat in the Ambassador Hotel. He did it up for the hotel and in return sleeps there when he is in N.Y. Rather too much, but pretty. Blue roses on everything, floor, ceiling, walls, beds and lamps! His living room white and black, with velvet cushions in reds, pinks, oranges. It's large and light so not too bad!

Early supper with Tommy and Mary. Sally in pyjamas awed by her toy donkey on wheels. She was quivering with delight and touched it very lightly. And said ooh. I adore her.

I heard the Queen and thought of you. I blubbed at the sound of Big Ben!

1956

The year began with a 'pea-souper' fog, one of the last to smother London after the Clean Air Act banned coal and wood fires.

4 January [1956]   Cambridge Square

Darling Joyce,

'I've nothing new to tell you, the fog goes drifting by . . .'[1] Yes, it's foggy, & groups of high-minded volunteers have been pacing the streets with Geiger counters, to see what dire chemical content the fog contains. The joke is that the City, which is a smokeless zone, is far worse than anywhere else!

We go to Omlet tonight. I hope we don't have to walk there.

[1] 'There is nothing new to tell you, I've said it all before', song written by Joyce in 1943.

7 January 1956   Hotel Laurelton

Darling Ginnie,

At 8.45 a.m. Leonora rang.[1] She talked till 9.30 and I swear I only said 'Oh' 'really' 'well' 'I'm quite sure'. It was highly entertaining, very scandalous, dangerous, witty, wicked and not above egotism. The start of it was an invitation to a tiny dinner of ten for the Windsors the night before I sail. The answer was No. The Abdication was a long time ago, but I just couldn't. I'm too patriotic.[2]

I lay limply till it was over. At first it was fun and I was amused by the wickedness and slight of tongue, but then it got out of control and I was simply the wastepaper basket into which she was pouring and I felt a bit tarnished. But she *is* funny, and she is dangerous, and I'd rather have her on my side than on the one opposite. For ridicule is a deadly weapon. Oh, she said, she was *very* relieved that Noël was using Lauren

Bacall as Slavia in his spectacular T.V. production of *Blithe Spirit* on Sat. because she was *deadly*.[3] She'd dreaded it might be Lucille Ball who *is* good.[4] Leonora said she was glad Noël hadn't offered her the part again as she knew she couldn't ever have been as good as everyone said she was then – 'No one could have been' – and that she knew when to stop. Which wasn't true of her conversation this morning. She also said 'I told Ed. Sullivan you were madly in love with him and warned his wife that tall cool English women were *very* dangerous!' As Ed. takes things pretty seriously I must be *very* stately indeed tomorrow!

[1] Leonora Corbett (1907–60) was a British film actress famous in the 1930s.
[2] The Duke and Duchess of Windsor often visited New York.
[3] CBS television production starred Noël Coward who described Lauren Bacall (1924–) as 'perfect'.
[4] American comedian (1911–89).

7 January [1956]   Cambridge Square

Darling Joyce,

We have just returned from a most unexpected ordeal – the Harrods Sale! Forgot it was on, but were determined to press on – I don't know how many old ladies I have stamped underfoot or how many Gent's macs I have torn off their hangers. We are absolutely bruised and panting now.

Winifred[1] came to lunch with Joyce [Carey] and talked about the fish she keeps in two shallow pools. 'We found they *must* have shade,' she said, & then, 'so now we've made a HUGE erection *covered* in everlasting pea!' There was a moment of staggered & silent horror!

Vic came to dinner and spent his time dissecting Dick's character, which he did with an objectivity which was rather frightening. To an outsider he might have been describing an enemy, & indeed I've often thought theirs is a sort of love–hate relationship. Tony got rather irritated (suppressed of course) for he has a nice healthy disdain for neuroses, & he doesn't think Dick ought to be quite so 'difficult' as he is. Nor Vic either. I think if he had his way he'd smack both their bottoms good & hard!

[1] Winifred Ashton, alias the writer Clemence Dane (1885–1965).

17 January 1956   Hotel Laurelton

Darling Ginnie,

Hi. Now the final rush is on and I am panic stricken. I came here with six pieces of luggage. I return with twelve!!! One whole box full of books and pictures. It is ghastly to contemplate.

Last night George Bauer, pianist, took me to Birdland where we stayed thirty minutes in reverent attention to the rest of the fans listening to very hot and very wonderful brassy jazz. It's a smallish cellar and the noise is terrific. We then went on down to the village and attended the Bon Soir. But wasn't good. Pity. Terribly noisy there too. Bed at two. Whew.

It's funny about Vic talking so about Dick, for I always think Vic is the real problem and the real neurotic. Oh D. is in a way but basically he is secure, whereas basically I always feel Vic is a bit not.

I'll be home in a minute. Cor. So much to do for the last 24 hours, so forgive telegraphese. I've shopped and seen taxmen and bank and coped with packing and telephoned kind friends and written thank you's and I'm dizzy. I look forward to the boat and rest.

JAN 18 AM 11 1956   HYDE PARK LONDON

JOYCE GRENFELL SS QUEEN MARY
COME ON BUCK UP HURRY ALONG DONT KEEP US WAITING LIKE
THIS   GIN

18 July 1956   King's Road

Darling Ginnie,

Lord's was rained off, so loads of Grenfells came to tea.[1] Hilda was wearing a mauve scarf, red straw hat, green dress, and another green jacket, and spent her time sitting on a sofa hemming some net curtains for a bathroom! Eccentrics add flavour. The whole handwork came in a crumpled carrier bag and, of course, within five minutes at least two guests were doing the job for her.

I'm meeting my little deaf old man (the one who fell down) at a bus stop near Regent's Park on Weds. afternoon for a little sit in the Park. He doesn't want a drive.

Fine for the party in Onslow Gardens. It was a slightly Eng. Lit. and Art party. I talked to Alec Waugh[2] and John Nash.[3] R. talked to Peter Ustinov's father and loved him. He is four foot high and bonny. The garden had Japanese lanterns and evening primroses and was quite enchanting with a little discreet flood lighting in bushes. Home by twelve. Very civilised.

[1] Every year Reggie's father hired a horse-drawn coach (minus horse) at Lord's and assembled his family with picnics to watch the Eton versus Harrow school cricket match – part of the 'social season'. Most male Grenfells went to Eton.
[2] Novelist and travel writer (1898–1981), brother of Evelyn.
[3] Painter and war artist, member of the London Group in 1913 (1893–1977). Brother of Paul Nash.

28 August 1956   King's Road

Darling Ginnie,

Let's skip the weather, hein? Ectually it is quite bright today with a
little gusty zephyr or two, but not SAFE.

Yesterday I filmed.[1] The morning went by slowly with some
crossword and feet up.

After lunch we were shot and shot and shot. It was gruelling. A most
difficult, sort of slapstick scene in which Lady Paulet, if you please, sits
on a cream cake! Reactions, laughter, the lot. Spontaneous laughter to
the point of helplessness is *very* hard to do. I got sort of hysterical with
tiredness and I can but hope that helped. It was a *long* scene with about
five different angle shots, many close-up. They called the extra hour and
I crawled home at 8.15.

August 29th, 1956

I write from the Studio where I arrived at 8 a.m. I was in the first
shot at 9, since when I have read *The Times* from A to Z, done all I can
(threequarters) of the crossword, and now I'm writing to yew.

Yesterday was recovery day from a real battering on Mon. All that
spontaneous laughing – I told you. My fan came to tea. Carole is a very
attractive, intelligent Jewish girl, with stage and T.V. ambitions. She has
real talent for mimicry and observation and can talk exactly like *me* for
one. Horrifying. And of course all her form, and staff and her mother's
friends. I met her when she interviewed me for a Younger Generation
radio prog. at the St Martin's about two or three years ago. She has a
very nice and rather remarkable mum who runs the sweet shop and
stationery near Shepherd's Bush and who has brought the girl up
wonderfully well. She has no accent of any sort, which is remarkable
since she is at a public school in W.14. She's just passed G.C.E. very
well. Age 17.[2]

Yesterday's tea was entirely taken up with deciding what she
should do if she goes in for an audition, so I was shown all the
voices and characters she can do, and they are apparently quite
endless.

This morning an extra told me her husband hadn't had a
bath for over two years. 'But,' she said, 'he's clean with it.' She's
never been in love with him but 'we rub along all right – I like
a quiet life'. She talks of him in the most frighteningly remote
way as if she saw him outlined but didn't bother beyond that.
The things people tell one! Really. I listened to her and a picture
of her married life formed in my mind and is so awful and so
bleak that I feel I'm reading one of those awful novels you think I
never read.

later

Since lunch we've been seen in close up in a theatre box on the first
night of the *Good Companions* London production, John le Mesurier[3] and
me in one, and next door Ralph Truman[4] and a blonde. She is said to
have been a telephonist at the B.B.C. and I'm afraid it is all too possible.

Aunt Nancy rang up yesterday. She was very funny and rather
wicked about her relations. I said 'You sound in good form', and she
said 'Oh I am *much* better' and paused, then 'You know what's wrong
with me? I'm just *mean*.' And she roared with laughter.

[1] *The Good Companions*, based on the novel by J.B. Priestley (1894–1984).
[2] Carole become a successful character voice-over and comedy actress known as Cass Allen.
[3] British actor (1912–83).
[4] British stage actor (1900–77).

After ten years living over a sweet shop in King's Road, Joyce and Reggie found a
new home in Chelsea. The large Victorian family houses of Elm Park Gardens had
been converted by the council into modern flats. The Grenfells rented a spacious
top-floor flat, with an attic study. Overlooking plane trees and tennis courts, they
lived there for the rest of their lives.

Joyce and Reggie returned to the USA for three more Ed Sullivan shows and a
five week concert tour.

Saturday, 22 September 1956   Cunard Line – RMS *Mauretania*

Darling Ginnie,

It's been very rough. The boredom of a rocking ship makes me cross.
One has no control over it and being rolled from side to side in the
bunk, willy nilly, is faintly irritating.

At the movie yesterday, when the storm was at its height, there was
a resounding broadside crash from a giant mountain wave and *all* the
chairs, except the back row where R. and I were sitting, fell over in the
same direction slowly spilling the audience in heaps.

R. has been robust throughout eating caviar and grouse and
generally enjoying the luxury. He's like a small boy about it all. Never
misses his 11 o'clock broth, reads the sheets avidly, and goes on
explores to report back to me the news and views.

There is a party of Russians – peasant types with little wooden
children in thick knitted stockings and round heads, there are five R.C.
priests who seem to be smoking cigars made from camel dung – whew,
and a party of six unattached elderly ladies who sit near us and delight
us. They talk cooking and clothes and the weather and are nice to each
other and funny to our ears, and I love them.

24 September [1956]   Cambridge Square

Darling Joyce,

The decor for our new flat is coming on. The 'den' is going to have Aubusson-blue curtains with lime green walls(!) – my invention – We've decided on an extraordinary pale sheeny salmonish pink for the hall walls, a lemon yellow carpet, & some reds for the chairs.

Had to leave the sunshine & go & see quite a good French film. But oh, how did I ever do this for 10 years? After last week's lot I came to the conclusion that if the entire national press went down on its knees & asked me to be a film critic again I'd say NO!

Liberace[1] appeared on our shores wearing a tweed suit threaded with gold. He has now gone to Paris where a wasp has stung his throat.

[1] Wladziu Valentino Liberace (1919–87), American pianist noted for his extravagant clothes and decor.

28 September 1956   Hotel Laurelton
                                                       New York

Darling Ginnie,

Mary is *enormous*. She wants me to be with her when the baby comes so I only hope it is punctual. She kinder feels close to me and needs a female hand at the crucial time. My niece Sally *heavenly*.

Afternoon with Ed. Sullivan and I'm to do the new Little Talk about Not Eating Eggs. He was most friendly and warm to me and we talked of integrity. I heard him say 'I'll call my lawyer' into the telephone, over Orson Welles who it seems owes him two or three programmes that he was paid in advance because he couldn't pay his Income Tax. It is such a fantastic world all that.

Opposite our room about a block away is a huge building full of studios and flats, and I can watch ballet dancers and singers and pianists and a huge white kitchen full of chefs.

My Fair Lady[1] is superb. I feared it couldn't be after all we'd heard, but by golly it is. We had a heavenly time. It was Julie Andrews' 21st birthday, so we were asked by her ma who was in our row and who I knew in London (war time B.B.C.) to go backstage and have a piece of her cake. The girl is so pretty, so unspoilt and so good. Rex Harrison[2] is so brilliant and so cocksure that it rubbed me the wrong way, but there is no denying his talent. We really had a huge evening of delight.

[1] By Lowe and Lerner, adapted from Shaw's play, *Pygmalion*, starring Julie Andrews (1935–) First performed in March 1956.
[2] British actor who could not sing so spoke his songs (1908–90).

11 October 1956   Hotel Laurelton

Darling Ginnie,

Mary has had a son. He is very large, 7 lbs. 11 ozs., and was
most elegantly rosy, not red, with large ears like my dear Pa,
very wide apart eyes and a wide smile! All this at ten minutes
old. I'd never been in on a birth so closely before and it really
is a most remarkable business. Very miraculous really. I was
with M. for all the prelim. labour and found it very interesting.
'Sometimes beautiful, always erroneous!' She had a toughish time
but it was only 2^12 hours actual labour, tho' she swears *never
ever* again. The boy is to be Thomas Langhorne[1] Phipps. Lang
I expect.

Maggy Sullivan did a spectacular disappearing act the day
she was due to do a play on T.V. Radio and press had it and a
breakdown was feared. Now a statement to say she felt she was
not right for the part, says she *told* the director she couldn't return
and meant it! Whether she'll be sued by C.B.S. is still not known.
Oh dear, what a mess egotism lands one in. For sheer selfishness
that sort of behaviour takes the bun. The show was of course
cancelled.

[1] Langhorne was the surname of the maternal grandfather of Tommy and Joyce.

21 October [1956]   Cambridge Square

Darling Joyce,

We went to Manchester on Wednesday & saw *Nude with
Violin* which was not very good I fear.[1] Quite pleasant & mildly
entertaining until the end when it sags dreadfully. Joycie [Carey]
is excellent, Sir John [Gielgud] all wrong somehow – not that
it is quite his fault. It's just that the worldly-wise valet is no
longer a character one can believe in – besides being rather
suspect. We implored Joycie to have lines removed. He says
he was imprisoned for 'an offence unspecified' – twice. There
aren't enough good jokes & it's old fashioned, but Noël can't
actually write a bad play & in a gentle way I enjoyed myself. Tony
didn't. Manchester was blazing in the sun, but looked hideous of
course.

Victor's new 'Under £5' dresses are selling well. He says
it's like cricket scores – the latest score is placed on his table
at intervals! About 3,000 so far & the big stores haven't got
going yet.[2]

A lot of excited speculation here about Poland & Hungary. It's rather wonderful how you really can't abuse people for more than a certain time, & we're all full of admiration but are perhaps veering towards over-optimism, & tend to think they have come over to us, which of course they haven't.[3]

[1] Noël Coward's latest play was on a pre-London tour. Directed by and starred John Gielgud.
[2] Stiebel had left Jacqmar and opened his own couture house.
[3] The Soviet army had just invaded Hungary after the Budapest uprising. By mid-December 11,000 Hungarian refugees had arrived in the U.K. Virginia helped the WVS run the national relief appeal.

27 October 1956   Hotel Laurelton

Darling Ginnie,
    I'm on Ed's tele show tonight with Elvis Presley. Never seen him and only just heard of him. Have you? *The* teenagers' idol. Sings rock'n'roll and wears sideburns.[1]

[1] Elvis Presley arrived in a white Thunderbird car which became covered in pink lipstick kisses. Joyce found him 'a pasty faced plump roly-poly boy, a good singer of his sort of hill-billy songs'. Presley called Joyce both 'Ma'am' and 'Honey'. As a contrast to Presley, Ed Sullivan invited Joyce to perform the song she wrote with Richard Addinsell about a privileged upper-class woman, 'The Countess of Coteley'.

31 October [1956]   Cambridge Square

Darling Joyce,
    Your itinerary appalls me!
    The world news is so dire & so complicated, not to mention frightening, it is hard not to be in a bit of a gloom.
    Tony is being wonderfully blimpish – he is so convinced that neither England nor the Conservative Party can do wrong – & he is all for us occupying the Canal Zone (which I imagine we are doing at this very minute) & to hell with UNO. He may be right, but I can't see how we can avoid becoming bloodily involved. And if we're going to mow people down in Port Said I can't see we're much different from the Russians in Budapest.[1]

[1] President Nasser of Egypt (1918–70) had just nationalised the Suez Canal Company, which had been owned by British and French shareholders. British Prime Minister Sir Anthony Eden (1897–1977) had ordered British and French forces to occupy the Suez Canal without consulting the USA. This was condemned by the United Nations and many Britons.

216

Joyce Grenfell Requests the Pleasure had been the last show Joyce did with other performers – apart from a pianist. From now on her career was as a solo actress.
The stage requirements of Joyce's 1956 US concert tour asked for:

Grand Piano (STEINWAY preferred), stage right, *MUST* be properly tuned on day of performance.
Lights should be focused to give the stage a warm, overall light. (Use flesh *pink* gelatins, *NO AMBER*.)
IMPORTANT
Please make arrangements to have a qualified woman available *at least two hours* prior to performance to press Miss Grenfell's four gowns.

A sketch shows the positions on the stage of the grand piano, prop table, decorative chair 'high enough for Miss Grenfell to lean on if sitting on it back to front', pouffe and hat stand.

1 November 1956   Actually at Ann Arbor
                                                              Michigan

Darling Ginnie,
    Briefly. Left N.Y. Monday to Atlanta. Was met by a T.V. news reel camera, two reporters and a still photographer. Sat in strip lit airport smiling rather too long.
    Next day, Tues, I was faced with a prog. that was laughable in its demands, but I did it, praying and surviving perfectly. Between 9 and 1 I was on five T.V. programmes as guest, being interviewed; I gave two press interviews and did one broadcast!
    At 6 went to the Tower Theatre. Big. 1800. We had a *lovely* house – warm, responsive, quiet, listen-y and kind. George accompanied me very well, at last. (He used to tug a little in opposite directions but that concentrated week of work in N.Y. has helped.) Nice Connie, my stage manager, was efficient and calm and helpful.
    We are now in the heart of Michigan University. The young mill round in pale beige macs and flat shoes (girls) crew cuts (boys). Serious and earnest and friendly when spoken to. The Eng. Dep. arrange all the 'lectures' and I'm one of those along with Clem Attlee (January) and economists and poetry readers!
    The news is so awful and we listened to Eisenhower's excellent and unpolitical speech before going to dine. Sobering. From here I feel Anthony Eden is *dotty*. Why *not* have consulted with the U.S. first – or have warned them? I gather Canada sides wholly with the U.S. Wish I knew what to think. My *feeling* is always against force and I see absolutely no good in this action unless the U.S. is with us in it from a moral p. of v.[1]

[1] British and French bombers had attacked military targets in Egypt,

2 November [1956]   Cambridge Square

Darling Joyce,
    I tried *not* to think or talk about Suez all day long – we mercifully
left off it at dinner. But I lunched with a gaggle of ladies & of course we
thrashed about like Puzzled whales. Most people seem to be shocked &
depressed, & even the most pro agree it's *got* to be a success. Whatever
'it' is. Do we stay there for ever? Do we go & come back? How do we get
rid of Nasser? Will they fight Israel *through* us? It's all so confusing.

5 November 1956   The Windsor Arms
                                                     Toronto

Darling Ginnie,
    Came to Canada yesterday.
    Well, I'm still in one piece after the first week – thanks to God. For
it *is* taxing and tiring. But amusing and interesting and stimulating
too. You know it's just as well that I *really* do know about not being a
person and not having to do the show or be an entertainer. If I didn't
I'd be very swellheaded because they all treat me so prettily and say
such things. But truly I am untouched by it in any essential way. Or
rather – I see it in proportion and rejoice that fun is being had.
    As for the world news – a hollow ha-ha. Interesting to read the
Canada press after the U.S. So much saner and on our side! It's like
coming home to be here, and yet I'd rather live in the U.S. I *think*. Easy
to make a statement like that since I only landed on Sat. night and
have, so far, seen nothing except that dear little lake and twelve very
nice middle aged people (our age and our kind).
    I've got a huge gerbe[1] of lemon yeller and orange pink crysanths
from a girl I was in Paris with in 1927!

[1] Sheaf or large bunch.

6 November 1956 2 a.m.!   Cambridge Square

Darling Joyce,
    This has been a truly *appalling* week. What with us in Egypt &
the Russians in Hungary, & England deeply & emotionally divided –
the House a bear-garden, mass meetings, everybody talking, talking,
arguing, arguing, trying to keep the edge off the voice, grateful in a
despairing way to be able to switch from Suez to Budapest, soul-searing
though all its last messages were – it's been simply *AWFUL*.[1]
    What with minding it all so much – either for one reason or another

– we feel exhausted; exhausted & touchy & *careful*. I've managed to get above it all at times, but really one would have to be a recluse not to get verbally involved at any rate.

I haven't the faintest idea which side I'm on re Suez – I think it's nice to get rid of a bellicose dictator but I'm averse to killing people.

And so you go on, love, with WHAT a start to your tour! T & I couldn't *believe* the first day's schedule. Quelle stamina!

We went and saw your new flat on Sunday – Reg there with a ruler measuring things & being sweet. It's going to be a treat. Your bedroom wallpaper is gay & dazzling.

[1] British and French troops landed in Port Said on 5 November.

8 November [1956]   Cambridge Square

Darling Joyce,

None of us much in the mood for entertainment these days – a bit fatiguéed from our emotions, & an uneasy background feeling that we're not remotely through the wood yet. Rumours flying hither & yon – that the Russians are pumping planes into Syria, or Egypt; that we shall now have to forget the Jews because they won't go back; a heavy feeling of guilt about the Hungarians whom we certainly shan't help, or if we do it means Armageddon. A light smell of fear in the air, in fact, & it's a relief to remember (as I do, but not nearly often enough) that there is nothing but God & its manifestations in the universe.

To is off to shoot in Scotland for a week.

9 November 1956   The Lord Elgin Hotel
                                                        Ottawa

Darling Ginnie,

Last night's audience in Toronto was terrific. We were sold out and they added a hundred chairs in places where no one could see a *thing*. We're sold out here too, and in Montreal and in Toronto.

Our departure from the Windsor Arms this a.m. was hilarious. Orders were left in writing for 6.45 calls. At about 7 a foreign voice, the night porter, rang up and said 'Six-forty-five – *six-forty-five now*'. A dotty man was in charge of the bills. He had no change and has given us all IOUs for our return! Between our bills a frantic Swedish traveller tried to pay his and get the key to his car he'd handed in to reception. It was nowhere. The foreign (Pole?) porter said 'In de gar-age. Not oben dill 8 tirty'. The poor Swede was desperate.

Our egos are all a little deflated here. We weren't met. We can't *trace* the management! The auditorium where we play is expecting us and is sold out for both nights, but it is a little bleak to be so very abandoned after all the loving attentions of elsewhere. Good for us no doubt; but bad *business behaviour*. These local managements are making vast sums out of me for, because I was unknown, I get only a set fee and can't join in the harvests they are all reaping. So it is a little galling. I shall be a little distant when the manager finally turns up. If he does.

The war/world news is awful. And riots in *London*. Horrid.

12 November [1956]   Cambridge Square

Darling Joyce,

Almost forgot to congratulate you *hugely* on your success. It *doesn't* come as a surprise.

The Astors have been getting a wigging in the Beaverbrook press. The *Observer* carried a hair raising article against Eden on Sunday – people cancelling their subscriptions right & left (or right anyhow) – & Jakie has raised his voice in the House. The *Express* says '. . . Bill[1] has inherited his title from his father, David[2] has inherited his paper from his father, Jakie[3] has inherited his seat from his mother', implying they've not done a thing on their own.

Don't pay too much attention to riots in London. There have been anti-Russian processions & one big anti-Tory meeting in Trafalgar Square where youths shouted '*Law* not War' & hit a few policemen on the head.

[1] 3rd Viscount Astor (1907–66) succeeded his father Waldorf Astor in 1952.
[2] His brother David Astor (1912–) editor of the *Observer*.
[3] His brother Jacob Astor (1918–) MP for Plymouth (Sutton).

15 November [1956]   Buffalo Airport

Darling Ginnie,

Canada was wonderful to me with a mildly anti-climactic finish at Niagara last night, where only 300 came to the show. But they were a very *nice* 300. However the promoter was very disappointed and both George and Connie don't like it on my behalf when it isn't HUGE. As it was everywhere else.

R. called me this morning as the piano had been taken down the stairs at 149 by Harrods and a bus had bumped into the van! *Lovely* to hear him.

The world news continues to rumble and so far I have not been hissed as English. I feel strangely withdrawn. When you are *here* you think it's a miracle that *anything* is ever done with unanimity. It is all so foreign and different – so Jewish – Italian – Irish – German. Most of them aren't a bit interested anyway. The U.S. is so big and so far off, or so they think.

15 November [1956]   Cambridge Square

Darling Joyce,

Victor has moved into his new flat and already it looks *ravishing*. Really, the old boy's colour sense is something out of this world. He's got red velvet curtains lined with yellow, & a series of wildly clashing red chairs, a blot of lavender blue, a magenta cushion or two – all the maddest things, & *perfect*.[1]

Dick proposes to buy a flat in Brighton.

Your flat is progressing like anything. I went & found Reg & Mrs Gabe contemplating your piano & three exhausted men. It appeared to be impossible to make the last flight without removing the banisters, but then next day one vast man heaved it onto his back & charged up the stairs with it!

Winifred dined last night – *very* lame, but beautiful.

[1] Victor Stiebel and Virginia and Tony were moving to new flats near Hyde Park Gardens.

1 December 1956   Hotel Laurelton
                                                                 New York

Darling Ginnie,

Thrilled to hear from R. that real progress is being made in your flat too.

Well here it is, the last day of the tour and Town Hall looms tonight. It's been a heavy week but now it's over from the travelling point of view, and that is joy. We did Wash. on Mon. and it was gorgeous. Weds. was Springfield, Mass., and oh so dull. A huge audience of dim respectable un-thinking New Englanders. It's so odd when the words simply don't penetrate *at all*. And such hard work for me. To my vast amusement the lady in charge said to George and Connie afterwards that I must be *delighted* by all the wonderful laughter. Not a titter.

On Thurs. we flew from Springfield on one plane, got into a helicopter at La Guardia and flew over N.Y. to Newark Airport, and then into another plane for Bethlehem, Penn., which was bliss. A heavenly host of enthusiasm. A taxing day. But the helicopter was fun. We saw the sights from 1000 feet up and it was so unbumpy and still and made ordinary flying seem awful. I loved it.

One of the hit songs here is called 'Throw Momma from the train a kiss'!

3 December 1956   Hotel Laurelton

Darling Ginnie,
So typical of life that when one has one's greatest triumph there is no one there to see it! Town Hall on Sat. was really huge. I've never had such a reception ever. And none of the loved ones except T. and M. were there. Nor were the press. For I seem to fit no category in the Town Hall. I'm not theatre there, nor am I music.
Yesterday the Phippses, and I went to a Sunday matinee of Judy Garland[1] at the famous Palace. She is plump, can't sing much any more from having yelled eternally, but is wonderfully good even so. She had three of her children on the stage with her and it was fairly nauseating but fascinating. The eldest, a girl called Liza aged about 8,[2] is plain and gangling but has some of Judy's early talent and will grow up into a charmer I think.
This may be the last letter before I sail. Maybe not. You never know.

[1] Judy Garland (1922–69), American singer and actress.
[2] Liza Minelli, aged ten. Daughter of Garland and Vincente Minelli, became cabaret artist and musical show singer.

5 December [1956]   Cambridge Square

Darling Joyce,
Newswise it's altogether a wretched Wednesday morn – petrol up to 6/- [30p] a gallon, bread going up, dollar reserves down a whump, a promise of increased income tax. It really does seem to have been a disastrous enterprise, & even Tony, who has been staunchly pro Eden, is beginning to feel it wasn't *quite* the most brilliant idea he ever had. Still, nobody's getting killed at the moment, which is refreshing![1]
I'm just off to sort clothes for Hungarians. Reg dines tonight.

[1] British and French troops were withdrawn from Suez and Nasser continued as President of Egypt until 1958. Eden won a vote of confidence and went on holiday to Jamaica.

1957

The Grenfells and the Thesigers both moved into their new flats in early 1957. Tommy and Mary Phipps came over from New York to stay with the Grenfells.

2 May 1957. Day off   Flat 8 34, Elm Park Gardens
                                                              Chelsea SW10

Darling Ginnie,

I am *appalled* by my horrible selfishness. Here I am counting the
hours till the flat is ours again. I don't think I can put my sense
of irritation down to either tiredness or the Change. It is just plain
unvarnished self, hating having its privacy invaded. They are *so* sweet,
so appreciative, but our rhythms are different and I am, of course,
long lost in living in *my* way, in *my* privacy. It is disgraceful and I am
really very ashamed. R., who probably feels it even more than I do, is
angelic and saintly and appears to do it all so gaily and easily. I *do* it,
but the burning irritation shows I know, and I'm sure I'm a horrible
hostess.

It isn't as if I didn't like them. I *do*. It's just plain resentment of *my*
privacy being invaded and I ought to be spanked. Hard. Brrrrr. There, I
feel better.

I filmed all yesterday and it was delicious for the sun shone and
we worked out of doors.[1] I finished early so I went on to watch
Laurence Harvey[2] working in *The Truth About Women*. This is a grand
technicolour epic, clothes by Cecil Beaton, in which L.H. has six or
seven different leading ladies in each episode. Among them are Mai
Zetterling[3] and a lot of lesser lights like Joan Collins' sister Jackie,[4]
etc. etc.

We went to see Robert Morley[5] on Tues. and it was *ghastly* – really
terrible. One of the major disappointments. His entrance and opening
number were very promising but after that it was disastrous. The
material was all really bad. I fear he had written it himself. He seemed
very nervous and he had *every* reason to be.

[1] *Blue Murder at St Trinian's*.
[2] British film actor (1928–73).
[3] Swedish actress and director (1925–94).
[4] Joan (1933–) British film star, and Jackie (1939–) actress and romantic novelist.
[5] British comedy actor (1908–) at the Café de Paris.

25 July 1957   Haus Thomas
                                                                       Austria

Darling Ginnie,

Frau Hirth arranged for us to go to the Folk tanze festival! Boys
slapping their thighs very skilfully in ancient lederhosen. I was longing
to join in the minuet but R got extra English and wouldn't.

Mr Owsley from California is a camera fiend and there seems to be a monologue about such a one. He never sees *nature*, all he's interested in is a wide lens view. He takes dozens of more and more boring views, of painted houses and streets – not because he thinks they are pretty and interesting but because they fit his lens. But he is so nice and not at all a bore. Far too shy to bore. Simple, happy people, and extremely kind and generous in asking us to 'ride' with them in their Mercedes.

Neuschwanstein is beyond any joke. A great Disney-Grimm affair perched on a peak and visible along the wide valley for miles. Never finished and of a hideosity. Do you remember German illustrations to medieval fairy stories in our youth? Well it's that. The candelabra in the throne room is a vast brass crown about 10 feet across, studded with great coloured glass jewels. I think Ludwig was there for eight days in all.[1]

We managed to drive up behind two fine fat horses: and down. Both had major motions both ways. Must be a sign of something, or else we are just useful as a sort of syrup of figs.

I've had a gruelling time thinking of a suitable tribute for the visitors book. I've now done a drawing of my dear old face and one hand holding a fistful of accurately drawn mountain flowers!

[1] Mad King Ludwig (1845–86) built the castle with a bribe from Bismarck in 1871.

28 July 1957   6 Hyde Park Gardens
                                                        London W2

Darling Joyce,
    Had a grovelling letter from *Young Elizabethan* magazine because one of their readers, a boy aged 12, has won a competition – with a poem of *mine*! Very enterprising of him, don't you think? And quite flattering.
    I've been doing chores, such as going to an *undertaker*, to get a low marble surround for our hearth. And consulting with the Paddington Rodent Officer about our mice. A chap in a peaked cap is here, hurling arsenic round the kitchen to catch the growing family – *wee* some of them are, rather sweet.

In August Joyce began planning a new tour of solo performances in Dublin and Britain. Her piano accompanist from now until her retirement was William Blezard (1921–).

24 August 1957   Elm Park Gardens

Darling Ginnie,

I've done a useful session with Bill this morning and now he and R. have gone off hand in hand to Mr Trumper [barber] to see if he can do something masterly about Bill's hair. It is of the baby silk variety and straight as string. He feels that it must be left long at the sides so that he can brush it back but of course when he gets carried away at the keys down it all falls like a pair of little curtains and he looks most odd, if endearing. Anyway we hope that a clever cutter, like R's friend at Mr Trumpers, is going to work a miracle.

My beautiful black velvet beret is here and R. approves. Can't wait to wear it but as my only outing in view is the Lyric Hammersmith tonight I don't see that I can for it is of the voluminous type and I will be asked to kindly remove it. No I shan't. I will be kindly asked to remove it.

Laurier and his stop watch were here for a long session yesterday and we made some tentative running orders. I am trying to arrange it so that I can sit down every now and then! It was all going to be so easy but I see I have given myself a good deal of exercise. In fact it all promises to be an active evening if you count singing at the pitch of your lungs in Joyful Noise[1] as activity, and I do.

I have listened to two ravishing morning recitals from E'burgh. Do you ever go to morning concerts? I think it is a wonderful time for music and Bach at eleven is just about perfect.

[1] Song about lady choristers, singing up to top F in the Albert Hall. Music by Donald Swann,

25 August 1957   Elm Park Gardens

Darling Ginnie,

To continue from yesterday: R. returned with Bill shorn of his long locks and looking wonderfully spruce and improved. He was *delighted*. Couldn't get over the barber's skill and artistry, and is now, for ever, bound to Mr Trumpers. So that was good.

In the evening to the Lyric Ham. for *Share my Lettuce*. I should have known not to believe a word of either Dick or Vic! So well directed and so quick and so young and fresh, that I agreed with the press boys for once. There are dire moments but Kenneth Williams[1] is very funny. Maggie Smith[2] isn't. I am announced in disastrous lettering in the foyer! Must have that dealt with.

[1] Actor (1926–88) best known for his parts in *Carry On . . .* films.
[2] Dame Maggie Smith, British actress (1934–)

31 August 1957   Stratford-upon-Avon

Darling Ginnie,
   The Tempest is tremendously exciting. I've never seen such an
imaginative production. Peter Brook[1] really is a sort of genius I think.
He was there looking like a little Jewish watchmaker on a Scottish
holiday, in the roughest of tweeds. He is getting plump on all his hard
work. John Gielgud is at his best. That lovely voice rolling out into
the theatre in a way none of the others can find at all. It is a bad play
except for Prospero and Ariel. And the comics, for once, are hilarious.
But it's P. Brooks' night – decor, music, costumes – the whole thing. We
saw John for a minute afterwards and I told him how enormously you'd
loved the poetry reading. He was delighted. 'She's very critical, isn't
she?' he asked. '*Very*' I said.

[1] Theatre director (1925–)

Sunday, 1 September 1957   Stratford-upon-Avon

Darling Ginnie,
   As You Like It was very enjoyable. I loved the look of it and thought
Peggy [Ashcroft] enchanting as Rosalind.
   As we drove into the car park the attendant, who is a friend since
my week here with *J.G. Requests T.P.*, whispered 'Sir Laurence has
just arrived', and there just opposite us in the restaurant sat Laurence.
[Olivier], Vivien [Leigh] and her mum. In silence. We said hello and
'welcome back' to V. and sat down, determined not to look or listen.
But of course from time to time the eye roved though we couldn't in
fact hear that far. It was, clearly, a strained meal. She was in a petunia
red silk duster and heavily be-jewelled. She is very puffy and plump and
has a sort of blurred, hot look. We spoke briefly after the play, going
round to see Peggy. Larry sat throughout the play with a set, grim,
unentertained look, and only applauded faintly. I thought he looked
wretched and I thought she was behaving in a very controlled enamelled
way, but I sensed no ease anywhere and felt great sympathy for all
concerned, particularly her mother who was obviously there as a sort of
bolster. Looks very like Viv and not all that much older.[1]

[1] The actors Laurence Olivier and Vivien Leigh were divorced three years later.

226

15 September 1957   Shelbourne Hotel
                                                                   Dublin

Darling Ginnie,
    No news yet, darling, except we're sold out for tomorrow and an
advance on £1,200, which is said to be v.g. Today we do lighting 2.30,
I record an interview, and we dress rehearse at 5.
    The theatre is chaotic still. It's been taken to pieces to install heating
and *safe* electricity. (It used to be held together with string and was
condemned!) They've preserved the charm of the interior, for it riots
with plaster and gilt and is one of the most attractive theatres in the
world. It's first class for sound too.
    My old red velvet curtains from *J.G. Requests* look lovely, but in order
to get a contrast I have to begin in the green dress – suitable for Eire –
because the flame one is almost too much of a tone-in for a first dress.
That new white fichu is a great help on the pink, but it is still not quite
right, I gather, and the black velvet will be a good idea.
    I've got a radio in the wall and feel very spoiled. Several
Ambassadors are attending tomorrow night! I forgot Dublin is like that.
R. is wearing his green tweed and looks very handsome.

15 September [1957]   Hyde Park Gardens

Darling Joyce,
    Had a heavy-ish session in church today. The Second Reader is a
wonderful Cunard liner Captain who shouts the Bible as though from
the bridge, only with a tremendous amount of expression. I still find
Church a bit depressing (though *not* C.S.), All the people I have known
since I was 12 appear one by one in various stages of decrepitude, some
limping, some in dark glasses, some bowed over or leaning on the arms
of friends . . . it saddens me, though I know it has nothing to do with
the truth of the matter – rather the Mind!

18 September 1957   Shelbourne Hotel

Darling Ginnie,
    Better last night. *Much.* The whole thing rose up and went like a
bird. The new running order is an improvement.
    Here is wet of an immense wetness. My room is full of flowers and
it has become Home in that strange way hotel rooms can. I always
instantly make a nest and love it wherever I am, even in Manchester.
    Yesterday I saw the Book of Kells, which is hideous – the
illuminations I mean. Little squirmy tortured Celtic designs, and I don't

care if they are 8th century they are boring and ugly. I did not say so.

23 September [1957]   Hyde Park Gardens

Darling Joyce,
   We went & saw Joycie [Carey] fly off to the U.S. last evening.
VIP treatment, in that modern lounge with all those free drinks. She
reminded us of the story of Noël's mother who, when asked after her
first flight, whether she'd been afraid, answered quite seriously, 'Good
heavens no, why should I be? I used to swing *very* high as a girl.'
   We went to a Thesiger wedding on Saturday – bride marrying
a sweet looking Australian. The piece de resistance was his Mum.
She wore a pink tweed coat & skirt onto which she had pinned a
whole gladiolus, top bud at the ear & base of stem at the navel!
Touching, rather.

26 September 1957   Newcastle-upon-Tune

Darling Ginnie,
   Wondering so much how Tommy's play went.[1] Not a word so far.
I wonder. Oh dear. New York is so tough. I'm glad I wasn't there!
Torture.
   Have you bought a 'sack' yet? Nor me. Nor, I swear, will I ever wear
a sack. How silly can you get? I've never seen such joke fashions.
   I wonder how I can remember to buy some Lux tomorrow? Such a
difficult sort of thing to remember.

[1] Tommy Phipps's first play on Broadway, *Four Winds*, starred Ann Todd, directed by
Guthrie McKlintic.

30 September 1957   Glasgow

Darling Ginnie,
   The first perf. tonight was not very good. They were tough and quite
cool at first. I dried in one song and made a mess of it, which was a pity
and shook us all! However I got back into my stride and the second part
went well, and they were warm at the end. But I somehow think the
press will be critical. I wonder if I'm right to be doing this sort of show?
I've always half wanted to so now I am doing it, and if it's no good,
well there we are.

30 September [1957]   Hyde Park Gardens

Darling Joyce,
    Had a brief word with Reg last night and I gathered all was well,
except perhaps for poor Tommy. I gathered from snippets in the papers
that Tommy's play was beautifully written, beautifully acted, but
boring. Surely a contradiction in terms? 'Boring' is the most stinking
comment, and terribly off-putting. I can't see it bearing any relation to
T. either – surely the least boring of men? I could understand it being
practically anything else – facetious, cynical, whimsical, or even too
profound, but boring amazes me. Hope it will be all right. Anyway, it's
quite a feat having a play on Broadway at all.

2 October 1957   Glasgow

Darling Ginnie,
    Yesterday one of the stage staff said to me 'Ye've got some bonnie
crits.' (Nice notices to you.) And they were. It made the spirits soar and
I walked for miles, uphill, after ordering a tweed length for R's birthday:
a lovely mud colour.
    R. had such a brave battered letter from poor Tommy. Such things
are hard to take dammit. He says it is the more baffling because there
were twelve curtain calls and *cheers*. That on Broadway is very rare.
Mysterious. It can't be as bad as all that, surely. *So* many intelligent,
worldly wise people had faith in it.
    I had such a terrible nightmare last night of R. choking that I woke
up thudding and soaked! Even in my dream I prayed like mad. Had
to do a lot more when I woke up and only iron control prevented me
ringing him up to see if all was well. It was horrid. Bah.
    Poor Dick (sh-sh) has had a vile press after some fool played
'Warsaw' in a prog. including Chopin and Liszt. He is bruised of course.
Also a lecturer used 'Warsaw' to illustrate what bad music is! It's so
b——y unfair, for it wasn't written as *good* music – it was a pastiche
of a piano concerto for a film. They are beasts. No one mentions how
beautifully D. sets songs – 'Three Brothers' and 'Time'. They are first
class of *their sort*. They aren't meant to be Schubert.

1958

After the success of Joyce's visit to America in 1957, she was invited back to
tour and perform a new show on Broadway. Although Atlantic flights were
becoming more common, Joyce preferred the rest that a boat journey allowed

her. Also on board the *Queen Mary* was her aunt Nancy Astor, then aged seventy-nine.

14 January 1958   RMS *Queen Mary*

Darling Ginnie,
Boat drill. *Damn*. Have to go . . .
Being a good citizen I went and learned the ropes. Coming away I found Nancy in the lounge reading a book on calories. She must lose a stone, she says. Can't find caviar in her list so will just carry on. It's *so* typical of my family that the rules *never* apply to them, so none of them went to boat drill. I sat at the Captain's table once and he said it really was rather b——y minded of the smarties *never* to go. If there *is* a fire or any trouble they are no help, and so with that in my mind I now always go and find out my station and how to get there.
Aunt N. is rather dotty I fear. But very sweet. Except that she must be in on everything including bridge which she can't play but which she says she wants to learn. This is not a success with the bridge players. She's a spoiled child really. But it's very sad.
My *St Trinian's* is on tonight!

17 January [1958]   Hyde Park Gardens

Darling Joyce,
I've been recording this morn at the BBC – & *who* should be on the same programme but youdle! Talking about the things that make you cry. Very good I thought it was. I was a bit provoked because they had to go through the whole programme twice – everybody else was pre-recorded but me, or rather pre-pre-recorded, & I'm a *busy* woman, Miss G.!
The galleys of *Cockney in the Country*[1] have just arrived & I am postponing taking to the floor with them. We really enjoyed *St Trinian's*. Thought you were smashing good in it. We laffed.
Loving pensées, your Gin

---

[1] Book by Virginia, 'dedicated to Londoners who are forced either by good manners, family ties or the boiler blowing up to go to the country.' It includes chapters on how to cope with cows, trees, and the sky.

22 January 1958   Hotel Laurelton
                                                   New York

Darling Ginnie,

Tonight I went to Church. Somehow away from home it is far more enjoyable. Over here the C.S. Church is just part of the scene and not something odd. They take it in their stride and the meetings are remarkably gay!

Saw *West Side Story*[1] and was much excited by it. It's rather horrible, the Romeo and Juliet story in terms of West Side juvenile delinquents versus Puerto Rican ditto. But oh the direction, the dancing and the score by Leonard Bernstein. We were in the 16th row and it was all right and the best available even with pull.

[1] Opened three months earlier at the Winter Garden. By 1960 Joyce had seen this show five times.

Joyce's tour began in Canada with George Bauer, pianist, and Connie Alderson, stage manager.

4 February 1958   Winnipeg
                                                   Canada

Darling Ginnie,

A rosy fingered dawn over this vast sprawling completely flat city. Not pretty re buildings but sort of friendly. I was here as a child in 1913, I think, and do you know I actually remembered the fact that the railroad was near the hotels. It was here that I used to scuff my feet along the carpet and then touch the corner of the brass bed and make sparks!

Canada is like coming home. Yesterday's show was preceded by a five min. Committee Meeting of the Ladies Music Club and the Queen. I surged. Her picture is everywhere and I like that very much. It's a wonderfully uniting influence.

George and Connie are so nice to be with. We laugh a great deal and they look after me so sweetly. We're being very grown up and all telephone calls go to Connie first – she is screening me!

In Vancouver the Women's Pen Club entertained in my honour – sherry in a member's house. Nice cosy, dowdy ladies – very like the members of my own dear old Soc. of Women Writers and Journalists![1]

The show was a wow, it really was. Sold out well in advance and they said it could have been trebled, easily. I was expecting rather a quiet reception – but it was Tremendous. God Bless Ed. Sullivan I think, and British movies.

11 February 1958   San Francisco

Darling Ginnie,

I particularly liked getting your birthday cable a day late because I know you have a problem – or as the natives here would say, a 'block' about my birthday.

No time to write here. It's a whirl. Gay too.

In brief. My advance is 6,000 dollars, which is thought to be jolly good. Hooray. Did press lunch conference today. I am off to a do at the English Speaking Union now. Saw Vera Lynn[1] for five secs at her theatre today. *Have* to go to her first night tonight. My press boys insist. After which I have to see Carol Channing's[2] show at midnight. Ye gods.

Next day

Noël's first night went off all right. *Nude [with Violin]*. But I was acutely conscious of it being a near thing. It is *so* wordy, so over written, all the characters talk like Noël, and tho' I laughed a little it wasn't ever very spontaneous any more. Oh *dear*. He looks old and worried and that's no fun to see. I like idols to stay up on their pedestals.

Carol Channing is the zany daughter of a late C.S. lecturer and she has gone a *long* way from the nest of her origins. Very tall, thin, with endless arms and a huge mouth; her hair dyed *grey* is in wisps à la Anita Loos only more of it. She has a certain talent but it's undisciplined and wild and very crude indeed. The audience ate her up in mouthfuls.

To my horror George had said it was my birthday and she had a cake delivered to our ringside seat and a spot light put on me. I was glad no loved ones were around. She's a warm hearted trouper. We had to go up to her room afterwards and the cake was sent up. No knife so I sliced it with a wire coat hanger. Bed at 3 a.m. I do hate being up late. I've got caught in a sort of obligation round of social engagements.

14 February [1958]   [Hyde Park Gardens]

Joyce darling,
    Ta for your Valentines – you *funny* you. 'Granny' indeed!

16 February 1958   Beverly Hills

Darling Ginnie,
    Leonard[1] met me and drove me out here via all the stars' houses.
Fred Astaire lives there – Janet Gaynor[2] – Tony Curtis[3] – etc. etc. It is far
prettier than I expected. More colour. Greener grass. Heavenly weather.
    Leonard's house is small with a big main room. White with gay bits
and pieces in it. A little chi-chi but cheerful. And *comfy*.
    Leonard has a button on his vast white car, with red lining, and at 50
yds distance can open his garage door as he approaches. Some sort of ray
operates it! His bed can raise its head or its feet at the touch of another
button. He has moved out of his room for me and he is in the guest room.
Such kindness and such thoughtfulness and generosity. He is *taking* 30
people tonight to see me and giving a party afterwards in my honour.
These include – Claudette Colbert,[4] Janet Gaynor, Judy Garland (if well
enough), Tony Curtis, etc. etc. A sink growls and chews up all the orange
peel and rubbish except tins! A button turns the heating on at sunset. I
write in a pale lemon yellow room with one orange-pinky chair.
    San Fran. was *so* lovely. I did vast business – the audiences were
lovely to work for.

[1] Leonard Gershe, film and television script writer, wrote *Funny Face* starring Fred Astaire
and Audrey Hepburn. Joyce first met Gershe in London with Richard Addinsell.
[2] Mitzi Gaynor (1931–), American musical star.
[3] American film star (1925–), father of Jamie Lee Curtis.
[4] French-born leading lady in pre-war American films (1905–).

19 February [1958]   Hyde Park Gardens

Darling Joyce,
    Victor had a splendid opening yesterday. Lovely friendly well-wishing
atmosphere, ravishing clothes – one of his best collections, & the
room elegant beyond words. He was so clapped he had to take a
bow, & turned quite pink, dear boy. It was Princess Margaret's first
time to a public dress show. The gang sat in two rows facing each
other by the fitting room. My, we do look pretty archaic now. Diana,
Kay, Gladys, looking at me, Winifred and Dick. Fair gave me the
creeps![1]

[1] Diana Cooper aged 66, Kay Hammond aged 51, Gladys Calthrop aged 61, Clemence Dane
aged 73, Richard Addinsell aged 54 and Virginia aged 48.

20 February 1958   Beverly Hills

Darling Ginnie,
    Well it went off very well on Mon. The Press has been wonderful.
Houses not full. It is not a theatre town and the ones who come rave
and yell and it is fun to play, but, as I say, small.
    Leonard's party on Mon. was so nice. Thirty of us and among them
Claudette Colbert who is very friendly and nice, Gladys Cooper – who
sent flowers, Janet Gaynor, charming and tiny, husband Adrian, nice.
    We go to see Judy Garland and children on Sunday. Stravinsky[1]
came to the show. Didn't meet him, alas. The days whizz past.

[1] Russian composer (1882–1971). Naturalised American 1942.

22 February [1958]   [Hyde Park Gardens]

Darling Joyce,
    Dick gave a huge party for Winifred's 70th birthday last night.
Winifred wasn't at all well & she'd been pumped full of things to keep
her going – she even retired to the kitchen & had a shot of penicillin
mid-stream. But it went with a marvellous swing, there being enough
of every station to cosset itself, including lots of 'potter's' in folk-weave
scarves. There was a glorious Floris cake with the names of all W's
plays & books inscribed on it.
    I'd bought W. a very chi-chi present: two gold bows with a toilet roll
suspended between them & a toothglass holder to match!
    T. hated every minute of it of course, & this *always* irritates me
though the poor lamb has every right to dislike parties if he wants
to. He moons after me with home-beseeching eyes, & last night I was
maddened!
    I envy you meeting Judy G., unless, of course, she's doped or drunk
in which case I don't!
    Darling, will I need an evening dress? Vic is concocting me a
décolleté black marocain & silk number for evenings in the country –
would it do for your first night on Broadway? I'm having all my skirts
shortened – 17″ from the ground – *yards* of leg, I look quite ridiculous!

25 February 1958   In the air to Chicago from Los A.

Darling Ginnie,
    Well, that was Hollywood. I must say I enjoyed it enormously
because of staying *so* comfortably and quietly with Leonard. It never
got less fun. It was peaceful and civilised and his kindness and

234

thoughtfulness never ceased. The week of work was fun to do tho' we never had a full house. But it went with a swing. I should have done two shows at most in a bigger hall perhaps. Never mind. I enjoyed it.

Yesterday I went to F.C.C.S.[1] Beverly Hills. It's a huge Church. Pale blue carpets. I expected it to be very glossy and unreal, but it was full of nice quiet looking people. They took me to meet Doris Day[2] afterwards. She's a C.S. and a nice uncomplicated schoolgirl type. Very wholesome – in fact just what you've seen in the movies. Her husband is called Monty Melcher and he is nice. Their house is brand new, modern. Huge spacious white living room with lemon yellow sofas – big as beds and deep. She showed me her clothes *room*. Twenty feet long, eight across, and hung *full* of clothes in great order. Also a sweater cupboard with at least fifty sweaters in it. And the shoes. As a star she has to have a great variety. And she *is* a big star here. One of the few whose pictures always make money.

We went to see a Jap. house on a peak belonging to a very frightening little man who was dressed in a heavily embroidered white shirt with an ivory *Buddha* on a chain round his open neck. He was like a very *pretty* Max [Adrian] – with an endless totally meaningless smile. He's a complete phoney.

[1] First Church of Christ, Scientist.
[2] Flm actress (1924–).

26 February 1958   University of Wisconsin
                                                                      Madison

Darling Ginnie,

This is so different from Hollywood and *so* much nicer. There is a flabbiness there that begins to affect you after a while and it is good to be back in more difficult country among northerners with a definite outline and morals etc. For instance *almost* everyone – male – that I met in Hollywood was the non-marrying kind. They are, as we know, easy to get on with, good company, kind, gentle, etc. But . . . nothing very visibly vicious but soft and unreal. The streets are full of golden Adonises in sweat shirts, gold hair and gold skins. By the dozen. Frightening. Where are all the lovely girls I was told would serve in shop, soda fountain and hairdresser? I saw none. What I saw all wore pony tails and tight slacks – contradiction in terms – and they had a shelacked hardness unlike the east of this country. They go to the main centre of the town like that. It's all part of the easy living and it makes for soft core.

The impression is that life is *easy*. And yet it is far more complicated mentally than anywhere else I've been. Women seldom wear roll-ons or corsets – physically or mentally.

Do you know you will be leaving in three weeks! Thrilling. Now about clothes. You won't need a full evening dress unless anything very odd happens, but you'll need a short sleeved low*ish* necked short dinner dress, black if you like. (It's almost a uniform here.) All cabs, cars are heated – shops to bursting point. Bedrooms are warm.

3 March [1958]   Hyde Park Gardens

Darling Joyce,

You aren't half bounding about.

Interesting about Hollywood, & rather surprising – in fact very surprising, because all the stars *appear* to be their own sex & look blooming & *rugged* even. Pretty boys, & girls with horses manes I find ultra-astonishing.

Love and whoopee from Maggie

19 March 1958   Boston

Darling Ginnie,

Yesterday I went to the Mother Church.[1] I sat in the Gallery, sun poured in and I was really so pleased to be there, and then suddenly in the hymn I burst into tears! Can't think why. But it wasn't sad – Joy, I suppose! Anyway a great surge. Wet.

I met several of the bodies on the Board[2] after my show and was so amused to note the ones who are apparently sort of embalmed in 'Lurve' and Old C.S. folklore and the ones with seeing eyes and clearness and no-person. So there *are* some of those! Good. And Thank God.

Now New York. Canada tomorrow.

And next week – YOU.

[1] The First Church of Christ, Scientist established by Mary Baker Eddy in Boston in 1879.
[2] The Christian Science Board of Directors.

Virginia and Tony joined Joyce for a month's holiday in New York and North Carolina. Joyce then began a four-week run on Broadway.

21 April 1958   Hotel Laurelton
                                                          New York

Darling Ginnie,
   I went out twice last week after the Show. Once to a very fascinating
modern young T.V. Group's party where jazz musicians played and
made a jam session. There were actors and models and Sugar Ray
Robinson[1] and T.V. 'personalities' and Peter Ustinov and Richard
Rodgers[2] and the funniest collection of very chic *Vogue* dressed girls
with funny mask make ups on and long thin shoes and idiotic little
knee length shifts. They looked idiotic. Many of the gents were queer
so it didn't matter, and the whole thing was very brittle and odd and
amusing to watch for an hour.
   The other night I went to an arty Greenwich Village coffee bar with
Norman Newall, H.M.V. record manager.
   I close on Sat. (Hooray!) And R. comes (Hippity Hip). Tho' I hate
leaving Connie and George to whom I am genuinely devoted.

[1] American boxer (1920–89), six times world champion.
[2] American composer (1902–79), wrote the musical *Oklahoma*.

Saturday 26 April 1958   Hotel Laurelton

Darling Ginnie,
   Lovely to see R. today. He beamed in, brown and bonnie, with his
pockets full of letters from you and Viola and Dick and sweeties from
Mrs Gabe.
   Guess what? Yesterday I was principal guest of a distinguished Very
Chic club called the Escholiers – composed of successful theatre men. I
wore Vic's pink suit, my mink and my please-don't-eat-the-daisies hat.
   I sat on the right side of the Pres., Bobby Clark, and who was on my
other side . . . ? Maurice Chevalier![1] I loved him. He is as nice or even
more so off than on. Modest, charm, gentle, quiet. He saw the show and
said *very* nice things. We talked shop and had a fine time. It was on the
roof of the St Regis–Penthouse. Very gay. I had fun.
   Now I must go and carol with George. It's sad, but I am a leetle tired.
And now for the hols!

[1] French actor and singer (1888–1972), just appeared in *Gigi*.

7 May [1958]   Hyde Park Gardens

Darling Joyce,

The country's getting into a bit of a pickle at the moment – bus strike on, underground doing a sympathetic go-slow, a serious threat of a railway strike. The streets are wonderfully empty in spite of an expected 30,000 more cars.

Did Reg know his letter was in *The Times*? Couldn't understand *one* word of it, the clever fellow!

7 May 1958   Hotel Laurelton

Darling Ginnie,

Went to a gala ball (charity) called the Lunt-Fontaine Ball.[1] Tickets $35 each. The Lunts made an entrance in a spotlight, we all rose and roared. This was very moving somehow. They looked so small suddenly, and vulnerable. Mary Martin sang a song in their honour. A few speeches, food and dancing. Bed at 2.30.

On the T.V. is a group of twenty male voices in identical suits with identical handkerchiefs in their breast pockets singing a song called 'Tie me to your apron strings again'! What would Freud and the psych boys make of that one.

---

[1] Called after the actors Alfred Lunt and his wife Lynn Fontaine.

Virginia and Tony were staying with the Thesiger family in Scotland when Tony's mother died. His father was 99 years old.

19 August 1958   Elm Park Gardens

Darling Ginnie,

Lovely to talk to you this morning. I will be thinking of you this afternoon at two-thirty, and I hope those rods of rain will have abated, or anyway that To has found some huge umbrellas to cover you both. I have been wondering if you had a black hat with you and think that the sort you might find in Strathdon might add cheer to your wardrobe. Darling, it all sounds most tiresome.

I do hope the old man won't mind any of it too much. Thank goodness you can now shut some windows and have a fire when you need to.

Hancock's Half Hour or Church? Difficult decision.

19 August [1958]   Bellabeg

Darling Joyce,
    Well, darling, it's all over, & we are all feeling much better. I really
think funerals are so barbarous – all that kefuff over an insensate body
that I get cross every time I go to one. And yet I suppose one must do
something. Bundling people away with nary a word or a flower would
be ill-mannered perhaps. The coffin was submerged in flowers, heaved
onto the shoulders of two game keepers; the Scotch mist swirled about,
the sheep looked over the wall, the maids howled, the pipes skirled &
the Minister committed Mrs T. to a heather lined hole. I was in a tearing
rage, but I think everybody loved it!
    It's curious what a deep affection Mrs T inspired in all her menials.
They really loved her, & yet she was always very autocratic, ringing
bells incessantly & bawling for them, & they lived in perfect austerity, on
hard beds in dreary cold rooms. It's so mysterious.
    Mrs Ritchie has asked if she can stay on when the old Mr T dies
and look after Alec.[1] Terrific relief all round. The old man is admirably
untouched. Smoking a Burmah cheroot & talking about grouse.
    I need friends, flowers, movies, plays, music, laughter – beauty and
noise in fact. Pity I don't like nature – there is such a *lot* of it here.

[1] Tony's brother (1904–71). Their mother had had German measles while she was pregnant
and Alec was born with learning difficulties so was unable to work or live alone.

22 August 1958   Elm Park Gardens

Darling Ginnie,
    The rain in the night was like the pattering of very *large* feet. All
night it seems to have pounded down. Plane tree leaves are stuck as if
pressed on the pavements.
    Yesterday lunch with Dick who arrived full of the L.P. record which
has complications – mild – about the 'sleeve'. He was shown the front
but not the back, and remembering the absence of his name on my
L.P. very naturally wishes to see a proof before it is finished. But no one
wants to show one. Oh you know, all the inter-departmental excuses.
Tiresome. He is philosophic, quite, but cross too.
    He had, unofficially, seen Winifred.[1] She says *of course* it was not
thrombosis – 'they' are all wrong. And sadists to try and keep her in
bed etc. She is frustrated because her play is due to go into rehearsal
and she can't go to prelim. discussions. I think this is probably
a good thing all round. Authors are best kept away, particularly
overpowering ones.

We had a hilarious supper with the Col. and Hilda [Grenfell]. They had driven up in a 1925 Rolls they bought for £80, driven by an Italian who has never been in London and speaks no English. Ye gods. They were in excellent form and brought me flowers. We bought the meat course and Hilda had 'salad from the garden' and packet soup. We found the Italian, a big jolly outdoor country Italian, in the kitchen trying to sort out this menu. The food was remarkably horrible.

Today I fitted a little dining suit Virginia is building me. It has, am I mad? – a sort of *bolero* jacket. The thing is my waist is all I have to offer and these square jackets are ghastly on me. Anyway I'm happier nipped in, fashion or no fashion.

[1] Winifred Ashton/Clemence Dane, had had a heart attack.

24 August [1958]   Bellabeg

Darling Joyce,

Togo is out shooting every day next week, which is marvellous. I have discovered why this house is so soul searing. Not one single pretty or elegant object in it. Everything is serving a useful purpose in hideous mahogany. 'A thing of duty is a joy for never' I cleverly said to myself in bed this morning. The eye is constantly offended.

Interesting money situation. Mrs T will have left about half a million. £300,000 of this will be taken by the Gov. When the old man dies, they will take about half of that, leaving £100,000 to be divided into three, which is £35,000. Very nice, but a somewhat peculiar residue from half a million! I think it's just as it should be, but it's a bit hard on Donny[1] if he wants to keep this place going.

[1] Tony's eldest brother (1901–78).

26 August 1958   Elm Park Gardens

Darling Ginnie,

Ta for your Sunday letter. 'A thing of duty is a joy for never.' Very good. Though not strictly true if you count duty as obeying the voice of God! But in the context of mahogany velly good.

Viola, R and I went to Regent's Park and meandered among some tremendous borders crammed full of exotic and entirely unknown flowers. We talked at length about Class. It seems to be on every tongue. The *D. Mail* is running articles on it, the B.B.C. have a series about it. Fascinating subject and for once some truth is being forced out. People like class distinctions. Of course the upper crust stay silent. The interesting thing is that the top and bottom get on well together and easily. It's the middle and lower that don't jell but grate. The middle – the lower middle – are my unfavourite group. The working classes are clearer cut and safer in their solidarity plonk on the bottom. Once they start shifting up they are never quite so sure. But I do like the possibilities, don't you. On T.V. a young working class scholar at Oxford, son of a Glos. miner, spoke most eloquently about his problem at New College. His friends were often from Eton and Winchester and in Oxford all was at ease. But when his girl came to see him she was miserable, his friends were awkward and he, loving both and seeing all sides, wasn't happy either. He offered no solution. Individuals can escape their stations but their backgrounds can never go with them it would seem.[1]

Today I'm to meet Mr Clews at the 74 bus terminus in Camden Town.[2]

I walked for a while all round Ranelagh Gardens and thought of my childhood and the deep emotions I went through in those sooty environs. Now all is flowers and a garden house with benches, and the shrubberies are cleared so one couldn't hide in them much. I was a Brown Bean there. Also a Follower of Bonnie Prince Charming. Both secret societies, and I was torn by loyalties to both. I remember a certain mauve linen dress I rather liked except the neck was too tight.

[1] Twenty years later Joyce had mellowed and stated that she hated the habit of judging people by their class.
[2] Joyce found Mr Clews when he had 'come over all queer' and fallen down in the street. For several years until he died she subsidised his pension and took him out from his men's hostel for picnics.

1959

Joyce joined Reggie at the copper mine in South Africa.

12 February 1959   Messina

Darling Ginnie,

Good honest sweat is pouring off my forehead, down my cheeks and between me boosoms. I don't mind it, leading the life I am, but to work in, have babies in, live in – NO.

Our social life begins on Mon., and then wham – buffets, sun-downers, teas. But that's what Miriam [Grenfell] and I are here for so no complaints. But . . .

My birthday was unmarked and, except for your letter, nothing happened at all, and idiotically I rather minded that R. did nothing. You know how good he is about presents, so you will understand my sense of let down. I didn't want a *present*. I wanted either an orange pulled off the tree or a joke from the Limpopo Novelty Dept. or a private toast when he drank his old gin and lime, but I didn't get any of it, so there it was. Stupid to mind. I'm too old to be *so* silly I know. Oh I know. But it doesn't stop one minding au fond. And I did. He knew it, too, because I told him when we went to bed! And then *he* minded and I wished I hadn't. Did you ever read such a silly montaigne out of a petit mole hill?

We all went down to the open air Bio to see *Cockleshell Heroes*, which is very good and awfully funny. The stars overhead were so compelling that I left the dull bits of the film and gazed upward entranced. Of course they are all in the wrong place but so brilliant and so *close*.

16 February 1959   Hyde Park Gardens

Darling Joyce,

Oh mysterious Africa! We really must come & have a look one day – it sounds so awfully . . . well, *different* from Bayswater Road.

That *was* a queer business about your birthday! It's so terribly unlike Reg I can scarcely believe it . . . but I know only too well how childishly disappointed one feels. One knows it is silly & it doesn't mean anything, & yet one can't help feeling one deserves that little extra effort.

I shall be interested to see what happens on March 9th – our wedding day – without you to spur Tony on! We shall exchange the brooch which I shall have paid for, but *flowers* do you think?

We are getting all titched up for tea party at Buck House tomorrow. I varnished my toenails last night, just in case the Queen should ask to see my feet, & To is wearing some new pants, just in case . . .

Room at the Top is first class.[1] Instead of coming home to tongue we thought we'd eat out, but the Aperi, Monsigneur & Capri were shut, so we ended up at the Ritz. We were *completely* alone. There were no guests of any sort, *anywhere*, just a gorgeous gilded waste of emptiness! Haven't been there for years, & it really is a scrumptious place – so clever of them to have left it untouched, pillars, & fountains & vast statues & palm trees. Delicious food too. But *nobody* staying there.

---

[1] Film starring Laurence Harvey, directed by Jack Clayton.

[18] February [1959]   Hyde Park Gardens

Darling Joyce,
   Ta, ta, *ta* for your cable. It cheered us up no end. We were sitting
there, two bundles of nerves, & it reminded us that we were really very
lucky people, & were not going to our executions! Needless to say all
our aches & pains left the moment we reached Buck House.
   It certainly is quite an experience, innit? You know thc form, so I
won't describe every detail, but a brief résumé:
   The Queen wore dark blue velvet, I had ten minutes *alone* with her
on a sofa – talked about giggling at the opera, her experiences in a
hurricane giving a Colour to the Navy – very gay, she was, much more
animated than I had imagined, & one quite forgets who she is until
suddenly she looks across the room with that *eye* – that extraordinary
Royal eye. I loved her. My only criticism was the standing. Wow, my
feet! We looked at the pictures for nearly two hours.
   There was another giant pea-souper [fog] last night, which when we
emerged had become a choking Jaeger blanket.

25 February 1959   Messina

Darling Ginnie,
   This is such a country of contrasts. *So* beautiful and so beastly.
One sees the point when Afrikaaners resent British investment
and withdrawal of wealth in the past, but it's no longer possible
by law. What is made here must be spent here. And rightly I
think. But the Afrikaaners go on fighting the Boer War. Like
elephants they never forget. And it's a waste of time. They are
as narrow as Calvin – indeed the Dutch Reformed Church *is*
Calvinistic. Totally un-loving, bitter, old fashioned. And it dictates
the mood, which is hate of and determined destruction of everything
British.

8 May 1959   Bellabeg House
                                                                Strathdon

Darling Joyce,
   Scotland is the only place in which I Mitty.[1] I find myself concocting
schemes in which I buy a beautiful Georgian house in Hertfordshire
– & convert it into elegant flats for you & us; & I go deeply into the
colour schemes & worry about Ascot water heaters & who's going to
have first go at the broad beans. Tony is dead against the country, &
laughs uneasily at my Mitty-ing, but I have a real feeling I'd like to do

something different one day, such as dig in a garden, or count the petals on a primrose![2]

Tony is so sweet with the old man.[3] There is a dressing crisis every morning – this morn he put his vest on *over* his shirt; & I am touched by T buttering his toast & cutting it up into little fingers – he looks heartbreaking doing it, somehow.

Men are so much less demanding. We sit for hours in gorgeous silence. The old man is really hardly ever awake now except at meals when he eats hugely.

A X for Reg

[1] To fantasise, after the fictional character Walter Mitty, played by Danny Kaye.
[2] From 1967 the Thesigers rented one wing of a Queen Anne house in Hertfordshire as a weekend retreat.
[3] Tony's father Percy was now blind. He died three months later.

Joyce and Reggie went to stay for a few days in the Lake District. They loved it so much that they visited the same village every year for the next twenty years.

13 May 1959   Scale Hill Hotel
                                                                   Loweswater

Darling Ginnie,

The Lakes are very glamorous and glassy with *exact* reflections. There is a fine rain and a brilliant light. Most extraordinary and very beautiful. And then, finally, this blessed valley – so quiet, so unspectacular, and so full of curlew and lambs and bluebells and the scent of pines in the wood nearby. Only a small, underpressing copse of them but such a Pong.

A great welcome from Mrs Milburn, the hotel's owner. Her husband was drowned last summer in a fishing accident when the water got into his waders and held him under water. Ghastly. A nice man and she loved him so much. But she is coming to and is so nice and so quiet and patient. It is very simple but very comfy, beds, boiling water, smiling helpers, flowers, good nursery foods, and the peace and quiet are healing in themselves.

Books, birds and a little bubbling river to sit by. A flotilla of baby ducklings upstream.

15 May [1959]   Hyde Park Gardens

Darling Joyce,

I visited Bridget Lenihan[1] in hospital last night – womb removed & out of parlour-maiding till August. Damn. I'd never been in a public ward before: not nearly as bad as I expected, but I imagine the incessant noise must be terrible. Bridget, who is an ardent Catholic, & of a goodness unsurpassed, told me that as she had not led a fast life she supposed it was God's will for her to have a growth. I did *not* suggest that in that case it was blasphemy to have it removed.

[1] Alec Thesiger's parlourmaid.

15 May 1959   In a field – Loweswater

Darling Ginnie,

Ta for yours. Can't explain the 'spiritual home' feeling of this place. I had it at Nannau too – I mean at once, not after association. It got me here from the word go.

We are in a field with a panoramic view of far off mountains, and cuckoos are shouting and larks rising and praising the Lord en route, and there is a dandelion clock in front of me waiting to be blown. There is a banana for R. and a napple for me in my plaid bag. The scent of pines on a far off hill wafts around us, duck fly past, and the birds sing. It's GOOD.

17 May [1959]   Hyde Park Gardens

Darling Joyce,

We went to see the Marilyn Monroe film.[1] It has Jack Lemmon & Tony Curtis dressed as women, & really is awful, but irresistibly funny. Much too long of course, but for most of it we were in fits. There is nothing so enjoyable as laughing against one's better nature, & those boys really looked so *funny*, darling, there was no gainsaying them.

We went in the morning, because I was sure the evening's audience would consist of teddy boys making kissing noises.

It is curious how very rich people of my neighbour's ilk put one's back up, & it would be interesting to be psycho-analysed on the matter, don't you think? Is it just jealousy? or something to do with class? Or simply that they always seem to behave so badly?

These reflections are caused by Mrs D having a cocktail party for 400 today, & I find I am secretly pleased it is raining! So unfair, as I don't know the woman – still, it's so nice to know there's something she *can't* buy. She has built a huge marquee over the terrace, which goes right over the bedroom windows of the basement flats. For nearly a week Mr Gomme & Mr & Mrs Kay have had no light or air, & as she repaired to Ireland no action could be taken. It is wonderfully thoughtless, isn't it?

[1] *Some Like it Hot*, directed by Billy Wilder.

[May 1959]   Hyde Park Gardens

Darling Joyce,
    Another lousy day, darling.
    Hilarious news of Mrs D's party. Mr Gomme, incensed by being
caged in under the awning, spent the evening cooking kippers &
onions, & Mrs D's guests were all but asphyxiated. Mrs D's cook also
misbehaved, drinking a whole bottle of whiskey, & our Mr Rolfe had to
be summoned to carry her to bed. Oh what times we have in H.P.G.!

In June Joyce set off for her first trip to Australia for a twelve-week tour with William
Blezard. All Virginia's letters from this period are lost.

3 July [1959]   Macleay Regis
                                                       Macleay St
                                                          Sydney

Darling Ginnie,
    Oh your flowers! Thoughtful, kind, dear thing to do, and I love them.
I'm a *leetle* confused as to which they are but am pretty sure they are
the mixed gerbe of anemones, jonquils, pinks and gladioli? Anyway they
are heavenly.
    At first I was a bit apprehensive about this building and the flat on
the 8th floor. But then I saw the view and the absolute magic of it has
completely won me over and above the decor. Such a vast sweep of
harbour, full of little and big boats, like little white butterflies. Hills with
houses surround the harbour and it is gay and cheerful and indeed
absolutely fascinating. The decor is quite hysterical – one green, one
grey, one greenery yallery, wall with a scarlet chimney breast. It is
straight Great West Road, including the furniture and lamps.[1] But it's so
comfy and so peaceful and so cosy and this GLORIOUS view. I am very
lucky and grateful. Also I'm glad not to be sharing. It's bliss to be able
to potter alone and I rejoice about all that.
    Bill has got a flatlet nearby and it suits him and his pocket, so that
is good.
    I'm to have a cleaning lady weekly, and groceries are delivered. One
of the great Sydney characters is a journalist called Dorothy Jenner[2]
who lives in the block. Writes a gossip column as if she knew one very
intimately and is widely read and held with affection. She it was who
made up the bed for me and did the flowers. Cosy. She told me of Toni
the grocer – Greek with five children.
    The theatre is perfect size for me. Rather square, three row circle.
    Yesterday was all press. I seemed to have talked and posed from 12

on. The clear air and sun made my recovery quite quick, and I endured the gruelling very well.

People are well disposed towards me via radio, films, records. I hope I can live up to it. We open in 10 days.

[1] The Great West Road (now the A4 west of Hammersmith, London) was lined with Art Deco factories built between the wars.
[2] Dorothy Jenner was known to Australian radio audiences as 'Andrea'.

9 July 1959   Sydney

Darling Ginnie,

I usually get to the theatre by 11 when I exercise my voice and then do some work with Bill for an hour or so.

I am incensed by a really horrid, sly interview written by a man ordinarily thought to be nice, trustworthy and decent, but this time he evidently didn't like me so wrote a sort of sneery article – full of inaccuracies too. Mercifully it appeared in a very little read periodical. I was so cross I nearly wrote a reply but had enough sense not to. Far better ignore it. The Theatre is so distressed for me! It's not that important.

Otherwise the press has been friendly and nice. Not overdoing it, just civil and friendly.

Mary O'Hara[1] came to tea. She's very refreshing. A touching creature. She is a genius. It is the loveliest performance you ever heard and saw. Pretty as paint, young and *very* talented. She sings to a little Irish harp. Rabid R.C. but I must say it gives her great joy and support. She was only married for a year to Richard Selig, the American poet, and he died of some very rare disease. She is absolutely undaunted. 'God looks after me.' And why not.

[1] Mary O'Hara (1935–), Irish singer and harpist. Soon after this she became a nun in a silent order. Then, twelve years later, she came out and resumed her career as a singer. Joyce kitted her out with stage dresses.

13 July 1959   Sydney

Darling Ginnie,

Last night I was on T.V. in *Meet the Press*. It seems to have been rather a big success. *Very* nice reaction. What amuses me is the constant amazement when they say 'But you are so *natural*.' What else can one be?

After the prog. we – the panel and chairman and me – went to the chairman's house for a drink and Danny Kaye came in. Pale tweeds and those extraordinary space shoes we used to see in N.Y., remember. Very clumsy but obviously bliss for the toes. He was cordial and guarded at the same time! We sang close harmony on a sofa for about ten minutes and he said I'd been very good on telly. I find him a little scaly – lizard like – but not bad. At least he plays friendly this time. When I met him before he was *so* bored at meeting another entertainer. It was quite funny.

I've suddenly tumbled on a truth I really should have discovered before. Namely that the Australian accent is *not* a class thing. We equate it with suburbia because of our home associations, but it means nothing here and one suddenly hears erudition, wit, quality talk in that accent and realises one has been *unconsciously* feeling slightly superior! I was appalled when I realised this. And ashamed.

I grow increasingly ashamed of the way we all treat Colonials, discriminating and all. And they sense it. I've been able to talk pretty freely to one or two people and it's interesting. This is a good country and I am longing to see more of it – the country places.

15 July 1959   Sydney

Darling Ginnie,

Morning was full of chores. I needed a coat to use for 'Boat Morning' and was sent to the 'Opportunity Shop', which is second hand clothes of the top group sold for a kindergarten fund! Got a v.g. sort of gabardine raincoat for a fiver.

My dresser, Irish Olga, is grey haired (well coiffed), smiling and nice. Efficient too. My stage manager is from the Hebrides. Electrics is called Arnaud and the Spotman is Tony, a huge bruiser with a rather twisted face. All are as nice as can be.

The set is very pretty. Based on the London one – dark ruby velvets and a chandelier. But, an innovation, they have got a very long venetian blind that stretches full width behind the velvets and we open up to show it, slats open and blue lit, for 'Songs My Mother Taught Me'. It suddenly becomes open air in a pleasing way.

We had an invited audience of hairdressers, cabdrivers and wives, secs. from theatre suppliers etc. They were wonderful. So it was a useful experience and enjoyable too. Tonight is the night.

17 July 1959   Sydney

Darling Ginnie,

Well it went off very well as R. will have told you. V.g. notices too. The house was really rather too much, in saying it as I shouldn't.

Hysterical and smart, and busy showing how much they understood. Typical first nighters I'd say – revue that is. It was like the N.Y. opening and I found it frightening because of this wildness, and felt that it would alienate the quieter element there and probably the critics. But they got a little quieter – exhausted maybe?

Anyway it sure was BIG. I didn't give a very good performance altho' it was a controlled one. But we couldn't get our phrasing going with any glow because they laughed too much and were so eager. But kindly. Very neighbourly place this.

22 July 1959   Sydney

Darling Ginnie,

Being Abroad you won't have heard of all our Dramas down under! In brief – there were conflicts between the Board of Directors of the Phillip St Theatre and Bill Orr who runs it. He is a little cocky but he is also head boy there and has done a very remarkable job with it and is much respected and applauded.

Well, on Mon. the Board sacked him! For the most trivial reasons – petty slights they felt he'd done to them etc. Oh all so silly. Great dramas though and hurried meetings and resignations and press interviews with directors.

Then last night I went to the theatre at 7 and the theatre's solicitor told me the show was cancelled. The staff, loyal to Bill Orr, felt this would achieve something. So Bill Blez. and I left to come home.

There were scenes at the theatre and an emergency directors' meeting summoned, and Bill Orr was reinstated! I was not involved and felt beautifully calm and remote till the *Syd. Morn. Herald* had a banner headline 'Comedienne walks out of theatre'.

Up rose my rage. 'Walking out' is a bad thing to say of a *nactress*. It implies stamping of feet, righteous indignation, offended ego and cetera. Also, more important still, a great sense of irresponsibility. So – in went a statement.

Got the press agent to handle it, who gave it to the papers, and kept *beautifully* mum otherwise. But I cabled Reg. to explain all just in case some fool Ass. Press message might leak into local papers and distress him. I think the theatre staff was right to strike last night and am glad Bill Orr is back on the job. He needed a whip crack but not the sack. This has now turned him into a martyr-hero.

Tempis – how is that written – tant pis maybe – I'm to play tonight, the sun is out, I love the stage stuff, love the theatre, we're sold out for weeks, so God's in His Heaven, as always. And am I tired!! Not too bad actually.

Last night there was a press photographer lurking in the doorway –
11.45 p.m.! I covered my face with my arm and got in un-caught, and
felt so wobbly as if I'd done a great crime. Did you ever.

Bill Blezard is a good steady pillar to lean on and we laugh quietly to
ourselves at all the Brouhaha!

24 July 1959 Sydney

Darling Ginnie,

Half the Board has now resigned. But peace reigns. It was all *so* petty
– childish – unnecessary. Such emotions, such goings on.

Today I got a retraction on T.V., radio and in print as well as letters
from enraged Sydney-ites who felt the city had let me down. So now all
is in order. The business is wonderful. Long queues and the advance
piling up. Lovely enthusiastic audiences who listen and laugh and
applaud all the proper places.

I've got Mary O'Hara, Irish folk singer, in the spare room. In a burst
of enthusiasm I offered it to her and here she is. She's a nice creature
– practically a nun really. She's just off to *Saturday* mass at 12.10 with
nothing but a drop of coffee in her stomach. She's deeply involved
with her Church and is doing her tour to raise funds for a home for
old people. No one is doing anything, so she arrives in small towns
unheralded, unknown, and plays to empty halls. Such a waste. She is a
superb artist and had a terrific time here where the publicity was good.

She is an easy guest and very quiet, so no complaints except that
I really like it best when I'm here on me own. *Selfish* to the core,
that's me.

On Sunday I went to my Church. Mary O'Hara took a tennis racquet
to hers in the hope of a tussle with a Holy Father after Mass!

Bill came to tea and Mary sang 'She moved through the fair' for us
unaccompanied, and it was so remarkable and touching that we were
both quite cold with wonder.

21 August 1959 Sydney

Darling Ginnie,

I'm progressing. It's been rather tough. A chesty cold. Cough.
Thickness. I sound as if it had been endless. I'm not low. Just BORED.

I managed the show by not singing at all. I spoke the story songs,
cut out all the 'Songs my Mother Taught Me', 'Joyful Noise' and ended
part one on 'Learn to Loosen', about being a Great White Horse. Apart
from a great moan of sound it wasn't too bad. But I have asked for
boosters for tonight – two shows.

I saw half a matinée of the Bolshoi Ballet dance yesterday. They danced with enormous skill but such awful dances, clothes, music, and it was all strangely out of touch. Some of it was unintentionally very funny. Very arch – very naive. 'Ocean' was a muscled young man with silver in his green tinsel shorts and lots of pale green chiffon, for waves I suppose. He danced miraculously but his clothes!

P.S. I wrote a new Nursery School this week.
Love to To. And youdl.

24 August 1959   Sydney

Darling Ginnie,
Two lully letters today. And two from R., Vic and Dick and Viola – such an endearing account of her morning with you and To. She loved it and wrote so well describing you. 'Gin had made it a treat day by ringing up the day before so I was looking forward. The mixture of that and a still, fresh park in the sun, only a few specialist sunbathers finishing the white bits, out early, and the T. apartment all glowing in peach softness and a sun-flooded balcony in a ring of willing petunias, all was like a special extra present for a feast. And that's what it was. I am grateful for their thoughtfulness.'
So am I. Yesterday I saw Bondi Beach. A wide – mile? – shallow curve of palest sand, then blue Pacific rolls in. There were fifty or more bathers surfing on boards and it looked so wonderfully easy and is *impossible* – like ballet.
The voice is there again in all but the very middle. An odd soggy patch. But with the wonderful mikes and with Bill's *really* remarkable swiftness in transposing everything to any key at a minute's notice, I am able to do all the songs now except 'Joyful Noise'. That will be back in a day or so. So lots to Thank God for. In particular Bill Blezard. He really is a most remarkable musician.

9 September 1959   Sydney

Darling Ginnie,
Even at my teeny little theatre I make over £500 a week – Australian £1=16/-. Can't work it out but it's good money I think. Though God knows I earn it too!!
I've written a lyric for Bill to 'put a tune to' as a surprise for the last night. They make a big thing of last nights. It's just a thank you song to Phillip St., which I really do love so it's easy to say. It's the nicest theatre I ever played in.

Yesterday the Overseas League lunch. Such dear funny British faces under the funniest Australian hats. They all (hats) look as if they'd been made in a mould: the felt has a sort of solid look. And all in bright colours with something to shine somewhere. A buckle, or three diamonds sewn on in front. Never a lapel without a sparkler. And the teeth are always borrowed or else gold filled. Not very pretty. Rugged faces but nice. There were about 95% women, eating sandwiches and acorn coffee.

A chord on a pale yellow upright piano, not remotely in tune, and everyone stood and belted out the Queen. Somehow remarkably moving as well as comic. I fought a lump and giggle equally, and mastered both.

It is absolutely fascinating and I think thrilling that the tribute paid to me is 'we left the theatre feeling so much better than when we came in!' 'Such a sense of happiness' and *never 'You* are such and such!' I think that's entirely as it ought to be from a C.S. point of view and it lifts the burden. I know *I'm* not that good so it all falls into place, and the success of the thing ceases to be anything that could make me conceited. (I'm not honest. Really.) I'm just grateful that it all works and apparently gives real pleasure.

It's lovely to know R. will be here in a few weeks – then the hol. – then *HOWME*. My Australian accent is getting quite *promising*.

P.S. I have put clean sheets on today – a tremendous chore I always think. Daily I simply pull the bed up and tuck in. I sleep that tidily I don't need to do more. I'm amazed at how tidy I sleep really. Just slide in between the sheets like a bookmarker. And yet I do starfish all *over* the bed at night. But not a sign.

16 September 1959   Sydney

Darling Ginnie,

Shirl Conway, who is doing Auntie Mame here, was on T.V. on Sun. – said she thought Australian men didn't know how to talk to women and didn't know how to behave to them either. The press rang me next day for my view, so cagily I said it was up to women to make their conversation so interesting that men would want to talk to them. This came out as: 'J.G. says Australian women must rub the rough edges off the men'!! I was enraged. I'd been *so* careful what I said so as not to offend. Now this! You can't win with the press.

Sunday 20 September 1959   Sydney

Darling Ginnie,
   I've been creatin' – oh for some time and oh so slowly. It's a
monologue, in that very rich American idiom. It begins to move but I
long for some lovely inspired surprises. They are the hard bits. I mean
like the line in 'Life & Lit.' which knocked me side ways when I first said
it, quite spontaneously and unworked out:
   'I was awfully surprised when he became a nun.' Those gems don't
come often, alas.
   Bill too is creatin'. It's a big orchestral overture and the theatre
resounds all day with monumental dissonances, rather good I think,
and he is very caught up in it.
   Did I tell you? A wild oldish Sydney Psychiatrist who grows them
sent me 16 *branches* of orchids! They watch me in a very oriental way.
Not sure I like it.
   Ten days from *today* R.P.G. is due . . . !!!

30 September 1959   Sydney

Darling Ginnie,
   Yesterday a highly enjoyable lunch with young students at the Univ.
who bade me join them there. The Journalists Club. They were very
bright and all current and gay as grigs. Very nice to me and they laid
on a slap up sit down white damask tableclothed repast with a waiter
and two buxom waitresses in the Union Building. About twenty of us.
Lots of sun and laughter, and they gave me an impression of vitality,
wit and world awareness, which is an encouraging feeling. They know
all about everything like Stephen Potter – Drop of a Hat – Tom Lehrer
– Nicholson & May. They read *Punch*, the *Spec.*, the *O.*, and know every
note of Bernstein. All about 19–21.[1]

---

[1] Clive James (1939–), television presenter and writer, was one of these students. They were
very surprised that Joyce accepted their invitation. This was the beginning of a friendship
which continued when James moved to London and Joyce described him as 'my wild,
Australian boy'.

2 October 1959   Sydney

Darling Ginnie,
   Tonight's the night – R. is due at 9.45, but you know what Air
Britannia is – 'Round the world in eighty delays'. I've been doing the
journey with him ever since he took off Weds. and am fair tuckered up!

It *is* exciting. The bed is made, the floors are polished, every pot, jam jar and vase has flora on it.

4 October 1959   Sydney

Darling Ginnie,
    The boy is here. Lovely it was.
    We took Peter Ustinov to lunch and are now by the fire, reading. P.U. is here to make *The Sundowners*.[1] He was so funny about his visit to a masseur – no a *masseuse* – in Tokyo. The lady, strong, met him in a bra and transparent shorts and ignored him as a man, dealing coolly and superbly with his body as if he were a race horse. She saw a toe nail that didn't please her so clipped it neatly. Tucked a bit of his beard in where it sprang out, and sent him forth feeling 100%. He is very good company. We left him to face the press.

[1] Film directed by Fred Zinnemann, also starring Robert Mitchum and Deborah Kerr.

12 October 1959   Sydney

Darling Ginnie,
    The last night and party went easily and we ended with Bill and me improvising opera quite brilliantly! I astound myself sometimes when this sort of thing comes off! We changed keys in mid air and *never* faltered. You can't think how intoxicating it is to do. One needs no audience. It's sheer self indulgence, and we agreed afterwards that it is our favourite form of art.
    I'm glad I came. I've grown really fond of the place and my nice pals here. But oh for London . . .

18 October 1959   Eidsvold
                                                                           Queensland

Darling Ginnie,
    Goodness me, how little one knows about Australia. It's so much lovelier than anyone ever tells you. The enormousness of it and the sense of age and timelessness at once make it very unlike anything we are used to. And the flowers and the birds are so lovely and gay. I expected a cattle station to be rather bare and brown.
    This is what it's like: mile on mile of hilly, rolling land, trees, meadows (measured in miles and called paddocks), and rivers and little townships consisting of a single row of houses.

The birds! – parrots, bee-eaters, canaries. R. is out with book and glasses and so happy. The peace, the space, the beauty of it.

R. and I each saw kangaroo today. Huge 'old man' kangaroos six feet tall! They loped away in enormous hops and stood like stone staring at us. Silly heads and flipper arms and big bat ears.

If I was young and liked country life I'd come here. No question of it. As it is I'm more for S.W.10.

24 October 1959   Melbourne

Darling Ginnie,

Two lully letters. Thank you, love. Sorry about your dottiness but I know it all too well. One of my blanks was to carry a pair of stays – roll-on – all the way to the lift in Sydney when I'd meant to put it in a drawer! It would have looked interesting in the street I fancy. Really tho' it is a bit potty. Part of you-know-what no doubt. I go on getting huge flushes but they are of no worry and keep me warm when it's nippy. This new tropical clime R. tells me, is due for twenty more years! Will our characters change with it? Interesting to see.

Melbourne is much more English than Syd. and flatter too. This old rather grand hotel has noble old porters and nannies to do the rooms.

The Connie Jeffries family do on Sunday was a big success. Do you remember her? Parlour maid of ours, sister of Bert who was a Cliveden chauffeur, daughter of old Mr Jeffries who gardened the Long Garden at Cliveden? He was a great character. I don't believe he could read much but he could grow anything. They had a *tiny* cottage up a lane. No mod. cons.

Now Connie and her four children are Australians (since 1949). Tom her husband is dead (May), and one son is an Anglican clergyman: her daughter married and followed her out, and they have built a really charming modern little house with fridge, washer, T.V. Austin is in the P.O. and taking his architect's diploma on the side. Another son is doing very well in timber, the baby is 16 and helps Connie in the café milk bar they built. They all have good cars, paid for. All this in 10 years. They work very hard but can make such progress here.

1960

Joyce returned to New York for a television programme and ten-week tour.

28 January 1960   New York

Darling Virginia,

Not a word from either Dick or Victor. I don't know why I mind but I do. They are so touchy about being remembered and *usually* remember others. I'm not touchy. But I'm a little sad. Not *really* of course. But I wish they *had* thought to send a telegram.

Yesterday I baby sat for Mary who is working. She's being fitted now for the shows next month.[1] Nanny has a cold and went off to a women's hotel to have it in. So Tante had to take over.

The children were wild as birds for the first ten minutes and had me foxed, did they but know! However I stood firm and was severe enough to cause them to take notice. Both are very bright and so over endowed with vitality that it is startling to an elderly aunt. But it was endearing as I left to have Sally hug me and whisper 'I'm sorry I was naughty.' I melted.

The rush in N.Y. is not just a myth. One is driven as if one was a Ferrari – or is that an electric fire? The beauty of this city and the horror of its attitude of mind to most things combine to be rather bewildering. At night it is really wonderful to see. But the streets are still rough and full of holes and the crowds are not pretty. Individuals are often endearing and attractive. I'm glad I don't live here.

Funny how much freer one feels here about being a C.S. It is accepted as normal and one isn't a freak. I do like this I must say.

Much love and to To.

[1] Mary Phipps was a fashion model.

[January 1960]   Hyde Park Gardens

Darling Joyce,

I went to Kirk, & found m'mind straying a bit, a whole section gone on wondering if a woman's hat was really her hair or vice versa. Came to *no* conclusion. Rousing hymns, & my tenor was pretty smashing today. It varies rather.

We are slowly recovering from the office dance which was very testing to our physique. A five course dinner – each course was 'played in' on a clarinet & saxophone, a new innovation & not wholly successful – & then hours of hectic dancing. Most of the dances were in the nature of games, such as dancing with a stick of spaghetti joining the mouths

of partners! It was very gay & rock & rolly, & quite *fantastically* noisy!
Now we are both crippled.

5 February 1960   New York

Darling Ginnie,

I'm lying in bed somewhat sleepily after doing the prog. latish last
night for some friends of T's and George's as a sort of dress rehearsal. It
went far too well! But old war horses me now recognises the problems
in halls and theatres. One works so much in a vacuum.

Had them all in floods of tears with Boat Train. Did you ever. I was
most beautifully un-involved last night. Totally impersonal and perhaps
that is why it went so well. I wore my new Victor apple green paper
taffeta and felt shapely.

Talked to Aubrey Blackburn[1] this a.m. about the St Trinian's film.
The money isn't enough considering they seem so keen to have me
and I don't want to do it! They may get Sellers[2] – but I doubt it. I've
said I'll do it if they'll pay more *and* have a really good man in it!
Subconsciously I hope they'll say no – I think.[3]

[1] Joyce's theatrical agent.
[2] Peter Sellers (1925–80), British comedy actor.
[3] Joyce did appear in *The Pure Hell of St Trinian's*. George Cole took the place of
Peter Sellers.

5 February [1960]   Hyde Park Gardens

Darling Joyce,

Your itinerary has come, & positively appalls me! I suppose you will
survive, but *heavens*!

We finally weakened before a mysterious onslaught from Maureen
Dufferin[1] – she asked us to three things in a fortnight! So we went &
dined. An enormous dinner party in honour of the Head of Columbia
pictures, only he didn't happen to be there! But a host of elegant types
were. We chatted to Osbert Lancaster,[2] & gaped around at the diamonds
splashed on every bosom.

Yesterday presented a different picture, as I spent most of it in King's
Cross goods yard, distributing *Christian Science Monitors*![3] Never knew
such dirt, squalor & general slumminess still existed. But one of British
Railways employees, an enormously stout woman in blue trousers
& a bursting red jersey, with dyed hair, followed us out & asked if
we could get her a Bible, as she'd never read it. So you never know,
do you?

I ought to be writing a 'satirical Valentine' for BBC's *Woman's Hour*.
To work, to work.

[1] Maureen, Marchioness of Dufferin and Ava (1907–).
[2] British cartoonist (1908–86).
[3] Daily newspaper, published in Boston, USA with a British edition.

7 February 1960   New York

Darling Ginnie,
   In brief. Princeton was very good. Pretty day. T. lent us his station
wagon and George drove. The piano was a brute. We made a stink:
a better one – slightly – was produced. So wearing. Such ignorance.
Dammit.
   It's odd that authorities think any old piano will do. Glad to say my
agent was there and saw first hand, so now a letter is to go out to *all*
my dates impressing them with the need for a really first class piano.
Various friends came round afterwards and lots of strangers. Why oh
why do I attract *so* many queers? They *flock*! Isn't it odd.
   R. cabled and sent flowers. These arrived in a six sided cellophane
box and was a purple orchid in a pink tulle frill, and all was sprinkled
with gold dust! So wonderfully unlike R. – or me.
   Verily Anderson[1] who writes those funny books – *Beware of Children*
etc. – is here for the first time. Coming here for lunch today.
   Much love darling.

[1] British author (1915–), recently widowed. They first met when Verily Anderson
interviewed Joyce for the Girls' Friendly Society magazine. From 1960 they became close
friends in London and Joyce helped to support her five children, one of whom edited
this book.

10 February [1960]   Hyde Park Gardens

Darling Joyce,
   Today is your birthday & I am thinking of you with great love &
affection, & wishing like anything I was bringing you a cake, sparkling
with 21 candles. You're getting a big girl now, & frankly I'm proud
of you. You do me credit. If you're as nice when you're 50 as you are
now, I shall know everything has been worth while. Joking apart, my
blessings.
   How maddening the piano was so awful. I would have thought
it was elementary to provide a chanteuse with a decent one – not to
mention poor George. As for there being so many queers fluttering
round your candle, I can only assume your maternal attributes

outweigh your sexy ones! Also, I suppose, they are perceptive & sensitive?

We are quiet & snug – T asleep, & me having just whanged out a silly poem for *Punch*.

14 February 1960   Washington

Darling Gin,

Ta, you clever postal type, you. Keep on writing, eh?

Eight inches of snow. White and wonderful and *so* inconvenient. I flew in from Ann Arbor, where I'd had a really sensational recep. in the vast Hill Auditorium – over 3,500 people there! And such a response. They tell me I've improved and have developed! – deeper and ranged wider. Encouraging. It was wonderfully exciting and fun. I felt totally un-responsible hooray.

This week is high pressure so could you please call Mrs Gabe to say I loved my Valentine and will write from Florida next weekend. Love, love.

17 February [1960]   Hyde Park Gardens

Darling Joyce,

Yesterday I went & visited one of the F of P homes[1] – oh, so touching! I do think old age is heartbreaking. There were these dear old things with the salvaged remains of their lives crammed into little rooms; Mrs Reed showing her late husband's *Punch* cartoons; Miss Maud poring over a map to see where her nephew had got to in Africa; Mrs Hudson painting frail water colours; & Mrs John, aged 92 sewing Cash's name tapes into her pillowcases. All shawls & little clawing hands.

[1] Virginia was on the committee of the Society of Friends of the Poor and Gentlefolk's Help, a charity which housed elderly people. Princess Margaret was the patron. The society shared an office with the Disabled Soldiers Embroidery Industry in Ebury Street, London.

19 February 1960   Charlotte Airport

Darling Virginia,

Please share this letter with Dick and Victor and ask their forgiveness but NO time for letters and I do want to tell you about this week.

I discovered an old lady who'd been at school nearby with my Ma. She remembered her as 'the most glamorous girl in the school, and with the prettiest legs'. Also the most amusing and flirtatious.

After the show in Staunton – a good one – I was swept off by a

committee lady followed by Connie and George in our hired fine red
Ford. They slid gently into a drift and had to be rescued by the Police,
so never got to the very nice little gathering in such a pretty old
Colonial house. I didn't stay late, worrying about Geo. And Connie.
Outside the house I saw a white moon and stars, the huge box hedges
loaded with snow like Christmas puddings with icing that one sees in
drawings and never in life. Connie and George had taken refuge in an
All Nite Laundry and eaten cookies and cokes from slot machines on
the wall!

Our next destination was the astonishing Bob Jones University
in Greenville. We were a little wary of it since Connie had so many
letters from them stressing that as they were a religious institution I
must clean up my material, not wear low cut dresses, etc. 'Bob Jones
University' has 3,000 non-denominational Prot. students from all over
the place. No smoking, dancing, drinking or going to the movies! No
Jazz! Bob Jones is 79 now and an old time Evangelist. He's now a tired
old man, very repetitive and can't listen to anything once he gets off.
Clichés flew from him – 'If God meant man to smoke he'd have given
him a chimney in his head'. He was full of the Blood of the Lamb,
hell-fire, and it was fascinating but *awful*.

Money has poured in to build this pale brick campus – hideous –
and equip it with its own film studio, own radio station, and the best
equipped auditorium in the country! We are in very comfy guest rooms.

Geo. and Con. had to smoke in the W.C. Huge No Smoking signs
everywhere. We ate with the old man, Mrs Jones, and grandson Bob the
3rd, and young Mrs Jones, in a room off the vast hall where students,
faculty and their families all eat in shifts.

The young Bob Jones the 3rds are just married – Dec. They live in
one room in the married students' dormitory and eat *all* meals in the
dining hall with grandpa and grandma, pa and ma (when they are
there – now crusading or art buying in Europe). So the young Bobs are
never alone, no cooking, no quiet life except bed.

Hymns, prayers, and rather dull food. The students sang 'Come out.
Come out' to me and I had to show myself at the door. Applause! This
before the show.

The auditorium is vast, 3000 seats, and purple throughout. It is used
as a church and a concert hall, and has revolving stages, trap doors,
trick lighting, etc. etc. George's rhythms had 'em worried I think, but
when I announced him I mentioned the magic word 'Julliard School of
Music' and they accepted him! (They were so silly.)

The Art Gallery was an eye opener. Picture the campus a nightmare
of square cheap yellow brick buildings linked by concrete paths. Very
big. No taste, no sign of quality anywhere. But the Gallery! I'd heard

it was valued at $200,000 but queried it. It was in fact *wonderful*. A collection of religious pictures including Rubens, Botticelli, Tintoretto, to name but a few! Also a fantastic collection of icons. I was astonished, room after room. No one knows where the money comes from but the Lord provides!

Everyone I know (from Tryon, only 40 miles off), wanted to come. Dear, kind, generous, Christian Bob Jones Univ. wouldn't let them in. Finally I persuaded them to allow me *one* pair of tickets! I must admit the place was full. 3,428 came, they turned away 350, we were told. It was amusing to discover that my show was compulsory for students.

Connie was rung up by the Costume Dept. to say did the dresses need pressing. She said no thank you, and the lady pressed on saying it was policy – she had to *see* the dresses before the shows. We realised she had to make sure my dresses *weren't* cut low!

Geo. and I were nervous as witches. Vast place and all these restrictions, added to which the students came 'formal' in evening dresses and dark suits! But it went very well, much bowdlerised and all my favourites cut – 'Life & Literature', etc. etc. Afterwards five calls and then dozens came back stage to say thank you. Very formal and somehow touching. When we left the theatre we saw the dating couples walking in pairs – a few feet behind each other, along the concrete paths. This, we realised was their only social chance to dress up. No dancing, no parties. They all have a slightly luminous elation and ask have you been saved, at the drop of a hat.

Somehow it was a very depressing place because so narrow, chilly, un-loving and afraid. Discipline, it seems to me, is no good unless it enables one to behave under all circumstances. This was like Communism or Nazism.

We were glad to get away, loaded with tracts.

Queen Elizabeth II gave birth to her third child, Prince Andrew Albert Christian Edward.

24 February [1960]   Hyde Park Gardens

Darling Joyce,

It's a boy, as you will have gathered! Enid Blyton[1] has written verses to be sung to Over the Sea to Skye, & I have been hours trying to make the words fit. They are all about spring & fluffy ducks, & I can only suppose she follows a different version of the time to what I do.

---

[1] Author of *Noddy* children's books (1897–1968).

27 February 1960   En l'air

Darling Ginnie,

Palm Beach is extraordinary. It is like a sort of super American version of upper-crust Virginia Water cum Ascot[1] in a tropical setting. Very manicured gardens, palms, and such luxury. It's a club settlement. You have to be proposed and passed and finally elected before you may buy and build. Of course no Jews. I'm appalled really and can't imagine why they like being here, except that it's exactly like Long Island and their life there only in the sun. All elderly of course. And a lot are very bien tho' some are merely moneyed. The keynote is Success. They are *literally* all millionaires.

We went to a terrible dinner dance last night, all tycoons. I was amused and appalled by the people there. So rich, so spoiled, so diamonded and dyed, so un-happy looking. Old ladies who should have been knitting cosily somewhere bursting out of topless satin, with blue hair, and facials, and such jewellery. Lots of unsavoury Extra men. A dinner jacket and a reasonable appearance are a passport for any man, I'm told. I met several such, often queer, and all on the make, at a simple little floodlight pool side buffet supper dance in my honour after the show on Sun. night. Not very attractive. Molluscs.

An amusing lawyer told me 'Hobe Sound is a lot of old crumbs of the upper crust held together by dough.' Very neat.

I really cannot take elderly tycoons and their boring ladies. It is always so interesting to realise that these men *must* have brains or, surely, they wouldn't be millionaires now? But they bluster, roar with inane laughter, slap each other on the back, pay utterly un-meant compliments to the ladies, haven't ever read – or can't read – books, know *nothing* of Eng. Lit. or Amer. Lit. or the Arts, and are godawful BORES. Today, four pairs of elderly crashers drank – stiff martinis – for an hour and finally got to the table at 1.50. Delicious lunch and a lot of hilarity and noise. I got quieter and quieter and rose above the heavy handed jokes about fishing, clubs, shooting parties and talk of business. I don't believe any of these men *really* like each other, but all are BIG tycoons – millionaires all, still like small boys showing off. Their wives hang on, with hideously set modern diamonds (good) and neat hair-do's and pastel dresses.

I must tell you about the petit point cushion I saw on a yacht at Hobe Sound. It was embroidered in quite petit petit point with this subtle legend: 'This is our boat and we do what we damn well please on it'!! That sort of adolescence here makes me writhe. The skipper is a millionaire, a crude, yelling, back slapper, full of boyish animal spirits that caused me to cringe. His wife looked rather worn.

Princess Margaret and Tony Armstrong-Jones is *fascinating.*[2] I am *so* surprised. As you know I've been photographed by him for the past five or six years and I like him. Gay and amusing and Bohemian. Always *late* for everything, spontaneous, creative. But not, I'd have thought, at all likely to conform, and I'm amazed at him giving up his freedom and very successful career, so I'm hoping it MUST be love. I shall write to them.

It is just such a breeze that will freshen up the Royal Circle. They do hate the ranks being invaded, don't they?

[1] The 'stockbroker belt' south of London.
[2] They had just become engaged. Anthony Armstrong-Jones (1930–) was a well-known photographer, later Earl of Snowdon.

29 February [1960]   Hyde Park Gardens

Darling Joyce,

WELL! *What* about our Princess? Fascinating here, because these old types think it is a real disaster, & they feel it *keenly.* They don't like him being a photographer, they are convinced he is a pansy, they don't like his father marrying for the third time, & to an air hostess. And they really & truly mind, just as much as though she were their own daughter. Well, I honestly can't see that it matters, can you? I mean, the chances of him being King of England are pretty remote, & if the poor girl's in love with him . . . anyway, I've been fighting on the lad's side. And now I'm already fed to the teeth with the whole darling romance.

Wouldn't it be nice if P.M. got the wedding dress from Victor? It would cheer him up no end.

Mrs Westaway is here now! Mrs Horne[1] had to gallop off to look after her sister, so we've kicked Mrs W out of retirement, & there she is, in a very starched white coat, knocking up some pretty smashing pancakes.

[1] Mrs Westaway was Virginia's retired cook, Mrs Horne her cook until 1963.

9 March 1960   Hotel Sir Francis Drake
                                                              San Francisco

Darling Virginia,

This *is* an attractive city. And a real city. Not just a big town. Lots of 'bien' about and oh it does make a change. Smartly dressed too. Not just flashy.

I had a killing fan letter – pages of praise and one criticism. In 'Antique Shop' the lady writer felt I'd not used the right word when I make the lady say 'Do come in. How sweet of you to come and see my terrible little DUMP.' This word, the lady said, was wrong. 'I feel,' she wrote, 'the word you want is *establishment*.'!! I love it when they miss the whole point. My new Nursery School sketch is tremendous now. I suppose I've learned how to do it. Anyway it is BIG and I'm told it's the best of all of them.

Oh *dear* – I see Hartnell is doing the dress.[1] I could SPIT. Why couldn't she let Vic do it? It is tough; altho' I expect he was pretty certain he wouldn't get it? Or did he hope? Is he better? Oh poor.

Nice articles on me on Women's Pages today – Victor's clothes featuring. Wore his grey outfit for interviews.

Incidentally – a secret I expect – Britten has asked Viola to work on the amenuensing part of his new *Midsummer Night's Dream* because Imogen Holst[2] is ill. Very flattering. It is sad for poor I. Holst, but it is very exciting for Viola.[3]

Thank God for God.

[1] Norman Hartnell (1901–79), dress designer to the royal family, knighted in 1977.
[2] Musician and folk song arranger (1907–84) daughter of composer Gustav Holst (1874–1934).
[3] The opera *Midsummer Night's Dream* was one of Britten's important works, with Peter Pears singing Oberon.

12 March [1960]   Hyde Park Gardens

Darling Joyce,

Victor lunched yesterday – in the throes of designing P.M's going-away dress, & has done no fewer than 32 sketches! The Press badger him so much that he is hiring a press agent to tell them what kind of braces he wears & if he likes soup. Seems he *was* disappointed, *very*, about the wedding dress, because there were definite rumours. All the same, I don't quite see how she could have given Hartnell such a slap in the face, do you?

16 March 1960   Seattle

Ginnie Darling,

Your aim is so accurate. A letter for me today. Thank heaven Vic is to do the going away dress. That's *something*.

I'm so glad you are writing again for *Punch*. That's good. I really wish I was. Maybe I'll try. Everyone who has seen previous progs. thinks I'm *so* much better – *deeper*, more profound! What, one wonders, can I have been like before when the praise comes so thick *now*?

A gossipy lady asked Connie last night if it was true that I had married Stephen Potter! This so infuriated Connie and gave her the giggles at the same time so that she nearly choked, and startled the busy lady a great deal.

25 March 1960   The Drake
                                                                Chicago

Darling Ginnie,
     Iowa city was unexpectedly good. The West has real charm. What an amazing country – continent – this is! So huge for one thing. We met some really attractive and intelligent professors and had 2,000 heavenly people in the Union Hall. They were *so* appreciative it was a joy to do the programme.
     A pleasant little party afterwards at which I was introduced to Lady Janet Shipton – 'her father was Prime Minister of England'. She was very squirmy and shy and I couldn't place her. Attlee![1] 'And this is her husband Dr Shipton', and there was that hilarious looking little man with the fan of teeth that I suddenly remembered from his wedding photographs five years or so ago! Do you remember him? He is a very brilliant scientist it seems. Has a tiny beard as well as these teeth. Is nice, too. But it is a *very difficult* appearance.
     Did I write all this to you? I wrote it to Dick I think, but now I'm confused and don't know if I told you too? Forgive your dotty friend.

[1] Clement Attlee (1883–1967), Labour Prime Minister of Britain from 1945 to 1951.

28 March [1960]   Hyde Park Gardens

Darling Joyce,
     I am onto the last address on that itinerary of yours, & I can hardly believe it – Lord, Love, you really are a tough baby. You ought to give a testimony about it when you get back: 'How I sang in 50 places in 60 days'!
     Yesterday I tottered up Wigmore Street in a wild wind. I went to try on m' new chiffon semi-evening affair. Smashing, it is, very simple, in a sort of thunder colour. Stiebel's was a *hive*. A lovely sound made – buzz buzz & little muffled cries and the pattering of feet galloping on errands. It seems fearfully dotty, but the Royalty are wearing long dresses, & the rest short!
     Tremendous drama at yesterday's meeting of the FoP.[1] One of our old types has just died and left £30,000! He said he only had £400 a year, & told a naughty wicked lie! Pity he didn't leave it to the Society – though that might have looked even fishier.
     I was furious with Dick today because he says he is going to put

a marvellous dye called man-Tan on his face: it doesn't wash off. He was quite *serious* about this. I once had a similar argument with him regarding a toupé. Rather touching the way he longs to be young & beautiful, but I am also slightly shocked.

[1] Friends of the Poor.

1 April [1960]   Hyde Park Gardens

Darling Joyce,
    Rather a wobbly hand this morn, due to a late night on some very slippery tiles! After a Charity film – P.M. and A.A–J[1] there, so we were all tarted up – then on to refreshers. Absolute hell. All ladies with bee-hive hair-do's, diplomats, Lords, Cary Grants. Lots of famous faces. The only people we knew to *talk* to were Noël & Joycie.[2] Noël ha. been ill,[3] & has become a little old man, with the remains of his hair rubbing off in places like a sad wee mat. It was appallingly congested, and not easy to get away, as our hostess stood bang by the front door.
    Victor dined, in happier form. The *Express* is going to give him a very large sum to design a going-away dress for the proletariat – paper patterns provided & all![4] Trade is booming, with heaps of Duchesses queuing up for ball gowns. Poor Hartnell is apparently having a truly ghastly time, as the bridegroom is having 'ideas'. Sequins or anything glittery are definitely out, & that for Hartnell is a major disaster.

[1] Princess Margaret and Anthony Armstrong-Jones.
[2] Noël Coward and Joyce Carey.
[3] Coward had phlebitis – inflammation of the veins in his legs.
[4] In 1954 Victor designed a New Look dress for Joyce which was offered as a paper pattern in *Everywoman* magazine. 'The top of Miss Grenfell's dress is in grey silk jersey, with a skirt of grey and white lace over two underskirts of grey and pastel pink net. It has the new hip-length bodice.'

6 April 1960   The Windsor Arms
                                                   Toronto

Darling Virginia,
    Three gorgeous missiles here from you. TA oh TA. You know it is a joy to see your old blue envelopes with your dear old fist on them. Thank you for all gossip, darling.
    Montreal went very well. It is rather an attractive city but so priest ridden and covered in convents it gets one down after a while. I had a house full and they were wildly enthusiastic. I mean wild. They cheered, they roared. I kept feeling – 'Now, children, quiet or there'll be tears before bedtime' but there wasn't. I don't like quite so much success.

It seems to be too easy and I don't quite respond to it – feel I want to withdraw.

6 April [1960]   Hyde Park Gardens

Darling Joyce,
    General de Gaulle,[1] the pompous old drip, is here, looking a bit toffee-nosed & pulverising the traffic, but being a huge success. One doesn't quite know, of course, whether the crowds aren't out to look at Queenie, whose first appearance it is since her babe, but anyway the route was thickly lined yesterday and the Mall all titched up. There was a firework display in St James' Park with the largest crowd since the Coronation! 100,000 they estimated.

[1] President of France from 1959 to 1969 (1880–1970).

7 April 1960   The Windsor Arms

Darling Virginia,
    Ooer – I've *lost* my voice. Absolutely. I just made last night's show – oh only just. Agony it was. Not so physically, although it wasn't exactly fun, but the fact of being out on a stage without equipment and an audience of 100s sitting there is a real nightmare. It's just one of those rare deep seated colds I seem to get periodically. This one is a lulu as they say! Dammit. We have cancelled tonight's and it looks as if I'll have to cancel Saturday's too in New York. It really is enraging. I've done nearly nine weeks without any troubles and now on the very last lap – this.
    It seems just about the hardest nut to crack in C.S. – this voice business. I suppose if I was a dancer it would be me feet. The monotony of a one tone range is so constant that I bored myself last night.
    Connie is here now answering the telephone talking to New York and generally coping. When she told Klaus Kolmar, the N.Y. Agent, he at once said 'You know a lot of money is involved in this for the sponsor'! As if I'd done it on purpose. Connie was furious. 'She is not doing this for fun' she said. He was more reasonable after this.
    Isn't it all maddening But I've had a cable from R. saying he is on his way.[1]
    I hope to write you a gayer letter next time! I don't feel low. After all it is not very important in relation to the rest of the world. It is merely tiresome for us personally involved. So damn damn.
    But lots of love darling.

[1] Reggie had been in South Africa.

Joyce and Reggie were invited to Princess Margaret's wedding on 6 May in Westminster Abbey. Joyce sent Victor a cable asking him to design her a suitable outfit.

16 April 1960   New York

Darling Gin,
    Vic sent over sketches and I've chosen a dark leaf green chiffon that will be good for evenings later. It seems very silly to put on such a garment for a morning wedding but I suppose he knows best. I've written to find out what colour I am expected to wear on my head hands and feet as I'm a bit foxed. Green shoes maybe. White hat, gloves? Beige? It's so complicated.
    I ordered a tray for P.M. only to learn Vic has done so too. Never mind she'll have two. Mine is larger and painted cream with strawbs. and lilies of the valley and his I gather is black, so that makes a change.

Good Friday   Hyde Park Gardens

Darling Joyce,
    We've had a late breakfast & eaten very hot, frightfully cross buns which are now expanding like India rubber in our tums.
    On Wednesday we rushed off to see *Look on Tempests* because Gladys had told us Vanessa Redgrave was so marvellous in it.[1] And by heaven she was! And so was Gladys Cooper. Haven't seen such satisfying acting in years, & we adored it. Unfortunately its theme, the effect of discovering a man is homosexual on a mother & wife, has failed to attract the British public. The man himself does not appear, so the would-be titillated have scorned it, & it's not a 'family play' of course. But oh dear, what a pity. Such *magic* acting.
    Went up to Hampstead Heath & tried our luck at the coconut shys. Oh the lads & lassies there! *All* the boys wear those tremendously long pointed shoes, & what with drain-pipe trousers, string ties & long hair, they positively alarm. The girls simply look mad – unwashed rag-bags.

[1] Gladys Calthrop had been to see this play by Joan Henry with Noël Coward.

17 April 1960   Hotel Laurelton

Darling Ginnie,
    Easter and a pretty day it's been. We walked down to see the Easter Parade on Fifth Avenue and it really is a sight to see. Hats! Joke hats, pretty hats, hats to catch the eye for photographers, hats on dogs, hats

a yard wide and covered with roses, and we saw one on a poodle – only this was a sort of diamanté tiara! This town is full of exhibitionists and screw balls and this seems to be their day. And all the amateur photographers are hat conscious and click away in the face of total strangers. But they are out to attract attention, so deserve it. They close the street to traffic for three hours and everyone walks in the middle of the road. The extraordinary sound of high heels clicking.

Lunch at Mary's where she and Nanny gave us a huge turkey. We had an egg hunt and Sally sang us a song about four poor crows full of woe and disaster, and we all got hysteria and Sally was furious. Lang is absolutely enchanting at the moment. He sings long calypso like songs to himself about *everything*.

I've recorded almost every monologue in the repertoire – stock piling. They only use four on one disc. There is a great market for monologue records here and I've fought it for so long, but now, mixed with the songs, I've compromised.[1]

We saw Mary Martin in *The Sound of Music* and of course we enjoyed it.[2] It had a bad cynical press who were bored because it is all clean fun concerning nuns, children, yodelling and Mary Martin. A combination guaranteed to succeed. As one of the columnists said 'Nuns are always sure fun, so are children, so is Mary Martin – all three together just aren't fair' – or words to that effect. And it's true. It's a sort of super Novello show and I loved it. Mary is actually a little too old to play a girlish novitiate, but she does it nicely and has a scrubbed wholesome air that suits the piece. It was crammed out with children and grannies. It's a huge sell out.

I got a *pretty* hat for the wedding. It's made of green petals of all sorts and goes with the pattern Vic sent. And I've got shoes being dyed to match, so I'm set thank goodness.

My word I've got you a pretty present. It's blue, and it is . . . No I shan't say. Much love and to To.

[1] Joyce rarely recorded her monologues until she had stopped performing them live.
[2] Musical by Rogers and Hammerstein, just opened in New York.

On Joyce's return to London, she started filming *The Pure Hell of St Trinian's* while Virginia was on holiday in France.

13 June 1960   Shepperton Studio

Darling Gin,
    Up at 6 today. The rushes today were of the recorder playing sequence and because everyone laughed so much *in* the studio I was a

little apprehensive about the filming of it. I am, obviously, trying really hard to play it right and that is what is so funny. Cecil Parker's[1] look of rapt attention slowly fading is pretty funny too.

I'm all ready in my policewoman's uniform to be whipped over to Walton Police Station to be photographed running in the door there waving a newspaper. Can't remember quite why but it's a linking shot.

Viola seems to have done very well at Aldeburgh. She is playing the celeste and the harpsichord and the piano in various operas and is deeply involved in their productions too. It's lovely. *At last* – some official recognition of her very considerable talents. Of course Ben B[ritten] is famous for hot weather friendships that cool in a trice and out goes whoever is the victim. But let's hope it's different this time. Why not?[2]

---

[1] British actor (1902–73).
[2] This was the beginning of a long and fruitful musical relationship between Viola Tunnard and Benjamin Britten.

15 June 1960   Elm Park Gardens

Gin Darling,

It was quite a day. We were in a big disused sand pit near Woking. It was being the Arabian Desert no less and very effective if shot down on so that all edging green was eliminated. Cameras were on the little cliffs as it were, 10 or 12 feet high, shooting down on us. Donkeys with Arabs, and a goat helped the atmosphere.

George Cole[1] and I sat in his car for hours because the sun was fitful and huge thunderstorms broke at intervals with theatrical effects and such wet. Poor Ascot ladies.

Later – on the set, which is The Emir's Palace. Lots of Arabs and girls in chiffon trousers and yashmaks, and I am in a striped bernous with a chiffon head scarf to be worn as a yashmak. I'm at the tail end of a line of 6 *houris* all of us carrying a part of a Hoover. I pause for identification with a broad wink just in camera! All lovely subtle stuff you see.

---

[1] British comedy actor (1925–).

270

24 June 1960   Elm Park Gardens

Darling Ginnie,

John Gielgud is having a party at the Nat. Film Theatre on Mon. night to see two very old Shakespearean films of 1911 and 1913! We hope to go if I finish here on Mon. as at present scheduled. You never know with films. Yesterday we did twenty one set-ups in one day, and Cecil, George and I were in nineteen of them! All little linking shots of great boredom but very necessary.

We spent most of Thurs. and Weds. in an Arab Cafe scene with the smoke machines on. The eyes watered, the throat burned. Hell. The second day was better when they used incense instead of burning paper. We also did a pure Marx Bros. sequence that felt terribly funny, tho' whether it will be – who knows. Into a *tiny* back stage dressing room, about 3 feet wide, came crowding Cecil, George Cole, Nike P., Cyril Chamberlain, Monte Lairds, a girl dancer and a *very* fat lady being an Arab dresser – and me. We all kept moving as we came in, in a sort of circular dance. They say it looked wonderful and it felt *so* funny we were hard put to it not to giggle. I may say this film will need the abandoning of *all* critical standards to be enjoyed. But I rather *think* it *is* funny on a sort of wild level.

I've got a poem coming out in *Punch*! After all these years. I've written several in the past week but mostly no good for publication.

31 July 1960   Lawford Hall
                                            Manningtree
                                               Essex[1]

Darling Ginnie,

This is me writing you a Fan letter. Because in this pretty Adam green bedroom I have lain in the four poster bed, reading the collection of your poems 1939–1945 and they *are* so good. And so moving. It is a most remarkable evocation of a period and a mood – moods – and recalls those difficult days with real power. You are a clever gal. So I write now, fifteen years later, to say thank you darling.

Last night we played Likes & Dislikes, in which you list five things you genuinely like and five you genuinely dislike. Among his dislikes Martin put 'Watching other people enjoying themselves'! Phillys [Nichols] liked freesias and Reggie liked being up after getting up early. A young woman called Alva Elrith, who dined, disliked bus conductresses and liked Soho. I put 'hairy legs' as one dislike and didn't dare look to see if Jojo's were – I rather think they may have been.

What a pretty house this is. Phyllis heard wild evil music in the room next to hers two nights ago. It was on a piano. There is no piano next door to her room! It is a ghostly place. R. slept in the big double bed with me though, which was nice.

[1] Home of Sir Philip and Lady Nichols (Waldorf Astor's niece).

Joyce went to Harrogate for a performance in the Royal Hall.

21 September 1960   Hotel Majestic
                                                            Harrogate

Darling Virginia,
     Who *is* Lord Greville?[1]
     I do NOT love him.
     He has the suite below me and at 1 a.m. turned his radio on F.F.F.[2] for bongo rhythms, and shot me awake. The night porter went to try and locate the sound when I telephoned. Reported it was Lord Greville and he would request him to lower the sound. He did, a little. But it was still very audible. I telephoned, in all, four times before I could get silence. It seems his Lordship was not alone and it was 'a little awkward'. Awkward? It was bloody awful. I was shaking with rage and *wide* awake. I kept trying to love the situation and saying to myself: it doesn't matter if you sleep or not, just lie still. But you know . . . The night porter was free with names and told Lord G. it was me, at which he, Lord G., is alleged to have said he would make less noise. But that wasn't enough. I demanded silence. If I hadn't looked so peculiar in rollers and a pigtail and a pink furious face, I'd have gone down and thumped on Lord G's door myself. Wasn't it lucky I didn't.

[1] Ronald Fulke Greville was an unmarried gentleman of private means (1912–87), the last of his line.
[2] Fortissimo – very very loud.

22 September 1960   Hotel Majestic

Darling Virginia,
     This *is* a funny hotel. I'm overhearing two ladies talking about maids. 'She *thinks* she turns out but I have to do it all over again.' 'We don't use furniture polish – just a damp leather.' 'She sees a blur on the furniture, but *never* notices a dirty sill.'
     The audience was a little slow but I was nanny and urged them along gently till they could stand alone, and they ended up bright as buttons! I've got fresh carnations from a fanatical young man who

came back stage and kissed my hand and said 'Aim a Scot – fra Edinburgh – and you are a wonderful woman'. He was all of 25.

Lord Greville is big boobyish blond and queer, and didn't play his radio last night. I think he was tight. He is with a pale friend – for two weeks – cure I suppose.

Cheeri-bye jest now.

1961

Virginia and Tony went on holiday to Portugal.

23 April 1961   Elm Park Gardens

Darling Ginnie,

I would just like to say that while my true self knows it is all one whether you are in Lisbon or London, my lesser selfish me wishes you were still in London. I miss our morning talks: I missed being able to consult you over yesterday's crossword which foxed us no end, though we got on better with struggle: I miss *you*. Interesting that one is far closer to close friends than to kith and kin, or to *some* close friends.

Kenneth Williams' revue started *so* well that we were convinced the critics had been wrong. Then it sank slowly. He *is* funny and makes the most of nothing. Paddy Stone has done a good slick job of direction and invented some good dances for Irving Davies[1] to do. But Irving is on far too much and, good as he is, one tires of rhythm, teeth, jive movements and whirling. It looks very good. Some sort of slide is thrown on to the skycloth at the back – from the back? I think it must be that way because the actors never get between it and cast shadows. There is imaginative lighting in a dance about being followed by one's shadow. The girls are sex-y and lack talent. A sort of poor man's Joan Sims cum Dora Bryan is too small in her ideas. Called Sheila Hancock.[2] Music totally un-memorable. So it's all rather sad. Kenneth W. repeats the old formula with new words.

[1] Welsh dancer who was in *Joyce Grenfell Requests the Pleasure* in 1954.
[2] Cockney actor (1933–) went on to become successful television comedy actress.

26 April 1961   Elm Park Gardens

Gin Dearest,

Today I went alone to see *The Devils* at the Aldwych.[1] Very good and very horrible. It really is a rather revolting wallow in sex disguised as a piece of history! How they do get away with it! It's about nuns who

get delusions? of sexual rapture – ecstasy – and it's blamed on Satan
via a priest who is a bit of a lecher but *not* with nuns. Dorothy Tutin[2]
is wonderful but it is very farmyard to see her having a sexual spasm
from a – z all over the stage. There really are no holds barred now. Just
because she isn't having all this at the hands of an actual partner (but
only through a mental) it gaily passes the censor.

I hope all is peaceful for you? France is having a hummocky time.[3]
Tiens. All love.

[1] Play by John Whiting, based on Aldous Huxley's book *The Devils of Loudon*.
[2] British actress (1930–).
[3] Algeria was in the throes of a civil war over independence from France.

Joyce was appointed a member of the Pilkington Committee under the chairmanship
of Sir Harry Pilkington, glass manufacturer. This was set up to advise the
government on the future of British broadcasting. For two years the ten members
met representatives of all walks of radio and television before submitting their report.
One of the members was Richard Hoggart (1918–), author of *The Uses of Literacy*.

Thursday night, 27 April 1961   Elm Park Gardens

Darling Virginia,

Still no word from you. I do hope all is well? Maybe you are in some
remote hut being held by brigands? Tiens.

Tonight we had Richard Hoggart and his wife and the Assist. Sec.
Miss Fisher for supper. They were all so nice. We talked about letters
and what fun it would be to make an anthology of very good ones.
Richard is Prof. of Eng. Lit. His wife used to teach it too. Miss F. is very
well read, and of course R. and I are wizards! Anyway it was very lively
and I enjoyed it.

Rain is expected tomorrow. R. has had his hair cut.

28 April [1961]   Palace Hotel
                                                   Bussaco

Darling Joyce,

I'm ashamed at my ignorance of all things Portuguese. I commented
on a church being decorated with lavatory tiles, but I had no idea that
every church was, & that tiling is famous here, brought over by the
Moors. Pretty ugly, *ekshurly*.

I am feeling miles better, sweats & flushes quite gone. I'm also
beginning to 'take notice' again, which is a great relief, for though being

insensate sounds refreshing, it isn't. I think from a C.S. point of view, one ought to love & enjoy all things, don't you? Not give a damn one way or another?

29 April 1961   Elm Park Gardens

Darling Ginnie,

Yesterday was another all day Pilkington. We saw Sir Ian Jacob, former Director-General of B.B.C., we saw Commander Cox who runs Independent Tele news. The first was dull, the second was *so* enthusiastic, naval, and all's-well-with-the-world-of-I.T.V. that we felt he must be disguising something! Maybe not. After lunch it was Granada and there we had three henchmen. They were enjoyable because genuine and capable and, again, enthusiastic. Granada is a good company and their range is from comedy to highbrow lectures, so they at least exercise their viewers a bit. It was all very concentrated.

I went to the New Opera Co. at Sadler's Wells to see Viola's new translation of Ravel's *L'heure Espagnol* and *loved* it. Ravel's music is gay and witty, and Viola's libretto matched it beautifully. She knows singers so has skilfully put only the right vowels in the right places, and she's matched every note as in the original very tidily and un-contrivedly. It was a big success. Huge house, great applause. She stood at the back of the circle beaming away, and when we saw her afterwards she was still glowing most becomingly.

She had been very quiet about it. I'd no idea it was going to be so successful. Isn't it lovely. Rave notices today and *The Times, Tele.* and *E. News* all praise her new version by name. She is *very* pleased. So am I.

It's a very grey day and I wish it wasn't. Athene has rung to say please save *May 31* for our lunch party and will I tell you to do so too please. Beau is 80.[1]

[1] Every spring Athene Seyler held a lunch party for her closest friends to celebrate her husband Beau Hannen's birthday.

8 May 1961   Scale Hill Hotel
                                                                 Loweswater

Darling Virginia,

Muncaster yesterday to see Rhodos and Azaleas and while I *admire* I do not *love* them. They were magnificent and so was the lawn terrace. The plastic mac'd public, spike heeled and toffee papered, came in numbers.

We are always pleasantly and lightly involved with the Vicar,

Geoffrey White, and this means, out of courtesy, we go to his church. Evensong was in a *tiny* little church at Buttermere. *So* endearing. 'The Day Thou Gavest Lord' and two nursery hymns. Ten of us and an harmonium. The bell rung by a teeny little very old Arthur Rackham tree-and-root woman. Flowers fluting out of little vases everywhere. I loved it and thought my own thoughts.

10 May 1961   Loweswater

Darling Ginnie,

All is nature so no news, but at 11.10 we went out into the night to look for the U.S. Satellite which passes overhead regularly, and there, dead on time, it was 15,000 miles up and moving stately through the dark, brighter than a star. And its light is simply the reflection of the sun. It was very strange and interesting.[1]

A curious nameless depression smote me yesterday and was hard to shift. End of hols? Man's foolishness? The horror world? Or a *slight* headache? The lot I expect.

[1] Either *Mercury Freedom*, the USA's first suborbital manned flight carrying Shephard or an early satellite recording the weather.

10 July 1961   Westone Hotel, Weston Favell
                                                      Northampton[1]

Gin Darling,

The Pilkington firm Rolls fetched us and Sir Harry [Pilkington] was there to welcome us. The house, Windle Hall, is about 175 years old and been tampered with. Sir Harry Pilkington is *very* difficult to describe. Everything one says sounds so awful but he *isn't*. He is hearty, extrovert, goes everywhere by bicycle without a coat, a sort of muscular Victorian Christian. But he is also brilliant, kind, perceptive and, I find, touchingly vulnerable. Interesting that he is perceptive *and* sometimes insensitive too. He is always four moves ahead of everyone else and has a grasp of situations and problems much sooner than the rest of us – and not only me. I think he is a v.g. Chairman.

Someone asked me if he was an intellectual, but I'm really not quite sure if I know what a real intellectual is, do you? I know people of intellect – you! People who *like* intellectual things – me. But neither of us *are* intellectuals, are we? I asked Viola her view and she said she thought a real intellectual was also widely cultured as well as brainy. Now Sir H.P. isn't that. He's a Handel, Gilbert & Sullivan, no modern art man; keen gamesman and good mixer.

We worked all day, then saw round the glass works – fascinating.

We saw so many nice people doing enormously skilled work very well, and that is always satisfying. I must say we did a lot of useful work and have come to two or three final decisions. Secret of course!

At breakfast we shared a table with a complaining engineer and 'nice little' wife. It was non-stop moaning. We just wouldn't play and I was a b-y little ray of sunshine and made Pollyanna remarks quite deliberately to see if it could turn the tide, and it did! He too was counting blessings by the time we left.

I have three days of Pilk. including one in Belfast, so it's a busy month.

¹ The Pilkington Committee stayed in this hotel to meet at Sir Harry Pilkington's home, Windle Hall.
  As well as the Pilkington meetings, Joyce fitted in some performances in local theatres.

14 July 1961   Westone Hotel

Darling Virginia,

Yesterday was a mat. and evening, and both went well in different ways. The ladies at 2.30 were numerous but mouse quiet. I had to fill all the gaps, and a series of 'Tsts Tsts' accompanied almost every remark I made. It is so funny to me to be funny to silence! But they applauded a lot at the end. I felt like a nanny. As if I had to cherish them and *explain*. I spoke loud and clear and SLOWLY. Oh it was funny. I caught Bill's eye at one point and nearly gave way. It isn't that one feels superior, one feels *responsible*.

Guess who walked in to the theatre tonight? Elliott Coleman! When I came back to my dressing room to make a quick change there was a note – 'I'm here'. I was very glad to see him but would have preferred almost *any* other time, for I'm doing two shows tomorrow. However . . . Now he's telephoned and has a whole free day at my disposal! Oh well. I'd planned a little tennis with the others, an early lunch, sloop, and then the 5.30 and 8.15 shows. But I must change my plan! We will do *something* and lunch, and then get rid of him. How ungracious I sound – *am*. The trouble is that professional life simply doesn't go with old amours and the strength has to go to the *job*.

17 July [1961]   Scotland

Darling Joyce,

It was a most un-concentrated afternoon today. After writing a couple of *Homes & Gardens* articles, I went to the village shop and bought a rubber ball, price 1/9d & bounced it up against the wall! I made To play hockey with me after tea, with walking sticks, & then cricket with the seat end of a shooting stick!

21 July 1961   Elm Park Gardens

Darling Ginnie,

I meant to get a word to you yesterday but was faced with two days accumulation of mail, some of it urgent. ('No, I *won't* open your Autumn Fayre.')

Ulster was full of interest. We saw several witnesses in groups. Our favourites though were the Union of Small Shopkeepers, who were four little olde worlde Dickens' characters who stood up when spoken to! One, when asked why his Union hadn't objected to some practice they were complaining about, said 'If we'd of done so they'd of just said: "Pew'Pew to you".'

Our new Zephyr car is a dream of dark grey and gleaming chrome and we *love* it. We've got safety belts and non-draught windows and it purrs in silence and has a great beating powerful heart under all that quiet. A dream to drive and no bigger than before. First outing we collected Winifred for Victor's soirée later. Kept thinking of Hugh Walpole's remark on seeing Winifred: 'She'd strip awkward'. She negotiated the car well, really, much hampered by flowing chiffon, spanish shawl, nylon net gloves and stick, and we made it. She is in very good looks.

Vic's show is lovely. Lots of suits – none very new but very wearable and a bit easier with some swing in the skirts. Evenings of course *superb*. All the loved ones knee to knee in Privilege Corner, with Athene and Beau added. Huge crowds of press ladies, and it went well.

Much love, love, and how I larffed about you bouncing that ball. *Good* sign. See you Tues. Hooray.

Social Life. You are dining here on Tuesday.

Goody gum drop.

The Pilkington Report was published in June 1962, after two years of committee meetings and interviews with experts, broadcasting professionals and users. Some of the daily newspapers were enraged about the report's criticism of ITV quiz shows, but the Sunday papers approved of the recommendation to widen networking.

15 September 1961   Taynuilt
                                                                           Argyll[1]

Darling Ginnie,

We got here about 2.30 and found Frances in the garden cutting flowers for our arrival. She is such a remarkable and dear creature.

She and Patrick were really happy. Perhaps because of this she goes on being so warm and relaxed and cosy and easy. She talks about him absolutely naturally and roars with laughter about things they did and laughed at.

Yes, I know how empty it is without the husband-boys. I suppose unconsciously one's life *is* geared to that evening return and when that doesn't happen there is a void. I detest it. I get *used* to it, but I don't like it.

I've done a lot of re-writing and re-shaping of my T.V. play[2] and now it's almost all typed. Roughly. But at least it's in a readable form and I can get a better idea of it. John Kennedy is not cheerful about the world. He thinks Khrushchev will do a Pearl Harbor and drop a huge bomb on the U.S.![3]

I do hope – and think – he's wrong.

[1] Home of Reggie's sister Frances Campbell-Preston and her four children. Her husband, Patrick, had died the previous summer.
[2] A play about a bishop which was never performed.
[3] J.F. Kennedy (1917–63), President of the USA, was convinced that if Cuba had nuclear missiles, the Soviet Union would use them against the USA.

1962

Virginia went with Celia Johnson to Burma to meet up with Tony who was working there. They stopped in Beirut and Hong Kong where Celia gave poetry recitals.

8 February 1962   Elm Park Gardens

Darling Ginnie,

Last night was the Royal Gala perf. of Tyrone Guthrie's production of *H.M.S. Pinafore*[1] at Her Maj. in the presence of Her Maj. I thoroughly enjoyed it and so did the Q. Dick and I sat in row D. and had a lovely time. It is the vitality of the writing that stands up so strongly, isn't it – words and music. Earlier I sold progs. in the first six rows and filled my little tin with crisp notes. I believe £6,000 was raised for Pensions for Actors. Anna Neagle, Miriam Karlin, Mai Zetterling, and I were among the Thespians who sold. Anna and Miriam were smothered in not terribly white, white fox. Mai wore a white lace tennis dress, and Miriam admitted she had nothing on under her silver sheath as we stood waiting to be presented to the Q.

The Queen looked radiant and was lit by a mass of diamonds everywhere. On her bust was a skating rink sized single stone with slightly smaller drop pendant from it. 'Everyone' was there. Edith Evans with a grey Dutch cut bob, Bea Lillie, and a mass of managers including one who refused to pay 5/- for his prog.

This catty little account will now cease. I wore my very old dark red satin stage dress and me mink.

I should be working on my new Shirl which needs improvement.

¹ Operetta by Gilbert and Sullivan.

February [1962]   Riviera Hotel
                                                               Beirut

Darling Joyce,

Hilarious welcome here. No fewer than four gentlemen & a crowd of reporters to meet us at the airport. There was a tremendous moment when I stepped out of the plane, & there was a barrage of flashlights! They were all expecting Mrs Fleming, & everywhere they think it's me! Must be my red coat. The dear girl is certainly very shy & tongue tied with reporters. She's very sweet & easy; I foresee no emotional difficulties at all.

The only people in the restaurant besides us were an elderly man & a junoesque blonde. Towards the end of dinner *she* sent over a note which read 'Didn't you go up the Nile in 1936? Angela Forbes.' Rang no sort of bell, but she'd recognised me, knew my name, etc. Aren't people marvellous? Or can it be my darling face hasn't changed *one* little bit?

Next morn.

F . . . K! The road to Baalbek is wedged with snow, so we can't go there.

10 February 1962   Elm Park Gardens

Darling Ginnie,

Your birthday card was beautifully organised. Mrs Gabe hid it till today. Ta darling v. much. I laughed. Mrs G. put a note by my bed last night DO NOT OPEN UNTIL BREAKFAST. So I didn't. In it was another. HAPPY BIRTHDAY. LOOK UNDER *RED CURTAIN* IN PASSAGE. I did. There were three daffodils in a pot, and under-cooked pale pink tulips, your card, and a package from Vic with two enchanting Victorian books about birds in it.

Later Viola & I went to Kew. It was so exciting – snowdrops in masses, magnolia buds made of grey fur and camellias OUT. Birds yelling and the whole place stirring deep. As we left who do you think we saw limping in alone? Oswald Mosley.[1] I was his bridesmaid, aged 8, but don't tell!

Guess where *I'm* off to? Horrids.[2]

[1] Sir Oswald Mosley (1896–1980) married Cynthia, daughter of Marquess Curzon in 1918. In 1936 he married Diana Mitford. He was leader of the British Union of Fascists and an admirer of Hitler. He and Diana were imprisoned in Britain from 1940 to 1943 as sympathisers. They moved to France in 1951.

[2] Harrods department store, where that day Joyce bought a sponge bag.

18 February 1962   Elm Park Gardens

Darling Ginnie,

Supper last night with Viola, and then to the Festival Hall together with a capacity house to hear Ella Fitzgerald.[1] We had to sit through 45 mins. very boring hot trumpet and cocktail bar type piano (nice as a background but hell in a concert hall. It *goes* nowhere.) We writhed in boredom. Then Ella and her trio – piano, double bass and drums – splendid. Plain and lumpy with straightened auburn hair. But she can sing. Lovely oldies – 'Someone to watch over me' – 'Foggy Day' – 'Just one of those things'.

[1] African-American jazz singer (1918–96).

22 February [1962]   Repulse Bay Hotel
                                                                Hong Kong

Darling Joyce,

We had a very social day today, starting with luncheon with Sir Robert Black, the Governor. I was glad it was lunch because I gather the evenings are very stiff & protocolaire; & they insist on long dresses & gloves.

We were nine only – wife, daughters, ADCs, etc., & yet we were met in the hall by the ADC bearing a board with the place names attached, & he said 'You will proceed to the left of the dining room, Mrs Thesiger, & be sitting on his Excellency's left, & you, Sir, will proceed to the right & take your place on Lady Black's right . . . that is here, Sir, on the chart. You, Mrs Fleming, will also proceed to the left . . .' We stood, on our high heels, gloved, hatted, & smelling of Je Reviens, & our mouths fell open *wide*.

Anyway, when we'd done all this 'proceeding' we had a delightful luncheon, stuffed tomatoes & apple crumbly.

Celia's recital was a huge success. She reads with passion, emotion, sensitivity, as well as humour, & one wonders which the real C is!

She couldn't be a nicer travelling companion, is invariably pleasant & unselfish & thoughtful, & enjoys everything to the full. But I know her no better than when I started – and yet there's obviously a great deal going on inside. Strange. Or perhaps just English.

Joyce and William Blezard went on tour with a new solo show *Seven Good Reasons* directed by Laurier Lister before it opened at the Theatre Royal, Haymarket.

6 March 1962   Elm Park Gardens

Darling Ginnie,
     Birmingham Town Hall was agreeably crowded with kindly people. Bill and I were unaccountably nervous. Took us time to settle in. One is terribly exposed in Town Halls. Backed by empty steps on which (at other times!) choirs are massed and with no merciful wings or curtains, it is fairly testing. They thought I was funny and were *very* generous, so it was comforting. Laurier came and took notes and was useful. The new pieces went *very* well and that was nice. He tots up laughs and lists them, and to my amazement told me that 'Dumb Friend' – new dog one – had about seven more than old regulars like 'Life & Lit.' and 'Nursery School' which are usually top laugh makers. Hope it goes in London. I thought I did it so badly last night. L. thought it so good. I don't believe we artistes ever do know!
     Bill played a spirited solo by Rimsky-Korsakov[1] and brought down the house.

[1] Russian composer of opera, symphonies and piano pieces (1844–1908).

11 April 1962   George Hotel
                                                          Huddersfield

Darling Ginnie,
     Last night I was in a huge and very deep bath when the telephone went, so I dripped over to it and there was Bill Blezard, very gloomy: 'No one in this pub has heard we are coming here. No one has seen a poster or a mention in the press.' This cheering news made me laugh by its sheer depression. There are in fact two posters outside the Town Hall, although there was nothing in the list of local entertainments. Well, we shall see.
     Huddersfield's an interesting solid town with a noble pile of a station, black and porticoed. All of Huddersfield wears a white trim to its solemn black. The excretion of millions of starlings. They have edged everything with their droppings.

It will be interesting to know if we have an audience tonight. Maybe not. Very good for us not to be so successful perhaps!

18 May 1962   Scale Hill Hotel
                                                    Loweswater

Darling Ginnie,

Four a.m. is a beautiful time to rise if, as we had yesterday, 'the moon on the one hand and the sun on the other', but I didn't feel the moon is my sister nor the sun my brother – really. Do you remember that song? My ma used to sing it self-accompanied.

We went, at *last*, to Wordsworth Cottage in Grasmere.[1] Very touching and evocative. The lady in a thick beige coat and strong Cumbrian accept was reeling off the facts when she paused suddenly – 'You aren't J.G. are you?' I said 'Yes'. She blushed, smiled, went into excited raptures and had to be lured back to William and Dorothy by me on account there was a very earnest American lady of no light touch at all who (a) had never heard of me, (b) didn't want to hear of me, and (c) had come to hear about the Wordsworths, probably a *very* long way. It is an astonishing thing that meeting a voice you've known on radio can give such crazy pleasure. She was totally re-charged and said 'I can't wait to tell my daughter.' What little lives we lead and what little things make a difference.

It is absolutely Arctic and *wildly* beautiful. The smells and the air and the sound of distant sheep and curlew and the QUIET – oooer. I love it. And you. All love.

[1] Home of the Romantic poet William Wordsworth (1770–1850) and his sister Dorothy (1771–1885).

Joyce and Reggie went for the first time to the Aldeburgh Music Festival which began in 1947. They then went every year until Joyce's death. The Aldeburgh Festival was run by Benjamin Britten (1913–76), the composer, and Peter Pears (1910–86), the singer, who lived together in the Red House nearby. Imogen Holst helped to run the festival.

16 June 1962   Wentworth Hotel
                                                    Aldeburgh
                                                    Suffolk

Darling Ginnie,

I do love this Festival and this hotel. *Everyone* is concerned in the goings on and there is the sea and yesterday the sun shone. 'Amadeus' last night in a packed church. R. says he liked it. Liked the slow movement of the Mozart best. Then back to the church for the Deller Consort doing very early Flemish music. Ooh such sounds. Marvellous squeezed harmonies and cool soaring sounds rising out of richness. I thought it marvellous. The church floodlit, a moon and a warm night to walk it.

16 June [1962]   Hyde Park Gardens

Darling Joyce,

No news. Must go & get m'jewels out of the Bank, as I want something dainty to dazzle an American couple we are meeting for luncheon at the Savoy. Oh dear, it is *so* difficult to get to the Savoy these days! Never mind – *courage.*

17 June 1962   Aldeburgh

Darling Ginnie,

Life here is delicious. Yesterday, wearing twelve year old trousers and feeling a proper Charley in them, we collected victuals from a grocery and drove to Orford Quay to join the birding launch. Such a funny lot.

One old man of 83, who was immobile as a tree like my pa was, had to be lowered to the boat. He was, I fancy, an ex-Judge or Q.C. He and an elderly Jewish gent exchanged legal gossip in the boat and their elderly wives carried picnic bags.

There were two young*ish* women, teachers? unsuitably clad in vivid cottons, white 'cardigans', plastic macs and thin shoes; a trio of open-air middle-agers, and a Mrs Bridgeman in windcheater and tiny sailing hat that looked glued on. I would have put her down instantly as Yacht Club, bridge club, golf club, and not all my dish. But not a bit of it. Not only was she bird mad but sailing crazy, and spends time voluntarily teaching the young to sail under a Government Scheme. She was amusing and unlikely.

We saw nothing but sky above pale bending reeds. We saw marsh harriers (only two pairs in *all* England and Scotland and Wales), and bearded tits and beautiful giddy coloured redstarts. Etc.

Today is Blythburgh and some *Tchaikovsky*! Tonight harpsichords in the Parish Church. R. is bearing up well.

18 June 1962   Aldeburgh

Darling Ginnie,

Came across Hans Keller, the musicologist, and his artist wife in a state of panic – they had no transport and he *had* to be at Blythburgh to supervise the concert, being broadcast by B.B.C. So we took them over, taking a picnic with us. Heavenly church. Full of light it was and radiant. Lovely concert. Tchaikovsky *and* Mozart – interestingly unexpected mixture. Nobly I think I must give up the morning Debussy I crave and go early with R. to Minsmere for birds.

In the autumn Joyce and Virginia went to the USA together for a holiday where they stayed with the Phipps in their new house on Long Island.

1963

Joyce and William Blezard returned to America to appear on television. They stayed with Dorothy Hammerstein, the widow of Oscar, in her New York apartment.

28 February 1963   Greenwich
                                                              Conn

Darling Virginia,
    I had a nice elderly woman across the aisle from me on the 707 who'd never flown before, so I was able to cosset her a little and help with forms etc. She lost her husband last year or she'd be celebrating her golden wedding this. She was very nice and rather lost, and I was glad to see her son and daughter-in-law were safely there to collect her when we arrived. Very English but in a little American hat.[1]
    Trevor Howard was on the 'plane, in first class, and when we were waiting to go in to Immigration he spied me. He doesn't really know me at all, but cried out 'Darling', and embraced me in a very alcoholic hug repeating over and over 'Bless your Chinese heart'! He also said 'You look 35 – *marvellous* – Bless your Chinese heart', and went on about how he'd *never* forget me with that dog that day in the restaurant. He'd remember where it was in a minute . . . He didn't. Wonder who he thought I was? He's here to tape *Disraeli* for T.V. He is *so* unattractive when tight but such a good actor. My heart bled for the agent who was meeting him.

---

[1] This woman was probably the inspiration for Joyce's sketch 'First Flight', first performed in 1969.

5 March [1963]   Hyde Park Gardens

Darling Joyce,

Again a brilliant day, with just a twitch of warmth. We've been out in the Bentley, to visit Alec & Co.[1] They all seemed exceptionally happy, largely because the cat had died! He was a 14 year old Siamese & what with clawing & messing, was more or less wrecking the house. Maids wildly relieved he has been gathered, & even Alec, no longer smothered in beige fur, all smiles.

Took Victor to lunch at the Apéri – he looked pretty awful, but says his heart is better. He said he might have to avail himself of my offer to pay the week's wages. This is *very* entre nous, darling, & of course it may not happen – all depends on who pays her bills today & tomorrow.

I bought T an elephant that blows bubbles for our anniversary present! From Hamleys. (Embarrassing innit?)

Incidentally, a bit of my plumber-poem was quoted in *The Times* 4th leader today![2]

[1] Tony's older brother Alec lived in Kensington with a tutor-companion and several servants.
[2] *The Times* leader 'referred to the news that Scottish plumbers no longer had mates'. Virginia's poem first appeared in *Punch*:
  'Ah! with what choking love I do survey/ This crouching paragon, this non-pareil!/Bless him, ye gods, with opulence and fame,/This artisan who said he'd come, and came.'

6 March [1963]   Hyde Park Gardens

Darling Joyce,

I *have* got to pay the wages for Victor this week, but never mind . . . I am fearfully rich! It seems business really is perking up, & the old boy doesn't seem too despondent. Home bearing a divine coral chiffon shirt, which V says both I & Tony are to wear!

10 March 1963   Madison Avenue
                                                          New York

Darling Virginia,

It was a long day. I had my hair done, then we 'blocked' the programme from 2 till about 4. Then a pause, we did a dress rehearsal after this, then made up, then at 8 we taped. Connie – my ex-manager was there and saw it both live and on the monitor sets and said certain angles weren't my best! I have a feeling this is an understatement and I probably looked awful.

I very much enjoyed the people I worked with over this T.V.

Particularly nice and sensitive, and good at their jobs too. Bill B. was given a pale blue shirt to wear and I sprayed his very wild hair to keep it from flapping. He made one false note in the intro. to 'Time' and was sad about this, but only I could have told and he mended it *instantly*.

Before leaving Britain, Joyce had recorded a radio appeal for the Friends of the Poor charity, which raised over £2,000.

12 March [1963]   Hyde Park Gardens

Darling Joyce,
    Oh Lord! I meant to thank you right away for your Appeal. Came over beautifully, & everybody is fearfully pleased. Money is already coming in. You are a NICE, GOOD, LOVING, DEAR girl to help us in this way – & someone will tell you officially, but I want you to know *sub rosa*.
    Just talked to Vic. He'd lunched with Hardy Amies,[1] who is on top of the world at the moment, so he found it a bit much, poor old boy! He's engaged in frightful retrenchment plans – one workroom of 20 girls is being scrapped & various others will have to go. Darling, *nobody* knows of this, so shhh.

[1] British dressmaker (1909–) by appointment to the Queen.

In spite of Virginia's rescue package, Stiebel's couture business closed down. He had multiple sclerosis and his health was deteriorating. Virginia bought him a flat near hers and from now on Virginia, Joyce and Reggie supported him. His friend Richard Addinsell had a weak back and chronic hypochondria.

7 May 1963   Loweswater

Darling Virginia,
    The whole valley is in a tizzy about the proposed building of a hideous waterworks with a plant and two cottages, right at the entrance of this enchanting vale. B.B.C. and I.T.V. have been there photographing and interviewing and helping to protest. I'm called in to support by talking to local press. The vicar goes on I.T.V. tonight and has been here for me to coach him and we've *all* told him what to say and how to say it. It is a National Park and was bought to keep safe for ever. That's what is so dastardly. There *is* an alternative site and that is what we are plugging for. The water is needed for Manchester but it really mustn't be taken at the expense of ruining this very special and, so far, totally unspoilt bit of country. No one is allowed to build *anything* here to mar it. The electricity board had to do its job underground to bring

light to the valley, so the water board *must* help, too, and take the alternate but less immediately easy site. At least that's the hope.

I try to love the W. Cumb. Water Board and I am *sure* they are all men of integrity, taste and good to their families, but it would be nice if they'd see our point and put their building in another place. Joe Colthard, my old gardener friend, 80, was on T.V. saying he 'thowt nowt of t'plan to ruin the valley'. He was very salty.

R. bought another supply of Allen & Hanbury's blackcurrant lozenges which he loves and lives on since he stopped smoking.

The campaign to preserve the environment was successful and the water board had to modify their plans.

2 May [1963]   Hyde Park Gardens

Darling Joyce,

Went in a *bitter* wind to a service for the FoP[1] at St Mike's, Chester Square. The prayers always touch me to tears, but their dreadfully trustful simplicity – for our gracious President (pause of 3 seconds), for the Staff (another 3), for the Home Superintendents (3 more) & I long to know what everyone is really *thinking*. I mean, does the *Church* still believe in a personal God? I dare say lots of old ladies think he is 'up there' somewhere, ticking off the items, & perhaps saying 'Hein? not so *fast*, please! What was the last one . . . ? the Committee members?' but does the *Church*?

Then we all went round to Ebury Street for a bun fight. Tony had tea with P.M. [Princess Margaret] & fell for her completely. She was looking lovely in a scarlet coat & black velvet Spanish hat, & he drowned in her eyes & returned to me looking *ever* so flushed! They talked about you and Snowdon's photographs.

[1] Society of the Friends of the Poor and Gentlefolk's Help.

23 July [1963]   Hyde Park Gardens

Darling Joyce,

I talked to Reg last night, also Vic who was having quite a battle with his *Vogue* article. I hope he keeps it *simple*. Young authors will try to find sparkling similes which only sound phoney, won't they, & the language of couture is phoney enough anyhow!

Darling, aren't we *lucky* to be creative? I was thinking of some of our lady friends who have nothing on earth to *do*. I suppose there are thousands of women, most of whom fill their time with good works, but some simply don't know *how* to fill the hours. It must give one such a frightful feeling of futility. And yet our mothers weren't constructive & led reasonably futile lives & were apparently satisfied. Perhaps women really were content then to see that their homes were well run, & to run out to DH Evans one day and Peter Jones the next?[1]

[1] London department stores.

Joyce and William Blezard flew to Australia for a second tour of three months.

2 August [1963]   Hyde Park Gardens

Darling Joyce,
    Stephen Ward has taken a huge overdose of sleeping pills & is in a coma.[1] Great efforts are being made to revive him, so that he can be put in prison! (He's been found guilty on 2 counts.) Man's inhumanity to man *depresses* me sometimes.
    Heard a Keeler joke about TIM [speaking clock] on the phone 'At the third stroke it will cost three pounds four shillings and sixpence.'
    Ward is obviously going to die & suddenly everybody seems a bit sorry for him! I think the whole thing got well out of proportion. When one considers those people who ran brothels and beat up the tarts who didn't pay up, Ward's activities are mild, & yet the publicity defies comparison.
    We were rather pleased & surprised with *Cleopatra*.[2] Of course it's far too long – we were nigh crippled after 4 hours – but it is also beautiful. We thought they had been unkind to Elizabeth Taylor – well, I mean, she *hasn't* the wherewithal at all, of course, isn't sexy enough or intelligent enough, but she was much much better then we thought she could be. And it isn't all that vulgar – a few dotty touches such as Cleo's bath sponge being a square yellow Woolworth's sponge, with a carved gold plastic handle glued to its top, but on the *whole* it's quite good taste.

[1] Stephen Ward had been found guilty of living off the immoral earnings of prostitutes, including Christine Keeler who slept with both John Profumo, Conservative cabinet minister and Secretary of State for War, and a Soviet Embassy official. Profumo resigned on 5 June, admitting he had lied to the House about knowing Keeler.
[2] Epic film, starring Elizabeth Taylor (1932–) and Richard Burton, directed by Joseph Mankiewicz (1925–81).

9 August 1963   Adelaide

Darling Virginia,
    Yesterday Prue Holden and daughter Belinda, who is 22 and wears a

thick white make up and sooty eyes, came with me to see a pre-view of that film I made last year *The Old Dark House*.[1] It is beyond words awful! Boring, bad and of incredible slowness. Do not let any sort of loyalty on your part lure you anywhere near it. I look even *older* than Aunt Nancy, and it is vulgar, dull and *unforgivable*! I was deeply ashamed at being seen in it. They are using my current season (successful) to advertise the film and I feel guilty! Golly it is a brute. I wrote to R. and told him he *must* prevent me doing these things!

[1] Remake of 1932 classic horror based on J. B. Priestly's novel *Benighted*. Directed by William Castle, starring Robert Morley and Fenella Fielding.

12 August [1963]   Hyde Park Gardens

Darling Joyce,

A Scottish couple came to be interviewed today.[1] How times have changed! Hatless, lounging back in the best armchairs: takes one a-back for a moment. Marvellous references & they both seemed very nice, though the eldest, the cook, obviously fancies herself a bit of a *character*, which might be a bore. The cook said she wasn't much of a cook, the house-parlourmaid half, a gentler type, had never waited at table or done any valeting. They shall come & have a bash at it in September. I worked so hard, & was so charming I had to lie down on the sofa afterwards!

I've just been to Church, parked the *wrong* side of the meter & got fined ten bob!

Tony, reading *The Times* this morning at brekker, has just said to me 'Who on *earth* are Prince Charles & Princess Anne?' You must admit I have, on occasion, to be alarmed? But I *know* I mustn't be.

[1] Virginia's cook and parlourmaid were leaving.

13 August [1963]   Hyde Park Gardens

Darling Joyce,

I must say this doctor business is a racket! First one doctor tells To he has low blood pressure and sends him to another doctor to have a blood count. He sends him to another one to have a complete overhaul. This doctor tell To he has low blood pressure and 'endogenous depression',[1] which is simply 'The Change'. He sends him to a fourth doctor for an X ray! Surely it's possible for one doctor, or at the most two, to have enough equipment to do the job? Oh how gorgeous, gorgeous, gorgeous not to be in their hands! Still, here's hoping their pills will cure my boy. One of the doctors said he'd be fighting fit in five weeks.

Incidentally, the Scotch types *are* going to have a bash at it! I feel that even if they won't 'do' in the end, it's restful to know there are these two amiable types to come soon. They have a budgie.

Marvellous fan letter from Basil Boothroyd[2] about my Mrs Mitty article in *Punch*. I am particularly enchanted with a sentence beginning 'technically so frighteningly adroit . . .', for my technique is entirely intuitive, & I haven't a clue what he means! But I'm glowing all the same.

[1] At that time depression was attributed to either 'internal or 'external' factors. Tony's symptoms were fatigue and forgetfulness.
[2] Assistant editor of *Punch* (1910–).

27 August [1963]   Edinburgh

Darling Joyce,

We've had a happy day. We started off by visiting the Modigliani & Soutine Exhibition, where we incidentally encountered the Princess Royal[1] & had to bob & bow . . . 'very interesting' said P.R. looking at a tremendous nude.

Then we visited Coldstones, the house that Tony gave to the WVS.[2] It is being converted at the speed of a paralysed snail into 10 flats for 10 WVS old ladies. The architect was there & we made polite gurgling noises at him, & T exclaimed over bits of old wallpaper.

Tony is eating much better, & sleeps enormously but has awful nightmares. He often cries out & whimpers, & last night he woke me up by playing the piano, with great verve & gusto, on my behind! I worry at him being so fearfully tired. People keep kindly telling him how ill he looks, which doesn't help.

[1] Princess Mary, Countess of Harewood (1897–1965), sister of George VI.
[2] House near Edinburgh which Tony's father bought for use in the Easter holidays for golf.

29 August 1963   Windsor Hotel
                                                                    Melbourne

Darling Virginia,

Last night I did *Meet the Press* and it seems I was a wow, which fascinates me because I am not very *clever* (quick yes, but not educated), and I seemed to hypnotise the three journalistic gents. They seemed to think I was of real interest. I felt a bit of a fraud but it was very nice to be looked at with such respect. Even awe! I daresay it was partly surprise that Miss Gossage or that policewoman in St Trinian's could actually put two words together or think *at all*.

I must quote to you from two cosy local letters.

'The football team I coach are playing in the Grand Final on Sunday afternoon and all the players and supporters are coming back to my home for a barbecue tea at 5, and if you feel inclined to pop along it would be a delight.' Welcoming and *kind*.

And a schoolgirl who is playing Gossage in *The Happiest Days* has rehearsed for six weeks and 'we are now just improving our character interpretation and expression. Our director is a woodwork teacher, which is very handy for our scenery.'

Sir Robert Menzies[1] was going into the hotel as I got there last night and we had a big reunion. He's a fan – as well as P.M. of Australia! Dame Patty, his wife, is a darling and has come down from Canberra with him for two days entirely to visit my Show. Tiens.

All love and to To. So glad he put on 3 lbs. I gather R. has too! Plump hubbies for us.[2]

[1] Prime Minister of Australia 1939–41 and 1949–66 (1894–1978).
[2] Neither Tony nor Reggie ever became plump.

7 September [1963]   Bellabeg

Darling Joyce,

It's so damp here but T doesn't seem to be suffering from exposure. I don't know why he hasn't got foot-rot or rust or scrut or some other soggy sheep disease! He says he feels 'just about the same' as when we arrived.

Christine Keeler has now been arrested for perjury! Allowed out on bail but I guess she'll end up in jail, poor ass.[1]

[1] Keeler received a six month sentence for conspiracy to obstruct the course of justice and perjury during the Ward trial.

15 September [1963]   Hyde Park Gardens

Darling Joyce,

Well, the new maids seem very nice indeed – extremely willing & eager to learn. Marion has never waited before, so it's a bit confused & wobbly, with the thumb *in* the vegetable dish, but what the hell!! The point is they're NICE, and full of surprises. Christina is polishing the front door handle – she's the *cook*!

In my beige tweed I was taken today by my spouse – you can see how much better he feels – twice down the Big Dipper & once down the Water Chute at Battersea Fun fair!

While Joyce, Reggie and William were in New Zealand they stayed with Reggie's youngest half-sister Laura. Her husband Brigadier Bernard Fergusson was New

Zealand's Governor-General, as his father and both grandfathers had been. News that the Queen was expecting her fourth child in March 1964 had just reached British diplomats.

17 September 1963   Government House
                                                        Wellington

Darling Virginia,

Isn't it nice about the Queen? Bernard told us last night before *you* knew. He'd had a coded telegram early yesterday and as it was to be told to the world at 6 p.m. last night your time he thought it safe to tell it to us then. Very nice.

Well, here we are in a very comfortable Government House. Big, with red carpet on the stairs. It's grand luxe, with a nice housemaid called Joan from Yorkshire whose passion is washing. R. and I are in the Duke's suite, so called because done up for Prince P.[hilip] at some point. Large double, R's dressing room and a vast *salle de bain*.

Bill Blezard is staying here too and was a little scared, but it was all so easy and cosy that he is relaxed. He's very well-informed and a darling, so it wasn't difficult for him once he saw the form. Later

Wellington is saying: Spring! Laura and Bernard are a huge success here. I've already heard it on all sides. And the glorious part is that they are enjoying it all so much.

Either I never knew or else I'd forgotten you'd given so many wonderful things from Kitty's flat to the Fergussons. Laura pointed out lamps, tables, pictures, etc. etc. and said it really had been the saving of their lives at the very moment when you did the great giving and was still being so *deeply* appreciated, and they were so thrilled about it. Well done you.

17 September [1963]   Hyde Park Gardens

Darling Joyce,

We saw *Birds*,[1] which was very good & rather horrible: T didn't think it was all that special – he admired the technical brilliance, but it didn't frighten him. Frightened me. Vic sat most of the time with his eyes shut!

[1] Horror film directed by Alfred Hitchcock.

18 September 1963   Government House

Darling Ginnie,

How *can* Bernard and Laura endure the ardours of their life? Since
yesterday we have had staying that smiling Samoan Prime Minister
and his Aide, and now the Maharajah of Mysore who is large and soft
and covered in beautiful rings, sounds exactly like P. Sellers, and has
three wives none of whom speak. Bernard is a marvel. Remembers *all*
the Indians he knew when there in the 1930s and in the war. Keeps
bravely on through long silences.

We had a splendid time with the Samoan P.M. yesterday. Peter
Gibaut, the Naval A.D.C., is very good, gay and efficient, and to make
chat in a pause asked who the little girl had been who had greeted him
at the Airport with the lady?

Bernard, laughing, said 'A.D.C.s should *never* ask who ladies
are who greet guests at Airports as You Never Know!' Laughter all
round. The Samoan said the little girl was his daughter and the lady
her auntie.

'Oh,' said Laura, 'she *must* come to tea tomorrow. You must be
longing to see her.' The A.D.C. then asked who the small boy was who
had been there too.

'My son.' 'Oh,' said Bernard, 'he *must* come up tomorrow too. And,
Sir,' he added, 'you must give their schools a special holiday in honour
of your visit.' No one else noticed the Aide's look of suppressed giggles
but later he told Peter Gibaut that Auntie was, of course, the mother of
the Prime Minister's two illegitimate children before his marriage! The
P.M. never batted an eyelid.

20 September 1963   Government House

Darling Virginia,

Last night after dinner Bill did his stuff on a rather uncertain old
Bluthner, on which Padereski[1] once played. He was in top form and
quite brilliant. He improvised. He played two tunes at once, one in each
hand, he lay *under* the piano and played the minute waltz (Chopin) from
that position! and was really terribly funny and dear. Bernard adored it.
So did we all. And then he produced a piece he'd found in an old music
stool. It was a descriptive piece about sixty years old called 'The Relief
of Delhi', with the description printed above each section, such as 'Col.
Wilson approaches', 'The marauders retire', 'The bugles announce the
retreat', etc. etc. It really was one of the best turns I ever heard and we
cried with pleasure.[2]

When I did the Y.W.C.A. coffee morning on Tuesday the Chairman said to me 'Our secretary is very shy. Such a nice woman, *always* happy. She's a Christian Scientist.' This was a pleasant surprise because sometimes Y.Ws. don't let C.Ss. in as we're not supposed to be Christians!

Laura's wearing one of my old Victor suits made in 1955! It still looks marvellous! It's dark green with pleats at the back.

[1] Ignace Jan Paderewski, Polish pianist and composer (1860–1941).
[2] Blezard later included this in Joyce's shows.

30 September 1963   Government House

Darling Virginia,

Just before supper Bill and I produced our surprise – a song In Homage to Their Excellencies, set to a splendid Scottish type tune with a bagpipe drone introduction and a lilt. The big moment came at the very end when we produced little N.Z. flags hidden under our jackets and waved them! I wrote the words going up in the plane to Auckland last Sunday and Bill set it a day later, and we rehearsed ever since. Bill and I shared the singing! Here it is:

Och, it's good to be at Government House
With His Excellency and his Excellent Spouse.
And his excellent Geordie, and excellent crew –
Virginia and Tim and Peter, too. (A.D.Cs.)
And Mike and David and all their brood (Sec. and Comptroller),
And the excellent, excellent, excellent food.
And och – the hospitality!
And och – the jolly gaiety!
We drink a toast in gin – or juice
For it's guid to be at Government Hoose.
God Save the Queen, Hip Hip Hooray,
And her Representatives here today,
For it's grand to be – yes, it's grand to be
With His Excellency – with Her Excellency –
With Their Excellencies at Government House.

Full operatic finish and then a further Hip Hip Hoorah and out with the flags. Of course we did it *several* times and a gay evening was had. Then there was a further operatic hour in which we all improvised a really very surprising Handelian piece on the words 'Today is Sunday'.

All my love darling, and to To. (It's lovely to be with R. again. He is very bonny.)

18 October [1963]   Hyde Park Gardens

Darling Joyce,

Joycie [Carey] & I went to *The Sound of Music*. She thought it
nauseating, but I *loved* it. We were surprised that things hadn't gotten
worse than they were – it started in May 1961! People weren't over-
acting or being sloppy, & it was *packed*.

The papers are playing up dramas behind the scenes in the Tory
Party! Today's betting is on Alec Home,[1] whom the *Express* & *Standard*
have taken to calling 'the 14th Earl' in a sneering way. Obviously
Macmillan thought he would be an uncontroversial figure, but he
has been proved lamentably wrong! Tho' I'm sure he is both capable
and GOOD, I wouldn't think he was quite the right 'image' for the
Conservative party at this moment? Wonder how Libby[2] will like it! Oh
Ta to Diem our boys aren't politicians!!

Personally, I think they are all as boring as boring can be, but as
they won't get in again, I guess it doesn't matter much!

[1] Sir Alec Douglas-Home (1903–96), Conservative Prime Minister 1963–4. Harold Macmillan
resigned as Prime Minister on 10 October due to ill health. Douglas-Home disclaimed two
hereditary peerages in order to become Prime Minister.
[2] Douglas-Home's wife, Elizabeth, a step-cousin of Reggie and friend of Joyce and Virginia.

19 October 1963   Queensland

Darling Virginia,

I know you'll be cross with me but Aubrey just cabled to say will
I do a week's work in Hollywood for an M.G.M. film playing Julie
Andrews' tweedy crazy mother! I may.

Yesterday was the Country Women's Assoc. meeting, and I had
giggles over the demonstration and talk on Tupperware. It's plastic
and made into containers for food storage. It's airtight and when you
seal it you must 'burp' the air out of it 'as you would "burb" a bieby'.
Her Australian accent was a beaut. We had a competition and were
awarded points as follows:

Those wearing high heels scored 10, low heels 25. If you wore any
buttons each scored 1 point. If your ears were pierced you scored 1
point. And if you had 'Lice on your Petti' you scored 20. (Lace on your
petticoat.) It was just my dish. I did Shirl's 'Foreign Feller' and they
were very giggly. All pretty dressy, some with hats, and some with
gloves, quite a lot of grooming.

Goodness you do write enjoyable letters. I've just been re-reading
some in a tidying up spree and I can't tear one up. Dammit. You are
funny and good and kind and I love you very much.

25 October [1963]   Hyde Park Gardens

Joyce Darling,

Three letters from you this morning: my impression is that I
get *several* every day, but though you write fast & fluid-like I don't
expect you could *ekshually* pen me 4 times a day, hein? But that's my
impression & a *very very* lovely impression it is too, darling. Wasn't
all that fond of the one about you going to Hollywood, but I am only
superficially cross, on selfish grounds. Basically it's a wizard idea. Will
you a) buy me a white nylon shirt (40 bust) and b) take care not to
over-caricature the tweedy mother? They'll try & make you say 'By
Jove' or 'Dontcheknow what?' & you must *resist*, please.

Lord Beaverbrook[1] has decided to love Alec Home & the papers are
full of his charm, simplicity, honesty, integrity, etc. ROT to say he
wanted to be P.M. He was obviously reluctant to take the job, and I
don't suppose there's ever been a more selfless man. It's just a shame
he's a peer – or rather was a peer. Goodness, isn't it EXTRAORDINARY
how things have changed – even in our lifetime!

[1] Canadian-born British newspaper magnate (1879–1965), owner of the *Daily Express* and
Evening Standard.

25 October 1963   Hairdresser's
                                                         Sydney

Darling Ginnie,

Two fat letters waiting for me. Also a *long* letter from Vic *without*
mention of his ills. The handwriting was good and was full of chat
about Alec Douglas-Home and his distress at his election when he
feels a newer image should appear. I think I agree, much as I love and
admire Alec. But he is the establishment, and while Glos. and Wilts. will
love him for that I fear Staffs. and Lancs. won't? Poor Libby. What a
hell of a life. Out here no one credits that he is doing this because he
feels it's right and a duty. They are all sure it's for his own self interest.
If ever this was NOT the time it's now with Alec. Or so I'd stake my
life. Agree? He is one of the old public servant types who *serve* without
thought of self. I'd say his *sacrifice* to this job is big. He's about to lead a
defeated Government, has given up a title of great historic interest and
all his private life – and *not* for self.

A travelling salesman spotted me as we arrived and gave a yell.
'Where's the hockey stick?' Oh that image! I'll never be rid of it, will I.

26 October 1963   Sydney

Darling Virginia,

I've read the script and have said I'd do the film. It's totally unlike anything I've ever done before. It's called *The Americanization of Emily* and is by Paddy Cheyevsky,[1] with James Garner[2] and Julie Andrews.

It's a 'black' comedy I suppose – a savage attack on the behaviour of top brass in 1944 D. Day period, satirised mercilessly. It's brilliantly written and I should think would be controversial to the point of explosion. Mrs Barham (my part) is Emily's mother – dotty in that she won't accept the deaths of her husband and son. She's attractively non-sequestering, and her chance to accept the situation is going to be a hell of a 'challenge'!

It's a small but effective part and the whole film is very strong and often hilarious in a very broad way. I decided it would be an 'experience' and mercifully a brief one so I'd do it. I suppose the message is that the glorification of death is dishonest – wrong? Being Jewish, Cheyevsky holds that life is simply full blooded vitality and there's no hint of any spiritual quality. But I go with him in his horror of slaughter. Emily is a W.A.A.F. driver and a bitter young war widow. There's an ironic twist but a vaguely hopeful ending. So there we are, and I couldn't be more surprised!

I do enjoy your letters, luv. Ta. I feel in contact and it's a good thing. What a lot people miss who don't use letters to communicate by.

[1] Film writer (1923–81) best known for *Altered States*.
[2] American actor (1928–).

2 November [1963]   Hyde Park Gardens

Darling Joyce,

We've been entertaining a cousin of T's called Mabel, she's 88, lives in St Leonard's and all she wanted to do was go along the M1 – so that's what we did – scorching along at 85 m.p.h.![1]

You'll now be packing, on your way, a step nearer home. Hurray *Hurrah*! You really HAVE overdone it a bit this time, hein?

[1] This, the first motorway in Britain, was opened in 1959.

7 November 1963   Beverly Hills

Darling Ginnie,

I made it. Whew.

Leonard's [Gershe] new house is so pretty and gay. Blazing lights and full of colour. I have a T.V. that operates by remote control from a small device in the hand – no wires. Miraculous. Roger [Edens] says my picture is a 'prestige picture' and 'important'. Friday

Called by agent's office youth where I met 'the boys'. These are identical youngish Jewish gents in a sort of Madison Avenue uniform, all of whom said 'It's nice knowing you' after two minutes of assessing me, and left!

At M.G.M. I met the producer, Marty Rasmahop, whom I like. NOT too busy being BIG, but intelligent, quite humorous and very quick witted. He then sent me with his assistant, girl called CoCo Morris, wearing tight white linen pants, ankle boots in soft white leather, bright green sweater and no make up, to meet the director Arthur Hiller.[1] He is small, dark, youngish, clever and I liked him. While I was there I watched Julie Andrews and James Garner make uninhibited love in a close-up lying on a hotel bed. Can't *think* how they do it while so closely observed but it was a very good professional job.

After lunch a long session at wardrobe trying on clothes that are to look good but worn – it's 1944 and rationing is on.

The part is full of meat and jolly difficult. They think it will only take *eight* days! I can't see how it can.

[1] Previously a television director, best known for *Wheeler Dealers*. Also directed *Genevieve*.

10 November 1963   Beverly Hills

Darling Virginia,

This is a fantasy world! Yesterday L. and I had a lovely morning swimming in his *heated* pool and drying off in hot sunshine. Then lunch on his terrace in our terry towelling 'robes'.

We called on Edie Goetz. She is Louis B. Mayer's daughter, social queen of the area and loaded. Wears a vast diamond ring. And her pictures – *all* the Impressionists are represented; also three blue period Picassos, a Berthe Morisot, Latour, Modigliani, and the Degas dancing child in bronze. etc. etc. The house is vast and has that curious hush that rich U.S. houses have. Comes from so much upholstery and deep carpets.

All the furniture is *vast* and the library *so* full of vast tomes and the sofas so wide and wonderful that, at least, one feels quite small. Edie Goetz is small and neat, very chic, Balenciaga dresses her, and she is also straight New York West Side Jewish, which is somehow endearing. Her sentences are inverted. She says things like: 'So I am thinking to myself . . .' But she's warm hearted and dear and Leonard is very fond of her. He told me rather a good anecdote about her. She read the *Life of Freud* and when she finished it she sighed and said 'What a *mind*!'

I don't see how the movie crowd are expected to be normal. It's all so over life size and there's no reality or values. I'd find it hard to retain a sense of proportion if I was young here.

13 November 1963   On the set

Darling Virginia,

Over the sound of mechanics floats Julie Andrews' voice singing for no particular reason. Nice voice. Here I am in a sort of portable dressing room on the set. I've got sewing, a drawing book and some writing paper for there are sure to be long periods of inactivity.

I have to overcome a distaste amounting to phobia about cigars. (I've just heard the two still photographers talking about Julie and James Garner: 'We'll get 'em in one of the cabins and have them clown around for us'!) Everyone smokes them or so it seems.

The *poisonnel* I deal with are all very friendly – wardrobe, hair, make-up. The chief assistant is a big burly old man and he's inclined to put his arm around me whenever he sees me, which is wearing. I ooze away as imperceptibly as possible and maybe soon he'll get the message.

I must now wander over and watch the scene preceding mine and get in the mood. Yesterday my stills were done in the house of Mrs Barham (me), a middle class-upper-ish-lady with an Army background. I almost died when I saw it. Straight Balham![1] As tactfully as possibly I told the Producer who was *very* grateful – '*Please* help us – tell us'. So I did. The aspidistras and lace mats have gone and the 'suite' of chairs will *have* to do. It's in black and white so won't look *so* bad.

[1] Working-class area of Victorian terraced houses in south London.

15 November 1963   Beverly Hills

Darling Virginia,

Yesterday I had to do a scene ranging from the fey brightness, through realisation (false in our view of course!) of the full horror of war, to tears. I almost managed to produce real tears. My eyes stung and I *felt* teary, but they wouldn't show so I had to have some eye drops and that set me off a little. I dread the rushes. I abandoned all thought of looks and just blubbed in VERY close close up!

Yesterday's *Hollywood Reporter* had five full size pictures of the five principals, one to a page – J. Garner, J. Andrews, Melvyn Douglas,[1] James Coburn[2] and me. Mine was taken while I was talking and is all lines and blurs, and I look not 53 but 75 and *so* like Aunt Nancy! Leonard is furious! I don't see it matters. It's a character part of a dotty lady. The studio people are all so thrilled at the coverage and say it doesn't matter at all what the picture is *like* as long as it's IN.

I've got to like and know both James and Julie. He's quite funny and we all laughed a good deal together, and Julie and I sang in harmony between takes and it was enjoyable.

[1] American film star (1901–81).
[2] American film star (1928–).

18 November 1963   Beverly Hills

Darling Ginnie,

Today on the set it's one long rush and a very complicated scene with lots of movement.

A big Sunday night supper party (sixteen) at Edie Goetz's. After the food the drawing room became the Curzon Cinema – a whole *wide* screen came down out of the ceiling at one end, a whole panel with a Manet, a Monet and a Cezanne on it went up, like an eyelid, and revealed projection holes. An Indian movie was shown.

Very difficult scene today because it's all done in movement and I'm bad at remembering moves and lines at the same time.

Did I tell you Mrs Gabe *is* going to marry her Reg? And continue to work with us from Edgware, or some such? Did you ever. She sounds radiant.[1]

Julie *is* to do the movie of *The Sound of Music* and it *is* good casting.

Later – I've just done a complicated scene with James Coburn. Nice. He was in *The Great Escape* and looks like a slit in an orange. Charm. And a *good* actor. Now for a scene with him and Julie.

[1] Mrs 'Gabe' (Anna Gavrieldes) had been widowed in 1960. She continued to work for Joyce until 1964.

20 November 1963   Beverly Hills

Darling Virginia,

Apart from re-shooting a lot of the first scene I *think* I've finished. But you *never* know in movies.

I have a yellow cab every day and I can't tell you how nice the drivers are. All very different, ranging from actors and lawyers to lady drivers and casual labourers who feel like sitting down at last.

All are talkative in an agreeable way and I find them fascinating. Very 'philosophe' and for the most part thinkers.

Two have told me they couldn't manage without their belief in God, so of course they were in! This morning's was a construction engineer, i.e. builder's labourer. But the heights and the weights got too much for him.

Yesterday's was a 6 foot 4 actor with a splendidly resonant fruity voice. 'But I'm too tall for it,' he said ruefully, 'until I get a chance to prove I'm good in spite of it. It's all right to be tall if you are the lead but you can't humiliate the star by topping him.' He just missed good looks.

Leonard and I communicate by note, for I leave the house at 7.15 before he's up. Last night he said 'I'm so sleepy tonight I shan't write you a note', but on my breakfast tray was a piece of music paper with a crotchet and the message 'I couldn't resist this note, see? Love L.' He is a really very dear creature.

22 November [1963]   Hyde Park Gardens

Darling Joyce,
    I gaily rang up the lads – they are at Brighton – to be greeted by the news that President Kennedy had been shot & was critically ill! Since then I've been sitting with the wireless on. That the poor man had died came quite early on, yet I have felt drawn to go *on* listening, to hear the details, to hear the comments, & then hear them all over again. I imagine that U.S. is in complete turmoil. Oh dear. *What* a violent age this is.
    I'll come & meet you in the Bentley.

President John F. Kennedy was assassinated in Dallas, Texas.

23 November 1963   Beverly Hills

Darling Ginnie,
    Yesterday's ghastly tragedy knocked everyone sideways. I'd been up early and went in an M.G.M. car to get my clearance permit from the Internal Revenue Building in L.A. – an hour away. I was starting to pack about 10.30, chatting to Leonard, when the telephone rang. His neighbour said his maid had heard it on the radio. We switched it on at once and it was a terrible twenty five minutes from the first announcement to the confirmed report of Kennedy's death. We felt quite ill and looked it I think. Ghastly. Such a waste. I was a great admirer.
    L. took me in to Beverly Hills where I went to see Julie Andrews and

her baby. Leonard went to be with Pat Lawford, Kennedy's sister, and stayed there till evening. *Very* close chum.

After lunch I was in the Beverly-Wilshire Drug Store when my name was called on the loudspeaker! How the studio found me I can't imagine, but they did, and I had to rush out for a re-take. It was for an alternative reading of a line they *might* want to do.

It was Arthur Hiller's [director] birthday but no one felt festive, as you can imagine. All the crew and set men were wretched and sober. Jim Garner couldn't do his comedy scene and went home. Julie asked Arthur and his wife and me to have supper in her sitting room at the Beverly-Wilshire, and it was *very* nice and quiet and cosy. When I got back Leonard and I talked about it all.

I hated saying goodbye. I do dig in when I'm fond of anyone!

1964

Joyce and Reggie went to South Africa for a month.

3 February 1964   Hyde Park Gardens

Darling Joyce,

I really DON'T like you going away – and this time you seem to have CREPT somehow – without any chat or I-wonder-what-I'll-take or please-ring-up-Viola-sometimes etc. so that I feel *amazed* to find you weren't here. It was like a very very slow take!

Intensive Telly-watching tonight – *Black and White Minstrel Show, Perry Mason, Dr. Finlay's Casebook* and *Monitor* – whew!

The *Standard* is *full* of the perils of night club life – in the middle of the front page is a palm in which lie a cluster of 'purple hearts', and the reading matter tells of *hundreds* and *hundreds* of teenagers who stay awake whole weekends, eating a pill or two when the arms of Murphy should claim them! This is all in Soho, I may say!

7 February 1964   Hyde Park Gardens

Darling Joyce,

Tojo arrived back from the office soon after luncheon yesterday looking truly ghastly – like a very old candle – and feeling quite *desperately* tired. He's staying home today – he's rather a better colour this morning.

Celia came to tea – she was up for a Mother's lunch.[1] She said it was absolutely *hilarious* – everybody taking everybody else's name down in a little book, and a woman called Lady Roberts, who lived in Norfolk and had already brought out two girls, saying to C. 'Oh you must have special *trains* you can't do it unless you have special trains!'

C. was so aghast at all this – she says she can't organise even a bridge four – that she went right off to a firm called Party Planners, and *they're* going to 'do' the dance. Peter wants 400 people, Celia 300!!! Kate popped in to fetch her Ma to go off to a cocktail party – *ravishing* she is, with her vast eyes and huge lashes, and now a little lipstick.

I must nip out now and do a few desultory shoppings in Harrods.

I took Kay [Hammond] to see *Dr Strangelove*[2] yesterday. It was good, but not *all* that good. I thought Kay loathed it because it caricatured Americans to such a *degree* – they were all either mad or ineffably stupid – and she became quite exasperated and only her innate good manners prevented her from exploding! *Wonderful* bad taste joke at the very final sequence – cloud upon mushroom cloud billowing across the screen while Vera Lynn sings 'We'll meet again, don't know where, don't know when'.

[1] Celia Johnson was arranging the 'coming out' in the London social 'season' of her seventeen-year-old daughter Kate.
[2] Film about a nuclear bomb, starring Peter Sellers and George C. Scott, directed by Stanley Kubrick.

10 February 1964   Messina

Darling Ginnie,

Two letters and a splendid cable came for my birthday. The weekend at the ranch was *lovely*. I fear you might not like it there owing to wild life and nature and the odd insect and the outdoor existence.

We love it for it is such a paradise of birds and butterflies and peace, and although I'm not one for beetles and moths and creepers I don't mind them there somehow. The rondarvels are very spare. Just good flat beds, a chest-of-drawers and one chair. A flaring paraffin light at night.

As the birds came to see us we just sat in canvas chairs under the huge shading trees. The young zebra wandered among us. There are the three cheetahs, grown too large and athletic to be free, poor things. And a young leopardess, hand reared but very treacherous and menacing and now no one can handle her at *all*. The boys hate her and she hates back, hissing and spitting. Harold says she must either be given to a zoo or else destroyed, for she is really dangerous. We've seen any number of leaping impala looking like *Radio Times* cover designs.

R. has given me a book on Shakespeare and some scent and a telephone trunk call code number so I can ring from *any* where – even here – and be charged on my own bill. Glad To feels a bit better. I'm sure the lecturer is right. 'There's no discouragement *can* make him once relent to be a Pilgrim.'

10 February 1964   Hyde Park Gardens

Darling Joyce,

Happy B'day, darling! You're noticed in *The Times*, I may say! 'Joyce Grenfell, 54' it says! Both of us slept like tops (which, in case you aren't as cultured as you make out, comes from the French word *tope* – mole!).

I joined Georgina Coleridge[1] at Worth's,[2] where she was watching her daughter being fitted with a wedding dress – haven't been to Worth's since I got my first coming-out dress – white chiffon it was, with petals all of different lengths. We had interesting discussions about where to put granny's Brussels lace and what to wear on the head, etc. Then she and I lunched at the Connaught – scrummy and expensive.

The long day's journey moves into night and *Panorama* – and I am now 11 stone 1lb – and the tulips are dead – and I really am *quite* depressed, but only objectively so, in a curious way.

Love to everybody please.

[1] Editor of *Homes & Gardens* magazine.
[2] Couture house, established in nineteenth century.

12 February 1964   Messina

Darling Ginnie,

This morning – it's 6.45 – the lawn is a billion diamonds. Such a dew. We had an arduous evening. A buffet dance for twenty two. Mostly perfectly agreeable if dull. The Afrikaans ones mostly have chips on shoulders and are of a bone dullness. One soon exhausts food and clothes and children as topics, and one subject one longs to go into – Apartheid and all its horrors – is an absolute tabu. This is because it is not politic for us as visitors to show what we are known to feel. Bad manners enter into it too! And of course I'm constantly haunted by the conscience of getting our living, and a very good one too, in a country where such awful things go on. The only good thing is that this mine is most beautifully run and conditions are really good. Even so blacks are kept very black. We are thought to be very subversive and even communistic when we shake hands with Africans.

It's true that although the servants here are so gay and charming and friendly it is not at all certain how loyal they'd be if roused. Look what happened in Kenya. All the same one must go on hoping and behaving as if one believed all is well.

Back to our evening. I was glad when the gramophone began and
I forced R. to whirl me onto the floor of the stoep, cleared of furniture,
where we pounded round to lovely old tunes.[1]

[1] Before they were married, Joyce and Reggie won a prize for their dancing.

13 February 1964   Hyde Park Gardens

Darling Joyce,
I've just got home from lunching at the Brompton Grill – Dick, fresh
from Brighton, was there with Joycie – and find Tony has come back
from the office, having been too wobbly and tired to complete the
day there. He is half asleep already, and very fed up with things, poor
darling. I must say it is pretty maddening to have been given a clean
bill of health – and yet to feel so rotten. Jane writes and suggests T.
should have needles struck in his head by a Chinaman! Oh the things
that have been suggested!
I ate a large fish cake & parsnips, followed by treacle pud. Had such
a lot of indigestion on the way home, I nearly had to stop the car – but
I kept on saying 'God was there, in that place, *long* before the treacle
pud' and the pain eased off.

15 February 1964   Hyde Park Gardens

Darling Joyce,
Patrick[1] popped in on his way to Victor. He is dissatisfied with T's
improvement, and so has given him some *different* pills. Seems there's a
tiny portion of his brain not getting enough nourishment. Very good,
Patrick is about saying that dozens and dozens of people have this, and
it's not remotely what can be called a mental illness etc.

[1] Dr Patrick Woodcock, a London GP from 1952 to 1985 whose patients included Victor
Stiebel and Noël Coward.

26 February 1964   Jo'burg

Darling Ginnie,
I have just had an unusual experience. My tum felt a little odd so I
looked and there was a grapenut in my navel!
I'm so exercised about Apartheid and all the conflicts here. Cape
Town paper is very anti-it and goes on nagging. So do the brave Black
Sash women, an organisation dedicated to righting the wrong, but how?
Lunch with Ruth Neale of the Institute of Race Relations, Jo'burg,

who is first class and very clear in her mind. It's a hair raising country and the strain of living in it and doing her sort of job is terrific. She made me feel if I did come out and play here next March, to benefit her Institute, it would be a good and useful thing to do. I don't in the *least* want to do it, that's a fact. But I think I probably should . . . It's a hellova situation and if one can even ease tension *that's* something. Or so she says. Bishop Joost de Blanck says that laughter is in very short supply. So we'll see.

I've been encouraged by the enormous amount of protest going on within S.A. and there are those who think they'll win in the end. I wonder if there's time? Still, they are protesting and acting. It takes guts too. Love to you both.

Joyce agreed to do five performances on condition the audiences were racially mixed. However, the cultural and economic sanctions against South Africa prevented William Blezard, a member of the British Musicians' Union, from performing in South Africa until apartheid laws were changed, so they did not go.

23 March 1964   Elm Park Gardens

Darling Ginnie,

I rather envy you in the clean cold if damp air up there. It's mild and muggy and weighs a ton here.

Today will work on the sketch I suddenly wrote on Friday in the bath. I tried it on R. and he thinks it's got something.

Now I must put on all clean unders on account it's (a) Monday and (b) I'm fitting!

Keep writing, darling Nanook, and give my love to your friend. Lots of blubber to keep you warm. All love.

P.S. John (Beatle) Lennon's nonsense poetry book is so wonderfully silly.[1] I dote on it but defy you to ask me why. It's crazy, man. Crazy. But I larf.

[1] *A Spaniard in the Works.*

24 March 1964   Bellabeg
                                                         Scotland

Darling Joyce,

An unbelievably ghastly day today, snow still lying in strips on chocolate earth (oh the poet in me!) and I doubt if we go out – well, I suppose we'll have to; one almost always does, it's something to do with having a nanny, I imagine.

I *do* think people's attitude to writing is funny – even one's loved ones! I sat writing an article yesterday evening and T. came and went on various errands, telephoning the office, talking to the workmen, going to the johnny, putting in a new light bulb, and each time he came in he talked to me merrily, apparently absolutely *unaware* that writing needs a weeny bit of concentration. Not that it mattered in the slightest, as I have all the time in the world, but isn't it odd? If I'm reading the Lesson he's quiet as a mouse . . . but I believe this is a universal blank spot, his cheerful disregard for the creative arts.

To is entirely swathed in wool, flannel and tweed.

Going to have another whack at the article now . . . Doesn't cleaning the bath make one hot?

22 April 1964   Elm Park Gardens

Darling Ginnie,

Channel 2 was great fun last night.[1] A superb production of *Kiss me Kate* sung with gusto and good voices. The picture was quite wonderfully clear. We saw fireworks to finish with and a news report at the end done in a direct but somehow fresh and young wąy! It was all very young but disciplined and intelligent. I'm full of hope for it.

I love names. Today's S.O.S. police message on the air at 8. was for a man called 'Tootsie Stranger'. He's a travelling salesman.

I retrieved my (from you) umbrella from Baker Street Lost Property. What a sight it is. All those hundreds of brollies labelled with where they were found and when. I was *so* glad to see mine again. I get attached to inanimate objects and once nearly cried over a sponge I lost.

[1] BBC 2's first night.

23 April 1964   Boston Hotel
                                                                      Rome

Darling Joyce,

Rome is looking splendid. The Spanish steps are entirely flanked, banked, reaped and moulded with huge white and pink azaleas – such a sight – a smile! Hundreds of people strewn around them, Americans, mothers feeding babies, beatnikky students, Germans, Chinese, dowagers, tramps, priests, swarms of photographers, and a warm sun setting on all.

Am *furious* the crossword is all Shakespeare today.[1] I am so uncultured I don't know the answers to any but the most obvious clues, and I've been sitting here having a bash at inventing them. I first invented 'Portia's legal name' as Brassamio, and then I decided it was Baldesare, and now it ends in R, so I'm completely foxed!

Oooh, this is a *pretty* place. I love it. But oooh, too, the traffic. I don't know *how* old ladies ever get across the road: the only system is to step smartly off the kerb and hope the cars stop in time!

Tojo is in fine form, and *terrifically* energetic compared to a few months ago!

¹ William Shakespeare's 400th birthday. Both Virginia and Joyce were keen *Times* crossword puzzle solvers.

27 April 1964   Elm Park Gardens

Darling Ginnie,

Yesterday I joined the huge crowds going in for the service to honour Shakespeare organised by The Poetry Society. I was representing the Society of Women Writers and Journalists. A heavenly day, and the Abbey glowed pale gold. Michael Redgrave read from Ecclesiasticus – 'Let us now praise famous men', and Cecil Day Lewis gave a *superb* address. A grand service with copes and lots of redundant priests hovering. Lovely choir. Absolutely out of contact with Reality and Truth as I see it but very well done!

Brief tea in a restaurant near Whitehall with the S.W.W.J. and then I went to see Vic who had sounded *so* low. Vic did his usual remarkable performance of courage and gaiety. How I do salute him. His lovely enthusiasm is equally remarkable.

When David Attenborough was controller of BBC2 he introduced viewers to performers who had not previously appeared on British television. Joyce was among these, and made her first appearance on British television.

9 August 1964   Hyde Park Gardens

Darling Joyce,

You were absolutely *smashing*. The soft light of BBC 2 was beautifully flattering – you looked younger and gayer than ever – and absolutely *ravishing* when you were doing the foreign lady being interviewed:¹ this was a *real* triumph, close-up like that, with the camera trained on every movement of muscle and quaver of eyelash. We were both awfully moved by it – it's the dignity of the creature which catches at the heart, and that attractive accent, which is completely right for somebody who's lived here for thirty years.

And now I'm going to bed, on account my hubby is waiting in it for me!

[1] 'Life Story', first performed in 1959, about the wife of a famous musician.

25 August 1964   Elm Park Gardens

Darling Ginnie,

A lead heavy damp difficult Monday. After lunch I got at a vile pile of duty mail: sixteen proper letters, four p.cs. and some bills. I was absolutely poggled.

On Sunday, I think it was, Malcolm Muggeridge[1] was on BBC 2 talking to a group of young anarchists. At first they seemed to be the usual weirdy-beardies in clouds of unsuitable hair. Then they began to emerge as actual thinkers. Their view of what anarchy is amazed me because it turns out I'm one too! They believe in man's individuality as a divine thing and that he is capable of controlling and governing himself. They seek only this sort of liberty. They don't wish to kill kings or overthrow governments, but to awaken everyone's latent potential to an inheritance already his if only he'd recognise it! Very close to home, hein?

Instead of making me rage, as I'd expected it to do, I was astonished.

Last night's telly had Danny Kaye with Johnnie Mills[2] and Hayley,[3] and the three of them did a dance routine that was unintentionally *very* funny indeed. Oh Les Anglais when they go rhythmic! Hayley must stick to acting – & so must her Daddy. And they were useless in a sketch. No sense of comedy, of improvisation. But Danny was in very good form.

The boys are back from Brighton today. Oh Lor, I must order some flowers for Vic. I bought a girdle at P.J. All love darling and to Ole Todl.

R. is yelling . . . Must go.

I do miss you and our morning talks.

[1] British journalist (1903–90).
[2] British film actor (1908–).
[3] His actress daughter, aged eighteen. She had just appeared in the play *The Chalk Garden*.

27 August 1964   Bellabeg, Aberdeenshire

Darling Joyce,

Lully to hear your voice – tho' you sounded as tho' you were
in Africa!

T. looked utterly deflected, and I had to give him a tiny pep talk –
because I think one must *look* fairly cheerful, for manners' sake – and
he said 'Oh it's quite fun really!' in a doleful way!

When I returned he was quite bonny again. I don't quite know what
to think about his giving up shooting – I mean, we shall *have* to come
up here every year, for Mrs Ritchie's, if not for Alec's sake – and it does
give him something to *do*. He does so little now – no golf or tennis or
fishing – and he is interested in absolutely nothing (except me!) that I
have a feeling ANY activity should be fostered. If I thought he would
give up shooting in favour of botany or bird-watching . . . but I can't,
at the moment, see him being interested in anything. I rather dread
the thought of him taking tiny walks, and dropping off over a book! Of
course, I can see what's got to happen – I shall have to take up fishing
and golf and botany and bird-watching, and make him help me!

I wrote most of the morning, interrupted by Alec, who after his mad
morning bicycle race up the valley, settled down opposite me with a
book, from which he occasionally raised his head to say 'D.d.does your
Church have a Ch.ch.ildren's Service?' and 'D.do.do you like macaroni
cheese?'

3 September 1964   [London]

Darling Ginnie,

I'm under the dryer, newly cut and permed. At 11.30 I go to D's
to hear the setting he's done for my new out-of-the-blue, and possibly
useless, lyric that begins:

> I wouldn't go back to the world I knew,
> I wouldn't go back for a day!

It's difficult to describe. Hope you'll like it.[1]

Yesterday was another beauty. Home all a.m. practising, doing
words, then a call from R. saying 'Who's for tennis?', so after a little
more practising I donned me white and we had a grass court and it was
very soothing.

Church. I spoke. About the way love heals atmospheres. Told of that
encounter with rough brute Customs man in New York some years ago

and how I refused to accept his attitude and met him in the only place where both of us actually have our being – love. It worked perfectly and we ended buddies!

¹ 'I wouldn't go back to the world I knew' was first performed in 1965.

4 September 1964   Elm Park Gardens

Darling Ginnie,

I had lunch with Joanna Scott Moncrieff¹ and we talked a great deal about God. She said: 'Do you know any *good* Christians?' We laughed about this rare species and decided we knew many actual Christians who weren't churchgoers and were good-ish. She needs to know some articulate ones for her new job – Religious Broadcasting.

¹ Deputy editor of *Woman's Hour* and then in BBC's Religious Broadcasting.

6 September 1964   Elm Park Gardens

Darling Ginnie,

Out early to Olympia where I sold pieces of rich fruit cake in aid of Oxfam at the International Food Fair. I was in my smart creamy flannel suit and fair melted. But I must have taken £10 in thirty minutes, all in bobs, so it was worth the sweat.

Viola's been conducting the rehearsals of *Screw* and *Lucretia* and *Herring*¹ and hands over on Monday to Ben B. and Merideth Davies and the orchestra. She's determined it shall be first class for Russia, as they are representing intimate opera – never yet seen there.

I wrote a holy pome and am still polishing it. It's called 'The reason for Joy'. D. has set another 'Song to make you sick' called 'I doan't say nowt', to be sung rustic. I love it!

¹ Ben Britten's operas *Rape of Lucretia* (1946), *Albert Herring* (1947), *The Turn of the Screw* (1954).

Joyce and Reggie went to Canada and the USA for a tour of performances. Virginia and Tony planned to join Joyce and Reggie in New York, after the tour.

17 September [1964]   Hyde Park Gardens

Darling Joyce,

Shall be thinking of you on Sunday, with R hooking up your dresses . . . do you have to iron them, I wonder? . . . you'll have a Beatle success I know.

312

Last night T let drop, by mistake, that he felt a bit fey during the day. After only four days back in the office!! He could have bitten out his tongue, poor boy, & made very light of it, but I *did* feel oh dear.

18 September 1964   The Berkeley Hotel
                                                            Montreal

Darling Ginnie,
     By sheer chance I discovered Bill's name is not on the bills or on the programme. Ye gods. I really was *so* mad. There has been endless fuss about Bill being an integral part of my show. What do I *pay* these agents for? When I discovered it I rang Ottawa and Toronto and clearly they'd neither of them got his name anywhere. Isn't it maddening? These things are so important not only to Bill but to the whole project. It looks so b-y conceited to have only one's own name in the bill, and anyway Bill's contribution to the programme is *very* considerable not to say vital.
     It *isn't* my job *every time* to see to these details. So you see I was *kloss* and it's such a waste of energy.
     It is so *wonderful* to have R. here. Makes the *whole* difference. Not only because 'he is here' but because he is *so* helpful. Will do all the managerial chores that Connie did for me. All love to you and To.

19 September 1964   Montreal

Darling Ginnie,
     Bill woke in the night and suddenly realised he'd left the copy of the piece he does in the programme called 'The Battle of Delhi'. The point of it is its great age and tattered condition, for he found it in an old music stool. He uses it to convince the audience of its authenticity. It's a story piece with spoken narration. He instantly rang Joan in Barnes – oh miracles of science – she made sure the copy was there, and left her with the task of getting it to him *somehow* and soon! Then he got up and wrote out the whole thing as far as he could remember it. It lasts four minutes!

20 September [1964]   Hyde Park Gardens

Joyce Darling,
     This is to tell you we are NOT coming, after all. I came home just now & found To had left the office at 1.30 & been sleeping ever since, & he obviously *isn't* well, isn't fit enough to do a long sociable motor

trip. He's been fighting this damned feyness & exhaustion since he got back from Scotland, and been pretending everything was OK, but I truly think it would be a foolishness, & pointless, to bring him on a US trip he wouldn't enjoy. So I've persuaded him to call it off & I think he's relieved. For my part, I am at the moment too disappointed to *speak*. I've been looking forward to this for such ages, & I find it hard to *believe* it isn't going to happen!

Ta for your two letters. How maddening about the billing – there's nothing so infuriating than inefficiency, is there?

22 September 1964   Lord Elgin Hotel
                                                                Ottawa

Darling Ginnie,

I had a rave review in the evening paper for Sunday's show but a carping one in the morning one, complaining of my gentleness and the size of the hall. This was fact, but when I read that my cockney was more convincing than my upper class English I realised the critic needn't be listened to too closely!

Bill told us yesterday of a piano he once met in Wick, where he was for years in the R.A.F. in the war, that had three mice in it living in a nest made of torn up cloakroom tickets!

Bill goes over huge here and is beaming and very endearing.

23 September [1964]   Hyde Park Gardens

Darling Joyce,

I am keeping my thinking very clear at the moment, refusing to accept any of these lies, or be discouraged. I have got over the first pangs of bitter disappointment (at 53 one does that rather easily, I find!) & tho' everything seems a bit flat now, it brings with it a certain sense of rest too – two absolutely empty weeks.

25 September 1964   Toronto

Darling Ginnie,

Oh the *disappointment*. But of course you are right to take this decision and you are always at liberty to change your mind just supposing T. feels more like it. Darling, I do mind for you, very much. It's damnable T. having this sickness and he must be freed of it – or proved free of it to our view, for of course he is nothing less than whole now. Please give To a huge kiss and tell him we miss him and you no end already.

This is just a little love note to say boo-hoo and hard-cheese and damn it all, and to say we think of you endlessly and get home soon and don't be down-hearted. It's only a passing phase, as Patrick says, and To must just relax and lean on Love.

I'm thinking of you, darling, *so* much.

26 September 1964   Toronto

Darling Ginnie,

R. has been doing my tax, coping with our flight to N.Y., and generally being a super manager. Darling – I do wish you were both coming.

Last night was 'fab'. The most attentive and responsive audience. R. at the controls *most* effectively. We'd rehearsed the lighting for 'Life Story' – widow and journalist who is to write her late husband's life – and it is total stage darkness and one fierce stop light on my chair into which I walk. The light was dead on my chair but when I walked into it, it only lit up to my knees! I sat there and the spot man did nothing so I had to bend down into the beam and wave him up a bit. This was of course a big laugh and the whole purpose of this sombre light change to induce a new mood was *somewhat* lost. But I got it back by refusing to respond to the comedy of it, although I was dying to. It *was* very funny but I just had to hang on or the number would never have worked.

It's been fun and as always when I finish I am torn by relief and the wish to go on. It seems so silly *not* to work! I wonder how long I'll feel like this?

Keep writing and rest up, ole To, and, darling Nanny Gin, take care of yourself as well as To, because we love you.

Oh I do *wish* you were coming.

27 September [1964]   Hyde Park Gardens

Darling Joyce,

You were on the telly last night, luv – very nearly perfect – my only criticism being for the orchestra or mebbe the producer who hadn't got it balanced right & tended to swamp you at moments. You looked fine, darling. You were frightfully moving in Boat Train. Of course, hopeless bravery is my Achilles Heel, tear-wise, so I cried, & went to bed with that bad cold I always get.[1]

It is yet another caramel day – we are almost bewildered by this endless succession of edible days. Tojo sends his love or rather says 'Tell her I love her with a passion that is not wholly pure!'

Writing this on m'knee with the News, which is such a bore these days, nothing but politics, first the P.M. being scornful about Labour, then Harold[2] being snide about the Tories, then Jo[3] slanging both of them.

By the way, darling, can you remember to put our flat number (7) on the envelopes? & also, perhaps refrain from putting S.W.10. which delays things a soupçon?!![4]

[1] Tear-jerking poem about a mother seeing off her emigrating son and family.
[2] Harold Wilson (1916–95), leader of the Labour Party.
[3] Jo Grimond (1913–94), leader of the Liberal Party.
[4] Hyde Park Gardens is in W2. Joyce's home was in SW10.

1 October 1964   New York

Darling Ginnie,

Ta for yesterday's letter. So glad that To is bit more rested. When is the op.?

Yesterday morning I had 10.30 'breakfast' at the Plaza with a man from M.G.M. to talk about promoting the two films I made for them – *Emily* and *Yellow R.R.* Actually we ended in talking about the publicity man's life and problems handling Shirley Maclaine – rather difficult. I was sorry to hear S.M. had become tricky for I dote on her, but she is *so* much in demand and so spoiled now that she's become a little madam, I gather. His real passion is poetry – he has sold fifteen in his life – so he finds film promotion quite tough. He's a dear little man called Mike de Lisio. Tactful and gentle and just what he's doing in the film world seems mysterious. It's money I daresay.

R. and I saw the matinée of *Hello Dolly*, which we loved. It is so beautifully done with real style and freshness. Carol is funny and oversized and right for Mrs Dolly Gallagher Levi. She's a big broad type of star and gives out in a big broad way. Waved to us in the third row and called out 'Hello Joyce' as she took her calls! R. enjoyed it as much as I did and we had a good time.

1 October [1964]   Hyde Park Gardens

Darling Joyce,

We are *both* rather whacked today as we spent our 'one night out a week' with Mr Osborne at the Royal Court.[1] If only he would cut his stuff! The amount of verbiage which pours out of the mouth of his hero is battering to a *degree*. Half way through the last act I stopped listening

– my ears *numb* from the noise of words – & seeing T's pale, luminous face beside me, I dug him in the ribs, & we left! There were a great many other seats thumping up, but I *was* a bit ashamed.

Osborne has such a gift for dialogue, but this isn't a play, it's a monologue with diarrhoea!

When T & I were dining at the Royal Court Grill Room before the show, I told him of the way I was thinking of him – as made by God, so absolutely perfect & spiritual. He was rather eager to hear this, & then said, touchingly, 'I suppose I could almost think that God loves me so much he couldn't let me be ill?' & I said 'You're absolutely on the right tack, darling', but isn't it funny how people cling to the idea of a personal God?

Joyce [Carey] & I lunched at the Brompton Grill yesterday. Joycie was describing the teleplay with Vanessa Redgrave to Noël & said 'Vanessa plays the part of an artist who has one leg shorter than the other . . .'

'My *dear*,' he said, 'how fortunate it isn't *longer* than the other.'

---

[1] *Inadmissible Evidence* by John Osborne, directed by Anthony Page and starring Nicol Williamson.

5 October 1964   New York

Darling Ginnie,

Truman Capote[1] came to lunch at Tommy's and is *so* extraordinary that no word can accurately capture him. He is very small and rather muscular, with a boyish hair cut and a pale face. He has an exaggerated sibilance in his speech and waves his arms when he talks as if he was doing a joke cissy – but it's for real. And he is highly intelligent, amusing – and somehow nice. He wore a round necked fair isle sweater, rather crumpled dungaree type trousers and pale blue tennis shoes. R. couldn't believe his eyes.

Yesterday afternoon I had my hair washed, and high time too. I heard a riveting conversation in the next cubicle.

'I *told* you it would be a shock at first but it's beautiful.'

'I don't know . . .'

'It's champagne colour and it blends *beautifully* with your own grey. It's really stunning.'

'But it's so *light*.'

'You just live with it for a week and then if you don't like it I'll rinse it darker, but you'll *love* it.'

'I don't know . . .'

Of course I couldn't wait to see the lady and when she walked by, very tall and slight, my age, I thought she looked marvellous!

Incredibly natural, silvery-grey and very becoming. She looked so uncertain.

Took herself to the door to see it in daylight, came back – 'I don't know . . .'

Couldn't resist it, so I said: 'If you will excuse a complete stranger I'd like to say I think it looks *lovely.*'

'Oh *do* you?' she said. She was very shy and unsure. 'Thank you,' she said, 'I feel much better.'

---

[1] American novelist (1924–84).

7 October [1964]   Hyde Park Gardens

Darling Joyce,

It was a real happiness to yell at you types. Ta ta ta for ringing.

We've been mucking about today, doing dunny things, & it's been ever so pleasant (this sounds like the diary of a homosexual prostitute, doesn't it & it's fortunate I know you to be 'pur, pur, pur'!).

This morning, I was battling with an eggy sort of holy poem, & I had just written down 'There is no little place where God is not', when Christine burst in to tell me the kitchen sink had overflowed all over the floor! I had to give a great guffaw of laughter – which she failed, naturally enough, to appreciate – & I amended my verse to 'There *is* a little pipe where God is not.'

We would be sitting at Heathrow now, contemplating the mist. Tojo looks a bite more rested, but he says he's *awfully* glad he's not flying to the U.S.

Oh my *word*! I wish we were almost with you . . . have a lovely time, darling, & miss us frightfully, hein?

11 October [1964]   Hyde Park Gardens

Darling Joyce,

I caught a glimpse of our future leaders on the telly – people like Mr Callaghan,[1] & Mr Healey,[2] & they looked *horrid*, all of them enormously fat & flabby with wet mouths & boot button eyes! I shall be glad when this election is over. Labour is now ahead, if one can believe the polls, though why anyone wants to consult them I can't imagine, as I told you all that Lab. would get in, ages ago. Anyway, I'm fed up with all the vituperation & smearing & jeering; & now gangs of young have taken to shouting Conservative speakers down, so that no-one can hear a word of their ridiculous speeches. What with this & the gross discourtesy to the Queen in Quebec, the air has a tetchy smell to it this week.[3]

[1] James Callaghan (1912–), Chancellor of the Exchequer under Wilson, later Prime Minister.
[2] Denis Healey (1917–), Secretary of State for Defence in 1964, later Chancellor of the Exchequer.
[3] French Canadians had demonstrated against the Queen.

14 October [1964]   Hyde Park Gardens

Darling Joyce,

Out on the tiles last night with Dick. We ate at the Ivy, & then strolled along Shaftesbury to see the Aloin Dayley dancers. They were no good at all, & we couldn't see how they had got such wonderful notices. They were hideous, & somehow that intense jerky dancing is so old-fashioned. So we left in the interval. As I was driving him home down the Cromwell Road, we saw lots of people standing about – Ah! we said, the Queen![1]

So we stopped, and stood in the crisp night air – forming a somehow tremendously touching line, thin as a whisper, all down that boring old road. There were some young in open cars in the middle of the road, & when Q. came, in a lit up car, they honked horns & all we elderly types rushed forward, waving our hankies & shawls and crutches – & then, we all burst into tears and went home. Seems there was also a lovely turn out at B.P. [Buckingham Palace] Everybody's so furious she's been subjected to this humiliation, & each wanted to say Well, *I* love you anyway!

[1] Cromwell Road leads to Heathrow airport. The Queen was returning from Canada.

16 October 1964   New York

Darling Ginnie,

Back in N.Y. for a few hours. The prettiest fall colours of *all*!

The election is over and as far as the N.Y. papers and radio know it's Labour with a very narrow margin.[1] So there we are and I'm sure we'll get used to it, and let's just hope it works. The Stock Exchange has plunged already, I gather! You must be so glad it's over, and when you get this the post mortems will be over too, I trust. Geoff said last night 'How I envy you – missing your election!'

Last night we saw young Robert Kennedy[2] on T.V. and Reggie thought he was delightful, charming, courteous and good and civilised.

But Tommy, who knows him, says he's an arrogant, tough, brutal and ruthless pusher and politician! So *how* do we know *anything*?

During a big family lunch, Lang surprised us all by knowing all the planets.

We saw Joan Sutherland[3] on the *Sullivan Show*. Singing superbly of course and looking quite well too. Also on it were a beat group from London – the Animals? – or the Beasts? And four young men from the Cambridge Revue, who are a big hit here in *Cambridge Circus*, did a piece from their show that proved them to be endearing and quite talented.[4]

[1] Labour won the general election by five seats and Harold Wilson became Prime Minister.
[2] Brother of John F. Kennedy (1925–68), US Senator, ran for President. Assassinated in California.
[3] Australian opera singer (1926–).
[4] Peter Cook (1937–95), Dudley Moore (1935–), Alan Bennett (1934–) and Jonathan Miller (1934–).

16 October [1964]   Hyde Park Gardens

Darling Joyce,

We didn't stay up late for the Election, but we saw some Mods (or Rockers) swimming about in the fountains of Trafalgar Square in the pouring rain & listened for a while to assessment & prognostications & trends & swings etc – doled out by dear Mr Dimbleby[1] & his troupe.

Since last I wrote I've really done nothing but sit in a train. I bumbled all the way to Malvern to see some old ladies. I bought some lavender bags & a hot water bottle cover, had a cupper with Mrs Dyson Perrins, who gave us this home. She is one of those marvellous women dedicated to unselfish acts – check tweed suit, fawn silk stitched hat, hair cut by rat's incisors, tiny brown wrinkled face. Looks like a temporary cook, and has a fortune, made from *sauce*.[2]

To has ordered me a new Mini for Christmas! The very latest model. Exciting, hein?

My love to anybody who happens to be handy.

[1] Richard Dimbleby (1913–65), television journalist, father of Jonathan and David.
[2] Lea & Perrins Worcester Sauce.

21 October 1964   New York

Darling Ginnie,

One more letter just to tell you that Barbra Streisand[1] is really enchanting. She's got such comedy, a long thin body, long neck, arms, legs, and beautiful long thin hands – all of which she employs to emphasise and point with. She moves funnily but never gawkily unless it's deliberate, and then it has a sort of grace! And I'm mad for her singing, as I think you will be too. It's dead on, clear and malleable, and she can belt but without losing the musical sound: and she can sing small like a lullaby singer. She's got an extraordinary face – full of pathos and charm and plain too – jolie laide. Her nose and forehead are in one like an Egyptian drawing. Not nearly as good looking as Nefertiti but there's a resemblance! We adored her and enjoyed *Funny Girl* like anything.

We had lovely seats, and right across from us was Audrey Hepburn.[2] She looked so pretty and quite unspoiled. White brocade from neck to toe, one of those severe Givenchy jobs, straight as a narrow, with matching white brocade shoes. Hair done up in a huge sort of bun and scraped back. Recognised by *everyone* and respectfully treated.

My Fair Lady film opens tonight and I think she may get a bit of rubbing for it because the 'on dit' is that although she looks superb in the grand parts she never convinces as a cockney waif, and there is widespread feeling that Julie [Andrews] *should* have had the part. Not Audrey's fault but she *may* have a rough time.

This marvellous series of indulgences must soon cease and we'll be back in the harshness of home life! We are enjoying it all very much. See you soon darling. Lunches? Dinners? All love and to To.

[1] American singer and actress (1942–).
[2] Belgian-born film actress (1919–93).

1965

Joyce had written a new solo show with songs by Richard Addinsell, which she and William Blezard took on a tour of England.

16 March 1965   Queen's Hotel
                                                           Cheltenham

Darling Ginnie,

Oh dear. Dick's name is *not* on posters or on throwaways for the Brighton show on Thursday. It *should* be. He is *sad*. I'm enraged. This is the agent's job. Oh damn as well as oh dear.

R. is home, brown and bonny.[1] It is very nice to have him home, I can tell you. I've done 'Eng. Lit.' to him and he likes it a lot. We've told each other all our news, such as it is, for we write daily so there isn't much unwritten.

We rang Vic to sing 'Happy bidet to you'.

I believe the booking is good. It's my world première of 'Lally Tulett',

'Hymn', 'Eng. Lit.', 'Wouldn't go back to the world I knew', 'Bring back the silence', and 'It's made all the Difference' (the football pool one). I had to type it all out (lots of inaccuracies) for the Lord Chamberlain. *Everything* has to go to him.[2]

All love to you, darling, and to Ole To.

[1] He had been to South Africa.
[2] Until 1968 the Lord Chamberlain had to certify that all public theatre performances were not blasphemous, obscene or subversive.

17 March 1965   Queen's Hotel

Darling Ginnie,

Isn't this pretty paper.

The new stuff went very well and 'Hymn'[1] stopped the show. In fact they laughed so much that many of my verbal gems were lost. But a nice fault. Part 1 is good, but I'm not a bit satisfied with Part 2, and I think after tomorrow at Brighton, we must reconstruct it.

Quite a long day it was! Bill and I rehearsed to the accompaniment of hammering as men took down the all-in-wrestling platform. Then I came back here for a working-kip. In this I lie flat, toes on a h.w.b., black scarf over the eyes, and I go through all the words of everything in a comatose but restful fashion. It took me one hour and fifteen minutes!

And there you are.

[1] Song about a woman who leaves her soup boiling while she is at church.

11 May [1965]   Bellabeg

Darling Joyce,

A curious coincidence. I was nattering to To on the river bank, telling him the last time I caught a trout was when Bim Northampton handed me his rod to hold, way back in '28, when T. handed me *his* rod to have a practice with ('Now UP!' he cried) & there was a fish on the end! It was all of 1 lb, but felt like a whale. I've just eaten it for my brekker.

Oh the silence! isn't it intoxicating? We're beginning to feel so Victorian in this heavenly hush.

I haven't a wit, a tittle or an iota of news for you.

15 May 1965   Scale Hill
                                                              Loweswater

Darling Ginnie,
    Bill and I had a difficult audience in that it really didn't always
know we were intending to be funny. Later I learned that Carrs Biscuit
Factory had made a big block booking of fifty and that this was Carrs
first visit to Rosehill[1] ever. I think it was also the first visit to any live
entertainment for this group too, for they were like a movie audience:
no sense of *their* responsibility, thus we hardly got enough applause at
the end of items to allow us time to move to the next. I exaggerate, but
it was hard work. And then, at the interval, enormous applause. In the
end they sat there clapping their little hands together till they must have
been scarlet.
    I've finished my season and as always feel a mixture of sadness
and relief.

[1] A small private theatre owned by Sir Nicholas Sekers.

19 May [1965]   Hyde Park Gardens

Darling Joyce,
    Nothing from you for two days, which is mysterious, but I imagine
I should be informed if you'd sprained your wrist falling down a fell,
& that this silence merely denotes happy relaxation from the cares of
friendship?
    T is going to see another doctor who has cured a friend of Sheila's
of melancholia in 10 days. Patrick [Woodcock] perfectly approving,
though he said the only tricky thing about these sort of doctors is they
are apt to try shock treatment. And he doesn't think To would like that
one little bit. Anyway, he will talk to this doctor & urge him to stay his
hand. I think it's a good thing to give an impression, at any rate, that
somebody is doing something. Vic thinks it excellent that To should
have 'settled' for feeling tired, but sometimes I think he has settled for
feeling tired for life! Don't write a word of this to me.
    There's so much to see on telly tonight – *University Challenge*, football
final, *Z Cars* – we're giving ourselves a tongue on a plate on the knee!

21 May 1965   Loweswater

Darling Ginnie,
    Yesterday was a great success – the village fete.[1] Sun shone and
a record attendance came. Tea on two very long trestle tables: two

shillings a head and lashings of scones, sandwiches, cakes all home made. £160 resulted, so smiles abounded. R. helped shift chairs and then ran the spinning wheel – à la roulette – for bottles ranging from booze to Brylcreem. For a gimmick I wore my Picture Postcard hat and explained it in my speech. Then I charged one shilling for snapping me in it and this little attraction made £4.0.1d!

There was fishing for bottles with curtain rings, bouncing ping-pong balls off a board into a bucket, pacing out what you thought was 22 yards and sticking in a little label to mark your guess – I was within five inches, and there was darts, and throwing pennies into a bucket of water to try and cover a half crown lying on the bottom. Ella's plant stall was lovely and sold out fast.

Last night after supper Tim Armstrong, the woodsman, took us to try and see a badger and we did! Wearing layers on layers of wool we sat on some stones in the river and as it got dusk (10 p.m.) out came a striped nose from a big hole in the bank opposite. We watched him clearly for quite a time and then he shambled off on a hunt. It was lovely.

I must put you right about my taste in country. I, too, am very much for lush but I like wild tops above my lush and the call of flat dune-y bits and estuaries is purely ornithological and not aesthetic. The reason (hush) I'm not in favour of Scotland's endless drear hills is their bareness and all that heather. What I love about here is the valleys full of green fields and trees and little cottages etc., but most of all trees. I don't want to live surrounded by them so I can't see out, but I do wish to be able to look up or down on them. See? Lakes are o.k. to visit but too much flat water is not for I. But gurgling brooks *are*.

---

[1] Occasionally, Joyce agreed to one of the many invitations she got to open fetes.

21 July 1965   King's Lynn

Darling Joyce,

A superb concert last night, in St. Nicholas' – Rostropovitch[1] and a few lads playing Vivaldi, Tartini and Boccherini concertos. R. half turning round to conduct them and then embracing his cello with warmth and really staggering brilliance.

Queen Mum and party came, of course – the same as every year: David Cecils, Duke of Wellington, et cetera, but with the addition of Noël! Noël spotted us both coming up the aisle and going down it, and gave us two superb theatrical faces, almost, though not quite, blowing us a kiss. Very friendly of him.

The Royal party has 10 free seats every night, but they haven't *once*

Joyce and Richard Addinsell on *RMS Mauretania* crossing the Atlantic to New York, September 1955 (*Courtesy of Claremont Fan Court School*)

Joyce brings her Christmas shopping back from New York on the *Queen Mary*, December 1957 (*Courtesy of Claremont Fan Court School*)

Joyce helps in a nursery school in Oldham, Lancashire, 1952 (*Courtesy of Claremont Fan Court School*)

Joyce, Reggie and Miriam Grenfell birdwatching in South Africa, 1955 (*Private collection*)

Joyce and Virginia in a meadow near Brighton, Easter 1956 (*Private collection*)

Virginia on her way to Scotland in 'Gussie' the Bentley, September 1955. Photo by Tony (*Private collection*)

Reggie and Joyce and their new Ford Zephyr in Elm Park Gardens, July 1958 (*Private collection*)

Christmas with the Grenfells, 1961. Reggie, Richard Addinsell, Joyce, Virginia and Victor Stiebel. Photo by Tony (*Private collection*)

Joyce rehearses with William Blezard at the Theatre Royal, Haymarket, 1962. She is wearing a silk frock designed by Victor Stiebel (*Private collection*)

Joyce reads Beatrix Potter on 'Jackanory' children's television, 1969 (*Courtesy of Claremont Fan Court School*)

Virginia, Joyce and Reggie in Austria with Tony, 1957 (*Private collection*)

Dilys Tugwell on Virginia's balcony at Hyde Park Gardens, 1970 (*Private collection*)

Joyce with her niece and nephew, Sally and Lang Phipps, in their New York flat (*Courtesy of Thomas Phipps*)

Paul Paget marries Verily Anderson, 1971, with his best man John Betjeman.
Eddie gave his mother away, attended by her daughters Alex, Janie and Marian
and new son-in-law, Charles Hampton. Photo taken by Joyce (*Private collection*)

Joyce, Virginia, Simon Bowes-Lyon and his aunt, Queen Elizabeth the Queen
Mother, at St Paul's, July 1972 (*Private collection*)

'Face the Music', BBC2, 1976. Joseph Cooper, standing, with producer, Walter Todds. Sitting beside Joyce are Robin Ray (left) and David Attenborough (right).

Virginia and Athene Seyler reciting an ode composed by Celia Johnson at Joyce and Reggie's golden wedding party in Virginia's home, 17th November 1979. Joyce died two weeks later (*Private collection*)

remembered to bring their programmes! That means they've had forty already!!

¹ Russian conductor and cellist (1927–).

5 August 1965   Shrewsbury

Darling Joyce,

We lunched badly in Welshpool, and then went to see Powis Castle, a thing I've always wanted to do. If I had married into Powis I should have, with your approval I know, cut my throat *right* away – Stygian dark rooms crammed full of stuccoed ceilings and Genoese velvet chairs: a proper castle, in fact, VAST, with battlements and towers. Its beauty lies in its situation, which is high, and in its garden, which is *fab*, going down down down in floral terraces to a *huge* expanse of lawn. It is funny, but we go so rarely to stay with anybody these days – that one rather *forgets* about gardens. This one smelt so heavenly, of limes and honey and cherry pie, and was so buzzy with bees and a distant lawn mower, I had a sudden nostalgia for those exhausting weekends one used to spend in one's youth – like at Cliveden! I suddenly expected someone to come out of the house dressed for tennis, or to turn a corner and find Lady Ilchester.

A happy day . . . To sends his 'passionate love'. He seems quite well, and is in excellent spirits, though hugely ga-ga!

5 August 1965   Elm Park Gardens

Darling Ginnie,

I really hate it when you are away. I know we don't meet all that much, but there we are at 8.20 a.m. with the blessed telephone as a glorious link. Mornings without our call are very incomplete.

Bill Blezard for tea and a moan about Marlene¹ and her total egotism and the ghastly time he had at the Theatre Royal, Brighton, with his strings in the Outer Hebrides (a box) and his trumps in the Azores (the opposite box), and *he* can't hear Marlene and Marlene can't hear him and when vexed always races away regardless of tempo or his beat, and it is hell. Until now he's been on stage behind her. Says he'll issue an ultimatum before Birmingham next week! Poor Bill.

Did I tell you about the quote I found in one of those little 'boxes' in the C.S.M.? 'Joy doesn't happen. It is the inevitable result of certain lines followed and laws obeyed.'

¹ William Blezard was musical director to singer Marlene Dietrich.

19 August 1965   Bellabeg

Darling Joyce,
I'm doing a lot of 'everything's enjoyable' this trip to counteract To's
feeling that everything is a bore. I expect it is if one's feeling awfully
tired, but I've told the old boy we must not only count, but be *actively*
aware of our blessings.

22 August 1965   Elm Park Gardens

Darling Ginnie,
Off to the Festival Hall for the Bolshoi finale. While waiting we had
a very diverting time awarding people marks out of ten for eccentricity,
comedy, beauty, happiness. Plenty of the first: very few of the latter two.
We began with my favourite 'Ballet School' and some of the grander
ladies were to be seen getting crumbs out of teeth as they did the
barre exercises. They hadn't had time to freshen up much after the
matinée and hair was very whiskery and make-up far from matte. But
I don't think lack of time was the reason for the beautiful and talented
Plitskaya's[1] *very* dirty neck! It contrasted strongly with her rather
china pink and white face, and on closer inspection through my birding
glasses my suspicion was clearly proved to be right. But she can dance
like an angel.
It was a very exciting performance and everyone danced just that
much more somehow. The leaps all seemed longer and higher, the
ladies kicked with such freedom and grace, and the men did even more
entre chats and span like tops. It was *very* exhilarating indeed, and
when Mr and Mrs Vaslou did their fantastic waltz and she ran and
threw herself at him horizontally from at least eight feet, we all gasped
and wept and roared. Lovely creatures both.
Dick is so thrilled because *at last* Vic has agreed to using a chair[2]
and they had a splendid walk down the High Street looking at shops
and people. Vic's first street level peregrination in *eight years*. It's always
been a car and no slow tempo. D. was touchingly pleased. It opens new
vistas he says.

[1] Russian ballerina (1925–).
[2] Victor Stiebel had multiple sclerosis.

23 August 1965   Bellabeg

Darling Joyce,
I don't believe in the Virgin birth, do you? I mean, only *one* woman

in all this time? I shocked T. frightfully when I said this a few days ago: 'But that's the whole *point*' he said. If she did do it all on her own she is just as, if not more of, an interesting character than J.C. as she must have *perfectly* seen what creation is & what man is. The Catholics worship her, of course, but we & the Anglicans think of her, if at all, as a mum first count. I wonder what Mrs Eddy *really* thought.

Isn't it delightful the way one can ponder on matters at 9.35 a.m. in the morning?

24 August 1965   Elm Park Gardens

Darling Ginnie,

The Virgin Mary. I don't think it matters much whether she was or wasn't, and it *may* simply be a poetic way of underlining her enormous purity and spirituality? She was aware of what she'd done, I think and that must have given her a special aura. But you know it is impossible to rationalise the whole story: it is too remarkable, too important and *is* magic, so mebbe Mary was kind of special?!

R. tried to put up a shelf and left it very wonky. (I'd forgotten that word. Wonky. Isn't it period? I used to use it a lot when I wore a cloche hat.)

After lunch I made my selection of five books for a 'Celebrity Choice' Exhibition the National Book League are to hold in 1966, and the reasons why I chose what I did. *The Brontë Story. Call the Dance* (Agnes de Mille). *Edward Marsh* (C. Hassall). *The Secret Garden*, always my top favourite childhood book and it still holds. And Richard Hoggart's *Uses of Literacy*. I deliberately left out books of poems and essays as I felt it a bit showing off, and as *S. & H.*[1] is my top favourite book after the Holy Bible I'd just let the thoughtful area go!

[1] *Science and Health, with key to the Scriptures*, Mary Baker Eddy, 1875.

30 August 1965   Elm Park Gardens

Darling Ginnie,

You never answer questions or comment on my letters, which leads me to suppose you don't look at them again before answering. I'm not *insulted*! It's only that sometimes I ask a question wanting an answer and I feel a discussion might be of interest.

Isn't it a *relief* that the Gemini boys are down and well.[1] I get quite edgy thinking of them up there, do you? Claustrophobic. It seems that getting rid of excreta is one of the problems of space travel. Now it can be put out of the capsule in some way but is, presumably, now whizzing round in space . . . nasty to step out in your space suit for a bit of space walking and get a smack in the face from you know what whizzing by!

Verily came by to collect the old bookcases from Parr's for her Norfolk life and I had done a big clothes clear out for her too. She can wear my shoes, which is very useful for I'm such a bad shoe buyer and often make mistakes, and these somehow fit her.[2]

Ta again for the grouse – much enjoyed. Love to T. Love to U.

---

[1] American spacecraft *Gemini V* had orbited the Earth 128 times in 190 hours with Leroy Cooper (1927–) and Charles Conrad (1930–) who became the third man to walk on the Moon in 1969.
[2] Joyce and Reggie had bought and renovated a house for Verily Anderson and her family. Janie converted many of Joyce's frocks into mini-skirts and flared trousers. Joyce and Verily both had large feet – size $7\frac{1}{2}$.

31 August 1965   Bellabeg

Darling Joyce,

Funny you should say I never comment on your letters, as I never think you comment on mine! Certainly you never answer any questions! Well no, now I come to think of it, you *did* comment on the Virgin Birth, but that was a bit unusual (both for you & Mary).

Hordes of people, largely called Forbes, but occasionally Wallace, came to tea – there were enough cakes to feed a whole regiment of Gordon Highlanders.

In October Mrs Gabe left Joyce to spend more time with her elderly husband. For twenty years she had been a 'friend cum sort of nanny cum cook cum carer of our hearts and house'. Her ex-sister-in-law Mrs Agos, originally from Cyprus, took over and also stayed about twenty years – until shortly before Reggie died.

Joyce went to America to stay with the literary editor of the *Christian Science Monitor* in Boston, Massachusetts and visited the Mother Church.

26 October 1965   19 Brimmer Street
                                                                  Boston

Darling Ginnie,

A quickie to tell you I'm having such a good time here and enjoying the whole C.S. set up and atmosphere. I wasn't aware of the new feeling of air let in to the movement! The general view is that for a century we have been talking to ourselves, learning about C.S. Now our task is to share this marvellous thing and new ways are being sought and found. To start with there are meetings with other churches now (once impossible) and the subject is healing. We are to stop being so damned exclusive and mix more etc.

I seem to have done a lot of talking and listening and I'm a little dazed by it, but it has been rewarding. A holy story I like is of the two men meeting on board ship and from certain things said each began to think the other must be a C.S. but didn't like to ask outright. Then they found themselves at the rail watching a sunset. One said 'Are you leaning on the sustaining infinite?' He was.

Tommy is angelically meeting me at La Guardia. A great help.

Now I'm going out so olive oil to you.

1966

Joyce, William Blezard and Diana Lyddon, her British stage manager, were marooned in a blizzard during a short tour in the spring of 1966.

2 April 1966   Yorkshire

Darling Ginnie,

The snow is still hurtling down and lies six inches deep. We are twenty one miles from Richmond and I rue the day when I *idiotically* said I'd stay here and not in a hotel on the spot. I never *do* stay with people when I'm working and why I had to say yes this time I don't know. *Much* kindness and certain creature comforts but a huge house with no heating in the bedroom, and a vast but warm bathroom and along a corridor. Oh you know – from the houses of our youth.

One of the reasons I don't stay with kind friends is that one simply *has* to make some effort and while I'm on this job I really do need the absolute nothing of being alone. I'm rehearsing my new monologues and am hoping to be brave enough to try them tonight. I think I've got a good title – 'The Past is Present'. This is a group title and can include 'Lally Tullett' as well as the lady at Waterloo meeting her old flame after forty years. And the Old Girls' Reunion. This last is *awful*. I love it!

Richmond is full of charm, isn't it. The local stage manager was arranging a great gerbe of arums and forsythia *on* stage, and I had to say I'm so sorry but I'm afraid I can't have flowers on the stage. Too fussy, and in this tiny space too bulky. It was all right – no offences taken. The theatre is enchanting I must say. The new Steinway came on Thursday and Steinway's man was vetting and tuning. It's a *beauty* – Bill is thrilled.

Diana Lyddon went to stay the night with friends up in the hills, and I am trying not to worry about whether she can get to the theatre today, for she has my make-up and jewels and props with her. Damn the snow. April.

Wasn't it interesting that there were no new working class Labour candidates – all were professionals – teachers, doctors, lawyers, etc. This is good and less likely to have chips on shoulders I'd guess. I'm quite hopeful really. Glad the boredom is over, aren't you. Wonder if the economy is as bad as it's hinted at? What does Wilson do next, je me demande.[1]

[1] The general election held on 31 March increased Labour's majority to over 100 seats.

[April 1966]   Hyde Park Gardens

Darling Joyce,

Oh these church flowers! Mrs Grieves, who has pink pink cheeks & snow white hair, and has had lessons in flower arrangement, does them for Sunday, & I do them for Wed. It took me half an hour to disentangle her tortured effects from the miles of rabbit wire. I have *eight* vases to do, one if you please, for the Second Reader's room – just in *case* he might pop in on a Wednesday evening! I gave him three very old tulips & a crumpled carnation today. It seems that once upon a time an usher was healed by looking at a bunch of asters, but even so it's silly.

Tonio is tired tonight – he says he is definitely better. I think he worries about his memory – and yet he doesn't want to try gimmicky aides like I do: I mean, I remember the Bentley's heater has to be pulled out two stops for HOT by thinking of a Boy Scout rubbing TWO sticks together & making FIRE! Of course, I dare say if I couldn't remember what a Boy Scout was, I'd give up too.

11 April 1966   The Cavendish
                                                    Eastbourne

Darling Ginnie,

This is a very good hotel by any standard. Little touches *do* make a difference. Blotter full of paper and envelopes, two kinds of loo paper. Flowers. 'Lanaircel' blankets. And cetera.

Last night we had a trio to play to us through dinner. Mercilessly they sawed on through a selection of dimly remembered musical comedy scores, and that was rather enjoyable in spite of the actual sound. Best of all was the lady pianist, mid forties, dark with rimless glasses that she whipped off after every 'selection' before she unsmilingly acknowledged the applause (considerable). She had on such a splendid dress. Cloth of gold with *dark brown* wings of floating net, floating free under her arms and falling alongside her piano stool.

The net had been artfully carried forward across her bust and there held by a lozenge of orange red net! The effect was rather like one of those moths on Barbara's carpet. She played deftly with crisply curled fingers, and she and the elderly fiddler ended most precisely together and made their little accelerandos with perfect co-operation. The cellist, living in his own world, sawed on, basically sound and in the strictest tempo. We had *many* old Gershwins, and selections from very early *revues*. No Gilbert & Sullivan and no recent gems – *West Side Story*. or *Sound of M.* So that made a change.

Do you hate tipping? I never know how much to give, and when they charge 10% on the bill does one have to make it up to 15%. I'm endlessly pressing florins into palms for tiny jobs and feel foolish.

13 April [1966]   Hyde Park Gardens

Darling Joyce,

A fine letter from you today describing the joys & perils of the Cavendish. Oh that pianist! Her dress sounds almost exactly like the one I wore when I was a bridesmaid to Elizabeth Vesey!

To has a terrible tummy ache, but the doc doesn't know why. D'you know, I think one of the joyful things about C.S. is its simplicity. The confusion of materia medica is so fantastic, its complexity of symptoms, its hysterical escalation of pills (each new one designed to offset the side-kick of the last), the whole sort of enslaving kerfuffle makes one feel absolutely bewildered. All concocted to help, of course, but oh Pouf! lemme out of here!! Such a GLADNESS not to be *encumbered* innit?

All the same, I wish To would go in for some more simple diseases, like measles or mumps – he seems to specialise in mystery illnesses, don't he?

We are settling in for some very intensive watching – Richard Briers, *Bewitched*, & *Dr Kildare*. There are 12 worthy patients waiting for his kidney machine, Joyce, and only *five* of them can be taken; it is absolutely *ghastly*! The suspense is killing us.

16 April 1966   Elm Park Gardens

Darling Ginnie,

Noël's play has good notices in *Times* and *D Mail*.[1] The Somerset Maugham story really – disguised homosexuality unveiled by blackmailing earlier affair (Lilli Palmer) when he tried to be normal.

R. thought it better than I did. He was entirely held, thought it so well written, etc. And it *is* but . . . The subject calls for depth and depth is the one thing Noël doesn't have. Noël always strikes me as being almost entirely without *real* compassion. Surface stuff, sentiment – yes. But deep selfless caring? (How *does* one *know* though? So easy to say these things but as N. is always surrounded by yes-men and as far as one can *see* has never done an unselfed thing for anyone, the impression is that he is incapable of really profound selflessness.) I do sometimes see *tiny* signs of mellowness a-growing!

I felt it could have been really important if it had been by Shaw. But as it is I think it is quite Noël's best play for years, full of vigour and sinew and less trivial than usual. Dieu merci. I'm sick of trivia except as a decoration and *this* he is a master of, of course. You will enjoy it because it is so well done.

Theatre full of people who crave gracious living and lovely clothes. Went back stage afterwards too. 'My' room at the Queen's has been done up for N. in very gay green and white chintz and was full of scarlet flowers. The Master looked a good deal older off than on when he was made up to look eighty!

My Aquascutum suit has come and I *love* it. The tweed looks like powdered sugar on soft brown earth! General effect: light.

Love to you, girl. Love to Old To too.

---

[1] *A Song at Twilight*, directed by Vivian Matalon, written by and starring Noël Coward, with Lilli Palmer and Irene Worth. Coward was simultaneously rehearsing his next play, *Shadows of the Evening*, due to open two weeks later, while also recovering from a perforated intestine.

17 April [1966]   Bellabeg

Darling Joyce,

It's after dinner, 8.20 to be exact & To has gone off to bed! What I must guard against now, & think about, is despondency – not in the *least* essential, is it? I just caught a glimpse of another four years of being careful & quiet, of never going out without knowing To is longing to get home. All stupid thoughts, because there's no room for improvement in a divine idea, and I must concentrate on this & not get side-tracked by my dear one's appearance, which looks as though it will take for *ever* to get plump & pink again.

It's really most awfully difficult to love Aberdeenshire – I am trying like mad and have found some very nice lambs and have some delicious water to bath in, beef, drop scones & my bedroom wallpaper. I am loving them all *passionately*, so that I don't scream! Now to holy thoughts!

Interesting how life forces one to turn more to God, innit? I find myself alone in a cold house with a sick man – no friends near, everything deathly quiet, indoors and deadly ugly out – feel a bit frightened, you know, about To, going on being ill, so I HAVE to pull myself together, don't I? And isn't it rewarding when one does?

Ring me up as often as you can.

12 June 1966   Wentworth Hotel
                                                                 Aldeburgh

Darling Ginnie,

Lovely day yesterday ending with an accolade: 'Will I do another programme here next year for the new hall at Snape and the 20th Festival?' 'Yes, Ben.' At once, sitting in the Parish Church at 10.45 hearing but not I fear listening to lovely early Byrd (ha ha), I was panicking about new material for the event!! It is flattering and I'm *very* pleased.

Am much amused by the funny little behaviourisms of the Big Guns here.[1] They are at a disadvantage in being so recognisable, so evidently the reason and the centre of it all, and they have cultivated ways of seeing and not getting involved. During a boring endless slow Danish encore sung by the little sailor-suited Boys Choir I amused myself by writing a jingle on this subject:

> Ben smiles,
> Peter smiles,
> But Imogen lowers her head
> And scurries.
> The festival weighs a ton on her,
> I mustn't add to her worries.
>
> Ben smiles,
> Peter smiles,
> But Imo avoids recognising
> Saving herself – for what? one wonders.
> Her modesty *is* surprising.

Absolutely unpolished and bitchy. But private. It is funny to see her *not* seeing me! And this goes for everyone.

[1] Benjamin Britten, Peter Pears and Imogen Holst.

14 June 1966   Aldeburgh

Darling Ginnie,

After lunch we went to Snape to look at the Maltings and discover which bit of it is to be the new concert hall. The roof is off and it looks ready to start. Big and very well placed. One end of the big building will be a restaurant.[1]

Yesterday drinks with Ingaret and Laurens van der Post[2] to meet J.B. Priestley and Jacquetta Hawkes.[3] J.B. Priestley is not attractive. To start with he is anti so much. This is unappetising. Being pro too much may be tiresome but it's infinitely more endearing than the stultifying narrowness of being anti. This means mind closed. The other is less constipating.

Jacquetta Hawkes is very anti too. Anti Rhodesia for one thing, so we couldn't talk about Laurens' first class article in yesterday's *S. Telegraph*. *Really* interesting. They met us at the door and hissed 'don't mention the article', so we didn't. But it is so good. And unexpected. He feels Rhodesia is doing the workable thing to benefit all Rhodesians, black and white. For a very anti apartheid South African this is interesting.[4] Did you see it?

Mrs Priestley has very narrow lips and doesn't look one in the eye. Clever, yes. Shy, perhaps. But not cosy. J.B.P. paints rather well. Took it up ten years ago. It was a really very perceptive sketch he showed us done in forty minutes that morning.

R. says 'Come on'. Sorry. All love to both.

[1] New Maltings concert hall, originally an agricultural barn, being built to seat 830.
[2] South African-born travel writer (1906–96).
[3] John Boynton Priestley (1894–1984), English novelist and playwright, author of *The Good Companions*. His wife Jacquetta Hawkes (1910–), science fiction writer and archaeologist.
[4] Ian Smith (1919–), Prime Minister of Rhodesia, had unilaterally declared independence from Britain. This maintained the supremacy of Europeans and non-suffrage of Africans.

17 June 1966   Aldeburgh

Darling Ginnie,

I went to hear Imogen Holst give a lecture on 'What is Musical History?'.

Dull you might think? It was utterly fascinating and absolutely first class. She came on trippingly, head down. Not a trace of powder or lipstick on that 15th century head painted on wood. A pale beige dress blending in with face and hair. Almost invisible really. And then she began. It was a miracle of erudition, simplicity, interest, passion and *wit*. Haven't enjoyed anything more during the whole festival, and it's been a very good festival.

When Ben was nine years old and at Prep School he went to a music shop in Lowestoft, and he found an early two part song for women's voices by Gustav Holst. It was his very first contact with modern music. She was caustic about critics who write of 'tendencies' and say that a composer is 'paving a way' etc. 'What they are doing' she said 'is making music . . .' (or words to that effect) 'not creating tendencies.'

She made us all sing a ten part round, and that was a triumph for we did – first time.

Doris[1] has written a long and *very* good letter on the subject of B.B.C's attitude and has come to the same conclusion quite independently as I have that the Established Church is the real block to religious tolerance here! We must dissolve it!! Did you know the C. of E. still put out pamphlets against us full of actual lies and distortions, and ignore any letters of protest from the C.S. Church?

If only the religious boys would take the trouble to find out what C.S. is really about it would be simpler. But as it is they believe all the bad stories and none of the true.

Doris says it seems incredible that the Q. of E. [Queen] is explicitly forbidden by law to recognise or accept the teaching of C.S.! We are linked with Jehovah's Witnesses of all ignominies. This is supposed to be Christianity in action. It is the Middle Ages. It doesn't matter in the end but it is wrong: just as hanging is wrong and freedom is right.

[1] Christian Science practitioner commenting on the BBC's attitude to Christian Science.

19 June 1966   Aldeburgh

Darling Ginnie,

Yesterday was lovely. It really was. A *lovely* association.[1] Huge gathering of greyheads but with a sprinkling of younger people and a very alert and lively atmosphere. Ralph[2] was in top form, full of vigour and humour, and I found it thrilling. How I do bless M.B.E.[3]! The theme was on 'Our leader and her works' and was most fascinating. Total acceptance of her revelation includes her great contribution to history and it's no use trying to separate them. Many resent the idea (a) of a woman being a revelator and (b) anyone mentioned in the same breath as Jesus. I enjoyed the whole day in spite of a cracking headache which ultimately wafted off unnoticed.

Came back in a carriage with two marvellous old Colonels Marriott and Miller. They boomed about Lord's and the hardness of the seats, and about their need to know how to cook! I joined in and egged them on. Their wives won't let them get near their stoves and yet when the wives go away they are left helpless. It was finally decided they'd get on to the W.I. and arrange for lessons next winter.

The Festival Party in the Jubilee Hall was really great fun. Julian Bream[4] played some jazzed up Bach – superb. Surprise item Peter P. singing 'The Owl and the Pussy Cat' in an amusing setting. Then a jam session with Emanual Hurowitz (first fiddle of orchestra), Julian B. and a double bass, and, unrehearsed, Peter, doing 'Night and Day'. His rhythm was appalling! No feel for the beat at all. Wasn't it interesting. A gay evening.

Aldeburgh has been *such* fun. Best year so far for weather and birds and music.

---

[1] Meeting of Christian Scientists who have studied together under one teacher.
[2] Ralph Schofield, joined the Church in 1907 and passed on in 1976. A Christian Science practitioner and teacher, Joyce was a pupil in his class – a series of meetings for in-depth study of Christian Science.
[3] Mary Baker Eddy.
[4] British musician who reintroduced the guitar to classical concerts (1933–).

Joyce and William Blezard went on their third theatrical tour of Australia and New Zealand. Reggie took time off from his job to accompany them.

21 July [1966]   Hyde Park Gardens

Darling Joyce,

I went off this afternoon, a tiny tin of tongue, a pie, two tins of peaches & some biscuits clasped to my bosom, to call on your Alicia,[1] & I'm sorry to tell you, darling, she died last week! Quickly & *peacefully*. 'It breaks me heart' the matron said 'seeing all those postcards and letters coming in from Miss Grenfell – but I HAVE written to her about it.' She has passed on your sheets to the sick room, and has swiped your photograph 'I hope she won't mind if I keep it?'

Victor is disgruntled & depressed about Mr Wilson's Crisis measures[2] – 'I simply can't AFFORD any increases!' he says, which I find *funny*! His horror of being dependent on us is so acute he has Mitty-ed himself into forgetting that he is – I've noticed this before, have you?

---

[1] Alicia was one of Joyce's fans whom she visited regularly.
[2] Prime Minister Harold Wilson had introduced stringent national economy measures such as frozen wages and increased taxes, to improve the British economy.

25 July 1966   Windsor Hotel
                                                     Melbourne

Darling Ginnie,

Perth went with a fine flourish. I took over 16,000 dollars! in nine performances. That's £6,000 English and not to be sneezed at. And such a reception. Tears to the eyes. Oh those waves of affection pour forth and the generosity of heart that starts it off. I am most marvellously un-responsible for I do know that it is simply manifestation of the One Mind. And very nice too. It's the custom to send last night flowers and I had such lovely ones. Just as well I made a lot of lolly because our hotel bill for the suite was colossal. I don't think I'll tell you! HUGE even by Claridges standard I'd guess. But *worth* it. And that's all that matters.

Perth Airport was a sight yesterday morning. Five thousand young things arrived to greet a local Pop hero called Normy Rowe. No difference in their appearance from our little horrors except that in Perth they go barefooted! But the boys are long haired and pin toed, and the girls have undone hair and tight tight pants. They look rather nicer than ours because they are far less sophisticated and the clothes are a uniform rather than an attitude of mind. Normy, the usual very ordinary lad with a fringe, got off the plane two hundred yards away and was whipped into a bus and away! Groans from the fans.

I dreamed I saw a man conducting an orchestra with a very funny ribbon bow on the end of his baton and I laughed so much it woke me up! It really was a very funny sight. A sort of cartoon drawing of a bow with a life of its own! Love to you. Love to your feller from us both.

31 July [1966]   Hyde Park Gardens

Darling Joyce,

Our weekend has been spent, almost exclusively, watching the World Cup final & recovering from it! Our nerves were all a-jangle for, as R will know, but you won't, Germany scored an equalising goal 30 *seconds* from the end!! So they had to play extra time & it was all absolutely hair-raising & 'emotional' & I died a thousand deaths. It was so important we should win – to at last, once again, be tops in *something*, and I must say judging from Bayswater Road last night, our morale has been boosted to hysterical heights. When the dreadful equalising goal was scored I could feel the blood draining from my face with shock – I might have been told you were run over – and then I became absolutely furious with the England team & at the height of my rage, Victor rang up & said in a high tense voice: 'Oh God! Why did you introduce me to this *bloody* game?'[1]

[1] At full time the score was England 2: Germany 2. England scored two more goals during extra time.

1 August 1966   On the way to NZ

Darling Ginnie,

En route, en l'air, and this little item gave me a good deal of unkind amusement.

'DIETARY NEEDS – RELIGIOUS PREFERENCES.

For Roman Catholic Passengers on Qantas Flights, a Special
Dispensation has been granted by The Sacred Congregation of the
Council of the Holy See from the Law of Abstinence on Fridays and all
other Obligatory Days.'

I think it is very splendid. How *can* they take it seriously? What *do*
they think God is?

5 August 1966   United Services Hotel
                                                                Christchurch

Darling Ginnie,

After last night's performance, the evening paper had rather a
stinking notice headed 'Miss Grenfell strives too hard for laughs'! It was
very patronising and I wished I'd remained a gracious drawingroom
figure and didn't notice, but it drew the loyalest rage from Bill and
all the stage staff at the theatre! It seems the writer is a well known
grouch, elderly and unpleasable! He only mentioned 'Eng. Lit.' in order
to give away the final line, touched on the anti-Muzak song, and was
tolerant about 'Nursery School'. I do resent the pirating of my good
lines, using them wrongly and thus neatly ruining the joke.

Poor Bill, again, had a big hit with the audience and not one word
in the press. That's the sort of thing I get a bit down about. He really is
the best accompanist in the theatre business and I do love him to get
recognition. Sometimes an adverse criticism from a well known grouch
can be interpreted beneficially – as we used to do with Bernard Levin.[1]
Of course one is a bit dampened by such a notice. I mean it comes as a
slap in the face after such a particularly warm reception. And one does
wonder, of course. *Am* I *striving* for laughter? The answer is: No, I'm
not! So there we are and business is healthy and a happy surprise to all
concerned.

[1] British journalist and theatre critic (1928–).

[10] August [1966]   Bellabeg

Joyce! have you still got your belly button? Mine fell off last week; at
least, it came to pieces in my hand! It's been slowly dying for decades, &
latterly was withered & sear, so I feel I've probably had a demonstration
– on the other hand perhaps I've lost something precious? Certainly
irreplaceable. Anyway, it looks *miles* better now. But possibly abnormal?
T says he still has *his*. I've just got a dear little hole.

Masses of love to Reg Pascoe, please.

11 August [1966]   Government House
                                                              Wellington

Darling Ginnie,
     Seven Bishops for lunch yesterday and not too many *seemed* to be at
all spiritual.
     Today I wrote to the only critical letter writer out of a hundred and
sixty of my broadcast on prayer, it questioned my Christianity since I
didn't mention Jesus. I took enormous loving trouble in writing back to
say I felt that my point of view was entirely the result of J.C's teaching
and in four-and-a-half minutes it had to be kept very clear etc.etc. All
love darling to both.

12 August [1966]   Turnberry

Darling Joyce,
     The Glorious Twelfth, he! ha! and Donny [Thesiger] rang to say
there are literally *no* grouse, so there will be no shooting. Tonio says he
doesn't mind one little bit, but oh men! they are such funny creatures!
In the same breath he said 'I don't expect you'll want to stay there for
three weeks now, will you?' as though the shooting was the cause of all
Aberdonian pleasure for *me*. Personally I am absolutely delighted there
won't be any of those terrible shooting lunches in those chilly butts, & I
only hope To won't be too bored with *nothing* to do.
     Your letter about the stinking notice also drew loyal rage from me.
No, you are not striving to be funny – but isn't it odd how criticisms
such as this pull one up short sort of, & make one re-appraise? Because
Mrs 'Silence Home-Forum' said just the same thing to me, & I was
astonished. And yet, thought I, maybe it's true – maybe I've been a
'humorous' writer for so long, my humour has become forced, & I can't
write what is known as a 'light' article without dragging in something
funny. But you don't do that – of that I am sure – except I suppose
you have a punch-line or two, & of course you caricature, as does any
'artiste' who seems to be acting 'naturally'. Oh well, I daresay a knock
or two is salutary – makes one tighten up etc.

20 August 1966   Auckland

Darling Ginnie,
     It was arctic in the theatre last night and rather a slow house,
needing love and encouragement. I had to wear a cut-down woollen
spencer [vest] to keep warm.
     A new hazard has revealed itself. A discotheque just behind the
theatre that plays its bloody discs F.F.F. so that one really does have

to pitch up to combat it. I had to fight rage and irritation (a) with this and (b) the ponderous slowness of the house, but Love Conquers All, and by golly the house came to and were so responsive and I grew used to the b–y discs. Also my body mike is too big and gave me a bruise on me bust bone between the bosoms! I've learned to wodge it with cotton wool and it hurt less, but I do NOT love it as I love my own little lipstick mike.

I took to holy thoughts and scientific facts about harmony being continuous etc. and I was able to rise above it completely! A real triumph. For some odd acoustical reason the sound didn't get into the auditorium but remained a stage horror.

I'm worried to death about your belly button! Heavens. I'll look at mine tonight and report later. I should think if yours was so sere and withered you are better without it. I have just had the most uncontrolled, enjoyable, exhausting, furore about your letter. Oh dear. How lovely it is to lose control – as well as belly buttons. A very good letter. (How Bar Bev. would have loved this.)

R. has read your b.b. letter and folded up with giggles too. Funny fliend. Now R. wants to post this. So ta ta for now. All love to both. Oh your b.b.

24 August [1966]   Bellabeg

Darling Joyce,

How you have time to write to me so much *beats* me – I know that tiny hand flows along with great speed & felicity, but with all the other letters you have to write & all the things you have to do, I still don't see how you do it. I hope it doesn't press on you, luv, or hang over you?

I adore your letters, as you know, but I'd hate to think you EVER thought Oh *Hell*! Now I must write to Gin!

T is in wonderful form, cracking jokes and laughing – I am pleased.

Bridge [maid] was relating the iniquities of the gardener to me, how he only gives her half dead flowers to arrange (in the manner of all gardeners) . . . and then she ended up '*Whell*! We'll just have to leave him to God!' 'Yes, we WILL, Bridget' I said. I wonder what the Catholic way of doing this is?

31 August 1966   Windsor Hotel
                                                                         Melbourne

Darling Ginnie,

Yesterday morning was an occasion about which I could have *no* pre-conceived idea. All I knew was that the U.S. Ambassador wished to make a presentation to me and the press were alerted. Dear heaven!

I walked into the 'lounge' as instructed, and found four T.V. Cameras, the press from three papers and their camera men, the U.S. Consul, the U.S. P.R., and others. Soon Ed. Clark,[1] who is a joke man from Texas, arrived. Big, lisps, cordial o.k., but seems to be nit-witted. Is he? Can he be? He's very rich like all Texans one supposes. Oil? Don't know. He embraced me as a close loved one. Then handed over a 'gift wrapped' package. On the word go I was to open it up. Under the gay paper and cellophane ribbon was a huge and good bird book (which we already possess!). On camera I had to draw it out, open the fly leaf and read out the inscription. This was very flowery and ended: 'I tip my Texas hat to you. – Sincerely, Ed. Clark'. He then read it out *again*! By this time I had become *so* internally giggly I didn't know where to look.

We went on being snapped talking about birds 'with feathers on' (oh Gawd) and he was extremely friendly and fulsome and I felt as if I was in Wonderland. Now what *do* you suppose it was all about? Anglo-American relations? But why, in Australia? Just a personal fancy? Anyway it got big coverage and the Heading in the *Evening Herald* says: 'Joyce Grenfell outwits the U.S. Ambassador'. *Not* very difficult to do.

[1] Edward Clark (1906–), US Ambassador to Australia from 1965 to 1967, was a lawyer and banker.

6 September 1966   Windsor Hotel

Darling Ginnie,

Last night a hail storm hit the theatre as I was about to do 'Learn to Loosen' and it made such a tremendous row that I couldn't hear Bill play! So I said to the audience let's wait a second, and to fill in we'll do 'Oh what a Beautiful Morning' – Evening. (I didn't really have to hear him for this.) The audience laughed, and I sang and they came in with the chorus. We were getting to the end of the second chorus where it says 'Everything's going my way-ay'. I sang, quite un-prompted by thought, 'Everything's going *a-way*', and at that *exact second* the hail stopped as if it had been turned off by a switch! The timing was really so extra-ordinary and the whole thing *so* neat and tidy that Bill laughed, I laughed and the house roared. Wasn't it splendid?

We got back to the programme after that and it had become a cosy party. Well, it often does that, but this was rather special.

8 September 1966   Windsor Hotel

Darling Ginnie,
    This cable came last night:

Is there a way to make you reconsider the possibility of returning to London
via New York October 3 – November 2 to do Blithe Spirit I guarantee
delightful rehearsal period with no strain Dirk Bogarde Rosemary Harris
Rachel Robert and Noel Coward join me in urging you to reconsider George
Schaefer.[1]

    Nice to be asked! The answer is No, for a plethora of reasons. (A)
I don't want to. (B) I'm working here till October 8th. (C) We have
a lovely holiday planned and R. is panting for it. Me too. And (D) I'd
be no good in acting Ascati. It's *so* old hat and so worn out. I have
cabled regretfully, of course, and pointed out dates don't fit, and ended:
'Frankly you are lucky because I can't act, only entertain'. But, as I
said, *very* nice to be asked.[2]
    Verily wrote such a dear letter saying she felt now was the time to
tell me how her whole life had changed from when I told her about
C.S. in the hospital that Christmas time three or four years ago.[3] She
is a very remarkable woman and I am so pleased she has this lovely
continuity to lean on – fly with – be because of.
    Leading one's social life only in the morning is quite a job because
there are so few mornings and we seem to know so many nice people
we really want to see.
    Last night the Governor and Governess Delacombe came, so I
suppose we must go and sign their book. They asked us to dine *before*
the show! Really the *ignorance* of theatrical life!! *Before* the show. I
wouldn't have gone after the show, so I don't know why I fuss.

[1] American film and stage director (1920–).
[2] This production had to be cancelled because of Coward's poor health.
[3] Verily Anderson was in hospital for several weeks in the winter of 1963. During this time
Joyce visited her every day and helped take care of her children.

11 September 1966   Hyde Park Gardens

Darling Joyce,
    I was waiting to watch a telly programme on Buddhism, about
which I felt ashamed to know nothing (*still* don't know much!) and I
was regaled by a bedtime story about Jesus, for tiny tots, read by a

peroxide blonde, and acted by glove puppets, two Koala bears, a sort of lion, a duck, & a mouse in a burrow! None of them ekshually Jesus, but his family, preparing to go on oh such a lovely expedition to Jerusalem: oh what fun, a picnic! And Jesus gets lost . . . where can he be? Oh what can have happened to Jesus? squeaked by tiny voices & with a great flapping of furry ears. He was in the Temple, talking to the Elders . . . transformation scene, with Koala Bears in robes . . . yes, he's a very clever boy. Then everybody saying our prayers with weeny paws (when available) over glassy eyes. QUAINT ideas people have.

Patrick called yesterday morn & looked at T's hernia & said it was a straightforward cobbling job – they push it back & sew it in – & he'd be in hosp. around a week to 10 days. The surgeon will be the chap who already copes with his piles, and the hospital he usually functions at is the Westminster – not conspicuously handy for visiting wives who live in Bayswater, but still.

10 September 1966   Windsor Hotel

Darling Ginnie,

We saw me on T.V. last night. It looked very funny here because our huge old T.V. set has no visible means of altering the picture and instead of my long horse face I appeared broad and flat topped, and because I had my fringe down, for a change, looked rather like Lucille Ball! This was quite a curious experience to see how odd one *can* look on T.V.

14 September 1966   Hyde Park Gardens

Darling Joyce,

Wonderful self-control of yours not to be flattered into filming *Blithe Spirit* – but I'm sure you're right. And as you say, NICE to be asked.

Dire news today. When I came panting home from standing on my head counting electric light bulbs in the basement of the Church, Marian, looking ashy pale, said she'd been trying to tell me for *ages* . . . they were leaving! Seems her sister in Canada has been iller than she supposed, & she & Christine, after fearful heart-searchings, have decided they must go & help her run her home out there; for a year at any rate. They'd had sleepless nights about it 'and when you told me Mr Thesiger had to have an operation I felt like cutting my throat!'

Isn't it a bore? Although they're both profoundly irritating at times, they are friendly & amiable & clean, & they like each *other*, which is such a help. Oh well! I don't seem to be wildly depressed: though of course one hates *change*. I wonder if there ARE any maids in the world

343

ekshually? Never mind. I *know* I can fry an egg & I can LEARN to grill a steak.

18 September 1966   Windsor Hotel

Darling Ginnie,

I doted on your description of the religious puppet play! It was hilarious. Oh dear, what *do* people think religion is for.

I finished up with a huge flourish last night. I don't know if your *Daily Express* has reported the case of the man in Melbourne who nailed up his wife in a cupboard. It happened here. Well, in my Nursery School sketch I have the line: 'Dicky – we *never* shut people up in cupboards'. I've been saying it all week and I *never* thought of the case, but last night a sort of roar went up as I said it and the penny dropped. When it finished I said: 'except in Melbourne', and off they went again. It was quite hard to get back into the sketch.

Since my mum died I've never thought I'd want to boast quite as much as I do at this moment, and only you, I think, can be boasted to in her place! But come to think of it it isn't *boasting* – it's really the most marvellous sense of *gratitude* for the acknowledgement of what we as C.S.s stand for. Last night I had from the stage staff, Hetty my dresser, and various others the most living tributes of affection summed up in 'You've made such a lovely atmosphere in the place'. Tears came into eyes, words like 'grand' and 'goodness' and 'sincerity' were used, and I stood there each time silently thanking God and rejoicing that this manifestation is *shared* – recognised and acknowledged.

Thought you'd like to know.

23 September 1966   Hyde Park Gardens

Darling Joyce,

Tonio had a better night, & is now rather cross because everybody told him it wouldn't hurt & it does! He was much more rational today – yesterday he was really very dotty (anaesthetic, I suppose?) & Sister Evans was a soupçon worried because nobody had told her about T's trouble . . . 'he seems a trifle disorientated, we find, & keeps on trying to get out of bed during the night.' When I arrived last night at 5.15 he was telling the nurse he was *sure* we were supposed to be dining with someone!

Vic lunched, & we had a gorgeous laugh about the *myriad* tales of disaster – everybody has half a dozen pals in dire distress.

Victor has just rung to ask how To is & to tell me that a specialist came to see Dick last night & he HAS got a couple of crumbling vertebrae. This means that he must stay in bed for 3 to 6 months, being pumped full of calcium. Apparently it was a dramatic session, & Dick was very upset but *very* good about it. I must say it's a fair bugger innit?

Oh!! Viola rang last evening – just to ask after To. Wasn't it sweet of her? We had quite a long talk, & she admitted she was busy, but not fearfully happy: would like a year's sabbatical to 'replenish'. I suppose the gal's exhausted, pore ole thing.

8 October 1966   Sydney

Darling Ginnie,

We've just watched a big white liner arrive from Southampton. Our hearts bleed for emigrants arriving at dusk on a grey stormy evening and probably going to a hostel. After being safely cared for so long (four weeks?) on board it must be a bit bleak to arrive and be launched as it were. Between shows

So L.B.J.[1] is to visit Australia. Well that is a good thing I think for it is really U.S.A. and Australia that belong together now, geographically anyway. The climate and way of life – informality – is much more American now than English, and the conventions and social carry on are really more suburban U.S. We no longer have such a social set up – women's clubs, societies, committees. Charity is social here – I mean almost entirely so. Balls go on nightly in aid of causes and are very smart and flashy and, I assume, *ghastly*.

You've no idea just how feted I am here! I'm *really* considered special, and there were fifty people at the stage door after the matinee. I *couldn't* see them all so just went to the door and waved!! In addition a party of forty rather dull schoolgirls were there and I had to go and wave at them too. (Why, I wonder?)

I've tipped the staff.

Given Bill a fat bonus.

    "   Simon a thinner bonus.

    "   present to Sylvia who dresses me.

Now let's get the final programme done and get to bed!

[1] Lyndon Baines Johnson (1908–73), President of the USA 1963–9.

14 October 1966   Hyde Park Gardens

Darling Joyce,

To went to the office, which he found very exhausting, though he can't have been there more than an hour, but then it's the mental attitude, of course, the feeling that it is work!

I podged through Derry & Jones & Barkers; such interesting shops, can't have been into either for 20 years, & I don't fancy anybody else has either, as they were dead empty!! I must confess that all I could find to buy was 9 nailbrushes for the church's cloaks!

David Frost's[1] programme is v. *serious* now & there was a proper ding-dong going. The camera was trained on the audience at the first night of *US*, the controversial play on Vietnam, & there were actors groping around the auditorium with paper bags on their heads! Then Peter Brook saying how despicably sad it was that nobody had put out a hand to help these stumbling people – which I thought extremely unfair as one would surely presume a cast didn't need any help from an audience – I mean, that this was part of the play? Then everybody had a whack – two incensed Americans, Peter Cook, Ken Tynan – & they'd all thought the play bad for different reasons, either not partisan enough or too partisan, and they were thoroughly het up and annoyed by what they'd been through. *Good* television – I was RIVETED – because people *cared*.

I haven't done any tatting[2] for weeks now – it's absolutely *divine*. I either read *The Wind of Change*, or M. Muggeridge, or M.B. Eddy, or else look steadfastly, and unthinkingly at the telly – with both eyes. I'm not *sure* I shall *ever* tat again!

T. sends 'passionate love', he says.

[1] British television presenter and chat show host (1939–).
[2] Virginia's word for tapestry, which she did a lot.

Joyce had planned to visit a friend in Colorado, and Virginia spotted that Joyce had given her the wrong address.

OXFORD STREET LONDON PO
24OCT 66
DONT GO NEAR ARIZONA YOU LUNATIC WOMAN YOU WANT
844 HUMBOLT STREET DENVER COLORADO ALSO A NANNY PRESUMABLY
LOVE GIN

Monday, 24 October 1966   Hyde Park Gardens

Darling Joyce,

I always *love* it when people are out of character, don't you? And I find it *utterly* endearing of you to have forgotten where you are going – not only the street, but the town & the state as well! It is NOT like you, Joyce, my old RELIABLE friend, & I wouldn't want this vagueness to become a habit; but just once, like this, it is enchanting!

We went to the flicks & saw *The Russians are Coming*,[1] with Tessie O'Shea in the part they wanted you for. Have you seen it? You wouldn't have been happy in the role . . . tied to a not very attractive comedian, first back to back, then bust to bust, rolling over & over each other on the floor, then hopping down a perilous looking staircase & ending up all which ways in the road. I should definitely have grieved for you in these predicaments.

[1] *The Russians are Coming, the Russians are Coming*, film directed by Norman Jewison starring Carl Reiner and Eva Marie Saint, 1966.

25 October 1966   Sydney

Darling Ginnie,

How I laughed at your cable. 'Lunatic woman' – yes *indeed*. And, guess what? my air ticket is made out to Phoenix too! Mental aberration of a strange sort. Just imagine if I'd flown off to Phoenix and planned to look Edna up in the local book on arrival! Well, the Lord provides and I have been saved *that*.

R. left yesterday and I hated that. But this has been the most marvellous time and I really can't be greedy nor am I ungrateful for every minute of it.

Do you know that in spite of pining to see you and Tommy and my flat etc. etc. I really hate leaving lovely Sydney. I can see that if one was in a hotel and didn't have the pals and know the houses and gardens one might not love it, but seeing as I do I love it deeply. Am homesick for it now!! Yesterday the Australian Fleet with G.B. and N.Z. vessels 'exercised' in the Harbour, all 'dressed' with white clad tars. Moving and pretty.

I'll soon be back. Goody. For I have A Friend – not only in Jesus but also in You.

Joyce came home via Beverly Hills where she stayed with Leonard Gershe.

2 November 1966   Beverly Hills

Darling Ginnie,

California *is* cloud-cuckoo land. For a holiday it is amusing and I indulge in it, but the idea of living here is impossible. Values don't exist as we know them and it is all so vast. Yesterday Leonard, who is the most darling host, took me to a new shopping area in a place called Tarzana. It is a huge air conditioned building, containing big department stores at either end and a couple of wide arcades on two levels with shops in there of *all* kinds and qualities, even an international self serve Cafeteria flanking an enclosed ice rink! We had Chinese food and watched a lot of gangling and pretty-to-see children skating.

Somehow the whole place is fraught with danger one feels. The Speedy Fairways where cars go at a uniform 65 are terrifying to me. Leonard drives like an angel, but the idea of being at the wheel myself causes me to palpitate! I find I have to work in Science here as nowhere else simply to maintain equilibrium. The values, as I say, don't exist and it is hectic and false. '*Sometimes* beautiful but always erroneous.' The pleasure *seeking* is pitiful.

Last night Mia Farrow,[1] who looks like a Kate Greenaway child with her cropped hair and sexless little figure, came here with Roger for drinks and sandwiches before we all drove in her Jaguar across Los Angeles on a series of the pacey fairways to see her mother Maureen O'Sullivan open in *The Subject was Roses*. It was in the round – completely – and sound was so amplified that any contact of hand on paper, glass on table, slap on back resounded through the place.

Mia was besieged by fans and her manner was very nice to them. She is a mixture of self-conscious little girl (an image I can see she enjoys and heaven knows she looks about ten) and unselfconscious young woman. Spoilt, I *think*, and full of a sense of power (and this is the *self* destructive quality that they all get here when they are about to command such attention and money) but friendly and modest. I found her unselfconscious little girl *act* a little too much of a good thing. She flings her arms round people and stands on tip-toe, and I thought: Oh hell, come off it Mrs Sinatra, you're a big girl now. Her mother is dear, quiet, and not all that confident, and that is endearing. *Quite* a good actress. The play is almost very good and certainly holds the attention almost all the way.

[1] American film star, then aged twenty-one, recently married to Frank Sinatra thirty years her senior. They divorced two years later and she went on to have children with André Previn, composer, and Woody Allen, film director, and adopt eleven children.

4 November 1966   Hyde Park Gardens

Darling Joyce,

Audrey Hepburn is staying beneath us – the maids watched her going out in a huge beetroot red Rolls . . . trés flambouyant.

We've just been for a walk, to Peter Pan & round,[1] and scuffled the leaves with our suede shoes – it was rather nice. I've been to Church this morning, to beat some chrysanthemums with a hammer & slit the stems of anenomes & arrange same in a maze of tortured rabbit wire

– it all felt rather un-Christian somehow. This evening I'm on duty [in church].

¹ Statue by the Serpentine lake in Kensington Gardens.

1967

When Joyce was invited to a private party to meet Prince Charles and Princess Anne, Virginia bet her £5 that they would ask her to do a monologue.

January 1967   Hyde Park Gardens

Darling Joyce,
    Never be it said I do not repay my debts of honour – but I think it's absurd of them not to have asked you to perform!!
    X GIN

The housing charity Shelter benefited with Joyce's win. She was often asked to perform for charities. If it was one of which she especially approved, she would do it. She would not raise money for medical charities and she would not perform in cabaret. Save the Children Fund was one of her favourites, and in Exeter she raised over £550 with one performance.

1 April 1967   Gypsy Hill
                                                               Pinhoe
                                                          near Exeter

Darling Ginnie,
    The concert was a big wow last night. A *vast* Great Hall indeed, very modern and good acoustics. Fifteen hundred there and all on my side. Lady Devon, who is as vast as the Great Hall, beamed on me out of a beaded baby pink evening sweater over an evening skirt.
    I'll tell you something nice. Yesterday morning I woke up with a blaze of sun rising smack into my room and, as I always do, I prayed and for the first time for weeks felt a sort of flood of joy about Miriam. A sense of well-being. Every time I thought of Mim all day this sense of joy was with me. Last night I recorded it in my diary. I didn't know till this a.m. when I talked to R. and learned it happened early yesterday morning.¹

¹ Miriam Grenfell died of leukaemia the day before.

Meanwhile Virginia was planning a country retreat in Hertfordshire, at the home of her old friend, Waldorf Astor's niece, Rachel Bowes-Lyon. Tony's health continued to deteriorate. His memory was failing, and he slept most of the time, though still went into the office for a few hours a day. Virginia found that socialising was the worst strain – she never knew what Tony might say next, or if he would ask his hostess who she was. Virginia's faith in Christian Science gave her strength, optimism and patience.

1 April [1967]   Brighton

Darling Joyce,

I see Miriam has gone. Wonderful quick really – I mean this last bit. I suppose she just drifted off into unconsciousness, quite unaware of the doom materia medica had arranged for her. I feel for you, luv. I know you two had lovely giggles together, & that is always a bond – besides it really gives one a *shock*, dunnit. I feel for her boys too, it is vile for them.

I've just written to Rachel who said that it would be difficult to tamper with the nursery floor at St Paul's, but that she'd love us to have the floor above. Tiny rooms, but it would be easy to knock down a few walls. We'd have the whole floor. There'd be room for three bedrooms, two bathrooms, including a 'suite' for the exclusive use of the Grenfells, if they will have it? Tony & I talked it over & it didn't take long, I can tell you, for us to agree that nothing would give us greater pleasure than for you to stay in this flat whenever you want – to treat it as your own pomme de terre.

I want to give it a whirl, if it's a failure and T actually hates it & I actually can't cook a sausage we can opt out – lovely to be rich enough to say that, hein?

Tonio sends his '*Great* love' (he *says*!!) He is faintly pink of brow & looks very handsome.

8 April 1967   [Elm Park Gardens]

Darling Ginnie,

How lovely about the attic-y flat. It sounds very good and you and T. are darlings to wish us to be part of it. Lovely idea. How about a cosy Christmas in which I teach you how to cook?!

29 April 1967   Eastbourne

Darling Ginnie,

A delectable morning all sun and haze and a silken sea. The pier is in silhouette against it like a piece of modern sculpture done in wire. The minarets of the main building seem noble instead of ridiculous, and the lovely light transforms all we look upon, including a riot of tulips and wallflowers massed fatly in a broad bed across the road.

R. and I went to the Private View at Burlington House and it never disappoints.[1] We watched the press watching the arrivals and knew at once which funny hat worn for just that purpose would catch the cameras. One young woman was in shocking pink from top to toe and the hat was a ten gallon Stetson. The widow Munnings[2] was in full fancy dress including a gauze turban over a wig of rich auburn-black curls. There was a hint of Mandarin coat, tinsel, velvet, embroideries and lace, and, oh *joy*, winter boots underneath. She sat dazed, poor old dotty.

A startling eccentric in a green deerstalker, huge red rose (real) in his corduroy lapel, was being a lively caricature of some recognisable but unidentified man with a Wellingtonian profile. There were 'students' in washed-out dungarees and Liberty flowered shirts. Very few mini skirts really but lots of hair everywhere. Isn't it interesting the way the Breton sailor hat survives year after year on the convenable ladies. Many were to be seen yesterday, white mostly, over neat navy two pieces. It was boiling in there and I congratulated myself in having left off my vest.

I thought there were far more attractive works than usual and fewer real horrors. I'm afraid the garish op. and pop canvases simply don't get through to me, but the quieter small pictures ring my little bell and I could have bought many. The encouraging thing, we thought, is the amount of really beautiful craftsmanship there still is. Really skilled performances, full of love and enjoyment. I suppose that is only one thing of the functions of art but it shouldn't be dismissed. If things *are* done – even unconsciously – to the glory of God I think this shows and communicates.

I got a girdle at M. & S. having bought two failures last week in Bournemouth! Owing to tempus fugit-ing I find a short girdle does more for the shape than a long one that pushes up the redundant and causes a roll. But I tend to forget this and go for long ones as I always did . . .

[1] The Summer Show at the Royal Academy, Piccadilly.
[2] Lady Violet, widow of Sir Alfred Munnings (1878–1959), sporting painter and President of the Royal Academy.

30 April [1967]   Bellabeg

Darling Joyce,

Driving rain and lashing wind, but we've had a few bonny days, so I for one shan't mind a nesting day.

We went over to Strathdon for lunch and nattered happily. I tried not to listen to To telling the same story twice! I now always have one ear cocked to hear what the darling is up to – and I'm sure I must heal myself of it: after all it is entirely based on fear, & I should loose him & let him go. Indeed I feel buoyant & calm – if one can feel both at once – & full of confidence that the truth *must* prevail.

Oh my heavens, it really is *SNOWING*!!

Loved your description of the Academy. I'd love to see all those peculiars, & poor Lady M. Does she still carry a stuffed Pekinese around?

2 May 1967   Churchill College
                                                    Cambridge

Darling Ginnie,

After writing a few letters, Clive James, my Australian, arrived, having walked out from the city. He was bidden to join the lunch party here for us to meet these young Drama Society boys.

I don't find any of the sense of separation between generations we are supposed to feel now. Perhaps because these are all *very* intelligent. They have more poise and vision and can see a bit further than the protesting young men who are simply trapped in their own immaturity? Anyway they were friendly and chatty and easy and nice. Not a 'gent' in sight, and I suppose the fact I didn't register this until now is a proof of the encroaching classlessness that, I must say, I do welcome, don't you. The meeting place is ideas. The language is interest.

The performance went well in the little theatre and it was agreeable to work on that scale again after the big barns. They were not a very responsive audience in that they were shy and possibly self conscious. Very few young there for it was 35/- to raise money for the charity, 'Lifeline',[1] and I know they must have been the kind who watch each other. I daresay academic circles are quite special and a bit enclosed.

Aren't Plymouth Council a mean lot to refuse Francis Chichester the freedom of the city when he returns.[2] The *Tories* won't have it. I'm never going to vote Tory again! I really do think they are a funny unpredictable lot. And they are very philistine about the arts, and at least Labour have done VERY well about this and realise the usefulness of *ideas*.

It's pretty at the moment. Green lawns in newly mown stripes, blossom, and a Constable sky with fat English clouds. What a sexy piece Ravel's Bolero is. It's on the Third Prog. and even at 9 a.m. it is pounding in the blood.

---

[1] Charity helping the 1,700 refugees still living in camps in Germany who could not return home to the Soviet Union. Later the charity helped other war refugees.
[2] Francis Chichester (1901–72) was the first man to sail solo around the world (1966–7). He was later knighted.

2 May [1967]   Bellabeg

Darling Joyce,

A hurricane wind sweeping thick veils of rain across an invisible landscape! I rather like a beastly day to be so beastly one can't possibly go out!

Another thought – utterly non sequitur, but you know how mercurial my wonderful mind is – may I please, plagiarise your idea of how delightful it is *not* to be an air stewardess, & write an article thereon? Say no if you feel like it – it won't be the end of a beautiful friendship. If however, you had the idea of turning it into a pome, SAY so, hein?

4 May 1967   Calverly Hotel
                                                                    Tunbridge Wells

Darling Ginnie,

I learned on the radio that today we can write the date like this: 4–5–67. Neat, eh?

We had a most wonderfully gay and quick and *unexpected* audience last night! It's been sold out for days and there was one of those pleasing airs of excitement about the occasion.

Bill and I were in good heart. Bill had a wonderfully funny experience. Arrived at the theatre he went to hang out his evening suit. No jacket! Desperately he went off to find a man's shop to see if he could borrow. Early closing! In his agony he stopped the first man for directions, and this man, forgetting early closing, directed him to a Burton's. (This was before Bill realised it too.) Coming back from a fruitless errand Bill met the same man and told him his quandary. The man looked across the street, hailed a friend, the friend was General Manager of the Assembly room, *exactly* Bill's size, and produced his dinner jacket! *Happy* ending.

I have a loyal fan, left over from the war, who lives here. Dr. Lucy Campion. She's a sort of 'Fern Brixton' character and obviously very nice and enthusiastic. I always get a note and flora. This time it was daffodils and a hand beaten silver hair-pin dish that she's hammered herself for me! It is actually very pleasant to see and handle. She told me no one wants doctors over fifty, so she's taken up silver smithery to fill in.

26 May 1967   Scale Hill Hotel
                                               Cumberland

Darling Ginnie,

Do you know dippers? They are very beguiling smallish birds, black headed with snow white bibs and chestnut under-bellies, and they stand on rocks in rivers and bow and dip. Little rotund waiters they are, and they streak along rivers and nest under overhangs of moss or rock or grasses.

I had a vivid and dotty dream in which Eliz Jane Howard[1] was to appear at a charity performance that was also being televised. Somehow R. and I were seated on stage and yet we saw it on T.V. too. She stood in the wings trying to attract the Compere's eye. 'Willy', she kept whispering, 'WILLY'. She had on a full length white evening coat tied with a little bow *at the knees*. Under this she wore scarlet trousers and a silver top. She said to Willy: 'All the women will *loathe* me but the men will like it.' She then came on stage to a warm welcome of hands and did a sketch about tennis far too fast and to few laughs. I burned for her in agony. It had to finish and she just went off to a very few handclaps. Now, Daniel, can you interrupt this dream? Isn't it rum.

Today I drew some Christmas cards. You heard me all right. I'm doing a few now just for fun.[2] When I looked at my self portrait again in the cold light of morning it was so awful I had to tear it up. But it was funny too. But vanity won.

[1] British novelist and playwright (1923–) at the time married to author Kingsley Amis (1922–95).
[2] Joyce planned Christmas for months ahead. She gave presents to over 100 friends and relatives, that year ranging from ten shillings to the postman to a dish-washing machine to Joan and William Blezard.

Benjamin Britten invited Joyce to perform in the opening week of Maltings, the new concert hall at Snape and celebration of twenty years of the Aldeburgh Festival.

1 June 1967   Wentworth Hotel
                                               Aldeburgh

Darling Ginnie,

Bill came to 34 and we rehearsed our 'Beer' song and the Duet. All of which took time. And then the loading up of the car! How I wish I knew how to travel light!

The Grenfell's Luggage! I have just counted THIRTEEN pieces – all of 'em full to busting – AND stage dresses AND four coats.

We came in via Snape and went to see the new Hall. It's so attractive. The walls inside are red brick and the wood appears to be blonde and unstained. The chairs are the same, with cane seats and backs. All so light and rural looking, without being in the least 'folksy'. *Very* spacious and gay looking.

We found John Piper[1] putting the finishing touches to some large posterish coloured panels in the foyer. All a bit garish. The place was stiff with people doing last minute jobs. Drink was being delivered to the fascinating restaurant with big windows looking straight out over the marsh. The B.B.C. were everywhere. So were the film boys who are making the documentary I'm to be in on Thursday.[2] We had a good look round while it was comparatively empty, for tomorrow's crowds won't allow much exploring and H.M.[3] will be in all the best places. I'd say it's a great success as a building – lots of parking space, a big lawn with a huge Henry Moore on it looks well, and the theatre skilfully built within the walls of the original Maltings.

[1] British artist (1903–92).
[2] Directed by Tony Palmer. Joyce was filmed doing two of her sketches. Shown again thirty years later at the fiftieth anniversary of the Aldeburgh Festival.
[3] Her Majesty the Queen.

5 June 1967   Aldeburgh

Darling Ginnie,

Bang-bang in Israel this morning.[1] Oh Lor' . . . Surely we won't have to go and meddle, will we? It's *so* ridiculous, isn't it.

I bought a little red sailing cap with a bobble on top to wear for 'Ethel' – the girl who goes mad at football games. I've revived it and it's really far more apt in 1967 than it was in 1954. Thank heaven.

My show is tonight and this a.m. Bill and I rehearse our Ben song at 10.30, and then at 12 go up to the Red House[2] and sing it to the Master himself. Bill spent *all* yesterday afternoon writing out his jazz accompaniment so he gets it right! I have *never* toiled, polished, worked on anything as I have on this ditty. Let us pray he likes it. I do! Bill does!

R. and I played tennis with van der Posts at 3.30 until poor Ingaret fell backwards and did herself an injury to her wrist. They are so strong at tennis. Laurens is very agile and accurate and moves like a boy. She, too, is unmarked by time, with a girl's figure and vigour. Astonishing vitality and zest. Like teenagers: bony, quick, accurate and *strong*! I was amazed.

R. and I plodded rather but were fairly accurate if dull. I mind not making contact, because it is so boring, but I don't care a jot – or a tittle – who *wins* so long as I am in the game, under some sort of control. Don't mind being out-played a bit. Do mind missing shots, mistiming and failing to *look at the ball*.

¹The Six Day War had broken out between Israel and Egypt.
²Britten's home which he shared with Peter Pears.

5 June [1967]   Hyde Park Gardens

Darling Joyce,

Oh LORD! Isn't this AWFUL? One simply can't *believe*, as one sits eating strawberries & cream & looking on that pretty Hyde Park that hundreds of people are being killed at this very moment. That all the dreary, frightening business of swooping sirens & air-raid shelters & rubble are happening NOW. Vietnam seems so far away, somehow, one can only grieve academically – but Israel & Egypt are on the doorstep, & somehow the *fatuity* of war is terribly vivid today, don't you find?

6 June 1967   Aldeburgh

Darling Ginnie,

At noon Bill and I went to the Red House and did the Festival song in praise of Ben to him and Peter. As we arrived the beautiful new Steinway was being returned to Ben's library-music room after being used at Blythburgh on Sunday, so we sat in the garden in *hot* sun with cool glasses in our hands talking Festival.

Then into the long room full of good modern pictures and soft light coming in from all sides – or that is my impression, probably wrong! I sang it well and the reaction was *so* extraordinary that I was quite flummoxed. Ben ran to me and embraced me, weeping! He was *very* touched and moved. It was very dear and *entirely* unexpected. Keep this to yourself because both Vic and Dick are very anti-Ben and would be snide about it. Somehow it was touching in itself. He was very flattered and clearly it *had* moved him. Peter too, but less obviously. So we were rewarded.

Permission granted, Joan¹ and Bill Blezard lunched and we had a tremendous discussion about treating creative artists. I said we *all* have a need for kid gloves – certainly in the early stages of work. Encouragement is vital at that stage and must come before criticism. Joan agrees with Viola that the *objective* is the point – the music in their instance – and this must always come first and, roughly, to hell with feelings of artists. But I know that unless the artistic creature is reassured (or this artistic creature, anyhow!) in the very early stages the objective isn't reached.

I rested after this, then Bill and I met at the theatre and worked. Under difficulties. The piano had no pedals! It had been moved in but not totally reassembled and the man responsible was not to be found. However dear Bert Pearce, Steinway's genius and charmer, came to tune it and got it together for us. There was a lot of dust about because tabs [curtains] were used that hadn't been used before and whoosh there were motes and beams everywhere.

The programme went well and our song was rapturously received. I was dying to sing it again but didn't feel there had been quite enough specific call for that! Later everyone said 'Why didn't you sing it again?' Damn. Lost me only chance. For it's a one occasion song.[2]

P.S. The war in the Middle East is so unbelievably wrong and *stupid* that I trust we will keep out of it? Deserts are the best places for battles.

[1] William's wife (1920–) an orchestral conductor and lecturer at the Guildhall School of Music.
[2] The recitative aria was full of puns on 'Ben' – bene, benefactor, beneficial, and began: 'How benevolent is the setting/Suffolk winds benignly blow/ Benefiting all who come here/ And to concerts go-o-o-ho', set by William to a swing tune. William and Joyce made a gramophone record of the song for Britten and Joyce delivered it to the Red House the next day. Britten found it, unopened, at the back of the hall cupboard five years later.

7 June [1967]   Hyde Park Gardens

Darling Joyce,

Loved your letter this morning – what a *marvellous* reaction, to the peaean, paean, pee . . . of praise! Could anything be more rewarding? No, I won't tell the boys about B's tears.

8 June 1967   Aldeburgh

Darling Ginnie,

Ta for your good letter and news of the metropolis. Thank goodness the war seems to be ending. One can't help being pleased about the Israelis, but I hope they'll stop soon.

Last night it was the new production of *A Midsummer Night's Dream*[1] at The Maltings. It's *very* good. Looks pretty and was beautifully directed by Colin Graham. (Again.) Viola is the repetiteur[2] and was at the harpsichord and celeste in the pit, looking very pretty in a black chiffon topped (loose) jacket over a straight dress. Have hardly seen her: she's been rehearsing all day and night.

This year is the longest holiday we've ever had. A week in Cumberland and very nearly three here. Good.

[1] Composed by Benjamin Britten in 1960, one of his major works.
[2] Chorus master for an opera.

15 June [1967]   Hyde Park Gardens

Darling Joyce,

We went to *Rosencrantz & Guildenstern are Dead* yesterday.[1] Enjoyed it *enormously*. Not quite the play to take To to, perhaps, as it is extremely muddly, particularly if, like him, you can't remember the plot of *Hamlet*! However it is beautifully acted by these lads. One, Stride, I've seen before. The other, Petherbridge (no, *not* ridge) is marvellous, looks & very much sounds like Scofield. It's light & pleasant and thoughtful – think you'd love it.

We're watching the Trooping [of the Colour]. The old familiar pattern unfolds before us – Queenie looking cross, & all the splendid gentlemen on horseback looking uneasy, & the band playing like billyo, & the sun shining, & the flags flying – HEAVENLY.

And certainly too distracting for letter writers.

Oh! the British Grenadiers!! *Tears*.

[1] Play by Tom Stoppard (1937–) with Edward Petherbridge (1936–) and John Stride (1936–) playing Hamlet's courtiers. Won the Tony Awards and New York Drama Critics Award.

19 June [1967]   Hyde Park Gardens

Darling Joyce,

On Saturday we went to Cliveden! Toe saw it was open in some paper, so I said oh all *right*! (only *not* like that) Needless to say it was completely depressing. There was just one other car in the drive, a leaden sky, cold wind, all the blinds drawn, a sad old gardener sitting on a chair by that big yew hedge, & not a *sound*. The silence was the worst. The ghosts were LEGION.

I hadn't been there for years & years, so my ghosts were all young, from us in our twenties & Jakie & Michael [Astor] racketing around with Nanny – all that *noise* there used to be, the comings & goings; & now this great big silent negative, this NO place.

We first went on to the terrace – no sweet-smelling things between the flagstones now, no Aunt Nancy doing mashie shots, no tea in the orangery. We then went in the house – just the front hall & the three main rooms are on show, & personally I think 2/- is a lot to ask for those, don't you? The books are still on their shelves, & there is a sad circle of grand chairs in the small room which used to be so full of photographs and pictures & life . . . oh *dear*! And what I missed most was the tray of drinks in the hall!

The sad gardener told us the Long Garden was no more, but the Water Garden was, so we hurried down the drive & went & stood contemplating those huge goldfish. I know I am especially susceptible to nostalgia, but I think that even you, who are so forward looking, would cry.[1]

I went to see the Italian film on J.C.'s life & hard times.[2] Unfortunately the tiny cinema was crammed with school-kiddies in blazers, which made it an extra restless experience! Anyway I was disappointed – lovely photography, the making of everyone simple & poor, & the scenery bare & unyielding, & the multitudes tiny: the smallness of the scale in fact – basically an excellent idea. BUT, the protagonist was so unlike what I imagine him to have been, I couldn't believe in him for a minute, not namby-pamby or mawkish, but completely without love, or even compassion. He had a face shaped exactly like a perfectly beautiful egg, & with no expression delineated on it at all. Very peremptory way of speaking, fanatical, but still with this cold basilisk countenance. In fact, he was unattractive, which I'm sure Jesus wasn't – I always think of him as a very vigorous, very warm, very happy person, don't you? This chap was far too solemn and dead-pan. The Virgin Mary was exquisitely lovely – and it all went so terribly slowly that I left before the Crucifixion. ('How does it end?' Toe asked me when I got home!!)

[1] Waldorf Astor had given Cliveden to the National Trust in 1942, with the Astors remaining as tenants. When William Astor, his heir, died in 1966, the Astors relinquished their lease. It is now a privately run hotel, owned by the National Trust.
[2] *The Gospel According to Matthew*, directed by Pier Paulo Pasolini (1922–75).

21 June 1967   Aldeburgh

Darling Ginnie,

I don't know about that holy film, do I? Sounds poor. Until you mentioned it I'd never thought of what Jesus looked like. I know what I think it *felt* like to be with him – confident, unafraid, happy, warm. But his looks? I suppose he was small. He was young, of course, and dark. Sort of straight featured, brown eyed, with an athelete's upright figure and beautiful bony hands!

24 June 1967   Elm Park Gardens

Darling Ginnie,
    Nice to hear you last night. Ta.
    We watched *Our World* with fascination.[1] Hope you saw it? It really
was thrilling and I thought the scenes of theatre in it well chosen and
full of interest – Zeffirelli doing *Romeo & Juliet* with two *baby* actors,
and both beautiful;[2] Bernstein rehearsing Rachmaninov; and Heather
Harper[3] belting out Wagner in Beirut. And all 'live'. It did give one a
sense of immediacy and small-world-ness, didn't it.
    R. is asleep and about to snore. I will whistle and that usually works.
Love to you'se both.

[1] The first live television link-up between European countries.
[2] Olivia Hussey, aged fifteen, and Leonard Whiting, aged sixteen.
[3] British soprano opera singer (1930–).

14 August [1967]   Hyde Park Gardens

Darling Joyce,
    I've been *very* low. I fancy I'm tired, the accumulation of little things
– the fact that T. can't remember where the glasses are kept, or indeed
practically anything gets me down, and today I've felt exactly as if I
was living in a vacuum with a child of two, & likely to stay that way
forever! I could weep. Perhaps I should. I haven't yet. But *no*, there's
nothing more boring than self-pity.
    After lunch I went & saw Audrey B[1] & we talked about steadfastness
& she told me to give Tony a C.S. treatment – ask him first, she said but
I'm sure he'll say yes, & don't worry about the pills he's taking as you
neither of you think they work: & if he's like a child now, that's OK by
Mrs Eddy. So, I've asked To & of course he's said OK, so I've been deep
in my thoughts & books ever since tea.
    Later – our dinner has done us good. To was far more perky than he
has been lately, & had spontaneous gaiety – very *happefying*.

[1] Audrey Butterworth was a Christian Science practitioner.

18 August [1967]   [Hyde Park Gardens]

Darling Joyce,
    Yesterday To was really quite talkative, probably because he's been
to see his Mrs Allen who massages his head. She's a dear girl, & today
she asked T to say a prayer every day. 'I have a wonderful prayer for

you' she said, 'and often my patients have been healed by it . . . oh!' she added turning to me, 'Christian Scientists don't believe in Jesus Christ, do they?' What QUAINT ideas people get! Anyway, she wrote out this potent prayer, and it reads: 'Oh Lord Jesus, Son of God, have mercy on me.' That's all. Still, I'm all for T doing a little self-help.

I make To say his 'prayer' in the morning, while I'm doing the lesson. He touchingly lowers Hammond Innes, closes his eyes & says 'Lord have mercy up me' & then picks it up again & goes on reading.

25 August 1967   Home [Elm Park Gardens]

Darling Ginnie,

Thank heaven it's been almost a week of sun. It certainly helps, don't it. We had a chiffon veil all day yesterday and it was a bit steamy and airless but rather pretty. Chinese water-colour with the sudden shock of a bright red bus as an accent.

I was at the B.B.C. all day taping *The Time of my Life*.[1] The war and ENSA was the most demanding, interesting and certainly the most educational time of my life. I don't go into the horrors – fears – courage – blitz – Churchill – Battle of Britain. It is simply the account of how one entertainer learned her job by doing it. The records and tapes I'm using are *so* nostalgic and good. Very moving to hear J.B. Priestley talking of the little boats after Dunkirk. Vera Lynn comes over as powerfully and attractively as ever. Edith Evans speaking the sonnet as she did in Diversion is *beautiful*. Etc. Hope you hear the programme.

Much amused and so was Joanna [Scott-Moncreiff] when she told me that one of her clergy colleagues said of my *Ten to Eight* 'It was much too theological for me'!! What a comment on the Church. I've had so many letters and most of them NOT from C.Ss., which is good. It is the others that one would like to communicate with and it seems to have happened. This morning's mail alone has brought me twenty odd letters, all of which must be acknowledged.

I found reliving the war years for that programme quite churning up. It was in so many ways a time of good things in that it brought out man's love for man as well as his inhumanity. There was so much sharing and caring, wasn't there. A feeling of all hands to the plough and, for me in that job, a feeling of being stretched and used to the full and for a good reason. No wonder I felt let down when I got home to drab tired out England. Unspinning in the grey was very hard to do. My job has been far more fun of course!

Twenty seven morning glories round the dining room window today. Oh it is *so* pretty.

[1] Home Service radio series in which celebrities chose records to illustrate an important time in their lives.

28 August 1967 Bank Holiday   London

Darling Ginnie,

Today was so pretty. Began with a bloom on it and a heavy dew, so our tennis balls got very dirty. I washed them in Fairy Liquid when we got in and baked them dry in the oven. They *look* beautiful now, all soft and fluffy, and R. says their bounce is all there. I got the idea from Mary Rox.[1] whose *maid* always washes hers – in Lux!

Did you hear the programme *Time of My Life*? To my amazement Reggie was visibly moved. Even I, who knew what I was going to say, had a funny feeling of emotion. R. was very encouraging about it. This was a relief because in all truth I had no idea if it was any good or not. Far too close and far too much involved. It was indeed *such* a time in anyone's life so that the atmosphere was charged with awareness and beauty was very hard to bear, wasn't it. I remember sitting in those bare rooms at the National Gallery with the outline of the removed pictures still on the walls listening to some Mozart and suddenly *knowing* that music is spiritual and therefore eternal, and even if every scrap of paper on which it is written, every fiddle, bow, brass or wood wind destroyed, music would still be there. These tiny foretastes of eternity were quite a help at that time.

We watched Judi Dench[2] in a play on Second [BBC2] called *If you ask me to I'll Sparkle* or some such unreasonable title. By John Hopkins. Very good. She is one of the very best actresses, don't you think? Totally *real*. It was a heart breaking play. About the need for real affection in families, I think.

Poor Mr Epstein.[3] Poor Beatles. Isn't it interesting about all this meditating. It's so near and so far from the real Truth. But they are hungry for something real to count on – the young, the Beatles, the Hippies. It is 'the sustaining infinite' they want to find and this half truth won't really nourish them, but it is infinitely better than L.S.D. The Garu[4] *[sic]* who they follow is interesting too. What the Garu is trying to say, I think, is that the Infinite is Good and eternal and available to us all at all times. Yes indeed. So as far as it goes it's useful. I was startled to see that the Arch. Bish. Ramsey[5] approves *too*! We always knew these little Beatles were after something true. I think that is their attraction. The rebellious element *is* a necessary one I think. Strange times.

I must try and catch up on the *Listeners*, *Punches* and *New Yorkers*. Why do we take them? Well, the *Listener* comes because I'm on the B.B.C., G.A.C.[6] The *N.Y.* is a Christmas present, and *Punch* is an old habit.

I must also start reviving monologues soon for the concert tour. Run through one a day is a good start.

[1] Mary, Duchess of Roxburgh.
[2] British actress (1934–).
[3] Brian Epstein (1934–67), the manager of the Beatles pop group, had died of a drug overdose.
[4] Maharishi Mahesh Yogi, a Hindu guru, taught Transcendental Meditation to the Beatles.
[5] Michael Ramsey (1904–90), one hundredth Archbishop of Canterbury and Primate of All England from 1961 to 1974.
[6] General Advisory Committee.

30 August [1967]   Hyde Park Gardens

Darling Joyce,

Oh *goodness*!!! Have I ever commented on your programme?? No, I haven't! What a FRIEND! Well, it was EXCELLENT – so fresh & invigorating. I cried practically the whole way through! *How* nostalgic and evocative those old tunes are!

As you say, isn't it odd, all this meditating? And all those thousands of young at Woburn, doing nothing, as far as one could gather, but tinkle little bells & hand each other flowers. The papers' main impression is one of intense boredom. What I've never gathered is whether these Flower Children do anything *else* – I mean, are they clerks or bus drivers as well as being psychedelic? Is it a philosophy or a career? Because the world wouldn't run if nobody works. But oh this hunger for something lovely 'outside'! It is terribly touching, isn't it? Though why one has to wear such incredibly mad clothes & paint one's face like a savage to find it, I can't fathom.

I can't fathom all this bish-bashing outside (& inside) embassies! I'm fed *up* with all this violence, aren't you?

To is hoping that this holiday in Scotland will cure him completely. Pore old thing. If he had any memory he would know he'd been up here seven times since he started feeling woolly – so in this case it is lucky he hasn't! Mustn't it be HELL, feeling ill & tired & muddled for *years*?

4 September 1967   London

Darling Ginnie,

I've rehearsed my script for *Woman's Hour* birthday week.[1] I've set
myself a task for I do seven or eight different voices all on top of each
other and no pause to consider. I'm announcer and questioner and
answerer. I worked on it yesterday and it's falling into place. I discover
pitch helps, Scots highish, Welsh middling sharp, and Yorkshire
basso, etc.

Went to church and sneaked out in last hymn in order to hear *The
Critics*.[2] Snooty they were. Katharine Whitehorn[3] was generous and
made me feel a little less misunderstood! Do you know I have *never*
found *any* disadvantage in being U – nor do I now on most things. But
there is a basic resentment of one's background. It's as if 'they' didn't
think you ought to be in the competition. There was some reluctant
admiration and I must admit they mostly rated me as a 'real artist' and
this is the accolade of course. But by golly 'they' don't like what isn't
familiar and I sense a suspicion that it's not fair for me to be U *and* an
artist! When you think of it I'm not as U as all that. Good yeoman stock
on Pa's side – grandpa in trade! a merchant. And Ma? an attractive
line of English emigrants to Virginia I suppose. *Gentle* people and my Pa
educated but no noble lineage. I'm not downcrying, just looking at it
clearly.[4]

How one does justify oneself, nicht? When 'they' said it was time I
re-thought my material I sort of sank in despair. When I think of the
difference between, say, 'Useful and Acceptable Gifts' and 'Lally Tullett'
and 'Eng. Lit.' I wonder if I'm in the delusion.[5] They *are* very different.
Come to think of it, the recent critics have said this – range widened,
deepened, etc., but I think casual listeners who have probably only seen
me once, possibly in a film, are stuck with the first image. Anyway,
what the hell . . . God is good, audiences still attend – so far!

[1] Twenty-first birthday.
[2] BBC Home Service radio programme reviewing Joyce's latest show. Joyce sometimes
appeared as a critic on this programme.
[3] British journalist on the *Observer*.
[4] Nora's father was a millionaire and although the lineage may not have been noble, Joyce
and her relations were all privately educated with good incomes.
[5] First performed in 1939, 1965 and 1965.

In September Joyce went on her fourth tour of North America with William Blezard as
her accompanist and Diana Lyddon her stage manager. This time, as well as her solo
performances, she took seminars with students at local colleges of all denominations.

8 October 1967   Southampton

Darling Gin,

I hope To is home again and that reports are going to be useful. I think of you a *great* deal. And To.

Had breakfast at a Nedick's counter and was amused at watching the coloured clients who outnumbered we Caucasians in a big way. Very varied income groups and very varied in their attitudes, clothes and manners. I notice that I *don't* notice the very educated well dressed Negroes any more – as Negroes. This is what will happen I suppose. And hope.

For the richest country in the world there is a *lot* of poverty.

I wing off tomorrow with Bill and Diana. I'm longing to begin now. Diana is full of confidence, thank heaven. Bill is here and rang last night in a fury over the inefficiency of the airport – customs, immigration, etc.

Hate to part from R. Horrid, horrid, horrid. He is so marvellously solicitous and does so much for me. I'm spoiled of course. R. has just called from the Air Terminal. He is a very saintly character and I love him very much indeed.

Bill was in a daze from the flight over and very sleepy. He had his shoes cleaned by a shoeshine boy on 42nd Street and was sitting there staring into space when Marlene [Dietrich] suddenly appeared by his side! She had tickets for him for tonight's opening and he is taking Diana. It's her first Broadway appearance. He says she seemed very calm.

8 October [1967]   Hyde Park Gardens

Darling Joyce,

Tony's been given some even stronger pills, which make him even more hazy. The general gist of his diagnosis is that there is something structurally wrong with his brain, that it has shrunk a bit (they *didn't* say prematurely senile) & that though his memory will never be first class again, these pills may make it better. What did interest me was Dr Williams saying 'What really interests me is the influence mind has on brain.' I longed to pursue this, but T was aching to go, but isn't it fascinating that even the medics now think there is a mind somewhere influencing a brain?

Here is the simplest poem EVER!
XXXX GIN

THE HEALING
After so long, so long
in my tight prison,
with my familiar shackles
heavy on head and heart;
after so long, so long,
suddenly I see the bars
with the eyes God gave me,
and suddenly, suddenly,
(oh, my heart flies out of the dream
like a singing bird!)
Suddenly there is freedom.

Virginia Thesiger

Tony had received various diagnoses including acute depression and poor blood circulation in the brain. He probably had Alzheimer's Disease. Athough Alzheimer had described the disease in 1910, the term was not generally used even in the 1960s and 'pre-senile dementia' held a social stigma.

1968

As Tony's health deteriorated, Joyce loathed leaving Virginia while she went for a holiday in the sunshine of South Africa.

28 January 1968   At the airport

Darling Ginnie,

I'm thinking of you. I shall miss the sound of your voice of a morning. But, thank God, we do talk on paper and I can hear you in your writing. Ta for being you, oh admirable and loved friend.

30 January 1968   Hyde Park Gardens

Darling Joyce,

Ta for your farewell note. I love you *too*! It's lovely to know you mind, but you mustn't, darling. I am honestly *much* better than I was, inasmuch as I don't feel panicky any more, & it does seem, all fit, more removed from me. I have slight anger when we're with people who don't know, but this happens rarely, & anyway is based entirely on one not wanting one's dear ones to make fools of themselves. Most days now, I take it in my stride, and I really *am* helped by Audrey who is working for me twice a week, so that I don't have that feeling, *always* false as I well know, that it all depends on me. So don't worry the tiniest bit about me, luv – I shall be *cross* if you do.

Happy days, luv. X for Reg.

7 February 1968   Johannesburg

Darling Ginnie,

Back in urban life with a bang. Like New York – like Sydney –
London – everywhere, J'burg is building and all night long there was
the roar of some sort of machine.

R. found Harold [Grenfell] *very* low. A lot of small miseries added to
Miriam's loss are making his life a real hell just now. Business is fine, in
fact booming. But his very nice Cape coloured chauffeur is in hospital;
his eccentric African cook of twenty years, who treats him like a god
and irons his shirts like an angel, is a Tanzanian and all Tanzanians are
being returned to Tanzania, and he is difficult and old and there is no
work for him there. Sad.

I'm waiting for a call from Nadine Gordimer,[1] the S.A. writer, very
liberal and interesting and a friend of Laurens van der Post. Most of her
books are banned here! I've got lots of writing to do and I think I may
go out and look for a tidy linen dress.

[1] Novelist (1923–), won the Nobel Prize for Literature in 1991 for her books exposing
apartheid.

7 February 1968   Hyde Park Gardens

Darling Joyce,

I sent you a cable yesterday c/o Grenamms, & I gather Dick sent
you one c/o your Constantia Hotel. Hope mine gets there first!! Your
birthday duly noted in *The Times* today, luv. Ta for our Valentines,
which have come this morn . . . a tiny bit early, but it's nice to know we
have secret lovers, at *any* time. You *are* a thoughtful gal . . .

To has just come in to say he's off to meet a blonde at Swan
& Edgar's! Very gay. Actually I gather he is going to buy some
butterscotch in the village![1]

[1] Praed Street, opposite Paddington Station.

8 February 1968   Johannesburg

Darling Ginnie,

At 12 Alice Spence, the very attractive and nice Swedish wife of
the General Manager of Messina, sent her car and I joined her at the
hotel where she is perching with four children till she can find a house.
The office has moved here from Messina. I talked to Alice's chauffeur,
Nicodemus, and found he was a great reader. He prefers Maugham to
D.H. Lawrence, loves Guy de Maupassant and Chekhov, and said: 'All

the time I am travelling everywhere in my head.' It was a fascinating conversation. What folly this apartheid is. Idiotic.[1]

[1] This meeting with Nicodemus, a twenty-five-year-old Methodist driver, was the inspiration for '*Nicodemus' Song*' which Joyce performed later that year, to a syncopated drum rhythm slapped on her knees.

8 February 1968   Hyde Park Gardens

Darling Joyce,

Yesterday *Times* had a full page ad sponsored by lots of tycoony people like Lord Thomson ... & David Frost (!) telling people how they could help Britain – under separate headings – 'Elderly', 'Children', 'Motorists', 'Civil Servants', 'The Government', 'Housewives', etc. Rather a good idea, though Quintin Hogg[1] today says it's a rotten one because it's a mistake to try & save the situation for the government – that they must GO, not be boosted by our sacrifices! Anyway, under 'elderly', I see it says save bottle tops & newspapers, so that shouldn't test me too seriously![2]

Just been watching *Softly, Softly* – To. asleep all the way through, just waking up twice, once to say he was off to have a bath – you've *had* that, I said – once to say when was dinner – you've had *that*, I said. The News says 20% fewer deaths on the road, & Queen Mum visiting P.M. in hospital, where she's had her tonsils out!

X X X Gin

[1] Conservative MP (1907–).
[2] The 'We're Backing Britain' campaign was initiated by a group of secretaries who offered to work extra time for free, to help the British economy.

11 February 1968   Alphen Hotel
                                                             Constantia
                                                             Cape Province

Darling Ginnie,

Yesterday I had the most superb bathe in an aquamarine sea, clear as glass, from a white beach, and it was a joy. The long rollers lifted me up and I felt light as a feather – a dancer – a will-o-wisp. I was fancying all this in my little greeny-bluey bathing dress and a sort of rubber mob cap on my head when *wham*! a much larger and more powerful roller broke just where I was and threw me all over the place.

I needn't have worried about my figure on South African beaches! You never saw such 'stomicks'. Afrikaans ladies eat a lot of bread and cake and pastries.

In the afternoon we went to the Botanical Gardens on the slopes of Table Mountain. This is largely wild and huge. We saw sun-birds, took a good walk and in the car park ran into a coloured (mixed) wedding party that was the *prettiest* sight. Such colours as the ladies wore – lime, lemon, kingfisher blue, turquoise, white, scarlet, pink, orange – you name it. The bride was *beautiful* and had a gold lamé dress. They'd come to be photographed against the great blue mountain backcloth.

It's been nice not knowing anyone and being quite unrecognised. (No T.V. here and very few films.) I'm having to exercise *much* control and am doing it, you'll be glad to hear, for the talk of South Africans and the travelling British is *so* narrow, Tory, longing-for-the-old-days stuff that it makes your fliend want to vomit.

I find the oppressive feeling a great weight and rather wish I could talk to a really good with-it C.S. Doris' letter on the subject of not being nationalist, tribal etc. but only seeing that man is *only* the son of God, seems particularly necessary here with so much hate and fear about. What I resent is being made to feel so hateful too – of Afrikaaners and the skin-preserving Europeans as a whole who live here. Hate is too strong a word. A wish totally to disassociate from them is the feeling. As for the visiting English with their loud upper crust voices . . . So you see I need to learn to Love More! Yes, indeed.

Darling. You are a marvel.

I salute you.

Wish you were here.

13 February 1968   Hyde Park Gardens

Darling Joyce,

THAT was a super surprise, darling!! Many many thanks, luv. It was real joy to hear your dear old voice, & goodness, how marvellously clear & close! Science is pretty wonderful these days, innit it? I mean, the mind boggles at the mechanics of the thing dunnit? But it all proves that space & distance & time don't count any more.

14 February 1968   Hyde Park Gardens

Darling Joyce,

I'm just back from *Swan Lake*-ing with Vic, which was a *bit* agonising, as Fonteyn[1] has become 'simply wonderful for her age', & rather like Clara Schumann,[2] who used to get away with everything without playing a note in her old age, she gets away with everything without dancing. No, that *isn't* fair – she dances divinely most of the time, but the testing bits *are* a strain, & one sees those pore neck

369

muscles standing out & the smile frozen with the effort. Vic minded dreadfully. Rudy,[3] of course, was flowing & utterly graceful, & it was really very enjoyable, especially as we left before the last act!

Darling, I'm really absolutely OK 90% of the time, & the other 10% I'm not depressed or self-pitying, simply exasperated! I just indulge myself in a bit of irritation – completely invisible & inaudible, I *hope* – and then I pull myself together again. When I mutter to myself 'Oh fuck that buggering bunch of keys!' I feel a bit relieved, which shows, Joyce, that, as you may have suspected, I am delightfully human. Hein?

Church this eve, when I am on dooty.

[1] Dame Margot Fonteyn ballerina was then forty-nine years old.
[2] Pianist wife of Robert (1819–96), Clara Schumann performed for over seventy years.
[3] Rudolph Nureyev (1938–93), Russian principal ballet dancer.

20 February 1968   Johannesburg

Darling Ginnie,

In the mail was a film script with a fat part of an unappetising kind for me. *The Age of Consent*, starring James Mason,[1] directed by James Mason, to be made in Queensland, Australia. *How* I hoped it might be a good script – at last. But it wasn't. It's pedestrian, too facile, toys lightly with the real values and then goes soft on the whole thing. All the usual permissiveness and lots of excuses for nudity – he's a painter. She swims bare, etc. etc. My part is the type-stock spinster, with a little dog, who is so man hungry she suddenly goes for a confidence trickster and smothers him with kisses. *So* like your friend. So I've cabled no.

Nadine Gordimer came in to have a drink with us. This time she seemed even tinier, beautifully made and fragile. I suspect she's strong as wire, like H.M.G.![2] She wore a purple linen shift, lovely bare feet in orange sandals, and she looked good. She has a Nefertiti's head and a hairdo that adds to this impression. We talked endlessly about Africa and mutual friends and writing and books, and suddenly after a second whiskey she really opened up.

I think I've got a flea. Two little groups of three bites on me body!

[1] British stage and film actor (1909–84).
[2] Reggie's step-mother, Hilda Mary Grenfell.

20 February 1968   Hyde Park Gardens

Darling Joyce,

Georgina [Coleridge], looking vast & wearing the maddest hat I have ever seen, multi-coloured gros-point crown slitted on to a butcher blue band of knitted wool with tassle, came to luncheon. We nattered & laughed, & finally commiserated with each other – because her husband has high blood pressure & is always collapsing!! WHO is well, one wonders?!

We've got *Beachcomber* on the telly tonight – I find the spoof advertisements in it so *marvellously* funny I roll about on that yellow sofa in paroxysms!

1 March 1968   Messina

Darling Ginnie,

I began on a *Ten to Eight* for Joanna [Scott-Moncreiff] in a series called *The Debt I owe my Parents*. Not easy, even though I do owe mine a huge amount, simply because if one says 'I owe my humour, brains, beauty, talent, etc. etc. to my ma or pa' it really comes out as a list of one's own qualities! Instead I'm going on the lines of having learnt by example. And this is true. Both my parents were loving and generous, and this climate of freedom made it possible for us to live and develop without frustrations.

And I'm working on a song and I rather like it. But there is a lot more work to go into it. The idea is quite pleasing. I think the first line will be: 'It was hell living in Mulgarth Street', and it's about an East End woman who has been rehoused in a lovely block of new Council flats and misses the feelings of life in the street below. It's got a sort of wistful cum resentful feel about it I think! Anyway I'll go on with it and see how it comes out. Don't read that to Vic if you *do* ever read my letters to him because I find that it's a mistake to quote one's work until it is really ready – except to you. And Dick always minds if I show a lyric before *he's* seen it! Oh les boys![1]

[1] 'Mulgarth Street' ended up as a monologue, first performed in 1971.

2 March 1968   Hyde Park Gardens

Darling Joyce,

A spot of food shopping in Harrods. They've got one of the space capsules set up in that middle bit – yes, a *genuine* one – & if you want to peer into it you can queue up & climb a little staircase.

My writing life is considerably confused at the moment, on account of how I am writing what happened in the *past* each month for *H & G*[1] – sort of Nelson was born & Bach died & the first atom bomb was exploded stuff – and also what *happens* each month in England for the [*Christian Science*] *Monitor*. You would think it was easy to keep them separate, yet for each there has to be a wee preliminary canter i.e. 'This is the month when everybody goes on holiday' or 'April is the cruellest month says T.S. Eliot', & it is in these, in this fruit salad of the Derby & Agincourt, the opening of the Royal Academy & Blondin crossing the Niagara that I become confused, in the scene *setting* as it were.

[1] *Homes and Gardens.*

9 June 1968   Wentworth Hotel, Aldeburgh

Darling Ginnie,

We went to Lettice Colman's – full of young men in partly fancy dress. One had a polo necked shirt made of pink gingham, another had exaggerated bell-bottom trousers. There was long hair. All were very pleasant and friendly, and Luci looked entrancing in a skin tight black silk polo necked sweater and very tight black levis. Around her waist – no, low on the hips – a Victorian gilt chatelaine!

I've flinched from Birtwhistle's[1] new opera *Punch & Judy*, which is 'not suitable for children'! Or me, then.

We saw John Gielgud at Snape and discovered he was alone, staying here too, so we asked him to join us for dinner. He was in good form and very pleasant and funny. Full of theatre anecdotes. Rather a bitchy story about Emlyn W.[2] who went back stage to see Gladys Cooper somewhere on tour, quite lately. He passed two very elderly ladies as he was going into the stage door and one said to the other: 'I wish I hadn't let you see her, she *used* to be so graceful.'

Another about Noël telephoning across the Atlantic to California to sympathise with Clifton Webb[3] over the death of Mabel, his extraordinary million years old mother. Clifton Webb was famous for being very stingy. He was crying down the telephone to Noël and Noël said: 'Clifton if you don't stop crying I shall reverse the charges'! Not very kind but funny. John was, in fact, rather mellow and kind in most of his stories. Very affectionate about Winifred, Zena Dare,[4] Lillian Gish,[5] among others. Said they all had great qualities of goodness to others – 'Dear women'. We enjoyed our evening. He is doing his Shakespeare programme tonight and we attend.

[1] Harrison Birtwhistle (1934–). English composer. *Punch & Judy* was a new composition in a severe, severed form.
[2] Emlyn Williams (1905–87), Welsh actor, dramatist and director.
[3] American character actor (1893–1966). Had been in Coward's plays.
[4] Zena Dare (1887–1975). Actress who starred with Noël Coward.
[5] Lillian Gish (1896–1982). American silent screen star.

11 June 1968   Aldeburgh

Darling Ginnie,

Later, re your phone call. I think the answer to your question, 'What is the good C.S.'s purpose in life?' is really answered by 'What is life for?', and this I think is true for *everyone*: 'Life is for finding out what God is.' Literally that. The dedicated C.S. doesn't have to be a practitioner or a nurse. If one seeks to practise C.S. in one's daily life then the rest is added unto you. Some *are* called as preachers etc. Luke, isn't it? The only essential is that one must *practise* what one believes. There are lots of dedicated holies[1] who really are only *fulfilled* by this calling. Fine and dandy. But I think a very good architect, for instance, expressing his understanding is an essential member of society. It is how C.S. informs our lives that matters.

Here endeth the lesson.

I used to get deeply depressed about my pa. And I remember much earlier depressions when we first lived at Cliveden, in Greenwood Cottage before Parr's was done up for us. I felt that life was *all* hell and there was no way out. I wasn't unhappy – in love with anyone (except R.), just horrified and submerged. And yet I knew, and it was a sheet anchor, that all was well even though, pro tem, I couldn't seem to *feel* it. I suppose this *is* 'leaning on the sustaining infinite'.

Well, our hectic life of Pleasure and the Arts, mingled with Sport continues.

We were bowled over by *The Prodigal Son*[2] and Orford and the dusk and the setting. It was a heavenly occasion. A pretty dove coloured evening – into – twilight. Soft and subtle. The air tense with the excitement that Ben's new works always bring with them.

All the regulars were there in force and we had wonderful seats. When it was over there was a *long* sustained and powerful silence. It's a lovely piece. Peter Pears was the Tempter-narrator and looked rather awful in a high black (net and wire?) hat as if made of petals in flame shapes. He had an eye mask and a blond wig and beard and was not exactly tempting! but very evil. Alas, I detected rather a sign or two of wear in that remarkable voice, and after hearing the young ones in such form it showed rather. *Sad*. But he was, as always, such a real craftsman that one was full of admiration. It is full of invention and movement. We loved it. Many are saying it's *the* best. I still love *Fiery Furnace*, but this is a very close second.

R.'s *real* enjoyment of the concerts and events here is one of the most lovely bonuses to have. He gets enormous delight from *watching* even when he isn't interested in the sounds.

E.M. Forster[3] and William Plomer[4] lunched next to us. We walked down the High Street with Desmond Shaw Taylor.[5] The place hisses

with the sibilance of highly intellectual non-marryers. They seem
to swarm here, all shapes, sizes and ages. While I was listening
desperately to the very advanced horror music of the piano piece
this morning I made myself laugh with an obituary I thought all too
possible:

'She died from opening her mind too far.'

Funny, eh?

[1] Joyce and Virginia's word for Christian Scientists.
[2] New opera composed by Benjamin Britten.
[3] Edward Morgan Forster (1879–1970), novelist, best known for *Howard's End*. Wrote
libretto for Britten's *Billy Budd*.
[4] British writer (1903–76).
[5] Music critic (1907–95).

16 June 1968   Aldeburgh

Darling Ginnie,

I've had a lovely mail with nothing requiring an answer except a
request from A.P. Watt & Son[1] to write an autobiography. I suppose
I get an average of two requests a year from agents or publishers,
and fortunately I have a stock answer: I have already promised
that IF I ever *do* write an autobiography it will be done by Rupert's
Company. This is a fact. He, anyway, would see it *first*. But I doubt if I
do one.[2]

Last night there was a party sitting at the next table to us.
Alfred and Clementine Beit[3] and Vivienne Mosley,[4] who was
my bridesmaid. She looks intelligent and nice; large, busty and
handsome, with a low voice that carries, but it was Clementine's
that rang out and shamed me! There was a lot of loud chat about
music, and it was *so* funny and so insensitive to give free opinions
F.F.F. in the diningroom of the Wentworth in Festival Time! Ears
were on stalks all round, and when Alfred said Britten can't write
a tune I thought perhaps a thunderbolt might hit him! Sydney
Nolan[5] and wife were at the table the other side of the group and
could hardly eat for listening. They discussed modern art and I
dreaded they talk about Sydney, but they simply dismissed the later
Picassos, acclaimed Rembrandt, and then took to discussing their
friends.

They were really rather terrible and once again I felt ashamed of my
class and disassociated myself from it! It is the total disregard of other
people that is so unattractive. And so arrogant. I think, possibly, this
group was quite intelligent and not at all nasty, but they exposed their
folly so lavishly that even John, the head waiter, gave me a loud

understanding wink as he passed by! And I do think it's time there was a social change. Roll on the tumbrils.

[1] Literary agent, established in 1875. Joyce had been Mr Watt's client before the war.
[2] When Joyce did write her autobiography, Rupert Hart-Davis had retired as a publisher, but helped her edit it, and it was published by Macmillan.
[3] Sir Alfred Beit (1903–94), South African industrialist, married Clementine Mitford (1915–).
[4] Sir Oswald Mosley's sister (1915–).
[5] Australian artist (1917–94).

10 July 1968   London

Darling Ginnie,
    Yesterday I begun to sing again. A wheel wobble after such a long pause, for except on Sundays and Wednesdays [at church], I haven't sung since November. It's as if the elastic is gone loose, but it usually tautens again into a better instrument and I'm singing freely up on A^b, which isn't bad for fiftyeight.
    An actress 'new to C.S.' whose prac. suggested she should talk to me! rang and asked if C.S. helped my work. I said: 'It is the very centre of my being and informs everything I think and do.'
    A member of F.C.[1] decided she must be more loving and friendly and was shopping in the King's Road when she realised she'd cut some elderly woman she vaguely realised she knew. So she went back to remedy the slight and discovered it was her own reflection in a mirror! I love it. Love, darling, and to T.

[1] First Church of Christ, Scientist, Sloane Street, London.

Joyce began an eight-week tour of Britain with William Blezard.

2 October 1968   Robin Hood Hotel
                                                              Newark-on-Trent
                                                                        Notts

Darling Ginnie,
    You know that old question they used to ask in radio interviews: What was your most embarrassing moment? I had a lulu last night and got such giggles all by myself. The Music Club for which we did the show last night gave me a big bouquet of fat headed crysanths in autumnal tints and they came swathed in cellophane with a pink plastic paper ribbon. I was to be photographed *before* the show with the head girl of the school (where the concert was) presenting me with the flowers. Cellophane glares in flashlights and I hate flowers in it anyway, so I decided to free them from their encasement. And as I tore off the

stuff I saw the flowers weren't in a bunch at all but had been laid on a paper background and tethered in place by the damned cellophane. The whole thing just fell apart and the 'medical room' where I was dressing was covered in petals! Somehow I forced the stiff brutes into a bunch and tied them up with the unyielding pink 'ribbon' *just* before the head girl and the press man arrived. I was very hot and bothered.

Earlier in the day I overheard a row between a Spanish or Italian chambermaid and a Scots ditto in the corridor outside this room. They screamed and growled and then there was a little pause after which the Latin type said:

'And now weel you kindly b–y b–r off.' It was the kindly that corpsed me.

Word has got out among the chambermaids that I'm me and one by one they come in with various excuses to have a look! One is Danish, said she liked me VERY much, I am so foony. Last night's girl, a pretty blonde, is a homesick Cockney, said it was lovely to see me in the *flesh*. It always sounds so awful, don't it. Up I must get. All love darling, love to T.

19 October 1968

Duke's Head Hotel
Tuesday Market Place
King's Lynn
Norfolk

Darling Ginnie,

It was specially nice talking to you this morning. I had a slight sense of isolation in spite of having had a good long gossip with R. last night. Perhaps it was because literally no one came back stage last night and this is *so* rare and very anti-climactic. One doesn't actually want *praise*; one wants contact! The 'praise' *is* in the sense of communication, the laughs, the silence when it's needed, and of course in applause. There was plenty of all these. But it's a bit like broadcasting: you do it and off it goes and you don't know where it went and a friend coming round afterwards just proves it has arrived somewhere. What egotists we artisticals are!

Have you heard 'Those Were the Days'[1] sung by the little Welsh girl the Beatles have found? Catchy. But she's got *no* voice. Mary Hopkin – she's got a sweet little thread of a child's voice. Maybe that's the appeal. All love, darling. Love to T.

[1] Written by Gene Rankin.

Sunday, 27 October 1968   Hyde Park Gardens

Darling Joyce,

Silly to write when I'll be seeing you at lunch so soon, but I will all the same.

We've just been watching the shenanigans on TV.[1] The major procession, which steered for the Park, quite orderly one gathers, but the lads who split off & went to Grosvenor Square getting a *mite* obstreperous. They've been cooped up in the square for about 2½ hours − & it's an amazing sight, for the police are standing in front of the Embassy 20 *deep*: taken from above their helmets look like stars (their silver badges is what I mean, you fool!) and somehow it's rather wonderful & British that there isn't a tin helmet or a bayonet or any tear gas or mace, certainly no *tanks* in sight. I may be speaking out of turn, of course.

[1] Students demonstrated outside the US Embassy against the war in Vietnam.

1969

In early 1969 Joyce read Beatrix Potter's stories on the children's television programme *Jackanory*. Virginia was inspired to write her this poem.

> A POEM FOR JOYCE FROM GIN
> Here I sit, grey and fat and bit sad,
> listening to you, Joyce,
> reading Peter Rabbit on the television.
> As I watch you, dear friend,
> and listen to that familiar voice
> reading those innocent words,
> slowly you turn into Nanny Radford,
> and I into a little girl,
> very perky, in a starched petticoat,
> waiting to have her knees washed
> before being carried down
> those long cold stairs
> into the drawing-room.
>
> One last look at the liberty bodice
> hanging over the fender
> and then down down to the grown-ups,
> to the heat and the heavy carpets,
> to the silver tea things and the remains
> of the buttered toast,
> to the little Waterford pot
> for the Tiptree's strawberry jam,

and to Perrin in muslin cap
staggering out with it all on a butler's tray.

Down I go to the paternal watch
which opens when you blow,
to games on the rug in front of the fire,
and then, over-excited,
to maternal arms and the book you are reading now.

I am a pale little girl,
with flaxen curls
and pure white socks,
and you, Joyce – strange I never noticed before –
are *exactly* like Nanny Radford
(all that rough cherishing
and those clucking noises
and that grey alpaca skirt
and those comforting arms!)
Lord! I wish it were true,
and you would soon be coming down
those long cold stairs
to carry me, screaming with rage,
up to my bed.

V.G.[1]

[1]Later published in the *Christian Science Monitor* for which Virginia wrote articles and poems until 1991.

24 February 1969   Red Studio
                                                  Aldeburgh

Darling Virginia,

As I arrived Peter [Pears] was out exercising his miniature dachshund. He looked marvellously handsome with his white hair blowing and his good bones and that attractive smile. He had on a long scarf like an undergrad, and there is a sort of eternal undergrad something about him, isn't there. I think it is because he has, with all his enormous scholarship and maturity, kept his first enthusiasm. That's one of the most attractive qualities anyone can have, don't you agree?

Last night Ben [Britten] dined. He is so strange. One gets *fairly* near but as with all people of genius there are whole areas of total privacy. He is also fairly confident in B.B. in *some* ways and *not* in others. He is very concerned at the number of appeals for musical help from young composers; from teachers about young pupils; from mothers about young talented offspring. The demands for time are increasing and persistent – time to look at scores, hear performances, see and talk to budding artist/composers. Etc. IF he gave up composing and conducting he might be able to cope but as it is, the things pile up; scores arrive and sit unopened, etc.

It really is a problem and I suppose a common one for anyone of his stature and known interest in young people. He is, as he says, pleased to be asked. He had a lot of help when he was young and I think he feels bound to do the same for other people. There is a faintly – and I meant faint – malicious streak that is apparently latent in a lot of these rather feminine men. I think that he could be ruthless, merciless? It is part of the insecurity of such a position, no doubt. He is very agreeable to meet; generous about talent in others – he spoke enthusiastically of Heather Harper, of Viola and all her work.

When I sit to Att[1] she is so concentrated that we don't talk much and it's a marvellous opportunity to work in C.S. God, Mind, is actually *there*. At all times. What is the quotation? 'Where the Spirit of the Lord is, there is liberty.' Something like that. *Marvellous*.

R. writes from S. Africa of having solved a lot of local problems of a purely domestic nature and he feels a lot easier. He is itching to get home and I share the itch. Talking of which do you find you get itchy in the winter? Att and I were saying that we find we need quite a lot of enjoyable – well rubbing is more like it – after removing the girdle and before taking the bath. I use a delicious body oil after the bath and that is very pleasant. I feel quite Roman rubbing myself down. Itching sounds very unattractive and unclean and I don't mean that, really. Just a sort of wintry feeling that one needs oil.

Verily writes to say she's got R. and me in her latest book, disguised, and what shall she call us?! It's all about the building of the house which as you know is secret. So that does need thought.[2]

[1] Mary Potter, ex-wife of Stephen, was painting Joyce's portrait. Attenborough was her maiden name, which stuck as a nickname.
[2] Joyce was called 'Kate' and Reggie was 'Tom' in Verily Anderson's book *Scrambled Eggs for Christmas*.

5 February [1969]   Hyde Park Gardens

Darling Joyce,

Ta for another lovely letter. Glad the Potter is coming up to your liking. As you know, I'm not terribly pro Potter, as she's so terrifically pastel, but I'm all set to heal myself of this condition!

My lunch party was v successful – Sheila with pink camelias, Bungs with a potted primula & Louise came back to hand round the Sole Ritz! It was her day to do the clothes, & I think she enjoyed seeing the old faces again. We ranged over God, Illegitimate children, Biotex (which apparently washes one's smalls *and* ormulu with shining success), computers, why the backs of our necks stay dirty however much we wash, & burglars. Rose[1] has been burgled – they took all her good bits of china, leaving the mended pieces. They wrapped everything up in her napkins, not leaving one, which was an added inconvenience.

To has been much better these past days, quite often smiling. This, actually, is considerably more heartbreaking than when he's a pudding, as I'm sure you can understand; one of my comforts is that he is almost unrecognisable most of the time.

Got to go out to dine tonight. I forgot my 'jools' are in the bank, so I can't pin sapphires to my corsage to distract the eye from my avoirdupois. But who *cares*?

[1] Lady Rose Baring (1909–95), lady-in-waiting to the Queen.

Saturday, 7 June 1969   Wentworth Hotel
                                                           Aldeburgh

Darling Virginia,

A feast of Purcell, Mozart and Schubert with the Amadeus. What a dream of a hall it is. The Trout quintet as a finale with Ben at the piano. It was magical. The whole thing rose and flew – or maybe *swam* is a better verb. Anyway a lovely treat.

R. has gone to collect Bill, who was doing a T.V. *Play School* all day.

Many old faces, all looking splendid, which is comforting. Lady Dashwood in purple, still *mooerning*, do you suppose? Sunday

We heard the news of the fire at 8 a.m. on our radio and can hardly believe it. There it was yesterday, so beautiful, so airy, so absolutely the dream of what a concert hall in a country place should be. Now . . . The mind boggles at the mammoth task of coping with all of us and our tickets for concerts at the Maltings. R. has gone down to offer our help in any clerical or practical way as needed. Someone will have to cope with the crowds and the reorganising. Ben was up all night of course. Peter, too, no doubt.

Most of the concerts, and all of the big drawing-power events, were to have been at the Maltings. Orford and Blythburgh are to be used we heard but they don't hold the numbers. I think there will have to be parallel concerts to absorb us all – while some go to Orford others will be in the Jubilee? or that awful W.I. hut place in Thorpeness? It's a task all right.

I don't think Lady Dashwood is *moo-erning* the late lamented Sir

John, for last night she was in white with a vibrant magenta shawl like a Casa Pupo rug.

We were to have gone to the Maltings for a huge choral concert with Ben and Peter tonight . . . Tell you wot: I wish you were here. Love. Love.

I'll telephone later.

7 June 1969   St Paul's
                                                                                                                  Hertfordshire

Darling Joyce,

I have re-read your letter & it's sad to read about the joys of the Maltings concert hall, having seen those leaping flames on the telly last night – oh DEAR. But of course it will rise again – & everyone will rush to give money; even, perhaps, the insurance? But still . . . the *effort*.

It seems EVER so strange without you two here. I expect one of your dear old faces to come round the door at any minute, or the squeak of grapefruit knife accompanied by tinned Vivaldi from the kitchen, or Reg booming brilliantly on half a glass of sherry. There is nary a sight nor sound. Disappointing.

11 June 1969   Aldeburgh

Darling Ginnie,

I have told Ben I'd do a show for the funds when I'm home from Australia.

To Blythburgh [church], where a real job has been done in two days to turn it into a concert hall. Amazing. Carpenters and elecs. have worked *all* night; wardrobe, too, I believe, and we were given an impeccable performance of *Idomeneo*.[1] It is full of such *beautiful* music and of course Ben got every nuance out of it. I found the whole occasion such a triumph of *spirit*. Very moving to know how hard people will work when they feel it is *needed*. A great tribute to Ben and all who have made the Festival such an *actual* thing. Marvellous. I couldn't see Viola and her harpsichord but acoustics are lovely in Blythburgh and I heard her beautifully. Heather Harper sang like an angel.

Viola is Continuo in *Idomeneo*; in *Prodigal Son* as assistant to Ben; in two or three concerts as duet partner with Ben; and as accompanist to Peter P. So she's got a very full plate. She looks better but still walks badly although she says her leg starts to *feel* better.

[1] Opera by Wolfgang Amadeus Mozart (1756–91).

12 June [1969]   Hyde Park Gardens

Darling Joyce,
    Tonio is eating better. I have to give it to him mouthful by mouthful.
I realised last night the food does go down better if it's placed in the
mouth. I can foresee this posing tiny problems – such as me never going
out to any meal ever again – but doubtless love will find a way. Such
as, feeding To at outlandish times. He goes driving with the policeman
this afternoon.
    Dilys goes for her hols tomorrow, to Yugoslavia, & Hilda has
suggested we should employ, in her absence, an ex-house-parlour *man*,
called Fred, who used to be, as she was, with Dirk Bogarde. He is tiny,
sixty-one, & very clean & neat & makes the beds & dusts with the best of
them. OK, I said, call in Fred![1]

[1] Christine and Marian had recently retired and been replaced by Hilda and Dilys. Louise
still came to iron.

12 June 1969   Aldeburgh

Darling Ginnie,
    Yesterday we both helped in the Festival Office for a couple of hours
in the morning, addressing envelopes for receipts of money sent in
for the Maltings fund. They have had a wonderful response and such
dear letters. One woman, either elderly or ill or both, or poor? wrote
to say she had never been to Aldeburgh or the Festival and didn't
suppose she ever would but wrote that she was so grateful for Ben's
music and Peter's singing that she was enclosing £3. The local Borough
Council, who are a bit jealous of the Maltings and haven't been very
co-operative, have relented and sent £1,000 interest free loan. There is
a lot of Love generating around the whole place.
    We drove home in an exquisite 'crepuscule'. A rosy sunset, deep
masses of cow parsley and white may trees.
    It is being a lovely time and I've hardly thought of Australia and all
that lies ahead.
    I feel *very* guilty at having all this freedom and fun while you are so
tied; and you are so marvellous about it, darling. I love you very much
and admire you *more than I can ever say*. All love, darling.

13 June [1969]   St Paul's

Darling Joyce,
    It has been such a perfect June day here I have become very

382

depressed. My role of companion-nurse stands starkly out in all its fathomless boredom when placed against the ephemeral loveliness of such a day. I am haunted by all the ghosts of those spinster saints who have dedicated their *lives* to looking after the old & feeble. Oh the tedium of it! How did they ever survive – without love to help – though I suppose there was Love?

As I slowly put strawberry mousse into Tony's mouth – 'Open wide ... that's it' the whole nostalgic thing of a summer country week-end makes me triste as anything. I ought to be thinking holy thoughts, I know, but I sometimes get quite bored with doing that too!!

The fire at Aldeburgh was caused by an electrical fault and insurance covered the cost of rebuilding the Maltings concert hall to the same design as in 1967. A further £80,000 was raised to improve fire precautions, wiring and the dressing rooms and the new concert hall was opened once again by the Queen in 1970.

Joyce, Reggie and William went to Australia via Hong Kong on a five-month tour. Tony could no longer speak or feed himself – and Virginia phoned Joyce often.

9 July 1969   Sydney

Darling Ginnie,

Poor Marianne Faithful[1] is desperately ill here. She and Mick Jagger[2] arrived in full fancy dress the day after we did, and my heart bleeds for her, virtually alone out here in a big hospital. If I didn't *have* to go to Adelaide today I'd have forced my way in to hold her hand and speak to her in a London voice. Poor little thing. The radio just says it's a collapse. I fear it may be to do with drugs, but whatever it is – *poor* little thing.

Sad to hear To was less well. Oh darling, this is when I wish I was nearer. But it is a very silly wish because there is no separation in Love and none of us are anywhere else. I do find this a help.

The T.V. interviews asked all the same questions about Mick Jagger-as-Ned-Kelly, nudity and permissiveness. Difficult finding new ways of answering same questions.

To the theatre to test mike. It worked like a dream and we were *so* relieved, when, suddenly, it picked up a police car. This cut me out entirely and the theatre was filled with a whine of a voice on one note describing a wanted man! So we are using the very good foot mikes. They always used to work pre 1963, so why not now?

I think of you, darling, *so* much. All love.

[1] Pop singer (1947–) and girlfriend of Mick Jagger. She had attempted suicide while on drugs.
[2] Lead singer of the Rolling Stones (1945–). In Australia to star in *Ned Kelly*, directed by Tony Richardson.

15 July [1969]   [Hyde Park Gardens]

Darling Joyce,
    Another horror of a day. Tony never speaking, just nudging
& waving. I really get *maddened* by this – and I know I shouldn't.
Altogether I'm perfectly fed up with everything this evening – but I shall
simmer down soon, & I'll get out my holy books & holy thoughts & take
my stays off.
    Aren't the young *pathetic* these days? Brian Jones on the bottom of
the swimming pool,[1] & now Marianne Faithful, & the Beatles – *they're*
a morality play if ever there was one, those bright bouncing boys with
their clean hair & joyful faces, now utterly corrupted by money – except
for George Harrison,[2] who seems to be quiet & reclusive.
    The heat wave continues. Yesterday it was 86° in London. Everybody
looks remarkably sweaty. Also nude! Extraordinary, when you think
back, even a few years, that now one hardly remarks on six out
of seven British workmen being shirtless in London – *all* builders &
roadmenders are stripped to the waist, bless'em – I rather like those
bronzed torsos, if YOUNG and not too hairy.
    I might go & sit on my balcony for a few mins prior to going to bed –
it's that hot. On the other hand, in my night attire, I might inflame the
passions of passers-by in the Bayswater Road . . .
    Love to you both, old socks
    from Grumpy Graham

[1] Guitarist with the Rolling Stones, drowned while on drugs.
[2] Lead guitarist with the Beatles.

Joyce, Virginia and 600 million other people watched as Americans Neil Armstrong
and Edwin Aldrin were the first men to walk on the Moon.

22 July 1969   Melbourne

Darling Ginnie,
    8.30 a.m. for a bedside interview with photograph. I'm all prinked up
in my pretty white and pale blue polka dotted bed jacket. By mercy of
heaven I *always* do my face *first* thing, so I wasn't caught 'underwears'!
    Oh the moon men! Were you as glued to T.V. and radio as all
Australia has been – is? For they aren't home and dry yet. I thought
the worst part was waiting for them to join up. It was only an hour ago
– 7.30 a.m. here – and I was doing my hair and face and praying as
the long pauses between announcements from Eagle and Houston came

through. It *is* a feat, isn't it. How could they *endure* it. Interesting that all the astronauts are believers, isn't it. Bet they were praying, too! The whole of yesterday was one long look and listen in. My morning radio tape was postponed till 1 o'clock and even then we could only tear ourselves away from the studio set after we'd seen the boys bouncing on the moon's gritty crust.

Darling, you sound *so* fed up and I don't blame you. It isn't right and it *mustn't* be accepted. *Please* consider a trained helper, a nurse. I know To may not like it at first. He'll get used to it. But it is wrong that you should have to cope with the *whole* weight. You have done *so* marvellously for *so* long and there are trained helpers who don't have the added problem of heart tugging in dealing with such a situation. *Please do this.*

23 July [1969]   Hyde Park Gardens

Darling Joyce,

It was WIZARD talking to you this morning. So clear I was tempted to dally & tell you what I was having for luncheon!

Did you see the moon landing? I saw it about four times yesterday, with that showy leg waving about, & those jumps, & the flag. And now we've got to get prepared for that splosh in the sea, I suppose.

One day last week there was a threatened Underground Strike & the Buck House Garden Party (so awful traffic jams). Anyway, Princess M & Lord Snowdon & party were going to a film premiere & dressed to the nines in tiaras & all, abandoned their cars at Knightsbridge & went by *Tube* to Leicester Square, & walked from there! *Wish* I'd seen them. I don't expect P.M. had ever been underground before, do you?

Must run now, darling heart.

25 July 1969   Melbourne

Darling Ginnie,

What a relief to have the moon boys safely down. It's been quite a week for them, hasn't it! How incredible it all is. One is already taking it for granted. Thank God it all worked so wonderfully. It really is a feat of endurance, of planning and of scientific know how. Whew!

Our chamber maid came to see my show and says it was all lovely and how did I *remember* it? I must have a real brain!

I write you very dull letters, darling, but they are bung full of love.
P.S. Very good notice in the *Sun*. Headline 'Re Joyce: we rejoice'.

5 August [1969]   Hyde Park Gardens

Darling Joyce,

You'll be pleased to hear that last night I decided it was nurse-time
– but in point of fact To has been *so* ill today my plans may have to
change. He can't swallow a thing, & he has this deep cough & looks
dreadful, poor darling.

A nurse comes tonight, so I shall feel more relaxed. I hope the nurse
is hefty as To can't turn over in bed without help.

10.15 Darling, To got much worse. I got Patrick [Woodcock] round
& To's got pneumonia. P asked me if I wanted him to give anti-biotics,
& I said oh *please* not. So I gave P a gin & tonic, then he went off to the
theatre with Joycie. I tried not to cry.

I fancy I MIGHT have a good cry when I get into bed – I believe it
might do me good – but again it might not. I am so longing for To to
drift away, & I feel his resistance must be low as can be, but I know,
too, that strong Thesiger heart . . .

Darling, I have put through a call to you – debated whether to do
so, but decided it was really *good* news, though you will be frustrated by
being so far away. But please don't be. I feel your thoughts constantly
with me – I really do. Victor has already rung twice this evening &
said, 'I hope you realise how wildly frustrating it is being a cripple at a
moment like this. I want to *run* to your side.' What's going to KILL me
is people being sweet & kind! Audrey has promised not to be!

6 August 1969   Melbourne

Darling Ginnie,

Did you know that 85% of Australians live in cities? Anyway they
are, for the most part, totally unaware of country life and they abuse it.
It's such a beautiful and strange country and this is the one flaw. But
it *always* is! man is a destroyer. He may build Versailles with one hand
but he pollutes rivers, makes dust bowls, and cuts down forests for the
Daily Mirror and *News of the World*. I suppose it is all part of the process
of finding out that materialism can't win happiness in the end? There is
a huge need for conservation in Australia because of the limited areas
where water supplies are available.

But I *love* it here.

I've been awarded The Nicest Listener radio award for the week
as the Nicest Person! Some small commercial station has this award
and my certificate came last night. The letter that came with it says
awards are given in recognition of 'extraordinary achievements, acts of
kindness, heroism and service to the public interest'. So there.

Darling, I think of you so often and so much.

6 August [1969]   Hyde Park Gardens

Joyce Darling,
    To is not really here. The day nurse is Australian & *far* taller even
than me, thin, beautiful face. Incredible what she did to To this morn –
washed him from top to toe & then gave him a manicure & a pedicure,
& then a shave. Pourquoi, je me demande?
    Dilys gave me an enormous hug & a kiss this morning. I had a nice
good cry over the gingerbread – unpleasant, somehow, not having
control, innit.

6 August 1969   Melbourne

Darling Ginnie,
    This is the second letter I've written to you today. We have just
spoken and I am with you in spirit as never before. I've been thinking
so strongly of man's freedom and I realise it is of To's freedom I am
really thinking. I got a sense of no beginning, no ending, only being.
    Of course, humanly, I'd like to be there with you, able to do chores
and telephonings, etc. But I know you are surrounded by love and
Audrey's support, and I am so grateful, darling, that you know what is
real and whole and always True. I salute you with all my heart. Love.
    Darling, I'm right there with you. All love.

7 August [1969]   Hyde Park Gardens

Darling Joyce,
    It's 5.30 & the sweet Australian nurse has shut the door of To's
room, herself inside, so perhaps he has died. When I came home
from lunching at Carlton Towers, she told me it was very near. I then
suddenly had a *terrific* crying jag – my bedroom – recovered, mopped
up, powdered nose, emerged from room, met Hilda in the kitchen, & the
whole thing started again!! Isn't crying peculiar? Why at one moment
& not another? Hilda & the nurse terribly sympathetic & loving, which
made it far worse – & was escorted, as though crippled, in here & given
the inevitable cupper.
    Then Hilda popped her head round the door & said 'I do hope I
haven't done wrong, madam, but I've rung Miss Butterworth, & she's
coming round.' *Dear*. I think I'd really rather cry alone really. However,
Audrey appeared, & was a help – just by being very ordinary & talking
about the Lesson & how to make raspberry tart.
    It is still radiant weather – what a summer!! In every sense!

Flowers from Violet Thesiger today – the others are holding their horses.

I do miss you, darling. Still, I feel you are near-*ish* . . . thought has no boundaries after all.

I forgot to say that this morning the man from Chubbs came to see about putting in alarms, & there was a macabre ballet of him, the nurse, Patrick, Hilda, Dilys & me weaving in & out of rooms & each other!! How *funny* life is!

7.45. Old To *still* hasn't died.

My tummy is *pretty* collywobbly I can tell you.

XXX Gin

8 August 1969   Melbourne

Darling Ginnie,

How odd are the ways of the human mind. I caught myself feeling guilty yesterday because I was having a good day at the new Art Centre here while you are going through this hell in England!

Of course Tony, or anyone else, has never been in *this* life anyway.

I wrote to Dick yesterday and I was saying that when I went through the blackest time of my otherwise pretty sunny life (and that was when my ma left my pa), I used to be so grateful to look out of the window and see people living ordinary lives while I seemed to be held in hell. I remember sitting in the train to Paris with my pa when we went in search of my ma and thinking as we sped past lightened windows: 'in *there* everything is light and cosy and safe'. And I envied it. What a change since I have learned that there is only one place of security and we are all, spiritually, contained in it, free and light and complete.

I send you great waves of support and love darling.

9 August [1969]   Hyde Park Gardens

Darling Joyce,

Tony is with us still!! Or at least *not* with us, but he is a bit of a skunk, I *must* say! I feel quieter today, less strained.

He's been 'very near the end' for days now, but his heart goes on & on. 'What a constitution!' says Patrick. Patrick says nearly all deaths are like this, & that really it's a *process*, like birth, & couldn't really be tampered with.

It's been a hot, *steaming* day. I went & had my hair washed & called in on Riem for a moment. 'Promise me, Ginnie,' she said, 'that you will break down.' 'I HAVE!' I answered crossly.

Do you know, love, I believe I'm going to find it quite bonny – when

I think of To – to see him as he was, when he was bonny. Isn't that nice? Even now I can disassociate To from his face & form of these past years, & see those blue eyes & that charm, & hear the things he said . . . but not, as it turns out, without crying a little!! So perhaps I'll stop doing it & watch some football instead.

I think I'll come & join you in the States in November. Is that a nice idea?

10 August 1969   Melbourne

Darling Ginnie,

We finished in high style with three mammoth performances. Please keep this to yourself because it isn't done to tell figures, but R. tells me I have *averaged* just under £1,000 a performance in Melbourne and am up 5,000 on all previous records! I get a nice comforting percentage of it and no complaints. The quality of the audience has been perceptive and warm and generous. I think there is a real hunger for Love today and it seems this aspect is to be found in the programme. And the sheer affection of the backstage staff when they said goodbye last night makes me know that this isn't ME they seem to love, it is Love itself. This can't be said to anyone but a C.S. but you know what I'm on about.

All my love darling Gin. Love, Love and Love.

After writing this letter, Joyce decided to phone Virginia. Tony had died a few minutes before aged sixty-three.

10 August [1969]   Hyde Park Gardens

Joyce Darling,

What LOVELY timing!! Hearing that dear old voice just when I need it most. Wish you could have transmitted that dear old face too. I dare say they'll get around to that one day hein?

Except for feeling appallingly loved, I haven't felt anything else very much today, which I don't quite understand – except, I suppose, that darling To died such a long time ago? Or I'm sort of punch-drunk? Maria & Patrick came quick as they could after my summons, & P wrote out the death certificate on the dining room table while I was eating the boiled egg Hilda insisted on cooking for me.

The undertakers came round at 10.30 & while I discussed the thisses & thats with a sombre gentleman in a black tie, To was quietly taken away. Then loads of phoning, to bonny Scotland mostly & endless cups of tea.

I spent the afternoon going through To's papers & two of his dressing table drawers, separating the pennies from the golf tees etc –

& wondered what one earth one does with ivory backed hairbrushes. I don't seem to mind a bit seeing his clothes. Maybe it's being aware of God's wholeness & inseparability. I sometimes forget that Science works! And what is so lovely is that again today, when I think of To, I see him as he was before he was ill – it's as if these terrible years have been swept aside, or really melted into the native nothingness.

Patrick has been *so* wonderful. I thought of giving him T's Leica camera.

In bed, 11 p.m. 10 August 1969   Sydney

Darling Virginia,

The more I think about To the more lovely things I remember about him in the good days. He was so gentle, so funny; so gloriously silly; and he had charm enough to call the birds off the trees. He was also *good*. I think of him at Parr's Cottage so long ago and of our tennis playing, à quatre. And what fun it was to dance with T. who was such a gay dancer. I remember *vividly* dancing with him on the first evening we met him. Here was the young man who somehow managed to lure Gin *out again* of an evening once she'd got home! I said something to draw him out about you and I remember he said you were very attractive, and I glowed and was *sure* there was something going on.

I remember his affection and his quickness and his funny nonsenses; and in particular the day I said I'd put a green pea up his nostril in the dining room at Cambridge Square and when I did it how he became absolutely *helpless* with giggles and just sat there shaking and gasping.

His total adoration of you needs no underlining. Oh darling you have been such a wonderful and loving wife and he was so very right to woo and win you. I hope so much that soon this long nightmare will vanish into thin air where it belongs and that you will find To as he was/is at the very peak of his best.

Your marriage has meant a great deal to your friends. I think there is a special benison that happy marriages confer on *other* people. 'Gin-and-To' became one word and it added up to felicity.

I hope these next weeks won't be too awful and the next few days not too agonising. You really have had to do with too much of distressing deaths, haven't you. All those nearest and dearest to you have seemed to go through *bad* times and I think your remarkable and constant poise is very wonderful. You are, 'bar chaff', a *real example*, my darling Gin. You really are.

Now, love, you must go easy and recover some of the quiet and peace. Living for yourself, as it were, will be odd and maybe hard. But you have great patience. In a way you've been alone for *so long*.

I was so glad to hear you this evening (morning for you) and *so* grateful that this long and gruesome vigil is over for you.

Oh *how* I wish I was there to be of some use as a nanny. That's a fact. Yes, I do.

I hope you got the cable. You get *all* our love which is considerable. My darling Ginny, I think of you with supporting prayers and love. Darling friend, I salute you, and I remember To with huge love.

12 August [1969]   Hyde Park Gardens

Darling Joyce,

I LOVED hearing you, too. But, Mrs Grenfell! considering my present financial plight – I have only got about £112,000 in one bank & a similar amount in another – I'll thank you not to reverse the charges when you call me from Australia!! 'Would you like to know the cost of this call?' the man said. 'Not very much,' I answered, 'as I didn't make it.'

'Well, we're charging you £6.' 'Are you indeed?' I said.

I'm only JOKING, love, I'd pay £600 to hear the old voice really.

I'm going down to St Paul's tomorrow alone to lay a few ghosts & see if there is any marmalade.

Have a gorgeous first night in Sydney, darling.

13 August 1969   Sydney

Darling Gin,

It was a *lovely* call last night (yesterday morning for you). I felt such a huge sense of gratitude for your serenity and great big bottomless well of joy for the knowledge that life *is* the continuity of all good.

I felt very close and it was blessed to know you were so supported not only by Love but by loving friends too.

Just off to do interviews and work with Bill at the Theatre. I send you so much love and joy.

The Thesiger family and their domestic staff came down from Scotland for the funeral.

14 August [1969]   Hyde Park Gardens

Darling Joyce,

Whew!! This really HAS been a day, darling!! But here I am, well survived, sitting with my shoes off in a mass of flowers & letters & holy cards, ALONE at last!!

Donny, Alec, Nina [Thesigers] & Mrs Ritchie got here at 7 a.m. off the train from Scotland. Then Cathie & Davis appeared & took Alec off for a drive. Gorgeous flowers kept on coming all morning – 40 or 50 'tributes' – so many we needed a 'floral hearse' – & I somehow couldn't *settle*.

The cremation was a bit of a shambles really – not only were we packed like sardines in the pews – but a great many men had to STAND. Wasn't it *awful*? An excellent clergyman, who read out my bits in a nice voice, & as if he meant them. For a while the front pew on the other side of the aisle was empty – and just at the last minute, evidently bludgeoned or pushed into it came Audrey & three of my holy pals. And I must say I rather adored having four holies sitting in a row just next to me. Alec broke down in the service, and cried all the way home too.

After tea at home we discovered Donny could get into To's shoes, *and* the jackets of his suits, so we had a terrific trying on bee. I've kept two *very* soft cashmere sweaters for Reg & also To's tweed overcoat, if he wants it.

In the staff sitting room there was the merriest wake going on – screams of demonic laughter.

And now everybody has gone. I have rung up Victor & told him 'all about it' – I find it irksome not to be able to tell To who was there & how greatly he was loved & how the chapel *overflowed*. And I did miss *you* darling, & that sweet Reg too. I had such an angelic letter from him.

I had a tremendous sense of *life* today – we all sang 'The King of Love my Shepherd is' at the tops of our voices, & there being lots of men they made a merry bellow – & like you at your Dad's funeral, I had to restrain myself from grinning! Isn't C.S. MARVELLOUS?

Darlingest Joyce – I love you dearly – feel your thoughts close pressed to me.

14 August 1969   Sydney

Darling Ginnie,

Do you know I see Tony, too, as he was at his very best. So that *is* good. And eternal, too.

The A.B.C. have just been here with a pile of equipment, two engineers, a producer and two interviewers. I taped *fifty* minutes off the cuff, talking about Life, touring, writing, comedy, Life, home, birds, Australia, Life, and what Ellis Bain called my 'philosophy'! For those with ears to hear it was patently clear what I was really talking about. For the rest it was probably just words.

Yesterday was geared to the gala charity performance and it was a very useful dress rehearsal for the official opening tonight when the critics come.

It was a very dressy Gala; a top social Event, with talk in the press on who was going to wear what! Dinners being given everywhere, so I must say I dreaded the whole thing because you know how a good dinner can deaden an audience. But all was well. They weren't all that bright but they were very civilised and well mannered, and in part 2 they forgot their hairdos and let rip and we ended in a *truly* gala spirit.

The entire thing was an *invitation* affair. You were invited to take seats and they sold out before they got to the end of their address list, so there has been some 'feeling' among those who didn't get a chance to pay £3. for a back seat! Social life it seems, really *still* operates here. Hairdressers were booked out all day and the whole thing struck me as quite dotty, but as it made a lot of money for the two charities, a Nursery School and a Nursery Training School, it was useful. They will each clear £1,000!

P.S. I thought of you at Golders at midnight our time and 3 o'clock your time, and I am very glad that is now over for you, love. Too late I realised I hadn't asked anyone to send flowers for us and I could have kicked myself. Darling, I am sorry about that. Very silly of me.

Today you are going to St. Paul's if all has gone according to plan, and you and Audrey can have a really quiet and restful time. How *good*.

15 August [1969]   St Paul's

Darling Joyce,

I had a real tear-jerker of a letter from you today – cried like anything over it, as it was so swell remembering how funny and attractive To was – the pea in the nose & the way he danced et al. You do write *good* – too good in this instance, luv! It's a letter I will always treasure – I think probably the darlingest I've ever had in my life. I'd like to read it again, but I can't yet, as I'd only blub again, & Audrey is sitting opposite me, stitching the top of a nightgown.

In the night I thought about To walking round Nymphenburg with a Baedeker in the top of his trousers because they were too large for him. I am rather appalled at my feeling of release & . . . well, *happiness*. It seems so dreadfully unnatural. And yet, goodness knows I loved him. And yet again, I suppose he had died for me ages ago – the moment you can't communicate with a person . . . oh well, I don't know! But you can see it rather *shocks* me!

I have a photograph of him on my writing table, in uniform, looking frightfully good-looking, & there's a beginning of a smile & every time

I look up I catch that look in his eye & can't *help* grinning back. It makes me feel a bit MAD – that's the only drawback – the being so happy. Elizabeth Basset, who came to tea said 'But it seems to follow up everything you've told me about C.S. I don't know why you're so surprised!' Nor do I know.

It has been what they call a 'long haul', hasn't it darling, but on the whole 10 years seem to have evaporated . . . still I *am* tired.

No sooner had Virginia buried Tony than her old friend Riem died of lung cancer and a month later Bungs (Catherine Kennedy) died of a heart attack while on a family picnic.

Although she hated Scotland, Virginia visited the Thesigers in Aberdeenshire. Alec's family and his domestic staff were relieved when she offered to take over legal and practical responsibility for her brother-in-law, now sixty-five years old.

In October Virginia and Joyce met up in New York for a month's holiday together before returning to London.

1970

Joyce did not publicise the fact that she was a Christian Scientist – she believed in spreading the word by example. Only her closest friends and relations knew, though she did not deny it if anyone asked. She often gave religious radio broadcasts and church sermons, but she concentrated on the universal truths of Christianity – Love, goodness, forgiveness – and avoided mentioning her own church. Then, when she was sixty years old, she decided that the time had come to tell the world that she was a Christian Scientist. She chose to do it on the BBC Radio 4 morning programme *Ten to Eight*, which later became *Thought for the Day*.

Soon after Tony died, Virginia bought a flat in Chelsea for her friend Audrey Butterworth, a Christian Science practitioner. During Tony's illness Virginia had missed the pleasures of leisurely sightseeing in foreign parts. She and Audrey took many holidays together.

20 January 1970   Elm Park Gardens

Darling Virginia,

Hope your skies are as blue as this paper. Ours are navy blue (it's dark: see). It is good to think of you congenially holidaying abroad, although frankly I miss you and feel funny not talking to you on the telephone.

Encouraging results – or rather reactions to the broadcast have come in including a call from the Librarian in the City R.R.[1] yesterday afternoon to tell me a man had come in and said he and his wife had always enjoyed my broadcasts at 10 to 8 and now they knew what it was all about and he wanted to know more. I feel so grateful if it reached *anyone*, and so this is a little warm contact with the outside as it were. The faithful write in generously and at the A.G.M. last night I had many *grateful* little bits handed on. I'm surprised at the number who say how *courageous* it was to do it when all I feel is a sense of gratitude that somehow takes care of all those previous faint fears. I think things happen at the *right time* if one is being honest and trusting.

Two anti-C.S. letters – a Jehovah's Witness and a cross C. of E.[2] lady full of arrogance and references to blood and lambs . . . Oh and one crackpot, on a p.c., who believes I'm a communist and wish to destroy civilisation.

I wrote 32 pieces of mail yesterday, many on p.c.s. but quite a lot fairly full letters.

[1] Christian Science Reading Room.
[2] Church of England.

26 January [1970]   St Paul
                                                           South of France

Darling Joyce,

Lully letter awaiting here. You sounded gay & rather enjoying your correspondence re the broadcast – SIN included!

Audrey is busy with her holy books.

Let me tell you that *I* once went on the Giant Dipper at Wembley with Prince Chichibu – together we were, screaming, & he, as I remember it, in a bowler hat! Is he the Emperor now, do you imagine?[1]

Last night, after supper, we put on a record that you and I made! Round about 1946 I should say! Do you remember it? I wrote a carol, with funny words, & on the other side there's 'I'm in love with a gentleman'! I'd clean forgotten its existence, it was such a droll experience – you sang DIVINELY darling – not that you don't *now*, but I'd forgotten you did *then*. It seems we made it in some studio in Cavendish Square. If cross-questioned by the Gestapo I'd have remembered a booth in Bond Street! I'm sure we did something in one.[2]

[1] Prince Yasuhito Chichibu-no-miya was the second son of Emperor Yoshihito of Japan (1879–1926). He studied in England from 1925 to 1927 and died aged fifty-one in 1953.
[2] Records could be cut in recording booths, rather like modern photograph booths.

Joyce was about to set off with a new solo show for charities with William and Diana when Apollo 13 was launched. The next day the astronauts – John Swigert, James Lovell and Fred Haise – were in trouble and the planned Moon landing was abandoned. The whole world waited to see if they would survive the journey back to Earth.

16 April 1970   Elm Park Gardens

Darling Virginia,

The astronauts: golly. One is conscious of the spiritual being quite
unconnected with all those in spite of one's heartfelt compassion and
agony for all those who love them, as well as for the men themselves.
'No place' – no thing – only Mind. It includes space of course. I miss
you when all this kind of thing exercises me so. Long to talk to
those I love.

This morning Viola rang up and with the utmost difficulty and in
such a heavy disguise virtually asked me to set about finding out
about C.S.[1] I felt quite breathless. She said she couldn't understand
any of it – she'd have to be taught and guided by a teacher, etc, etc.
I said I thought it would best help to read the book first and with an
open mind. Pause. Quietly she said 'I will try'. I said I'd try to think of
the right practitioner for her to go and talk to. It is such an infinitely
precious moment, this, and I feel the delicacy most firmly. Protect it,
love. It is such a step forward.

Viola said 'Perhaps Ginnie may know someone.' If you felt like
ringing her up in the ordinary way – maybe suggest lunch?

---

[1] During 1969 Viola Tunnard had had difficulty walking and began playing wrong notes
on the piano. This was later diagnosed as Motor Neurone Disease, a rare, incurable
degenerative disease. She was unable to continue working, but hoped to be able to coach
musicians.

17 April [1970]   Brighton

Darling Joyce,

I'm not at all certain where the precise danger lies for the astronauts.
I *think* they are going to have to rely on the baby bit of space ship, the
landing bit, for electricity to get them home? Oh dear.

I wonder if there's a phone by your bed. I better ring Reg . . .
no reply; he must be dining with a blonde. I'll try & get him in the
morning.

18 April 1970   Hastings

Darling Ginnie,

The relief of that landing! Isn't it marvellous. There was a T.V. in the
White Rock Pavilion but I was half made up when I heard about it so
I stayed where I was and prayed, while Bill and Diana watched it all
with awe. When I went on stage I had a friendly welcome and I said
that it was good to be back at the Pavilion (it was) but before we began

the show I felt I wanted to add my gratitude to theirs for the wonderful news of the safe landing, and we *all* clapped!

I think of the astronauts returning to their families and rejoice. What an episode. I think it is a very difficult problem knowing whether to go on pouring money into what seems to me a pointless but politically important project (if the U.S.A. don't do it the U.S.S.R. will), or do something about people – housing, schools, integration. It all takes money. I see the drive behind wanting to go with the space programme but it does seem so silly. Just because it's there they have to go and touch the moon.

20 April 1970   Canterbury

Darling Virginia,

It was a *very* gala show. One of the winged ones. The Marlowe is an old movie house so it's long and narrow with a gallery climbing to the roof, but good for sound. John and Alison Ward[1] sat on a bench (padded) in the wings and professed they'd enjoyed it more from there. Can't believe it. Except when I was young and used to sit in the wings to watch Ruth [Draper] there was a sort of added magic in being so near: almost part of the thing.

It seems Aunt Nancy [Astor] was responsible for First Church here. Gave it to them. Have you ever been there? It is housed in a 12th century Dominican priory or abbey or some such. It sits on the edge of the river and is impossible to find. Hidden, it is, in a derelict bit of the City.

The magnificent crypt is ice cold and empty. The impression was of very senior citizens and a twenty year old usher in a green mini skirt and white lace tights. The hymns were murmured. I had to reign in my singing but couldn't resist a tenor part in the last verse of the final hymn. I thought: we have the one answer to today's problems and we aren't reaching people with it. This set up, so archaic to *look* at, couldn't really appeal to anyone unless they were desperate and listening with all their ears, eyes and heart. But what is the answer? They were all so happy and proud of the white elephant Aunt N. crushed them with!

[1] Watercolour artist and member of the Royal Academy, and his wife, mother of six. The Grenfells commissioned him to paint many of their favourite views and people.

21 April 1970   Robin Hood Hotel
                                               Newark-on-Trent
                                               Notts

Gin Darling,

After talking to you I went into the very warm and cosy T.V. lounge
to wait for Diana and I caught Benny Hill[1] on I.T.V. He had a blonde
wig and false teeth and was *very* funny indeed doing the Catherine
Boyle job on a Eurovision song contest, talking to the competing
countries. 'Come in France. Entre Frornce.' And in came Germany. I
find him funny, do you? At one moment a verra Scots voice came on
saying: 'Grreat Brritain ten votes, Gairmanny ten votes, etc. etc.' And
then Benny Hill: 'Thank you Northern Ireland.' It was simple fun but he
has style and this flourish that make it work for me.

Heaven knows what tonight will be like in the big de Montford Hall
set in a park in Leicester. It wasn't fun to play in five or six years ago.
This one is for the Royal Commonwealth Society for the Blind and they
usually do a very good job of organising, so let's hope. They get mayor
and civic dignitaries and make an Occasion. We cleared £1,400 at
Stratford-on-Avon in 1968, enough to build and equip an eye clinic for
Nigeria.

In 1949 or 1950 I was there for *Penny Plain* and it was remarkably
uninspiring, so it must be *loved*.

Must pack. All love. See you Thursday.

[1] British vaudeville comedian (1925–92).

6 May [1970]   London

Darling Joyce,

I'm writing to you in BED – which is a pretty peculiar state of affairs.
I'm propped up on a veritable invalid's mound of pillows – don't know
how you can write so much in bed; it's SO uncomfortable!

Vic not too well today – but in marvellous spirits! We had a cosy
lunch and talked about Carol Channing, about old age & friendship, &
the debs of 1928, which was when I came out. I also did a tremendous
'ziggy' dance to see if my new toupé would stay on! Well, it stayed *on*,
but heeled right over to one side.

8 May 1970   Greenway Hotel
                                                  Shurdington
                                                  Glos

Darling Virginia,

Thank you for a good letter. Wonder why you find writing in bed is uncomfortable. It could be that you put your knees up and try to write on them? As an expert this is how I do it. Put something flat, such as Noël's *Song Book*, against your upper leg with knee slightly bent. This makes a sort of desk, see. If you haven't got Noël's *Song Book* with you – and I don't advise it, it weighs a ton – you must get something flat and wide instead. A blotter. An upturned tray. I write from a semi-supine position with lots of lovely pillows surrounding me as it were, rather than pushing me from the back. In this position writing letters to A Friend is nothing but *plaisir*.

I started learning some of Noël's songs from the Aldeburgh programme. *So* much to learn. *So* many tricky verses. And his ranges are really very tough. Top G down to low Ab in one song. Bill is helping me select keys I *can* manage.

A nice couple of fans said it was so interesting to learn that I was a C.S.; and they said it with real interest and not as a criticism! They were *not* C.Ss.

13 May [1970]   Hyde Park Gardens

Darling Joyce,

I WAS sorry to miss you this morning.

I dined with Patrick [Woodcock] last night. He'd dined the evening before with John Gielgud and Joycie [Carey]. In the middle Patrick was wanted on the telephone. Of course he thought it was an urgent call for help, but it turned out to be L.P. Hartley,[1] very drunk, wishing to find out if Patrick had read about the locusts that are being bred to eat up the grass at Lords! P said he tried, as the others politely murmured, to make his replies sound medical . . . 'That doesn't sound too good . . . m'm . . . I shouldn't let it worry you . . . etc.'!

I've been to the ballet with Laurier [Lister] tonight. He sent you much love and deplored the fact he never sees you. He is extremely well, & so is Max [Adrian].

---

[1] Leslie Poles Hartley (1895–1972), British novelist, best known for *The Go-Between*.

Joyce planned another six-week tour of America with William and Diana but in a year the concert agent had only managed to book five concerts.

20 May 1970   Cumberland

Darling Virginia,

Ta for telephoning. Sorry I was still in bed. Since then a slow burn of ire over the American tour has grown, and I rang up Aubrey Blackburn who was equally astonished by the ineptness of the plan. I doubt if anything can be found at this late stage, but we are exploring. I did some work about the continuity of good; harmony being established.

As you know, my concern really isn't for me. I'm quite glad of a brief tour, but for Diana and Bill who (a) love it, (b) want it as a nice fat slab of income.

20 May [1970]   Hyde Park Gardens

Darling Joyce,

Good news. We are changing 'Friends of the Poor' to 'Friends of the Elderly'. At last! Enfin!! Not a frightfully stimulating letter heading, but we HAVE to say what we do, & we want to keep friends. I wanted 'Friends of the Elderly and Gentle', but was laughed out of court! Perhaps rightly. In brackets underneath will be (Formerly Friends of the Poor and Gentlefolk's Help). We have to bring in this old class distinction as we get our money almost entirely from the genteel, who feel 'there, but for the grace of God go I'. We hope, in a few years time to drop the Gentlefolk – it being presumed that there won't be any left!!

My love to old Pascoe please.

Saturday night, 23 May 1970   Llanarmon

Darling Virginia,

So glad F.P. will be F.E. Good idea.

I've just read the Lesson and after reading that bit about 'supernal freshness' and its implication of eternal youth I looked up and saw myself in the mirror opposite – tousled, specs on nose and an air of abandoned concentration that was so funny I laughed! I did NOT look either fresh or youthful, only *frubsy* and retired! But inside . . . oh that's different. Daisy fresh and so young. I'll do my face now, just to help.

I must either overcome the fantasy that tea keeps me awake or not have it. I could not get to sleep and R snored and snored, and when, finally, I had to go along the passage, he said he couldn't get to sleep either, and I laffed and laffed. You never heard such trumpetings.

[June 1970]   Hyde Park Gardens

Joyce Darling,

Kay [Hammond] has just been to lunch: very quiet & nice. But I had a difficult moment (one I've had before) when she said 'Really, Victor's finances intrigue me. How can he have enough money to live the way he does?' I was very good. I didn't let even the faintest look come into my eye. I said 'Well, I don't know: I always imagine Dick helps him enormously.' The trouble about saying this so vaguely is that of course I would know, probably, about V's financial set up. Anyways, I was completely dead pan, and then got off the subject!

But while we are on it: *Honest* old Vic has discovered my bank has paid him £146 odd in June instead of £66.17.6. 'You were an idiot to tell me!' I said. 'I would never have noticed!' I never think Banks make mistakes, do you? But I believe they *do* & one ought to keep more of an eye on them. Shan't, I don't expect!

The rebuilt Maltings concert hall at Aldeburgh was finished and Joyce was invited to perform a special opening concert of Noël Coward's songs.

3 June 1970 Evening   Elm Park Gardens

Darling Ginnie,

I went to work with Cleo[1] and Ben Luxon[2] at Richard Rod. Ben's.[3] The time was for 2.30, but found Richard *just* starting to make an omelette for Cleo and himself. Ben turned up about 3. I had said I had to leave at 5 (and did) but it wasn't very tidy, I thought, and no sort of suggestion that it was odd! I know I am too time conscious, but it was a little trying. But I was unruffled and we got a lot of good work done. Lots of practice needed.

Dick is avid for news about Cleo Laine. She had on a khaki Victorian cotton print (like early American cotton chintz) maxi dress with a green chiffon scarf, a tortoiseshell belt, and red patent leather boots! She now wears her hair à L'Afrique. Fuzzy. And she is *so* pretty.

I will have to hold the book of songs as I simply cannot guarantee to be word perfect in *fourteen* songs. Richard suggests that Cleo Laine and I should wear contrasting kaftans. Nice idea. Who will design? Where obtain? The only kaftan I've got is a very old and heavenly coloured-roses on emerald and veridian green leaves.

[1] Cleo Laine (1927–), British jazz singer.
[2] British singer (1937–).
[3] Richard Rodney Bennett, musician and composer (1937–).

5 June 1970   Aldeburgh

Darling Virginia,
  England at its perfect best. Suffolk is so pleasing to me; so is Essex,
and those little villages with pink and pale yellow washed houses
standing in gardens with peonies bursting into ruby red and pink and
white, and wisteria and laburnum drips. Chestnut trees can never have
had a heavier weight of candles. And not a cloud in the sky.
  The election news is a tremendous boring thing with which we've
got to live, I suppose. Wedgwood Benn's outburst against Powell is the
main topic on the air today.[1] It was violent and not at all adult. I'm
allergic to both Powell and Benn because they are unappetising to look
at as well as explosive. But I suppose they must be Loved! It is a BORE,
and if only they'd get together – Labour pool their real concern for the
quality of the life we are to live and the Tories to liberate commerce but
not allow commercial radio! I don't trust Tories, as you know! I don't
trust Orrible Arold, but I do like quite a lot of the others. And I think
their values are more real. Enough.[2]
  Viola is staying with very nice people called Cowan, who have
a house in Crabbe Street, Aldeburgh.[3] She was walking very badly.
Seemed to be all right but thinnish.
  Today to the Maltings to see the Queen and hear Ben conduct his
concert. It is lovely to be here again. We both start beaming as we get
into East Anglia and particularly in June for the Festival.
  Peggy Ashcroft arrived and we sat with her in the sun for a time.
She is astonishingly young looking for 63.

[1] Tony Benn (1925–) Labour MP, and Enoch Powell (1912–) Conservative MP.
[2] Joyce had voted for all three political parties, depending on their policies at the time.
[3] Viola stayed with Jean and Christopher Cowan until she died.

8 June [1970]   Bad Schachen
                                                              Austria

Darling Joyce,
  Audrey took me for a drive and I realise I am terribly nervous
driving with anybody else these days. It seems to have got worse since
Tony drove so erratically at the end of his days, though I've always
been rather curly-toed. Poor Audrey, who has been driving since she
was 16, decided this must be her first & last drive with me as passenger
– my oohs & ahs & flinchings quite unnerved her!
  I suppose B.B. and P.P. will mind about E.M. Forster? I hadn't

realised he'd only written *five* books. I protest – there is too much dying going on.

10 June 1970   Aldeburgh

Darling Virginia,

Cleo, in a camel hair trouser suit and white top, was at the Jubilee Hall, joined by Ben Luxon and our producer. Hard work was done plotting moves and getting used to the stage. Both Ben and Cleo do their thing so beautifully. His voice is a joy to hear and if he will stop *acting* the funny numbers a little and let them happen he'll be very good. Her singing of City and 20th Century Blues is marvellous. This is where Richard R.B. comes into his own with ingenious jazz accompanyings, and the result of this fusion with her blues singing is very enjoyable.

I am learning to move and sing at the same time. Not very easy but I *can*! When in doubt I sing in Yugoslav, as Liz Welch always used to describe her gobbledy gook in memory lapses!

Cleo is so pretty and we both like her very much. There is a quiet centre in her and a gentleness. And she is a real artist. She also loves her John Dankworth[1] very much, and her son and daughter. He is a *charmer*. They are a most attractive pair, very dear and real. She and I had an interesting conversation about racialism. She is very 'realistic' about her situation and quite without any chip. She said too much fuss is made about colour and 'difference' and if it could be let alone it would happen naturally that people would get to *know* each other as people and that is the way to heal this separation and fear. She is pale and only faintly negroid in appearance. Her hair is entirely African, but her eyes are light grey green, her mouth sensitive and wide, and she seems to me to be enchanting and funny and intelligent (very) and gay and warm. You'd like her. I now want to go to Ronnie Scott's[2] and hear her and J.D. do their music. It means sitting up *so* late though.

[1] Jazz musician and composer (1927–), Cleo Laine's husband.
[2] Jazz club in Soho, London.

12 June [1970]   Bad Schachen

Darling Joyce,

Wotcher think of the Election? Sounds a mixture of yahoo-ism & complete apathy. Can't make out whether to believe the Tories, who say things are ghastly, or Mr Callaghan who says they're OK. Yet I can't think owing £1600 million can be healthy, hein? By the way, Audrey was v. thrilled because her secretary sent her an absentee voter's card on which it was written that in case of blindness etc., a certificate must be got from a 'doctor or a Christian Science practitioner'. She thought that was a real break-through.

14 June 1970   Aldeburgh

Darling Virginia,

Cleo's singing of 'Chase me Charlie' stopped the show and justifiably. She's very gay and funny in it and adds all the sparkle it needs. Ben Luxon pulled off all his numbers wonderfully well. We had a big ovation, and I think lots of it is due to Colin Graham. Richard Rodney Bennett provided style and quality with his arrangements. Cleo's bright magenta and scarlet all over brocade-like cotton Kaftan was becoming and gay, and my bright turquoise and emerald stands up to it well.

I can see, egoist that I am, that I'd get very bored doing this sort of thing when I know that I *can* do better! But it is interesting to work with other people and good for one not to be centre at all times. But frustrating in a way and I don't think very rewarding.

I rang Viola last night and found her in a very low state, 'What am I going to do?' This sort of line from that stoic, strong character was terribly moving. She is in despair and feels poorly . . . It was so difficult not to call out – 'None of this is true, darling'. I refrained! She is terribly worried about her future in *every* way. I said: 'We will take care of your problems: R. will help you sort out the business side.'

16 July [1970]   Bellabeg House

Darling Joyce,

Yesterday was spent entirely in talking – to Mrs Ritchie, Bridget, Cathie, & her ma, Helen the gardener's wife. But they are dear people, & *gosh*, am I lucky! I might have spent all these years co-ercing Spaniards to look after Alec!

Watched telly. How dour [David] Frost was, interviewing Tennessee Williams.[1] How can you ask anyone what they think *love* is, & expect a satisfactory answer! Thinking of love, can you understand how sometimes I found To's complete absorption in me a burden? He used to say 'You are my life', & it sounds so lovely, but in fact imposed a heavy responsibility. I would have loved him to have had, like Reg, a bit of life of his own, to have stopped off at the Turf, or a picture gallery on his way home from work, & to have argued sometimes, or even suggested plans for summer hols. I wonder if it was my fault he was so dependent on me. Probably was. I daresay if I'd been a frail little flower he would have made all the decisions. What a darling he was – and so gay &

funny & utterly loveable. I'm not really being retrospectively critical as *no* gal could *ever* have had a better husband.

Alec looks extremely well – he has gone forth on his bike with a grocery order.

¹American playwright (1911–82), wrote *A Streetcar Named Desire*.

17 July 1970   Elm Park Gardens

Darling Virginia,

Must tell you how extraordinary is the power of Love – quite unknowingly. I went into Peter Yapps searching for a special shoe Viola wants to re-order. Sloane Street Branch. I was served by a young girl who said she loved my sketches and we had a chatty surface level conversation and no more. Next evening at church she came up to me and said: 'I can't tell you what you did for me in the shop yesterday simply by your friendly loving presence. Chaos has been reigning and I was in despair, ready to give in my notice. I had no time to get at my Bible (which I keep at the shop), but you brought with you such strength of Love and calm that I was quite healed.' Did you ever. She is a member of your church but visits mine sometimes.

18 July [1970]   Bellabeg House

Darling Joyce,

Everybody's gone to bed. It is just 9.30. Broad daylight too. Alec & I watched a bit of *It's a knock-out* – he laughed like a drain until it became his bedtime when, Cinderella-ish, he left – in the middle of a laugh. Isn't it curious the way routine makes him feel so safe?

Ta for yours love. You MUST start your auto-biography soon, on account you make characters so vivid. But I suppose 'doing' live people will be tricky?

I can see how difficult it must be coping with Viola's views on C.S. – intellectual argument always *sounds* so rational, & one's own, fey to the point of madness! And V. can be quite dogmatic can't she.

19 July 1970   Elm Park Gardens

Darling Virginia,

Aren't friends lovely to have. I start with you who are more than a friend for you've been there so long and so steadily that you can't be categorised. You are you!! I feel *so* rich in my friends. Not all are easy.

I think of Viola, D. and Vic! But *so* dear and so special and so worth the energy one needs to fit in with their idiosyncrasies.

There is no doubt about it – like everything else – one has to work at friendship, but the work is a joy and so rewarding. I always think it is the most rewarding of all human activities and it is of one's own choosing – or good fortune!

To answer your letter of July 16. I didn't see Tennessee Williams because of R's passion for Morecambe & Wise, but I've gone off Frost just now though I'm sure he'll do better again and forget *'fantastic'*!

Yes I *can* understand how you sometimes felt T's complete absorption in you a burden because there have been times when I shared this view although there has come about a lovely and increasing independence in R. that I cherish and rejoice in. I think the reason one doesn't like it is because it isn't, basically, what love is about. Love only really works between two people when both are revolving perfectly on their own individual axis and this makes the pattern into one large revolution. If one leans the structure wobbles.

I don't think it was your fault that T. was a leaner. I think he'd always been and he retained his small boy need of support instead of growing on his own feet. *Very* endearing and very understandable, but not *your* fault. Had he been tougher and more independent he mightn't have appealed to you. And, as you say, he was so enormously loveable and funny and gay and attractive and companionable. Human beings seem to be very mixed, don't they, and it's part of their charm.

I don't know how one weans a husband from loving and leaning too much. In my case the adversity of war separation and my own overseas experience and attractions forced the issue and have proved to be a blessing. A real one. I take *no* credit for it. I am grateful for it because R's independence is precious to me and very strong, and it in no way diminishes our love for each other. That is stronger than ever and increasingly wonderful.

It's another lovely morning after a misty start. The kind of day I remember from my childhood summers. Delicious scent of hot hay, hot pine trees. Bees. Ditches with poppies and toad flax and chicory in them. Lazy feeling days.

I've got ten concerts to do in England before we do the six in America.

Joyce flew to New York to appear on the *Dick Cavett Show* and the *David Frost Show*, followed by a short tour with William and Diana. She stayed with her old friend Milly Natwick (1905–94), an American film actress who played eccentrics.

13 October 1970   Hyde Park Gardens

Darling Joyce,
    Longing to hear how New York & its dear ones are faring.
    This afternoon I went to the Kinetic Exhibition at the Hayward
Gallery – highly recommended by Dick. So I have been groping about in
the dark with a lot of teen-agers with flashing lights, & mobile pieces of
steel, and distorting mirrors, & weird noises, & lots & lots of nails stuck
into circles whirling round us! Frankly I only found two things that I
thought had *anything* to do with Art, but then I am not really artistic &
I *know* it – so I won't be insulted. later
    I've had *such* a happy evening with your old man. We ate a socking
meal at the Savoy and then we dallied tremendously in the main hall
of the Savoy proper till the play. Which is very funny – almost entirely
because Alastair Sim is so divine. The audience was full of peers –
Harcourt, Rothermere, Leicester, Stockdale. Reg & I decided that when
they'd run through all the PLUs[1] – which won't take long these days –
the play would collapse, overnight!

[1] People Like Us.

13 October 1970   At Milly's, New York

Darling Virginia,
    Wednesday I see a man from the *David Frost Show* to discuss what
I do on *that*. I *think* I'll do 'Old Girls' School Reunion' tonight and
'Nursery School' for Friday Frost. There is chat, too.
    Birds are in transit south and New York is a migratory route, so
birders are all eyes just now. Milly saw a green humming bird last
week! Makes New York much nicer to know this can happen. Haven't
seen many midi skirts here yet. And no maxis. All is hip and thigh. All
love darling. Write soon.

14 October [1970]   London

Darling Joyce,
    Audrey & I have just been watching you doing your music quiz[1]
& you were wearing a green dress I've *never* seen. You were all very
clever again – the only one I twigged which you lot didn't was Norma
– on account I've got the record. *Why* does Robin Ray[2] know the opus
number of every bit of Beethoven? It's very impressive.

[1] *Face the Music*, on BBC 2, presented by Joseph Cooper, was an unusual panel game in

that it had no scores and no teams. The panel of one woman and two men, such as Joyce, Richard Baker and David Attenborough, answered questions on classical music. It began as a radio programme *Call The Tune* in 1956 with Joyce and Stephen Potter.
[2] British broadcaster and journalist, son of actor Ted Ray.

14 October 1970   New York

Darling Virginia,

The *Dick Cavett Show* last night was quite a time. Black Jazz players made an organised protest and stopped the show! Trevor Howard was in it – tight. But I was praying like mad and I was protected in that none of this happened until I'd *done* my bit and it was all neatly in the bag.

All seem pleased except me: because I *know* I *overdid* the 'Old Girls' School Reunion' and I *can* do it better than that.

15 October [1970]   London

Darling Joyce,

I had a terrible drama this morning!! Went out early to Selfridges, the bank, Marks & Sparks & when I returned home laden with things, NO BAG!! I had just cashed a cheque for Viola (£30) and me (£20), and it held my whole LIFE. I borrowed ten shillings from Hilda, hurled myself into Bayswater Road, couldn't get a taxi, *or* a bus, so ran, mac flapping towards Marble Arch. I eventually got a bus & pulled myself together & prayed – knowing all God's ideas were honest & that there was nowhere for a bag to go except in divine Mind – and THERE it was, sitting on the counter at M&S! It was surrounded by trade, women buying & selling, passing their purchases over its brown body, & it must have been there a good hour. Isn't God wonderful?

After this hair-raising interlude I visited Douro Place[1] & spoke of Christmas presents. Bridget has bought a record player, & asked for two records – one *The Sound of Music*, and the other, 'Gilbert & Sullivan, madam, *Pinafore*. But I *would* like it sung in English, please.'

[1] London home of Alec Thesiger.

15 October 1970   Greenwich

Darling Virginia,

I dressed myself in my purple stage dress ready to be collected. D. Frost sent a limousine and off I sailed with Lionel Larner, my agent. It was all far better organised than the *D. Cavett Show* – British influence?!

I was on first. Trevor Howard, again, on second, and I stayed on while he talked. D. Frost was very nice to me; not adulatory or smarmy and quiet and considered and *amused*.

The audience was *very* welcoming and when David asked me about the Nursery School sketches, there was recognition and applause and an 'I remember' feeling! I was amazed. Anyway I had a very long session, didn't do a monologue but quoted from various characters, and it was relaxed and *felt* all right.

David has asked me to come back again while I'm in N.Y. and I will. He was very friendly and is intelligent and has it more or less in proportion I think. He said: 'It is all going *amazingly* well', with a slight look of pleased surprise. He is bigger than I'd remembered – quite tall and heavy. He looks less nervous and pale than before. How can he endure the life I can't imagine. Trevor was sober, attractive, and did well this time.

Virginia and Audrey went to Stratford-upon-Avon to see Shakespeare's *A Midsummer Night's Dream*, directed by Peter Brook.

October 25 [1970]   Hyde Park Gardens

Darling Joyce,
The play last night at Stratford was quite *extraordinary* – like a clean, brilliant *Hair*,[1] with Oberon & Puck on trapezes, the trees a forest of tortured wire, Titania's bed a huge red ostrich feather, the rest of the scenery simply plain dead white walls topped with a parapet along which romped fairies in grey trousers & silver shirts. Ladders, fire crackers, orchestra, a Japanese juggler, lots of paper plates & Christmas decorations whizzing through the air – absolutely CRAZY, and yet very stimulating. Mercifully the text is fairly well untampered with. Why do you think Bottom, instead of having an ass's head, was changed into Mickey Mouse? It was ridiculous when he brayed! All the same it was quite a romp, & you couldn't help being galvanised, there was so *much* going on, one was sort of *roused*.

[1] The first British musical after theatre censorship was repealed in 1968, it had naked actors.

1 November [1970]   London

Darling Joyce,
Well, I've made it!! Unbelievably incredibly, amazingly, I'm 60! The sun came out especially to see how I was looking, the golden leaves

danced for my benefit, & Hilda sent me a card of a mermaid kissing a fish! She also gave me a hot water bottle in a camel hair coat; Audrey produced a gorgeous shantung scarf, Vic some soap, & YOU a kettle. It *is* such a joy, this kettle. TA.

I rang Viola to ask if I could stock up her larder, as I am going to Fortnum's anyway. She allowed me to get something to hot up for lunch. She says her legs are functioning better. And she's got a rush job on with a Scandinavian opera − writing the words under the right notes. 'Drop the Tippett' they said 'and do this by Sunday.' So I feel she feels *needed*.

The Fire Brigade are very despondent about Guy Fawkes night as they think it inevitable that the rubbish dumps will be lit. They are praying for pelting rain. In the meantime the dumps grow, the streets are filthy, & one definitely meets *smells*. The strike's been on about six weeks now, & some of the rubbish has been moved by private contractors & even the army. But lordy, today with all the paper & leaves swooshing round one's head in Mary Bakers [eddies], it was vile.[1]

I wish you'd come HOME. Why are you hanging about like this?

[1] The dustbin men's strike ended five days later, after a settlement of £2 extra pay a week and three weeks' holiday.

6 November 1970   At Milly's

Darling Virginia,

I did the *Frost Show* again last night and it was an anti-climax. Wish I hadn't yielded to flattery! First of all Frost was tired and not at all on the ball. He'd been to Boston *for the day* − done an appearance on the *Johnny Carson Show* at 6.30, and was thirty minutes late for his own programme. He had too many guests and we really didn't gel much − Harry Secombe,[1] Norman Wisdom,[2] Charles Aznavour,[3] a man called Kosh who wrote that script Orson Welles did on radio in 1939 about Martians landing here that threw the whole country into a panic[4] − and me. So no one had much time and I felt none of it got off the ground. Norman wasn't very good and he and I told about how we made the record of Narcissus and tried to illustrate but it didn't *really* work. Also the audience was of a dullness. Largely female − a whole row of hostesses in orange uniforms from an unknown airline filling the front row and not getting any of the points. Secombe, who is a nice man, sang three songs with rising finishes and got good applause, as tenors always do.

Aznavour pitied himself interminably, addressing a baby daughter who is going to grow up and leave him for a stranger, etc. etc.

Humourless and cloying and *very* skilled. He is six inches high. Like a small friendly insect. The only interesting thing was Kosh. I got in a few brief voices, reported on my tour. It was boring and uncoordinated.

I felt disgruntled, old spoilt brat that I am.

[1] Welsh comedy actor and singer (1921–).
[2] British comedy film actor (1920–).
[3] Armenian-American singer and film actor (1924–).
[4] Based on *War of the Worlds* by H.G. Wells. Orson Welles's production was so convincing that listeners believed that aliens really had landed on Earth.

[10] November [1970]   Hyde Park Gardens

Darling Joyce,

I've just been watching you in *Blue Murder at St Trinian's!*[1] Such a touching, nay heart-breaking policewoman! *Very* good you are in it – & oh boy, do you look young!!

Incidentally, Audrey met Elizabeth Winn[2] at her hairdressers yesterday, and E told her the Westminsters now have your Aunt Nancy's flat but they can't keep anybody to look after them as it is haunted! Apparently, the cushions are always on the floor in the morning and Aunt N's laugh can be heard ringing out at all hours. Isn't it BIZARRE? Audrey says she'd like to hear Aunt N's laugh again, but it could be spooky, all on its own, hein?

[1] Made in 1957.
[2] Cousin of Joyce. Audrey had been Nancy Astor's Christian Science practitioner.

1971

7 June 1971   Aldeburgh

Darling Virginia,

Yesterday was *so* lovely. All sunny and warm and encouraging. The rolling fields between Orford and Snape were smoky green of rising barley and all the pale plates of elderberry flowers were blooming together with the first wild roses. Enough to cause one to sing.

I spied Diana Cooper[1] in a beige picture hat. She is marvellously pretty but uncanny, and in the cruel grey light it was sad to see how forcibly stretched her poor face has been so nothing sits in quite the right place except those star blue eyes.

Verily Anderson and her cousin companion Paul Paget[2] joined us for dinner on Saturday. He is an architect. Not the marrying kind. A *dear* man. They are enjoying each other's company so much. It really is a most lovely thing for both. We all heard Peter P. sing 'Winterreise' to Ben B's superb accompaniment – an astonishingly clear performance.

Dinner with Laurens and Ingaret van der Post. Lots of metaphysical talk and I was trying hard to see where we match ideas. Quite often. She is a sort of spiritual counsellor, professionally. Very Christian and a bit psychological but there are some places where we coincide. He is a mystic and a dreamer etc. I like both very much.

---

[1] Lady Diana Cooper (1892–1986) great beauty in 1930s, was then seventy-nine years old.
[2] Paul Paget (1901–85), Surveyor to St Paul's Cathedral and senior partner of Seely and Paget after the death of his partner, John Seely, Lord Mottistone.

15 June [1971]   Hyde Park Gardens

Darling Joyce,

I've had *such* a day. I feel both over-charged & depleted in a curious way. Left here at 6.30 a.m. in Gussie[1] to collect Margaret.[2] She had a bath while I popped into Minnie[3] to get her Abbey ticket from the WVS. At 11 we all hatted & gloved and waited for the car I'd ordered. It never came, so at 11.30 I pushed Margaret into Minnie & scorched down to Westminster, parked on a double yellow line (told the warden she'd just have to fine me! – which she didn't) & ran to the Abbey!

It was a terrific service – the Abbey bursting at the seams, mostly us girls but also pals & politicians & 'other voluntary bodies'. Lady Churchill[4] – *beautiful* still – powdered her nose & did her lips all through the service! Gorgeous hymns, Lord Hailsham[5] reading the lesson, and then the WVS Roll of Honour was carried up the aisle & laid on the altar. When I saw the five middle-aged, bulgey, grey, *dear*, proud types I burst into tears. It was all so nostalgic – that absolute sea of beetroot & spinach from which emerged faces of forgotten comrades, caught up my heart most painfully. I cry now as I write. Oh *dear*.

I delivered Margaret back to Heathrow at 4 p.m.

I *do* feel sad tonight.

---

[1] Virginia's Bentley car.
[2] Margaret Peabody was a Christian Scientist flying from the USA for the day to attend a service at Westminster Abbey for the Women's Voluntary Service.
[3] Virginia's Mini Morris car.
[4] Lady Clementine Churchill (1885–1977) wife of Sir Winston, Prime Minister of Britain 1940–5 and 1951–5.
[5] Quintin Hogg had received a life peerage and was Lord Chancellor from 1970–74.

17 June [1971]   Aldeburgh

Darling Virginia,

Heather Harper and Janet Baker[1] sang duets by Tchaik. and Rossini and it was a delightful treat. Never can it have been sung like that. Both birds in perfect voice, perfectly blended, humorous/serious, very musical and wholly enjoyable. One sat and purred. Add Ben at the piano and you really could not have surpassed the experience. He is such a superb pianist and accompanies far better than anyone else living (and is said never to practise). Brilliant and witty and warm and tender. The piano ceases to be a percussive instrument under his hands.

Max [Adrian] writes from Southsea where he is filming *The Boy Friend* that Ken Russell[1] is directing and which I refused to be in. And am I glad. He says it is a long way out – 'often horrid' – and he is *not* happy. Oh dear. He says 'my silly old heart isn't enjoying the strain'. Poor Max. I think Ken Russell is sort of mad. How could he make that innocent little 'pastiche' into anything horrid I wonder? Daren't think!

Viola is plumper and bent and her fierce little hands, so wonderfully muscular and responsive to the piano, are pale and limp and very nearly no good at all. She seems calm and restful. Thanks be to God. They are *dear* people.

[1] Janet Baker, Australian opera singer (1933–). In 1974 she was made a Dame.
[2] British film director (1927–), best known for *Women in Love* and *The Devils*.

Joyce and Reggie set off for their annual stay in the Lake District.

2 July [1971]   Cumberland

Darling Virginia,

Did I tell you of my problem with the Chichester Theatre? They booked me for two nights in October at a *much* smaller fee than usual, so I spoke up. It seems they'd given the evening to the British Heart Foundation *without asking me*. I never do medical charities although I do work for the Blind – particularly the Commonwealth Blind – and although this is a very fine point I do find it is a very different thing. Quibbling? Possibly, but it's my view. Anyway I was furious. It was a 'liberty' to do this without asking. I *never* take a fee for a charity show anyway and the whole thing made me cross. So I said: 'get me out of it' whereupon Lady Woolton writes to say it isn't her fault, please will I do it, etc. I'm cross at being put in such a position. I must try and see that Love will find a way. I've written briefly to Lady W saying I understand Ian has written and hope she will forgive me. Oh Lar!

Is one right to stick to principle? this being (a) that I never take a fee for charity, (b) nor do I do medical causes? or should I give a free show for British Heart Foundation to placate Lady W.? Isn't it tiresome? And it's not my fault, that's what's so maddening!

All the same in a hundred years.

5 July [1971]   [Hyde Park Gardens]

Darling Joyce,

I saved your letter to the end of the morn, only when I'd finished mit bills etc., to give myself a treat.

It is annoying about Chichester. Of course I suppose most people would say you could take the fee & give it to the charity of your choice. But I do feel it's a mistake to get involved in *hearts*. You must draw the line somewhere, & I think hospitals & medical centres is *where*. I agree with you that the Blind are different. Though why?

Dilys has just been in to tell me you have written to her. 'Fancy writing to a char!' she says in awe. 'You are a friend,' I say haughtily.

5 July 1971   Cumberland

Darling Ginnie,

Church was touching. We had Joshua and those trumpets with the wall falling down and for the life of me I couldn't remember what the message is? Can you?

The choir is splendidly visible: five ladies in large summer hats and two older men. The sounds they produce do not blend. Miss Irwin on the organ has worn the same knitted hat for over fifty years and has never been seen without it, was bullied by a tyrannic old mum, until merciful if tardy death removed her four years ago, aged nearly ninety. Since then Miss Irwin's organ playing has vastly improved and so has her life. She goes on every outing, supports every coffee morning, all, on foot as far as a bus. No road to her cottage through which rain cascades. She trudges in gummers, cheerful since mum went, and has at last got a wireless.

Miss Irwin's organ playing *actually* tickles me – sends shivers of delight down my spine, for it is so tentative it only suggests she *may* have touched that note I half thought I may have heard! I do find funny sounds excruciatingly funny, don't you? Yes you do.

The Grenfells usually spent a summer weekend with their old friend Sir Rupert Hart-Davis (1907–) in the Yorkshire Dales. Joyce and Rupert had known each other since they were children, and Rupert's sister Deirdre was one of Joyce's bridesmaids. Reggie and Rupert had been at Eton together and both enjoyed watching sport on television. Joyce got on well with all his wives, especially his fourth, June, who he married in 1968. In 1971, Joyce began writing her autobiography *Joyce Grenfell Requests the Pleasure* and Rupert had offered to read the first draft.

9 July [1971]   The Old Rectory
                                                 Marske-in-Swaledale

Darling Virginia,

Oh England how I do love you. Swaledale is ravishingly beautiful because it is cultivated around the river in steep sloping fields, and above is wildness, fells and moors. In every bend of the shallow river Swale there were happy holiday-ers in deck chairs or sprawled on rugs, the children splashing in pools, the olders nodding off. All having exactly the time they'd hoped for in the sun.

A touching little letter from Viola in *pink* ink saying: 'This isn't a life; I had so much still to do.' She also said strawberries and sun were a help; so had been Wimbledon on TV, and all the loving kindness she met with. But it seemed so pitiful. I felt near tears to see the unrecognisable handwriting and this little burst of hopelessness. I wrote back affirmatively, firm in my certainty that nothing real can ever be lost or changed.

10 July [1971]   Marske-in-Swaledale

Darling Ginnie,

As you can imagine I'm longing to know what Rupert thinks of the m.s. I've brought to show him. He began it on Friday and was encouraging; had a good idea about the opening.

I'm trying to re-do the dull bit about my granny, but she was rather dull! Still it is very much part of the pattern of my growing up and there were many compensations such as food and her staff whom we much liked. Mrs Creed the cook, Griffin her maid, Mac the housemaid, Mr Parker the butler, and a series of faceless scullery maids and odd boys.

Saturday, 10 July [1971]   [Marske-in-Swaledale]

Darling Virginia,

Second letter today because I do want to tell you Rupert's verdict on my m.s. Encouraging. He says it is fresh and lively and entertaining and touching, and to get on writing much more and then we will see about shaping it. So I'm up again having felt very diffident and uncertain about the whole thing. *Quite honestly* I simply did not know whether it had any quality or not. Far too close to it to be able to see it. Rupert says it is very tight knit and none of it redundant. Ah me – now for the next stint.

Joyce's increasing openness about her faith in Christian Science and the success of her morning radio talks meant she began to be invited to give sermons in churches. The Rev. Joseph McCulloch had established lunchtime dialogues between the twin pulpits of his church, St Mary-le-Bow in Cheapside, London. Joyce enjoyed these discussions and relished the opportunity to share her certainty of the power of God to an interested but not always Christian congregation.

14 July [1971]   Elm Park Gardens

Darling Virginia,

I've left the proper writing paper in the drawing room, hence my holiday pad. I keep plain paper for answering fans on so as not to reveal where I live, see.[1]

I set off in my green and white voile, mit white collar and cuffs, to St Mary le Bow. The traffic just oozed in the Strand. So I got off the bus three stops early and arrived, heaving, five minutes late.

The dialogue went well. Subject, 'Beauty'. We talked of inner eye mostly but some outer eye aspects. Of people who are less than pretty or handsome and yet give off the impression of light that is beauty. I said what a difference an accent makes. You say in American:

'He's a *loverly* man' and it is risible.

You put it into Yorkshire

'E's a loovly man.'

and it is rich and true and acceptable of a fact. I went into what I mean by a 'lovely person' – one who is motivated, animated and demonstrating some sort of spiritual awareness of order and law. We agreed order came into beauty. It went on wings, there were laughs, they were responsive and very generous.

Joseph McCulloch said he had never seen so many young people there. As we walked into that luminous church the sight of all those radiant faces, open and welcoming, was absolutely *moving*. How they *listened*.

Helene Hanff[2] came at eight. She was good value telling of her self-education programme begun at eighteen. She wanted to be a writer so decided she must read some book about writing. Page 1 of the first book referred to *Paradise Lost*, so she went and got that out. And then Professor Newman, so she got *that* out. And Newman referred to various other people, so it was a year before Helene got beyond page 1 of *How to Write*. She told this very well, and then after dinner we drove to see the City and Tower floodlit.

[1] Joyce always carried writing paper, stamps and envelopes in her handbag in case she had a few moments to write a letter.
[2] American author of *84 Charing Cross Road*, visiting London for the first time. Joyce had enjoyed both her book and the play so invited Hanff to dinner.

16 July [1971]   Manor House Hotel
                                                   Moretonhampstead
                                                   Devon

Darling Joyce,
    Audrey & I have ekshually been out & about today & are QUITE
worn out by the novelty of it! WE drove to Plymouth, & first went to
look at the Astor House, which Audrey remembers with nostalgia &
affection. A nice caretaker sort of person took us over the house. It is
just as it was, except they have added a john in Lord A's room. Audrey
said everybody used the one lav. Nancy put in a bath for herself, but no
john, & Waldorf's bath was naked, plumb in the middle of his bedroom.
Nice furniture, all beautifully polished & cared for. It's used by the
Corporation to house visiting VIPs.
    I nicked a *Times* from outside someone's bedroom on the way out –
so I've got the Xword to do . . . goody!

20 July [1971]   Elm Park Gardens

Darling Virginia,
    I sit here 'teed up', scented, earrringed and all, at 9 a.m. waiting
for the T.V. cameras to come and record me speaking of Noël for a
documentary they are making about him.¹ At 11.30 Sybil² comes
over to be done too. I'm in my turquoise blue trouser suit with the
blouse-with-bow. The flat is looking a fair treat in the early sun and the
flower table is beflowered with love-in-a-mist, daisies, pinks, cherrypie
and some dark sweet-peas to pong the place. Later
    The producer was in a rose pink shirt, tie and pants. Very gentle and
friendly. The crew were all appreciative of the flat and my coffee.
    I spoke of meeting Noël when I was ten, when Mrs Patrick
Campbell brought him to lunch with my mother. She had on a big
black velvet hat and said to me in that big black velvet voice: 'Are
you happy?' (I used this, *years* later, when I wrote Fern Brixton piece,
only she said 'Are you heppy?') I talked about Dick and I writing
'Du Maurier' and how Noël directed me with gestures, moves, etc.
and how to this day, 25 years later, I still do the song and use his
movements.
    Sybil arrived and I plied her with coffee while she was made up. Pale,
frail, and bright as two new pins. She knew Noël as a boy and praised
him lavishly but said he was cruel. For one so Christian and obviously
admiring it was quite firm! And of course she is right about his high
tension. She was very dear and humble and remarkable and we all

loved her. We sat her in the green wing chair with the flower table *just* in, so she appears to be among flowers and looked ravishing.

Did you say you nicked a *Times* from outside someone else's room? I'm aghast!!

[1] Noël Coward had recently been knighted for services to the theatre.
[2] Sybil Thorndike (1882–1976), British actress, was then eighty-nine years old.

July [1971]   Devon

Darling Joyce,

We've had a happy day & I'm about to ring up Victor. He was feeling so rotten yesterday, & surrounded by the ill & sad – Dick, Joycie, etc. On the other hand I sometimes feel he & Dick faintly resent, no, not resent, but find it slightly tiresome we are so well! I think they only find us human when we have colds! The usual C.S. occupational hazard!

Don't be silly, it wasn't a *today's Times* I nicked, but an old one sitting on an old breakfast!

23 July [1971]   Elm Park Gardens

Darling Virginia,

I'm *very relieved* to know that *The Times* you nicked was second-hand and a day old! Somehow it was not like my friend to – er – nick. *Thank you* for telling me. I *might* have felt I had to have a Little Talk with you if I hadn't learned the truth!

The Palladium show, like Stratford, was 90 per cent U.S. The whole thing was taking money under false pretences. You never saw such a vapid *waste*. Tommy Cooper[1] stood and gagged *mildly*, and was fairly funny. Or one had to think so in a kind of despair. His non-conjuring *is* funny I think and he is obviously a warm friendly feller, but – oh Gawd. Other than his personality and gags about us having paid £1.50 to watch him (dangerous I thought!), there were some superb adagio dancers and a good tumbling act called The Stupids. A poor man's Barbra Streisand, Anita Harris, was so over-miked that one reeled back as she belted out familiar Streisand numbers. Pretty, good voice, dead in tune and flexible – but oh that mike. *Agony* Ivy!

Clive Dunn[2] from *Dad's Army* was very dear but mild and unsuited to that great barn. He did a sketch about a butler getting progressively tighter that had seeds of possibility but never flowered. Oh it was an arid desert of an evening.

[1] British comedian (1922–84).
[2] British actor (1921–).

418

The next day Joyce and Reggie were chief guests at the wedding of Verily Anderson's third daughter Janie, to art historian Charles Hampton. Their wedding present was a cheque for £117.50, to pay for 'a good coat and skirt'. It had been Joyce's idea that the eight bridesmaids and pages, aged two to seven years, should be held together in the church with a rope of wild flowers. Joyce changed at Sally Bean's, the house the Grenfells bought for the Andersons, named after an eighteenth-century smuggler who lived there.

24 July [1971]   Aldeburgh

Darling Virginia,
    Steamy hot as we left London for Janie's wedding to Charlie
Hampton in Norfolk. Picnic en route and we got to Sally Bean's. Chaos.
I never saw so many children. Verily and Janie had gone to Paul Paget's
to change. I changed in a room with 2 young girls busy with eye make-
up. Clothes on floor, tops of cupboards, everywhere. In the garden was
a picnic and tents in which various young had slept. Rachel's babies
and Marian's three & sundry others were getting ready as bridesmaids
– dark Liberty flower printed voile, daisy wreaths. Two pages in little
Augustus John shirts with draw string necks – same voile.
    The church was full of wild roses and hedgerow flowers. Verily had
put us in a special sort of royal seats facing sideways beyond the front
pew. Janie's home-made Botticelli Primavera dress was very successful,
with ivy leaves around her head and *Bare Feet*! Charlie was in an
Edwardian morning coat and wing collar. Verily in a long blue & white
dress & huge hat & I've never seen her more handsome & relaxed.
The party was at Templewood where Paul had put up an enormous
marquee. Janie & Charlie arrived in an open 1920s Rolls, sitting on
the top of the back seat as if they'd won an election! The guests were
a mixture of Norfolk County – top hats and modest silks – & Way out
King's Road – bare feet, fancy dress, long hair & sometimes tail coats
over collarless vests with tennis shoes.

Three weeks later Verily and Paul Paget were married at St Bartholomew's Church,
Smithfield which Paul had restored. Joyce was Verily's bridesmaid and John Betjeman
was Paul's best man.

7 August [1971]   St Paul's

Darling Virginia,
    I think when you are as close to an old friend as I am to you one
doesn't often enough say what one thinks about the other person's
achievements and character, so on this dark dank black morning I

write to say I think you are remarkable, courageous, good, funny,
full of charm and wit and warmth, and I not only love and like you, I
admire you! Your selflessness is an example. Your generosity endless.
Your imagination wide and deep. Added to which you are, as are we all
thanks be to God, unique only more so than most.

(A cracking thunder clap *very* nearby, with lightning.)

That's about it. I don't think it's enough to think these things; they
must be expressed. So thank you darling for being you!

Now I will write you a thankyou for our happy stay in the attic:

My dear Mrs Thesiger

It has been so delightful being here in your gracious and lovely home
and we do realise how blessed we are to have such a privilege. The grace
and felicity of the decor, the lovely appointments and the constant H. *and*
C. have all added to our enjoyment, and we write in gratitude for your
courteous kindness. When we are back in Minnesota we will often think
of the happy days in Herts.

Cordially

Ethel de Baskerville

and love, lots of it, from J

I think specially of you in August with its past, but I know that what
is time is now *only*.

Joyce went to stay at the Bishop of York's Palace for a charity performance in aid
of Feed the Minds. Her host was Archbishop Donald Coggan (1909–), Archbishop
of Canterbury from 1974 to 1980.

13 October 1971   Bishopsthorpe
                                                                      Yorks

Darling Virginia,

Variety is the spice of . . . From a tiny warm Trust House room to a
big airy (alas) bedroom in the Bishop's Palace.

The Arch. Bishop Coggan is plain-ish, very fair, with rimless glasses
and I suspect blond eyelashes. Friendly, and highly intelligent; also
spiritual – which makes a change among the clergy I tend to meet.

There are also the twelve wives of all the Northern bishops, all
pleasant. I've warmed particularly to Mrs Wakefield who has big bones
and teeth, vitality, warmth and an absolute faith in the good of God.
Also Mrs Manchester fat-friendly and bien.

It seems it is known I am a C.S., and I am particularly pleased about this because I was totally accepted as a fellow Christian and the Bishops' wives were not only amicable but several mentioned the *help* they'd had from my 'holy' 5 minutes on the BBC! When I left the Archbishop thanked me not only for the laughter and for doing the show for his 'Feed the Minds' charity but for my 'sense of true values and standing for good'. Tribute to C.S.

The morning meditation and prayer was very thoughtful and he said some good things but is well off the beam about what God is! (A sort of Superman.) He'd deny this, I'm sure, but his view that one *can* grumble to God reveals a lot. Very odd.

Interesting that you say no lecturer ever tells what C.S. *is*. I think I'd say it is the Science of Discovering what Man is and how to find this out.

A few weeks later, Reggie confirmed his love for Joyce by appearing at breakfast wearing, over his pyjamas, the morning coat he had worn at their wedding, forty-two years before – without mentioning it.

1972

This was the 'winter of discontent' in which the coal miners went on strike, and to conserve energy, electricity was rationed, television closed at ten o' clock and the national speed limit was reduced to 50 m.p.h. Also Joyce began to have trouble with her left eye.

15 February 1972   Crabbe Street
                                                                   Aldeburgh

Darling Virginia,
Thank you for calling. It was good to hear your voice, love. All is going well here and the lovely sense of appreciation and awareness of love that I find in Viola is very touching. She is quite helpless. Her hands lie curled in her lap. She tires of the chair after a time, so I gave her lunch in a recumbent position.

Viola read the *Guardian*. I folded it for her, pulled her legs up to lean it against, and then tried to anticipate when she was ready for a turn over. Meanwhile I dealt with a batch of sixteen letters, and in between we talked about this and that.

We saw *Face the Music* and I looked ninety seven and haggard. The lighting in my own shows was so careful and kind, but this fierce general lighting reveals all of the old face. I thought I was a bit down and I remember not feeling very lively when I did it.

16 February 1972   St Paul's

Darling Joyce,

Turned on the tele and the cut came. So off we went & filled bottles
& climbed into our beds! I must say it's mighty drear, reading by
torchlight, innit? Indeed the whole business which we are facing with
such stoicism, makes one wonder whether democracy is quite the
right answer! When we were suffering for the nation's survival in the
war the task was easy, but now we seem to be silently suffering, as we
watch the country brought to its knees. It's ridiculous that a quarter of
a million men should be allowed to paralyse the country, with all that
there coal just sitting behind gates which nobody dares open.

The circumstances, which are *cold*, demand that I go & eat some
toast.

XXX Gin.

7 June [1972]   Hyde Park Gardens

Darling Joyce,

Home now from seeing Marlene [Dietrich] with Audrey, to find
you rung, dammit. Well, it was really exactly the same old mixture
– FANTASTIC appearance, that vast yardage of white fox fur, & the
shining sheath of a dress ending in a diamond dog collar, & that
INCREDIBLE figure – and face for that matter. Still no voice, of course,
but every split second a 'performance', every sparse gesture making its
point. We both thought there were far too many tearful songs. One sees
how she feels she must act, seeing that she can't sing, but there was
a wodge of songs about soldiers returning from the war, crossed love,
Where have all the flowers gone, etc. all rendered in semi-darkness &
a variety of languages, all ending in muffled sobs & a discreet wiping
away of an invisible tear!!

A very extraordinary ending, with masses of shaggy young, in a
state of euphoria, racing down the aisle & laying bouquets at Marlene's
feet, reaching up their hands to touch her. She eventually shook hands
with some & put on the *coat* of one young man! Do you think this is
a gimmick that happens every night, or does donning a youth's velvet
jacket hot from his body, have some social significance? But isn't it
extraordinary how the young should adore her so? They were still
baying & drinking champagne with her when we fought our way out.

I like Princess Anne's derby hat, don't you? It seems very
unlikely, but she really does seem to have a dress sense, wouldn't
you say? Really, Hilda![1] watching the race! After Tottenham
Corner she was on her *knees* yelling 'Come on Lester!'[2] at the *top*

of her voice, her face scarlet with excitement. She stood to win all of 50p.

P.S. I spoke to Vic, & he tells me that Marlene's hysterical fans are *paid!* He insists that Peter Shaffer[3] was in M's dressing room after a show, & she refused to leave until the stooges had accumulated enough passers-by to jam the alley way! Oh well.

[1] Virginia's cook.
[2] Lester Piggot (1936–) jockey.
[3] Theatre director and dramatist (1926–).

11 June 1972   Aldeburgh

Darling Virginia,

Hilda[1] left us at 9 p.m. last night after rallying yesterday morning to a sort of consciousness in which she didn't speak, appeared to know Mary and was very peaceful. So thank goodness she's done with this long stress. One has felt her absence for *ages*.

I'm amused to find that the very *slight* irritation she has always roused in me persists in this situation. She was *so* wilful, always got her way, and now she's done it again! We have to leave here before the hol is over! It is *so* unimportant and I don't in the least mind really. I mean that. What I mind is the little triumph of summoning and being run to! But the whole thing is a mercy. I got to love her in a cool way. Admired her looks and guts and her intelligence. And she really did love R and Harry and treated them as her own.

A woman who worked under Hilda at the Y.W.C.A. remembered seeing her set off on her bicycle with her fur coat on back to front to keep out the draughts! I remember seeing her from a bus as I came from Piccadilly going west, H.M.G. free-wheeling south from Park Lane, wearing a yellow cycling cape and a sort of Mercury hat tied on by a chiffon scarf with floating ends. She was entirely oblivious of other vehicles and only angels could have got her through, but she never put on the lights of her bike because she saw the stars better without them.

Heather Harper has lost 32lbs. and looks quite *beautiful*. She's taken to wearing a pile up of hair à-la-Greq on top of her head at the back and she holds herself regally and is every inch a Big Star – and no longer a Big Fat Star. She is thrilled about her new look, and no wonder. It's stunning. And she is singing superbly.

[1] Reggie's stepmother, Hilda Mary Grenfell, aged eighty-six.

11 June [1972]   St Paul's

Joyce Darling,

I'm so glad about Hilda – you've been so good to her & I know it's been a worry & a weight. I imagine however old one is, losing a Mum is painful, even a step-Mum, & I hope darling Reg's feeling of relief isn't out-balanced by one of woe. I will write to him.

I've got one of my old press-cuttings books down here – to see if it contains any ideas I can re-hash, & I'm slightly dismayed at how unkind some of my film & book reviews were: *funny*, some of them, but *not* very loving. I think I certainly tried to find something constructive to say, & nearly every review contains praise for someone, but often hidden in a lot of punches to the jaw! Oh Dear. Incidentally, do you think a good C.S. can be a good critic? Mebbe? You're a good caricaturist & a good C.S. – I mean one can make a comment on the contemporary scene presumably, but without being unkind. That is your forte. I see it is not mine! Evidently I found it difficult not to be funny *regardless* . . .

I've come to the conclusion that my eyes don't look straight out of my head – that I have a swivel eye.

1) Is this true? 2) What do you intend to do about it?

14 June 1972   Aldeburgh

Darling Virginia,

Lovely letter again today. Truly it's worth going away to get your letters, they are so funny and warm and good.

About unkindness. That's difficult. It is so difficult to resist the funny line. I'm not *all* that kind if you really analyse some of my ladies. I've got kind-er with the years perhaps? I'm thinking, now, about material and I can't find anything funny that isn't a bit unkind, and I wonder if perhaps this means it *is* my time to stop?

R. is off early to Minsmere to talk some business with Bert Axell.[1] We are going to help them over a house to retire to and it needs careful thinking out how best to do it. We've managed to convince them it is a good investment for us! They are such nice people. A joy to be able to help a bit.

No, you have not got swivel eyes. Your gaze is steady and true and blue as can be.

---

[1] Warden of Royal Society for the Protection of Birds' reserve at Minsmere.

30 June [1972]   Hyde Park Gardens

Darling Joyce,
   Audrey is busy with her holy works, eyes sometimes closed, nose
sometimes held, she looks distinctly worn & I intend to pack her off to
bed early to 'knit up that ravelled sleeve of care . . .' Oh! one of Tony's
quotes, & it is his birthday today. I WOULD like to see him again,
wouldn't you? Sometimes I get quite exasperated about it – he was so
sweet & funny & heavenly to be with, dammit!
   What are the words of the hymn we had in church . . . de dah de-de
dah de-de, dah de de doh, de diddle de dah de doh? Thank you, I was
sure you'd know.

4 July 1972   Loweswater

Darling Virginia,
   What do you make of Mrs E's statement on P. 16 that 'a great
sacrifice of material things must precede this advanced spiritual
understanding'. I don't think it means we must give up living in
centrally heated flats, our cars, fur coats, T.V. and bath essences, do
you? I think the great sacrifice, and the most difficult of all, is the
material view of what we are.
   I notice there's a big emphasis on purity in the lesson this week and
that needs interpreting, too, doesn't it. I mean it has little to do with sex
or taking showers, but has everything to do with non-pollution of one's
vision of what God and man are. Purity is unblemished wholeness,
hein? You see I've been thinking! It's partly the weather and the waves
of low that come in with the awful news. Enoch Powell and Belfast.[1]
   Found a rare flower today and took it home to paint.

[1] Enoch Powell, politician, had made a speech supporting the deportation of immigrants,
and the civil war in Northern Ireland between Catholics and Protestants continued.

5 July [1972]   Hyde Park Gardens

Darling Joyce,
   My mother wouldn't have half bonked you one for picking the only
figwort in Cumberland, & I'm sure you've got a terrible conscience
gnawing at you.
   One set all, so I must concentrate on that . . . Goollie's win! Bang,
bang, *bang*, they went, bang, bang, *bang*! If you want a more detailed
description of the game consult your husband, hein? Wasn't he
watching? Oh . . . well, never mind.[1]

Yes, it's worrying to think of having to give up asparagus & cars & the theatre and one clings to the recollection that MBE doted on ice cream & ate gallons of it. But hair shirt stuff would be dishonest: just a gradual growth away from strawberries to more spiritual food should suffice!

I dined with Vic tonight – in his bedroom – & he was more serious & touching than I have ever known him. He confessed to being quite at the end of his tether & in despair, as his legs are getting worse all the time & he see no future apart from endless nursing & medication.

'I need help, Gin, I really do.' We had a very frank talk about C.S. and him. He has no faith, would be the worst possible patient as he couldn't learn anything or read anything. He knew how happy you & I would be if he tried C.S. & he couldn't bear to disappoint us if it failed! I said that no practitioner could actually treat him while he was stuffing himself with pills, simply because of the confusion of thought, and that, to be honest, he wasn't remotely interested in metaphysics, but simply in getting well (to which he agreed).

[1] Yvonne Goolagong playing at Wimbledon lawn tennis championship.

5 July 1972   Loweswater

Darling Virginia,
We watched *The Happiest Days of Your Life*[1] in a Margaret Rutherford tribute series of her old films. I looked like a stick of rhubarb. Thin as that lemon pastry, and was not a bit good. And so long! and so overstated. The clothes of the men date more than the dresses of the women. I'd forgotten about Muriel Aked. She was a joy. How time has changed one's humour. Sort of fascinating to see us all looking so young though. And ridiculous!

We went and found the Art Store in Kirkby Lonsdale – very attractive and doing well – children's books, holy books and some gifts. I don't know if I told you I lent it £100 to get it started? I met the young man at F.C.,[2] about five years ago, mebbe. He was full of enthusiasm and radiance, and when he wrote asking if I'd like to put a share in the store I said yes and forgot about it. When I walked in yesterday he welcomed me with open arms. He summoned his wife and two of their three babies, all pretty and attractive, and said 'I've been thinking of you today: I've got something for you.' Whipped out a cheque book and repaid me £40. Wasn't it good. And somehow so splendidly dovetailed my arrival on the day he'd thought to repay me. Saved a stamp, too.

Very much love, darling.

¹ Filmed in 1949.
² First Church (of Christ, Scientist in Sloane Street, London).

19 July 1972   Elm Park Gardens

Darling Virginia,

Today was our royal lunch at Clarence House and it really was a fair treat. We drove in through the gates and parked in the garden. Me in my grass green and white voile and R. in his dark suit with a lime green tie. The Q.M. was already on the lawn with two corgis, and we joined her on the edge of two vast plane trees underneath which lunch was laid. 'I do hope you don't mind a picnic,' was her opening remark!

Massed carnations of all colours in three bowls sat on a long narrow table laid with a white cloth. My word it was so *pretty*. Light through the leaves, the green lawn, the Q.M. in her lilac organza coat over the same print in silk and a lilac organza picture hat for the Garden Party later in the afternoon. (I'd asked if I need wear a hat and was told P. Alexandra was coming and *she* wouldn't wear one. So I didn't.)

We were a gay company. Q.M., Princess Margaret, Tony Snowdon (in khaki green *thin* linen-y suit, *pretty*), and their grins and lots of spirit. P.M. has lost *pounds* and looked really pretty – that lovely complexion and shining blue eyes. She's worked hard at it, she told me, 'no drinks'. Well worth it, I'd say. And she looks far more happier. So does he. I thought there was far more rapport between them and no strain. He'd driven himself in a station wagon and was taking them all back to Ken. Palace.¹

Noël [Coward] arrived after this and was very doddery. He walks in tiny faltering steps and one feels the least thing would send him tottering. But he was compos. and appreciative – laughed a good deal and seemed to enjoy it. Being out of doors makes the whole difference to a party. All the space and the air – even London air.

Celia [Johnson] arrived and, oh dear, she really was not well dressed for a summer occasion. Picture if you will a brownish-purplish-greyish print shirtwaist dress, with *black* stockings and shoes and gloves and bag, and a big shadowing straw hat (black) *and* black sunglasses. She looked a bit worn, darling C., but was in good heart and is mad about her granddaughter, Flora Laycock, who she says is ravishingly beautiful and good as gold.

Princess Alexandra was last to arrive, breathless, heartbreakingly pretty – like a flower; so vulnerable and tender and gentle. She had rather untidy hair, a bit blonded, no hat, and an apple green sleeveless shift with a round white collar and belt.

I wonder how much the staff like these fetes champetres [rural feasts]? There was a procession of red coated minions – decorative against the green lawn – and two or three butlers, in the traditional black tails. Good foods. Nearly hard boiled eggs on pâté for starters. Then roast chicken, beans and new potatoes. Then pale raspberry ice cream, with real raspberries with sponge fingers.

We talked across the table, the Q.M., Noël, and me about crying. 'I never cease' said Noel. The Q.M. said success made her cry. I told them Reggie wept at *all* nice-ness. The Q.M. said they showed *The Railway Children* at Sandringham and she cried a *great* deal but nothing compared to her son-in-law Philip. He gulped *noisily*. We all remembered crying at *Brief Encounter*.

We talked about Noël's early days as a 'dancing partner' at what became the Café de Paris. He did an exhibition with a Miss Edna something who had the very bright idea of singing a song at the close of their solo and it stole all the limelight.

I was sorry not to see in the house but it was so fresh and lovely out in the air and such a very pleasant surprise to find it was a 'picnic'!!

[1] Princess Margaret and the Earl of Snowdon announced their separation in 1976.

22 September 1972   Loweswater

Darling Virginia,

Oh, the Centenary Show at Loweswater! It was *so* enjoyable. The setting: three small fields on a hill in a wide bit of the valley with distant hills as the backcloth. Everything went on: cattle and sheep were competing in one field; ponies, shires and beautiful polished hunting horses in another. Little girls with poker backs, velvet caps, and huge numbers tied across their small persons. Hounds competing in trials, Russell terriers, Lakeland workers, and other dogs. Above all, the great marquee full to bursting with handiwork – wine, butter, rum butter, bread, cakes, shortbreads, iced cakes, eggs, fruit cakes, lemon cheese, etc. etc. And the sewing, knitting, tapestry, *velvet* quilted cushions, floral arrangements in various classes including one called 'Song Titles'. 'Stranger on the Shore' was an arrangement of two dahlias, a bit of driftwood, shells and grasses. The stranger? 'Ring a ring of roses' was just that!

The standard was very high indeed. Only the taste was abysmal. As for the icing – they did impossible things like writing out the history of the Loweswater Show in pale green script on a pale coffee iced top.

One lady carried off all the Firsts – Mrs Kirkbridge – she won for icing, a salad, a fancy cake, butter in a shape (crinoline as I recall, with lace), as well as flower arrangement and plain cake and shortbread! She's had the cup now for six years and is, evidently, the character I used to do in the little series of 'Speeches' who isn't present but I offer congratulations through her husband and 'all wishes to her for a speedy recovery from her total collapse'!

We did enjoy ourselves. The fresh air, setting, the sound of Cumberland voices, the excitement and the sheer skills. The old school house nearby had an exhibition called 'Bygones'. Treasures from local people – old smocks, sunbonnets, farm implements, family Bibles, a hip bath, group photographs, and above all my favourite Loweswater character, Miss Irwin, who plays the organ in church and who spins her own wool from bits she collects off barbed wire. There she sat on the platform in her inevitable hat, spinning on an ancient wheel, and by her side the rug she is making. Very cosy to the toes. In the war she and her ancient mother spun all their own clothes and *sent back* their coupons and got a certificate of recommendation and thanks from the Government!

The Vicar got a first for his eggs, so that's nice.

23 September 1972   Hyde Park Gardens

Darling Joyce,

Soon I'm titupping along the street to sup with Vic, but I've time to thank you for a superb letter about the Loweswater Centenary Show ... a hundred years of *what*, I wonder? being a lake? being a town? I can smell the squashed grass from here.

Private Lives was most enjoyable. Maggie Smith was what Vic would call deevine – marvellous timing, looking wonderful, was very funny. It's an idiotic play of course, & as Patrick said, if it's slowed up at all the characters suddenly strike one as being perfectly despicable – but it was funny, & we loved it.

Noël was there in a box with Diana Cooper and Gladys [Calthrop] & he had a great ovation. Patrick [Woodcock] says he is as spry as anything.[1]

Must go now, I LOVE you

[1] Sir Noël Coward died of a heart attack nine months later, in Jamaica.

Joyce's last theatre tour took her around southern England.

29 September 1972   Pratts
                                                            Bath

Darling Virginia,

It really is quite overwhelming to be *so* warmly welcomed as I was
last night by that audience. It was a sort of embrace. Affection of that
kind makes me feel very motherly toward the dear things.

I got two buttered buns from two over excited ladies in pink nylon
overalls in a weeny snack-bar near the Abbey. 'I was me, wasn't I?'
one asked. 'Yes,' I said. And the other said 'You're just like you are.'
It was a splendid encounter with lots of Tsts and 'I nevers' in broad
Somerset. I'm afraid *Face the Music* has made the face familiarer than
ever before, and it is actually a *slight* bore to hear one's name hissed
all up Melsom Street and in Boots and even in the Abbey as I sat
with eyes closed. But there it is and I disassociate from it as much as
possible. One very friendly woman, about forty, said 'I feel you are
a friend you see, so I had to speak.' I must say it is endearing and
heartwarming and I must be grateful. I *am* humble about it, knowing
as I do that it is the affection in them that acknowledges the affection
in me. And that's a fact.

12 October 1972   Home

Darling Virginia,

I think you might have enjoyed being a fly on the wall today while
I tried to learn my drum contribution in the Haydn Toy Symphony for
Sybil's ninetieth birthday concert. Coming in is *so* difficult. I had a score,
of course, and read it and counted and used a ruler as a drumstick and
haven't yet had a clear round . . . I was at it for ages, drumming to a
recording. It's *so* difficult. I'll be a figure of fun I fear. Tempis.

I plan to join you in the stalls after I've sung 'Time' and then, at the
end, I'll have to nip round to be in the finale.

John Betjeman's[1] appointment as Poet Laureate has had universal
welcome – I'm glad. Seems the right choice don't you think?

R's Christmas present to me is to be a re-designed kitchen. He
insists. He's in love with a new kind of gas stove and he had a young
planning man in to see how to reorganise . . . I'm completely contented
with what I've got but, clearly, my present to R. has got to be my
appreciation of the new design, to be carried out while we are away
either in S.A. or in Australia later . . .

[1] British poet (1906–84). Joyce went to school with Betjeman's wife Penelope and later
Betjeman and Joyce did several poetry recitals together. In 1947 Betjeman wrote a poem

for Joyce called 'Sylvia Paddington' about a woman who wore 'homespun and a necklace
of painted cotton reels'.

1973

As usual, Joyce and Reggie went to South Africa in January.

29 January 1973   Hyde Park Gardens

Darling Joyce,
    Lovely to think you have folded away that knitted suit for quite a
wee while! I hope Reg wasn't too paralysed from the knees down? I do
think height is nuisance in so many ways. In fact, except for looking at
processions, which isn't a frequent pastime in anybody's life, I can see
no virtue in it.
    I've just got back from seeing two Beckett plays at the Royal Court
& it has been a *very* peculiar evening. First Albert Finney,[1] marvellously
made up as an old tramp, listening to a tale he recorded when he was
39 – an incredible piece of acting, as he hardly says a word, but what
is it all *about*, what *for*, & why does a filthy tramp own a tape recorder?
etc etc etc??
    Followed by a MOUTH – Billie Whitelaw's[2] – spouting non-stop half
finished sentences for 15 minutes – absolutely hypnotising & terrifying
(have you ever seen a mouth on its own?) I think I shall probably have
DREAMS.

[1] British actor (1936–) in *Krapp's Last Tape*, directed by Donald McWhinnie.
[2] British actress (1932–) in *Not I*, directed by Antony Page.

1 February 1973   Johannesburg

Darling Virginia,
    I've felt wonderfully invisible except for a bossy English woman
who insisted on shaking my hand as if we'd met in the jungle. 'From
one English woman to the other' she said as she adjusted a pale
mink tippet and told us she'd been here for nine weeks visiting a
daughter.
    Then a woman came up to me and said 'You aren't Joyce Grenfell,
are you?', and I said 'No – I'm sorry . . .' and walked on!
    I went to the R.R. and read for half an hour. Met a very nice woman
working there and we sat and talked about the movement. Informal

services are continuing in the African township of Soweto. And there is, I think, one black C.S. practitioner–woman.

3 February [1973]   Hyde Park Gardens

Darling Joyce,
    YOU'RE on tonight. Doing what, I wonder? I'll tell you later.
    Didn't go out today but battled with a holy article while listening to the sad mooing sound of a saw cutting down yet another Elm tree in Hyde Park.[1]
    . . . Well THAT was very nice – you came *right* into my living room, & I liked you *very* much. You looked very pretty on my set and you performed a really smashing selection. Shall I tell you what you wore? But there is just one thing – I have never noticed before, & that is a fairly large gap between your teeth at the side! Is it really so, or an optical illusion? Of course the darned cameras are practically *in* your mouth.
    Shall I write again? No, I guess *not*. Be seein' yer, darling! *Goodie!*

[1] Dutch elm disease killed most of the elms in Britain during the 1970s.

6 February 1973   Messina

Darling Virginia,
    Large smiling Ralph the driver was at the air strip, and William the butler, and Robinson the cook, and a new maid Gertrude, greeted us at the house. Welcome cuppers on the stoep and then unpacking.
    Yesterday I wrote and wrote about my life and got sad about it! I don't intend using much of the early part but I felt I had to put it down. It isn't the parting of my parents that saddened me so much as my own inept insensitivity to the world around me. Such self-indulgence and acceptance of an order that I knew was not really right – the deep division of staff and master for instance. And the assumption of rights because of class. There was real poverty all round us in Chelsea and my Aunt Margaret as a Councillor, and then Mayor, was hard at work doing something about bettering housing conditions. God knows I do nothing now! But I'm aware of the needs and in our own tiny way we try to share a bit through the trusts R. has set up. True these only help our friends but it's a fairly wide ranging list and the best way we know how to do it.
    I wish I had your stylish writing manner. This is my problem over my book. When I try to write *well* I trip and fall. So all I can do is talk on paper and hope it lifts off when read.

At 3, I was told the nuns were in the pool if I wished to see them, so I donned my bathers and soon joined them. Sister Magdalene, Sister Ann and Sister Noreen (very young and pretty and newly out from Eire) were splashing and teasing and frothing up the pool. Hurling a big rubber ball, getting into rubber tyres and floating. Horse play of school girl ferocity. I sat on the edge and yelled at them, all deaf in their tight rubber caps. (I went in later.)

Virginia joined Joyce and Reggie for a holiday in the Seychelles.

18 May 1973   Scale Hill
                                                                Loweswater

Darling Virginia,

It's a sad, calm day with a heavy solid grey panoply over it. The cuckoo is shouting and there are other nice nature noises that were blown away yesterday.

The people who'd come to support World Life Conservation at the charity cocktail party near Keswick were universally worthy and square, I'd say. Lots of unmarried ladies in coveys who swooped on me with little cries of affection. One, in her confusion, said 'You are my favourite fan'.

Oh – the press camera man! Bearded, brown booted, seventyish, with his equipment in a *Gladstone* bag – and a flash light made of a tiny blue bulb on the end of a fishing rod. He didn't know why he was there or who he was to photograph, and said to me: 'I didn't know what to expect – I've just been sent – are you a T.V. personality? I never see T.V.' He asked Lady Rochdale what *her* name was, and used light meters and gadgets and took for ever to snap us in the hall. Very refreshing in a way . . . !

Later, over dinner, Lady Rochdale, a loyal C.S., told us of being in a bad car crash. She was told by the Orthopaedic Specialist and the Doctor she'd never use her knee again or see out of her eye if she didn't do what they said. And she knew she must get out and away. They said o.k. we'll give you two weeks to get right and then if you don't you must come back to us. And she was healed.

To my astonishment I looked over at R. and his face had gone hard with criticism! In the car he said he thought her *rudeness* to the doctors was inexcusable. That it was rude – and arrogant – to think they couldn't heal her. They'd devoted a life time to studying their job, etc. etc. etc. It was very difficult to explain that it wasn't rudeness to them but honour to God . . . Anyway he wasn't convinced. I was sorry about this. I think he has a slight smoulder of resentment at what he

thinks is our *arrogance* to the medical profession. It emerges from time
to time and I must somehow put him right about this. I think that it
is Love that makes them want to serve their fellow man and that this
is *good* and lovely; but that man is more than body and we believe
that acknowledging the spiritual results in healing and better health.
I must also know that R's resistance is merely a suggestion and not a
condition!

I can hear R. returning from his brekky – yes, and a letter from you.
Lovely. *Ta.* How good that Athene loves her colour telly.

In June Joyce's left eye became swollen and painful. During Ascot Week she gave her
last public performance for the royal family and fifty guests at the Waterloo Dinner
at Windsor Castle. For once Joyce broke her rule of not eating before performing,
and accepted the Queen's invitation to dine. Reggie, William and Joan Blezard were
invited too. Joyce wore a dress made of flame-pink Thai silk, the collar and sleeves
lined with moss green.

The following day Joyce agreed to see an eye specialist at Westminister Hospital.
Although Joyce was a Christian Scientist, for Reggie's sake she accepted treatment
with medicines, but refused surgery. By September she had lost the sight in her left
eye. The planned trip to Australia had to be cancelled.

3 July [1973]   Le Grand Bernard
                                                  France

Darling Joyce,

Hated leaving you, darling ole' thing, but I was encouraged to hear
you had a good night. All the same, luv, carry on with lots of resting,
won't you? You're being so brave about all this, & I do admire you:
it's a great big cracking tumble, I know, but only humanly speaking,
which is not speaking at all. I cling to the idea that actually nothing has
happened, it is just an illusion within an illusion, dammit. *Seems* real &
painful – I loathe you being in pain & I'm afraid I'm terribly glad you're
taking dope. It's just nothing, & you'll soon emerge from the maze-y
hazy mess of it & rise up singing – *and* seeing. I fancy my metaphors
are getting a trifle mixed, but what with Brahms & some French ladies
playing Scrabble . . .

I am thinking of you just off to see the eye doc. I know how you
must feel, darling, about all this, but you have done more GOOD with
your C.S. than anybody in the *world*. Think of all the letters that stream
in after every broadcast, saying how you have helped & comforted: and
you've never tub-thumped, like Aunt Nancy, or been arrogant in your
opinions. It is an *extremely* demanding religion, our dear old C.S., for
when you think every one of its platforms goes against the weight of
the entire world's thinking – no wonder there's a slip now & again. Be

of good cheer, darling heart – you've done so magnificently, & I'm so proud of you.

4 July 1973   Elm Park Gardens

Darling Virginia,

Last night I had a hired car to take me to Richmond Green to see the eye man. He is pleased with me. Says the pressures are down. But on I'm to go with the pills and drops . . . Ugh.

It is such a curious experience and some day I'll tell you how I find that working in C.S. *does* counteract the drugs and that's *very* confusing! But I am simply staying quiet in the 'secret place' where nothing can touch the spiritual being.

I had a long and *dear* talk with Ann[1] who said Aunt Pamela had been so muddled and *so* discreet about me that she really couldn't make head or tail of it all! People are *so* dear. R's sister Frances wrote me such a letter of love and gratitude for my faith and what it's meant in the family. Everyone says 'I'm so glad you aren't going away.' So am I! But the reason is a bore.

[1] Ann Holmes, a Phipps first cousin.

5 July 1973   Elm Park Gardens

Darling Virginia,

Days go by and really nothing happens, and this b–y 'suggestion' stays stubbornly the same although the man says the pressures are less. It's no good talking about it. All I want to do is to be free of the pills and drops and back with C.S., but to be fair to R. I can't yet for he feels I must give 'them' a chance.

I quite see why the mixture of C.S. and medicines don't work because they pull apart, though I suppose if one saw clearly enough the healing would supersede the medicines. I don't – yet. Thank God Mrs Eddy put in that bit about help for pain because it really is a tough one without. I'm not good at it. Can't think with it, just go round in rings and that's no use, so I'm grateful for the pills at that point . . . The eye man says this is a very slow business and I think I've been accepting it. Time to stop that. Such a *waste* for one thing.

For the first time since I began keeping daily diaries (before the war) I simply cannot be bothered. I don't want to record all this boring waste of time.

If only I can remember to do so I plan to enclose a ravishing picture

435

of carthorses cavorting in the sun for your delight. It's the sort of picture To adored. It's in Wednesday's *Times*. I *must* remember to send it to you. I *must*. I HAVE.

31 August [1973]   Hyde Park Gardens

Darling Joyce,

A very neat and tidy bit of biro work this morning! Not that I find it at *all* difficult to read your writing. Do other people? I expect so. It must be quite a challenge meeting new people. All that concern that is hard to cope with, because you have to answer it lovingly. Sorry the Viola situation was rather fraught.

You know how I can never remember what I've written? Thought I'd go mad in church tonight. One woman came up & said 'I simply adored your thing, about the apples & bananas!' (The WHAT? I thought.) Hotly followed by a man, in fits of laughter, 'Much enjoyed your articles, particularly the one about the toast!' (The TOAST? When have I written about *toast*!!) Followed by another woman talking about chocolates (chocolates?). I was completely bewildered. But it's true – my last *Monitor* article was about being sorry for left-over apples & toast & chocs that nobody's eaten.[1]

I really must take a pull.

Audrey has been to sleep, looking like a pretty dormouse under her rug, but now she is wide awake & gone off to give treatments.

I must go off into the garden now, Maud.

All love, darling. I think of you such a lot, & with so much admiration. You've faced all this with such courage & . . . well dignity, & though I'm not at all surprised you've behaved so beautifully, I'd just like to mention it's been noticed.

---

[1] Virginia wrote poems and articles for the *Christian Science Monitor*, sometimes using her married name, until she was eighty years old.

6 September 1973   Auchairne
                                                             Ballantrae
                                                             Ayrshire[1]

Darling Virginia,

Those girls' names in Numbers! Milcah, Noah, Mahlah, Hoglah and Tizzah. They sound a bit butch to me. Except for Mahlah maybe. She must have been the dainty one, do you think? The rest were doggie ladies in tweeds I fancy. I'd no idea there was this stand for equality so early in the day, did you?[2]

I've been reading my 1939 letters to my ma on how I got into the theatre. It is the coolness of the way I played it that astonishes me. And my great humility! (Thank God.) I was *so* far from being cocky but not in the least alarmed or unconfident. It was simply an experience to be gone through.

---

[1] Home of Reggie's sister Laura, and Bernard Fergusson, retired Governor of New Zealand.
[2] The five daughters of Zelophehad asked Moses if they could inherit their father's property as there were no sons. Moses asked the Lord, who said they should. Numbers 27: 1–10.

11 September [1973]   Hyde Park Gardens

Darling Joyce,
    Nought from you today, so perhaps the bombs have affected the mails, eh? (What *would* posterity make of that sentence, I wonder – bombs? England at war in 1973?)[1]
    No sign of Hilda [cook] yet, who went to Manchester. Dilys came in & pulled down the sunblinds & watered the flowers when she was meant to be on holiday! What *devotion*. I don't think Hilda can have been blown up at one of the stations.
    Hilda has just rung from Euston to say *she* can't get out & I wouldn't be allowed in!! I suggested she tries the underground & I'll pick her wherever she lands up.
    . . . Hilda has arrived. I've cooked her an egg & listened to the tales of her nephew's funeral and the *mile* of flowers (or was it mourners?).

---

[1] The IRA were targeting railway stations in England with parcel bombs.

14 September 1973   Howick Grange
                                                        Howick
                                                        Alnwick
                                                        Northumberland[1]

Darling Virginia,
    Over dinner we discussed a Happening – all night Sit-in – held in Liverpool Cathedral, with a smoking area, booths to give out literature for Oxfam, Shelter, Family Service Units, etc., and a supply of balloons was let loose. There was also much dancing and singing. Trevor Huddleston[2] thought it marvellous! I said, firmly, it has nothing to do with spiritual awareness. It is animal spirits, unthinking gut stuff. Oh yes – and there was a touch-in, and eyeball to eyeball looking at each other till all self-consciousness had been shed . . . Isn't it *pathetic*. I've always known Father Huddleston was *foolish*. He's a sort of saint but idiotic too. I said: 'Where is "Be still and know that I am God" in all this

noise and excitement?' Molly and Polly agreed but felt that the fact that the young are concerned at all is a good thing. O.K. But the Jesus People may have freaked off drugs and on to Jesus – and bully for them – but, so far, there hasn't been much evidence of more than emotion and soft centre. No discipline, no self-denying.

My eye is still sensitive to light! And it gets a bit runny and is happier closed. It really doesn't hurt. It is tender, that's what it is.

I am treasuring the lesson, aren't you. Mrs Eddy says the answer to healing is 'Love, Love, Love and more Love'. I'd add practice, practice, practice and more practice. And a lot less skidding off. Perseverance.

I must wash me smalls. Very much love darling friend.

Darling *best* friend.

P.S. R. says he's seen a bit of blue sky. Can't think where – the windows are solid grey, lashed with tears.

---

[1] Home of Molly and Polly – Lady Mary Howick, Reggie's first cousin, and Lady William Percy.
[2] Anglican priest who worked for many years in Soweto township, South Africa and campaigned against apartheid (1913–).

1974

In the spring of 1974 Joyce was fitted with a cosmetic contact lens to cover up her blind eye. She soon lost her self-consciousness and could wear it comfortably all day. She and Reggie went to their favourite valley in the Lake District, while Virginia held a dinner party for twelve in London. This was prior to a ball at the Hyde Park Hotel, hosted by Joyce's cousin Phyllis (Wiss) Astor, wife of Gilbert James Heathcote-Drummond-Willoughby, the Earl of Ancaster.

30 May 1974   Cumberland. In a Druid's wood while R. birds

Darling Virginia,

I think of you in London, your feet off the ground perhaps in preparation for la petite Wiss's ball; the table pretty for your dinner party, places marked, and your dress on a hanger pressed by Dilys, and your heart in your satin slippers? *Deep* sympathy from up here; and selfish gratitude at the thought of eggs and bacon for supper in Ella's kitchen as the sun goes down behind Low Fell, the friendly hill on which the windows look. There was an age when I loved the whole gala feeling of A Party . . . Long, long ago. The gay city life is a nice long way away as I sit in the woods.

We are still looking for the pied fly-catcher and, so far, not a peep out of one. Cuckoos are monotonous in their persistence, and a green woodpecker makes his yaffle laugh. Bluebells and new bracken and khaki moss on rocks and grey lichen on trees. It is *so* beautiful here it hurts. What a contrast to Belfast and Edgware Road and Dockland and New York.

We are donating an electric stove to the ex-vicar for his new house and R. has got brochures to study.

31 May [1974]   Hyde Park Gardens

Joycie dearest,

Well!! I really believe you & Reg would have enjoyed it. We got there far too early – 10.30 & there was a vast acreage of empty ballroom flanked by tables. It probably cost Wissie about £10,000 – 600 guests, no supper just cheese & wine. Wissie told me she'd ordered 96 lbs of cheese and 60 lbs of chocs.

Gradually people seeped in – all the old faces you can think of – Cavendishes, Cecils, Princess Alexandra & Angus [Ogilvy], Astors galore – everybody dressed in flowered chiffon, & all the boys in black ties & dinner jackets, nary a fancy coat in the place! At about 11.15 *Joe Loss*[1] took over – can you beat it? And oh, what a marvellous band! All the old tunes danced by all the old people – it was tremendously nostalgic. Heaven knows where the young were – in the discothèque I suppose or milling around the bar. A few appeared & tried to dance in their mad fashion round & through the elderly. I had a whirl but otherwise I paid little visits to other tables.

Wiss had got mixed carnations & sweet williams garlanded up the pillars – very pretty. The noise was absolutely terrific & my voice gave out completely.

[1] (1909–90), big band king of the ballroom in the 1940s.

16 June 1974   Wentworth Hotel
                                                        Aldeburgh

Darling Virginia,

When I got to Liverpool Street Station, after a leisurely bus ride for free on my O.A.P. ticket,[1] there was still forty minutes to go. I was chatting to a fan ticket collector, when there was an excitement – 'Clear the station, it's a bomb scare.' So we all went out into the street. I went up a side turning and did some praying. No bomb and after twenty minutes the police allowed us to go in again.

What a phlegmatic lot we *appear* to be. We all stood about in the street, some with luggage, and no one spoke! I chatted to a woman and her son about to take a train; all she had to offer was 'Tst – tst – I'm fed up with the lot of them.' The Irish, 'Them', all that make life so difficult, were embraced in that tetchy reaction.

Had a carriage to myself. Wrote a quiet, reasonable and infinitely patient complaint about the filthy condition of the Ladies at Liverpool Street Station, and sent it to the Stationmaster, misnamed Mr Savoury. What foreigners would think of it all. Definite evidence that we are a third rate nation . . .

Wild roses festooned the embankments as we got into the country.

---

[1] Joyce was worried at first about using her free bus pass, as it revealed her age. But she soon used it every day.

17 June 1974   Aldeburgh

Darling Virginia,

Viola is much frailer. It can't go on for ever. It is *very* demanding. They are all saints.

Murray Perahia[1] is very young and a joy to hear. Long arms and huge hands and a grin like the slit in an orange. Charm and modesty and oh! the *talent*. Evidently Ben and Peter think so too. This was his first appearance as accompanist to Peter and it worked marvellously well. A formidable technique. Viola says his right hand is less good than his left but I can't say I noticed it. The programme was broadcast and she heard it with great attention. It was a lovely concert and a good start for *our* festival.

---

[1] Jewish-Mexican concert pianist, aged twenty-seven. Won the Leeds International Piano Competition in 1972.

19 June [1974]   Hyde Park Gardens

Darling Joyce,

The day Thou gavest, Lord, is ended & I am now in bed – more or less with a rather tiresome uninvited bluebottle.

You rang up there . . . NICE.

Vic has just rung again – asking for sympathy – as he so hated leaving Dick in Brighton. I suggested he went & lived there with him, & he laughed & said it would be a disaster! He said he felt extraordinarily better.

'I feel I ought to thank somebody,' he said. 'Well you ought to,' I said, 'God.'

Hurry home, luv.

22 June 1974   Aldeburgh

Darling Virginia,

Janet has been with Vole this afternoon. She told me they had talked
about God. I knew she was a believer, Anglican I imagine, and that she
feels selected to make a joyful noise and does so to the Glory of God,
but I wonder what Janet means by 'God'. She and Keith[1] take a secret
hide-out cottage while they are here, to avoid the inevitable adulation J.
arouses and the social life she can so easily do without. But, it does give
her pleasure when people go back after a performance: I agree, it does.
Or, oh joy, it did.

Do you know, hand on heart, Guides honour and no toes or fingers
crossed, I am actively enjoying NOT being a worker, not being in the
act. No regrets, no wistful longings as I smell the size back-stage.[2]
Freedom. And gratitude.

Viola was argumentative – good sign and we talked about creativity
and the curious number of homosexuals who are geniuses, particularly
musical geniuses. We talked about the masculine qualities in certain
music and had an interesting discussion on the making of programmes
– the balance of ingredients, etc. She is very bright, informed and
usually right about these things. I learn as I go.

[1] Janet Baker's husband since 1957, Keith Shelley.
[2] Stage scenery paint is mixed with size, a type of glue with a distinctive smell.

23 June 1974   Aldeburgh

Darling Virginia,

It is a dish-water sea today. In the middle there was a blue time.

In the evening it was sackbuts and crumphorns and such, under
the charms of David Munrow.[1] Ever seen him? Four feet high and
cherubic, cheeks puffed out as he blows away at a variety of ancient
instruments and enhances the whole thing with his verve and drive and
skills. We began very early – twelfth century and there were Gershwin
syncopations hard to sit still to. R. and I met David Munrow when he
was on *Face the Music* last year and we took warmly to him.

I think modern music makes no sense to us *now* but is it, perhaps,
like the case of Dickens and Thackeray and others being repelled by the
brutality in the face of the boy Jesus in Millais' *In the Carpenter's Shop* –
that gentle, almost saccharine picture of Victorian realism? And, again,
of the cacophony Victorian hearers heard in Tschaikowsky's music.
All the same I still think Stockhausen is phoney and *nothing* to do with
music. With maths and computing perhaps; a fascinating exercise for

thems as understands such things, but not music. Noise is not music. Music is sound.

We went up to the Artists Bar afterwards and to my amazement there was Ben,[2] who asked me to sit with him. He looks thin and bronzed. So down I sat and he spoke of wishing he had more feeling of hope and faith. 'Progress is so slow.' I said I'd found marvellous support in my little trouble from the realisation that nothing fundamental changes – one is untouched by what goes on. 'Yes,' he said doubtfully, 'but I've lost confidence.' Then he said: 'I went to see Viola and her liveliness was so astonishing it really helped me.' He said something about faith and that I had it. Yes, indeed. 'I am working at it,' he said.

[1] Musician (1942–76) who rekindled British interest in medieval music and presented *Pied Piper*, Radio 3's most successful regular music series.
[2] Britten had received open heart surgery in May.

Viola Tunnard died on 12 July, after five years of illness.

13 July 1974   Elm Park Gardens

Darling Virginia,

Your offer to cancel the weekend and stay here with me was *very* dear and touched me deeply; so did the pretty basket of flowers. Thank you, darling, so much. I am absolutely o.k. Truly. The sense of joy/relief at Vole's freedom is real. And the joy is the paramount one. I have an image of her, dark haired again, walking with her back to us all, forward into light.

What a remarkable character! Difficult – ye gods. But a contributor and a strong clear identity. She had an extraordinary effect on people. The land is strewn with people weeping about her. They ring me and are *desolate*. Well, she was unique. Such a funny combination of the endearing, funny, 'whimsical' in the non-arch meaning, quirky, original, serious, passionate – very, and a great fighter *for* her friends as well as (in an unserious way) against those who loved her most! Jean and I came in for a lot of that but it would not change our love for her.

I always felt she was my 'child', and at one time, in inverted commas, she called me 'maman'. I think that is why I could take the rough treatment.

But what a good companion. Demanding, intellectually, and that made going to concerts or plays with her particularly enjoyable. She taught me a great deal and it was she who started me off observing nature! I'd always people-watched a hundred percent but hadn't paid much attention to birds and wild flowers and the light on hills. When we went on top of a bus together she always noticed the architecture of the building above the shop windows – above a Woolworths or a Boots. And she taught me to listen to music in quite a different way; very much more rewarding than that sweep-over I'd settled for.

At almost our last conversation together about two weeks ago I said: 'Oh I wish I knew how to heal you and set you free', and after a pause she said (hardly able to speak above a whisper) 'Perhaps I'm free now'. I treasure this. Was it a glimpse of the fact that her spiritual being was not in her helpless body? Was she trying to comfort me? I very much doubt that because I'd never known her do it before! No, I think it was a little sign of her being in a new place – or seeing *towards* it.

And now, at least, she is free of that impedimenta of lead body. I sense her being cherished and supported. I *wonder* what it's like, don't you? But I bet it's good.

I write all this more for myself than anything, but I want you to know how much I loved your loving concern and how glad I am that we are B.Fs. [Best Friends].

Darling B.F. I love you very much. TA.

15 September 1974   Aldeburgh

Darling Virginia,

Thank you so much for coming down for Vole's thanksgiving. It made the *whole* difference to me having you there. And thank you for your help, too. When I heard the 'Idomeneo' being rehearsed just before the service it overwhelmed me with tears – of self I suppose. It always is for oneself that one cries; one's own point of view of something sad or beautiful. I enjoyed the service so much. Real quality music, wasn't it. And such a united sense of affection for that strange loveable, talented, difficult, original creature. She touched so many people in so many different ways.

Bernie Dickerson, the tenor who sang so beautifully told me that the only way he got through singing his Bach was by hearing Viola's voice saying to him 'What on *earth* made you choose something so high and so difficult'! I took warmly to him.

Over two hundred were in the church, so it really was an occasion, and oh *how* surprised she'd have been. Was? Doubt if she knew about it though heaven alone knows what the time scale is or the consciousness after that experience.

Ben was there – I'm so glad. That was the real love of Viola's life – in a totally non-sex way I mean. His was the talent and the approval that meant most to her.

Viola's friends set up a memorial trust to provide student bursaries at the Britten–Pears School for Advanced Musical Studies at Snape Maltings.

1975

When Joyce and Reggie flew to South Africa for their annual visit Joyce took her half-written autobiography with her to work on.

20 January [1975]   Home

Darling Virginia,

Every time I left England during the war and afterwards for the US, Canada and the long Australian trips I always wrote you a farewell letter and left it in the bank to be delivered in the event of my departure for other realms. Time and again I tore them up. This time I'm writing, not via the bank, but direct to my Best Friend simply to *record the fact* of my gratitude and appreciation for ALL she does for me day in and day out, with imagination, selflessness and just straight loving-kindness.

If I appear to take it all for granted this letter is to assure you I DON'T. I'm AMAZED and moved and delighted by all the good that comes my way through you, darling. And TA for it ALL.

How rich we are to have this kind of long-lasting friendship and affection. What a marvellous thing it is and what a cause for re-joicing and thanking-God-for.

At this moment, 1.30 pm we are packed but not yet into our tropical wear.

It really is a stinker, innit. Rain in rods.

Love and thoughts and certainly about you and your Life and well being. Mine too – and all of us – thank God.

21 January [1975]   Hyde Park Gardens

Darling Joyce,

It is a lovely thing to have a best friend, & it's nice, looking back, to see there has never been the smallest strain between us – at least I can't think of one, can you? Just years of love & joy & laughter, & a feeling of perfect safety. Ta, ta, TA.

Edward Heath (1916–), MP and former Conservative Prime Minister, lost his position as leader of the Conservative Party when Margaret Thatcher, MP (1925–) contested the leadership and won the ballot, the first woman leader of a British political party. She was Leader of the Opposition from 1975 to 1979 and then Prime Minister until 1990.

5 February [1975]   Hyde Park Gardens

Darling Joyce,
   WELL!! Mr Heath is out! It's bye-bye to all that podgy pinkness & the open vowel sounds! Seems QUEER, after ten years, & I can't help feeling sorry for him – politics are a cruel business. However, some say he is responsible for all our troubles, so I mustn't be sloppy.
   . . . 9 o'clock news & Mrs Thatcher answered questions in a very dignified, quiet way, but she is so much the prototype of middle class Conservatism, so pink & white, & with all those hats, she seems, for all her reputed cleverness, a joke. Not that it matters as I don't expect a Tory government to get in for decades, if ever again, do you?
   I shall now fill my hot water bottle & go to bed.

11 February 1975   Messina

Darling Virginia,
   We've just heard about Mrs Thatcher. I'm AMAZED. Can't say I'm absolutely delighted but I don't see who else was a possibility. She looks so very Tory. She's so bland and controlled and suburban-smart. I cannot see her rallying the ranks, can you?
   But it is good that it is a woman and I'm all for that.
   It became very hot indeed and I sat on the stoep with drips falling off my nose onto the pad as I tried to compose a light hearted speech for Manchester City lunch club.
   A dove is saying 'I'm-an-executive' over and over and over. I'd never noticed it doing that before but it's quite clear that is what it's saying.

16 February 1975   Cape Town

Darling Virginia,
   Half a moon, the wrong way round, in a starry sky.
   I had a go at trying to write something about Ma and Lefty. The real pleasure and sense of joy they created at Little Orchard is vividly remembered with great appreciation by so many Tryonites. Baxter told us last year my ma was the key into a whole new world and that for a small town hick boy as he was it was a university education! How he went to some golf tournament with Lefty and Ma where a lot of VIPs were gathered and Condé Nast (of *Vogue*) came up to greet them and Ma said 'You know Baxter Haynes of course' and Condé Nast, ever the worldly editor said: 'Of COURSE' and shook him warmly by the hand! Bax said he grew INCHES from that moment and never looked back.

R. is as keen as mustard on editing and it is so interesting that he should be so good at it. Helps what I've written a very great deal.

21 February [1975]   Hyde Park Gardens

Darling Joyce,

Derek Nimmo,[1] sued for non-payment of rates, has taken a huge box of rubbish from outside his house in Kensington or Chelsea, & emptied it onto the desk of a Councillor! Lady Birdwood is also refusing to pay her rates because of the condition of the streets.

We had porridge for supper, I do recommend it.

[1] British comedy actor, author and producer (1932–).

Joyce returned from South Africa and continued writing her autobiography, with advice from Sir Rupert and Lady June Hart-Davis in Yorkshire.

26 May 1975   Marske-in-Swaledale

Darling Virginia,

Rupert went through my MS with R and me and only had about a dozen alterations to suggest, but he wants me to cut more foreword and say that I am a student of C.S. He says my book is the best evidence of C.S. that could be found! He found the foreword smug, but he was encouraging.

I don't really like my title – *J.G. Requests the Pleasure*; R. does. Rupert isn't strong in any direction about it but feels it will do if we don't find a better. June suggests 'A Kind of Sharing' and I like it. Rupert says it doesn't mean anything until you've read the book but isn't this always the case? Well, we'll see.

Am I to call you Virginia throughout, or Ginnie? I suppose it will be Virginia since that is your real name and looks prettier on the page. Do you have a view on this? Though I call R. Reg in real life, I don't in the book.

The air smells are good and the wild flowers profuse. There is a day old baby donkey in a field. Before lunch I made apricot, tangerine jelly and ice-cream mousse for our supper, and behold it was very good. Later in the day

June says she's so out of depth with some of the high-powered Eng. Lits who turn up and IGNORE her. There was an expert on Coleridge here a week or so ago who really didn't take any notice at all and never helped with a finger! Aren't people rum? June was very funny about it and gave me a really very entertaining account of a day when three separate people sat and talked about three of his other wives and how wonderful they were without it occurring to any of them that she might feel a little out of it! First someone – forget who – praised Comfort and Rupert agreed. Then Edith Evans, who was staying here, went on about Peggy [Ashcroft] – and Rupert agreed – and finally a nephew of Ruth's had his say about Ruth. All of this in ONE day. June said she couldn't help being amused rather than hurt. That is her great strength. But it can't have been easy.

We have talked at length about what Rupert is to do with his library and all his correspondence. They should be kept together. It is possible to sell the lot to a US university library AND retain possession till his death. Rupert thinks our correspondence should be offered to the British Museum![1]

[1] Hart-Davis' library and correspondence have been left to Tulsa University, Oklahoma, USA. Joyce and Virginia's letters have been given to Lucy Cavendish College, Cambridge. In 1968 Joyce became the first Honorary Fellow of this college for mature women students.

29 May [1975]   London

Darling Joyce,

Re your book, luv. Lovely news that Rupert has so few criticisms. I DON'T like the new title 'A Kind of Sharing'. It sounds like a quotation from an author I wouldn't like (Don't say it's Shakespeare! Or you!!). Why not have JOYCE GRENFELL in big letters with Requests the Pleasure in smaller ones beneath it. Everyone will say 'I want Joyce Grenfell's book' anyway, so I should pretty well call it that. And yes, darling, I think I better be Virginia. It is a much prettier word than Gin!

Sunday, 1 June [1975]   Cumberland

Darling Virginia,

Don't worry. We are sticking to *J.G. R. the P.* for title. I laughed when you said 'A Kind of Sharing' sounds like the kind of book you wouldn't want to read and I know just what you mean! And I agree about 'Virginia' rather than Gin. (Do you remember how Leonard used to send his love to Gin and Tonic?)

Are you as fed up as I am with the Referendum on radio? Every time I turn it on, there is Wedgie or Enoch or frenetic Barbara Castle[1] screaming about Britain bleeding to death. AND using Beethoven to emphasise their solid Britishness. I don't know what is going to happen but unless we stay in Europe our non-existent grandchildren aren't going to have much of a chance. Identity is another thing – this is the point, isn't it? The Britons stay Britons, the Huns STAY Hunnish, the French etc. no matter WHAT community they live in. Thank God!

What is a 'moue'? I'm often asking you what things are but you don't tell me, and you so much better educated than what I am.

Love darling friend of my youth – middle and all ages. What luxury.

[1] A national referendum was called to decide whether Britain should remain in the European Community. Anthony Wedgwood-Benn (Labour MP), Enoch Powell (Conservative MP) and Barbara Castle (Labour MP) were all opposed to Britain's membership.

4 June 1975   Midland Hotel
                                                        Manchester

Darling Virginia,

The recording of last night's *FTM* [*Face the Music*] was a cosy one and had all the right feeling of warmth and some wit, I think. We had a new question to do with initials of composers and titles of their works, and in his zeal to aid us with a hint Joe said: 'You need a P.' Of course, AS he said it he realised what he'd said and didn't turn a hair, nor did Robin, Brian Redhead or me, but the audience began to giggle and as they did so ALL of us, VERY briefly, collapsed with pent up reaction – and straight on to the next question without much pause. Oh, but it was enjoyable – and R. says it was VERY funny because of the delayed action. Do hope they won't cut it. We were all pretty knowledgeable but I failed on a Gil and Sul, question. I simply do not know my Gil and Sul.

We had a LONG supper and all longed to get away but because of a new ruling by BBC all bills have to be paid individually, and then submitted for repayment and it took forever to get it sorted out. We must find a new way. It was a silly waste of time, tempers and energy. No-one was cross but it just was SILLY.

R. says they all (who know) said my new eye is a complete success. I did the show sans specs.

13 June 1975   Aldeburgh

Darling Virginia,

What a morning. The sea is a shimmer of sequins on palest blue under a hazy sun. The Q. Mum is forcing me to put on a skirt for her concert at 3!

Ben is very lame – one side hardly functions – but he looks marvellously well in the face and IS working again. He moves slowly and it must be SO frustrating.[1] Peter looking beautiful, a little tense and tired I think.

[1] Britten had had a stroke.

15 June 1975   Aldeburgh

Darling Virginia,

The skies are thick grey and the sea, though flat, is a menacing colour – old armour.

I've just read *Rosie*.[1] Whew! And of course every word is TRUE. You can hear Rose's voice throughout and not one single word is made up. It makes fascinating reading when you know the cast list and I suppose it will be lapped up by the public who can't in any way balance all Aunt Nancy's rudeness, sharpness, unkindness, with her equally real thoughtfulness, generosity, kindness, and above all her humour – or, more accurate, her comedy. Which is different.

R. and I were saying that there is no reason why Rose shouldn't have told it all. It IS interesting, as human frailty always is, but she might have thought of the effect it will have on those who loved Aunt N. in spite of her frailties. But doesn't it show how impossible it is to know what people are REALLY like from reading about them? Aunt N's attitudes to servants and Royalty and the powerful are not attractive and can't be whitewashed. But her very real generosity, even if some of it was a Lady Bountiful form of egotism, DID bless and help.

I've just sent it to Tommy who will not like it any more than I do.

[1] *Rose – My Life in Service*, by Rose Harrison, Nancy Astor's personal maid.

17 June [1975]   Hyde Park Gardens

Darling Joyce,

Just about to buy the *Sunday Times* to read the Rose extract. Oh dear. It's a lesson to one, I mean, when one dislikes people in biographies one should remember one hasn't heard their voices or the way they said things – as you say, one can't know what they are really like by reading about them.

17 June 1975   Aldeburgh

Darling Virginia,
    In the afternoon Bill Blezard and I attended a talk on *Death in
Venice*[1] – masterly it was – by Colin Graham.[2] Scene by scene, musical
treatment explained – links pointed out – themes shown. It was also
a clear delineation of the Mann novel and the psychological sexual
images and, as I felt when I first saw it, it is really a justification of
homosexuality as a creative force. It's the battle between Apollo and
Dionysius in which Eros – and his eroticism – are cited as the true
power. There is a growing tendency around, I find, to celebrate the 'new
freedom' and flaunt the 'gay'. Lindsay Kemp's show on Sat. Night is,
apparently, straight homo-wallow and it has offended a lot of people.
Peter P. told me it was brilliant and original. He agreed it has longueurs
but was, I thought, on the defensive about it. Someone told us the show,
done in mime by Lindsay Kemp and 2 other transvestite fellers, was
done nude in London! We were spared that, thanks be.
    Colin's exposition of the opera was really quite remarkably
concentrated, clear and good. I just don't like the subject – decadence,
rotting flesh, the lust that is taken for love. It's such a dark story and so
tragic. Peter is MARVELLOUS in it. You will find it fascinating but one
emerges feeling a bit guilty – no, dirty.
    Oh FRUSTRATION. STILL no letter. Goes to show that they DO hold
up the $5\frac{1}{2}$p ones.

---

[1] Britten had composed this opera in 1973.
[2] Colin Graham (1931–), opera producer.

19 November 1975   Midland Hotel
                                                                    Manchester

Darling Virginia,
    Today's programme was a friendly one. André Previn[1] was a good
guest, articulate and funny, intelligent and not conceited. He was on the
train travelling with his manager trying to catch up after a 19-concerts-
in-28-days-tour of Japan . . . got back Sunday and still dazed.
    Robin [Ray] always sits for hours in the restaurant car and imbibes
an entire bottle of red wine. I wish he'd cut out some of his excesses.
He's so nice, very bright, *funny*, etc. and his non-stop fleshpots are a
pity. He doesn't get stoned . . . all the same.
    Richard Baker[2] is nice as ever with appalling clothes. This time a
wild silk jacket in pale string plaid pattern with green shirt and a fancy
tie and rather crumpled tan pants. Robin in dark suit for once and

André very dapper in black and white checked shirt. My lime green striped caftan was a mess. Too bulky and I felt uneasy thinking of Vic and Dick criticising! Colour lovely, but a mess.

Joe [Cooper] was bonny and did a nice job. I knew my answers and it was good to be with the old regulars again. Tonight David Attenborough, Robin and a composer I'd never heard of.

In spite of all these complainings I'm OK and about to go out in the rain to M and S to buy a pair of step-ins. Guess what? Mine FELL OFF in the street. Rather enjoyable somehow. Plastic hood, evening dress over arm, crouched under umbrella with producer's secretary, stepping out of panties into a puddle. It cheered us all up – Walter Todd was with us and nice Robin Lough, son of 'Oh for the wings of' Lough. VERY attractive charmer who now directs us.

Thank you for your continuing love and help which I APPRECIATE very much indeed.

---

¹ British composer and conductor (1929–).
² BBC television newsreader (1925–).

1976

25 January [1976]   St Paul's

Darling Joyce,

Deadly cold again. I had my electric blanket on all night and I like its overall warmth *enormously*. It's rather like God, there is no place where it is not.

Lunched with Victor yesterday and talked about Dick's back, which is unbelievably bad, and Rose Harrison and how loyal she was about the happy household at Cliveden. And about Princess Margaret meeting Elton Johns [*sic*]. Know the name, but neither of us could remember who he is. Something to do with pop?

Victor says everything in his body is going wrong. He's very despairing about this deterioration. Patrick rang me later to say that his heart is very dicky and this may be 'it'.

Victor Stiebel had been in a wheelchair for over ten years and his multiple sclerosis had worsened. Richard Addinsell's weak back prevented him from caring for Victor.

3 February 1976   Skeerport
                                                   South Africa

Darling Virginia,

How out of it you are. Elton Johns [*sic*] writes quite pleasant songs
and sings them wearing exaggerated butterfly or diamanté edged
glasses.

Suddenly all my tops and trews look a bit tatty and REALLY I'm
only seen at my best in the evenings and in my kaftans. But I really
don't care any more and there's freedom for you! An eccentric, retired
entertainer turned writer – I'll play up the eccentric. Dare say you think
I do already!

6 February [1976]   Hyde Park Gardens

Joyce Darling,

Vic died early this morning, very peacefully. He spoke to Dick before
he sank into unconsciousness. So ends another chapter.

Endless talks with Dick, who doesn't want any letters from loved
ones. 'I hope I'm going to manage alone – I think I am,' he said in his
red kaftan, 'but I know I *couldn't* face letters.' Patrick called in here &
Hilda gave him some gin. One mustn't forget that he has lost a very
good friend too.

The cremation is to be next Tuesday – just me and Kay.

7 February 1976   Lanzerac
                                                   Cape Town

Darling Virginia,

Ah me – and what a gap the dear fellow leaves . . . I rejoice that
it was so comparatively short but it's been a hellova long haul and
how GOOD he has been. Are you writing a piece for *The Times*? I hope
you will.[1] He was a remarkable, brave character of great vitality and
interests and a capacity for friendship.

All the good qualities he displayed are so clear: the interest in
his friends and their lives; his affection, loyalty, rejoicings in their
happinesses; concerns in their times of trouble. He had an astonishing
capacity for friendship and 'special relationships'.

Isn't it strange the way one particularly loves and remembers those
one laughs with. I have laughed a good deal with old Vic and he was
fun to tell funny things to, wasn't he? I'm so glad that YOU had the
most special of all his relationships with him and one unfraught with
anxiety. He loved and CARED for Dick, but he was a constant worry

and that made it all a bit hard going. My, we'll miss him. I do already. A gap in the ring. But as Tony has, he will become as he already is, part of us all.

You have been such a darling loving pal and I know his gratitude was colossal. You were (as always) the best friend in the world. And I know what I'm saying. Also you were his guiding light, his tower, and his way to God!

We often sang your praises together. God bless you, him, Dick, and all of us!

[1] John Betjeman wrote an obituary for *The Times*, with an addition written by Joyce and edited by Virginia.

8 February [1976]   Hyde Park Gardens

Darling Joyce,

I spent the day organising & saw the undertaker from Kenyons – the minimum funeral, which Vic wanted, no extras, smallest chapel, no music, no anything, costs £251.50. Whew! It's when one stops that one suddenly realises one won't ever see the old boy again: God knows he was a terrible tie, & I shall be much freer (*and* richer) without him but I'm bound to feel a bit of a draught. Dick is being extraordinary – I know people do get euphoria after deaths; but today he sounded as gay as a grig!

Be careful of JAWS, please, when swimming in the Indian Ocean.[1]

[1] The film *Jaws*, about a killer shark, directed by Steven Spielberg, had recently been released.

10 February [1976]   Hyde Park Gardens

Dearest Joyce,

I'm just back from Golders Green, darling. A darling service, read by a *Methodist* minister! The non-sectarian gentleman we'd ordered had fallen by the wayside. The minister was a large, comfortable, dear man & he read two psalms, two bits from the New Testament & some thoroughly perfect prayers about God's love, & eternity, & the joy of it all. Very comforting & he really sounded as though he believed every word of it. I suppose it took about 10 minutes & then the dear old friend slid away for ever – *never* like that bit, do you? I usually shut my eyes.

St Valentine's Day   Cape Town

My darling dear Gin friend

How's that for twee? I just wanted to be sure you knew I cherish you a great deal and you are all those things – darling; dear; Gin; and My Friend, so it's all TRUE, see?

The posts are really *trying*. Your excellent letter of Feb 10 after the Golders bit has come. I'm so pleased it all went well and I love the dear Methodist for being so warm and trouble taking. Up to a point I'm all for Methodists; they do believe in Love. Trouble is they also believe that Jesus is THEIR friend – I don't mean He isn't ours, I mean Jesus is an actual pally presence to them.

Thanks for telling, darling. I am appalled by the bill from Kenyons! Do we *have* to be 'done'? What happens if we settle for a pauper's grave in protest? No wonder undertakers are so rich. What a wicked blackmailing business. Whew. Yes, love, you will be a bit richer. So will Reg.

About Dick – what I find sad – and I mean sad – is that I no longer feel as I once did even though the heart IS willing, IS full of compassion and SOME understanding of his dotty, muddled carrying-on. There is no doubt about it: gentlemen of his persuasion are NOT normal. I have never yet met one who was. Foibles, allergies, all are perverse; and you may remember that 100 years ago homosexuals were called perverts. (So were those who defected to the church of Rome!) I'm afraid D. is no longer a part of my daily thinking as once he was. What a strong character he has. I've always been a bit scared of him, editing what I say, not always revealing what I feel. But he was such enjoyable company and so sensitive and imaginative and CREATIVE.

18 June 1976   Aldeburgh

Darling Virginia,

The shootings at Soweto are so horrifying.[1] Despairing. What IS the future? The radio report says the hate felt by the children is a revelation to the S.A. government. What do they expect when communications explain plainly that there IS another way of life – freedom IS a right – and they aren't being allowed to find it.

Harassed letter from Mary [Phipps]. Lang is getting together a band. Rehearsals FFF go on in the playroom by the garage. POOR Mary. She's nearly desperate. And it will go on ALL summer long. The JOY of not having children!

The light on the marsh is breathtaking. High tide and the reeds still

green. (The rest of the country is biscuit-coloured. Today's local radio
says don't flush EVERY time . . .)[2]

Because I have taken so against the *Daily Mail* we got a *SUN* to see
how it works. GHASTLY. A full frontal bust on p.3. practically life-size.
Bombers.

[1] South African police had open fired in Soweto township on black schoolchildren protesting
against compulsory use of Afrikaans in schools. At least 600 black demonstrators were
killed during riots in 1976.
[2] Britain had a national drought in 1976.

Joyce spent the summer publicising her first volume of autobiography, *Joyce Grenfell
Requests the Pleasure*, which soon reached the top of the bestseller list. In the autumn
Joyce and Reggie went to South Africa and Australia to publicise the book. This was
their last trip to South Africa as Reggie, now seventy-one years old, was retiring
from the Messina company.

26 October 1976   Johannesburg

Darling Virginia,

TWO lovely letters and your splendidly bad taste card were here to
greet me this morning. Marvellous!

Leaving Messina this morning WAS a trifle poignant. Those smiling
black faces fell when told of R's retirement. It was VERY touching. SO
many memories surged up – Miriam in the early days when it was all
new and spick and span: she made all sorts of improvements every time
she came out. And now the green striped curtains are beginning to fray.
No-one knows how much longer Messina will go on. The mine itself, I
mean. All mines finally get worked out.

R. said 'This is the last time I shall bath in this bath. I've been using
it on and off for 26 years.'

Very dear excitement up at Messina re my book, and it is arranged
for the company buyer to get copies for me to sign.

26 October [1976]   Hyde Park Gardens

Darling Joyce,

One of the Friend of the Elderly committee rang me to say she'd read
your book & spent three evenings with one of the nicest people in the
world. She quoted me large chunks & was full of questions & couldn't
get over your *goodness*. 'Oh she's all right', I said grudgingly!

I rang Dick & the nurse said he'd had a bad night but had listened
to the gramophone. I really feel he's subconsciously opting out, can't
go on facing life without Vic & has nothing to look forward to. I feel he

might go, simply for the reason that you are out of the country. Your
absence has a mysterious way of tidying things up life-wise!

6 November [1976]   London

Darling Joyce,
    You'll be sorry to hear I've been had up for speeding! Isn't that a
bind? I've driven for 49 years without getting anything but a couple of
parking tickets & I feel quite SAD at blotting my copybook. Apparently I
was doing 80 on a nice clear, but small, road. I couldn't think why the
car behind me kept flashing its lights. Nice policeman, looked about 16.
I may get an endorsement. Well, that'll teach me.

18 November 1976   Skeerport

Darling Virginia,
    Today I have a small twist of turquoise blue pinned to my lapel and
it stands for 'in favour of peaceful change'. I suspect this movement is
inspired by those brave Ulster-women. It is growing here and has men
in it as well. The poverty of black shack homes is shocking.
    From Happiness House, where Tape-Aids operates and does talking
books for the blind, I was driven to a morning 'cup' party – wine
cup and pâtés spread on French loaf. A gathering of about 110 and
several MEN.
    There was a very nice looking man, again of my age, who came
over and said: 'I have waited 34 years to say thank you for coming to
India in 1944. I was in Barrackpore hospital, very low and homesick,
and your visit made the whole difference, and I've *never* forgotten it.' He
was quite moved, very English, and I kissed him on the cheek. His wife
nearby said she didn't mind (I'd asked her!) and that all he'd said was
true. Funny coincidence that there was ANOTHER man there who had
also seen me 34 years ago in India!
    SAD you were fined for speeding. I am afraid you do go too fast.
DON'T DO IT AGAIN . . . PLEASE.

30 November [1976]   Hyde Park Gardens

Darling Joyce,
    I simply can't BELIEVE it! Wallace Brothers are *bust*! Isn't it sad?
Thank heavens To is dead. But oh, when I think of those old gentlemen
(Mrs Thesiger's father & two uncles) who went off to make their
fortunes, one to India, one to Burma, one to Siam, & came home to
found this family business – such a solid, respected family business . . . !!

Mercifully I've only got around £5,000 worth of Wallace shares left from the marriage settlement. I did have *thousands*. It's like Rolls-Royce foundering. Isn't it incredible how unstable everything is? I suppose it's happening everywhere – old businesses closing down, & people getting thrown out of work. I must lift up my heart, & stop *glooming*.[1]

By the way, while I was having my hair done today I read *Queen* & you are listed, with only a few other women, as being 'really witty'. You are quoted as being the first person to say 'a village fete worse than death'. I don't think you can be, can you? I'll *pretend* you are, but I seem to remember my father saying it when I was on his knee!

Oh I haven't given you a death today! How about Dorothy Mary Baring-Gould of Aldeburgh? Any good?!

[1] Wallace Brothers was taken over by the Standard Chartered Bank.

25 November 1976   Mandarah
                                                                    Australia

Darling Virginia,
Yesterday was HUGE, but all of it went well and I was stretched but not worn out. 2 press, 2 radio, 2 TV interviews and long signing sessions in 2 book shops. Such nice people of all ages.

A kuckaburra is chortling at us out of a gum tree. R says the TV interview we watched last night was a good one.

This is a charming city – or more of an overgrown market town. One of the nicest ideas is to grow climbing geraniums up telephone poles and electric lamp standards along wide suburban streets.

4 December [1976]   St Paul's

Darling Joyce,
You will know, even in darkest Australia, that Ben Britten died today.[1] Only news so far is that Peter Pears 'his lifelong friend' was with him. It really is a loss, dammit. He must have had another decade of triumphant music in him, at *least*. Wonder if Aldeburgh will survive?

While I'm on music, a brother & sister act were on TV last night – they are called The Carpenters,[2] are American, ever so soigné looking, he at the piano playing pseudo Bach accompaniments, to her singing slushy songs. All very 'thought out' & a mite pretentious. *Well*, the boy part, wearing a white satin suit – looks like a pansy – played the Warsaw Concerto in toto! It's apparently on his latest record & Dick is very pleased & it seems The Carpenters are becoming *the* thing.

In the scandal line we have had, on a family programme around 6 p.m., a punk rock group called the Sex Pistols who used so many four letter words & were so drunk & drugged & obscene that the telephones were jammed for hours.

All your interviewing does sound exhausting, but I suppose you can say the same things in each place?

Yesterday a Piper plane radio'ed there was a pink pig flying in the sky above – 'ground' paid no heed. Soon afterwards a charter plane radio-ed there was a pink pig heading east, going very fast. So reluctantly the airports sent out a message to all planes, about this pink pig. Meanwhile some pop group were in a fearful tizz, their vast pink pig against which they were being photographed in a field, having escaped its moorings. Eventually one of its trotters sprang a leak, & it came down. Nice tale, eh?[3]

I've sent flowers from you to Ben's funeral.

[1] Britten, who had received a life peerage in the summer, died of a heart attack.
[2] Richard Carpenter (1946–) and his sister Karen (1950–83), who was already suffering from anorexia nervosa from which she died.
[3] The pop group was Pink Floyd.

6 December 1976   Melbourne

Darling Virginia,

Oh DEAR – Ben. What will happen to the Festival? So long as Peter Pears is there it will of course have a special quality, but oh the feeling of loss they'll all entertain. But Gratitude too.[1]

Darling, under drier. Rush job at 8.30 before a live radio show with an outspoken Gorgon lady, so they tell me. Nous verrons. I'm NOT tired. It is all very stimulating and so affectionate and warming to the cockles. But tightly packed. No strain because all journeys are prepared and coped with.

[1] The Aldeburgh Festival continues to thrive and in 1997 celebrated its fiftieth anniversary.

9 December [1976]   Hyde Park Gardens

Darling Joyce,

Been to another memorial today – Edith Evans,[1] at St Paul's Covent Garden. I corralled Celia & Audrey into the same pew. It was jam-packed. As C said 'For somebody who's supposed not to have had many friends . . . !' but then a lot of people, I imagine, C & myself included, *weren't* friends – just there for the party! Not a very good one really. It's a beautiful church, but so shabby – almost derelict – with single bulbs hanging at different lengths & the walls streaky & grey, &

terribly cold. Michael Redgrave read 'Earth has not anything to show more fair',[2] followed by us singing To Be a Pilgrim, followed by Peggy [Ashcroft] reciting & some prayers & an address by Bryan Forbes.[3] He had three nice anecdotes. One about E.E. saying 'God has been very good to me: he has never allowed me to go on tour.' When a young actor on a first night said to her 'Good Luck', she said 'For some of us it isn't luck.' And lastly, when Bryan felt he should tell his daughters that Edith was very old & tired & would probably die quite soon, one of them said, 'Oh I don't think she'll die – it isn't her style.'

I think all the stage were there. Except that the sun was shining brilliantly there wasn't any feeling of warmth or love. Except perhaps from Bryan Forbes, yes assuredly from him.

[1] British actress, died aged eighty-eight.
[2] *Composed upon Westminster Bridge* by William Wordsworth. 1802.
[3] British film producer (1926–) and biographer of Dame Edith Evans.

12 December 1976

Koombahla
Mansfield
Victoria

Darling Virginia,

Yesterday we took a huge pavlova, iced cake etc. to an old age pensioners' party and I was introduced to the ladies who made excited bird noises and I felt a pig not to 'do' something for the guests, but I didn't. Don't think I could remember a whole monologue though I can still do bits.

Now, Sunday, I'm going to indulge myself on this pleasing paper. Today is our 47th wedding anniversary and the skies are wild. (It was wild on Dec: 12th 1929. Remember?)

Your last letter was a real winner. Dec: 4th. You began with the sad news of Ben's death. The Carpenters make rather pleasant noises as I remember – shows that people are turning to gentleness.

I didn't get too tired doing the promoting because there was such an affectionate feed-back. Signing is the hardest part because each one is a little encounter, a little starting again from scratch. And I had a great deal of it. And they certainly went well . . . ye gods. Also I did some thinking in advance.

We laughed at your account of Edith's memo – she was a crusty old thing and NOT easy to like. The reason so many went to the church was historic/snob value I'd guess. She was OUR greatest actress wasn't she, and her going needed to be marked.

19 December 1976   Sydneeee

Darling Virginia,

Your ravishing robin on his nest has come and is our pride of all cards. A beauty. You are so CLEVER to find such a love of a card. Made me purr and make little appreciative moans!

R. and I waited in for a call from Bernard Braden[1] in London. He is working for a new conference centre just opening in Wembley and he wants me to play there in March. Would I? Alas, no, I said. But ta for asking. I was firm though flattered. Nice to be asked but I've no wish to work that way again.

Just seen the most splendid Christmas card. Picture if you will a very gnarled old ENORMOUS oak tree. Against it is a photographed a not young woman in a red velvet coat, waisted, white fur trimmed, as is her red velvet pointed cap-hat; white hair bouffant, smiling and with stomach held in as she poses. Guess who. Mrs Santa? No, *Barbara Cartland.*[2] And underneath states that Queen Elizabeth I did something or other under it – killed a stag, or sat. How Vic would have loved this card!

We've just read of the hideous cold you are having . . . Frozen sea. I've written to Mrs Agos to turn on her fires. Please URGE her. Tell her my book has made lots of lolly and I can afford for her to keep warm. And if she won't do it tell her to move into the flat and get warm there.

[1] Canadian television presenter.
[2] British romantic novelist (1901–) step-grandmother to Diana, Princess of Wales.

1977

After Christmas in Australia, Joyce and Reggie returned home via Mauritius. Virginia continued to give lunch parties, write articles, shop at Harrods and staff the Christian Science Reading Room. At weekends she hacked brambles and 'nested' by the fire with Audrey Butterworth at St Paul's in Hertfordshire.

21 January 1977   Morne Brabant Hotel
                                                                     Mauritius

Darling Virginia,

Leaving Sydney was a real wrench. You know how I put down roots and they have had footing there ever since the first visit and I love it increasingly for its beautiful setting and because of the people I love who live there.

I WISH it wasn't so far away because I know you'd LOVE so much of the things we love there; but I can't be sure you'd love the rest – the strange country and the bush and the birds and the uniqueness of the Australia that I find so enormously enjoyable.

I am trying to realise that this might be the last time we'd come out here and hoping it isn't, for I truly love it and the special friends who make it so special. No real reason why we shouldn't. Rich enough – so far.[1]

I dipped in sea that was absolutely clear (huge starfish on the bottom) and actually too warm. The scene was like a Chinese painting on silk. Sea a shining flatness, the mountain opposite washed in a smoky grey-blue to indigo. An Indian couple, young, were making love in the shallows, nose to nose! Today we were given bright lettuce green water snail shells and two striped conical ones in bright colours. How can one not believe in a divine Principle? What symbols of variety and beauty they are.

Met a young wife of about 25, very worried because she isn't pregnant . . . gets ill each month with disappointment, poor luv. Did you mind at first? I did.

R. began work on re-condensing my book for BBC serial.[2] They sent me a version, cut to bits with all the best left out and R. is putting them back in the exact proportion of the original.

R. says buck up, time for supper.

[1] This turned out to be their last visit to Australia.
[2] For *Woman's Hour*, read by Joyce. Broadcast in 1977 and again in 1996 for the fiftieth anniversary of *Woman's Hour*.

22 January 1977   Mauritius

Darling Virginia,

A basket of fruit appeared in our room with a card saying: 'I hope your stay on the island gives you as much pleasure as you have given me in the past – sincerely Gerald Durrell.'[1] Turns out he's here on a conservation trip and he knows answers to all our bird, and some fish questions. Sitting on our verandah after lunch, painting, I heard a flip flap as of feet walking on the water, and looked up to see a lovely little stitched pattern of flying fishes coming across the lagoon in front of us. Pale they were, and about 30 inches long (guess). Gerald Durrell's eyes widened. He hadn't seen them before. They were stretching for about 100 yards, in and out. SO pretty.

G. Durrell is bearded, agreeable, interesting and amusing. A nice encounter and he bids us visit him in Jersey.

The spots on this page are marmalade.

[1] British conservationist and author of *My Family and Other Animals* (1925–95).

461

Joyce began work on the second volume of her autobiography, *In Pleasant Places*. Wherever she went she visited bookshops and signed copies of her first book.

16 June 1977   Aldeburgh

Darling Virginia,

Lunch at Westleton in the little pink cottage, one of a cluster, that we bought and rent to Bert and Joan Axell. It is full of clutter. Bird pictures – birds stuffed – bird books – bits of African pottery – patchwork – mats – ashtrays – and etceteras. Both are very welcoming and love the little house, so that is v.g. . . . Bert has just produced a book about Minsmere for the RSPB and Reggie says it is very enjoyable. Bert has an easy way with people and made a colossal success.

We were warmly greeted with: Now you're here it's a proper festival! The programme cover is a charming coloured photograph of Ben taken last year with a fistful of roses.

There was a good deal of emotion at Peter's first appearance, and it must have been hard for him to take, but he has an heroic quality of bearing and a great deal of faith, and it seems he came through with great dignity and calm.

Dear Imo – in a black top and 3/4 skirt – danced her way through an exquisitely performed little suite of charming music, her pa's Brook Green suite. I like Holst, don't you?

I am longing to write about Aldeburgh for my next book. The festivals have been such a very enjoyable part of our lives, and Ben's invitations for me to do my programmes were the highest accolade I've ever been awarded. This certainly is one of my Pleasant Places. R's too.

Bear hug from Clifford Curzon[1] in the lounge last night. He plays tomorrow. He hates Aldeburgh, he says. Bleak, bare, hideous and snobby. I was very surprised by the vehemence!

[1] British pianist (1907–) had just been knighted.

16 June [1977]   Portmeirion[1]
                                                              North Wales

Darling Joyce,

I am looking at a pretty turquoise & pink dome out of one window & a lot of hugging trees on the other. We set off in Wuff[2] & had a truly gorgeous drive. Wales is the *prettiest* country.

Sir William Clough-Ellis [sic] was at luncheon, with a very very very old lady we supposed to be his wife. Sir W had on his usual canary stockings, but I must say he looked older than time & had to hang onto the sweet trolley, thumb in the orange mousse, in order to leave the dining room.[3]

Believe it or not, I've been weeding the tangled bed outside our hotel room! Audrey thinks I'm mad. Don't much want to go home – one feels so delightfully in cloud cuckoo land here & neither Oakeshotts nor the Bayswater Road beckons.

[1] Italianate village, designed by the architect Sir Clough Williams-Ellis (1883–1978).
[2] Virginia's Rover car.
[3] Sir Clough Williams-Ellis was ninety-four years old. When Joyce met him in 1941 he was wearing 'tight fitting corduroy breeches and hand knitted mustard yellow stockings'.

19 June 1977   Aldeburgh

Darling Virginia,

It seems that Clifford Curzon, *before* a concert, is a fiend. Nothing is right. He rages and hits out and is well known for so this no-one is upset by it. Bert, who is in charge of the Steinways, told us that the sequence of events goes like this:

'The piano is useless – appalling, old, finished.'

'The piano is getting under control.'

'The piano is the best I've ever played on.'

I thought he was a bit harder than I expected him to be in the Beethoven, but otherwise I found it clear and splendid. Brahms was lovely. Though a lot of intermezzi together seem to add up to a thick wodge of sonorous sounds. And you?

Joyce and Reggie went to stay with Verily Anderson and Paul Paget in their mock-Palladian house in Norfolk which Paul had built for his uncle, Samuel Hoare.

26 July 1977   Templewood
                                                              Northrepps
                                                                 Cromer

Darling Virginia,

So cross with myself for forgetting to leave for you a pre-publication copy of *George-don't-do-that*.[1] It came yesterday. Dammit. Anyway I've got it for you. The cover picture is one of those that my ma wouldn't have liked – being the teacher and *saying* 'George – don't do that . . .' and DECIDEDLY plain. But the little drawing I made of John Ward has come out quite well. The copy of the book is somewhere in the flat should you go there at any time. (Don't put flowers there next week, love – I'm sure we'll bring some from Loweswater. You mustn't do it *every* time. There was never such a friend. NEVER.) It might be in the bathroom, on top of the little book case. R put it there so I could look at it from the bath!

E. Anglia looking as I best love it – straw-coloured and wreathed in wild flowers. Ditches thick with them. Paul Paget says it's because the saving of fuel by local councils means that they haven't mown down the verges. The clashing of bright pink rosebay willow with poppies is splendid. Nature note over.

[1] Six of Joyce's nursery school sketches, illustrated by John Ward, published by Macmillan. These began in the 1944 radio programme *How to . . . Talk to Children*, written by Joyce and produced by Stephen Potter.

27 July 1977   Templewood

Darling Virginia,

Good morning. We slept v. well in our charming Napoleonic beds with ample downy pillows.

The King's Lynn occasion went well AND I was able to wear the contact. This was a joy because it meant no explaining.[1] Verily's son, Eddie, drove us there (V., E. and me) and a few miles out of K.L. we went up a side road, they tactfully strolled down the hill while I popped it in, blinked and knew it was OK. It was the original one, and smaller and more easily dealt with. I was SO grateful.

I spoke for 25 minutes and there was a warm response from over 200. In the car Verily and I sang the old Girl Guide song about 'marching on the King's Highway with a heart that is light/and a step that is gay'. I only knew the first half but she knew the whole. During my talk I sang a bit as an illustration and when I got to the end of the bit that I knew, Verily, far end of room, jumped up and sang the last lines! It was SO funny. Perfect timing – total surprise and made all present and me laugh a good deal. She has a strong clear deep contralto voice and took the chorus an octave lower than I did!

[1] When Joyce did not wear the cosmetic contact, she wore a pirate's patch over her blind left eye.

29 July 1977   Templewood

Darling Virginia,

After a walk in the woods we drove to the little house we bought for Verily, Sally Bean's, and picked raspberries. The house has been such a happy success. It rescued V. when she was in a dire spot. Then we let Paul buy it back (for her) at the v. low price we gave for it and now it is her dower house and in constant use by her children, friends,

honeymooners, etc. When we were walking Verily and I got ahead
and she said she owed ALL her happiness to us! By some heavenly
dispensation I had entirely forgotten the various deeds R. had done in
her times of need and was amazed! Because of Sally Bean's she met Paul
etc. etc. Wasn't it nice? It made me realise the importance of knowing
that sharing isn't bestowing and one can let it go completely.

We've had such a truly pleasant time with Verily and Paul. The
feeling that a happy outcome is being lived out in a pretty place for two
very dear creatures who are GOOD makes it all the pleasanter.

Progress being made but freedom [from pain] not yet attained –
dammit. Sleeping well.

Virginia went to the Soviet Union with Audrey for two weeks.

2 September [1977] and you are due home   Elm Park Gardens

Darling Virginia,

Rang Dilys to check on the scene and all is in order. 'But I won't
be happy till Mrs Thesiger is back. I don't like her being in Russia. Not
Russia.'

Yesterday, sunny, was very crowded indeed. Between 11am and
12.12 I signed *170* copies of *George don't do that* at Selfridges. Absolutely
non-stop. Such nice people. Families, Aussies, Canadians, Americans,
young and old, and Britons. Reeling, I left the 4th floor where I'd been
set on a dais facing cruel baby spot lights focused straight on my face.
Interesting that dazzling light contrives to make one slightly deaf! I
found, not being able to see faces on account the blaze, I couldn't hear
their names! But I got used to it and signed away.

Having a tough time just now with bloody old rheumatism in eye,
and difficult to use contact. R. wants me to see a specialist. Our man is
ill and can't see me. I'm in good heart.

Joyce and Reggie went on a six-week tour of the USA for the English Speaking
Union. In each town she gave a talk about her life, illustrated with excerpts from
her monologues. The purpose was to raise money for the ESU, which sends young
people on work experience visits all over the world. Joyce's niece Sally Phipps had
been working in a women's refuge in London and returned home with them.

6 September 1977   In the air

Darling Virginia,

I knew there was something I wanted to tell you today. Last night
I rang Dick & we had a long, logical, affectionate, dear talk. I told him

that Macmillan were thinking of doing a collection of our songs with music. 'I'd like that,' he said.[1] Before we rang off I said 'I love you. And I'm grateful to you for so much.' 'My dear,' he said 'I love you too.' It was so touching and real and I was glad about it.

We've all got aisle seats which is a help. The head steward said the Captain would like a visit and it's manners to go. Also Sally was dying to go up front. Never had. Capt. v. nice. Only 3 men run this vast Boeing or whatever it is . . . Rolls Jumbo?

We didn't stay long but availed ourselves of 1st class loos and met Margaret Thatcher, the Chairman of the Conservative Party, en route to do a big address in Houston – also for the ESU. She was most friendly. Smaller than I expected, better looking and no make-up. Looked fresh and spry in a neat little print. Suitable. I mentioned I'd read a letter about her support for Mrs Whitehouse in today's *Times*; said I supported both of them (against licensing sex with children!!). 'Isn't it INCREDIBLE?' she said. 'Something must be done.'

[1] *Turn Back the Clock*, with Joyce and Addinsell's songs, was not published until 1983.

17 September [1977]   Hyde Park Gardens

Darling Joyce,

Don't mind about Callas,[1] do you? Mind more about the young giraffe in the Winchester Zoo who somehow skidded up while making love to his wife, & now cannot get up again. His back legs are spreadeagled & *everybody*, including firemen, have shoved & pushed & pulled – to no avail. Seems that a giraffe's ribs are too frail to crane him up. Victor, as he is called, is becoming exhausted. All England is on tenterhooks. His photographs show him feeding daintily from a bowl full of vitamins, while in the distance his wives are paraded, winking their long-fringed eyes at him, to encourage him.

I was in Audrey's room asking if she wanted beans or sprouts & I overheard her conversation with a patient in which A. was saying all sorts of helpful things about Love and Truth, & then there was a pause, & she said . . . 'Yes, of course that would be very helpful for the giraffe too!'

I've been working on the words for your record sleeve. I find it rather hard on account I love you so much – if you get me?[2]

From lovely London to the Sundown Kid.

[1] Maria Callas, Greek-born opera singer had just died, aged fifty-four.
[2] *The Joyce Grenfell Collection*, produced by Norman Newell, for EMI.

20 September 1977   Hyde Park Gardens

Darling Joyce,
    The giraffe has died, alas. Had a heart attack, the cissy thing, from
the shock of being hauled to its feet by a crane. We're all immeasurably
grieved, the whole country (perhaps the whole world?) having been
involved, with the wildest suggestions for getting Victor on his feet
again. One man suggested letting loose a lion in his compound. We're
a *peculiar*, but dear people, aren't we, smacking babies with one hand &
loving giraffes with the other?
    I tried on a corselette[1] at the shop by Harrods & I really believe
that taking off all one's clothes & putting them *all* on again is the most
unhappy thing to do mid morning. And mid afternoon too.

[1] Unboned corset.

25 September 1977   Hyde Park Gardens

Darling Joyce,
    Just been reading the *Sunday Times*. *George Don't* . . . has dropped
from 3rd in the best-seller charts to 5th, beaten by the *Twentieth Century
Dictionary!*
    Kay [Hammond] lunched. She looks real freaky now, poor soul – so
mauve & white & purple, with big rings under her eyes and everything
caved in.[1] *Sad*, because she minds. And since she minds it seems
impossible to say 'You look absolutely ghastly!' Such a trim figure, &
chic clothes. Isn't it funny that she can't see that caked liquid powder
under heliotrope rouge is a pity? She is compensating for her white hair
with *broad*, jet-black eyebrows, only attached here & there to her natural
ones. We must keep an eye on each other!

[1] The actress was then sixty-eight years old, a year older than Virginia.

29 September 1977   Nashville

Darling Virginia,
    I was interviewed for local press by a friendly woman who again,
had never heard of me. Good for the ego! It has been stroked so much
of late that it needs some neglect for a while. R. is appalled by the huge
wealth everywhere, as I am. Appalled? No, that's not right. But there
is an insular smugness about it – unreal – stifling. And somehow it
irks us.

To my inner rage I learned that the Nashville Branch of the ESU is *purely a social society*. They don't send scholarship boys and girls or do anything except meet twice a year and have parties with a speaker! I explained quietly and with an air of bewilderment, that I thought I was there to help publicise the ESU and raise funds for the purpose of providing scholarships. The new president, who is a King Boy Scout, and obviously has a conscience, took notice, looked a little ashamed, vowed *he'd* change things. Later he said he'd mentioned my point to 4 or 5 people and they agreed they ought to do more . . . I wonder if they will.

The surprise of finding that I can speak Virginian appears to give pleasure. The talk improves each time. Clearer!

You can see my ego has been stroked a good deal. Heady stuff! But I am actually still your old friend as you know her!

R. and I decided that this whole trip has been *enormous* fun. It went so smoothly too. We met such kindness and generosity everywhere.

See you SOON! Goody. How about lunch on Sat or Sun or BOTH?

4 October 1977   St Paul's

Darling Joyce,

Rachel [Bowes-Lyon] has had a happy time with the Queen Mum at Balmoral – they both caught some fish. I said to Ray what a pity it was the Q. Mum couldn't ever go blackberrying, & she said she could if she wanted to; & added that Queen Mary's[1] unattainable desire had been to climb over a fence!! What a picture that conjures up!

Whitworth parish magazine is going to town on the idea that schoolchildren are now allowed to do their maths with Ready Reckoners,[2] & may soon be allowed to do their exams that way!! I expect this will frighten you to death.

After yesterday's Friends of the Elderly meeting I nattered with Eliz.[3] who said she'd just been to another meeting, about battered babies, the members consisting of *very* important, *very* rich people in high positions, & that *nothing*, literally *nothing* was decided about *anything*.

Took a bus home, the conductor of which was the dearest middle-aged Cockney you ever did see. He mothered everybody, especially a crazy Swedish lady who wanted to go further than our bus did.

'Wait till we're round the corner,' he said '& then pop on the bus behind.' Well, she *didn't* wait, got off, ran round the corner, & then got onto our bus again, which promptly started. 'It's all right dear,' he said. 'Sit down now & we'll take you to Bond Street, & we can try again.' He was so nice to everyone that the whole bus responded & was wreathed in smiles . . . I MUST smile more!

Kay tells me Dick's mind is becoming more unbalanced. He frequently thinks he's in Ireland & is very poorly.

[1] Victoria Mary Augusta Louise Olga Pauline Claudine Agnes, wife of King George V (1867–1953).
[2] Calculator.
[3] Lady Elizabeth Cavendish (1926–), daughter of the 10th Duke of Devonshire and companion to John Betjeman from 1951. She was the Chair of the Friends of the Elderly and a Justice of the Peace.

Joyce was in London when, a month later, Richard Addinsell died, aged seventy-three.

1978

Joyce and Reggie took Tommy and Mary Phipps on a two-week lecture tour of the Mediterranean by cruiser, organised by Swan's Tours.

15 April   SS *Orpheus*

Darling Virginia,

We had 5 lectures yesterday and a gala dinner. Did you know that when the King of Greece got married in the mid 1800s Queen Vic gave *him* 7 Greek islands, then under our flag, as a wedding present?

Canon David Jenkins[1] sat at our table tonight. Charming, warm, light in hand and obviously a GOOD man. I feel I should be at his communion tomorrow at 7. . . . He ordered a bottle of red wine for dinner, shared half with T. and R and M and his wife, and saved the rest for the service!

Down pours the rain . . . Sea green tweed carpet to match sea green tweed upholstered edge to our bunks. It's not a large ship and compared to the *QE*[2] across the harbour it is a toy. SHE is colossal, and has splendid lines. We think of her pricey world-cruise clientele and prefer our motley lot, all of whom are thrilled to be on it and of a mature type. Old raincoats come into play.

Many professional types of both sexes; ladies in pairs, some soloists with chipped off grey hair and a look of wholemeal bread and pottery about them. And several like us – just middle-aged couples on holiday, some ladies in trousers and one or two snazzy with hats and heels. The common denominator is 'civilised', decent, and probably intelligent and, certainly, interested.

[1] Professor of Theology, and classicist (1925–) Bishop of Durham from 1984 to 1994, also a lecturer with Swan Hellenic.
[2] *Queen Elizabeth II*, Ocean liner.

Sunday, 16 April 1978   St Paul's

Darling Joyce,
   Audrey & I've had a crack at watching Clive James and Gore Vidal[1] arguing about whether Christianity has been worth while! Both of them are atheists, but James seems to be pro-Christianity – for the culture promoted – & Vidal is anti. We were terrifically annoyed – they are both so clever & nasty!

[1] American novelist (1925–).

16 April 1978   SS *Orpheus*

Darling Virginia,
   Everywhere is a sea of flowers and because of late rains the greenness is a joy.
   Oh Delphi! Straight to the litle round temple of Athena below the main site and a walk uphill to the spring.
   What a place it is! Up at the top it was quiet and magical and very beautiful indeed: in spite of the rain there was a good view and the setting alone is awe-inspiring. It really is quite a story, isn't it? The centre of the universe and that oracle, high on some leafy drug perhaps, pronouncing views in a state of trance!
   In the beautiful little theatre I sang a bit of Dido's lament but could only remember 'When I am laid – am laid – in earth' and 'Remember me'. I wished Janet Baker could have been there to do it properly.
   The cuckoo calls in the gorge and gold finches abound in flocks. Mary spotted several new birds and she is in her element of joy.
   As we climbed up the ruins a Briton saw me and said: 'Fancy seeing you here. I won't say a word. But there are lots of natives around.' And there were. Very nice they looked, professional types who knew their stuff – and me. As I was posing for a snap by R. some ladies spotted us and all said 'Oh, it's Joyce Grenfell', and they all clicked their cameras at me and said 'We saw you in Solihull – in Stratford in London' and were really very endearing and friendly, so I couldn't mind too much.
   Looking round last night in the café I was reminded of how hard it is to see the Christ in one's fellow man! The chewing, loud-mouthed American with his noisy women; the very plain Teutons; the complacent looking Swedes; and the dear dowdy Britons . . . But there is this miracle of mankind, and we were deciding, last night, that it must be a sign of progress that it really is quite hard now to decide who is a native of where. The uniformity is increasing. Is this progress? I suppose it is, really. The young are absolutely interchangeable – dungarees, hair, feet, and, the girls, un-made up.

At ten we started through the Corinth canal and were given the facts about that astonishing feat. Now R. is in the bath.

April 18th at Kos

Today dawned hopefully after a very rolling night. While we sat at dinner there was a sudden spectacular roll and wine bottles, cutlery and everything shot off one table. Upstairs in the Taverna the entire buffet – 30 foot long – loaded with dishes and cutlery simply shed its entire contents all over the floor and any customers who were nearby at the time!

We walked to a very ancient plane tree – said to have been sat under by Hypocratus[1] – he of the medicine man's oath – but surely NO tree has ever lived since 1400 BC! Still, it is big as a summer house. There Canon Jenkins, who is funny and informed and friendly, told us about the Aescapapius' (wow, is that right?)[2] psychiatric rest cure hospital. Here the first psychosomatic practices began – some of it faith healing. Lots of auto-suggestion (the docs bellowed through holes in the roof of the sleeping hall in the voices of gods declaring the patient well). Opium sleeping pills gave them rest and there were mud baths and purifying fountains.

We have also learned how 'theatre' came into being. Originally high art was monologue (please note), slight descent with dialogue and total decadence with chorus.

I'm appalled by the British botanist-gardeners. They pilfer – plunging trowels under rare orchids and anything else they see. The others pick posies, all of which die in the hot sun. Where is conservation?

[1] Hippocrates was a member of a family of priest-physicians, 460 BC to 375 BC.
[2] No, Asclepidae.

[April 1978]   St Paul's

Darling Joyce,

I am so enjoying the Rupert-G.L. letters.[1] What incredible erudition, & yet what a lovely light touch. And what a man's world! About once every three months a woman is mentioned: 'I went to my wife's step-father for the day', but not a woman has a thought or an opinion – a beautiful cerebral arrogance with females in their proper place, mutely serving in the background. (I know you're mentioned – but not really as a *person*, hein?)

[1] *The Lyttelton–Hart-Davis Letters*, edited by Rupert Hart-Davis. The letters were written between himself and George Lyttelton, his former teacher at Eton, and published in six volumes between 1978 and 1984.

27 April 1978   Naples

Darling Virginia,

We went to both theatres – Roman (crude) Greek, far more exciting.
I remembered how Viola and I had visited, alone with a driver, in 1944,
Salerno – very ghostly, landings on the beaches of a very inhospitable
shore. This whole visit to Sicily and Italy has been unexpectedly moving
to me because of my times here, and it evoked the atmosphere of
courage and humour we found in the hospitals both in the Syracuse
area and in Naples.

You can imagine how the blood rose when the Italian guide said
'That is where the AMERICANS landed' and didn't mention the 50,000
Britons – some of whom were in the bus – who had done just that. We
lost 2000 men.

Now it's the last morning. We are ready to Leave for Pompeii and a
plane home. Mr Swan himself is here now. He is marvellously efficient
and seems to be everywhere seeing that we get going.

It's been such a LOVELY time, especially having the Phipps too.
I'm sad it's over but look forward to settling down to Vol 2 again
next week.

Love darling friend J

Joyce finished writing *In Pleasant Places* the following February and it was published
in August 1979.

1979

Joyce and Reggie had enjoyed their Swan tour of the Mediterranean so much that
in February they went on a Swan tour of Egypt.

7 February 1979   Meridian Hotel
                                                                          Cairo

Darling Virginia,

Fellow tourists 80% or more from the US. Lots of the chosen. Those
we've spoken to are friendly.

The pyramids are very large, very splendid and still unsolved.
The braver fools among us bent low and went inside and down the
claustrophobic tunnel that emerges by the Sphinx. The Sphinx has
always been a 'she' to me but I'm wrong. later

It was thrilling to see the Tutankhamun stuff. Such enchanting
objects – such as a sort of greyhound with huge ears and a fox's tail
mummified and painted black. And the jewels. And the GLOVES.

I'm seeking to find Alphonse Alexan who was in the little social circle in which I moved in 1944 and '45. A Copt, who squired Viola and me about in his open touring car and gave parties in his comfortable airy flat. He is one of the few who stayed on here after the 1952 revolution. A man who runs the antique cum gift shop by the museum who knows Everyone, is sure he can find Alphonse for me.

It must be quite dodgy carrying metal bars to be cemented in (I think) while you are wearing a ground length striped garment, as the workmen are doing alongside the coach.

Here comes the rain!

8 February 1979   on board the *Delta*
                                                         Aswan

Gin Darling,

Twenty minutes to Aswan and there moored at the far end of the town, painted white and ablaze with lights, sat our pleasant, squat *Delta*. Cabin 114 has good beds with red headed head boards.

After lunch in a fellucca: delightful, slow, silent, warm with zephyrs. Our pilot was Tomas, beautiful and aquiline in coffee and white caftan. We went gently to the Botanical Gardens started by Kitchener on Kitchener Island. Pleasant oasis of huge trees and shrubs and flowers and a café. Parties of young Arabs singing to a guitar.

The history is very confusing to us and we let it slide. Dr Walters, a short-sighted youngish man and a jokey manner, message was not to try too hard to understand what we are seeing. 'Let it soak in.' And if we don't feel strong enough to see everything, 'stop'. Comforting.

17 February 1979   on board the *Delta*,
                                                         the Nile.

Darling Virginia,

The dust is quite fierce. I've used a chiffon hanky as a yashmak. After lunch – big moment – DONKEYS. The ride felt perilous but not uncomfortable, and I loved the feeling of going through the villages with only the tittup of donkeys' feet and the children for once not begging, but all saying 'Hullo' in the most charming flute noises. SO pretty they are – good teeth and, though grubby and poor, all are well fed. No sores. No rickets. Rather too many children SEEM to have only one eye functioning. I sympathised. Their colour sense is ravishing. A lot of crushed velvet shawls with fringes in orange

and red and pink, over patterned dresses of other oranges, reds
and pinks.

18 February 1979   [Hyde Park Gardens]

Darling Joyce,
    Evening paper just come & Pud Grosvenor[1] has died. A nice man.
His son, the new *dook*, looks a mite wet, don't you think? He's worth
circa £500 million, poor lad, What a *Burden*. Nice if you're fond of
caviar, tho'.

[1] 5th Duke of Westminster, born 1910. His son Gerald, (1951–) inherited valuable estates
in Chester and central London. Gerald's mother (one of four 5th Duchesses of Westminster)
was a cousin of Reggie's stepmother.

20 February 1979   in the plane en route for home

Darling Ginnie,
    Sadly Alphonse was away on business . . . sad. But a relief too!
He has cotton fields and factories and when last seen was svelte and
handsome and very civil and attractive.
    Oh Ginnie, shades of the past . . . In the afternoon we went on a tour
of mosques and a bazaar; and up on the ramparts of what is I think, the
Mohammed Ali Mosque. I suddenly realised, as we gazed onto the whole
panorama of Cairo from the slums to the skyscrapers to the pyramids,
that it was there I went in 1944 with Prince Aly Khan who produced
from his pocket a selection of gold and diamond earrings for me to
choose from. I protested 'I can't'. 'You must – just as a token etc.' I took
what I hoped were the cheapest and they were very pretty – flowers
with a diamond dewdrop. I expect I showed them to you at the time?
I kept them for years – never wore them – and finally off loaded them
at Phillips. Oh the guilt and the feeling of shame! And I'd done *nothing!*
I suppose for most people that sounds unlikely, but as you know it is
the truth. God certainly looks after fools. Standing up there just before
sunset last night it all flashed back to me and I was very entertained
and glad not to be vulnerable or young any more.

At the time of his proposal of love, May 1944, Prince Aly Khan, heir to the Aga
Khan and leader of Ismailia Muslims, was married to Joan Yarde-Buller. In 1949
he married film star Rita Hayworth. He was killed in a car crash in 1960.
    In March, Joyce travelled to Newcastle-upon-Tyne to record a television pro-
gramme about her heroes.

25 March 1979   In the night train from Newcastle

Darling Virginia,

Yesterday was a mammoth day. I caught the 10 to Newcastle from Kings X. I spied Melvyn Bragg,[1] who was to do his *Heroes* programme at 3.0: mine was at 6. He joined me in the very empty train. He is very nice; our wavelength. We're in tune about a lot of things including the failure to like or appreciate *Pennies from Heaven*.[2] He is first a writer and second a TV presenter. He lives in Hampstead with his family and also has a cottage in Cumberland where he writes his novels.

I always think he looks a bit pasty and somehow a little guarded on the box, but face to face he has a good colour, is a far taller man than I expected, and he is open and friendly. Decent. Real values. He chose heroes from his childhood – Stanley Matthews and such like, and then to my surprise, Clement Attlee! He said he was the only honest, humble, and visionary P.M. we'd had in our time – a man of moderate views for *everyone*. I welcomed this new idea of the 'sheep in sheep's clothing'.

He was interesting about the adult concept of heroes. He suggested that the idealists who ran the 1914–18 war were falsely labelled heroes – and all idealists are a menace! Hitler, Mussolini, Stalin etc.

Oh God. DONCASTER. And a long pause.

No tea.

Poor R. will already be at Kings X and there is NO way of telling him I'm still in Yorkshire. Dammit.

For my heroes I chose D'Alvaraz the tennis champ of the mid 1920s. Spoke about Sinatra's phrasing and Gertie's style. I spoke of my Pa's influence and quoted Bonhoeffer, and I read a paragraph from *Persuasion*.[3] I tried to underline the difference between heroes and the rest. And said that style was one of the things I chose heroes for. Asked if I had any villains I said no personal ones, but I am very against those who use class as a divisive weapon, & I dislike party politics & am neither Right nor Left but somewhere in the reasonable middle.

[1] Presenter of *The South Bank Show*, arts television series, and novelist (1939–).
[2] Television musical drama serial by Dennis Potter.
[3] Joyce's heroes were D'Alvaraz the Spanish woman tennis champion; Frank Sinatra (1915–), the American actor and singer; Gertie Lawrence (1898–1952), the English actress; Dietrich Bonhoeffer (1906–45), the German theologian who was hanged by the Nazis; and Jane Austen (1775–1817), the English novelist.

Tuesday 3 April [1979]   Home

Darling Virginia,

We saw Margaret Thatcher make her 5 mins answer to Callaghan's attack last week. It was truly masterly. Very low key. She was pale and in black! Voice low. She put her view of the future and her hopes and plans. It won't be easy but we need to find ourselves as a nation – our talents, our adventurous spirit etc. I thought it VERY good. R. was in tears! She really did show signs of leadership. What's more she said: 'And I promise not to make any promises that I can't fulfil' or something to that effect.

Nature note – GPO man seated on a little stool before one of those metal boxes, weaving telephone wires into some sort of fair-isle pattern out of hundreds of fine coloured telephone wires. He had a knitting pattern manual on his knee to refer to.

Joyce was a member of the Council of the Winston Churchill Memorial Fellowship Trust which provided travelling grants for people of all ages to go overseas. From 1977 she was the chair of the Crafts and Teachers of Crafts panel which involved travelling to Northern Ireland to interview applicants. She had 675 applications to read, from which she had to choose ten people, and she read all of them through, twice. The Conservative victory in the general election had led to an increase in the activities of the IRA in Northern Ireland and Belfast was suffering from more bombs.

21 April 1979   Belfast

Darling Ginnie,

I often wondered as I looked through the patterns of chintzes and materials for making curtains who on earth bought those midnight blue satiny stuffs patterned in overblowing beige and old-roses in explosions. Now I know. DEAR KIND Olwen and Raymond of 34 Cadogan Park, Belfast. Their house is of the LMS railway type hotel. Carpets are so deep and loose and you are very likely to break a leg in crossing one. The bathroom wall paper is made of huge kelly green and royal blue flowers in a rich man's version of William Morris.

All Heathrow is carefully guarded. No one much comes in or out unless vetted. We went through a road check near by. Belfast is very sad and poor and much is boarded up. The Centre is a no-go area for vehicles. And ANY car parked in an unscheduled spot is liable to be blown up. So risks in parking are NOT taken.

From discussions I learn the sense of fear has been grown used to but people don't go to theatres much or into the city at night. There were many burnt out buildings and more caged-in police depots.

22 April [1979]   St Paul's

Darling Joyce,
That's *two* nights gone in Belfast, thank heaven. At least I hope it's thank heaven. I meant to tell you to go *straight* to bed & not to meander around the shops.

I thought Belfast looked horribly bleak on the telly – raining & the streets deserted on account the bomb having gone off in a stationer's in the centre of the city. And then the main line out of Dublin blocked by a bombed train. I hope you're flying.

10.50 p.m. *That* was a nice surprise!! Put my mind beautifully at rest, hearing you. And obviously it's being a tearing success & you've conquered Belfast.

Joyce and Reggie went on their annual holiday in the Lake District.

22 May 1979   Scale Hill
                                                                 Loweswater

Darling Virginia,
Last night when we were going to bed, R. asked me how my eye was (it's been a b–y bore for days). I said it was so-so. Am I being conned into a sense of failure because of the non-healing? The thing has gone on for so long, and is SO uncomfortable at times that it is a bit discouraging. Of course I don't study nearly enough – 'in depth' that is. Must mend my ways. At the moment it is patchwork; the thing has puffed up again . . . But I sleep well – far TOO well – am well.

As you know – I hope – all the gratitude I feel for you as my oldest and truest and best friend grows daily. Never was anyone more conscious of the riches of such a friendship than I am. So we're quits!

26 May 1979   Loweswater

Darling Virginia,
I had a terrific dream, in which a lot of people – mostly MEN – came to tea; and one of them was David Hicks![1] I went down to an immense kitchen to put on a kettle. Couldn't get to the tap for piled up crockery. Every bowl on the plate was full of CONCOCTIONS – marshmallow soaking in RUM, etc. etc. I cursed Mrs Gabe, who was apparently in charge, but out. Only a packet of broken biscuits and eight people for tea. And there was a figure from my early youth, Olivia James, in a large black velvet hat! Interpret all that if you can! I awoke in a state of frustration and angst!

I don't dream much up here – or anywhere else except the Attic – but the night before I had one in which R. came into the room with a vast, elaborate antique *sword* and said he was going to hang it up on the wall. Nay, I said, you don't. And I woke up.

A ghastly air crash in Chicago. Think of the horror of clearing it all away . . . 289 . . . Well, don't then.

---

[1] British dress designer (1929–) and son-in-law of Earl Mountbatten.

May [1979]   [Hyde Park Gardens]

Darling Joyce,

I'm so sorry about your eye, darling. You're so wonderful about it & I know how discouraging it must be. I wonder if Reg is right about the guilt thing. Interesting. But isn't it difficult – to know if the faithful would be depressed to see you in an eye patch or be encouraged to find that you can also falter & not *mind*.

27 May 1979   [Loweswater]

Darling Gin,

Good to hear you last night. I hate waiting for mail. Do you remember we used to have 5 deliveries in London a day when we were children? And the last mail was collected at 11 pm from the corner of St. Leonard's Terrace and Smith Street. I used to hear the heavy door bang shut.

What a world. Surely things WERE better when the post office services worked and we didn't discuss homos on the radio, and saw them in plays on ITV. OR is it better for it all to be seen and then seen *through*? Probably. But uncomfortable. But then so it should be.

The presence of far too many rhododendrons is, to me, very downheartening, even when, as now, they are full of pink and purple. I always equate them with rain drips. And a certain Victorian/Edwardian solidarity and ugliness of stone and brick – and Tory thinking! (The fascist kind I mean!)

I'm a little shocked at you watching turned off sound TV horse jumping to that divine Mozart! But then I am totally baffled by your passion for sport. Still, I love you VERY much and it takes all sorts to make a world.

Joyce went on a tour of British bookshops to promote *In Pleasant Places*, to be published in August. Marina Warner, British writer and journalist (1946–) was promoting her book about Queen Victoria's sketch books.

25 June 1979   Queens Hotel
                                                              Leeds

Darling Virginia,
    Marina Warner and I sat in the comfortable train that took us
across country from Glasgow to Leeds, the most GLORIOUS country,
in sunshine. The elderberry blossom is only just out so is still a greeny-
white, and my favourite moon daisies are freshly laundered and crisp
and clean. How beautiful is England – and the north of it in particular.
    It was a journey to think of and treasure; just like journeys used to
be with pauses at quiet stations and the sound of sheep not far off. Very
restoring. I learned a lot more about Marina including the sweetness
of her nature and her kindness to me. She overheard the porter at the
Central saying he had no-one to send to fetch my bag, so she simply
came up to my room and carried the bag down herself! She wishes
deeply she had a private income and didn't have to do writing 'jobs'.
She is highly intelligent and giggly, too, which I find attractive.
    She gets better and better telling about her Victoria's sketch book
and every time adds more interesting facts. Do you know why little
boys wore dresses for so long in Victoria's days? Because until they were
potty-trained it was easier to change their nappies under a skirt! She is
NOT used to speaking but is so good at it. Keeps it fresh.

Once a year Queen Elizabeth the Queen Mother went to stay with her sister-in-law
Rachel Bowes-Lyon at St Paul's. Virginia went to St Paul's to relax, so she avoided
these social weekends, but Joyce was happy to be invited for the Saturday
night dinner.

9 July 1979   St Paul's

Darling Virginia,
    We had a blissful afternoon on our own in your happy living room.
The detective and footman are in our bedrooms. I wonder where the
two extra footmen are sleeping? One wears the dark blue battle dress,
with red piping, as they do at Buck House.
    It was a lively church service for the first 20 minutes and I thought
hooray – then into the long long long Communion Service with lots of
ritual, fetching of wines, wiping of goblets, giving it to himself and two
servers and then, eventually, up trotted the QM and then the whole
congregation except me.[1] Ah me. Lots of time to think and rejoice and
know and think of all that is true and good and eternal. The QM was
in turquoise with a fetching hat decorated with velvet ribbons. Pretty
contrast.

479

QM is very out-spoke. Very much dislikes the wrecking of valuable grammar schools, and feels that instead of easing class conflict has exacerbated it. She is glad she never went to school. She hates the idea of being crowded as one must be in a school. She is a funny mixture of folly and charm and prejudices.

The weekend has been quite enjoyable thanks to the weather, agreeable party, and the QM's pleasing nature. She *said* she loved being here; it was so restful. I asked if she'd enjoyed it when she lived here as a child. 'It was blissful.'

Bade the Q. adieu last night and to my surprise she kissed me!

[1] Christian Scientists celebrate communion through silent prayer and Christian living, and not in the form of ceremonies with bread and wine.

Joyce recorded a new series of *Face the Music* and publicised her new book with press and radio interviews, bookshop signings and literary lunches.

In the autumn of 1979 Joyce's eye started 'playing up' as she put it. She agreed to be examined by eye specialists before she and Reggie set off for a six-week visit to South Africa and Australia. The doctors advised that her blind eye should be removed, and to placate Reggie, Joyce agreed to the operation.

16 October 1979   Moorfields Eye Hospital

My Darling Ginnie,

Been visited by the doctor who does the job tomorrow; and the one who did the scan. The Irish matron's assistant is my avid fan. The anaesthetist and the registrar have all inspected me.

R. minded leaving me here this morning but was better at the second visit. I feel very removed and that is cause for immense gratitude.

The thing is, I'm truly grateful for the sense of Love I find everywhere and realise it is God in action. ALL good is always a proof of God's presence.

At a time like this one longs to make sure that those one loves really know just how much they are loved. In the case of R. and you it is 100% plus. More reasons for gratitude. Indeed 'the lines are fallen unto me in pleasant places.'[1]

Much love darling best friend. J

[1] Psalm 16, verse 6.

The eye was successfully removed, but the operation revealed that cancer had spread from Joyce's eye to her spine. Reggie was advised that Joyce probably had less than a year to live but to continue with the planned trip. Joyce was not interested in the medical diagnosis, and Reggie agreed with Virginia not to tell her. Joyce bought new clothes, had a new eye fitted and accepted invitations to preach in churches the following year.

Virginia organised a surprise party to celebrate Joyce and Reggie's forthcoming golden wedding anniversary. All the surviving 'old favourites' were there including Athene Seyler, Reggie's sisters, Verily Anderson, Mrs Gabe, William Blezard. I was the only young guest and, overawed by so many famous names, I sat close to Joyce for comfort.

'Come on Joyce,' shouted William from Virginia's grand piano. 'Stand up and give us a song.'

'I'll sing from here, but you must all join in,' she replied in her best headmistress tone.

Everyone sang with gusto, but I noticed that Joyce merely mimed.

'My neck's giving me hell,' Joyce whispered to me.

'Have you tried aspirin?' I asked innocently.

'It's well passed the aspirin stage, my old duck,' she said firmly.

Within a few days Reggie was nursing Joyce in bed and the Australia trip had to be cancelled. During her last week she overcame the pain with medicines and her strong faith. She continued to talk to friends on the phone and open her mail. On 19 November 1979, a letter arrived from 10 Downing Street saying that the Queen planned to make Joyce a Dame Commander of the Order of the British Empire in the 1980 New Year Honours list.

Joyce died on 30 November, just twelve days before her golden wedding anniversary. A memorial service was held in Westminister Abbey in February 1980 to which several thousand fans came. Joseph Cooper arranged the music and Paul Scofield read the lesson. Reggie asked me to wear the straw boater with pink roses which Joyce wore in *Picture Postcard*. I felt very self-conscious, but hoped that Joyce would have liked it. Reggie sat facing the other mourners and wept unself-consciously throughout the moving service.

Reggie continued to live at 34 Elm Park Gardens, changing nothing. His youngest sister, Frances, moved in and they cared for each other for over ten years. Both Reggie and Virginia found the gap left by Joyce hard to fill. Virginia lived on in Hyde Park Gardens, writing, entertaining and going to the theatre. In 1991 Dilys Tugwell retired after twenty-two years working for Virginia. Audrey Butterworth had just died so Virginia moved into her smaller flat in Chelsea. Dilys taught Virginia how to heat up food from Marks & Spencer.

In November 1992 Frances organised a joint party for Reggie's eighty-ninth birthday and Virginia's eighty-third. Three months later Virginia died of a stroke, followed the next month by Reggie, in the same room as Joyce had died.

> If I should go before the rest of you
> Break not a flower nor inscribe a stone
> Nor when I'm gone speak in a Sunday voice
> But be the usual selves that I have known.
> Weep if you must,
> Parting is hell,
> But life goes on,
> So sing as well.
>
> Joyce Grenfell (date unknown)

Biographical Notes

These friends and relations are in alphabetical order by first name, as used by Joyce or Virginia. The full name then follows.

Mrs Agos, Merope Gavrieldes, then Brimm, Joyce's cook-housekeeper from 1964 to 1980.

Alec Thesiger (1904–71). Tony Thesiger's older brother. He had learning difficulties caused by his mother having had German measles during pregnancy. He lived in London or Scotland with a domestic staff of cook, chauffeur, two maids and tutor-companion.

Athene Seyler (1889–1990). Actress and silent movie star. Her husband **Beau** Hannen (1881–1972) had been an architect with Joyce's father before he became an actor. They formed part of the 'Magic circle' of Joyce and Virginia's close friends who met every year for a Spring lunch.

Audrey Butterworth (–1990). Christian Science practitioner and Virginia's teacher. Close friend of Virginia after Tony died. Virginia bought her a flat in Chelsea. She founded Bow House for retired Christian Scientists, which Virginia helped her run. She often stayed with Virginia in the country, treating her patients over the phone, or by prayer.

Ben, Benjamin Britten, later Lord Britten (1913–76). Contemporary composer of operas (*Peter Grimes, Curlew River*) choral works, music for films and stage plays, etc. Started the Aldeburgh Music Festival in 1947 and lived in the Red House with **Peter** Pears (q.v.). A friend of Joyce from 1962 when she and Reggie began attending Aldeburgh Festival annually.

Bungs, Catherine Fordham (1910–69). Friend of Joyce and Virginia from Mme Ozanne's finishing school in Paris. Married Major-General Sir John Kennedy, Governor-General of Southern Rhodesia 1946–50.

Davies Alec Thesiger's chauffeur. Mrs Davies was Alec's cook.

Dick, Richard Addinsell (1904–77). Composer of film music including *Goodbye Mr Chips*, *Blithe Spirit* and *Beau Brummel* and the Warsaw concerto for *Dangerous Moonlight*. Also wrote theatre scores with Clemence Dane. Collaborated with Joyce from 1941 and accompanied her on British ENSA tours during the Second World War. For twenty years he was an invalid, suffering from a weak spine and hypochondria. In later years he could not cope with Joyce's success and energy, but shortly before he died, they made friends again.

Dilys Tugwell. Virginia's parlourmaid and then her cook cum housekeeper from

1969 to 1991. Her husband David was part-time handyman after they moved into Virginia's service flat.

Edy, Virginia's Morris Minor.

Frances Campbell-Preston, née Grenfell (1918–). Reggie's sister. Mother of four, widowed in 1965. Lived with Reggie in Chelsea after Joyce died. Lady-in-waiting to Queen Elizabeth, the Queen Mother.

Mrs Gabe Anna Gavrieldes (*c*. 1905–85). Joyce's cook-housekeeper at Elm Park Gardens from 1946 to 1964. Sister-in-law of Mrs Agos.

Ghulam Mahd. Bearer and servant to Joyce and Viola during their ENSA tour of India in 1944.

Gussie, Virginia's Bentley.

Harold Grenfell (1905–85). First cousin of Reggie Grenfell, manager of Messina Copper Mine in South Africa, owned by the Grenfell family. Joyce and Reggie visited Messina every February from 1956 to 1971.

Hilda Grenfell, née Lyttelton (1886–1972). Reggie's stepmother, married his father Lieutenant-Colonel Arthur Morton Grenfell when Reggie's mother died in 1910. She looked after her two stepsons, Reggie and **Harry** (1905–85), her stepdaughter **Vera** (1902–86), and had four more daughters, **Mary** (1910–95), **Katie** (1912–), **Frances** (1918–) and **Laura** (1920–79). Hilda and Arthur lived in Chesham Place, Belgravia, London and later in Eastry, Kent.

Hilda, Virginia's live-in cook from 1969 to 1978.

Imo, Imogen Holst (1907–84). Musician, musicologist, organiser of Aldeburgh Festival. Daughter of Gustav Holst.

Lang, Langhorne Phipps (1956–). Joyce's only nephew. Born and lives in USA.

Lefty, Maurice Flynn (1880–1950). Joyce's American stepfather. A glamorous man who had been a professional footballer. Married Nora Phipps, her mother, in 1931.

Ma, Nora Phipps née Langhorne (1880–1955). Joyce's mother, youngest sister of Nancy Astor. A society beauty, she was one of the original American Gibson girls, portrayed by her brother-in-law the portrait artist Charles Dana Gibson. Married to Paul Phipps from 1909 to 1930 in London and to Maurice Flynn from 1931 in America. Struggled to be a Christian Scientist.

Maria, Mary Brassey (1910–88). One of Joyce and Virginia's oldest friends. She devoted her life to good works and Christian Science. In her *Times* obituary Virginia wrote: 'She managed to be extremely efficient, even if she occasionally lost all the files.'

Minnie, Virginia's mini-car: 'an animated hip bath'.

Miriam Grenfell (*c*. 1912–67). Wife of Reggie's first cousin Harold. When at

Messina, it was the duty of Joyce and Miriam to entertain local farmers and dignitaries with 'tea potties' and 'sundowners'.

Nancy Astor (Aunt N.) (1879–1964). Joyce's maternal aunt, wife of **Waldorf**, Lord Astor of Cliveden. Was Britain's first woman member of parliament, a Unionist for Plymouth (Sutton) from 1919 to 1945. Mother of five sons and a daughter. Before the war she lent Joyce and Reggie Parr's Cottage on Cliveden estate. Very generous to Joyce, but also quite frightening.

Noël Coward (1899–1973). Film (*Blithe Spirit*), and theatre dramatist (*Private Lives*), artist, actor and songwriter ('Mad Dogs and Englishmen'). Joyce first met Noël as a child and then appeared in his 1945 revue *Sigh No More*. They remained friends, though Joyce never approved of his style of high living. Knighted in 1970.

P.M., Princess Margaret (1930–). Sister of Queen Elizabeth II. Virginia knew her through working with the Friends of the Elderly and Gentlefolk's Help housing charity of which she is Patron. Joyce first met her when she was invited to perform privately for King George VI. Both Joyce and Virginia were fervent royalists.

Pa, Paul Phipps (1885–1956). Joyce's father and a Christian Scientist. An architect, who studied under Lutyens. Half American and half English, he was brought up in England and worked in Canada during the First World War. He designed extensions to two of Joyce's homes – St Leonard's Terrace and Parr's cottage – and designed the Church of Christ, Scientist, in Bow Street, London.

Peter Pears (1910–86). Tenor singer, partner of Benjamin Britten, helped run Aldeburgh Music Festival.

Reggie, Reginald Pascoe Grenfell (Reg, R., Pascoe) (1905–93). Joyce's husband for fifty years. His mother was Victoria Sybil, daughter of Earl Grey of Howick. An accountant and director of Messina Copper Mine in Transvaal, South Africa. His hobbies were bird-watching and supporting Joyce's career.

René Easden. Joyce's cook for five years before the war at Parr's Cottage.

Rupert Hart-Davis (1907–). Publisher and editor. Rupert and Joyce's parents were friends, and his sister Deirdre was Joyce's bridesmaid. Reggie and Rupert were at Eton together. Joyce and Reggie stayed often with Rupert and his fourth wife **June** in the Yorkshire Dales. Rupert edited both of Joyce's autobiographies.

Sally Phipps (1954–). Joyce's only niece, on whom she doted. Born and lives in USA.

Stephen Potter (1900–69). Writer (*One Upmanship* series) and broadcaster. Joyce collaborated with him on the BBC radio series *How to . . .* They opened the Third Programme – the classical music channel – with *How to Broadcast*. Joyce and Stephen drifted apart after the war though she remained friends with his first wife, Mary (**Att**) Potter, a painter.

Tommy Phipps (1914–). Joyce's only brother, four years younger. Stage and television dramatist, lives in Southampton, New York with his wife **Mary** (1922–). Joyce stayed with them every time she visited the USA.

Tony, Antony Frederic Lewis Thesiger (Tojo, T, Todle, To) (1906–69). Virginia's husband. Managed a teak plantation in Burma until 1939. Then in anti-aircraft unit in Bristol during the Second World War. Joined his mother's family firm of Wallace Brothers, traders in India, Burma and Thailand, as a head-hunter for managers for the Far East. Retired in 1968 with Alzheimer's disease.

Verily Anderson (1915–). Author and journalist. First met Joyce in 1951 when she was pregnant with her fourth child, Janie. After she was widowed, Joyce helped to support the family. Married **Paul Paget**, architect (1901–85) in 1971.

Victor Stiebel (1907–76). Society dress designer. Worked for Jacqmar before setting up his own couture house with investments from Virginia. Designed most of Joyce's stage dresses. Virginia supported him from his retirement in 1963 until his death from multiple sclerosis.

Viola Tunnard (Vole) (1916–74). Musician and pianist. Accompanied Joyce during the war on ENSA tours of Middle East and India. Became successful repetiteur for Benjamin Britten. Lived in Aldeburgh during her final years with Motor Neurone Disease.

Waldorf, Lord Astor of Cliveden (Uncle Waldorf) (1879–1952). Inherited wealth from his father, an America property tycoon. MP for Plymouth (Sutton) until he inherited his father's peeerage, then Mayor of Plymouth. Husband of Nancy Astor.

Mrs Westaway. Virginia's cook in the 1950s.

Winifred Ashton (1885–1965) alias Clemence Dane. Novelist and dramatist, wrote *Will Shakespeare* and *A Bill of Divorcement*. Joyce met her through Noël Coward in the theatre.

Houses

Joyce's Homes

Most of Joyce's life was lived in Chelsea, London.

8 Burton Court, Chelsea. Joyce's home up to age nine.

28 St Leonard's Terrace, Chelsea (1919–29). Joyce lived here from age nine until her marriage. Near King's Road, opposite Burton's Court, a garden square. She attended Frances Holland School and then Clearview, a Christian Science boarding school, which later became Claremont Fan Court School.

21 St Leonard's Terrace, Chelsea (1929–36). Joyce and Reggie were given this four-bedroomed house as a wedding present, cost £3,500. They added two bedrooms and a sitting room for their two maids.

Parr's, Cliveden Estate, Bucks (1936–42). Nancy Astor lent this cottage to Joyce and Reggie in exchange for social duties when required at Cliveden. Nancy employed Joyce's father to renovate the old butler's cottage and gave £100 for furniture.

Beaufort Gardens (1942–5). Home of Pauline Spender-Clay. Joyce and Reggie stayed here whenever they were in London.

12 Rectory Chambers, Old Church Street, Chelsea (1945–6). Small rented flat.

149 King's Road, Chelsea (1946–56). Flat over Mr Kent's toy and sweet shop.

34 Elm Park Gardens, near Fulham Road, Chelsea (1956 until their deaths). Third-floor flat with attic study, owned by Chelsea Borough Council.

Virginia's Homes

All Virginia's homes were close to Marble Arch, London.

5 Montagu Square, near Oxford Street. Virginia's parents' home until her father died in 1937, when it was sold to pay death duties. From here she attended Notting Hill High School.

40 Orchard Court, Portman Square, near Oxford Street. Virginia's mother's home.

32 Cambridge Square. House near Bayswater Road bought by Tony's parents for £3,000 on their marriage in 1939.

Druid's Garth, near Bristol. House with tennis court rented during the Second World War.

7 Hyde Park Gardens. Overlooking Bayswater Road and Hyde Park. Virginia and Tony bought this large flat in 1956. Tony died there. Virginia left in 1991.

Whitelands. Flat in Chelsea bought by Virginia for her friend Audrey Butterworth. Virginia lived there from 1991 until her death.

Other houses

Cliveden. The principal home of Nancy and Waldorf Astor, near Windsor overlooking the River Thames.

4 St James's Square. The Astors' London home where Joyce and Reggie stayed before the war if they were going to a dance.

Nannau, North Wales. House often rented by the Grenfell family for holidays before the war.

Little Orchard, Tryon, North Carolina. Joyce's mother's home, bought for her by Nancy Astor.

Wentworth Hotel, Aldeburgh, Suffolk. Joyce and Reggie's favourite place at Aldeburgh from 1962.

Scale Hill Hotel, Loweswater, Cumberland. Joyce and Reggie stayed here every year from 1959 until the summer of 1979.

Bellabeg House, Strathdon, Aberdeenshire. House owned by Tony Thesiger's parents for grouse shooting, used in August and September. The laundry was sent up here from London throughout the year to keep local staff employed. Tony's father also bought Coldstones near Edinburgh for Easter golfing holidays, which Tony then gave to the Women's Royal Voluntary Service.

Books and Films

Books by Joyce Grenfell

Nanny Says, Dobson, 1972

By Special Request, Macmillan, 1973
Joyce's first autobiography, covering her life from birth up to 1954.

George, Don't Do That, Macmillan, 1977
Collection of Joyce's Nursery School sketches.

Stately as a Galleon, Macmillan, 1978
More theatrical sketches.

In Pleasant Places, Macmillan, 1979
Joyce's second autobiography, covering her life from 1954 to 1973.

Joyce by Herself and her Friends, Macmillan, 1980
A collection of portraits by old and young friends, relatives, with her poems.

An Invisible Friendship, Macmillan, 1981
A collection of letters between Joyce and Kathleen Moore, an English teacher and poet whom she never met.

Turn Back the Clock, Macmillan, 1983
A collection of performance sketches, poems and songs.

Darling Ma, Letters to her Mother, 1932–1944, edited by James Roose-Evans, Hodder and Stoughton, 1988

The Time of my Life, Entertaining the Troops – Her Wartime Journals, edited by James Roose-Evans, Hodder and Stoughton, 1989

Books by Virgina Graham

Heather Mixture, London, 1938

Say Please, illustrated by Osbert Lancaster, Harvill Press, 1949
'A book on Etiquette for Ladies, which will not help you to be a lady.'

Here's How, Harvill Press 1951
Amusing instructions on how to knit, plumb, garden – none of which Virginia ever did.

Nikki, London, 1956

Sahara Boom-de-ay, London, 1957

A Cockney in the Country, London, 1958

The Story of the WVS, Country Life, 1959

Everything's too Something, Country Life, 1966 Illustrated by Haro.

A Book on Casino Gambling, New York, 1978

Novels translated from the French: *I Said to my Wife*, 1953; *To the Gondolas*, 1958; *The Sky and the Stars*, 1956; *Say I'm in Conference*, 1959; *Daybreak*, 1959; *The Spanish Tulip*; 1959; *Ready Revenge*, 1960.

Films in which Joyce appeared

The Lamp Still Burns, 1943, directed by Maurice Elvey, starring Rosamund John. Propaganda war film in which Joyce played a lecturer on blood donation.

This Demi-Paradise, 1943, directed by Anthony Asquith, starring Laurence Olivier, Margaret Rutherford, George Cole. Joyce played a young English society girl.

While the Sun Shines, by Terence Rattigan, 1946, directed by Anthony Asquith, starring Ronald Howard. Joyce was 'an ex-deb ninny'.

Poet's Pub, by Eric Linklater, 1949, directed by Frederick Wilson. Joyce played a folk song enthusiast.

The Happiest Days of Your Life, 1950, directed by Frank Launder, starring Alastair Sim and Margaret Rutherford. Joyce played gym mistress Miss Gossage with the immortal line 'Call me Sausage'.

A Run for Your Money, 1949, directed by Charles Frend, starring Alec Guinness. Joyce was a sales lady in a dress shop.

Stage Fright, 1950, directed by Alfred Hitchcock, starring Marlene Dietrich, Alastair Sim, Sybil Thorndike, Jane Wyman and Michael Wilding. Joyce played a lady running a shooting gallery at the Chelsea Theatrical Garden Party.

Laughter in Paradise, 1951, directed by Mario Zampi, starring Alastair Sim. Joyce was a lady army officer called Fluffy.

The Magic Box, 1951, directed by John Boulting, starring Laurence Olivier, Michael Redgrave and Maria Schell.

The Galloping Major, 1951, directed by Henry Cornelius. Joyce was a Cockney milk bar maid.

The Pickwick Papers, 1952, directed by Noel Langley, starring James Hayter. Joyce played Mrs Leo Hunter ruling the waves with a papier-mâché trident.

Genevieve, 1953, directed by Henry Cornelius, starring Kay Kendall, Kenneth More, Dinah Sheridan. Joyce played a hotel proprietress, with limited hot water.

The Belles of St Trinian's, 1954, directed by Frank Launder, starring Alastair Sim, Margaret Rutherford. Joyce was a policewoman disguised as a gym mistress.

Forbidden Cargo, 1954, directed by Harold French, starring Nigel Patrick. A documentary thriller about Customs and Excise, in which Joyce played a bird watcher.

The Million Pound Note (The Man with a Million in the USA), 1954, directed by Ronald Neame, starring Gregory Peck. Joyce played an English duchess.

Blue Murder at St Trinian's, 1957, directed by Frank Launder, starring Terry Thomas, George Cole and Alastair Sim. Joyce played a policewoman in love with Terry Thomas.

Here Comes the Bride, 1957, directed by Roy Boulting, starring Ian Carmichael, Irene Handl and Athene Seyler. Joyce played the bride's aunt and improvised Lohengrin's Wedding March on the church organ.

The Pure Hell of St Trinian's, 1960, directed by Frank Launder, starring Cecil Parker, George Cole and Irene Handl.

The Old Dark House, 1962, directed by William Castle, starring Robert Morley and Fenella Fielding.

The Yellow Rolls-Royce, 1964, directed by Anthony Asquith, starring Omar Sharif and Ingrid Bergman. Joyce played Ingrid Bergman's Virginian lady travelling companion.

The Americanization of Emily, 1964, directed by Arthur Hiller, starring Julie Andrews, James Garner and James Coburn, in which Joyce played Julie Andrews' mother.

Index

Names and places marked with an asterisk* are included in the biographical notes on pages 483–6 or the list of houses on pages 487–8.